TEACHING STRATEGIES FOR ETHNIC STUDIES

SIXTH EDITION

James A. Banks
University of Washington, Seattle

Allyn and Bacon
Boston London Toronto Sydney Tokyo Singapore

Vice President, Education: Nancy Forsyth
Series Editor: Frances Helland
Marketing Manager: Kathy Hunter
Editorial Production Service: Grace Sheldrick, Wordsworth Associates
Manufacturing Buyer: Megan Cochran
Cover Administrator: Linda Knowles

Copyright © 1997, 1991, 1987, 1984, 1979, 1975
A Viacom Company
Needham Heights, MA 02194

Library of Congress Cataloging-in-Publication Data

Banks, James A.
      Teaching strategies for ethnic studies / James A. Banks.—6th ed.
          p.   cm.
      Includes bibliographical references and index.
      ISBN 0-205-18940-7
      1. Minorities—United States—Study and teaching.   2. Ethnicity-
  -Study and teaching—United States.   3. Pluralism (Social sciences)-
  -Study and teaching—United States.   4. Multiculturalism—Study and
  teaching—United States.   5. United States—Ethnic relations—Study
  and teaching.   I. Title.
      E184.A1B24   1996
  305.8'00973—dc20   96–11151
                                                                   CIP

Printed in the United States of America

10 9 8 7 6 5 4 3 2 1   01 00 99 98 97 96

*To the memory of Bob, my brother,
who shared my dream for a better world*

*and to Cherry, Angela, and Patricia,
my family*

BRIEF CONTENTS

CONTENTS

PART II
THE FIRST AMERICANS AND AFRICAN AMERICANS:
CONCEPTS AND STRATEGIES   135

PART III
EUROPEAN AMERICANS: Concepts and Strategies   251

8   EUROPEAN ETHNIC GROUPS: Concepts, Strategies, and Materials   253

9   JEWISH AMERICANS: Concepts, Strategies, and Materials   295

PART IV
HISPANIC AMERICANS: CONCEPTS AND STRATEGIES 329

10 MEXICAN AMERICANS: Concepts, Strategies, and Materials 335

PART **V**
ASIAN AMERICANS AND ARAB AMERICANS:
Concepts and Strategies 431

PREFACE

The accelerating demographic and economic changes within our society, the deepening racial divide, and the elusive quest for equality and justice make multicultural education imperative as we enter the twenty-first century. Since the fifth edition of *Teaching Strategies for Ethnic Studies* was published, the gap between the rich and the poor has widened, visible signs of the racial crisis have become stark, and the rate of increase of low-income youth and youth of color within the nation's schools and universities has continued to outpace the growth rate of Whites. Youth of color made up more than 30 percent of the students in the nation's schools in 1990; they are projected to make up nearly half of the student population by 2020.

Yet the American dream is alive, and our nation continues to make gradual steps toward its realization. The significant numbers of immigrants that settle in this nation each year are testimony to the vitality of the American dream. The continuing growth of multicultural education courses, experiences, and publications is also evidence that an impressive number of educators are committed to actualizing the nation's democratic principles. The major aim of multicultural education is to help the nation actualize its democratic ideals that are stated in its founding documents, such as the Declaration of Independence, the Constitution, and the Bill of Rights.

This sixth edition of *Teaching Strategies for Ethnic Studies* is designed to help teachers to conceptualize, design, and implement a democratic, thoughtful, and just curriculum that honors and reflects the experiences, hopes, and dreams of all Americans. It describes the knowledge, concepts, strategies, and resources that teachers need to implement a democratic curriculum by transforming the mainstream curriculum and incorporating content and concepts about diverse racial, ethnic, and cultural groups.

This sixth edition reflects current and emerging concepts, perspectives, and issues in the field. I have been able to incorporate detailed information from the 1990 census into this sixth edition. When I prepared the fifth edition of *Teaching Strategies for Ethnic Studies,* only preliminary data and projections were available from the 1990 census. The bibliographies have been extensively revised. They reflect the large number of materials and resources that have been published since the last edition was prepared. The rich resources and publications that now exist in ethnic studies, women's studies, and multicultural education are evidence of the growth and maturity of the field. I have also incorporated information from the *Handbook of Research on Multicultural Education* (Banks & Banks, 1995). Most of the books in this edition were not included in the previous one. Readers of this edition can refer to previous editions of this book for older but nonetheless important titles. Each of the chapters on all ethnic groups has been updated with new information and census data. Appendix B has been substantially revised to include new and exciting videotapes on U.S. ethnic groups.

Teaching Strategies for Ethnic Studies, Sixth Edition, is divided into six parts. Part I presents a rationale for incorporating ethnic content into the mainstream curriculum. Goals and key concepts for the multicultural curriculum are also discussed in Part I. The main goal of the multicultural curriculum should be to help students develop the ability to make reflective decisions so that they can, through thoughtful action, influence their personal, social, and civic worlds and help to make them more democratic and just.

Parts II through V contain chapters on the major ethnic groups in the United States. These chapters contain (1) chronologies of key events, (2) historical overviews of groups, (3) illustrative key concepts and teaching strategies, (4) annotated bibliographies for teachers, and (5) annotated bibliographies for elementary and secondary school students. Chapter 14 (on Arab Americans) is reprinted from another publication and has a different structure. This chapter is new to the sixth edition.

Recommended grade levels are designated for the student resources in the student bibliographies. Although the bibliographies are selective, no book is appropriate for all purposes and settings. You should examine each book carefully before assigning it to your students. The annotations can help in this screening process.

Part VI highlights and summarizes the major points discussed in the previous chapters and illustrates how you can use the information and strategies in Parts I through V to develop and teach multicultural units and curricula that focus on two or more ethnic groups. Chapter 15 presents the major components of a sample multicultural unit to illustrate the steps in unit construction. Annotated bibliographies of multicultural resources for teachers and students and techniques for evaluation are also included in chapter 15.

The appendixes are designed to help you obtain information and materials for classroom use. Appendix A is a chronology of key events in the history of ethnic groups in the United States. Appendix B lists videotapes suitable for teacher education and for student use. Appendix C lists books about women of color. Appendix D lists the Carter G. Woodson Award books; Appendix E cites twenty classic and landmark books in ethnic literature.

ACKNOWLEDGMENTS

I am grateful to a number of colleagues and friends for their help in the preparation of this sixth edition of *Teaching Strategies for Ethnic Studies.* Carlos F. Diaz contributed chapters 6 and 12. Virgie O. Chattergy updated the bibliographies in chapter 6. Jerome L. Ruderman contributed chapter 9. Chapter 14 was written by Patty Adeed and G. Pritchy Smith. I am grateful to the authors and their publishers for permission to reprint their work.

In undertaking a revision of this scope and magnitude, it is necessary to solicit the help and expertise of a community of scholars and researchers. I am deeply grateful to a group of distinguished scholars and able research assistants for their help in the preparation of this sixth edition. A group of academic specialists prepared perceptive and very helpful comments after reviewing the chapters on the various ethnic groups. Their comments strongly influenced the revisions of these chapters. I thank them for their help and expert guidance with the chapters designated:

Patricia Espiritu, University of Washington, Seattle, chapter 13

Yen Le Espiritu, University of California, San Diego, chapter 13

Evelyn Hu-DeHart, University of Colorado, Boulder, chapter 13

Gloria Ladson-Billings, University of Wisconsin, Madison, chapter 7

Oscar J. Martínez, University of Arizona, chapter 10

Carol Miller, University of Minnesota, Twin Cities, chapter 5

Sonia Nieto, University of Massachusetts, Amherst, chapter 11

Rudolph J. Vecoli, University of Minnesota, Twin Cities, chapter 8

Carlos J. Ovando, Indiana University, reviewed the previous edition and made helpful suggestions for this new edition.

I would like to thank the following individuals for their research assistance, support, and encouragement in the preparation of this sixth edition:

James A. Rodriguez, University of Washington, Seattle

Patricia A. Banks, undergraduate student

Angela M. Banks, graduate student

I wish to thank Lauri Johnson, one of my graduate students, for assistance in compiling the list of videotapes that constitute Appendix B. My thanks also to Grace Sheldrick, Wordsworth Associates, for her perceptive and expert editorial assistance. I am grateful to Cherry A. McGee Banks, University of Washington, Bothell, for nearly three decades of encouragement, caring, and intellectual support.

J.A.B.

REFERENCE

Banks, J. A. & Banks, C. A. M. (1995). *Handbook of Research on Multicultural Education*. New York: Macmillan.

GOALS, CONCEPTS, AND INSTRUCTIONAL PLANNING

P art I of this book discusses the basic instructional problems in teaching ethnic content and integrating it into the curriculum. Chapter 1 reviews some of the major trends in teaching ethnic content and argues for a need to expand the definition of ethnic studies and to include content about a range of ethnic groups in the multicultural curriculum. The problem of formulating goals for the multicultural curriculum and the interdisciplinary, conceptual approach to teaching are discussed in chapter 2. The author states that the major goal of the multicultural curriculum should be to help students develop decision-making skills so that they can become effective change agents in contemporary society.

To help students develop effective decision-making skills, the multicultural curriculum must help them master higher level concepts and generalizations. Chapter 3 discusses key concepts that can be used to organize a sound multicultural curriculum. The final chapter in Part I, chapter 4, discusses practical ways to plan, organize, and teach multicultural units and lessons. The actual steps to follow in order to gain the needed content background, to identify key concepts and generalizations, and to choose ethnic content are discussed. Valuing strategies and social action projects are also discussed in chapter 4.

1

THE MULTICULTURAL CURRICULUM

RATIONALE, TRENDS, AND GOALS

This chapter describes the nature and complexity of ethnic diversity in U.S. society. It also discusses emerging demographic trends, current developments in multicultural education in the nation's schools, and the goals of a multicultural curriculum. An important goal of the multicultural curriculum is to help students view events, concepts, issues, and problems from diverse cultural and ethnic perspectives.

THE PERSISTENCE OF ETHNICITY IN AMERICAN SOCIETY

Americans have always held tightly to the idea that ethnic cultures would melt or vanish. Consequently, a strong assimilationist idea has dominated American society since the British gained control of most American institutions early in the nation's history. The American assimilationist idea envisions a society in which ethnicity and race are not important identities. Group identities and affiliations would be based primarily on such variables as social class, politics, education, and other interests. The assimilationist idea that deeply influenced American life is symbolized by the melting pot concept. This concept was celebrated in Zangwill's play, *The Melting Pot,* staged in New York City in 1908.

Even though the strong assimilationist idea in U.S. society contributed greatly to the making of one nation out of disparate ethnic and immigrant groups, it has not eradicated ethnic and cultural differences and is not likely to do so in the future. Ethnic differences persist in U.S. society for several important reasons. Discrimination prevents many individuals and groups with particular ethnic, racial, and/or cultural characteristics from attaining full structural inclusion into U.S. society (Hacker, 1992; Cose, 1993; Feagin & Sikes, 1994; Winant, 1994). Ethnic cultures and communities often help individuals satisfy important human needs (Gay & Baber, 1987). Ethnicity also persists because of continuing immigration to the United States (U.S. Bureau of the Census, 1994).

Immigration to the United States has increased markedly since the Immigration Reform Act, enacted in 1965, became effective in 1968. Most new immigrants are coming from Spanish-speaking Latin American nations and from Asia rather than from Europe, the continent from which most American immigrants came in the past. Between 1981 and 1990, 87% of the legal immigrants to the United States came from non-European nations; about 10% came from Europe. Moreover, 87% of the immigrants to the United States during this period came from Asia (38%) and nations in the Americas (49%). Most Asian immigrants came from China, Korea, the Philippines, and India. Mexico and nations in the Caribbean were the leading sources of immigrants from the Americas (U.S. Bureau of the Census, 1994, p. 11).

The population of ethnic groups of color is increasing at a much faster rate than is the general population. If current trends continue, it is projected that the Asian American population will nearly double by the year 2000, whereas the total U.S. population will increase by 20% (Gardner, Robey, & Smith, 1985). The U.S. Hispanic population increased more than seven times faster than the rest of the population between 1980 and 1990. It increased 53 percent. Hispanics in the United States increased from 17.7 million in 1984 to more than 22.4 million in 1990 (U.S. Bureau of the Census, 1993b).

Although frequently done in the popular media, it is misleading to view Hispanics or Latinos as a single ethnic or cultural group because they speak the same language (Stavans, 1995). Extensive cultural, ethnic, and racial differences exist both among and within the various Hispanic groups, such as those from Mexico, Cuba, Puerto Rico, El Salvador, the Dominican Republic, Colombia, and Venezuela. Most Hispanics view themselves as Mexicans, Puerto Ricans, or Cubans rather than as Hispanics.

The Demographic Imperative

The ethnic texture of the United States is changing substantially. The U.S. Census projects that ethnic minorities—including Blacks, American Indians and Alaska Natives, Asian and Pacific Islanders, and persons of Hispanic origin) will make up 29.4% of the U.S. population by the year 2000 (U.S. Bureau of the Census, 1993a, p. 14). The changing ethnic texture of the U.S. population has major implications for all of the nation's institutions, including schools, colleges, universities, and the work force. These institutions must be restructured and transformed in order to meet the needs of the different kinds of peoples who will work in and be served by them. People of color will make up one-third of the net additions to the U.S. labor force between 1985 and 2000. By the year 2000, 21.8 million of the 140.4 million people in the U.S. labor force will be people of color (Johnston & Packer, 1987). Eighty % of the new entrants to the labor force will be women, immigrants, or people of color (Johnston & Packer, 1987, p. xx).

The demographic characteristics of the nation's student population is also changing greatly (Pallas, Natriello, & McDill, 1989). These authors project that by the year 2020 White students will make up only 54.5% of the nation's school population; students of color about 45.5%. Whites made up 73% of the nation's student population in 1982. Hispanics will constitute about 25.3% of the nation's student population in 2020; they made up 9.3% of the student population in 1982. The population of the nation's schools is also becoming increasingly low income. The number of children in poverty is growing in the United States and is expected to continue to grow in the future. The percentage of children in poverty increased from 14.9% in 1970 to 21.1% in 1991. About one of every five children below the age of eighteen was living below the poverty level in 1991 (U.S. Bureau of the Census, 1993a, p. 469).

American classrooms are experiencing the largest influx of immigrant students since the turn of the century. Between 1981 and 1990, about 7,338,100 legal immigrants came to the United States (U.S. Bureau of the Census, 1994, p. 11). A large but undetermined number of illegal or undocumented immigrants also enter the United States each year. The influence of an increasingly ethnically diverse population on the nation's schools, colleges, and universities is and will continue to be enormous. In fifty of the nation's largest urban public school systems, African Americans, Hispanics, Asian Americans and other non-White students made up 76.5% of the student population in 1992 (Council of the Great City Schools, 1994). In some of the nation's largest cities and metropolitan areas, such as Chicago, Los Angeles, Washington, D.C., New York, Seattle, and San Francisco, half or more of the public school students are students of color. In California, the population of students of color in the public schools exceeded the percentage of White students during the 1988/89 school year.

Students of color will make up about 46% of the nation's student population by 2020 (Pallas et al., p. 19). Most teachers now in the classroom or in teacher educational programs are likely to have students from diverse ethnic, cultural, and racial groups in their classrooms during their careers. This is true for both inner-city and suburban teachers.

A major goal of multicultural education is to transform the challenges of ethnic, cultural, and racial diversity into educational and societal opportunities. To reach this goal teachers will need to acquire new knowledge, skills, and attitudes. A major goal of this book is to help teachers attain the knowledge, skills, and attitudes they need to be effective in multicultural classrooms and schools.

Ethnic Revival Movements: A World Development

Many Americans think of ethnic and racial diversity as something uniquely American. Yet, most Western societies are racially, ethnically, and culturally diverse. Since the 1960s, ethnic revival movements have arisen in the United States, as well as in other Western nations, such as in Canada (Moodley, 1995), the United Kingdom (Figueroa, 1995), Australia (Allan & Hill, 1995), and several Western European nations (Banks & Lynch, 1986; Hoff, 1995). An ethnic revival movement occurs when an ethnic group initiates organized efforts to attain equality within a society, to eliminate discrimination toward its members, to attain structural inclusion into society, to legitimize its culture within the nation, and to shape a new, positive identity. Goals of ethnic revival movements are usually political, economic, and cultural. Ethnic revival movements tend to reinforce and intensify ethnic identifications and allegiances. Table 1-1 describes the phases that usually characterize ethnic revival movements in Western societies (Banks, 1985).

Ethnic revival movements tend to arise in nation-states that are ethnically diverse and in which ethnic stratification exists. Since World War II, the ethnic texture of Western European nations such as the United Kingdom, France, and the Netherlands has been enriched significantly by immigrants from their former colonies. Many immigrants from Southern and Eastern Europe have settled in nations such as Germany and Sweden in search of jobs and upward social mobility. Many nations in Western Europe, as well as Canada and Australia, are faced with the challenges and opportunities of educating diverse ethnic, racial, cultural, and religious groups, many of whom speak minority languages (Gill, Mayor, & Blair, 1992).

Diversity: An Opportunity and a Challenge

The kind of cultural, ethnic, racial, and religious diversity that the Western nations are experiencing is both an opportunity and a challenge to their society and institutions, including schools, colleges, and universities. When groups with different cultures and values interact within a society, ethnocentrism, racism, and religious bigotry as well as other forms of institutionalized rejection and hostility occur. Ample examples of these forms of group hostility and rejection exist in every nation characterized by racial, ethnic, and cultural

**Table I-I   PHASES IN THE DEVELOPMENT
OF ETHNIC REVITALIZATION MOVEMENTS**

The Precondition Phase

This phase is characterized by the existence of a history of colonialism, imperialism, an institutionalized democratic ideology, and efforts by the nation-state to close the gap between democratic ideals and societal realities. These factors create rising expectations among marginalized ethnic groups that pave the way for ethnic protest and a revitalization movement.

The First Phase

This is characterized by ethnic polarization, an intense identity quest by marginalized ethnic groups, and single-causal explanations. An effort is made by ethnic groups to get racism legitimized as a primary explanation of their problems. Both radical reformers and staunch conservatives set forth single causal explanations to explain the problems of marginalized ethnic groups.

The Later Phase

This phase is characterized by meaningful dialogue between marginalized and dominant ethnic groups, multiethnic coalitions, reduced ethnic polarization, and the search for multiple causal explanations for the problems of marginalized ethnic groups.

The Final Phase

Some of the elements of the reforms formulated in the earlier phases become institutionalized during this phase. Other marginalized cultural groups echo their grievances, thereby expanding and dispersing the focus of the ethnic reform movement. Conservative ideologies and policies become institutionalized during this phase, thus paving the way for the development of new ethnic revitalization movements.

diversity (van den Berghe, 1967). In several nation-states throughout the world—including the United States, the United Kingdom, and Germany—the incidents of bigoted attacks on ethnic and cultural minorities increased during the late 1980s and early 1990s (Banks & Banks, 1995; Figueroa, 1995; Hoff, 1995). Some observers linked the increase in overt bigotry to the serious economic transformations that are occurring in most Western nations.

Ethnic and cultural diversity is also an opportunity. It can enrich a society by providing novel ways to view events and situations, to solve problems, and to view our relationship with the environment and with other creatures. The exploitation of the environment is a serious problem in most developed nations, partly because of how Westerners have traditionally viewed their relationship with the earth. Traditional Indian cultures in North America viewed the earth as sacred and had deep reverence for other living creatures (McLuhan, 1971).

The challenge to Western societies and their schools is to try to shape a modernized, national culture that has selected aspects of traditional cultures coexisting in some kind of delicate balance with a modernized postindustrial society. In the past, in their singular quest for modernity and a technocratic society, the Western nation-states tried to eradicate traditional cultures and thus alienated individuals and groups from their first cultures and linguistic origins. This approach to shaping a unified nation-state has created anomie and alienation and has deprived individuals and groups of some of the most important ways in which people satisfy their needs for symbolic meaning and community. It has also resulted in the political and cultural oppression of some racial and ethnic groups within society and has consequently caused them to focus on their own particular needs and goals rather than on the overarching goals of the nation-state. Westernized nation-states will be able to create societies with overarching goals that are shared by diverse groups only when these groups feel that they have a real stake and place in their nation-states and that their states mirror their own concerns, values, and ethos. A multicultural curriculum, which reflects the cultures, values, and goals of the groups within a nation, will contribute significantly to the development of a healthy nationalism and national identity.

THE COMPLEXITY OF ETHNICITY IN AMERICAN SOCIETY

Ethnicity is an integral but complex part of American life. To acquire a sophisticated knowledge of the United States, students must master facts, concepts, generalizations, and theories related to the intricate nature of ethnicity in American society. Although ethnicity is a significant part of American life, there is a national American culture and identity shared by all groups in the United States. This national culture resulted (and is resulting) from a series of multiple acculturations (Banks, 1994). Diverse ethnic cultures, such as the Anglo-Saxon Protestant, the African, the Jewish, and the Mexican, influenced each other. The national American culture and identity consist of cultural components that have become universalized and are shared by most people within the nation. These universalized cultural components are products of the ethnic cultures in the United States and the American experience. Gleason (1980) describes the American national identity:

> To affirm the existence of American nationality does not mean that all Americans are exactly alike or must become uniform in order to be real Americans. It simply means that a genuine national community does exist and that it has its own distinctive principle of unity, its own history and its own appropriate sense of belongingness by virtue of which individuals identify with the symbols that represent and embody that community's evolving consciousness of itself. American nationality

...does not preclude the existence of ethnicity in the subgroup peoplehood-sense, but neither does the existence of the latter preclude the former. (p. 57)

In addition to the national American culture, there are ethnic and other subsocieties and institutions in the United States whose characteristics have not been universalized or become part of the shared national culture. The Anglo-Saxon Protestant subsociety, like other ethnic subsocieties, has cultural elements that are not universalized or shared by other Americans. Consequently, an individual American is ethnic to the extent that he or she functions within ethnic subsocieties and shares their values, behavioral styles, and cultures. An individual, however, may have a low level of ethnicity or psychological identification with his or her ethnic group or groups.

In Figure 1-1, the shaded area represents the American national culture shared by all ethnic and cultural groups. Circles A, B, C, and D represent ethnic subsocieties, such as the Anglo-Saxon Protestant, African American, Italian American, and Mexican American subsocieties. A major goal of the multicultural curriculum is to help students develop *cross-cultural competency,* which consists of the abilities, attitudes, and understandings students need to function effectively within the American national culture, within their own ethnic subsocieties, and within and across different ethnic subsocieties and cultures.

ETHNICITY AND INDIVIDUALS

Ethnicity becomes even more complex when we try to determine the ethnic group affiliations and identification of individuals. Many individuals in U.S. society not only perceive themselves as members of ethnic groups, but also are perceived as members of these groups by individuals outside their ethnic groups. This includes many, but not all, Americans who are Mexican, Polish, Jewish, and Vietnamese. The asterisks in the closed circles in Figure 1-2 represent individuals within these ethnic groups. However, these individuals also perceive themselves and are usually perceived by others to be American, as well as Mexican, Polish, Jewish, or Vietnamese, even though Mexican, for example, may be the first and most important identity for many Mexican Americans. Mexican Americans also share a broader American identity and the overarching idealized American values that cement the nation. Many Anglo-Saxon Protestants, such as those who are members of the Brahmin elite in Boston, also see themselves as members of a specific cultural group. Individuals represented by the asterisks in the closed circles in Figure 1-2 are clearly ethnic, from both inside and outside points of view.

Other Americans are more difficult to characterize ethnically because of how they view themselves and how others view them. These individuals are

Figure 1-1   ETHNICITY AND THE NATIONAL AMERICAN CULTURE

The shaded area represents the national American culture. Circles A, B, C, and D represent ethnic subcultures.

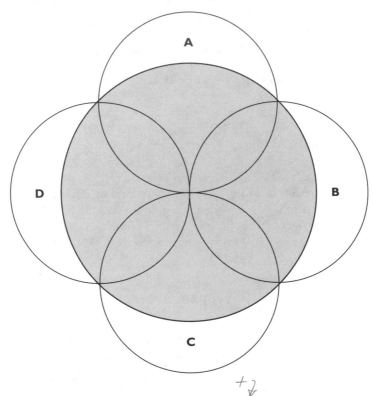

represented by the plus signs in Figure 1-2. They perceive themselves only as American and do not consciously identify with a clearly defined ethnic group. This group of Americans includes many third- and fourth-generation Irish and Scandinavians, as well as individuals with multiple European heritages. These individuals can best be described as mainstream Americans from sociological and psychological perspectives. Culturally, however, mainstream Americans share many characteristics with Anglo-Saxon Protestants because Anglo-Saxon Protestants have influenced the national culture more than any other American subgroup.

ETHNIC STUDIES: ASSUMPTIONS AND PRACTICES

Many educators realize the importance of ethnicity in U.S. society and the need to help students develop more sophisticated understandings of the diverse

Figure I-2 ETHNICITY AND INDIVIDUALS

The asterisks in the closed circles represent individuals who perceive themselves and who are perceived by other people to be members of clearly delineated ethnic groups. The plus signs [+] represents individuals who perceive themselves and are perceived by most other people to be merely *American*.

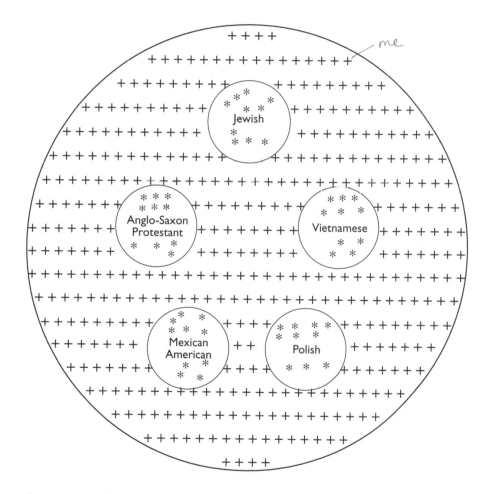

ethnic groups that make up the United States and a greater acceptance of cultural differences. Educational institutions at all levels have made some attempts to include more information about ethnic groups in the social studies, language arts, and humanities curricula. However, some assumptions about ethnic studies have adversely affected the integration of ethnic content into the curriculum. We need to examine and challenge these assumptions and related school practices and to formulate new assumptions and goals in order for the multicultural education movement to serve as a catalyst for curriculum reform and transformation. The greatest promise of ethnic studies is that it will serve as a vehicle for general curriculum reform and transformation. If ethnic content is merely added to the traditional curriculum, which has many problems (Pinar, Reynolds, Slattery, & Taubman, 1995), then efforts to modify the curriculum with ethnic content are likely to lead to a dead end. The total school curriculum should be transformed.

One pervasive assumption many educators embrace is that ethnic studies deals exclusively with groups of color, such as Asian Americans, American Indians, and African Americans. This assumption is widespread within the schools, and school programs often reflect it. In many school ethnic studies units and lessons little or no attention is devoted to the experiences of European American ethnic groups, such as Jewish Americans, Polish Americans, and Italian Americans. This narrow conceptualization of ethnic studies emerged out of the social forces that gave rise to the ethnic studies movement in the 1960s. To conceptualize ethnic studies exclusively as the study of people of color is inconsistent with how sociologists define ethnicity (Alba, 1992). It also prevents the development of broadly conceptualized comparative approaches to ethnic studies and multicultural education. Comparative approaches to ethnic studies are needed to help students understand fully the complex role of ethnicity in U.S. life and culture. Conceptualizing ethnic studies exclusively as the study of ethnic groups of color also promotes a kind of we–they attitude among many White students and teachers. Many students think that ethnic studies is the study of them (the Others), whereas American studies is the study of us. Many educators believe that ethnic studies has no place within an all-White classroom.

A related assumption, which educators often make about ethnic studies, is that only students who are members of a particular ethnic group should study that group's history and culture. Some ethnic studies units and lessons focus on one specific ethnic group, such as Puerto Ricans, African Americans, or American Indians. The ethnic group on which the units and lessons focus is usually either present or dominant in the local school population. Content related to diverse ethnic groups should be an integral part of the curriculum experienced by all students. *Ethnic modification of the total curriculum is essential.*

All students, regardless of their race, ethnicity, or social class, should study about the cogent and complex roles of ethnicity and ethnic conflict in U.S. society and culture. Most Americans are socialized within ethnic or cultural enclaves and are ethnically illiterate. Within their communities, people learn primarily about their own cultures and assume that their life-styles are the legitimate ones and that other cultures are invalid, strange, and different. The school should help students to break out of their cultural enclaves and to broaden their cultural perspectives. Students need to learn that there are cultural and ethnic alternatives within our society that they can freely embrace.

choice?

Many educators assume that ethnic studies is essentially additive in nature and that we can create a sound multicultural curriculum by leaving the present curriculum intact and adding ethnic heroes and heroines, such as Martin Luther King, Jr., Cesar Chávez, Sojourner Truth, Pocahontas, and Malinche to the list of Anglo-American heroes who are already studied in most schools. Conceptualizing ethnic studies as essentially additive in nature is problematical for several reasons. In too many classrooms throughout the nation teachers still emphasize the mastery of low-level facts and do not help students master higher levels of knowledge (Shaver, Davis, & Helburn, 1979).

Modifying the school curriculum to include ethnic content provides a tremendous opportunity to reexamine the assumptions, purposes and nature of the curriculum and to formulate a curriculum with new assumptions and goals. Merely adding low-level facts about ethnic content to a curriculum that is already bulging with discrete and isolated facts about mainstream American heroes will result in overkill. Isolated facts about Crispus Attucks and the Boston Massacre do not stimulate the intellect any more than do isolated facts about George Washington or Betsey Ross. To integrate ethnic content meaningfully into the total school curriculum, we must undertake more substantial curriculum reform. Adding facts about ethnic heroes and heroines and events of questionable historical significance is not sufficient. Transformation of the curriculum is essential.

An Expanded Definition of Ethnicity

Problems in teaching about ethnic groups result, in part, from the ways in which ethnicity and ethnic groups in the United States are often conceptualized and defined by teachers and curriculum specialists. They often limit their conceptualization of an ethnic group to an ethnic group of color or to an ethnic minority group. Teachers and curriculum specialists must have a more accurate and inclusive definition of an ethnic group in order to integrate ethnic content into the curriculum in more meaningful ways.

What is an *ethnic group?* Individuals who constitute an ethnic group share a sense of group identification, a common set of values, political and economic interests, behavioral patterns, and other culture elements that differ from those of other groups within a society. Members of an ethnic group have a shared sense of peoplehood, culture, identity, and shared languages and dialects. Alba (1992) states that Max Weber's classic definition of an ethnic group is still the most useful definition. Weber (cited in Alba) defines as ethnic group as a group whose members "entertain a subjective belief in their common descent because of similarities of physical type or of customs or both, or because of memories of colonization and migration.... It does not matter whether or not an objective blood relationship exists" (p. 575).

An individual is ethnic to the extent that he or she shares the values, behavioral patterns, cultural traits, and identification with a specific ethnic group. Many individuals have multiple ethnic group attachments; others consider themselves "American" rather than ethnic. In the 1990 United States Census about 90% of the population identified with at least one ancestry or ethnic group. About 59.9% reported a single ancestry, 29.7% a multiple ancestry, and 5.2% indicated that their ancestry was American or United States (U.S. Bureau of the Census, 1992, abstract, pp. III–1, III–4). Table 1-2 lists the most frequently reported ancestry groups:

Table 1-2 MOST FREQUENTLY REPORTED ANCESTRY GROUPS IN THE UNITED STATES, 1990

Group	Number
German	58 million
Irish	39 million
English	33 million
African American	24 million
Italian	54 million
Mexican	12 million
French	10 million
Polish	9 million
American Indian	9 million
Dutch	6 million
Scotch-Irish	6 million

SOURCE: U.S. Bureau of the Census, 1990 Census of Population Supplementary Reports. *Detailed Ancestry Groups for States.* CP-S-1-2. Washington, D.C.: Bureau of the Census. Issued October, 1992.

An individual's identity with his or her ethnic group varies significantly with the times in his or her life, with economic and social status, and with the situations and/or settings. Ethnicity is very important for some Americans and of little or only symbolic importance to others. Other groups, such as religious, social class, regional, gender, or occupational groups, are more important to many individuals. As members of lower socioeconomic ethnic groups attain more economic mobility, their social class interests often become more important to them than their ethnic affiliations.

In this book, ethnic studies is conceptualized broadly, as it is in the *Harvard Encyclopedia of American Ethnic Groups* (Thernstrom, Orlov, & Handlin, 1980). Information, materials, and strategies for teaching about White ethnic groups, such as Italian Americans and Jewish Americans, as well as about the experiences of ethnic groups of color, such as Mexican Americans,

Puerto Ricans, and Indochinese Americans, are included. To conceptualize ethnic studies more narrowly will result in curricula that are too limited in scope and that will not help students understand fully both the similarities and differences in the experiences of the diverse groups in the United States.

The multicultural curriculum should enable students to derive valid generalizations and theories about the characteristics of ethnic groups and to learn how they are alike and different, in both their past and present experiences. Even though it is neither possible nor necessary for the curriculum of a particular school or district to include content about every ethnic group in the United States (there are more than 100), each curriculum *should* focus on a range of groups that *differ* in their racial characteristics, cultural experiences, languages, histories, values, and current problems. By studying a range of ethnic and cultural groups, students will be able to formulate valid comparative generalizations and theories about the nature of race, ethnicity, and culture in U.S. society. The curriculum can be transformed only when events, concepts, and issues are studied from the perspectives of a range of cultural and ethnic groups.

Ethnic Minority Groups/People of Color

Even though an ethnic group shares a common set of values, behavioral patterns, culture traits, and a sense of peoplehood, an ethnic minority group can be distinguished from an ethnic group. An ethnic minority has unique physical and/or cultural characteristics that enable people who belong to mainstream groups to identify its members easily and thus to treat them in a discriminatory way. Jewish Americans are an ethnic minority group with unique cultural and religious characteristics. African Americans are an ethnic minority group with both unique physical and cultural characteristics.

An ethnic minority group is often a numerical minority and comprises only a small percentage of the national population. In 1990, ethnic minorities (including Hispanics of all races) in the United States made up 25% of the national population. However, as pointed out previously, the non-White percentage of the U.S. population is growing at a much faster rate than is the rest of the population. The U.S. Census projects that by 2050 minorities will make up about 49% of the total U.S. population (U.S. Bureau of the Census, 1993a, p. 14). The concept *minority* is becoming increasingly misleading and less useful in the United States as the population of people of color becomes closer to that of Whites.

In many school districts and schools, and in the school-age population of California and Hawaii, students of color constitute majorities. In part for this reason educators and social scientists are increasingly referring to groups such as African Americans, Hispanics, and Asian Americans as *people of color* rather than as ethnic *minorities*. Educators and social scientists are realizing that many terms and concepts used in the past do not accurately and sensitively describe ethnic, racial and cultural realities today. Table 1-3 shows the population of the major ethnic groups in the United States in 1970, 1980 and 1990.

ETHNIC STUDIES: A PROCESS OF CURRICULUM REFORM

Ethnic content should not be studied only by ethnic groups of color or be limited to specialized courses. Rather, ethnic studies should be viewed as a process of curriculum reform and transformation that will result in the creation of a new curriculum based on new assumptions and new perspectives. Such a transformed curriculum will help students gain novel views of the American experience and a new conception of what it means to be an American. Because the English immigrants assumed control of most economic, social, and politi-

Table 1-3 POPULATION OF ETHNIC GROUPS
IN THE UNITED STATES, 1970, 1980, AND 1990

Ethnic Group	1970 Population	1980 Population	1990 Population
Total	203,211,926	226,504,825	248,710,000
White Americans*	177,748,975	188,340,790	199,686,000
African Americans	22,580,289	26,488,218	29,986,060
Hispanics	9,072,602	14,608,673	22,354,000
Mexican Americans	4,532,435	8,740,439	13,496,000
Puerto Ricans	1,429,396	2,013,945	2,728,000
Cubans	544,600	803,226	1,044,000
Other Spanish Origin			5,086,000
Jewish Americans			5,981,000
American Indians	792,730	1,361,869	1,878,000
Eskimos		42,149	57,000
Aleuts		14,177	24,000
Asians or Pacific Islanders			7,274,000
Chinese Americans	431,583	812,178	1,645,000
Filipino Americans	336,731	781,894	1,407,000
Japanese Americans	588,324	716,331	848,000
Korean Americans	69,510	357,393	799,000
Asian Indians		387,223	815,000
Vietnamese Americans			615,000
Native Hawaiians	100,179	172,346	211,000

SOURCE: U.S. Bureau of the Census, *Statistical Abstract of the United States: 1994* (114th ed.). Washington, D.C.: U.S. Government Printing Office, p. 30.

*This figure includes the roughly 53% of Hispanics who classified themselves as White in the 1990 Census.

cal institutions early in U.S. national history, to Americanize has been interpreted to mean to *Anglicize*. During the height of nativism in the late 1800s and early 1900s, the English-Americans defined *Americanization* as *Anglicization* (Higham, 1972). This notion of Americanization is still widespread within U.S. society and schools today. Thus, when we think of American history and American literature, we tend to think of Anglo-American history and of literature written by Anglo-American authors.

Reconceptualizing American Society

Because the assumption that what is Anglo-American is American is so deeply ingrained in curriculum materials and in the hearts and minds of many students and teachers, we cannot transform the curriculum by merely adding a unit or a lesson here and there about African American, Jewish American, or Italian American history or literature. Rather, we need to examine seriously the conception of American that is perpetuated in the curriculum and the basic canon, assumptions, and purposes that underlie the curriculum.

It is essential to reconceptualize how we view American society and history in the school curriculum. We should view American history, literature, art, music, and culture from diverse ethnic and cultural perspectives rather than primarily or exclusively from the point of view of mainstream historians, writers, and artists. Most courses in the curriculum are taught primarily from mainstream perspectives (Applebee, 1989). These types of lessons, units, and courses are based on what I call the *Mainstream Centric Model*, or Model A (see Figure 1-3). Ethnic studies, as a process of curriculum reform, can and often does proceed from Model A to Model B, the *Ethnic Additive Model*. In courses and experiences based on Model B, ethnic content is additive to the major curriculum thrust, which remains mainstream-oriented. Many school districts that have attempted ethnic modification of the curriculum have implemented Model B-type curriculum changes. Courses on specific ethnic groups, such as African Americans and Mexican Americans, and special units on ethnic groups, are examples of Model B types of curricular experiences.

Teaching Multicultural Perspectives: A Model C Curriculum

Curriculum reform should proceed directly from Model A to Model C, the *Multiethnic Model*. In courses and experiences based on Model C, the curriculum is transformed and students study historical, social, artistic, and literary events and concepts from several ethnic, cultural and gender perspectives. Mainstream perspectives are only one group of several and are in no way superior or inferior to other perspectives.

Figure I-3   ETHNIC STUDIES AS A PROCESS OF CURRICULUM REFORM

Ethnic studies is conceptualized as a process of curriculum reform that can lead from only mainstream perspectives on our history and culture (Model A—*Mainstream Centric Model*), to multiethnic perspectives as additives to the major curriculum thrust (Model B—*Ethnic Additive Model*), to a completely multicultural curriculum, in which every historical and social event is viewed from the perspectives of different cultural and ethnic groups (Model C—*Multiethnic Model*). In Model C mainstream perspectives are among several and are in no way superior or inferior to other perspectives. In Model D (*Ethno-National Model*), students study historical and social events from the perspectives of groups in several different nations. Many schools that have attempted ethnic modification of the curriculum have implemented Model B types of programs. It is suggested here that curriculum reform move directly from Model A to Model C and ultimately to Model D. However, in districts that have Model B types of programs, it is suggested that they move from Model B to Model C and eventually to Model D types of curriculum organizations.

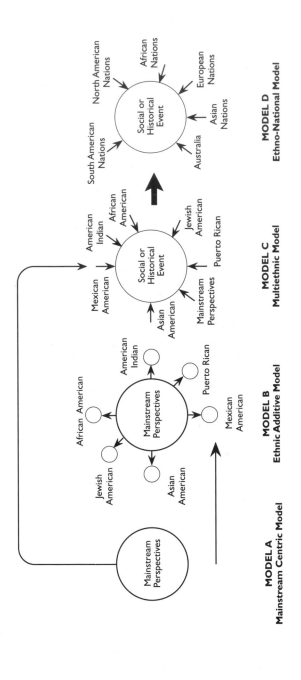

MODEL A
Mainstream Centric Model

MODEL B
Ethnic Additive Model

MODEL C
Multiethnic Model

MODEL D
Ethno-National Model

I am not suggesting that we eliminate or denigrate mainstream historians, writers, and artists, or mainstream perspectives on U.S. society and culture. I am suggesting that mainstream perspectives should be among many different perspectives taught in the various content areas. Only by approaching the study of American society and culture in this way will students obtain a holistic, rather than an ethnocentric, view of our nation's history and culture.

A writer's or artist's experience and culture, including his or her ethnic or community culture, cogently influences his or her works and views of the past and present. Feminists call this influence *positionality* (Code, 1991; Tetreault, 1993). Positionality is used to describe how race, culture, social class, and gender—as well as other personal and cultural factors—influence how we view our society and the world. However, it would be simplistic to argue that there is one mainstream view of history, art, literature, or contemporary events, or one African American view. Wide differences in experiences and perceptions exist both within and across ethnic and cultural groups.

People who have experienced a historical event or social phenomenon, such as racial discrimination or internment, often view and express the event differently than do people who have watched it from a distance. There is no one mainstream perspective on the internment as there is no one Japanese American view of it. However, accounts written by people who were interned, such as Takashima's powerful *A Child in Prison Camp* (Takashima, 1971) often provide insights and perspectives that cannot be provided by people who were not interned. Individuals who viewed the internment from the outside can also provide unique and important perspectives. Hence, both insider and outsider perspectives should be studied in a sound multicultural curriculum (Merton, 1972). Table 1-4 consists of a lesson that illustrates how to teach more than one perspective on an event.

Only by looking at events from many different perspectives can we fully understand the complex dimensions of American culture and society. Various ethnic and cultural groups are often influenced by events differently and perceive and respond to them differently. Important goals of the multicultural curriculum are to broaden students' conceptions of what *American* means and to present them with new ways to view and interpret American society, literature, music, and art. Any goals that are less ambitious. while important, will not result in curriculum transformation.

Ethnic Studies and Global Education

Students should also study world events, issues, and concepts from diverse cultural perspectives and points of view. The world studies program in schools is often characterized by a Model-A type Eurocentric approach. Events, concepts, and issues are viewed primarily or exclusively from the per-

Table 1-4 TEACHING MULTIPLE PERSPECTIVES:
CHRISTOPHER COLUMBUS AND THE ARAWAKS

The students are presented with the following excerpts from Christopher Columbus's diary that describes his arrival in an Arawak Indian community in the Caribbean in 1492. These are some of the observations that Columbus makes about the Arawaks:

> *They took all and gave all, such as they had, with good will, but it seemed to me that they were a people very lacking in everything. They all go naked as their mothers bore them, and the women also, although I saw only one very young girl.... They should be good servants and quick to learn, since I see that they very soon say all that is said to them, and I believe that they would easily be made Christians, for it appeared to me that they had no religious beliefs. Our Lord willing, at the time of my departure, I will bring back six of them to Your Highnesses, that they may learn to talk. I saw no beast of any kind in this island, except parrots.*

The students are then encouraged to view Columbus's statement from the perspective of the Arawaks. The Arawaks had an aural culture and consequently left no written documents. However, archaeologist Fred Olsen studied Arawak artifacts and used what he learned from them to construct a day in the life of the Arawaks, which he describes in his book, *On the Trail of the Arawaks*. The students are asked to read an excerpt from Olsen's account of a day in the life of the Arawaks and to respond to these questions:

1. Columbus wrote in his diary that he thought the Arawaks had no religious beliefs. You read about Arawak life in the report by Fred Olsen. Do you think Columbus was correct? Why?
2. Accounts written by people who took part in or witnessed (saw) an historical event are called primary sources. Can historians believe everything they read in a primary source? Explain.

SOURCES: Jan, C. (1930). *The Voyages of Christopher Columbus*. London: The Argonaut Press. Olsen, F. (1974). *On the Trail of the Arawaks*. Norman: University of Oklahoma Press.

spectives of mainstream groups in European nations and cultures. Model D (the Ethno-National Model) provides rich opportunities for linking ethnic studies and global education. In this model students study global events, issues, and concepts from the perspectives of ethnic groups within different nations, as illustrated in Figure 1-4. It is important to link ethnic studies and global education because they share several important goals and because the population of the United States is constantly being changed by the infusion of ethnic and immigrant groups from beyond its borders. Ethnic studies helps

Figure 1-4 MODEL D—THE ETHNO-NATIONAL MODEL

This figure illustrates how an event, problem, issue, or concept can be viewed from the perspectives of ethnic groups within several nations. A study of ethnic perspectives within other nations will help students gain a global framework for viewing and studying human events and problems.

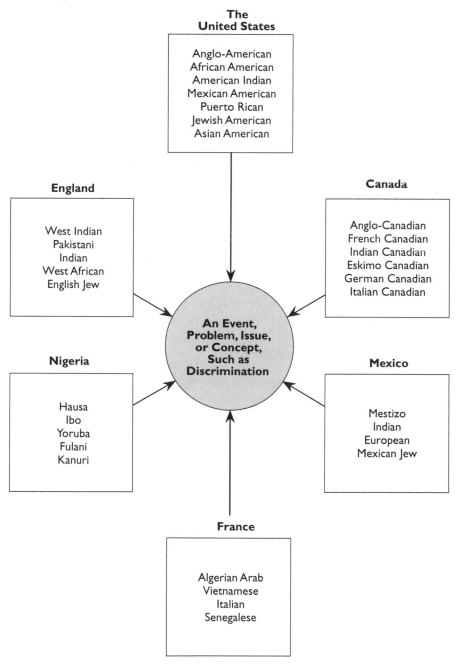

students better understand the lands and cultures from which these groups come.

Distinguishing Multicultural and Global Eduation

Although it is important to link multicultural and global education, it is essential that they not be confused and that one is not substituted for the other. Sometimes when teachers integrate Mexico, Japan, and Nigeria into their lessons they will claim that these topics constitute multicultural education. Global and multicultural education should be distinguished. Each makes unique and important contributions to the education of students. Multicultural education deals with ethnic, cultural, and gender groups within the United States (Banks & Banks, 1995). Global education deals with nations outside the United States and the interrelationships among nations (Merryfield, 1993).

The Canon and Curriculum Reform

A major reason that the curriculum in U.S. schools and colleges remains Anglocentric, Eurocentric, and male dominated is that the canon on which the mainstream curriculum is based is rarely made explicit, defined, or discussed. However, during the late 1980s and early 1990s a vigorous debate about the canon on which the mainstream curriculum is based took place. The dominant canon was questioned seriously by scholars of color and by feminists (Fitzgerald & Lauter, 1995; Tetreault, 1993). It was defended by mainstream scholars such as Cheney (1987), D'Souza (1991), and Schlesinger (1991). During the 1980s mainstream scholars established two organizations to defend the dominant canon—the Madison Center and the National Association of Scholars.

A canon is a "norm, criterion, model or standard used for evaluating or criticizing [and] a basic general principle or rule commonly accepted as true, valid, and fundamental" (*Webster's Third New International Dictionary,* 1986, p. 328). A specific and identifiable canon is used to define, select, and evaluate knowledge in the school and university curriculum in the United States and in other Western nations. This canon is rarely explicitly defined or discussed. It is taken for granted, unquestioned, and internalized by writers, researchers, teachers, professors, and students. It is European-centric and male dominated. It often marginalizes the experiences of people of color, Third World nations and cultures, and the perspectives and histories of women.

The struggle over the inclusion of ethnic content and content about women in the school, college, and university mainstream curriculum can best be understood as a battle over who will participate in or control the formulation of the canon or standard used to determine what constitutes a liberal education. The guardians and defenders of the established canon believe that it serves their interests and consequently the interests of the society and nation-state. They also view it as consistent with their experiences and perspectives and their visions of the future. People who criticize the established canon, such as many ethnic and feminist scholars, believe that it marginalizes their experiences and voices and results in a curriculum that largely ignores their histories and cultures (Graff, 1992; Fitzgerald & Lauter, 1995; Schmitz, Butler, Rosenfelt, & Guy-Sheftall, 1995). Critics of the established canon have established two national organizations, the National Association of Multicultural Education and Teachers for a Democratic Culture.

The people who formulate a canon or standard shape it in their own image and in ways that present their experiences, voices, and perspectives as essential parts of the human experience. The people who do not participate in formulating or shaping a canon are often marginalized or invisible in the curriculum that emanates from it. Students of color, such as African Americans and Mexican Americans, have been active voices on college and university campuses, demanding that the canon be transformed so that it recognizes and legitimizes their histories and cultures as essential parts of the United States and the world. Only when the canon is transformed to reflect cultural diversity will students in our schools, colleges, and universities be able to attain the knowledge, skills, and perspectives needed to participate effectively in the diverse society and world of the next century.

Approaches to Teaching Multicultural Content

Several identifiable approaches to the integration of ethnic content into the curriculum have evolved within the last two decades. The *Contributions Approach* to integration is one of the most frequently used. This approach is characterized by the addition of ethnic heroes into the curriculum. This approach to curriculum reform is usually a Model A (Mainstream centric) type of curriculum change because the ethnic heroes and heroines added to the curriculum are not only viewed from a mainstream-centric perspective but are also usually selected for inclusion into the curriculum using mainstream criteria. Consequently, ethnic heroes and heroines viewed positively by the mainstream society, such as Booker T. Washington, Marian Anderson, and Sacajawea, are most often chosen for study rather than are ethnic Americans who challenged the dominant class and social structure in society, such as W. E. B. Du Bois, Geronimo, and Angela Davis.

The mainstream curriculum remains unchanged in terms of its basic structure, goals, and salient characteristics. This is the easiest approach for teachers to use to integrate the curriculum with ethnic content. However, it has several serious limitations. Students do not attain a comprehensive view of the role of ethnic and cultural groups in U.S. society. Rather, they see ethnic issues and events primarily as an addition to the curriculum and thus as an appendage to the main story of the nation's development.

Content, concepts, themes, and perspectives are added to the curriculum without changing its basic structure, purpose, and characteristics in the *Additive Approach.* This approach is consistent with Model B, or the Ethnic Additive Model discussed earlier in this chapter. The content, concepts, and issues added to the curriculum are viewed primarily from mainstream perspectives. This approach is often accomplished by the addition of a book, a unit, or a course to the curriculum without changing it substantially. The Additive Approach allows the teacher to put ethnic content into the curriculum without restructuring it, which takes substantial time, effort, training, and rethinking of the curriculum and its purposes, nature, and goals.

The Additive Approach can be the first phase in a more radical curriculum reform effort designed to restructure the total curriculum and to integrate it with ethnic content, perspectives, and frames of reference. However, this approach shares several disadvantages with the Contributions Approach. Its most important shortcoming is that it usually results in the viewing of ethnic content from the perspectives of mainstream historians, writers, artists, and scientists because it does not involve a restructuring of the curriculum.

The *Transformation Approach,* which incorporates Model C, the Multiethnic Model, differs fundamentally from the Contributions and Additive Approaches. This approach changes the basic assumptions of the curriculum and enables students to view concepts, issues, themes, and problems from several ethnic perspectives and points of view. The key curriculum issue involved in the Transformation Approach is not the addition of ethnic groups, heroes, heroines, and contributions, but the infusion of various perspectives, frames of reference, and content from different groups that will extend students' understandings of the nature, development, and complexity of the United States and the world.

The *Social Action Approach* includes all of the elements of the Transformation Approach and adds components that require students to make decisions and take actions related to the concept, issue, or problem they have studied. Table 1-5 lists possible actions developed by a junior high school social studies class after studying a unit on the civil rights movements of the 1960s and 1970s.

The four approaches to the integration of ethnic content into the curriculum described above are often mixed and blended in actual teaching situations (see Figure 1-5). The move from the lower to the higher levels of ethnic content integration is likely to be gradual and cumulative. An important goal of teaching about racial, cultural, and ethnic diversity should be to empower students with the knowledge, skills, and attitudes they need to participate in

Table I-5 STUDENT ACTION

After a unit on the civil rights movement of the 1960s and 1970s, Mr. Carson's 7th grade social studies class made this list of actions they could take to help reduce discrimination in their personal lives, their school, and community.

1. Making a personal commitment to stop telling racist jokes.
2. Making a commitment to challenge our own racial and ethnic stereotypes either before or after we verbalize them.
3. Compiling an annotated list of books about ethnic groups that we will ask the librarian to order for our school library.
4. Asking the principal to order sets of photographs that show African Americans and other people of color who have jobs that represent a variety of careers. Asking the principal to encourage our teachers to display these photographs on their classroom walls.
5. Observing television programs to determine the extent to which people of color, such as African Americans and Asian Americans, are represented in such jobs as news anchors and hosts of programs. Writing to local and national television stations to express our concern if we discover that people of color are not represented in powerful and visible roles in news or other kinds of television programs.
6. Contacting a school in the inner-city to determine if there are joint activities and projects in which we and they might participate.
7. Asking the principal or the board of education in our school district to require our teachers to attend inservice staff development workshops that will help them learn ways in which to integrate content about ethnic and racial groups into our courses.
8. Sharing some of the facts that we have learned in this unit, such as that by the year 2000, one out of every three Americans will be a person of color, with our parents and discussing these facts with them.
9. Making a personal commitment to have a friend from another racial, ethnic, or religious group by the end of the year.
10. Making a personal commitment to read at least one book a year that deals with a racial, cultural, or ethnic group other than my own.
11. Do nothing; take no actions.

civic action that will help transform our world and enhance the possibility for human survival.

The Goals of the Multicultural Curriculum

Concepts, content, and teaching strategies cannot be identified and selected until goals are clearly defined. The development of decision-making and social action skills is the key goal for the multicultural curriculum presented in this book. The multicultural curriculum should help students develop the ability to make reflective decisions on issues related to ethnicity and to take

Figure 1-5   LEVELS OF INTEGRATION OF ETHNIC CONTENT

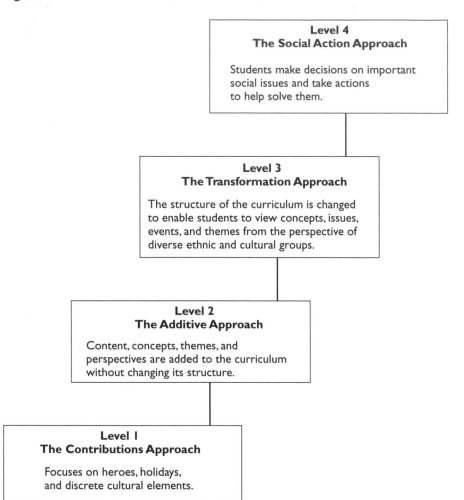

personal, social, and civic actions to help solve the racial and ethnic problems in our national and world societies. Effective solutions to the enormous ethnic and racial problems in our nation and world can be found only by an active and informed citizenry capable of making reflective personal and public decisions. Chapter 4 discusses decision making and its components in more detail.

The multicultural curriculum should also help students view historical and contemporary events from diverse ethnic perspectives, clarify their ethnic identities, and function effectively within their own ethnic communities. Individuals must clarify their own ethnic and cultural identities before they can relate positively to people who belong to different racial and ethnic groups. Educators need to foster the development of self-acceptance, but to discourage ethnic ethnocentrism.

The multicultural curriculum should also help individuals develop cross-cultural competency—the ability to function within a range of cultures. Although individuals within a pluralistic society must learn to accept their own ethnic and cultural identities and become comfortable with them, they must also learn to function effectively within other cultures and to respond positively to individuals who belong to other ethnic and cultural groups. They also need to learn how to interact with members of different ethnic groups and how to resolve conflicts with them.

Another important goal of the multicultural curriculum is to provide students with cultural and ethnic alternatives. Both the Anglo-Saxon Protestant and the Filipino American student should be provided with cultural and ethnic options in the school. Historically, the school curriculum has focused primarily on the cultures of Anglo-Saxon Protestants. The school was, and often is, primarily an extension of the homes and communities of Anglo-Saxon Protestant students. It rarely presents Anglo students with cultural and ethnic alternatives, thereby denying them the richness of the music, literature, art, values, life-styles, and perspectives that exist among such ethnic groups as Jews, Greeks, Puerto Ricans, and African Americans. Many behaviors and values within these ethnic groups can help mainstream Anglo students to enrich their personal and public lives.

The multicultural curriculum should also try to reduce ethnic and cultural encapsulation and enable students to understand their own cultures better. Individuals who only know, participate in, and see the world from their unique cultural and ethnic perspectives are denied important aspects of the human experience and are culturally and ethnically encapsulated. These individuals are unable to know and see their own cultures fully because of their cultural and ethnic blinders. The multicultural curriculum seeks to help individuals gain greater self-understanding by viewing themselves from the perspectives of other cultures.

The multicultural curriculum should also help students to expand their conceptions of what it means to be human, to accept the fact that ethnic minority cultures are functional and valid, and to realize that a culture can be evaluated only within a particular cultural context. Because cultures are made by people, there are many ways of being human. By studying this important generalization, students will hopefully develop an appreciation for the great capacity of human beings to create a diversity of life-styles and to adapt to a variety of social and physical environments. All students also need ethnic content to help them better understand themselves and the world in which they live. The ethnic experience is part of the human experience; education should deal with the total experience of humankind.

Another important goal of the multicultural curriculum is to help students master essential reading, writing, and computational skills. Multicultural theorists believe that ethnic content can help students master important skills in these content areas. Multiethnic readings and data, if taught effectively, can be highly motivating and meaningful. Students are more likely to master skills when the teacher uses content that deals with significant human problems, such as ethnicity within our national and world societies. Content related to ethnicity in the United States and in the world—and to the ethnic communities in which many students live—is significant and meaningful to students, especially those who are socialized within ethnic communities. Skill goals are extremely important in an effective multicultural curriculum.

EDUCATION FOR SURVIVAL IN THE TWENTY-FIRST CENTURY

The current school curriculum is not preparing most students to function successfully within the ethnically and culturally diverse world of the future. Many students grow up in middle-class, mainstream communities and attend predominantly mainstream, middle-class schools. Their world is very different from the world society in which they will be required to function in the future. The White race is a world minority. Two out of three people in the world live in poor and developing nations in regions such as Africa, Asia, and Latin America. Yet, the one out of three people in the world who live in the developed Western nations consume most of the earth's resources and exercise most of the world's political and economic power. The world is sharply divided between the few who are rich and well-fed in the Western developed nations—who are predominantly White—and the many who are poor and hungry in the developing nations, who are predominantly people of color. These sharp divisions also exist within nations.

Allport's seminal theory teaches us that people from diverse groups can work cooperatively to solve problems only when they function in equal-status situations and when they perceive their fates as shared (1979). We will not be able to substantially reduce ethnic, racial, and cultural tension in the United States and the world until most people have a decent standard of living and a modicum of political and economic power. Groups from different ethnic groups, races, cultures, and nations who have highly unequal amounts of power, influence, and wealth are rarely able to work cooperatively to solve difficult human problems. A major goal of education for survival in a multicultural global society is to help students acquire the knowledge, attitudes, and skills needed to participate in the reformation of the world's social, political, and economic systems so that peoples from diverse ethnic, cultural, and religious groups will be politically empowered and structurally integrated into their soci-

eties. Helping students to acquire the competencies and commitments to participate in effective civic action in order to create equitable national societies is the
most important goal for multicultural education in the twenty-first century.

SUMMARY

The curriculum within the nation's schools, colleges, and universities should
be transformed so that it will accurately reflect the ethnic, cultural, and racial
diversity within the United States. Schools, colleges, and universities are using
various approaches to infuse ethnic content into the curriculum, including the
contributions and additive approaches. Each of these approaches has important problems. To respond adequately to the ethnic realities within the nation
and the world, the curriculum should be transformed and should help students
to develop decision-making and social-action skills.

QUESTIONS AND ACTIVITIES

1. The melting pot concept does not accurately describe the nature of ethnicity in
the United States. React to this position by stating whether you agree or disagree with
it and why.

2. Make a list of the different ethnic, racial, and cultural groups that constitute
your ethnic heritage. Compare your list with similar lists made by other individuals in
your class or workshop. What conclusions can you derive about ethnicity in U.S. society by analyzing these data?

3. Study the results of the last national or local election. Note particularly the
voting patterns of predominantly ethnic communities. What generalizations can you
make on the basis of these data? What are the limitations of your generalizations?

4. Interview a curriculum coordinator in one or two local school districts. Ask
this individual to describe the school's efforts to implement multicultural education. If
the school focuses on some ethnic groups and not on others, ask for an explanation of
this practice. How do your findings compare with the trends described in this chapter?

5. According to the author, what should be the goals of the multicultural curriculum? Write, in one sentence or more, what you think should be the goals of the multicultural curriculum. Compare your statement with the goals listed in this chapter. In
what ways are your statement and the listed goals alike and different? Why? How are
your assumptions about ethnic studies and ethnicity similar to and different from those
of the author?

6. Divide into small discussion groups in your class or workshop. Appoint a
group leader and a reporter for each group. Discuss the following questions in your
groups. When the small group discussions have ended, the class or workshop should

reassemble. Reporters should give a brief summary of each group's discussion. The large group should then react both to the reports and to the following questions:

    a. Which of the Curricular Models presented in Figure 1-3 best describes the curriculum in your school or in a school that you have attended or in which you have observed?

    b. Do you think it would be desirable to help your school (or a school that you have attended or in which you have observed) move from one Model to another? (For example, move from Model A to B or from B to C.)

    c. What problems might you, as a teacher, encounter in trying to move your school (or a school that you have attended or in which you have observed) curriculum from one Model to another? (For example, moving from Model A to Model C.)

    d. How might these problems best be overcome?

    e. What benefits might result for both you and the students if your school (or the school that you have attended or in which you have observed) changed from one Model to another?

7. Define each of the following concepts and terms and tell why each is important:

the melting pot	Ethno-National Model
ethnic group	sense of peoplehood
ethnic minority group	contributions approach
people of color	additive approach
Mainstream Centric Model Ethnic	transformation approach
Additive Model	social action approach
Multiethnic Model	

REFERENCES

Alba, R. (1992). Ethnicity. In E. F. Borgatta & M. L. Borgatta (Eds.). *Encyclopedia of Sociology* (Vol. 2, pp. 575–584). New York: Macmillan.

Allan, R. & Hill, B. (1995). Multicultural Education in Australia: Historical Development and Current Status. In J. A. Banks & C. A. M. Banks (Eds.). *Handbook of Research on Multicultural Education* (pp. 763–777). New York: Macmillan.

Allport, G. W. (1979). *The Nature of Prejudice* (25th anniv. ed.). Reading, Mass.: Addison-Wesley. (Original work published 1954.)

Applebee, A. N. (1989). *A Study of Book-Length Works Taught in High School English Courses*. Albany, N.Y.: Center for the Learning and Teaching of Literature.

Banks, J. A. (1985). Ethnic Revitalization Movements and Education. *Educational Review 37*(2), 131–139.

Banks, J. A. (1994). *Multiethnic Education: Theory and Practice* (3rd. ed.). Boston: Allyn and Bacon.

Banks, J. A. & Banks, C. A. M. (Eds.). (1995). *Handbook of Research on Multicultural Education*. New York: Macmillan.

Banks, J. A. & Lynch, J. (Eds.). (1986). *Multicultural Education in Western Societies*. London: Holt, Rinehart and Winston.

Cheney, L. V. (1987). *American Memory: A Report on the Humanities in the Nation's Schools.* Washington, D.C.: U.S. Government Printing Office.

Code, L. (1991). *What Can She Know? Feminist Theory and the Construction of Knowledge.* Ithaca, N.Y.: Cornell University Press.

Cose, E. (1993). *The Rage of a Privileged Class.* New York: HarperCollins.

Council of the Great City Schools. (1994). *National Urban Education Goals: 1992–1993 Indicators Report.* Washington, D.C.: Author.

D'Souza, D. (1991). *Illiberal Education: The Politics of Race and Sex on Campus.* New York: The Free Press.

Feagin, J. R. & Sikes, M. P. (1994). *Living with Racism: The Black Middle-Class Experience.* Boston: Beacon Press.

Figueroa, P. (1995). Multicultural Education in the United Kingdom: Historical Development and Current Status. In J. A. Banks & C. A. M. Banks (Eds.). *Handbook of Research on Multicultural Education* (pp. 778–800). New York: Macmillan.

Fitzgerald A. K. & Lauter, P. (1995). Multiculturalism and Core Curricula. In J. A. Banks & C. A. M. Banks (Eds.). *Handbook of Research on Multicultural Education* (pp. 729–746). New York: Macmillan.

Gardner, R. W., Robey, B., & Smith, P. C. (1985). Asian Americans: Growth, Change and Diversity. *Population Bulletin, 40*(4), 1–44.

Gay, G. & Barber, W. L. (Eds.). (1987). *Expressively Black: The Cultural Basis of Ethnic Identity.* New York: Praeger.

Gill, D., Mayor, B., & Blair, M. (Eds.) (1992). *Racism and Education: Structures and Strategies.* London: Sage Publications Ltd.

Gleason, P. (1980). American Identity and Americanization. In S. Thernstrom, A. Orlov, & O. Handlin (Eds.). *Harvard Encyclopedia of American Ethnic Groups* (pp. 31–58). Cambridge: Harvard University Press.

Graff, G. (1992). *Beyond the Culture Wars: How Teaching the Conflicts Can Revitalize American Education.* New York: Norton.

Hacker, A. (1992). *Two Nations: Black and White, Separate, Hostile, Unequal.* New York: Ballantine Books.

Higham, J. (1972). *Strangers in the Land: Patterns of American Nativism 1860–1926.* New York: Atheneum.

Hoff, G. (1995). Multicultural Education in Germany: Historical Development and Current Status. In J. A. Banks & C. A. M. Banks (Eds.). *Handbook of Research on Multicultural Education* (pp. 821–838). New York: Macmillan.

Johnston, W. B. & Packer, A. E. (1987). *Workforce 2000: Work and Workers for the 21st Century.* Indianapolis: Hudson Institute.

McLuhan, T. C. (1971). *Touch the Earth: A Self-Portrait of Indian Existence.* New York: Promontory Press.

Merryfield, M. M. (1993). Reflective Practice in Global Education: Strategies for Teacher Educators. *Theory into Practice 32*(1), 27–32.

Merton, R. K. (1972). Insiders and Outsiders: A Chapter in the Sociology of Knowledge. *The American Journal of Sociology 78*(1), 9–47.

Moodley, K. A. (1995). Multicultural Education in Canada: Historical Development and Current Status. In J. A. Banks & C. A. M. Banks (Eds.). *Handbook of Research on Multicultural Education* (pp. 801–820). New York: Macmillan.

Pallas, A. M., Natriello, G., & McDill, E. L. (1989). The Changing Nature of the Disadvantaged Population: Current Dimensions and Future Trends. *Educational Researcher 18*(5), 16–22.

Pinar, W. F., Reynolds, W. M., Slattery, P., & Taubman, P. M. (1995). *Understanding Curriculum: An Introduction to the Study of Historical and Contemporary Curriculum Discourses.* New York: Peter Lang.

Schlesinger, A. M., Jr. (1991). *The Disuniting of America: Reflections on a Multicultural Society.* Knoxville, Tenn.: Whittle Direct Books.

Schmitz, B., Butler, J., Rosenfelt, D., & Guy-Sheftall, B. (1995). Women's Studies and Curriculum Transformation. In J. A. Banks & C. A. M. Banks (Eds.). *Handbook of Research on Multicultural Education* (pp. 708–728). New York: Macmillan.

Shaver, J. P., Davis, O. L., Jr., & Helburn, S. W. (1979). The Status of Social Studies Education: Impressions from Three NSF Studies. *Social Education, 43,* 150–153.

Stavans, I. (1995). *The Hispanic Condition: Reflections on Culture and Identity in America.* New York: HarperCollins.

Takashima, S. (1971). *A Child in Prison Camp.* Montreal, Canada: Tundra Books.

Tetreault, M. K. (1993). Classrooms for Diversity: Rethinking Curriculum and Pedagogy. In J. A. Banks & C. A. M. Banks (Eds.). *Multicultural Education: Issues and Perspectives* (2nd ed., pp. 129–148). Boston: Allyn and Bacon.

Thernstrom, S., Orlov, A., & Handlin, O. (Eds.). (1980). *Harvard Encyclopedia of American Ethnic Groups.* Cambridge: Harvard University Press.

U.S. Bureau of the Census. (1992). *Detailed Ancestry Groups for States* (1990 Census of Population Supplementary Reports, 1990 CP-S-1-2). Washington, D.C.: U.S. Government Printing Office.

U.S. Bureau of the Census. (1993a). *Statistical Abstract of the United States* (113th edition). Washington, D.C.: U.S. Government Printing Office.

U.S. Bureau of the Census. (1993b). *We the Americans . . . Hispanics.* Washington, D.C.: U.S. Government Printing Office.

U.S. Bureau of the Census. (1994). *Statistical Abstract of the United States* (114th ed.). Washington, D.C.: U.S. Government Printing Office.

van den Berghe, P. L. (1967). *Race and Racism: A Comparative Perspective.* New York: Wiley.

Winant, H. (1994). *Racial Conditions: Politics, Theory, Comparisons.* Minneapolis: University of Minnesota Press.

Webster's Third New International Dictionary. (1986). (Unabridged). Springfield, Mass.: Merriam-Webster, Inc.

ANNOTATED BIBLIOGRAPHY

Banks, J. A. (1994). *An Introduction to Multicultural Education.* Boston: Allyn and Bacon.

This brief book introduces preservice and practicing education to the major issues and concepts in multicultural education. It includes sample lessons, an evaluation checklist, and a bibliography.

Banks, J. A. (1994). *Multiethnic Education: Theory and Practice* (3rd ed.). Boston: Allyn and Bacon.

This book discusses the historical, conceptual, and philosophical issues in the fields of multicultural and multiethnic education. It includes an important chapter on "Reducing Prejudice in Students: Theory, Research, and Strategies."

Banks, J. A. & Banks, C. A. McGee. (Eds.). (1993). *Multicultural Education: Issues and Perspectives* (2nd ed.). Boston: Allyn and Bacon.

A group of scholars in multicultural education discuss educational issues and strategies related to ethnicity, race, gender, social class. religion, and exceptionality in this introduction to multicultural education.

Banks, J. A. & Banks, C. A. M. (Eds.). (1995). *Handbook of Research on Multicultural Education*. New York: Macmillan.

In forty-seven chapters and 882 pages, the leading scholars in multicultural education and related disciplines discuss the history, philosophy, practice, and future of the field. An important reference book for libraries and staff development collections.

DuBois, C. & Ruiz, V. L. (Eds.). (1994). *Unequal Sisters: A Multicultural Reader in U.S. Women's History* (2nd ed.). New York: Routledge.

An important collection of articles about women from diverse racial and ethnic groups.

Franklin, J. H. (1993). *The Color Line: Legacy for the Twenty-First Century*. Columbia: University of Missouri Press.

A noted historian describes the persistence of racism in American life and society.

Hawley, W. D. & Jackson, A. W. (Eds.). (1995). *Toward a Common Destiny: Improving Race and Ethnic Relations in America*. San Francisco: Jossey-Bass.

This edited volume includes chapters that deal with a range of issues, including interethnic and interracial relations, race and ethnic categories, ethnic identity and multicultural competence, and oppositional identity and African Americans.

hooks, b. (1994). *Teaching to Transgress: Education as the Practice of Freedom*.

bell hooks, the noted African American feminist, describes education as the practice of freedom in this book that describes a liberating pedagogy, a powerful strategy for multicultural teaching.

Loewen, J. W. (1995). *Lies My Teacher Told Me: Everything Your American History Textbook Got Wrong*. New York: The New Press.

The author critiques twelve leading high school American history textbooks and gives his own perspectives on historical events.

Okihiro, G. Y. (1994). *Margins and Mainstreams: Asians in American History and Culture*. Seattle: University of Washington Press.

The author documents how movements for human freedom often originated within the communities of people of color and of other groups on the margins of society. A thoughtful and stimulating book.

Rethinking Our Classrooms: Teaching for Equity and Justice (a special issue of *Rethinking Schools*). (1994). Milwaukee, Wisc.: Rethinking Schools.

This special issue of the interesting, informative, and teacher-friendly publication, Rethinking Schools, *includes many interesting ideas and suggested activities that classroom teachers will find helpful.*

Takaki, R. (1993). *A Different Mirror: A History of Multicultural America.* Boston: Little, Brown.

Takaki provides new perspectives on the development of America that are important for teachers and students.

Todorov. T. (1982). *The Conquest of America: The Question of the Other.* New York: HarperCollins.

A thoughtful and informative book that provides perceptive insights into Columbus, Cortes, and the concept of the "Other." An important book for gaining a new perspective on America.

2

DEVELOPING A CONCEPTUAL MULTICULTURAL CURRICULUM

The key goal of the multicultural curriculum should be to help students develop decision-making and citizen-action skills. The decision-making process consists of several components, including knowledge, values, the synthesis of knowledge and values, and action designed to implement the decision made. However, the knowledge that comprises reflective decision making must have certain characteristics. It must be scientific, higher level, conceptual, and interdisciplinary. Reflective decision makers must identify the sources of their values, determine how these values conflict, identify value alternatives, and choose freely from among the alternatives. They act only after identifying alternative courses of action, ordering them according to personal values, and expressing a willingness to accept the possible consequences of their actions.

This chapter focuses on the knowledge components of decision making. A presentation of the interdisciplinary conceptual approach is followed by a discussion of four categories of knowledge: *facts, concepts, generalizations,* and *theories.* You must be able to identify the categories of knowledge in order to structure interdisciplinary and conceptual lessons and units. Chapter 3 discusses concepts you can use to organize multicultural lessons and units. The valuing and social action components of the multicultural curriculum are discussed in chapter 4. Key issues related to the selection and evaluation of multicultural teaching materials are also discussed in chapter 4.

THE INTERDISCIPLINARY-CONCEPTUAL APPROACH

A decision-making curriculum is not only characterized by the sequential development of higher-level ideas; it is also *interdisciplinary*. In such a curriculum, concepts, when feasible and appropriate, are viewed from the perspectives of several disciplines and subject areas, such as the various social sciences, art, music, literature, physical education, communication, the physical and biological sciences, and mathematics.

It is necessary for students to view events and situations from the perspectives of several disciplines because any one discipline gives them only a partial understanding of issues and concepts related to ethnic and cultural diversity in society. Concepts such as *discrimination* and *ethnic diversity* are not merely sociological; they also have multiple dimensions. They have economic, political, legal, cultural, and moral aspects. The values and experiences of people of color are reflected in their literature, art, music, drama, dance, communication styles, and foods. Dominant ethnic groups within a society also express issues related to ethnic diversity and respond to these issues in their artistic and cultural forms. Students must view concepts and issues related to ethnic groups from diverse disciplinary perspectives in order to gain a complete understanding of the experiences of the diverse cultural and ethnic groups in the United States and the world.

STUDYING CULTURE: AN EXAMPLE OF THE INTERDISCIPLINARY CONCEPTUAL APPROACH

When students study a concept such as *culture,* they can gain a global understanding only by viewing ethnic cultures from the perspectives of the various social sciences and by examining the expressions of ethnic cultures in literature, music, drama, dance, art, communication, and foods. Content and insights from science and mathematics can also be incorporated into an interdisciplinary study of cultures. The next section discusses special issues involved in incorporating science and mathematics into the multicultural curriculum.

Concepts such as *culture* can be used to organize units and activities related to ethnicity that are interdisciplinary and cut across disciplinary lines. Other concepts, such as cultural assimilation, acculturation, and values, can also be analyzed and studied from an interdisciplinary perspective. However, it is neither possible nor desirable to teach each concept in the curriculum from the perspectives of all disciplines and curricular areas. Such an attempt would result in artificial relationships and superficial learnings by students.

There are many excellent opportunities within the curriculum for teaching concepts from an interdisciplinary perspective. Interdisciplinary teaching, however, requires the strong cooperation of teachers in the various content areas. Team teaching will often be necessary, especially at the high school level, to organize and implement interdisciplinary units and lessons. Table 2-1 contains key questions that students can pursue when they study cultures from an interdisciplinary perspective. Figure 2-1 illustrates the process.

INCORPORATING ELEMENTS FROM SCIENCE AND MATHEMATICS INTO THE MULTICULTURAL CURRICULUM

Incorporating elements from science and mathematics into the multicultural curriculum is difficult for most teachers. Issues related to science and mathematics can be incorporated into the multicultural curriculum in at least three ways: (1) ways related to content; (2) ways related to perspectives, paradigms, and concepts; and (3) ways related to equity issues (Banks, 1995b; Atwater, 1994; Secada, 1992; Secada, Fennema, & Adajian, 1995).

Some content related to science and mathematics can be incorporated into the multicultural curriculum. In science, the biological basis of skin color and the other physical characteristics of various racial groups can be studied. However, when the biological basis of race is studied, students should be helped to understand that race is largely a *socially constructed* concept or category even though scientists have attempted to formulate different racial categories (Banks, 1995b; Barkan, 1992; Gould, 1981). Health issues and diseases related to various ethnic groups are other appropriate subjects for science in the multicultural curriculum.

The experiences of various ethnic and cultural groups in science, in both past and contemporary society, is another appropriate study for science in the multicultural curriculum. The lives of African American scientists such as Daniel Hale Williams and Ernest E. Just should be examined in the scientific component of the multicultural curriculum. These individuals made significant contributions to science despite the blatant discrimination they experienced. Contemporary scientists from diverse groups should also be studied.

Content related to mathematics in the multicultural curriculum can highlight the role played by groups such as the Egyptians and Aztecs in the development of theory and practice in mathematics (Mason, 1962; Sertima, 1986). In the film *Stand and Deliver,* Mr. Escalante uses his knowledge of Aztec contributions to mathematics to motivate his Mexican American students to study calculus. Mr. Escalante reminds his students that their ancestors, the Aztecs, made significant mathematical breakthroughs. Students can also examine the experiences of mathematicians today from various cultural and racial groups.

Another important way to view science and mathematics in the multicultural curriculum is to examine the basic concepts, paradigms, and perspectives

Table 2-1 STUDYING ETHNIC CULTURES
FROM AN INTERDISCIPLINARY PERSPECTIVE

Discipline or Curriculum Area	Key or Focus Question
Social Studies	In what ways are the cultures of ethnic groups such as African Americans, Jewish Americans, and Mexican Americans similar and different? Why?
Reading and Literature	How do the fiction and other literary works by American ethnic authors reveal characteristics and components of their cultures?
Music	What does the music of an ethnic group reveal about its values, symbols, and culture?
Drama	What do plays written by ethnic authors reveal about their culture?
Physical Education	How do ethnic groups express their cultures, values, aspirations, and frustrations in their dances and creative movements?
Art	What does the art of an ethnic group reveal about its life-styles, perceptions, values, history, and culture?
Communication (Language Arts)	How does the language of an ethnic group express and reflect its values and culture? What can we learn about an ethnic group by studying its symbols and communication styles, both verbal and nonverbal?
Home Economics	What do ethnic foods reveal about an ethnic group's values and culture? What can we learn about an ethnic culture by studying its foods?
Science	How do the physical characteristics of an ethnic group influence its interactions with other groups, intragroup relationships, and its total culture?
Mathematics	What is the relationship between the number system used within a society and its culture? What do the symbol systems within a culture reveal about it? Historically, what contributions have different ethnic groups made to our number system?

used in science and mathematics and the influence these paradigms, concepts, and perspectives have had and still have on various ethnic and cultural groups (Banks, 1995b; Barkan, 1992; Gould, 1981). This can be done more readily in science than in mathematics. Darwin's theory of evolution as well as other scientific theories—such as the genetic theory of intelligence—have historically been used—and are being used today—to support scientific racism (Gould, 1981; Herrnstein & Murray, 1994). Students can examine scientific racism from both a historical and contemporary perspective (Banks, 1995b).

Figure 2-1 STUDYING ETHNIC CULTURES FROM AN INTERDISCIPLINARY PERSPECTIVE

This figure illustrates how a concept such as *culture* can be viewed from the perspectives of a number of disciplines and areas. Any one discipline gives only a partial understanding of a concept, social problem, or issue. Thus, multicultural units and lessons should be interdisciplinary and cut across disciplinary lines.

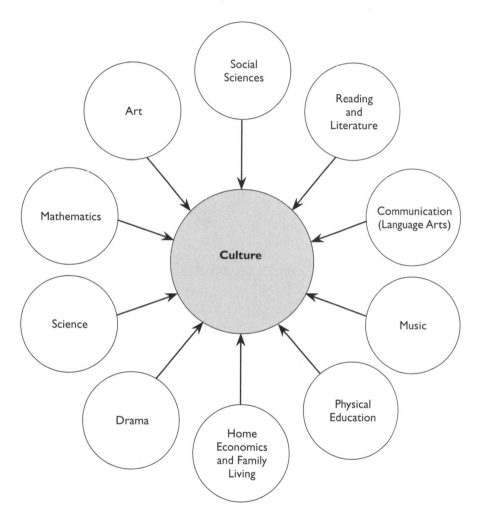

Levins and Lewontin, using a Marxist dialectic, argue that scientists act within a social context and from a philosophical perspective that is inherently political (1985). Students can examine the Levins and Lewontin thesis and determine the extent to which it is applicable to their science textbooks and readings. Students can also study such questions as these: What major assumptions, concepts, and perspectives do scientists use today that are related to the experiences of ethnic groups? What major influence are these assumptions, concepts, and perspectives having on the experiences of ethnic groups? Students can also examine how applied mathematics is being used to influence societal issues and practices.

When examining how scientists have constructed ideas about the low IQs of African Americans and other minority groups historically and today, the students can examine the arguments set forth by Herrnstein and Murray (1994) in *The Bell Curve* about the inferior intellectual abilities of Blacks and can discuss questions such as these: Why did Herrnstein and Murray create their theory? What groups in society benefit from it? What groups in society are hurt by it? Why are theories such as the one by Herrnstein and Murray created and popularized by the mass media when many scientists have serious doubts about them? The students can read critiques of the Herrnstein and Murray theory in *The Bell Curve Debate,* edited by Jacoby and Glauberman (1995).

A third and perhaps the most important way in which science and mathematics teachers can include multicultural content in their curricula is by examining equity issues in science and mathematics and by modifying their teaching techniques and expectations in order to enhance the academic achievement of students of color and of women. Researchers have indicated that students of color and female students often do not achieve as well as White males in higher-level mathematics and science courses (Belenky, Clinchy, Goldberger, & Tarule, 1986).

Students of color and female students also take fewer high-level mathematics and science courses than do White males. Researchers have suggested that these situations result in part from low teacher expectations and from the teaching styles used in science and mathematics courses that are inconsistent with how many students of color and female students learn (Belenky, Clinchy, Goldberger, & Tarule, 1986; Slavin, 1983). To make their teaching multicultural, science and mathematics teachers should encourage their students of color and their female students to enroll in higher-level courses, provide these students with support and encouragement, and modify their teaching techniques to make them more consistent with the learning styles of students of color and female students. Fullilove and Treisman (1990) have found that cooperative teaching and learning strategies can help students of color to learn advanced calculus.

THE FORMS OF KNOWLEDGE

I have illustrated how a key concept such as culture can be viewed from diverse disciplinary perspectives. To identify and select key concepts such as culture, you must be familiar with the nature of knowledge and its various forms—including *facts, concepts, generalizations,* and *theories.* These major knowledge forms and the contribution that each can make to an interdisciplinary and conceptual multicultural curriculum are discussed and highlighted next.

Facts

Facts are low-level, specific empirical statements about limited phenomena. Facts may be considered the lowest level of knowledge, and they have the least predictive capacity of all of the knowledge forms. In multicultural studies, as in all academic areas and disciplines, facts are the building blocks of knowledge. Students must master facts in order to learn higher levels of knowledge.

Examples of facts are:

- The Chinese immigrants who came to San Francisco in the 1800s established the *hui kuan.*
- More than 200,000 legal immigrants came to the United States from Mexico in 1992.
- Between 1981 and 1992, 986,200 legal immigrants from Europe settled in the United States.

A careful study of these facts about U.S. ethnic groups reveals several characteristics of factual statements. First, facts are *empirical* statements, or statements that can be tested with available data or data that can be obtained. By carefully studying and analyzing historical documents and statistical data, a social scientist can determine whether the Chinese immigrants who came to the United States in the 1800s actually established *hui kuan* societies. It is important to stress that factual statements are capable of verification or testing; however, many statements presented as facts, especially in multicultural studies, are on closer scrutiny normative or value statements that cannot be tested or can be tested only with great difficulty. An example of such a statement is "Indians were hostile." This statement is actually a misleading stereotype masquerading as a factual statement.

Because factual statements are limited in explaining causal relationships, students need to master higher levels of knowledge in addition to facts. Facts should not be the end goal of instruction because they are very limited. Many teachers end units by testing students primarily for their mastery of facts. Because facts, in and of themselves, do not encompass a large quantity of data, they have little transfer value, are quickly forgotten by students, and do not, if they are the end goal of instruction, help students to gain in-depth understandings of society.

However, to say that facts are limited in the contribution they can make to students' understanding of social events and problems is not to say that they are not important and that they do not have a proper role in instruction—quite the contrary. Factual statements are important in teaching. If you keep their limitations in mind and use them judiciously, they can contribute to student learning. Facts are the foundations of the higher levels of knowledge: *concepts, generalizations,* and *theories.* Without learning facts, as I later illustrate, students will not be able to master concepts and generalizations. However, you are justified in teaching facts only if they are used to help students develop higher forms of knowledge or to make decisions. Thus, for every fact you select for inclusion in the curriculum, you should have a concept, generalization, or theory in mind that the fact is intended to help the students develop. Facts taught randomly and in isolation have little instructional value. Yet, they can become powerful instructional tools if they are carefully selected and taught.

Concepts

Concepts are words or phrases that enable us to categorize or classify a large class of observations and thus to reduce the complexity of our environment. In structure and function, concepts differ from facts, generalizations, and theories. Both facts and generalizations are empirical *statements;* a theory consists of a system of interrelated generalizations and principles. However, concepts are special constructs because they are necessary for the formulation of the other categories of knowledge and are contained in all facts, generalizations, and theories. Because concepts are contained in all other forms of knowledge, students cannot understand a fact, generalization, or theory unless the concepts contained within them are meaningful.

The following are some of the key concepts discussed in chapter 3:

Cultural assimilation	Culture
Structural assimilation	Immigration
Acculturation	Power
Race	Values
Economic oppression	

Even though concepts are contained in all facts, generalizations, and theories, they are unique because they can also encompass a large range of facts and generalizations. A complete theory can be formulated about a single concept, such as cultural assimilation or discrimination. Some concepts are rather concrete, such as *street;* others are more abstract, such as *megalopolis.* Some concepts, such as city, are somewhere between these two extremes. We might call these kinds of concepts *intermediate-level* concepts. Thus, if we arrange these concepts into a hierarchy, it would look like this:

megalopolis

city

street

In this example, *megalopolis* is the highest-level concept because it consists of a region made up of several cities and their surrounding areas. *City* is the next-level concept because a city contains many streets. Of course, there are parallel concepts that are more concrete than *street*.

Concepts encompassing generalizations are often more abstract (or at a higher level) than are concepts that are contained in the generalizations encompassed. Also, the concepts contained in facts are often less abstract than those used to classify those facts. The same is true for theories. The example below illustrates how a higher-level concept, *immigration*, can be used to categorize a number of facts. The facts, of course, contain many concepts.

HIGHER-LEVEL CONCEPT: Immigration
Facts being categorized or grouped under concept:

- Between 1820 and 1979, 36,267,000 European immigrants came to the United States.
- By 1860, there were 34,933 Chinese in the United States.
- In 1900, 24,326 Japanese lived in the United States.
- In 1992, 77,700 Vietnamese immigrated to the United States.

Higher-level concepts can also encompass or classify generalizations (see discussion below for definition of a generalization). In the example below, the concept *culture* is used to categorize a number of generalizations at varying levels of abstractions.

CONCEPT: Culture

Generalizations being categorized or grouped under concept:

- An ethnic minority group usually acquires some of the values, behaviors, and beliefs of the dominant ethnic groups within a society.
- Dominant ethnic groups usually acquire some of the cultural characteristics of ethnic minority groups.
- African Americans have made a number of contributions to American music.

In many cases, some concepts are clearly at a higher level than are others. For example, city is a higher-level concept than street because a city contains many streets. However, because a concept appears in a factual statement does not necessarily mean that it is a lower-level or concrete concept. Study this factual statement:

More than 77,000 Vietnamese immigrants arrived in the United States in 1992.

This factual statement contains the higher-level concept, *immigrant*. As previously illustrated, the concept *immigration* can be used to categorize a number of facts. The distinguishing characteristic of a higher-level concept is that it is able to categorize a number of facts and generalizations. This is true even though that same concept may sometimes appear within factual statements. By identifying higher-level concepts, you will be able to help students relate discrete facts and data to form generalizations about ethnicity, which they can apply when studying ethnic and cultural groups both within the United States and in other nations. Table 2-2 illustrates how key concepts can be used to do a comparative study of ethnic groups within the United States and in other nations.

Table 2-3 illustrates one strategy for teaching a concept. This strategy is called "Lesson Plan for Attaining a Concept." Try teaching this lesson to a group of students or to a group of your classmates or colleagues in your workshop. After teaching this lesson, respond to this question: What are the advantages of using a conceptual approach to teaching?

Generalizations

A generalization contains two or more concepts and states the relationship between them. Like empirical facts, generalizations are scientific statements that can be tested and verified with data. Generalizations are useful tools in instruction because they can be used to summarize a large mass of facts and to show the relationship between higher-level concepts that students have mastered. Like concepts, generalizations vary greatly in their level of inclusiveness. There are low-level generalizations, which are little more than summary statements, and there are high-level generalizations, which are universal in applicability. To illustrate levels of generalizations, we study one fact listed earlier in this chapter and state generalizations at various levels that encompass it.

FACT: The Chinese immigrants who came to San Francisco in the 1800s established the *hui kuan.*

Lower-Level Generalization: Chinese immigrants in America established various forms of social organizations.

Intermediate-Level Generalization: All groups that have immigrated to the United States have established social organizations.

Highest-Level or Universal Generalization: In all human societies, forms of social organizations emerge to satisfy the needs of individuals and groups.

Table 2-2 A COMPARATIVE STUDY OF ETHNIC GROUPS IN DIFFERENT NATIONS

Key Concepts and Related Key Questions	Filipino Americans (USA)	British Pakistanis	French Canadians	Nigerian Ibos	Mexican Indians	French Algerians
Origins Is the group native or did it migrate or immigrate to its current location? If immigrant group, what caused the immigration?						
Discrimination Is the group experiencing discrimination? If so, what kinds? If not, why not?						
Culture What are the group's unique cultural and ethnic characteristics?						
Assimilation To what extent is the group assimilated both culturally and structurally?						

(Continued)

Table 2-2 *CONTINUED*

Key Concepts and Related Key Questions	Filipino Americans (USA)	British Pakistanis	French Canadians	Nigerian Ibos	Mexican Indians	French Algerians
Economic Status Is the group facing economic problems or does it have a secure economic status?						
Education Are the group's youths experiencing problems in the schools? Why or why not?						
Power What role does the group play in the political system? Has it been able to organize and to exercise political power effectively?						
Ethnic Revitalization Is the group experiencing or has it experienced an ethnic revitalization movement? Explain.						

Table 2-3 LESSON PLAN FOR ATTAINING A CONCEPT

1. Write "Rite of Passage" on the board. Ask the students to repeat the words.
2. List these examples of rites of passage on the board and tell the students, "These are examples of rites of passage":

Marriage ceremony
Christening ceremony
Funeral
Vision quest among the Zuni Indians
Baptism
Bar Mitzvah
Bas Mitzvah

3. Ask the students to describe what these examples of the concept have in common. Put the list on the board.
4. Help the students to identify and state the critical attributes of "rite of passage."
5. Ask the students to write a definition of "rite of passage" using the list of key attributes that they formulated above. Their definitions should be a variation of this one: "Ceremonies that mark a critical transition in the life of an individual from one phase of the life cycle to another."*

Follow-up Activity: Ask the students to interview parents and other family members to find out what rites of passages have taken place in their families. Ask them to share at least one family rite of passage in which they have participated or observed. Ask the students: "What important functions do rites of passage play for individuals, families, and societies?"

---

*This definition is from Theodorson, G. A. & Theodorson, A. G. (1979). *A Modern Dictionary of Sociology.* New York: Barnes and Noble, p. 350.

A study of these examples indicates that a generalization is a higher-level statement than a fact because a generalization encompasses a number of facts. The fact noted above tells us only that Chinese Americans established one kind of social organization, the *hui kuan.* The lower-level generalization in our example reveals that Chinese Americans established a variety of social organizations. Thus, the lower-level generalization encompasses not only the fact about the *hui kuan* but also the following facts:

- Chinese immigrants in America formed organizations called clans.
- The Chinese Benevolent Association is a confederation of clans and secret societies.
- Secret societies emerged within Chinese communities in the United States.
- The Chinese secret societies provided help to Chinese Americans and obtained control of gambling in Chinese American communities.

The next generalization in the example, an intermediate-level generalization, encompasses facts not only about Chinese Americans, but also about all immigrants and migrants in the United States. Thus, this generalization is at a higher level of abstraction because it encompasses more facts than the lower-level generalization. For example, the intermediate-level generalization, in addition to encompassing the facts about Chinese American organizations, encompasses the following facts:

- Puerto Ricans established the Puerto Rican Forum to help solve the problems of Puerto Rican migrants in New York City.
- Jewish Americans founded the Anti-Defamation League of B'nai B'rith to help mitigate anti-Semitism in the United States.
- In 1921, Spanish-speaking Americans formed the *Orden Hijos de America* (Order of the Sons of America) to train its members for U.S. citizenship.
- Japanese immigrants in America created the Japanese Association to provide services for its members.
- The National Urban League was founded in 1911 to help African American southern migrants adjust to city life.

The last generalization is the highest form of generalization possible because it encompasses all the other facts and generalizations above it, and it applies to all human societies in the past and present. Note that it does not contain a reference to any particular people, region, or culture. One way to determine whether a generalization is written at the highest possible level is to ascertain whether it is limited to a particular people, culture, or historical era. A generalization of wide applicability contains few or no exceptions and can be tested and verified, to varying degrees, within any human culture. The highest-level generalization in the example states that in every past and present human society, one can find examples of social organizations. This generalization has been tested and verified by social scientists. Whether they studied a preliterate tribe in New Zealand or the cultures in Medieval Europe, social scientists found types of social organizations such as the family and some kind of kinship system. It is true that the forms these organizations take vary greatly both within and between cultures, but nevertheless they exist.

It is necessary for you to be able to identify and write generalizations at various levels in order to incorporate ethnic content into the curriculum. During initial planning, you should identify generalizations of the highest order so that you can then select content samples from a variety of cultures to enable students to test them. If you start planning by identifying lower-level or intermediate-level generalizations, you will be greatly limited in the content that you can select to exemplify the generalizations. For example:

Chinese immigrants in America established various forms of social organization.

If you selected this generalization on which to organize instruction, you would not be able to help students derive generalizations related to the organizations that other ethnic groups, such as Anglo-Saxon Protestants, Mexican Americans, Jewish Americans, and Arab Americans, have formed in the United States.

You should begin planning by identifying high-level concepts and generalizations (often called key or organizing generalizations in this book) and then should select lower-level concepts and generalizations related to the chosen content *samples*. This type of planning is necessary in order to help students develop higher-level statements—one of the ultimate goals of instruction. Chapter 4 discusses procedures you can use to identify high-level concepts and generalizations that can form the core of a sound multicultural curriculum.

We have noted that generalizations range from the concrete to those that are universal in application. A fact related to a Chinese American institution, the *hui kuan,* was chosen to illustrate how a single fact can be encompassed by generalizations at three different levels. The choice of three levels was an arbitrary decision; generalizations at fewer or more levels could have easily been written. For example, Hilda Taba has identified four levels (or orders, as she calls them) of generalizations (Taba, Durkin, Fraenkel, & McNaughton, 1971). Because generalizations exist at many different levels, it is not necessary for you to spend undue time trying to devise elaborate schemes for classifying levels of generalizations.

However, to plan effective units and lessons, you should know that generalizations exist at many different levels, that all generalizations are at a higher level than facts, and that the highest-order or -level generalizations should be identified during the initial stages of unit planning.

Earlier in this chapter, I said that a generalization is a statement capable of being tested or verified. This is true; but because human behavior is so complex, generalizations in the social and behavioral sciences are always tentative statements and can never be proven 100% correct. Almost always, social science generalizations will have some exceptions. Because social science generalizations tend to be tentative and nonconclusive, they often contain qualifying words.

Study this generalization: *When an ethnic minority group is oppressed and it sees no legitimate ways to alleviate its problems, rebellions will sometimes occur.* The word *sometimes* qualifies this generalization because in many situations an ethnic minority group may feel oppressed and see no legitimate ways to alleviate its problems, yet ethnic rebellions may not occur. Japanese Americans, when they were forced to leave their homes during World War II and were sent to internment camps, did not resist or rebel as a group, although some individuals did resist internment. One social scientist has hypothesized that most Japanese Americans cooperated with the federal government because of the norms within their culture toward authority and because they did not believe that resistance would succeed (Kitano, 1976). On the other hand, many African Americans who felt oppressed in our cities in the late 1960s violently rebelled. The particular times, the culture of a group, and the group's perceptions of its social and economic status greatly influence how it will respond to an oppressive situation. This example is used merely to illustrate that students should be taught how tentative social science conclusions and generalizations are and *should learn that social knowledge is constantly changing and is never absolute.*

Generalizations are important in instruction because they enable students to make predictions; the predictive capacity of generalizations varies directly with their degree of applicability and amount of empirical support. Generalizations that describe a large class of behaviors and that have been widely verified are the most useful for making predictions. We have called these types of generalizations *high-level or organizing* generalizations. Generalizations enable students not only to predict behavior with a fairly high degree of accuracy, but also to solve problems in novel situations.

Theory

Theory is the highest form of knowledge and is the most useful for predicting human behavior. I stated that a *concept* is a word or phrase used to categorize or classify facts, data, and other forms of information and knowledge. A *generalization* is defined as a statement showing the relationship between two or more concepts that can be empirically verified. A review of the definitions of these terms is important because a theory consists of a number of interrelated generalizations. The generalizations within a theory constitute a deductive system and are logically interrelated. The generalizations contained within a theory are also high-level and *universal-type* generalizations; they are not low-level ones. A theory is called a *deductive* system because when several generalizations within a theory are stated, the concluding ones can be logically derived. In other words, when given some propositions within a theory, a conclusion can be derived from the stated generalizations. An empirical theory has the following characteristics:

- It consists of a set of interrelated lawlike propositions or generalizations that are testable.
- The propositions must show the relationship between variables or concepts that are clearly defined.
- The propositions must constitute a deductive system and be logically consistent: unknown principles must be derivable from known ones.
- The propositions must be a source of testable hypotheses.

The following example of a theory illustrates how the deductive process works. Gordon's (1964) theory of cultural and structural assimilation has heavily influenced the field of ethnic studies. Here are the four major generalizations within this theory:

1. With regard to *cultural behavior,* differences of social class are more important and decisive than are differences of ethnic group.

2. With regard to *social participation* in primary groups and primary relationships, people tend to confine these to their own social class segment within their own ethnic group, that is, the *ethclass*.

3. With a person of the same social class but of a different ethnic group, one shares behavioral similarities but not a sense of peoplehood.

4. With those of the same ethnic group but of a different social class one shares a sense of *peoplehood* but not behavioral similarities *[emphases added]*. (pp. 52–53)

Gordon's theory satisfies our criterion of a theory: *a system of high-level interrelated generalizations that constitute a deductive system.* In the first generalization in the theory, Gordon hypothesizes that in terms of cultural behavior, social class is more important than ethnicity. By cultural behavior, he means such things as the values a person holds, his or her speech patterns, and occupational aspirations.

This generalization suggests that an upper-class African American individual's clothing, values, and foods are likely to be more similar to those of an upper-class White than to those of a lower-class African American. The second generalization in the theory suggests that an upper-class Mexican American, while sharing cultural characteristics with White Anglo-Saxons, is more likely to participate in the private clubs and cliques of other upper-class Mexican Americans than in Anglo-Saxon private clubs and social cliques. The theory hypothesizes that even though upper-status individuals within different ethnic groups share similar values and behavior, their close, primary group relationships are highly confined to members within their ethnic groups of the same social class. This is also true for lower-class members of ethnic groups. Gordon presents much compelling evidence in his book to support the generalizations that comprise his theory.

Gordon's theory (1964) meets the criterion of a theory because when given generalizations one and two of his theory (presented above), one can logically derive generalizations three and four. To do so, however, it might be necessary to know how he defines two key concepts in his generalizations: *ethclass* and *sense of peoplehood*. He defines ethclass as the "subsociety created by the intersection of the vertical stratifications of ethnicity with the horizontal stratifications of social class" (pp. 52–53). Thus, lower-middle-class Vietnamese Americans constitute an ethclass. By *sense of peoplehood*, Gordon means "an individual's identification with a group that shares a common culture, religious beliefs, and values" (p. 23). He contends, for example, that African Americans in all social classes share an ethnic identification.

Grand and Middle Range Theories

Social science has few *grand* theories. Grand theories try to explain all of behavior. Freudian psychology is an example of a grand theory in social science. As Merton (1968) points out, most theories in social science are what he calls "theories of the middle range." Gordon's theory is middle range because it tries to explain only behavior related to cultural assimilation. Although Gordon's theory of assimilation has much explanatory power, it was created more than thirty years ago; ethnic and race relations have changed in some important ways since Gordon first constructed his theory. Gordon's theory needs to be examined in light of new findings and studies in social science. Heath and McLaughlin (1993), for example, found that for many of the teenagers they studied ethnicity or race was not their primary or most important identity. These youth often formed social groupings that cut across racial and ethnic lines.

Using Theories in Teaching

To help students fully understand the ethnic experience in the United States, you should, whenever possible, help them relate generalizations to a theoretical system. Generalizations have much more meaning when they are studied within a theoretical framework than when studied in isolation.

Because of their specialized structure and function, a complete theory can be structured around a single concept. Gordon's theory of cultural and structural assimilation is an example of a theory formed around the concept of assimilation. Cultural assimilation occurs when one ethnic group attains the values and behavior patterns of another ethnic group. Usually the ethnic minority group attains the cultural characteristics of the dominant ethnic group. Structural assimilation occurs when one ethnic group participates in the primary groups, such as private clubs and social cliques, of another ethnic group (Gordon, 1964). Gordon concludes that even though widespread cultural assimilation has taken place in U.S. society, little structural assimilation has occurred because ethnic groups within U.S. society, including dominant ethnic groups and people of color, participate mainly in the primary groups of their own ethnic communities. He maintains that our society has a high degree of cultural assimilation but is characterized by *structural pluralism* (Gordon, 1964). Although Gordon's theory probably explains large classes of ethnic behavior in the United States, the research by Heath and McLaughlin (1993) problematizes his theory.

AN EFFECTIVE MULTICULTURAL CURRICULUM

Major goals of an effective multicultural curriculum are to help students develop the ability to make reflective decisions on personal and public issues and to take successful action. Integrating the curriculum with ethnic content can be viewed as a process of curriculum reform. During this process, the entire curriculum is transformed to enable students to view events, concepts, and issues from diverse ethnic and cultural perspectives.

The multicultural curriculum is broadly conceptualized and includes the study of a wide range of ethnic groups. These groups are studied using a comparative approach. The multicultural curriculum is also conceptual and inter-disciplinary. Major concepts, when feasible and appropriate, are studied from the perspectives of disciplines such as the various social sciences, art, literature, communication, and the physical and biological sciences. Figure 2-2 summa-rizes the characteristics of an effective multicultural curriculum. The next chapter (chapter 3) discusses key concepts that can be used to plan and orga-nize a multicultural curriculum.

Figure 2-2   THE COMPONENTS OF AN EFFECTIVE
MULTICULTURAL CURRICULUM

The effective multicultural curriculum must be conceptual, broadly conceptualized, interdisciplinary, comparative, decision-making and social-action focused, and viewed as a process of curriculum transformation.

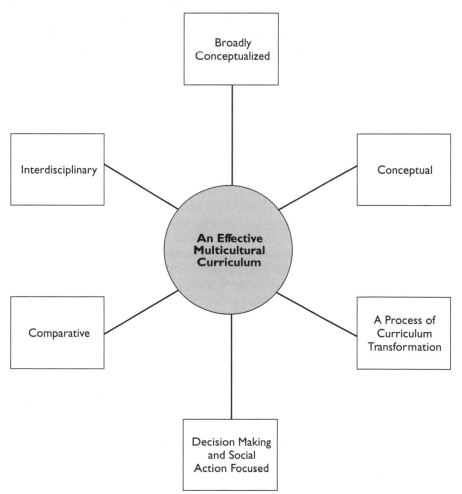

SUMMARY

The conceptual approach can best facilitate the integration of ethnic content into the curriculum and into the various subject areas. Using this approach, the teacher selects key concepts, such as culture, power, and discrimination, and then identifies content samples that can be used to help students attain these ideas. The conceptual approach allows the teacher to use content samples from several different disciplines and thus to teach in an interdisciplinary way.

When identifying concepts for a conceptual multicultural curriculum, you should make sure that a balanced approach is taken and that people of color are not depicted only or primarily as victims. They should also be described as people who helped to shape their own destinies, who built ethnic institutions, and who played major roles in attaining their civil rights. It is necessary to teach such concepts as prejudice, discrimination, and racism. However, it is also essential to teach such concepts as protest, empowerment, interracial cooperation, and ethnic institutions in order to portray a full and accurate view of the experiences of ethnic groups in the United States.

QUESTIONS AND ACTIVITIES

1. Label each of the following a fact, concept, or generalization and justify each label:

    a. Acculturation.
    b. In every human society there is a conflict between unlimited wants and limited resources.
    c. Assimilation.
    d. In 1827 Vincente Guerrero became president of Mexico.
    e. Ethnic cultures, values, and behavior are undergoing constant change.
    f. On September 22, 1862, President Lincoln issued a statement that has been called the Preliminary Emancipation Proclamation.
    g. In 1992, 213,802 Mexicans immigrated to the United States.
    h. During the 1960s and 1970s people of color strove less for cultural assimilation and more for cultural pluralism.
    i. Cultural pluralism.
    j. Ethnic group.

2. Here is a higher-level generalization: *Most foreigners who voluntarily immigrated to the United States were seeking better economic, political, and social opportunities.* Examine several of the books on ethnic groups contained in the bibliographies in Parts II–V and write several factual statements and lower-level generalizations that this generalization will encompass.

3. Examine several of the books in the bibliographies in Parts II–V and find a number of factual statements and generalizations that these concepts will encompass: cultural assimilation, structural assimilation, protest, discrimination.

4. Tell whether each of these statements is normative or empirical, and why:

    a. The American colonists should not have taken land away from the American Indians.

    b. Irresponsible African Americans rioted in many American cities in the 1960s.

    c. Many Mexican immigrants entered the United States illegally.

    d. Japanese Americans should not have been sent to relocation camps in 1942.

    e. Many Puerto Ricans migrate to the U.S. mainland each year.

    f. Many Chinese Americans live in ghettos in U.S. cities.

5. What do you think should be the role of the following categories of knowledge in a sound multicultural curriculum? Why?

    a. Facts

    b. Concepts

    c. Generalizations

    d. Theories

6. Examine several books dealing with people of color (see the annotated bibliographies in Parts II–V of this book) and identify a theory related to ethnic groups. Can this theory be taught to a group of elementary or high school students? Why or why not? If you think it can be taught to a group of students, develop a plan for teaching it. If you are a classroom teacher or a student teacher, implement your teaching plan and evaluate its effectiveness.

7. Make a list of your close friends. Note their ethnic, religious, and racial backgrounds. Compare your list with similar lists made by other individuals in your class or workshop. What conclusions can you make about structural assimilation in U.S. society on the basis of the responses made by you and your classmates or fellow workshop participants?

8. If your parents are first- or second-generation U.S. immigrants, make a list of their values and life-styles that are different from your own. If your parents are not first- or second-generation immigrants, interview individuals whose parents are and compare their values and life-styles with those of their parents. What tentative generalizations can you make about cultural assimilation in U.S. society by studying these data?

9. Define each of the following terms and tell why each is important:

knowledge	ethclass
reflective decision	cultural assimilation
fact	structural assimilation
concept	intermediate-level generalization
generalization	high-level generalization
theory	high-level concept
normative statement	low-level concept
empirical statement	

REFERENCES

Atwater, M. M. (1994). Research on Cultural Diversity in the Classroom. In D. L. Gabel (Eds.). *Handbook of Research on Science Teaching and Learning* (pp. 558–576). New York: Macmillan.

Banks, J. A. (1995a). Multicultural Education: Historical Development, Dimensions, and Practice. In J. A. Banks & C. A. M. Banks (Eds.). *Handbook of Research on Multicultural Education* (pp. 3–24). New York: Macmillan.

Banks, J. A. (1995b). The Historical Reconstruction of Knowledge about Race: Implications for Transformative Teaching. *Educational Researcher* 24(2), pp. 15–25.

Barkan, E. (1992). *The Retreat of Scientific Racism: Changing Concepts of Race in Britain and the United States between the World Wars*. New York: Cambridge University Press.

Belenky, M. F., Clinchy, B. M., Goldberger, N. R., & Tarule, J. M. (1986). *Women's Ways of Knowing: The Development of Self, Voice and Mind*. New York: Basic Books.

Fullilove, R. E. & Treisman, P. U. (1990). Mathematics Achievement Among African American Undergraduates at the University of California, Berkeley: An Evaluation of the Mathematics Workshop Program. *The Journal of Negro Education* 59(3), 463–490.

Gordon, M. M. (1964). *Assimilation in American Life*. New York: Oxford University Press.

Gould, S. J. (1981). *The Mismeasure of Man*. New York: Norton.

Heath, S. B. & McLaughlin, M. W. (Eds.). (1993). *Identity & Inner-City Youth: Beyond Ethnicity and Gender*. New York: Teachers College Press.

Herrnstein, R. J. & Murray, C. (1994). *The Bell Curve: Intelligence and Class Structure in American Life*. New York: The Free Press.

Jacoby, R. & Glauberman, N. (Eds.). (1995). *The Bell Curve Debate: History, Documents, Opinions*. New York: Times Books.

Kitano, H. H. L. (1976). *Japanese Americans: The Evolution of a Subculture* (2nd ed.). Englewood Cliffs, N.J.: Prentice-Hall.

Levins, R. & Lewontin, R. (1985). *The Dialectical Biologist*. Cambridge: Harvard University Press.

Mason, S. F. (1962). *A History of the Sciences*. New York: Collier Books.

Merton, R. K. (1968). On Sociological Theories of the Middle Range. In R. K. Merton. *Social Theory and Social Structure* (Enlarged ed., pp. 39–72). New York: The Free Press.

Secada, W. G. (1992). Race, Ethnicity, Social Class, Language, and Achievement in Mathematics. In D. Grouws (Ed.). *Handbook of Research on Mathematics Teaching and Learning* (pp. 623–660). New York: Macmillan.

Secada, W. G., Fennema, E., & Adajian, L. B. (Eds.). (1995). *New Directions for Equity in Mathematics Education*. New York: Cambridge University Press.

Sertima, I. V. (Ed.). (1986). *Blacks in Science: Ancient and Modern*. New Brunswick, N.J.: Transaction Books.

Slavin, R. E. (1983). *Cooperative Learning*. New York: Longman.

Taba, H., Durkin, M. C., Fraenkel, J. R., & McNaughton, A. H. (1971). *A Teacher's Handbook for Elementary School Studies: An Inductive Approach* (2nd ed.). Reading, Mass: Addison-Wesley.

ANNOTATED BIBLIOGRAPHY

Addison-Wesley Publishing Company. (1993). *Multiculturalism in Mathematics, Science, and Technology: Readings and Activities.* Menlo Park, Calif.: Author.

A worktext that is designed to help teachers integrate multicultural issues and topics into mathematics and science.

Banks, J. A. (with Clegg, A. A., Jr.). (1990). *Teaching Strategies for the Social Studies: Inquiry, Valuing and Decision-Making* (4th ed.). White Plains, N.Y.: Longman.

Chapter 3 of this book is a detailed discussion, with illustrations, of the nature and teaching of concepts, generalizations, and theories. Part IV discusses value inquiry, decision making, citizen action, and evaluation strategies.

Banks, J. A. (1995). Multicultural Education: Its Effects on Students' Racial and Gender Role Attitudes. In J. A. Banks & C. A. M. Banks (Eds.). *Handbook of Research on Multicultural Education* (pp. 617–627). New York: Macmillan.

This chapter consists of a comprehensive review and discussion of the research related to ways to help students acquire more positive racial and gender-role attitudes.

Davidson, N. (Ed.). (1990). *Cooperative Learning in Mathematics: A Handbook for Teachers.* Menlo Park, Calif.: Addison-Wesley.

Research indicates that cooperative learning can enhance the academic achievement of some students of color. This book contains twelve articles that describe cooperative activities teachers can use in mathematics.

Harris, V. J. (Ed.). (1992). *Teaching Multicultural Literature in Grades K–8.* Norwood, Mass.: Christopher-Gordon Publishers.

A useful and rich source for integrating literature from various ethnic groups into the curriculum.

Miller-Lachmann, L. (1995). *Global Voices, Global Visions: A Core Collection of Multicultural Books.* New Providence, N.J.: R. R. Bowker.

This fully annotated bibliography contains more than 1,700 books on ethnic groups in the United States as well as books about other nations. The books annotated in this book are both multicultural and global, despite the book's title.

Oakes, J. (1990). Opportunities, Achievement, and Choice: Women and Minority Students in Science and Mathematics. In C. B. Cazden (Ed.). *Review of Research in Education* (Vol. 16, pp. 153–222). Washington, D.C.: American Educational Research Association.

An excellent and comprehensive review of the research on the opportunities and achievements of women and minorities in science and mathematics.

Oliver, E. I. (1994). *Crossing the Mainstream: Multicultural Perspectives in Teaching Literature.* Urbana, Ill.: National Council of Teachers of English.

This book includes a rationale, resources, and strategies for teaching multicultural literature.

Saldaña, J. (1995). *Drama of Color: Improvisation with Multiethnic Folklore.* Portsmouth, N.H.: Heinemann.

This useful book for teachers contains stories from different cultures that can be used to integrate drama into the curriculum. Mexican American, Native American, Asian and Pacific Island, African, and African American stories are included. Teaching activities are also described.

Secada, W. G., Fennema, E., & Adajian, L. B. (Eds.). (1995). *New Directions for Equity in Mathematics Education.* New York: Cambridge University Press.

An excellent and thoughtful collection of articles that discuss many different issues and programs related to increasing the achievement of ethnic minorities and women in mathematics.

Sertima, I. V. (Ed.). (1986). *Blacks in Science: Ancient and Modern.* New Brunswick. N.J.: Transaction Books.

African contributions to astronomy, agriculture, architecture, engineering, mathematics, medicine. and other scientific fields are discussed in the articles that comprise this book.

Thomas, R. L. (1995). *Connecting Cultures: A Guide to Multicultural Literature for Children.* New Providence, N.J.: R. R. Bowker.

This book features more than 1,600 titles on ethnic groups in the United States and about other nations.

CHAPTER 3

KEY CONCEPTS FOR THE MULTICULTURAL CURRICULUM

The multicultural curriculum should help students to master higher levels of knowledge so that they can better understand race and ethnic relations and develop the skills and abilities needed to make reflective personal and public decisions. Sound multicultural lessons and units focus on higher-level concepts and generalizations and use facts primarily to help students to master higher forms of knowledge and to make decisions. Students must be able to make reflective decisions in order to take thoughtful personal, social, and civic action.

CRITERIA FOR SELECTING INTERDISCIPLINARY CONCEPTS

Within the various academic fields and disciplines is a wide range of concepts from which you might select when planning the multicultural curriculum. What criteria can you use when selecting concepts to organize multicultural units and lessons? First, you should consider whether the concept will help explain some significant aspect of the history, culture, and contemporary experiences of a range of ethnic groups in U.S. society. The experiences of ethnic groups in the United States have been characterized by a number of salient events, expressions, and themes, such as discrimination, protest and resistance, cultural assimilation, and acculturation. Consequently, these themes are highly appropriate organizing concepts for the multicultural curriculum.

Higher-level concepts that are capable of encompassing a wide range of data and information should also be selected for the multicultural curriculum. Culture is a more powerful concept than language because it can be used to organize and teach more information.

Concepts chosen for the multicultural curriculum should also be *interdisciplinary*. Interdisciplinary concepts are capable of encompassing facts, generalizations, and examples from several disciplines and areas. It is necessary to select interdisciplinary concepts because the curriculum should help students view and interpret events and situations from the perspectives of several disciplines. When students view events and situations from the perspective of a single discipline, they can acquire, at best, only a partial understanding of the event or situation they are studying.

When *social protest,* for example, is studied only from the perspective of political science, students learn that social protest occurs when alienated groups within a political system organize to push for political and social change. However, students need to study protest from other disciplinary perspectives to understand it fully (see Figure 3-1). During the civil rights movement of the 1960s, African Americans expressed protest not only in politics but also in their literature, songs, dances, art, and language. Thus, students need to examine social protest in these forms of communication to fully understand Black protest in the 1960s.

Some concepts are important to the structure of a particular discipline but cannot function successfully in an interdisciplinary role. Rhythm, melody, harmony, and tone color are important concepts in music. Key concepts in art include form, line, and shape. However, because these concepts are highly specific to their particular disciplines, they are not effective interdisciplinary concepts. However, both music and art, as well as dance and language, are forms of communication and culture. Music and art also have themes or convey central messages to the perceiver: so do a play, a dance, and many examples of human behavior. Consequently, communication, culture, and theme are effective interdisciplinary concepts because they are able to help students develop generalizations by studying examples drawn from the social sciences and the humanities.

When selecting organizing concepts for multicultural lessons, you should give some attention to the developmental level of your students. Young children can understand discrimination easier than they can understand institutionalized racism, in part because almost every child has been the victim of some kind of discrimination. He or she may have been the new child in the classroom, may be fat or thin, or may have had some other characteristic that other students singled out for ridicule. Young children can also understand discrimination more easily than institutionalized racism because discrimination is a more well defined, less abstract, and less ambiguous concept than is institutionalized racism.

In the primary grades, you should focus on concepts that can be taught using concrete examples, such as similarities, differences, culture, race, discrimination, and ethnic group. Open-ended stories and role-playing situations, many of which are described in Parts II through V, can make these concepts

Figure 3-1 VIEWING SOCIAL PROTEST FROM AN
INTERDISCIPLINARY PERSPECTIVE

This figure illustrates how a concept such as social protest must be viewed from diverse
disciplinary perspectives in order for students to understand its total political, social, and
artistic ramifications.

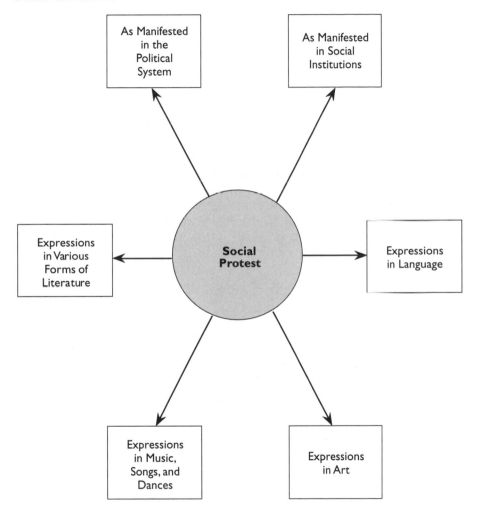

real and meaningful to young children. Children's books are also a powerful
tool for teaching concepts to students in the primary and intermediate grades.
A Jar of Dreams, by Yoshiko Uchida, is a moving story that vividly describes
examples of discrimination directed against eleven-year-old Rinko and her
family (Uchida, 1982). *Songs of the Trees* by Mildred D. Taylor can also be
used to teach discrimination (Taylor, 1975). Black language and cultural

expressions are salient parts of Virginia Hamilton's *A Little Love* (Hamilton, 1984). *Mountain Light* by Laurence Yep (1985), which enables the reader to experience the life of Chinese immigrants, can help make the concept of immigration meaningful and real to students. A number of outstanding children's books, annotated in Parts II through V, are available that you can use successfully to teach concepts such as cultural differences, prejudice, discrimination, and identity to students in the primary, intermediate, upper, and high school grades.

The student's previous experience with concepts and content related to race and ethnicity is an important consideration when selecting concepts for study. Concepts such as institutionalized racism, ethnic separatism, ethnic revitalization movement, and colonialism are so complex and emotional that they are often inappropriate for students who are studying race and ethnicity for the first time. More concrete and less controversial concepts are appropriate for such students. A student who is not familiar with such basic concepts as ethnic group, ethnic minority group, people of color, discrimination, and prejudice will have a difficult time understanding and appreciating abstract concepts such as institutionalized racism and ethnic separatism. These concepts should be studied only after students have mastered the basic concepts in ethnic studies.

INTERDISCIPLINARY CONCEPTS

Concepts drawn from various behavioral science disciplines that can be used effectively to organize interdisciplinary units and lessons are discussed below. The social and behavioral sciences are a rich source of interdisciplinary concepts because behavioral scientists study a wide range of human behavior. Art, music, dance, foods, language, and literature are expressions of concepts studied by behavioral scientists. Table 3-1 summarizes the major concepts discussed in this chapter. Table 3-2 illustrates how key concepts such as those in the following discussion can be used to plan and implement a comparative study of ethnic groups. Table 3-3 describes nine key concepts that can be used to organize a focused study of an ethnic group in the United States.

Culture, Ethnicity, and Related Concepts

Culture

Culture is the key concept in cultural anthropology. It is an essential concept in ethnic studies because an ethnic group is a type of cultural group. Culture consists of the behavior patterns, symbols, institutions, values, and other

Table 3-1 KEY CONCEPTS

Culture, Ethnicity, and Related Concepts	Culture
	Ethnic group
	Ethnic minority group
	Stages of ethnicity
	Ethnic diversity
	Cultural assimilation
	Acculturation
	Community culture
Socialization and Related Concepts	Socialization
	Prejudice
	Discrimination
	Race
	Racism
	Ethnocentrism
	Values
	Self-concept
Intercultural Communication and Related Concepts	Communication
	Intercultural communication
	Perception
	Historical bias
Power and Related Concepts	Power
	Social protest and resistance
The Movement of Ethnic Groups	Migration
	Immigration

Note: This table contains a list of high-level concepts that can be used to develop units and lessons that draw content, examples, and information from several disciplines. These concepts are defined and illustrated in this chapter.

human-made components of society. It is the unique achievement of a human group that distinguishes it from other groups. Even though cultures are in many ways similar, a particular culture constitutes a unique whole.

There is tremendous debate and controversy within anthropology about the meaning of culture. Some anthropologists contend that tools and other artifacts are not examples of culture but that the meaning and interpretation of these elements are what constitute culture. Bullivant (1993) defines culture as a program for survival.

The U.S. culture is comprised of many smaller groups. These microcultural groups share many characteristics with the common national culture but have some distinguishing characteristics that set them apart from other

Table 3-2 AN INTERDISCIPLINARY STUDY OF ETHNIC GROUPS

Key Concepts and Related Questions	American Indians	Mexican Americans	African Americans	Jewish Americans	Filipino Americans	Puerto Ricans
Culture: What ethnic cultural elements are present in the group's culture today? How is the group's culture reflected in its music, literature, and art?						
Ethnic Enclave: To what extent are members of the group concentrated within particular geographical regions?						
Racism and Discrimination: To what extent is the group a victim of racism or other forms of discrimination?						
Communication: To what extent do members of the group encounter problems when communicating with other ethnic groups?						
Self-Concept: How have the group's societal experiences affected the self-concepts of its members?						
Power: To what extent does the group exercise power within the ethnic community? Within the economic system? Within the larger society?						

Note: This table illustrates how a data retrieval chart organized around key concepts can be used by the teacher to plan and implement a comparative study of ethnic groups.

Table 3-3 ORGANIZING CONCEPTS FOR A
FOCUSED STUDY OF AN ETHNIC GROUP

The experience of each ethnic group in the United States can be viewed and compared using a few key concepts and themes. Below are nine concepts that can be used to view and study the experiences of an ethnic group.

Origins and Immigration

It is important to examine the origins and immigration pattern of an ethnic group in the United States.

Shared Culture, Values, and Symbols

Most ethnic groups in the United States have unique cultures and values that resulted from an interaction of their original culture with the host culture in the United States, from ethnic institutions created partly as a response to discrimination, and from their social-class position.

Ethnic Identity and Sense of Peoplehood

A shared sense of peoplehood and ethnic identity is one of the most important characteristics of an ethnic group in the United States. This shared sense of identity results from a common history and current experiences.

Perspectives, World Views, and Frames of Reference

Members of the same ethnic group often view reality in a similar way and differently from other groups within a society. This results largely from their shared sense of peoplehood and identity described above.

Ethnic Institutions and Self-Determination

Many ethnic institutions were formed by ethnic groups in the United States in response to discrimination and segregation. Many of these institutions continue to exist today because they help ethnic groups to satisfy unique social, cultural, and educational needs.

Demographic, Social, Political, and Economic Status

When studying about a U.S. ethnic group, its current demographic, social, political, and economic status needs to be determined. The economic and educational status of an ethnic group can change. New immigration can change the demographic and economic profile of an ethnic group.

Prejudice, Discrimination, and Racism

Prejudice, discrimination, and racism have been major themes and issues in the history and contemporary experiences of U.S. ethnic groups, particularly those of color.

Intraethnic Diversity

Even though ethnic groups share a culture, values, a sense of identity, and a common history, there are tremendous differences within ethnic groups. These important differences must always be kept in mind when ethnic groups are studied, or new stereotypes and misconceptions may arise.

(Continued)

Table 3-3 *CONTINUED*

Assimilation and Acculturation

The experiences of ethnic groups in the United States have been and still are characterized by widespread cultural assimilation on the part of ethnic minority groups and ethnic minority cultures. The influence of ethnic minority cultures on the mainstream culture should be examined as should the assimilation of minority groups into the mainstream culture.

groups. Thus, it is possible to describe the U.S. culture, as well as the various microcultures that constitute it, such as the Appalachian culture, the Southern culture, and the youth culture.

Ethnic Group and Ethnic Minority Group

Ethnic groups are types of microcultural groups within the United States that have unique characteristics that set them apart from other cultural groups. Many microcultural groups are voluntary groups, but an ethnic group is usually an involuntary group, although individual identification with the group may be optional (Banks, Cortés, Gay, Garcia, & Ochoa, 1991). An ethnic group has a historic origin and a shared heritage and tradition. The origins of the group preceded the creation of the nation state or were external to the nation state. An ethnic group also has an ancestral tradition, and its members share a sense of peoplehood and an interdependence of fate. It has some value orientations, behavioral patterns, and interests, often political and economic, that differ from those of other groups within society. Ethnic groups tend to have an influence, often substantial, on the lives of their members. Anglo-Saxon Protestants, Italian Americans, and Irish Americans are examples of ethnic groups.

An ethnic minority group is an ethnic group with several distinguishing characteristics. Although an ethnic minority group, like an ethnic group, shares a common culture, a historic tradition, and a sense of peoplehood, it also has unique physical and/or cultural characteristics that enable individuals who belong to other ethnic groups to identify its members easily, often for discriminatory purposes. Ethnic minority groups also tend to be a numerical minority and to exercise minimal political and economic power. Vietnamese Americans are an ethnic minority group with unique physical and cultural characteristics. Non-White ethnic minority groups, such as Vietnamese Americans and African Americans, are often called *people of color*. Jewish Americans, another ethnic minority group, are distinguished on the basis of their religious and cultural characteristics.

Culture, ethnic group, ethnic minority group, and people of color are essential concepts for the multicultural curriculum and should be introduced in the primary grades. You can introduce the concept of culture by showing the students a menorah, an engagement ring, and the numeral "5." By asking the students what these objects have in common, and by class discussion and the use of more examples, you can help your students formulate a definition of culture. When introducing the concept of culture, you should emphasize the *meanings* that artifacts and cultural elements have to individuals and groups and how they use and interpret them.

After the students have studied culture, they can then be introduced to the concept of microcultural group. Ethnic group and later ethnic minority group can be introduced using appropriate examples. When you introduce *ethnic group* you should help students to understand that individuals are members of many different groups, such as religious, kinship, and economic groups, and that an ethnic group is only one of the many groups to which individuals belong.

A person's attachment to and identity with these various groups varies with the individual, the times in one's life, and the situations and settings in which one finds oneself. Depending on experiences, social class, and many other variables, ethnicity may be important to an individual or it may be unimportant. Students should be helped to understand that just because they think an individual is a member of a particular ethnic group, that does not mean that the individual has a strong identity with his or her ethnic group or that ethnicity is important in his or her life. Ethnicity is rather unimportant in the lives of many highly assimilated and upper-status members of ethnic groups but tends to be a cogent factor in the lives of many lower-class ethnics.

Stages of Ethnicity

We often assume that ethnic groups are monolithic and have rather homogeneous needs and characteristics. Rarely is sufficient attention given to the enormous differences within ethnic groups. We also tend to see ethnic groups as static and unchanging. However, ethnic groups within modernized democratic societies are highly diverse, complex, and changing entities. I have developed a typology that attempts to describe some of the differences existing between individual members of ethnic groups. The typology assumes that individual members of an ethnic group are at different stages of ethnic development and that these stages can be identified and described.

The typology is an ideal-type construct in the Weberian sense and constitutes a set of hypotheses based on the existing and emerging theory and research and on my observations and study of ethnic behavior (Banks, 1994). The typology is presented here because it can be used as a departure point for classroom discussions of ethnicity. However, *its tentative and hypothetical nature should be emphasized in class discussions.*

Stage 1: Ethnic Psychological Captivity

During this stage, the individual has internalized negative ideologies and beliefs about his or her ethnic group that are institutionalized within the society. Consequently, the Stage-1 person exemplifies ethnic self-rejection and low self-esteem. The individual is ashamed of his or her ethnic group and identity during this stage and may respond in a number of ways, including avoiding situations that lead to contact with other ethnic groups or striving aggressively to become highly culturally assimilated.

Stage 2: Ethnic Encapsulation

Stage 2 is characterized by ethnic encapsulation and ethnic exclusiveness, including voluntary separatism. The individual participates primarily within his or her own ethnic community and believes that his or her ethnic group is superior to that of others. Many Stage-2 individuals, such as many Anglo-Saxon Protestants, have internalized the dominant societal myths about the superiority of their ethnic or racial group and the innate inferiority of other ethnic groups and races. Many individuals who are socialized within all-White suburban communities and who live highly ethnocentric and encapsulated lives may be described as Stage-2 individuals. Alice Miel (with Kiester, 1967) describes these kinds of individuals in *The Shortchanged Children of Suburbia*.

Stage 3: Ethnic Identity Clarification

At this stage, the individual is able to clarify personal attitudes and ethnic identity, reduce intrapsychic conflict, and develop positive attitudes toward his or her ethnic group. The individual learns to accept self, thus developing the characteristics needed to accept and respond more positively to outside ethnic groups. Self-acceptance is a requisite for accepting and responding positively to other people.

Stage 4: Biethnicity

Individuals within this stage have a healthy sense of ethnic identity and the psychological characteristics and skills needed to participate in their own ethnic culture, as well as in another ethnic culture. The individual also has a strong desire to function effectively in two ethnic cultures. We may describe such an individual as biethnic or bicultural.

Stage 5: Multiethnicity

Stage 5 describes the idealized goal for citizenship identity within an ethnically pluralistic nation. The individual at this stage is able to function, at least at minimal levels, within several ethnic sociocultural environments and to understand, appreciate, and share the values, symbols, and institutions of several ethnic cultures. Such multiethnic perspectives and feelings, I hypothesize, help the individual to live a more enriched and fulfilling life and to formulate more creative and novel solutions to personal and public problems.

Stage 6: Globalism and Global Competency

Individuals within Stage 6 have clarified, reflective, and positive ethnic, national, and global identifications and the knowledge, skills, attitudes, and abilities needed to function in ethnic cultures within their own nation as well as in cultures within other nations. These individuals have the ideal delicate balance of ethnic, national, and global identifications, commitments, literacy, and behaviors. They have internalized the universalistic ethical values and principles of humankind and have the skills, competencies, and commitments needed to act on these values.

Characteristics of the Typology

The emerging stages of ethnicity typology is an ideal-type construct and should be viewed as dynamic and multidimensional rather than as static and unilinear. The characteristics within the stages exist on a continuum. Thus, within Stage 1, individuals are more or less ethnically psychologically captive; some individuals are more ethnically psychologically captive than others.

The division between the stages is blurred rather than sharp. Thus, a continuum exists between as well as within the stages. The ethnically encapsulated individual (Stage 2) does not suddenly attain clarification and acceptance of personal ethnic identity (Stage 3). This process is gradual and developmental. Also, the stages should not be viewed as strictly sequential and unilinear. I am hypothesizing that some individuals may never experience a particular stage. However, I also hypothesize that once an individual experiences a particular stage that person is likely to experience the stages above it sequentially and developmentally. However, individuals may experience the stages upward, downward, or in a zigzag pattern. Under certain conditions, for example, the biethnic (Stage 4) individual may become multiethnic (Stage 5); under new conditions the same individual may again become biethnic (Stage 4), ethnically identified (Stage 3), and ethnically encapsulated (Stage 2). For example, many individual members of northern White ethnic groups became increasingly more ethnically encapsulated as busing for school desegregation gained momentum in northern cities such as Boston during the 1970s.

Figure 3-2 illustrates the dynamic and multidimensional characteristics of the development of ethnicity among individuals. Note especially the arrowed lines, which indicate that continua exist both horizontally and vertically.

Figure 3-2   THE EMERGING STAGES OF ETHNICITY:
A PRELIMINARY TYPOLOGY

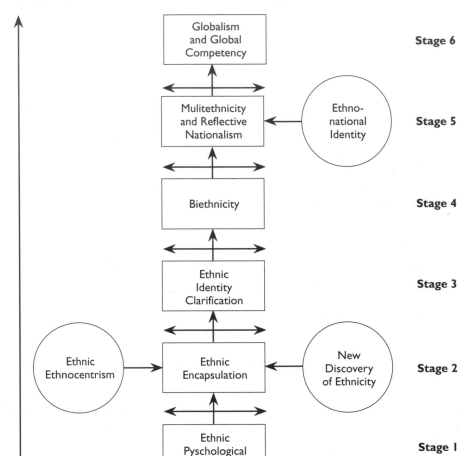

Ethnic Diversity

Students should learn that there are many different ethnic cultures in our society, and that these differences are not likely to vanish. Events cause them to emerge in each new generation. This concept is the antithesis of the melting pot theory. When studying about ethnic differences in the United States, students should be helped to understand that even though we have not experienced a true melting pot, most ethnic groups have acquired many mainstream American cultural characteristics.

Many ethnic individuals are *bicultural;* that is, they usually acquire culture traits of mainstream American culture but also retain many of their ethnic characteristics. Even though the more upwardly mobile members of ethnic groups tend to be less ethnic than are lower-class members, this generalization is nevertheless valid. A highly acculturated Chinese American, for example, will often marry a Chinese, eat Chinese foods, and belong to Chinese social organizations. Many ethnic youths attend public schools during the day and a language or ethnic school after regular school hours or on the weekend. Most African Americans who obtain college degrees speak standard English on their jobs and in other settings where it is appropriate to conform to the dominant society's norm. However, when socializing with less assimilated relatives and friends, they often use many words and phrases that linguists call *Black English or Ebonics* (Smitherman, 1994). Upwardly mobile Mexican Americans will eat "Anglo-Saxon steak" at fancy Anglo restaurants with their Anglo friends, but they often drive to Spanish-speaking neighborhoods to eat foods such as enchiladas and chilies rellenos.

In other words, ethnic individuals acquire those mainstream cultural traits necessary for them to survive in the wider society but retain many of the elements of their ethnic culture. The more upwardly mobile an individual is, the more likely he or she is to acquire mainstream cultural traits. The acquisition of mainstream Anglo-American speech, behavior, and values is necessary for upward mobility in the United States because mainstream Americans control entry to most social, economic, and political institutions.

When studying about ethnic differences, students should learn that cultural differences exist within as well as between various ethnic groups. Too many Americans think of ethnic groups as monolithic, and they find it difficult to understand why conflict exists within ethnic groups. *It is very important for students to study about the differences that exist within ethnic groups.* When many mainstream Americans are introduced to an African American or an Asian American, certain stereotypic images often emerge. They often assume that all African Americans know something about the Black ghetto because of their personal experiences and can tell them how the Black community feels about busing or interracial marriage. Many people assume that all Asian Americans are stoic, shy, and have a high scientific aptitude.

It is true that we can associate certain general characteristics with the various American ethnic groups. However, within these groups, individuals embrace these characteristics to varying degrees. Some deliberately attempt to reject them. When we meet an individual and know only that he or she is a Mexican American, and nothing else, there are but a few conclusive statements we can accurately make about that person.

Mexican Americans, like Asian Americans and African Americans, are a highly diverse group. Some Mexican Americans identify strongly with this group's political movement and wish to be called Chicanos. Others, especially those in the upper classes, tend to identify more strongly with their Spanish heritage and consider the word *Chicano* pejorative and insulting. Such individuals are more likely to prefer the term *Latin American* or *Spanish American* and to reject their Indian heritage. Some Mexican Americans consider themselves Spanish, even though their biological traits may be identical to others who consider themselves Chicanos or Mexican Americans.

The tremendous differences that exist within various ethnic groups often make it difficult for many mainstream Americans to understand why many Japanese Americans are anti-Korean, why the *Nisei* (first-generation Japanese American) often express disappointment about the values and life-styles of the *Sansei* (second generation), or why some upwardly mobile Mexican Americans disdain Mexican migrant workers. Intragroup differences and conflict exist within dominant ethnic groups as well as within minority groups. However, Americans tend to understand why a German American corporation president might disdain a German American dishwasher. The African American, however, who openly wonders about what life is like in the Black inner-city may be considered an oddity by many mainstream Americans. Class differences within the African American community are deepening as the income gap between those who are very poor (the so-called underclass) and the upwardly mobile Blacks increases.

Cultural Assimilation

When a member of an ethnic minority group acquires the behavior patterns, life-styles, values, and language of the mainstream culture we say that he or she has become culturally assimilated. *Cultural assimilation* is the process by which an individual or group acquires the culture traits of a different ethnic or cultural group. Because the dominant group controls most of the social, economic, and political institutions in a society, members of ethnic minority groups must acquire its cultural traits to move up the social and economic ladder. When studying this concept, it is important for students to learn that although people of color may become totally assimilated culturally (i.e., in cultural characteristics they may become indistinguishable from Anglo-Saxon Protestants), they will still be victims of discrimination and racism because of their different physical characteristics.

A widespread myth is that Mexican Americans and African Americans experience discrimination because they often have meager educations and live in barrios and ghettos. Even though it is true that many Mexican Americans and African Americans are members of the lower socioeconomic classes, and that all lower-class individuals are treated differently than middle- and upper-class people, it is also true that Mexican Americans and African Americans with high educational levels and incomes frequently experience discrimination because of their color. Because American racism is based largely on skin color, no degree of cultural assimilation eliminates it. A number of popular books describe the racism experienced by middle-class African Americans (Cose, 1993; Feagin & Sikes, 1994).

Some discussion of forced assimilation and cultural genocide should take place when students study cultural assimilation. Assimilation often occurs when a minority group "voluntarily" acquires the behavior patterns and life-styles of the dominant group in order to attain social mobility and occupational success. I use the word *voluntarily* here somewhat reluctantly because without some degree of cultural assimilation, a group that is very different culturally may not be able to survive in a particular culture. However, in the history of the United States, some forms of cultural assimilation that took place were totally nonvoluntary and might be called forced assimilation because the cultures of certain groups were deliberately destroyed (cultural genocide). These groups were forced to acquire the language, life-styles, and values of the dominant culture.

Individuals and groups who refused to accept the dominant culture were sometimes the victims of severe punishments, such as death. The cultures of African groups were deliberately destroyed by the slave masters. This cultural destruction began on the slave ships. It seems that systematic and deliberate attempts were made to destroy Indian cultures (Stannard, 1992). These efforts were highly successful. Many of the cultural elements of these groups now exist only in the pages of history, and sometimes not even there because they were often destroyed before they could be recorded.

Acculturation

When an Anglo-Saxon Protestant eats chow mein and a Chinese American sees a Shakespearean play, we say that acculturation is occurring because two different ethnic groups are exchanging cultural elements and complexes. Although the exchange of cultural traits is widespread within U.S. society, we often think of the cultural traits that ethnic minorities acquire from dominant ethnic groups, but we hear too little about the cultural traits that dominant groups have acquired from ethnic minorities. Since this is the case, you should highlight the ethnic minority cultural traits that have been acquired by mainstream Americans.

Students should study about the contributions African Americans have made to American music, especially their spirituals, blues, and jazz (Southern, 1983). American culture traits of Indian origin are rarely mentioned in schoolbooks. Indian contributions to American culture include the selection of sites for many American cities, as well as dress styles, tobacco, foods, and values related to the veneration and preservation of the earth. In two popular books Weatherford (1988; 1991) describes the contributions that Native Americans made to the world (*Indian Givers*) and to the United States (*Native Roots*).

All American ethnic groups, including people of color, have contributed material elements (such as foods and fashions), as well as nonmaterial traits (such as values and norms), to mainstream American culture. Students can use a data retrieval chart similar to the one illustrated earlier in Table 3-2 to record examples of contributions that various groups have made to American life. This type of chart is a convenient tool for studying cultural contributions as well as other aspects of ethnic group life in the United States.

Community Culture

Most Americans grow up in communities in which ethnic and cultural values, life-styles, language patterns, and behavior patterns differ from those of many other groups. This is as true for Puerto Ricans who grow up in East Harlem as it is for Anglo-Saxon Protestants who are raised in wealthy suburban neighborhoods such as Mercer Island, Washington, and Forest Park, Illinois. We usually do not think that middle-class or wealthy White suburbs have a unique culture because the culture within them constitutes the dominant one in the United States. However, Miel (with Kiester, 1967) in *The Shortchanged Children of Suburbia,* and Henry (1963; 1971) in *Culture against Man* and *Pathways to Madness,* describe some of the unique cultural traits of middle-class mainstream U.S. communities.

Because most Americans grow up in ethnic or cultural enclaves, they are *culturally encapsulated.* Ethnic minority groups, in order to attain social and economic mobility, are usually forced out of their ethnic encapsulation. However, mainstream Americans, who control entry to most social, economic, and political institutions, often spend their entire lives within their own unique cultural communities. The cultures of other groups remain foreign, nonhuman, and exotic to them. African Americans who grow up in small southern rural communities often think that everyone eats sweet potato pie, chitterlings, and hog head and black-eyed peas to celebrate New Year's Day. Without this kind of New Year's meal, bad luck will be imminent. When these African Americans migrate to northern and western cities and begin to participate in social institutions that have other norms and values, they discover, sometimes abruptly, that their world is not the entire world, and that not only do many people not eat sweet potato pie, but they have serious questions about people who eat hog intestines!

A sound multicultural curriculum should help all students—from both majority and minority groups—to break out of their cultural and ethnic enclaves and learn that there are many ways to live and survive and that because an individual has a different life-style, he or she is not inferior or superior. Many youths of color tend to devalue their ethnic cultures when they begin to participate in the mainstream society. Mainstream students should learn that there are different ways of living that are as legitimate and functional as their own. I am not suggesting that the school should attempt to force different life-styles on students. However, the school should help release students from *cultural* and *ethnic* captivity so that they can learn to appreciate cultural differences and thus learn how to live with people who speak a different dialect, eat different foods, and value things they may not value. We can learn to respect and appreciate different cultures without choosing to participate in them. Participation should be an individual decision. However, cultural understanding and empathy for other people should be fostered by the school.

Socialization and Related Concepts

Socialization

Socialization describes the process by which people become human. Sociologists, who use socialization as their central concept, assume that even though people are born with the physical capacities to become human, they are capable of becoming many things, including animal-like. Sociologists assume that people acquire human traits and characteristics only by interacting with the human group. The group makes use of norms and sanctions to ensure that the individual acquires the attitudes, values, and behavior patterns it deems appropriate.

Socialization and related concepts, such as values and norms, are important in multicultural education because they provide useful insights that help us understand how individuals acquire prejudices and ethnocentric values, and how people learn to discriminate against other groups. Socialization theory teaches us that children are not born with racial antipathies. Children learn these attitudes from the adults in their environment early in life (Milner, 1983). Modern sociological research and theory dispel old notions, such as the racial and cultural difference theory, which held that individuals have an instinctive fear and dislike of people who are physically and culturally different from them. Also discredited is the traumatic experience theory, which states that "racial prejudice emerges in an individual following a traumatic experience involving a member of a minority group during early childhood" (Rose, 1962, p. 77). Negative attitudes toward certain ethnic groups are institutionalized within our society. Children acquire them by interacting with "significant others" in their environment and reading books in school, watching television, and going to their place of worship. Most institutions within our society, including the schools, reinforce and teach negative lessons about America's ethnic minority groups. Students need to understand the relationship between socialization, prejudice, racism, and discrimination.

Prejudice and Discrimination

Prejudice is a set of rigid and unfavorable attitudes toward a particular group or groups that is formed in disregard of facts. The prejudiced individual responds to perceived members of these groups on the basis of his or her pre-conceptions, tending to disregard behavior or personal characteristics that are inconsistent with his or her biases. Individuals who are anti-Semitic will argue that Jews are loud and rudely aggressive no matter how many Jews they meet who do not have these characteristics. Prejudiced people see the world through a set of blinders and refuse to perceive people, incidents, and groups that do not reinforce their negative attitudes and stereotypes.

Although prejudice and discrimination are highly related and are usually associated, they are different concepts. Prejudice is a set of *attitudes,* whereas discrimination consists of differential *behavior* directed toward a stigmatized group. Rose has defined discrimination "as the differential treatment of individuals considered to belong to particular groups or social categories" (Rose, 1974, p. 102).

You can use Merton's typology (1949) with students in the middle, upper, and high school grades to help them to better understand discrimination. His typology makes it clear that a prejudiced individual will not necessarily discriminate and that an individual who is not prejudiced may discriminate. Merton's typology clarifies the extent to which discrimination is contextual, situational, and related to the social settings in which individuals function. Merton identifies four types of persons:

Type I: The unprejudiced nondiscriminator or all-weather liberal. This individual believes in racial equality and acts on his or her beliefs.

Type II: The unprejudiced discriminator or fair-weather liberal. This is a person of expediency. He or she does not have personal prejudices but will discriminate when it is easier or more profitable to do so.

Type III: The prejudiced nondiscriminator or fair-weather illiberal. This person does not believe in racial equality but does not discriminate because of laws or external factors that negatively sanction racial discrimination.

Type IV: The prejudiced discriminator or the all-weather illiberal. This is the bigot who is not ashamed of his or her attitudes and who acts on his or her prejudices and beliefs.

When using Merton's typology with students, point out that it is an ideal-type conceptualization. This means that no actual individual is a pure example of any of Merton's four types. Rather, the typology can be used to think of and to classify individuals who approach one of the types. Students can also use Merton's typology to describe individuals they encounter in their readings, media presentations, or in their social settings. They can use it to analyze and think about their own behavior and attitudes toward other racial and ethnic groups.

Race

Physical anthropologists attempt to divide the human species into subgroups on the basis of biological traits and characteristics. They use the concept of *race* to differentiate among the various human subgroups. However, anthropologists have had considerable difficulty trying to structure valid racial categories because of the wide variety of traits and characteristics that human groups share, the extensive mixture among groups, and because the racial categories they have formulated are socially constructed. Consequently, the schemes they have developed for classifying human races vary greatly in number and in characteristics.

Montagu (1974) classifies humankind into four major groups: Negroid or Black, the Archaic White or Australoid, the Caucasoid or White, and the Mongoloid. Oliver (1964) presents a scheme with seven major races: Early Mongoloid, Late Mongoloid, Negro, Bushmen, Australian, Pygmy Negroids, and White. Nine different racial types are identified in *Encyclopaedia Britannica* (1976, p. 350). There is considerable inconsistency in how physical anthropologists classify human racial groups.

Montagu (1974), who calls race "man's most dangerous myth," believes that the four categories he identifies can best be regarded as major *human groups* rather than as races. He seriously questions the validity of the concept of race and believes it has been a highly destructive factor in the history of humankind. He writes, "It is impossible to make the sort of racial classifications which some anthropologists and others have attempted. The fact is that all human beings are so...mixed with regard to origin that between different groups of individuals...'overlapping' of physical traits is the rule" (p. 7).

In most societies, the *social significance of race is much more important than the presumed physical differences among groups*. The social definitions of race also reveal the arbitrariness of the concept and why it might well be humankind's most dangerous myth. In the United States, any person with any acknowledged Black African blood is classified as Black, regardless of that person's phenotype (Davis, 1991). Many such persons, of course, look completely Caucasian and classify themselves as White. The majority of them accept the racial category imposed on them by society. We have no reliable statistics of how many such persons "pass" as White.

In early Mexico, the Spaniards invented so many concepts and terms for different types of racial mixtures that the cumbersome system of racial classification eventually became so complex and dysfunctional that it died of its own weight (Hunt & Walker, 1974). Partly as a result, the attitudes toward differences in skin color and in physical characteristics are considerably more flexible in former Spanish America than they are in the United States. In contemporary Puerto Rican society, for example, individuals with a wide range of skin colors are regarded as White. Other variables, such as social status, income, education, and hair texture are important in determining an individual's racial designation (Tumin with Feldman, 1971). In Mexico, the rural Indian can become a Mestizo by moving from the village to the city, becoming assimilated into the dominant Mestizo culture, and learning to speak Spanish (van den Berghe, 1978). By exploring the complex ramifications of the social meaning of race in both the United States and in other nations, students will be able to gain a better understanding of both the arbitrariness and political implications of race.

Racism

Racism is closely related to the idea of race. Racism is a belief that human groups can be validly grouped on the basis of their biological traits and that these identifiable groups inherit certain mental, personality, and cultural characteristics that determine their behavior. A corollary belief is that some biological groups, such as Caucasians, have superior mental and behavioral traits and that others, such as African Americans and Indians, are mentally and culturally inferior. Van den Berghe (1978) defines racism as "any set of beliefs that organic, genetically transmitted differences (whether real or imagined) between human groups are intrinsically associated with the presence or the absence of certain socially relevant abilities or characteristics, hence that such differences are a legitimate basis of invidious distinctions between groups socially defined as races" (p. 11).

Racism, however, is not merely a set of beliefs but is practiced when a group has the power to enforce laws, institutions, and norms based on its beliefs that oppress and dehumanize another group. Gay (1973) stresses the behavioral aspects of racism: "It is an extension of an attitude into an action. Although the focus of attention is on *behavior,* attitudes are of crucial importance for they are the motivating forces which determine the nature of the actions one takes" (p. 30). In a racist society, the political, economic, and social systems reflect and perpetuate racism; thus, racism is institutionalized.

Even though ethnocentrism is found in all human societies, racism is not. The kind of racism that exists in the modern world is a rather recent historical development. In the ancient world, different groups and peoples were often the victims of oppression or were enslaved. However, discrimination was rarely done on the basis of racial characteristics. Rather, it was usually based on religious, cultural, political, and social-class differences. Social scientists have noted that with few exceptions racism as we know it today was not practiced up through the seventeenth century (Montagu, 1974). According to van den Berghe (1978), however, racism "has been independently discovered and rediscovered by various peoples at various times in history" (p. 21). However, he notes that it was not until the nineteenth century that racism became an elaborate ideology distinguishable from ethnocentrism. Racism developed in the modern world to justify the exploitation and enslavement of aboriginal peoples by Europeans when they began their explorations into Africa, the Caribbean. and the Americas.

The European explorers and slave owners were Christians who needed an ideology to justify slavery when it began to be attacked. They needed an ideology they could view as consistent with both their religious beliefs and economic institutions. The arguments they structured eventually blossomed into an elaborate racist ideology. According to van den Berghe (1978), "Racism was congruent with prevailing forms of capitalist exploitation, notably with slavery in the [the Americas] and incipient colonial expansion in Africa. There is no question that the desire to rationalize exploitation of non-European peoples fostered the elaboration of a complex ideology of paternalism and racism" (p. 17). Montagu (1974) echoes the same point: "The idea of 'race' was, in fact, the deliberate creation of an exploiting class which was seeking to maintain and defend its privileges against what was profitably regarded as an inferior social caste" (p. 39).

When students study racism, they can try to determine the extent to which it is institutionalized within U.S. society, such as in the mass media or within schools and churches, and how racism is manifested in employment and in housing. The students can also discuss whether they are unconscious participants within an institutionalized racist system and what they might be able to do to change the system. Gay (1973) has distinguished *individual, cultural,* and *institutionalized* racism. Fruitful activities for students are to attempt to formulate working definitions for each of these concepts and to identify examples of them (Feagin & Vera, 1995).

Ethnocentrism

Most ethnic groups within a society tend to think that their culture is superior to the culture of other groups. This is especially true of the most powerful and dominant groups. In our society, Anglo-Saxon Protestants are the dominant group. Many of them feel that their culture is superior to the cultures of other groups and define culture as those aspects of *their* culture that they value highly, such as classical music and paintings by the European masters.

Students must understand *ethnocentrism* to comprehend fully the complex dimensions of American racism and the separatist movements that have emerged within ethnic minority groups. Although some minority persons, because of their socialization, tend to have low self-concepts and value the mainstream culture over their own, ethnocentrism among people of color escalated in the late 1960s. Some African Americans, Mexican Americans, and Asian Americans extolled the virtues of their cultures and demanded separatism and independent institutions. It may be that some degree of ethnocentrism is necessary for a group to attain cohesion and a strong identity, and that separatism is, as Sizemore (1972) has suggested, a necessary step toward inclusion within the larger society. However, you can ask students this question: How much cultural and political separatism can a society experience and remain cohesive? If this question is raised, several related ones should also be posed: If a society needs some common goals in order to survive, what groups within it should determine these goals? How might we change our society so that each ethnic group can influence policy that shapes common societal goals? At present, dominant groups determine most societal goals and the means to attain them. However, ethnic groups of color made it clear during the 1960s and 1970s that they will not accept this kind of power arrangement without protest and conflict. These kinds of questions and problems, related to ethnocentrism, should constitute a vital part of the multicultural curriculum.

Values

Those elements within a culture to which individuals and groups attach a high worth are called *values*. Within a social system are values that influence the group's feelings toward foods, human life, behavior patterns, and attitudes toward people who belong to outgroups. Sociologists have studied how values develop within societies and how they are inculcated by individuals in a community. Values, like attitudes and beliefs, are learned from the groups in which the individual is socialized; we are not born with a set of values and do not derive them independently. Groups use norms and sanctions to assure that individuals inculcate the pervasive values within their culture or microculture.

Even though there are some common values embraced by most U.S. communities (such as a respect for the lives of those regarded as human beings and loyalty toward national symbols such as the U.S. flag and the Constitution), these shared values are often defined and perceived differently within various ethnic microcultures, or they take diverse forms. Other values are important in some ethnic communities and largely absent in others.

The Nisei usually endorse many traditional Japanese values, including etiquette, personal control, the samurai ethic, a high respect for authority, the achievement ethic, and a strong sense of family obligation (Tamura, 1994). Family obligation in traditional Japanese cultures was often considered more important than personal freedom. Although many of the Nisei values have eroded among the Sansei because the Sansei are highly culturally assimilated, important vestiges of these values remain in Japanese communities today, especially among the aged. Some of these values, such as a high respect for authority and a strong sense of family obligation, conflict with mainstream American values. In mainstream U.S. society, authority is often challenged. It is rarely concentrated in one family member. Mainstream Americans also tend to be highly individualistic rather than group oriented.

Values in ethnic minority communities are often different from those in mainstream U.S. society. In the traditional Puerto Rican family, the girl was highly protected, and father was the undisputed head of the family. The family was also a highly interdependent unit. Uncles, aunts, and other relatives were often considered integral parts of the family unit. This type of extended family was also common among African Americans in the deep South. As African Americans and Puerto Ricans become more urbanized and more heavily represented in the middle classes, these aspects of their cultures diminish. However, the extended family is still a part of these ethnic cultures. Puerto Rican girls in New York City often do not have the same freedom to come and go with boys as do their Anglo-American peers.

When American Indians are studied in school, students are often introduced to certain stereotypic components of their cultures, such as tipis, baskets, canoes, or moccasins. These physical elements were parts of the cultures of certain American Indian groups, but they were by no means the most essential parts of them. Thus, students gain a superficial view of Indian cultures when they study only tangible cultural elements. *The essence of a culture can be understood only by studying its central values and their relationships to the daily lives of the people.*

The Indian view of people and their relationship to the universe must be studied to understand Indian values toward people and nature. Indian groups tended to look on the universe as a whole, with every object having a sacred life; to separate people from nature was antithetical to the Great Spirit, for to the Great Spirit all was life.

It is the values and related life-styles of ethnic communities that constitute their essence, not chow mein, basket weaving, sombreros, or soul food. These values and related behavioral characteristics and perspectives should be emphasized in the curriculum, not exotic cultural elements whose major outcome is the reinforcement of stereotypes. However, I am not suggesting that tangible cultural elements should not be studied, but that they should not be emphasized. Even though the study of ethnic values should constitute a large part of the multicultural curriculum, it is important to realize, however, that the values of all of America's ethnic groups are slowly changing, especially in urban areas. People of color are becoming urbanized at a faster rate than are mainstream Americans. It is also important to remember that highly assimilated and higher-status members of ethnic minority groups may share few, if any, characteristics with their more humble brothers and sisters. Despite these caveats, ethnic values are an integral part of life in the United States. They add strength and diversity to the U.S. national culture. This significant message should be communicated to students in all grades.

Self-Concept

An individual's feelings, attitudes, and evaluations of self constitute his or her self-concept (Lindgren, 1973). Each individual has a total picture of self that is largely a product of the individual's interactions within his or her social environment. How a person views himself or herself is cogently influenced by significant persons within his or her social world. Often individuals who exercise power over a person's life, such as parents and teachers, are important influences on the development of an individual's self-concept.

Many of the messages that youths of color receive from significant individuals and institutions within U.S. society regarding their ethnic groups are negative and dehumanizing. This fact has led some social scientists to hypothesize that youths of color internalize the negative images of themselves perpetuated by the larger society and thus have lower self-concepts than do White children. Prior to the 1960s, studies by researchers such as the Clarks (1940), Goodman (1964), and Trager and Yarrow (1952) consistently concluded that most Black children had lower self-concepts than did most White children. This research also indicated that African American youths make more incorrect racial self-identifications than do White children.

Researchers such as Baughman (1971), Larkin (1972), Spencer (1987), and Cross (1991) have seriously questioned the negative self-concept hypothesis. These researchers contend that the self-concepts of African American youths tend to be as positive as, and in some cases more positive than, the self-concepts of White children. Spencer (1987) has pointed that African American children who express a White preference (many do at a young age) often have a high self-concept. This is possible because *personal identity* and *group identity* are separate phenomena. Baughman believes that the African American child's positive self-concept is formed prior to his or her experiences with the White world. Research by Spencer (1987) and Cross (1991) has helped scholars to better understand the relationship between racial preferences and self-concept.

Intercultural Communication and Related Concepts

Communication

Social science literature is replete with definitions of communication. An actor whose behavior and symbols are perceived and interpreted by another individual are common to these many definitions. When an individual communicates, he or she uses symbols that are interpreted by the perceiver. Successful communication occurs when both the sender and receiver of the symbols interpret them in a similar way. Communication is unsuccessful when the sender and receiver of the symbols interpret them differently.

Individuals who are socialized within the same culture or microculture are more likely to have shared meanings of symbols than are individuals who are socialized within different microcultures, cultures, and nations. The wider the differences in cultures or microcultures between individuals, the more ineffective communication is likely to be. A middle-class Australian is less likely to interpret correctly the symbols made by a lower-class African American than is a middle-class mainstream American.

Intercultural Communication

In response to the increased communication between nations and world cultures (caused in part by new technological developments and a heightened interest in ethnic minorities in the United States), a new field, intercultural communication, has emerged. This field draws concepts and generalizations from various disciplines and studies the variables involved in communication across cultures. The field is also known as cross-cultural communication, interethnic communication, and transracial communication. Lustig & Koester (1993) define intercultural communication as "a symbolic, interpretive, transactional, contextual process in which people from different cultures create shared meanings" (p. 51). Communication often fails across cultures because the message producer and the receiver have few shared symbols and have been socialized within environments in which the same symbols are interpreted differently.

Intercultural communication is an important concept in multicultural studies. It helps explain many of the conflicts and misunderstandings that often occur between ethnic groups in the United States. During the 1960s, many African Americans interpreted Black power symbols positively and viewed them as symbols of racial pride and political efficacy. Whites often viewed Black power negatively and considered it threatening and a form of Black racism. In 1995, Whites and African Americans, as groups, viewed affirmative action differently. Most African Americans (82%) indicated that affirmative action programs were still needed. Whites, by a narrow majority (52%), indicated that affirmative action programs were no longer needed (Benedetto, 1995).

Cross-cultural communication can be improved when individuals from different cultures begin to interpret symbols in similar ways and when they have a strong desire to communicate effectively. When teaching about intercultural communication, you can identify many examples of barriers to effective communication across ethnic boundaries on radio and television news programs and in local and national newspapers and magazines. The class can use role-playing and discussion techniques to explore ways in which cross-ethnic and cross-racial communication can be improved.

Perception

Social scientists define perception as the "complex process by which people select, organize, and interpret sensory stimulation into a meaningful and coherent picture of the world" (Berelson & Steiner, 1964, p. 88). This concept helps us better understand the factors that influence how individuals come to know and interpret their physical and social environments. Many factors influence how people view their world. Social and cultural factors are cogent variables. In our society, race, ethnic group membership, and social class often influence how people see and interpret events, situations, and social issues. An African American civil rights leader and a mainstream U.S. corporation president are likely to view the high unemployment rate among African American youths quite differently.

Cultural, ethnic, and racial variables affect the perception of the historian, the writer, and the artist, as well as the layperson. Culture and ethnicity may have a cogent influence on a particular ethnic historian, writer, or artist, or practically no influence. The individual's level of identification with his or her cultural or ethnic group will highly influence whether his or her work will be affected by culture or ethnicity. Ethnicity tends to be a strong factor in people's lives in a society characterized by inequality and high levels of ethnic discrimination; it tends to be a less important factor in a society in which the various ethnic groups experience social and economic equality. The United States is highly stratified along racial, social class, and ethnic lines. Consequently, culture, ethnicity, and race are cogent factors that often influence members of both dominant and minority groups, including the members of these groups who are historians, writers, and artists.

Historically, American history and literature written by mainstream Americans have been mainstream-centric and have interpreted events and situations primarily from mainstream perspectives (Phillips, 1918/1966). Often, minority group cultures were not regarded as worthy of inclusion in literature anthologies, American history textbooks, and in music and art textbooks. Since the 1960s many mainstream American historians and writers have attempted to include more about ethnic groups in their works. However, often their interpretations of the experiences of other ethnic groups are mainstream-centric—although more benign than in the past. Since the 1970s, more historical, sociological, and artistic works by people of color have been produced (Berry, 1995; Franklin, 1976; Sizemore, 1972; Smitherman, 1995). Many of the perspectives presented in these works are refreshing. They add a vital component to our academic, artistic, literary, and social worlds.

Historical Bias

The social, cultural, and ethnic variables that influence how historians perceive their data result in *historical bias*. A historian's view of the past is influenced by his or her culture, personal biases, purposes for writing, availability of data, and the times in which he or she lives and writes (Appleby, Hunt, & Jacob, 1994). Because the historian can never totally reconstruct past events and is unable to report all the data he or she uncovers about particular events, he or she must use some criteria to determine which aspects of an event to report. The historian must also interpret historical events. History cannot be written without presenting interpretations and points of view. Because this is the case, it is important for you to teach students about the biases inherent in all historical writing and how to recognize and analyze them.

It is especially important for you to teach students how to analyze historical materials that are related to America's ethnic minority groups. Prior to the 1970s most histories of minority groups were written by mainstream historians. They often wrote histories of ethnic minorities that legitimized the dominant social and economic structure and that often depicted minorities negatively (Phillips, 1918/1966). Mainstream American writers and social scientists often perpetuated myths and stereotypes about ethnic minorities to explain why they "deserved" the low status in society to which they were most often assigned. Many of the stereotypes and myths that were constructed in early historical and social science research are still widespread within U.S. society; for example, African Americans were enslaved because they were uncivilized and lazy; slavery would not only civilize them, but would also deliver their souls to God; Indians were savages who had to be civilized by Whites in order to survive; Japanese Americans were a threat to national survival during World War II and thus had to be confined to relocation camps for national security. Some mainstream historians and social scientists are gatekeepers of the status quo; they generate research legitimizing the myths and stereotypes that dominant groups create about powerless groups to justify their status (Herrnstein & Murray, 1994; Jensen, 1969; Tucker, 1994).

Throughout human society, history has been written by the victors and not by the vanquished. Thus, most students in our schools study histories of American Indians and African Americans that were written by American mainstream historians who most often had little empathy or understanding of those cultures. Since this is the case, you should help students view the experiences of ethnic minority groups from their perspectives. I am not suggesting that the histories of ethnic minorities written by mainstream writers should be banned from the schools. However, the study of America must also be seen through the eyes of the vanquished, since students now study it primarily from the viewpoints of the victors. Even though both views can add to our understanding of the American experience, we must stress other viewpoints because mainstream views of American history are so widespread within our schools and the larger society. Only by trying to see this nation from the viewpoints of marginalized peoples will we be able to understand fully its complexity.

Histories and social science accounts written by ethnic minority writers, like the writings of dominant groups, reflect particular points of view and biases. However, students need to study these writings seriously in order to gain a "balanced" perspective on U.S. life and history.

Power and Related Concepts

Power

The ethnic experience within the United States cannot be understood without considering the role that the struggle for power among competing ethnic groups has played in shaping American history. History and contemporary social science teach us that in every past and present culture individuals have had, and still have, widely unequal opportunities to share fully in the reward systems and benefits of their society. The basis for unequal distribution of rewards is determined by elitist groups in which power is centered. Almost every decision made by people in power, including economic policy, is made to enhance, legitimize, and reinforce their power. Powerful groups not only make laws, but they also determine which traits and characteristics are necessary for full societal participation. They determine necessary traits on the basis of the similarity of such traits to their own values, physical characteristics, life-styles, and behavior. At various periods in history, powerful groups have used celibacy, gender, ethnicity, race, religion, as well as many other variables, to determine which individuals and groups would be given or denied opportunities for social mobility and full societal participation.

In colonial America, male Anglo-Saxon Protestants with property controlled most social, political, economic, and military institutions. These were the men who wrote the Declaration of Independence and the United States Constitution (Berry, 1995). They excluded from full participation in decision making those people such as African Americans and American Indians who were different from themselves. Our founding fathers had a deep suspicion of and contempt for individuals who were culturally and racially different. They invented and perpetuated stereotypes and myths about excluded groups to justify their oppression (Franklin, 1976). The United States, like all other nations, is still controlled by a few powerful groups who deny individuals opportunities to participate in society on the basis of how similar such individuals are to themselves.

Money and power in the United States are highly concentrated; the gap between the rich and the poor is widening. In 1959, the top 4% of families in the U.S. population earned as much as the bottom 35%. By 1989, the top 4% of families earned as much as the bottom 51%. In 1989 the top 4% (3.8 million individuals and families) earned $452 billion in wages and salaries, the same as the bottom 51%, which consisted of 49.2 million individuals and families (Barlett & Steele, 1992, p. ix).

When studying about power relationships in American society, students can be asked to hypothesize about how we can make our nation an open society and thus more consistent with our national ideology. They can define an open society as one in which rewards and opportunities are not necessarily evenly distributed, but are distributed on the basis of the knowledge and skills that each person, regardless of his or her ethnic characteristics, can contribute to the fulfillment of the needs of society. Students should be asked to discuss which of their hypotheses are most sound and how actions based on them might be implemented, and to state their limitations.

Social Protest and Resistance

Throughout U.S. history, movements have emerged within ethnic communities to protest social conditions, political policies, and economic practices that were considered unjust and unconstitutional. The types of protest have varied widely, from the actions of individual Japanese Americans to resist the internment during World War II to the race riots that occurred in U.S. cities in the 1960s. Groups tend to resort to extreme methods of protest such as riots and rebellions when they feel that the political system is oppressive, that there are no legitimate channels for the alleviation of their grievances, that there is some cause for hope, or that their protest movement might succeed. When studying about social protest, it is important for students to understand that such movements occur only when oppressed people feel that there is a cause for hope. For example, students can derive this generalization when studying the Black protest movements of the 1960s. This movement emerged partly because prior policies aimed at reducing discrimination had occurred. These included the desegregation of the armed forces by President Harry S Truman, the laws that desegregated many southern state universities, and the historic *Brown* v. *Board of Education* Supreme Court Decision in 1954, which legally outlawed *de jure* school segregation. These events were necessary precedents to the Black civil rights movement of the 1960s.

Many people think the ethnic protests of the 1960s were the first of their kind in U.S. history. Even though it is true that ethnic protests reached their zenith during these years, ethnic groups have protested discrimination and racism throughout U.S. history. Black protest actually began on the slave ships on the journeys from West Africa to the Americas. Slave uprisings and mutinies often occurred on these ships. Many slaves also committed suicide by throwing themselves into the Atlantic rather than acquiescently accepting bondage. Protest by African Americans continued during and after slavery. Slave uprisings, led by such individuals as Denmark Vesey, Gabriel Prosser, and Nat Turner, sometimes resulted in the mass murder of Whites (Aptheker, 1943/ 1987; Genovese, 1979).

Near the turn of the century, Black organizations emerged to fight systematically for civil rights, including the National Association for the Advancement of Colored People (NAACP) and the National Urban League. Other ethnic groups have also continually fought for their rights. Such organizations as the Anti-Defamation League of B'nai B'rith, the Japanese American

Citizenship League, the League of United Latin-American Citizens, and the Puerto Rican Forum were organized to work for the civil rights of various ethnic groups in a systematic way. Oppression of any human group is likely to lead to organized protest and resistance. Such protest and resistance have emerged within all of America's ethnic minority groups, although the forms and styles of that protest have reflected the unique cultural values, life-styles, and histories of the particular groups.

THE MOVEMENT OF ETHNIC GROUPS

Migration and Immigration

When individuals or groups move within a nation in which they are natives or citizens, we say that they are *migrants*. Individuals or groups who settle in a foreign country are called *immigrants*. Thus, migration describes the movement of individuals and groups within a nation, and immigration describes the settlement of people in a foreign nation. These two concepts must be studied in the multicultural curriculum because all groups that comprise the United States, except for a few such as American Indians, Eskimos, Aleuts, and Native Hawaiians, immigrated to this land from a foreign nation or migrated from Puerto Rico. We call Puerto Ricans migrants rather than immigrants because they became U.S. citizens with the passage of the Congressional Jones Act of 1917. Archeological theories and evidence indicate that American Indians immigrated to the Americas from Asia via the Bering Strait. Although this evidence is strongly endorsed by anthropologists, it is inconclusive. Many American Indians believe that they were created in the Americas by the Great Spirit.

When studying these two concepts, students can formulate hypotheses about why masses of immigrants entered the United States in the nineteenth century. Between 1820 and 1930, about 38 million immigrants came to the United States, most of them from Europe (U.S. Bureau of the Census, 1982). Students might hypothesize that many individuals and groups came to the United States to avoid religious and political persecution and to improve their economic conditions. When studying statistics on immigration to the United States, students can be asked to note the countries from which most immigrants came and to explain why. For example, between 1820 and 1979 6,985,000 German immigrants entered the United States. During the same period, only 3,038,000 immigrants came from the entire continent of Asia, and 36,267,000 came from the rest of Europe. Only 142,000 came from Africa. An investigation into why many more immigrants came from Europe than from Asia and Africa will lead students to discover that our immigration policies, until they were reformed in 1965, were designed to keep this nation largely White and to keep out non-Whites. Table 3-4 gives the numbers and

Table 3-4 IMMIGRANTS, BY COUNTRY OF LAST PERMANENT RESIDENCE: 1820–1979

Country	1820–1979, total	1951–1960, total	1961–1970, total	1971–1979, total	1975	1976	1977	1978	1979	Percentage 1820–1979	Percentage 1961–1970	Percentage 1971–1979
Total	49,124	2,515.5	3,321.7	3,962.5	386.2	398.6	462.3	601.4	460.3	100.0	100.0	100.0
Europe	36,267	1,325.6	1,123.4	728.2	72.8	73.0	74.0	76.2	64.2	73.8	33.8	18.4
Austria	4,316 {	67.1 {	20.6	9.1	.5	.5	.5	.5	.5	8.8	.6	.2
Hungary	}	36.6 }	5.4	5.8	.6	.6	.5	.6	.5		.2	.1
Belgium	204	18.6	9.2	4.7	.4	.5	.5	.6	.6	.4	.3	.1
Czechoslovakia	138	.9	3.3	5.0	.3	.3	.3	.4	.5	.3	.1	.1
Denmark	364	11.0	9.2	3.9	.3	.4	.4	.4	.4	.7	.3	.1
Finland	33	4.9	4.2	2.3	.2	.2	.2	.3	.3	.1	.1	.1
France	754	51.1	45.2	22.7	1.8	2.0	2.7	2.7	2.9	1.5	1.4	.6
Germany[1]	6,985	477.8	190.8	67.9	5.9	6.6	7.4	7.6	7.2	14.2	5.7	1.7
Great Britain[2]	4,914	195.5	210.0	121.5	12.2	13.0	14.0	16.4	15.5	10.0	6.3	3.1
Greece	661	47.6	86.0	87.7	9.8	8.6	7.8	7.0	5.9	1.3	2.6	2.2
Ireland[3]	4,724	57.3	37.5	10.6	1.1	1.0	1.0	.9	.8	9.6	1.1	.3
Italy	5,300	185.5	214.1	123.9	11.0	8.0	7.4	7.0	6.0	10.8	6.4	3.1
Netherlands	360	52.3	30.6	9.5	.8	.9	1.0	1.2	1.2	.7	.9	.2
Norway	856	22.9	15.5	3.5	.4	.3	.3	.4	.4	1.7	.5	.1
Poland[1]	520	10.0	53.5	32.5	3.5	3.2	3.3	4.5	3.9	1.1	1.6	.8
Portugal	453	19.6	76.1	93.3	11.3	11.0	10.0	10.5	7.1	.9	2.3	2.4
Soviet Union[4]	3,376	.6	2.3	28.4	4.7	7.4	5.4	4.7	1.9	6.9	.1	.7
Spain	262	7.9	44.7	37.4	2.6	2.3	5.6	4.3	3.3	.5	1.3	.9
Sweden	1,273	21.7	17.1	5.8	.5	.6	.6	.6	.8	2.6	.5	.1
Switzerland	350	17.7	18.5	7.7	.7	.8	.8	.9	.9	.7	.6	.2

(Continued)

Table 3-4 *CONTINUED*

Country	1820–1979, total	1951–1960, total	1961–1970, total	1971–1979, total	1975	1976	1977	1978	1979	Percentage		
										1820–1979	1961–1970	1971–1979
Yugoslavia	116	8.2	20.4	28.5	2.9	2.3	2.3	2.2	1.9	.2	.6	.7
Other Europe	310	10.8	9.2	16.4	1.3	2.0	2.0	2.5	1.8	.6	.3	.4
Asia	3,038	153.3	427.8	1,352.1	129.2	146.7	150.8	243.6	183.0	6.2	12.9	34.1
China[5]	540	9.7	34.8	96.7	9.2	9.9	12.5	14.5	12.3	1.1	1.0	2.4
Hong Kong	[6]200	15.5	75.0	109.5	12.5	13.7	12.3	11.1	16.8	.4	2.3	2.8
India	182	2.0	27.2	141.4	14.3	16.1	16.8	19.1	18.6	.4	.8	3.6
Iran	648	3.4	10.3	34.9	2.2	2.6	4.2	5.9	8.3	.1	.3	.9
Israel	690	25.5	29.6	34.2	3.5	5.2	4.4	4.5	4.3	.2	.9	.9
Japan	411	46.3	40.0	45.4	4.8	4.8	4.5	4.5	4.5	.8	1.2	1.1
Jordan	[6]41	5.8	11.7	24.0	2.3	2.4	2.9	3.2	3.2	.1	.3	.6
Korea	[6]276	6.2	34.5	235.4	28.1	30.6	30.7	28.8	28.7	.6	1.0	5.9
Lebanon	[6]58	4.5	15.2	37.3	4.0	5.0	5.5	4.8	4.8	.1	.5	.9
Philippines	[7]431	19.3	98.4	312.7	31.3	36.8	38.5	36.6	40.8	.9	3.0	7.9
Turkey	386	3.5	10.1	11.1	1.1	1.0	1.0	1.0	1.3	.8	.3	.3
Vietnam	[8]133	2.7	4.2	129.3	2.7	2.4	3.4	87.6	19.1	.3	.1	3.3
Other Asia	244	9.0	36.7	140.3	13.2	16.2	14.1	22.0	20.3	.5	1.2	3.5
America	9,248	996.9	1,716.4	1,778.3	174.7	169.2	223.2	266.5	197.1	18.8	51.7	44.9
Argentina	[9]97	19.5	49.7	27.2	2.8	2.7	3.1	4.1	3.1	.2	1.5	.7
Brazil	[9]59	13.8	29.3	16.4	1.4	1.4	1.9	2.2	1.8	.1	.9	.4
Canada	4,125	378.0	413.3	156.2	11.2	11.4	18.0	23.5	20.2	8.4	12.4	3.9
Colombia	[9]156	18.0	72.0	66.0	6.4	5.7	8.2	10.9	10.5	.3	2.2	1.7
Cuba	[10]539	78.9	208.5	249.7	25.6	28.4	66.1	27.5	14.0	1.1	6.3	6.3
Dominican Republic	[10]235	9.9	93.3	130.8	14.1	12.4	11.6	19.5	17.5	.5	2.8	3.3
Ecuador	[9]91	9.8	36.8	44.0	4.7	4.5	5.2	5.7	4.4	.2	1.1	1.1

El Salvador	[9]50	5.9	15.0	28.4	2.4	4.4	5.9	4.5	.1	.4	.7
Guatemala	[9]44	4.7	15.9	22.2	1.9	3.7	4.1	2.6	.1	.5	.6
Haiti	[10]89	4.4	34.5	49.8	5.0	5.2	6.1	6.1	.2	1.0	1.3
Honduras	[9]37	6.0	15.7	14.8	1.4	1.6	2.7	2.5	.2	.5	.4
Mexico	2,177	299.8	453.9	583.7	62.6	44.6	92.7	52.5	4.4	13.7	14.7
Panama	[9]51	11.7	19.4	19.8	1.7	2.5	3.3	3.5	.1	.6	.5
Peru	[9]52	7.4	19.1	25.1	2.3	3.9	5.1	4.0	.1	.6	.6
Other West Indies	758	29.8	133.9	237.4	22.3	27.1	34.6	33.5	1.5	4.0	6.0
Other America	695	99.2	106.2	106.9	8.9	16.1	18.6	16.4	1.4	3.2	2.7
Africa	142	14.1	29.0	66.7	5.9	9.6	10.3	11.2	.3	.9	1.7
Australia and New Zealand	123	11.5	19.6	21.6	1.8	2.5	2.6	2.5	.3	.6	.5
All other	309	14.0	5.7	15.8	1.9	2.2	2.2	2.3	.6	.2	.4

SOURCE: U.S. Immigration and Naturalization Service, *Annual Report*. Reprinted from U.S. Bureau of the Census, *Statistical Abstract of the United States, 1982–83* (Washington, D.C.: U.S. Government Printing Office, 1982), p. 89.

[In thousands, except percent. For years ending June 30 except, beginning 1977, ending September 30. Data prior to 1906 refer to country from which aliens came. Because of boundary changes and changes in list of countries separately reported, data for certain countries not comparable throughout. See also *Historical Statistics, Colonial Times to 1970*, series C 89–119.]

1 1938–1945, Austria included with Germany; 1899–1919, Poland included with Austria-Hungary, Germany, and Soviet Union.
2 Beginning 1952, includes data for United Kingdom not specified, formerly included with "Other Europe."
3 Comprises Eire and Northern Ireland.
4 Europe and Asia.
5 Beginning 1957, includes Taiwan.
6 Prior to 1951, included with "Other Asia."
7 Prior to 1951, Philippines included with "All other."
8 Prior to 1953, data for Vietnam not available.
9 Prior to 1951, included with "Other America."
10 Prior to 1951, included with "Other West Indies."

countries of origin of people immigrating to the United States between 1820 and 1979. This table can be the source of numerous inquiry exercises like the one suggested above.

A study of immigration to the United States since the Immigration Reform Act of 1965 reveals that the source of immigration to the United States has changed substantially since that time (see Table 3-5). Nearly 60% of the immigrants to the United States between 1951 and 1960 were from nations in Europe. Europeans comprised only 9.6% of the immigrants to the United States between 1981 and 1990. Asian immigrants to the United States increased from about 6% between 1951 and 1960 to 38% between 1981 and 1990.

During their study of the immigration and migration of ethnic groups, students can profitably compare and contrast the reasons that various groups migrated and the kinds of experiences they had in their new country. The special case of African immigrants to the United States should be highlighted. This group differed from all the other immigrant groups because their immigration was forced. They were also the only group enslaved on their arrival in the Americas. All the other groups of immigrants voluntarily came to the Americas, although many were escaping abject poverty, religious persecution, and dehumanization. Many of the early immigrants to the Americas were indentured servants who had few rights. However, most White indentured servants were eventually able to obtain their freedom.

When studying about the southern and eastern European immigrants to the United States, students can note how each group experienced discrimination and lived in urban ghettos, and how many of them eventually became culturally assimilated, attained social mobility, and moved to the suburbs of cities such as New York, Boston, and Chicago. Groups like Italians and Poles discriminated against African Americans and Mexican Americans when these groups started migrating to large cities after the two world wars.

European immigrant groups, especially the southern and eastern ones, were often the victims of discrimination and racist ideologies, but the racism they experienced never reached the proportions it did in the South against African Americans or on the West Coast when Asian immigrants started arriving there in the 1800s. It is important for students to realize that even though certain classes of European immigrants, such as lunatics, convicts, and idiots, were prevented from entering the United States in the 1800s, the first national group that was totally excluded from the United States was non-White. The Chinese Exclusion Act of 1882 completely stopped Chinese immigration to the United States for several decades. In the 1920s, the number of southern and eastern European immigrants entering the United States was reduced to a trickle because discrimination against them became intense and widespread. Non-White groups were virtually excluded from the United States. Only groups from northern and Western Europe were favored by the "national origins" quota

Table 3-5 IMMIGRANTS, BY COUNTRY OF BIRTH: 1971–1992

Country of Birth	1971–80, total	1981–90, total	1991	1992
All countries	4,493.3	7,338.1	1,827.2	974.0
Europe[1]	801.3	705.6	135.2	145.4
France	17.8	23.1	2.5	3.3
Germany	66.0	70.1	6.5	9.9
Greece	93.7	29.1	2.1	1.9
Ireland	14.1	32.8	4.8	12.2
Italy	130.1	32.9	2.6	2.6
Poland	43.6	97.4	19.2	25.5
Portugal	104.5	40.0	4.5	2.7
Romania	17.5	38.9	8.1	6.5
Soviet Union, former[2]	43.2	84.0	57.0	43.6
Armenia	(NA)	(NA)	(NA)	6.1
Azerbaijan	(NA)	(NA)	(NA)	1.6
Belarus	(NA)	(NA)	(NA)	3.2
Moldova	(NA)	(NA)	(NA)	1.7
Russia	(NA)	(NA)	(NA)	8.9
Ukraine	(NA)	(NA)	(NA)	14.4
Uzbekistan	(NA)	(NA)	(NA)	1.7
Spain	30.0	15.8	1.8	1.6
United Kingdom	123.5	142.1	13.9	20.0
Yugoslavia	42.1	19.2	2.7	2.6
Asia	1,633.8	2,817.4	358.5	357.0
Afghanistan	2.0	26.6	2.9	2.7
Cambodia	8.4	116.6	3.3	2.6
China: Mainland	[3]202.5	[3]388.8	33.0	38.9
Taiwan	([3])	([3])	13.3	16.3
Hong Kong	47.5	63.0	10.4	10.5
India	176.8	261.9	45.1	36.8
Iran	46.2	154.8	19.6	13.2
Iraq	23.4	19.6	1.5	4.1
Israel	26.6	36.3	4.2	5.1
Japan	47.9	43.2	5.0	11.0
Jordan	29.6	32.6	4.3	4.0
Korea	272.0	338.8	26.5	19.4
Laos	22.6	145.6	10.0	8.7
Lebanon	33.8	41.6	6.0	5.8
Pakistan	31.2	61.3	20.4	10.2
Philippines	360.2	495.3	63.6	61.0
Syria	13.3	20.6	2.8	2.9
Thailand	44.1	64.4	7.4	7.1

(Continued)

Table 3-5 *CONTINUED*

Country of Birth	1971–80, total	1981–90, total	1991	1992
Turkey	18.6	20.9	2.5	2.5
Vietnam	179.7	401.4	55.3	77.7
North America[1]	**1,645.0**	**3,125.0**	**1,211.0**	**384.0**
Canada	114.8	119.2	13.5	15.2
Mexico	637.2	1,653.3	946.2	213.8
Caribbean[1]	759.8	892.7	140.1	97.4
Barbados	20.9	17.4	1.5	1.1
Cuba	276.8	159.2	10.3	11.8
Dominican Republic	148.0	251.8	41.4	42.0
Haiti	58.7	140.2	47.5	11.0
Jamaica	142.0	213.8	23.8	18.9
Trinidad and Tobago	61.8	39.5	8.4	7.0
Central America[1]	132.4	458.7	111.1	57.6
El Salvador	34.4	214.6	47.4	26.2
Guatemala	25.6	87.9	25.5	10.5
Honduras	17.2	49.5	11.5	6.6
Nicaragua	13.0	44.1	17.8	8.9
Panama	22.7	29.0	4.2	2.8
South America[1]	**284.4**	**455.9**	**79.9**	**55.3**
Argentina	25.1	25.7	3.9	3.9
Brazil	13.7	23.7	8.1	4.8
Chile	17.6	23.4	2.8	1.9
Colombia	77.6	124.4	19.7	13.2
Ecuador	50.2	56.0	10.0	7.3
Guyana	47.5	95.4	11.7	9.1
Peru	29.1	64.4	16.2	9.9
Africa[1]	**91.5**	**192.3**	**36.2**	**27.1**
Egypt	25.5	31.4	5.6	3.6
Ethiopia	(NA)	27.2	5.1	4.6
Nigeria	8.8	35.3	7.9	4.6
Other countries[4]	37.3	41.9	6.3	5.2
Australia	14.3	13.9	1.7	2.2

SOURCE: U.S. Bureau of the Census (1994). *Statistical Abstract of the United States.* Washington, D.C.: U.S. Government Printing Office, p. 11.
[In thousands. For fiscal years ending in year shown.]
NA Not available.
[1]Includes countries not shown separately.
[2]Includes other republics and unknown republics, not shown separately.
[3]Data for Taiwan included with China: Mainland.
[4]Includes New Zealand and unknown countries.

system that was set up by Congress in 1921 and tightened in 1924. The quota was based on percentage of residents of a particular nationality in the United States in 1920.

The McCarran Act of 1952 relaxed some of the earlier restrictions but made the national origin parts of the law even more severe. Significant immigration reform did not occur until the Immigration Act of 1965, which amended the Immigration and Nationality Act of 1952. This act became effective in 1968. The 1965 act removed the national origin quotas and liberalized U.S. immigration policy. The Immigration Act of 1990 was another major overhaul of immigration law. It "increased total immigration under an overall flexible cap of 675,000. The 675,000 level to consist of: 480,000 family-sponsored immigrants; 140,000 employment-based immigrants; and 55,000 "diversity immigrants." The act also "revised all grounds for exclusion and deportation, significantly rewriting the political and ideological grounds." The act "repealed the bar against admission of communists as nonimmigrants and limited the exclusion of aliens on foreign policy grounds" (U.S. Immigration and Naturalization Service, 1993, p. A.1-20).

SUMMARY

This chapter has discussed a number of high-level concepts that can be used effectively to organize and teach multicultural units and lessons. I suggested that key concepts selected for the multicultural curriculum should be able to function successfully in an interdisciplinary role, should help explain some significant aspects of the cultures and experiences of ethnic groups, and should be able to encompass a wide range of data and information. When choosing concepts for the multicultural curriculum, you should also consider your students' developmental levels and their prior experiences with content related to race and ethnicity. Chapter 4 discusses ways in which the multicultural curriculum can be planned and organized.

QUESTIONS AND ACTIVITIES

1. Identify an ethnic problem in your community, such as a controversy over busing for school desegregation or affirmative action, the question of open housing, or discrimination in employment. List concepts and generalizations from several disciplines that might help students understand the problem. What strategies and materials would you use to teach the problem to students?

2. State the advantages of interdisciplinary multicultural lessons and units. What problems might you encounter in trying to structure these kinds of lessons and units? How might you resolve them?

3. Examine several of the books dealing with specific ethnic groups listed in the bibliographies of this book. Identify and list culture traits that are unique to different ethnic communities. What is the origin of these culture traits? Why do they continue to exist? Are they unique to particular ethnic groups or merely associated with lower-class status or a certain region? Explain your responses.

4. After reading a book on each of the major ethnic groups, make a list of the types of cultural and physical differences existing within them. Explain why these differences emerged and why they still exist.

5. Make a list of the major occupations in which most American Indians, Mexican Americans, Asian Americans, Puerto Rican Americans, and African Americans work (See a recent edition of U.S. Bureau of the Census, *Statistical Abstract of the United States*). Note the percentages of each group working in the major occupations identified. Carefully study the data you have gathered. What generalizations and conclusions can you make about the occupational status of ethnic groups of color in U.S. society? What factors explain their occupational status?

6. Using a map of your city or community, pinpoint the regions in which the various ethnic groups live with different colored markers to represent each major ethnic group. What conclusions and generalizations can you make about where different ethnic groups are concentrated in your community? What factors explain their location patterns?

7. Locate several conflicting accounts of slavery or the U.S.-Mexican War and develop an inquiry lesson to teach students how personal biases influence the writing of history.

8. Study the treatments of the major ethnic groups in your basal social studies, language arts, or other textbooks. What conclusions can you make? What materials and strategies can you use to extend textbook treatments of ethnic groups? How?

9. List examples of racial and ethnic discrimination you have seen and/or experienced. Why did the discrimination occur? How might this type of discrimination be reduced? How did you respond to it? Explain.

10. Watch several television programs during the week that have ethnic minority characters. Also study the treatment of ethnic groups such as African Americans and Mexican Americans in a newspaper or news magazine for a one-week period. Write a three- to five-page paper summarizing your observations about the treatment of ethnic minorities on television and in the printed sources you examined. Did you find any examples of racism? Explain.

11. Try to think of several examples of problems that result from communicating across different ethnic cultures. Develop and write a lesson plan for teaching the concept of intercultural communication to students.

12. Define each of the following terms and tell why each is important:

high-level concept, interdisciplinary, conceptual curriculum, microculture, ethnic group, socialization, intercultural communication

REFERENCES

Appleby, J., Hunt, L., & Jacob, M. (1994). *Telling the Truth about History.* New York: Norton.

Aptheker, H. (1943/1987). *American Negro Slave Revolts.* New York: International Publishers.

Banks, J. A. (1994). *Multiethnic Education: Theory and Practice* (3rd ed.). Boston: Allyn and Bacon.

Banks, J. A., Cortés, C. E., Gay, G., Garcia, R. L., & Ochoa, A. S. (1991). *Curriculum Guidelines for Multicultural Education.* Washington, D.C.: National Council for the Social Studies.

Barlett, D. L. & Steele, J. B. (1992). *America: What Went Wrong?* Kansas City: Andrews and McMeel.

Baughman, E. E. (1971). *Black Americans: A Psychological Analysis.* New York: Academic Press.

Benedetto, R. (1995, July 25). Affirmative Action Divides Blacks, Whites. *USA Today.* Section A, p. 1.

Berelson, B. & Steiner, G. A. (1964). *Human Behavior: An Inventory of Scientific Findings.* New York: Harcourt, Brace and World.

Berry, M. (1995). Slavery, the Constitution, and the Founding Fathers. In J. H. Franklin and G. R. McNeil (Eds.). *African Americans and the Living Constitution* (pp. 11–20). Washington, D.C.: Smithsonian Institution Press.

Bullivant, B. M. (1993). Culture: Its Nature and Meaning for Educators. In J. A. Banks & C. A. M. Banks (Eds.). *Multicultural Education: Issues and Perspectives* (pp. 29–47). Boston: Allyn and Bacon.

Clark, K. B. & Clark, M. P. (1940). Skin Color as a Factor in Racial Identification of Negro Pre-School Children. *Journal of Social Psychology 11,* 159–167.

Cose, E. (1993). *The Rage of a Privileged Class.* New York: HarperCollins.

Cross, W. E., Jr. (1991). *Shades of Black: Diversity in African-American Identity.* Philadelphia: Temple University Press.

Davis, F. J. (1991). *Who Is Black? One Nation's Definition.* University Park: The Pennsylvania State University Press.

Encyclopaedia Britannica. (1976). *Macropaedia.* Chicago: Author.

Feagin, J. R. & Sikes, M. P. (1994). *Living with Racism: The Black Middle-Class Experience.* Boston: Beacon Press.

Feagin, J. R. & Vera, H. (1995). *White Racism: The Basics.* New York: Routledge.

Franklin, J. H. (1976). *Racial Equality in America.* Chicago: University of Chicago Press.

Gay, G. (1973). Racism in America: Imperatives for Teaching Ethnic Studies. In J. A. Banks (Ed.). *Teaching Ethnic Studies: Concepts and Strategies* (pp. 27–49). Washington. D.C.: National Council for the Social Studies.

Genovese, E. D. (1979). *From Rebellion to Revolution: Afro-American Slave Revolts in the Making of the Modern World.* Baton Rouge: Louisiana State University Press.

Goodman, M. E. (1964). *Race Awareness in Young Children*. New York: Collier Books.

Hamilton, V. (1984). *A Little Love*. New York: Philomel Books.

Henry, J. (1963). *Culture against Man*. New York: Vintage Books.

Henry, J. (1971). *Pathways to Madness*. New York: Random House.

Herrnstein, R. J. & Murray, C. (1994). *The Bell Curve: Intelligence and Class Structure in American Life*. New York: The Free Press.

Hunt, C. L. & Walker, L. (1974). *Ethnic Dynamics: Patterns of Intergroup Relations in Various Societies*. Homewood, Ill.: The Dorsey Press.

Jensen, A. R. (1969, Winter). How Much Can We Boost IQ and Scholastic Achievement? *Harvard Educational Review 39*, 1–123.

Larkin, R. W. (1972). Class, Race, and Preadolescent Attitudes. *California Journal of Educational Research, 23*, 213–223.

Lindgren, H. C. (1973). *An Introduction to Social Psychology* (2nd ed.). New York: John Wiley.

Lustig, M. W. & Koester, J. (1993). *Intercultural Competence across Cultures*. New York: HarperCollins.

Merton, R. K. (1949). Discrimination and the American Creed. In R. M. MacIver (Ed.). *Discrimination and National Welfare* (pp. 99–126). New York: Harper & Row.

Miel, A. with Kiester, E., Jr. (1967). *The Shortchanged Children of Suburbia*. New York: American Jewish Committee.

Milner, D. (1983). *Children and Race*. Beverly Hills, Calif.: Sage Publications.

Montagu, A. (1974). *Man's Most Dangerous Myth: The Fallacy of Race* (5th ed.). New York: Oxford University Press.

Oliver, D. L. (1964). *An Invitation to Anthropology: A Guide to Basic Concepts*. Garden City, N.Y.: The National History Press.

Phillips, U. B. (1918/1966). *American Negro Slavery*. Baton Rouge: Louisiana State University Press.

Rose, A. M. (1962). The Causes of Prejudice. In M. L. Barron (Ed.). *American Cultural Minorities: A Textbook of Readings in Intergroup Relations* (pp. 77–80). New York: Alfred A. Knopf.

Rose, P. I. (1974). *They and We: Racial and Ethnic Relations in the United States* (2nd ed.). New York: Random House.

Sizemore, B. A. (1972, January). Is There a Case for Separate Schools? *Phi Delta Kappan 53*, 281–284.

Smitherman, G. (1994). *Black Talk: Words and Phrases from the Hood to the Amen Corner*. Boston: Houghton Mifflin.

Southern, E. (1983). *The Music of Black Americans: A History*. New York: W. W. Norton.

Spencer, M. B. (1987). Black Children's Ethnic Identity Formation: Risk and Resilience of Caste-Like Minorities. In J. S. Phinney & M. J. Rotheram (Eds.). *Children's Ethnic Socialization: Pluralism and Development* (pp. 103–116). Beverly Hills, Calif.: Sage Publications.

Stannard, D. E. (1992). *American Holocaust: Columbus and the Conquest of the New World.* New York: Oxford University Press.

Tamura, E. H. (1994). *Americanization, Acculturation, and Ethnic Identity.* Urbana: University of Illinois Press.

Taylor, M. D. (1975). *Song of the Trees.* New York: Dial.

Trager, H. G. & Yarrow, M. R. (1952). *They Learn What They Live.* New York: Harper.

Tucker, W. H. (1994). *The Science and Politics of Racial Research.* Urbana: University of Illinois Press.

Tumin, M. M. with Feldman, A. S. (1971). *Social Class and Social Change in Puerto Rico* (2nd ed.). Indianapolis: Bobbs-Merrill.

Uchida, Y. (1982). *A Jar of Dreams.* New York: Atheneum.

U.S. Bureau of the Census. (1982). *Statistical Abstract of the United States, 1982–83.* Washington. D.C.: U.S. Government Printing Office.

U.S. Immigration and Naturalization Service. (1993). *Statistical Yearbook of the Immigration and Naturalization Service, 1992.* Washington, D.C.: U.S. Government Printing Office.

van den Berghe, P. L. (1978). *Race and Racism: A Comparative Perspective* (2nd ed.). New York: John Wiley.

Weatherford, J. (1988). *Indian Givers: How the Indians of the Americas Transformed the World.* New York: Fawcett Columbine.

Weatherford, J. (1991). *Native Roots: How the Indians Enriched America.* New York: Fawcett Columbine.

Yep, L. (1985). *Mountain Light.* New York: Harper and Row.

ANNOTATED BIBLIOGRAPHY

Amott, T. & Matthaei, J. (1991). *Race, Gender, and Work: A Multicultural Economic History of Women in the United States.* Boston: South End Press.

An insightful and informative book on the experiences of women of color in U.S. labor.

Brooks, R. L. (1990). *Rethinking the American Race Problem.* Berkeley: University of California Press.

The author has crafted a thoughtful and informative examination of the race problem in the United States.

Franklin, R. S. (1991). *Shadows of Race and Class.* Minneapolis: University of Minnesota Press.

The relationship of race and class in the United States are perceptively discussed by the author.

Fuchs, L. H. (1990). *The American Kaleidoscope: Race, Ethnicity, and the Civic Culture.* Hanover, N.H.: Wesleyan University Press.

An eminent historian provides a sophisticated and perceptive examination of race, ethnicity, and the civic culture in the United States in this prize-winning book.

Gregory, S. & Sanjek, R. (Eds.). (1994). *Race.* New Brunswick, N.J.: Rutgers University Press.

This book includes essays on a range of topics related to race, including "American Racism: The Impact on American-Indian Identity and Survival," "Intermarriage and the Future of Races in the United States," and "Challenging Racial Hegemony: Puerto Ricans in the United States."

Hampton, H. & Fayer, S. (1990). *Voices of Freedom: An Oral History of the Civil Rights Movement from the 1950s through the 1980s.* New York: Bantam Books.

This excellent and comprehensive documentary history of the civil rights movement is a companion to the acclaimed television series Eyes on the Prize. *This is an excellent source to use with students.*

Milner, D. (1983). *Children and Race.* Beverly Hills, Calif.: Sage Publications.

The author discusses ways in which children acquire prejudices from society. He focuses on the racial situation in Britain but draws much of his research data from the United States.

Smith, L. (1949/1994). *Killers of the Dream.* New York: Norton.

This classic by the Southern White writer and activist is powerful and engaging reading. It provides keen insights that will help teachers think about racism today and the responsibility of Whites to help eliminate it.

CHAPTER 4

PLANNING THE MULTICULTURAL CURRICULUM

The multicultural curriculum should help students develop the ability to make reflective personal and public decisions. A curriculum focused on decision making must be conceptual and interdisciplinary and must be based on higher levels of knowledge. The preceding chapter, "Key Concepts for the Multicultural Curriculum," presents criteria and examples of concepts that you can use to organize multicultural units and lessons.

This chapter discusses ways to organize a decision-making curriculum after you have selected appropriate concepts and content. It also presents other components of an effective multicultural curriculum, including valuing and personal, social, and civic action. Steps you can take to master ethnic content and to select and evaluate instructional materials are also discussed.

IDENTIFYING KEY CONCEPTS AND ORGANIZING GENERALIZATIONS

When planning multicultural lessons and units that have a comparative approach and focus, you or a curriculum committee should start by identifying key concepts. These concepts should be higher-level ones that can encompass numerous facts and lower-level generalizations. They should have the power to organize a great deal of information and to explain significant aspects of the experiences and histories of ethnic groups. These concepts should also be able to function successfully in an interdisciplinary role.

After you or a curriculum committee has selected key concepts from several disciplines, at least one organizing generalization related to each concept should be identified. Each organizing generalization should be a higher-level statement that explains some aspects of human behavior in all cultures, times, and places. It should not contain references to any particular culture or group but should be a universal type of statement capable of being scientifically tested. Table 4-1 presents a list of key concepts and related organizing generalizations that can be used to plan a multicultural conceptual curriculum incorporating the experiences of a range of ethnic and cultural groups.

IDENTIFYING INTERMEDIATE-LEVEL GENERALIZATIONS

After an organizing (universal-type) generalization is identified for each key concept chosen, an intermediate-level generalization that relates to each organizing generalization should be formulated. An intermediate-level generaliza-

Table 4-1 KEY CONCEPTS AND ORGANIZING GENERALIZATIONS

Key Concept	Organizing Generalization
Acculturation	Whenever ethnic groups have extended contact, exchange of cultural traits occurs between minority and majority groups, as well as between different ethnic groups.
Intercultural communication	Individuals and groups socialized within different ethnic cultures are often unable to communicate effectively because they interpret the meanings of symbols differently. Ineffective communication frequently results in conflict between ethnic groups.
Perception	In a society stratified along racial and ethnic group lines, ethnicity and race tend to influence cogently how individuals see and interpret events, situations, and public issues.
Racism	Powerful groups that hold racist beliefs usually structure institutions, laws, and norms that reflect their beliefs and oppress the victims of racism.
Power	Within an ethnically stratified society, individuals and power groups struggle for power and influence. Power struggles often lead to social change.
Immigration–migration	In all cultures, individuals and groups have moved to seek better economic, political, and social opportunities. However, movement of individuals and groups has been both voluntary and forced.

tion applies to a nation, to regions within a nation, or to groups comprising a particular culture. Table 4-2 presents an intermediate-level generalization for *immigration–migration,* a key concept listed in Table 4-1. In an actual curriculum, intermediate-level generalizations would be identified for each organizing generalization selected and shown in Table 4-1. However, the example in Table 4-2 is limited to save space.

Table 4-2 GENERALIZATIONS RELATED TO IMMIGRATION–MIGRATION

Key Concept

Immigration–migration

Organizing Generalization

In all cultures, individuals and groups have moved to seek better economic, political, and social opportunities. However, movement of individuals and groups has been both voluntary and forced.

Intermediate-Level Generalization

Most individuals and groups who immigrated to the United States and who migrated within it were seeking better economic, political, or social opportunities. However, movement of individuals and groups to and within the United States has been both voluntary and forced.

Low-Level Generalizations

Indians: Most movements of Indians within the United States was caused by forced migration and genocide.

Mexican Americans: Mexicans who immigrated to the United States came primarily to improve their economic condition by working as migrant laborers in the western and southwestern states.

European Americans: Most southern and eastern Europeans who immigrated to the United States came primarily to improve their economic status.

African Americans: Large numbers of Blacks migrated to northern and western cities in the early 1900s to escape lynchings and economic and political discrimination in the South.

Asian Americans: Most Asian immigrants who came to the United States in the 1800s expected to improve their economic conditions and return to Asia. During World War II, Japanese Americans were forced to move from their homes to federal internment camps.

Puerto Ricans: Puerto Ricans usually come to the U.S. mainland seeking better jobs; they sometimes return to the island of Puerto Rico because of American racism and personal disillusionment experienced on the mainland.

Indochinese Americans: Most Indochinese Americans, unlike most American immigrant groups, came to the United States because of political developments in their native lands.

Determining Which Ethnic Groups to Study

Selecting a Range of Groups

When an intermediate-level generalization has been identified for each key concept, you must decide which ethnic groups will be selected for study. A range of groups should be included in comparative multicultural units and lessons in order to teach significant concepts related to American ethnic groups and to illustrate both the differences and similarities in their experiences, cultures, and histories. Groups that differ in racial characteristics, levels of assimilation, social-class status, and in the periods and circumstances of immigration to or migration within the United States should also be studied in the multicultural curriculum.

Units that include ethnic groups that have been successful educationally and economically, such as Jewish Americans and Japanese Americans, and those who still face massive social and economic problems, such as American Indians and Mexican Americans, can illustrate the enormous range in the experiences of ethnic groups in the United States. However, when ethnic groups such as Jewish Americans and Japanese Americans are studied, you should help students understand that although Jewish Americans and Japanese Americans have experienced tremendous educational and social mobility, members of these groups are often victims of discrimination and sometimes face identity problems related to their ethnicity (Klein, 1980; Tamura, 1994). Thus, these groups share some characteristics with lower-status ethnic groups such as American Indians, African Americans, and Mexican Americans.

Studying ethnic groups such as Chinese immigrants and Cuban Americans can illustrate the differences and similarities of two ethnic groups who came in large numbers to the United States at different points in history and for different reasons. The first Chinese immigrants came to the United States in the 1800s hoping to get rich quickly and return to their homeland. Most of the Cubans who settled in the United States between 1959 and 1970 came to escape a communist form of government (Olson & Olson, 1995). African Americans provide an interesting contrast to these groups. They were the only ethnic group that was forced to come to America. They came in chains.

The experiences of Jewish Americans in the United States have also been unique. Jews comprise a White ethnic, cultural, and religious group that has experienced high levels of educational and economic mobility but still retains significant aspects of their ethnic culture and identity. Many Jews still marry within their own ethnic group. Usually White ethnic groups become mainstream Americans when they attain high levels of educational and economic mobility (Alba, 1990). American Indians, Eskimos, Aleuts, and Native Hawaiians differ from most other ethnic groups because they can claim America as their native land. Indochinese Americans can be studied to illustrate the problems faced by ethnic groups displaced by a modern war and relocated in an alien and highly industrialized society.

Studying Groups That illustrate Key Concepts

No single multicultural curriculum can include a study of each American ethnic group. The number is much too large to be manageable. There are more than 100 ethnic groups in the United States (Thernstrom, Orlov, & Handlin, 1980). In addition to the groups of color who, since the 1960s, have urged educators to include more information about their histories and cultures in the curriculum, some White ethnic groups—such as Italian and Polish Americans—are also urging teachers to include the study of their experiences and histories in the school curriculum. Arab Americans—who numbered 870,000 in the 1990 U.S. Census (El-Badry, 1994)—also deserve attention in the school curriculum. Teachers need to help undercut the pernicious stereotypes about them that are institutionalized within the U.S. and other Western societies (Said, 1978).

A major goal of the multicultural curriculum is to help students master key concepts that will help them make better decisions and become more effective citizens in a pluralistic democratic society. *Thus, the focus should be on helping students master key concepts that highlight major themes in the experiences of ethnic and cultural groups in the United States.* Within a conceptual curriculum, which particular ethnic groups are selected for study becomes a secondary, though important, consideration. The experiences of the ethnic groups selected for study should be the best examples of particular concepts.

It is essential that students master certain concepts, such as *race, racism, prejudice,* and *discrimination,* if they are to gain a full understanding of American society and history. Racism has been a decisive force in our nation since its beginning and is still a major force in the United States today (Anti-Defamation League of B'nai B'rith, 1993; Terkel, 1992). Consequently, students must study this concept in a sound multicultural curriculum. When studying racism, students will need to examine the histories and contemporary experiences of ethnic groups of color such as African Americans, American Indians, Mexican Americans, and Asian Americans. Racism emerged to justify the enslavement of African Americans and was later developed into a full-blown ideology used to defend the exploration and exploitation of America and its native peoples (Banks, 1995).

Racism is still a major problem in U.S. society. A study of various ethnic groups that are victimized by institutionalized racism will help students develop a better understanding of this intractable problem and the ability to reason about it more intelligently. The different forms of prejudice and discrimination that exist in U.S. society also merit serious study by students in all grades—kindergarten through the university level. Research by Glock, Wutnow, Piliavin, and Spencer (1975) indicates that students who are more cognitively sophisticated and who can reason more logically about prejudice are likely to express fewer prejudices than are less cognitively sophisticated students. Gabelko and Michaelis (1981), influenced by the Glock et al. findings, developed a handbook of activities to help students reason more logically about prejudice and thus to reduce it.

A study of the experiences of Jews in the United States can facilitate an examination of the forms of prejudice and discrimination in contemporary U.S. society. Research indicates that anti-Semitism is widespread in the United States (Anti-Defamation League of B'nai B'rith, 1992). It warrants open examination by students within an uncoerced classroom atmosphere.

Concepts such as *cultural assimilation* and *structural assimilation* are also important in the multicultural curriculum. A study of groups of color, such as African Americans and Filipino Americans, can illustrate how some members of these groups have become *culturally* assimilated but have been denied *structural* assimilation, or the ability to participate freely in most U.S. institutions because of their physical characteristics. However, the study of White ethnic groups such as Irish Americans and German Americans can illustrate how these groups have attained high levels of cultural and structural assimilation. Often members of these groups are indistinguishable from other mainstream Americans (Alba, 1990).

When studying cultural and structural assimilation, students can also examine such groups as Polish Americans and Italian Americans. By studying these groups, students can see how some White ethnic groups are experiencing particular levels of cultural and structural assimilation but still retain many ethnic institutions. Individuals within these ethnic groups often participate in ethnic communities and institutions (Pula, 1995).

Other factors will also influence which ethnic groups you or the curriculum committee selects for study, including your interests and academic background and the ethnic groups represented in your class, school, and local community. However, units and lessons should not be limited to a study of local ethnic groups. Puerto Rican students should have the opportunity to study their own ethnic culture. They also need to learn about other ethnic cultures in order to understand more fully their own ethnic culture and the total human experience. Learning only about one's own culture is encapsulating and restricting. As Edward T. Hall has perceptively stated, "The future depends on [humankind's] transcending the limits of individual cultures" (Hall, 1977, p. 2).

IDENTIFYING LOW-LEVEL GENERALIZATIONS

When key concepts and organizing generalizations have been selected and the ethnic groups to be studied have been identified, low-level generalizations related to each ethnic group selected for study should be stated. Identifying a low-level generalization for each group will ensure that specific information about each group will be included in the teaching units and lessons that will be developed later. Table 4-2 presents low-level generalizations related to seven major ethnic groups and to the key concept, *immigration–migration.*

Organizing generalizations are universal statements that omit references to specific peoples, cultures, and places. Intermediate-level generalizations refer to a particular nation, to regions within a nation, and to a particular culture. Low-level generalizations differ from both organizing and intermediate-level generalizations. They apply to specific groups or microcultures within a culture and a nation.

CONCEPTS AND GENERALIZATIONS IN THE MULTICULTURAL CURRICULUM

To help you plan the multicultural curriculum, I have identified five key concepts related to ethnic groups and related intermediate-level generalizations. To save space, related organizing generalizations are not stated. However, these can be inferred from the generalizations given. For example, the first concept is *conflict.* The related organizing generalization, which encompasses the two statements below it, is: *Throughout history conflict has arisen between and among groups in all cultures.* Although organizing generalizations are not given below, they are important because they enable you to incorporate content from other nations for comparative purposes and to help students appreciate the power of high-level ideas. Table 4-3 shows how the students may use a data retrieval chart to study the key concepts below and *immigration–migration,* which is in Table 4-2.

CONFLICT: (The words and phrases in capitals are concepts; the statements that follow them are related generalizations.) Conflict exists among different generations and subgroups within ethnic minority groups. These conflicts are especially evident in values, goals, and methods of protest.

CULTURAL DIVERSITY: There is wide diversity among and within various ethnic groups. The extent of group identification by members of ethnic groups varies greatly and is influenced by many factors, such as skin color, social class, and personal experiences.

VALUES: Many values within ethnic minority communities differ from those of mainstream Americans, even though their values are changing, especially as people of color become more culturally assimilated.

SOCIAL PROTEST: At various times in history, movements within ethnic minority groups emerge to develop more pride in their groups, to shape new

Table 4-3 USING SELECTED KEY CONCEPTS FOR A COMPARATIVE STUDY OF AMERICAN ETHNIC GROUPS

Key Concepts	American Indians	Mexican Americans	African Americans	Jewish Americans	Vietnamese Americans	Puerto Ricans	Cuban Americans
Conflict: Within group: With other groups:							
Cultural Diversity: Within group:							
Values: Unique: Shared with others:							
Social Protest: Types used: Results of:							
Immigration–Migration: Reasons for: When: Results of:							
Assimilation: Cultural: Structural:							

identities, to gain political power and control of institutions, and to shatter stereotypes. The intensity, scope, and type of movements have varied widely from group to group and have been influenced by the unique histories, values, cultures, and life-styles of ethnic groups.

ASSIMILATION: As ethnic groups become more assimilated and attain higher socioeconomic status, they tend to abandon certain elements of their traditional cultures. However, they sometimes reclaim aspects of their cultural heritage once they are secure in middle- or upper-class status. This assimilation usually occurs in the third generation.

TEACHING STRATEGIES AND MATERIALS

Once you or the curriculum committee has identified the key concepts and generalizations that can serve as a framework for a multicultural curriculum or unit and has stated lower-level generalizations related to the experiences of ethnic groups in the United States, you (or the committee) can then identify the materials and teaching strategies necessary to help students derive the concepts and their related generalizations. A wide variety of teaching strategies, content, and materials can be used to teach ethnic content. The sample generalization about immigration–migration in Table 4-2 can be effectively taught by using content related to the forced westward migration of the Cherokee, which occurred in 1838 and 1839. This poignant migration is often called "The Trail of Tears." When teaching about Puerto Rican migrants, you can use Clara E. Rodriguez's (1991) excellent book, *Puerto Ricans Born in the U.S.A. A Historical Atlas of the Jewish People: From the Time of the Patriarchs to the Present,* edited by Eli Barnavi (1992), is a beautifully illustrated, richly informative, and excellent reference book for teaching the Jewish experience.

Walter Nugent (1995) examines European immigration from 1870 to 1914 in a well-written and revealing history, *Crossings: The Great Transatlantic Migrations, 1870–1914.* He discusses European emigration to Argentina, Brazil, Canada, and the United States. Ronald Takaki's (1993) *A Different Mirror: A History of Multicultural America* can help you and your students to rethink and reimagine the American experience. In *The Color Line: Legacy for the Twenty-First Century,* John Hope Franklin (1993), the eminent historian, describes the extent to which racism permeates contemporary U.S. society.

There are now excellent publications on women of color. You should make special efforts to integrate materials about women of color into the curriculum because they have been as invisible in minority history as they have been in White history. Well researched and scholarly historical works on women of color include *Black Women in America: An Historical Encyclopedia* (Volumes I & II), edited by Darlene Clark Hine; *The Montgomery Bus Boycott and the Women Who Started It,* edited by David J. Garrow (1987); and *Unequal Sisters: A Multicultural Reader in U.S. Women's History,* edited by Ellen Carol DuBois and Vicki L. Ruiz (1994). Darlene Clark Hine, with Wilma King and Linda Reed (1995), has edited an informative collection of articles on Black women history entitled *We Specialize in the Wholly Impossible: A Reader in Black Women's History.*

Simulation, role playing, as well as other strategies described in Parts II through V, can be used to teach effectively about immigration and other key concepts identified in this chapter. The six key concepts and organizing generalizations presented in Table 4-1 can be taught at every level within a spiral conceptual curriculum and developed at increasing levels of complexity with different content samples. At each level K–12 materials related to a range of ethnic groups should be used as content samples to teach students key social science concepts and generalizations. Figure 4-1 illustrates how six key concepts can be spiralled within a conceptual curriculum at eight different levels. This same curriculum design, of course, can be used in a K–12 program, an 8–12 curriculum, or with any levels.

Planning Lessons

To assure that every lower-level generalization identified in the initial stages of planning is adequately developed within a unit, the teacher can divide a sheet of paper in half and list the key concepts and the organizing, intermediate-level, and lower-level generalizations on one side of it and the strategies and materials needed to teach the ideas on the other half (see Table 4-4).

THE VALUE COMPONENT OF THE MULTICULTURAL CURRICULUM

Although higher-level, scientific knowledge is necessary for reflective decision making on ethnic and racial problems, it is not sufficient. To make reflective decisions, citizens must also identify and clarify their values and relate them to the knowledge they have derived through the process of inquiry.

Because many ethnic and racial problems within our society are rooted in value confusion, the school should play a significant role in helping students to identify and clarify their values and to make moral choices reflectively. Although the school has a tremendous responsibility to help students make moral choices thoughtfully, teachers often fail to help students deal with moral issues reflectively.

Some teachers treat value problems like the invisible person; they deny their existence. They assume that if students know all the "facts," they can

Figure 4-1 SIX KEY CONCEPTS SPIRALLED WITHIN A CONCEPTUAL CURRICULUM AT EIGHT DIFFERENT LEVELS

This diagram illustrates how information related to America's ethnic groups can be organized around key concepts and taught at successive levels at an increasing degree of complexity.

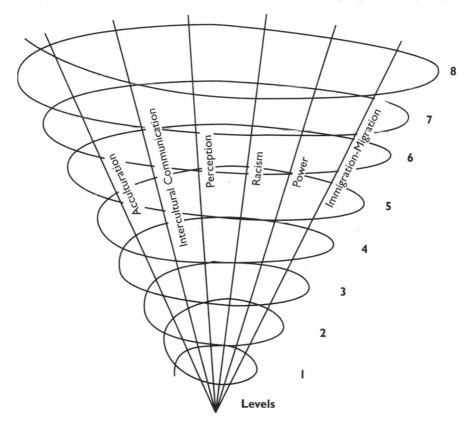

resolve value problems. Such teachers may be said to practice the cult of false objectivity. Other teachers use an evasion strategy: when value problems arise in the classroom, they try to change the subject to a safer topic. Probably the most frequently used approach to value education in the elementary and high school is the inculcation of values considered "right" by adults or the indoctrination of these values. Such values as honesty, justice, truth, freedom, equality, and love (as defined by teachers) are taught with legendary heroes and heroines, stories, rituals, and patriotic songs. This approach to value education is unsound and inconsistent with a culturally pluralistic ideology.

Although the school should promote the values inherent within the American creed, such as human dignity, justice, and equality, these values can-

Table 4-4 KEY IDEAS AND TEACHING STRATEGIES

Key Ideas	Activities
Key Concept: Immigration–Migration **Organizing Generalization:** In all cultures, individuals and groups have moved to different regions in order to seek better economic, political, and social opportunities. However, movement of individuals and groups has been both voluntary and forced. **Intermediate-Level Generalization:** Most individual and groups who have immigrated to the United States and who have migrated within it were seeking better economic, political, and social opportunities. However, movement of individuals and groups within the United States has been both voluntary and forced. **Lower-Level Generalization:** During World War II, Japanese Americans were forced to move from their homes to internment camps.	1. Reading aloud selections from Takashima, *A Child in Prison Camp.* 2. Discussing how Shichan, Yuki, and Mother felt when David and Father were taken away. 3. Viewing and discussing the drawings in *A Child in Prison Camp.* 4. Viewing and discussing the photographs in Conrat and Conrat, *Executive Order 9066: The Internment of 110,000 Japanese Americans.* 5. Hypothesizing about why Japanese Americans were interned. 6. Comparing textbook accounts of the internment with accounts in *Executive Order 9066* and *Within the Barbed Wire Fence: A Japanese Man's Account of His Internment* by Takeo U. Nakano. 7. Reading selections from the novel, *Journey to Topaz,* by Yoshiko Uchica, and discussing the experiences of the Sakane family during internment. 8. Viewing and discussing the videotape *Family Gathering* (New York: New Day Films). In this videotape, a Japanese-American woman comes to terms with her family's World War II internment. 9. Summarizing and generalizing about the forced migration (internment) of Japanese Americans during World War II.

not be taught in a didactic fashion. Didactic approaches to moral education, which many teachers use, are unsound because they fail to help students learn a process for handling value conflicts and dilemmas. Often, individuals must choose between two equally "good" values, such as between freedom and equality. In a democratic pluralistic nation such as the United States values such as freedom and equality are often interpreted differently by different individuals and groups. The values themselves are also often in conflict.

During the mid-1990s, Many African Americans, Mexican Americans, American Indians, and women argued that affirmative action programs were necessary for them to attain equal employment opportunities because of past discrimination. White males often opposed affirmative action and felt that it denied them equality and justice. In 1995, Governor Pete Wilson of California became a visible and influential leader in an anti-affirmative action movement that resulted in the end of affirmative action in the state's colleges and universities. Affirmative action became a highly contentious issue because of the different ways in which various interest groups viewed and interpreted it (Carter, 1991; Chavez, 1991; Ezorsky, 1991).

Because of the different ways in which various ethnic and racial groups often interpret the same values, such as justice, equality, and freedom, and because of the conflicts inherent in these values, teaching students in a didactic manner that they should value honesty, freedom, or justice is ineffective. Rather, students should be taught a *process* for identifying value conflicts, analyzing them, and for resolving value conflicts and dilemmas.

Students should also be helped to make reflective moral choices and learn how to justify their moral decisions. All values are not equally valid. Some values, such as inequality, racism, and oppression, are clearly inconsistent with human dignity and other American creed values that are set forth in the basic legal and constitutional documents of the United States. Although standards that guide a person's life must be freely chosen from alternatives after thoughtful consideration of their consequences, students who choose or hold values that conflict with human dignity and other American creed values should be helped to see how their values conflict with democratic values and ideologies.

Students should also be helped to understand and predict the possible consequences of the values they embrace. The major goal of moral education should be to *help students develop a process for identifying value conflicts, resolving them, and rationally choosing and defending their moral choices.* This is the only approach to value education that is consistent with our democratic ideology and that is educationally sound. Serious value problems arise in the classroom when ethnic groups are studied. Students of color often have important value questions about their ethnic cultures, their identities, and about effective strategies to use to effect social and political change. Public issues such as busing for school desegregation, affirmative action, and discrimination in housing and employment pose controversial and complex moral dilemmas.

APPROACHES TO MORAL EDUCATION

A number of models, approaches, and theories related to value education have been developed that you can use to organize and teach value inquiry lessons. These include the public issues approach developed by Oliver and Shaver

(1966) and Newmann (1970), the values clarification approach conceptualized by Simon, Harmin, and Raths (1991), and the cognitive-developmental approach developed by Lawrence Kohlberg (1975). The next section presents a brief summary of the cognitive-developmental approach developed by Kohlberg and a value inquiry model that I have developed.

The Cognitive-Developmental Approach to Moral Education

Kohlberg (1975) hypothesized that an individual's ability to reason morally develops sequentially in a series of definite stages and that these stages are found in all nations and cultures. He identified three levels of moral development: (1) the preconventional, (2) the conventional, and (3) the postconventional. Each level has two stages. The six stages constitute a hierarchy: each higher stage is a more sophisticated and more rational form of moral reasoning (see Table 4-5).

The theory assumes that an individual's stage of moral development can be determined and that moral education must be based on the student's stage of moral reasoning. A major goal of moral education, according to Kohlberg, is to stimulate students by using moral dilemmas to move to the next higher stage of moral development.

Kohlberg believed that students are not able to understand levels of moral reasoning that are more than one stage higher than their own. However, instruction below a student's stage of moral development will not stimulate him or her to think at the next higher stage. Kohlberg's research indicated that when students are engaged in discussions about moral dilemmas in which they are required to reason at one stage above their current stage, moral development and growth occur. Two basic assumptions of Kohlberg's theory are that an individual must proceed through the stages sequentially and that none can be skipped.

The theory assumes that there is an indirect relationship between chronological age and level of moral development. Very young children, according to the theory, tend to reason at the lower levels. As individuals grow older, they tend to reason at the higher levels. However, Kohlberg found that most individuals he studied were not able to reason beyond Stage 4. Kohlberg used open-ended stories that present moral dilemmas and discussion related to the dilemmas to stimulate students to think at higher stages of moral development. The nature and quality of the subsequent discussion are an extremely important part of this teaching strategy. Kohlberg used stories similar to the following one:

What Should the Vinsons Do?

Mr. and Mrs. Vinson are strong advocates of civil rights in the local community. Mr. Vinson testified in favor of school desegregation when the U.S. Commission

Table 4-5 A SUMMARY OF KOHLBERG'S
STAGES OF MORAL DEVELOPMENT

Level 1: Pre-Conventional

At this level an individual's moral reasoning results from the consequences of actions (punishment, reward, exchange of favors) and from the physical power of those in positions of authority.

Stage 1: Decisions result from a blind obedience to power, an attempt to avoid punishment, or an attempt to seek rewards.

Stage 2: Decisions result from a desire to satisfy one's own needs and occasionally the needs of others. Individuals view reciprocity as a matter of "You scratch my back and I'll scratch yours." Reasoning involves little consideration of loyalty, gratitude, or justice.

Level 2: Conventional

At this level an individual's moral reasoning involves consideration of the interest of others (family and peers) and a desire to maintain, respect, support, and justify the existing social order.

Stage 3: Decisions result from a desire to please and help others and receive their approval in return. Behavior is frequently judged by intention—"He means well" becomes important for the first time.

Stage 4: Decisions result from a desire to maintain the existing authority, rules, and social order. Right behavior consists of doing one's duty.

Level 3: Post-Conventional

At this level an individual's moral reasoning incorporates moral values and principles that have validity and application beyond the authority of groups. Moral reasoning becomes more comprehensive and reflects universal principles.

Stage 5: Decisions result from recognition of an individual's rights within a society that has a social contract. As a result the individual's reasoning emphasizes the "legal point of view," but with an emphasis on the possibility of changing laws.

Stage 6: Decisions result from an obligation to universal ethical principals that apply to all [human-]kind. The universal principes of justice, reciprocity and equality of human rights, and respect for the dignity of human beings as individuals serve as a basis for individual reasoning.

SOURCE: From "An Application of Kohlberg's Theory of Moral Development to the Social Studies Classroom" by Ronald E. Galbraith and Thomas M. Jones, 1975. *Social Education, 39*, p. 17. Copyright 1975 by National Council for the Social Studies. Reprinted by permission.

on Civil Rights held hearings on school desegregation in Northtown two years ago. A year ago the Northtown Public Schools were ordered by a federal judge to implement immediately a plan for desegregating its public schools. The plan was implemented when school opened in September. Lincoln School, which had been an all-White school, was the first school that African American students attended. These students are bused from the Vinsons' neighborhood.

The Vinsons' daughter, Tessie Mae, who is eight, is one of the students being bused to the Lincoln School each day. Tessie Mae gets up at 6:30 A.M. so that she can catch the bus in front of her house at 7:30 A.M. Last week, just one month after school opened, a ten-year-old African American girl was beaten by a White mob at Lincoln School. Rumors say that some White parents are coming to school with guns. The climate of the school is tense and hostile. A racial incident occurs at the school almost daily. Several days last week White parents greeted the buses bringing Black children to Lincoln School by throwing rocks and eggs at them. Anti-Black graffiti are on the walls of Lincoln's halls.

The Vinsons are worried about their daughter and are seriously considering taking her out of Lincoln School. However, the leaders of the National Association for the Advancement of Colored People (NAACP), who initiated the legal suit that resulted in the court order forcing the Northtown schools to desegregate, are strongly urging African Americans to keep sending their children to Lincoln. These leaders feel that if African American parents stop sending their children to Lincoln they will be doing exactly what many of the Whites want them to do and that they will be defeating the desegregation plan. The NAACP is urging the African American community to stand up for what it believes in: an equal education for African American children.

Question: Should the Vinsons take Tessie Mae out of Lincoln School?

A VALUE INQUIRY MODEL

I have developed a value inquiry model that is presented in detail in my book *Teaching Strategies for the Social Studies,* 4th edition (Banks & Clegg, 1990) that you can use to help students to identify value conflicts, to examine them reflectively, and to choose and defend their moral choices. The model is reprinted below (in list form), along with sample exercises illustrating how it can be used when discussing value problems related to race and ethnicity.

1. Defining and recognizing value problems: observation-discrimination.
2. Describing value-relevant behavior: description-discrimination
3. Naming values exemplified by behavior described: identification-description, hypothesizing.
4. Determining conflicting values in behavior described: identification-analysis.
5. Hypothesizing about sources of values analyzed: hypothesizing (citing data to support hypotheses).
6. Naming alternative values to those exemplified by behavior observed: recalling.
7. Hypothesizing about the possible consequences of the values analyzed: predicting, comparing, contrasting.
8. Declaring value preference: choosing.
9. Stating reasons, sources, and possible consequences of value choice: justifying, hypothesizing, predicting.

Value Inquiry Lessons: Examples

For value inquiry lessons, you can use case studies clipped from the daily newspaper, such as incidents involving controversy between police officers and various ethnic groups or cases related to busing to achieve racially desegregated schools, open housing, and affirmative action. Ethnic literature is an excellent resource for value inquiry. I use two examples to illustrate its use. Photographs, role-playing activities, and open-ended stories related to ethnic events can also be used effectively.

Example 1: Literature

A Child in Prison Camp by Shizuye Takashima (1971) is a powerful and poignant autobiographical account of the experiences of Shichan, a young girl in a Canadian internment camp during World War II. When the internment of the Japanese is studied, you can read aloud the following section from the book about the family conflict that occurred when the family was trying to decide whether to stay in Canada or return to Japan. You can then ask the questions that follow.

Spring 1944

The war with Japan is getting very bad. I can feel my parents growing anxious. There is a lot of tension in the camp: rumors of being moved again, of everyone having to return to Japan. Kazuo and his family leave for Japan. Many are angry they have left us. Some call them cowards, others call them brave! I only feel sad, for I like Kazuo so much, so very much.

Father shouts at mother, "We return to Japan!"

"But what are we going to do? You have brothers and sisters there. I have no one. Besides, the children...."

"Never mind the children," father answers. "They'll adjust. I'm tired of being treated as a spy, a prisoner. Do what you like: I'm returning!"

I can see Mrs. Kono looks confused.

"My husband is talking of returning to Japan, too. I think it's the best thing. All our relatives are still there. We have nothing here."

Yuki stares at her. "It's all right for you, Mrs. Kono, you were born there, but we weren't. I am not going. That's all!"

And she walks out of the house.

Mother gets very upset. I know she wants to cry.

"I don't want to go to Japan, either," I say. "They're short of food and clothing there. They haven't enough for their own people. They won't want us back."

(Reprinted from *A Child in Prison Camp*. Copyright © 1971, Shizuye Takashima, published in Canada by Tundra Books and in the U.S. By William Morrow).

Questions

1. What problem does the family face? (Defining and recognizing value problems)
2. What does mother want to do? What does father want to do? What does Shichan want to do? (Describing value-relevant behavior)
3. What does the behavior of mother, father, and Shichan tell us about what each thinks is important? (Naming values exemplified by behavior described)
4. How are mother's, father's, and Shichan's beliefs alike? Different? (Determining conflicting values in behavior described)
5. Why do you think that mother feels the way she does? Father? Shichan? (Hypothesizing about sources and values analyzed)
6. What are some other things that the family might have been able to do? Why? (Naming alternative values to those exemplified by behavior observed)
7. What might happen to the family if it stays in Canada? Goes to Japan? Why? (Hypothesizing about the possible consequences of the values analyzed)
8. What would you do if you were mother? Father? Shichan? Why? (Declaring value preference)
9. Why would you do what you said you would do? What might happen to you as a result of your decision? (Stating reasons, sources, and possible consequences of value choice)

Example 2: An Open-Ended Story

Open-ended stories present problem situations. If carefully chosen or written, they are excellent tools for stimulating class discussions of issues related to race and ethnicity, as well as other human relations problems. After reading an open-ended story to the class, you can have the students identify the problems within it, the values of the characters, the courses of action they might take to resolve the problems, and the possible consequences of the proposed solutions. The students can also act out or role play solutions to the problems.

Role-Playing in the Curriculum by Fannie R. Shaftel and George Shaftel (1982) includes several open-ended stories that deal with intergroup problems. The story reprinted below is from this book. Questions that can be used with the story are also provided.

Seed of Distrust

Betty was all excited when she ran into the apartment. "Mother, will you iron my green dress tonight?"

"I was planning to do it Saturday night, honey, so you'd have it for Sunday School."

"But I'll need it!"

"What's the rush?"

"Nora's invited me to a party tomorrow after school."

"Oh. I see," her mother said slowly, as if thinking hard. "Nora's the little girl on the second floor?"

"Yes. She's real nice."

Betty's sister Lucy, who was a sophomore in high school, asked. "Does her mother know?"

"Know what?" Betty asked.

"Nora's White. Isn't she?"

"Sure!"

"Does her mother know she's invited you?"

"Of course! I m-mean. I guess so."

"Does her mother know you're Black?" [Or Mexican, or Puerto Rican, etc.]"

"Sure!"

"You mean you think so?"

"Y-Yes," Betty stammered.

"Better make sure." Lucy said, and turned back to the math she was studying.

"I'll iron your dress, honey," Betty's mother said reassuringly. "You'll look real nice."

"Uh-huh." Betty said dully. "Thanks, Mom."

And then, next day, after lunch, the thing happened—Nora met Betty in the hall, outside the fifth-grade room.

"Betty. I've been hunting for you." Nora said urgently. "Listen. My Aunt Dorothy phoned last night. She's arriving today for a visit. My grandma's coming over to see her, and mother's making a dinner for the whole family, cousins and all. You see? We've got to postpone my party. Until next week, maybe. I'll let you know!"

Betty looked at her, blank-faced.

"Don't bother." Betty said. "Don't bother at all." And Betty turned and walked away, her back very straight. For an instant Nora just stood and stared. Then she ran. She caught Betty's arm and stopped her.

"Betty, what's the matter? Why're you talking like that?" (pp. 383–384)

(Copyright © 1982 by Prentice-Hall. Reprinted by permission)

Questions

1. What is the main problem in this story?
2. What do you think of these characters: Betty, Lucy, Nora? Why? What kinds of things and people do you think are important to each of them? Why?
3. Do you think that Lucy should have asked Betty if Nora's mother knew that she was Black? Why or why not?
4. Do you think Nora told the truth about the family dinner? Why or why not?
5. What are some courses of action that Betty can take? What should Betty do? Why? What would you do if you were Betty? Why? What might be the consequences of your action? Why?

PROVIDING OPPORTUNITIES FOR PERSONAL, SOCIAL, AND CIVIC ACTION

People of color in all regions of the United States are victims of institutionalized racism, poverty, and political powerlessness. When you identify concepts and generalizations, you should select those that will help students to make decisions and to take personal, social, or civic actions that reduce prejudice and discrimination in their personal lives, in the school, and, when possible, in the other social settings in which they function. Primary grade students cannot take actions that will reduce discrimination in the larger society. However, they can make a commitment to not tell or laugh at racist jokes, to play with and make friends with students from other racial, ethnic, and religious groups, and to read books that describe children from other racial, ethnic, and religious groups. Middle, upper grade, and high school students can also take personal and social actions within the school community to improve race and ethnic relations.

Teachers must play an active role in getting students to undertake personal and social action to improve race relations in their personal lives and in the institutions in which they function. To improve race relations in the classroom, you can structure interracial work and study groups, making sure that students of color have equal-status roles in these groups. Research has indicated that when students from different races and social classes have equal-status within interracial work and study groups, these groups can improve interracial attitudes and help students of color to increase their academic achievement (Aronson & Gonzalez, 1988). A number of researchers, such as Johnson and Johnson (1993), Slavin (1995), and Cohen (1994), have written publications that will enable you to structure cooperative groups that will help students develop more positive intergroup and interracial attitudes. If you structure groups within the classroom that improve students' interracial and ethnic attitudes, the students will be more likely to take actions in their personal lives outside of the classroom that will make their lives more interracial and intercultural.

After they have mastered higher-level knowledge related to racial and ethnic problems and have clarified their values, you can ask your students to list *possible actions* they can take to help improve race relations in their personal lives, in the school, and in the other institutions in which they function. Also ask them to list the *possible* consequences of each action they identify. Students should participate in action activities and projects only after they have studied the issues related to the action from the perspectives of the social sciences and humanities, analyzed and clarified their values regarding them, identified the possible consequences of their actions, and expressed a willingness to accept them.

Figure 4-2 is a graphic you can use when asking students to list possible actions and consequences they can take when planning action and participation projects and activities.

GAINING THE CONTENT AND CONCEPTUAL BACKGROUND

Most teachers, like most other Americans, have large gaps in their knowledge of ethnic and racial groups because content about these groups is not thoroughly integrated into the mainstream school, college, and university curricula. Within

Figure 4-2 POSSIBLE ACTIONS AND CONSEQUENCES

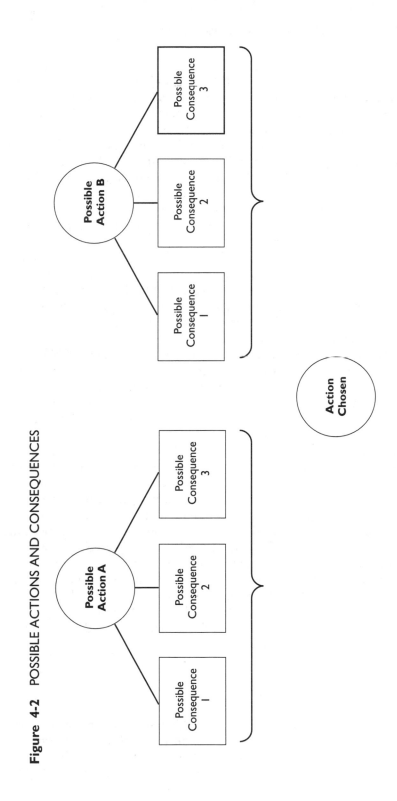

the last twenty years, many college and universities have implemented ethnic studies and/or multicultural education course requirements. Because of these requirements, most new and future teachers are more knowledgeable about ethnic and cultural groups than were most teachers of yesteryear. However, because ethnic and cultural content is still not fully integrated into the mainstream curriculum nor within the popular culture, current and future teachers need to increase their knowledge of the experiences of ethnic groups in order to become highly effective in today's multicultural classrooms and schools.

You need a working knowledge of the role of ethnicity and race in American life and about the histories and problems of the various ethnic groups before you can implement a sound multicultural curriculum. Even for the most ambitious teacher, acquiring the minimal knowledge needed to teach a multicultural curriculum is a challenging task. Although attaining information about American ethnic groups is challenging, it is equally rewarding. Ethnic content deals with the conflicts and dilemmas that have decisively shaped American life. It sometimes evokes anger and shame, but just as often compassion, admiration, and *hope.*

You should begin a reading program with one or two general books or comprehensive chapters that provide an overview of ethnicity and race in the United States. This type of book or chapter can provide you with a conceptual framework for interpreting and comparing the experiences of the various ethnic groups, as well as serve as an excellent source for concepts and generalizations that can be taught to students.

You should also read at least one general survey book or comprehensive chapter on each of the major U.S. ethnic groups. This publication should be a high-quality sociological or historical survey written from the perspectives of the group being studied. To become sensitive, you must learn to view events from the viewpoints of the victims of discrimination because for too long we have viewed U.S. history and culture primarily from mainstream American perspectives. Most teachers are familiar with mainstream perspectives on U.S. history, culture, and society. They need to become more aware of other ways to view America. The bibliography at the end of this chapter contains recommended books and book chapters that give general overviews of ethnicity and race in the United States, as well as survey books on each of the major American ethnic groups. Annotations for most of these books are found at the end of appropriate chapters in Parts II through V.

FINDING STUDENTS RESOURCES

Prior to the 1960s, the paucity of books for children and young people that dealt with ethnic groups was a serious problem for teachers and librarians. The number of books on ethnic groups increased significantly during the period between the late 1960s and the late 1970s. However, during the 1980s, the number of children's books published with ethnic themes and issues decreased, perhaps reflecting the general conservative mood in the nation during that decade. There are more books available on some groups than on others. A reasonable number of books on Jewish Americans and African Americans are still published each year. However, there is a paucity of new books for children and young people each year on Puerto Ricans, Mexican Americans, and Filipino Americans.

Evaluating books with ethnic themes is still a major problem; it is discussed later. How can you locate published books? The children's librarian in the public library and at the curriculum center of the local college or university are excellent resource people, as is the school librarian. Children's librarians receive a number of book lists and books from a wide variety of sources. They are usually willing and able to help you find books on a particular topic such as ethnic studies.

Hundreds of children's books are published each year. Consequently, you will find it necessary to rely on bibliographies published periodically by professional and ethnic organizations to locate the most recent books. Some of the best bibliographies that list books on ethnic groups are published by public and private organizations, such as state departments of education, school systems, civil rights organizations, public libraries, and professional organizations.

One of the most comprehensive periodic publications that contains critical reviews of children's books dealing with ethnic groups is *Multicultural Review,* published quarterly by the Greenwood Publishing Group, located in Westport, Connecticut. *Multicultural Review* also contains feature articles as well as review of videotapes and other audiovisual materials. *Multicultural Education,* a quarterly publication of the National Association for Multicultural Education, includes a column on "Multicultural Resources" that periodically includes a discussion of materials for students, including films, videotapes, and books. Most of the materials included in the column are for teachers and other professionals. *Teaching Tolerance,* a magazine published twice a year by the Southern Poverty Law Center, is distributed to teachers without charge. It includes helpful teaching ideas for teaching about diversity as well as books and other materials for use with students. The National Women's History Project in Windsor, California, publishes a periodic *Women's History Catalog* that includes some excellent materials on women of color for students and teachers.

Two book-length works that include valuable annotations and information on children's books about diverse ethnic groups are *Teaching Multicultural Literature in Grades K–8* by Violet J. Harris (1992), and *Culturally Diverse Library Collections for Children* by Herman L. Totten and Risa W. Brown (1994).

Rethinking Schools, an excellent and informative periodic publication targeted for a teacher audience, contains perceptive and serious reviews of both student and teaching materials related to diversity. Rethinking Schools is located in Milwaukee, Wisconsin. AACP, Inc., in San Mateo, California, markets books and materials on Asian Americans. It publishes a comprehensive catalog periodically. *Quarterly Black Review of Books* is published six times per year in New York City. It reviews books for children and adults. ABC Book Company in Oak Park, Illinois, markets multicultural books for children.

Social Education, the official journal of the National Council for the Social Studies, publishes an annual supplement on notable children's books. *The Booklist,* published by the American Library Association, the *Bulletin of the Center for Children's Books,* published by the University of Chicago Press for the University's Graduate School of Librarianship, *School Library Journal,* published by the R. R. Bowker Company, and *Horn Book* are periodic publications that contain reviews of children's books. *The Language Arts,* published by the National Council of Teachers of English, occasionally publishes articles that discuss children's books. The Council periodically issues special publications on books dealing with ethnic groups.

Magazines and newspapers, such as *Ebony* and *The New York Times,* also publish book lists and reviews of children's books periodically. You should check these sources. Finally, browsing in the children's section of local bookstores in large cities can lead to the discovery of a gold mine of recent children's books. The salesperson in charge of children's books is usually willing and able to help the browsing educator or school librarian.

GUIDELINES FOR EVALUATING AND SELECTING MULTICULTURAL MATERIALS

Some of the books and other materials on ethnic groups published each year are insensitive, inaccurate, and written from mainstream and insensitive perspectives and points of view. Nevertheless, good materials on each group are published annually. Identifying them requires a considerable amount of time and careful evaluation and selection. The criteria and examples of books below are offered to help teachers, curriculum specialists, and librarians evaluate and select ethnic studies resources for classroom and library use.

One useful way to select excellent books on ethnic themes for children and young adults is to examine carefully the new works of authors who have established reputations for writing sensitive and excellent books for children and young adults. African American authors, such as Lucille Clifton, Virginia Hamilton, Walter Dean Myers, and Mildred D. Taylor, have written excellent books that accurately depict African American culture in sensitive ways. Other authors of color have also written sensitive and powerful books about their particular groups, such as the late Yoshiko Uchida (Japanese American), Laurence Yep (Chinese American), Virginia Driving Hawk Sneve (American

Indian), and Nicholasa Mohr (Puerto Rican). Some writers who are not members of the ethnic groups they write about have also established excellent reputations for writing and editing outstanding books. Both Dorothy Sterling and Milton Meltzer have edited outstanding books on African Americans.

Books and other materials should accurately portray the perspectives, attitudes, and feelings of ethnic groups. Certain values, aspirations, and viewpoints are prevalent in American ethnic communities. Books should honestly and accurately reflect these perspectives and feelings, both through characters and in the interpretations of events and situations. One of the best ways to assure that books describe the perspectives of ethnic groups is to use books written by them. In *Thief of Hearts,* Laurence Yep (1995) describes how Stacy, a Chinese American girl, is torn between her Chinese and American cultures. In *My Life with Martin Luther King, Jr.* (1993), Coretta Scott King gives her perspectives on the important events in their lives. Yoshiko Uchida (1982) tells the powerful story of her family's internment in *Desert Exile: The Uprooting of a Japanese-American Family.* In her autobiography written for young people Rosa Parks (with Haskins, 1992) gives her view on her arrest that triggered the Montgomery Bus Boycott. Her account refutes often-repeated accounts that states that she did not give up her seat because she was tired.

Fictional works should have strong ethnic characters. Many books have characters of color who are subservient, weak, and ignorant. Papa, Mama, Aunt Waka, and Rinko are strong characters with whom the reader can empathize in *A Jar of Dreams* by Yoshiko Uchida (1981). The reader learns about the further adventures of Rinko in the sequels to this book, *The Best Bad Thing* (1985) and *The Happiest Ending* (1985). The reader comes to know and deeply care for characters such as Old Mary, Lali, Yolanda, and Rudi in Nicholasa Mohr's (1977) collection of interrelated stories, *In Nueva York.*

Books should describe settings and experiences with which all students can identify and yet should accurately reflect ethnic cultures and life-styles. *The Moon Lady* by Amy Tan (1992), *Finding the Greenstone* by Alice Walker (1991), *Drylongso* by Virginia Hamilton (1992), and *The Patchwork Quilt* by Valerie Flournoy (1985) each describe authentic ethnic cultures within the context of universal stories with which all children can identity.

The protagonists in books with ethnic themes should have ethnic characteristics but should face conflicts and problems universal to all cultures and groups. The characters in *Dragon's Gate* by Laurence Yep (1993), *The Best Bad Thing* by Yoshiko Uchida (1985), and *The Road to Memphis* by Mildred D. Taylor (1990) have authentic ethnic characteristics and values yet describe universal human problems.

The illustrations in books should be accurate, ethnically sensitive, and technically well done. Many books have beautiful photographs or drawings that are inaccurate. Excellent and powerful illustrations are in these titles: *Love Flute,* story and illustrations by Paul Goble (1992); *Lift Ev'ry Voice and*

Sing—The African American National Anthem, by James Weldon Johnson, illustrated by Spivey Gilchrist (1995); and *African Animals ABC,* written and illustrated by Philippa-Alys Browne (1995).

Ethnic materials should not contain racist concepts, clichés, phrases, or words. Many books contain words, phrases, and statements that have negative connotations even though these books might have many other strengths. Books on Eskimos sometimes present them as carefree, happy people who have no serious human problems. Some books on Indians either state or imply that all Indians lived in tipis, were hostile to European settlers, and were savages. Words such as *savage, squaw, hostile, primitive,* and *uncivilized* can alert you to a possibly insensitive book or resource, although their use in a book does not necessarily mean that it is insensitive. An author might use these words for the sake of historical accuracy, to depict the language of bigots, or for other justifiable reasons. The teacher or librarian must judge the use of words and phrases within the total context of the book or resource. Nevertheless, you should watch for these kinds of words when evaluating instructional materials. You should also be sensitive to stereotypes of ethnic groups that are subtle. Subtle ethnic stereotypes are more frequent in books today than are blatant ones.

Factual materials should be historically accurate. Books that present inaccurate information about ethnic groups confuse students and reinforce stereotypes. They can also be the source of misconceptions and stereotypes. Examples of accurate informational books about ethnic groups are *Jump at de Sun: The Story of Zora Neale Hurston* by A. P. Porter (1992); *Stubborn Twig: Three Generations in the Life of a Japanese American Family* by Lauren Kessler (1994); and *The Chinese American Family Album* by Dorothy and Thomas Hoobler (1994).

Multiethnic resources and basal textbooks should discuss major events and documents related to ethnic history. Events such as the removal of Indians to Indian Territory in the 1800s and the large migrations of Puerto Ricans to the U.S. mainland that began in the 1920s should be included in every multiethnic and U.S. history textbook. Key legal documents such as the Treaty of Guadalupe Hidalgo (1848) and the Chinese Exclusion Act of 1882 should be included. To be able to determine which key events and documents should be included in basic factual sources, you will need to read at least one general book and a comprehensive chapter on each of the major ethnic groups, as suggested earlier.

In addition to the guidelines suggested above, you should determine the age level for which a particular book might be appropriate. Both interest and reading level should be considered. Some books are excellent for adult reading but are inappropriate for school use; others are fine for older readers but inappropriate for young children. The type of classroom situation should also be considered when selecting multicultural materials. A particular book might be appropriate for use with some classrooms but not with others. You should bear in mind whether your class is, for example, all African American, all American Indian, all Asian, all White, or ethnically integrated. You should also consider how you will use each resource. Some books are excellent for basic information but will not give the students a feeling for the ethnic group. Other books have excellent illustrations but poor and distorted texts. Some excellent books, such as *Desert Exile* and *In Nueva York,* are not appropriate for all students, all purposes, and in all kinds of settings. You must exercise sound judgment, sensitivity, integrity, and insight when selecting and evaluating multicultural materials for class use. In the final analysis, only you can determine which materials can best help to achieve your instructional goals.

SUMMARY

This chapter has described the steps you must take to structure a multicultural curriculum focused on decision making. These steps include (1) the identification of key concepts and generalizations, (2) the formulation of intermediate-level generalizations, and (3) the identification of lower-level generalizations related to the ethnic groups selected for study. Once these steps are completed, you can then proceed to structure lessons and gather materials. When formulating lessons, you should make sure that lessons include value inquiry exercises as well as social-action and participation activities when these are appropriate. Examples of value inquiry lessons and social participation activities were discussed.

Prior to implementing a multicultural curriculum, you should plan a reading program that includes (1) one or two general books on ethnic groups in the United States, and (2) at least one survey book or comprehensive chapter on each of the major ethnic groups. Recommended books and chapters in both categories are in the bibliography of this chapter. The selection and evaluation of student materials is a challenging task. Guidelines and resources for completing this task were given.

Part I of this book deals with the goals of the multicultural curriculum and procedures for planning and organizing instruction. Parts II through V present historical overviews of ethnic groups in the United States and strategies and materials for teaching about them.

QUESTIONS AND ACTIVITIES

Respond to the following *Ethnic Literacy Test* and discuss your responses, giving reasons for them, with your classmates or colleagues. Determine your Ethnic Literacy Score by comparing your responses with the answers given at the end of the test. How might you use this test with your students to stimulate research and discussion? What sources might they use to check their responses?

Administer this test, in part or whole, to your class. Adapt it to your students' reading and grade levels. How well did they do on the test? Why?

Ethnic Literacy Test

Directions: Indicate whether each of the following statements is TRUE or FALSE by placing a "T" or "F" in front of it.

1. The percentage of Whites in the United States, relative to non-Whites, decreased between 1980 and 1990.
2. The first Chinese immigrants who came to the United States worked on the railroads.
3. In 1995, the population of African Americans in the United States exceeded the national population in Canada, as well as that of Australia.
4. Puerto Ricans on the island of Puerto Rico became U.S. citizens in 1920.
5. In 1990, Mexican Americans made up 61.2% of the Hispanics in the United States.
6. Between 1820 and 1930, 15 million immigrants came to the United States.
7. White Anglo-Saxon Protestants are the most powerful ethnic group in the United States.
8. Rosh Hashanah, which in Hebrew means "end of year," is a Jewish holiday that comes early in the fall.
9. Between 1971 and 1992 immigrants from the United Kingdom were the largest European group immigrating to the United States.
10. The first law to limit immigration to the United States was passed in 1882 to restrict the number of African immigrants.
11. Puerto Ricans in New York City tend to identify strongly with African Americans in that city.
12. Between 1980 and 1990, Asians and Pacific Islanders increased 108%, more than any other ethnic group.
13. Most African Americans came from the eastern parts of Africa.
14. The internment of the Japanese Americans during World War II was opposed by President Franklin D. Roosevelt.
15. In 1990, there were more than 20 million Hispanic Americans in the United States.
16. Almost a million (980,100) immigrants came to the United States from the Philippines between 1971 and 1992.
17. Congress passed a Removal Act that authorized the removal of Indians from the east to the west of the Mississippi in 1830.
18. A Japanese settlement was established in California as early as 1869.
19. The United States acquired a large part of Mexico's territory under the terms of the Treaty of Guadalupe Hidalgo in 1848.
20. Agriculture dominates the economy of the island of Puerto Rico.
21. The first Africans to arrive in North America came on a Dutch ship that landed at Jamestown, Virginia, in 1619.

22. The U.S. Census projects that by the year 2050 racial minorities will make up about 47.5% of the nation's population.
23. *Paper sons* is a custom that is associated with Chinese Americans.
24. In 1990, there were nearly two million American Indians, Eskimos, and Aleuts in the United States.
25. Some of the bloodiest riots involving African Americans and Whites occurred in the early 1900s.
26. About 227,800 immigrants from nations of the former Soviet Union came to the United States between 1971 and 1992.
27. The United States acquired the island of Puerto Rico from Spain in 1898.
28. There are only 438 Japanese surnames.
29. Chinese immigrants to the United States became distinguished for their outstanding work on truck farms.
30. The U.S. Census indicates that 192,000 Puerto Ricans lived in the Western states in 1990; most lived in California.
31. A third-generation Japanese American is called a Sansei.
32. About 233,800 Iranians immigrated to the United States between 1971 and 1992.
33. About one-fifth of Native Americans lived on reservations and trust lands in 1990.
34. Most Chinese immigrants to the United States came from western China.
35. Eleven Italian Americans were lynched in New Orleans in 1892.
36. Nativism directed against southern and eastern European immigrants was intense when the Statue of Liberty was dedicated in 1886.
37. In 1990 there were more than one million Cubans living in the United States.
38. More than 257,000 Haitians immigrated to the United States between 1971 and 1992.

Answers to Ethnic Literacy Test

1. T	2. F	3. T	4. F	5. T	6. F	7. T	8. F	9. T
10. F	11. F	12. T	13. F	14. F	15. T	16. T	17. T	18. T
19. T	20. F	21. F	22. T	23. T	24. T	25. T	26. T	27. T
28. F	29. F	30. T	31. T	32. T	33. T	34. F	35. T	36. T
37. T	38. T							

Note on Sources used in Constructing Ethnic Literacy Test
Most of the statistics in this test are from: U.S. Bureau of the Census (1994). In addition, Bateman and Egan (1995) was used in constructing Item 3. In 1990, there were about 30 million African Americans in the United States. The national populations of Australia and Canada were 17,746,600 and 26,521,000 respectively. (G. Bateman & V. Egan, eds. *The Encyclopedia of World Geography,* New York: Barnes & Noble, 1995).

REFERENCES

Alba, R. D. (1990). *Ethnic Identity: The Transformation of White America.* New Haven: Yale University Press.

Anti-Defamation League of B'nai B'rith. (1993). *Highlights from an Anti-Defamation League Survey on Racial Attitudes in America.* New York: Author.

Aronson, E. & Gonzalez, A. (1988). Desegregation, Jigsaw, and the Mexican-American Experience. In P. A. Katz & D. A. Taylor (Eds.). *Eliminating Racism: Profiles in Controversy* (pp. 301–314). New York: Plenum Press.

Banks, J. A. (1995). The Historical Reconstruction of Knowledge about Race: Implications for Transformative Teaching. *Educational Researcher,* Vol. 21 *(2)*,15–25.

Banks, J. A. with Clegg, A. A. Jr.(1990). *Teaching Strategies for the Social Studies* (4th ed.). New York: Longman, Inc.

Barnavi, E. (Ed.). (1992). *A Historical Atlas of the Jewish People: From the Time of the Patriarchs to the Present.* New York: Schocken Books.

Browne, P. A. (1995). *African Animals ABC.* San Francisco: Sierra Club Books for Children.

Carter, S. L. (1991). *Reflections of an Affirmative Action Baby.* New York: Basic Books.

Chavez, L. (1991). *Out of the Barrio: Toward a New Politics of Hispanic Assimilation.* New York: Basic Books.

Cohen, E. G. (1994). *Designing Groupwork: Strategies for the Heterogeneous Classroom* (2nd ed.). New York: Teachers College Press.

DuBois, E. C. & Ruiz, V. L. (Eds.). (1994). *Unequal Sisters: A Multicultural Reader in U.S. Women's History* (2nd ed.). New York: Routledge.

El-Badry, S. (1994, January). The Arab-American Market. *American Demographics,* pp. 22–30.

Ezorsky, G. (1991). *Racism and Justice: The Case for Affirmative Action.* Ithaca, N.Y.: Cornell University Press.

Flournoy, V. (1985). *The Patchwork Quilt.* Illustrated by J. Pinkney. New York: Dial.

Franklin, J. H. (1993). *The Color Line: Legacy for the Twenty-First Century.* Columbia: University of Missouri Press.

Gabelko, N. H. & Michaelis, J. U. (1981). *Reducing Adolescent Prejudice: A Handbook.* New York: Teachers College Press.

Garrow. D. J. (Ed.) (1987). *The Montgomery Bus Boycott and the Women Who Started It: The Memoir of Jo Ann Gibson Robinson.* Knoxville: University of Tennessee Press.

Glock, C. Y., Wutnow, R., Piliavin, J. A., & Spencer, M. (1975). *Adolescent Prejudice.* New York: Harper and Row.

Goble, P. (1992). *Love Flute.* New York: Bradbury Press.

Hall, E. T. (1977). *Beyond Culture.* Garden City. N.Y.: Doubleday.

Hamilton, V. (1992). *Drylongso.* Illustrated by J. Pinkney. New York: Harcourt.

Harris, V. J. (Ed.). (1992.). *Teaching Multicultural Literature in Grades K–8.* Norwood, Mass.: Christopher-Gordon Publishers.

Hine, D. C. (Ed.). (1993). *Black Women in America: An Historical Encyclopedia* (2 vols.). Brooklyn, N.Y.: Carlson.

Hine, D. C., King, W., & Reed, L. (Eds.). (1995). *We Specialize in the Wholly Impossible: A Reader in Black Women's History.* Brooklyn, N.Y.: Carlson.

Hoobler, D. & Hoobler, T. (1994). *The Chinese American Family Album.* New York: Oxford University Press.

Hoobler, D. & Hoobler, T. (1994). *The Italian Family Album.* New York: Oxford University Press.

Johnson, D. W. & Johnson, F. P. (1993). *Joining Together: Group Theory and Group Skills* (5th ed.). Boston: Allyn and Bacon.

Johnson, J. W. (1995). *Lift Ev'ry Voice and Sing.* Illustrated by J. S. Gilchrist. New York: Scholastic.

Kessler, L. (1994). *Stubborn Twig: Three Generations in the Life of a Japanese American Family.* New York: Dutton.

King, C. S. (1993). *My Life with Martin Luther King, Jr.* (rev. ed.). New York: Henry Holt.

Klein, J. W. (1980). *Jewish Identity and Self-Esteem: Healing Wounds through Ethnotherapy.* New York: The American Jewish Committee.

Kohlberg, L. (1975, October). Moral Education for a Society in Moral Transition. *Educational Leadership 33*, 46–54.

Mohr, N. (1977). *In Nueva York.* New York: Dial.

Newmann, F. N. with Oliver, D. W. (1970). *Clarifying Public Controversy: An Approach to Teaching Social Studies.* Boston: Little, Brown.

Nugent, W. (1995). *Crossings: The Great Transatlantic Migrations, 1870–1914.* Bloomington: Indiana University Press.

Oliver, D. & Shaver, J. P. (1966). *Teaching Public Issues in the High School.* Boston: Houghton Mifflin.

Olson, J. S. & Olson, J. E. (1995). *Cuban Americans.* New York: Twayne Publishers.

Parks, R., with Haskins, J. (1992). *Rosa Parks: My Story.* New York: Dial.

Porter, A. P. (1992). *Jump at de Sun: The Story of Zora Neale Hurston.* Minneapolis: Carolrhoda Books.

Pula, J. S. (1995). *Polish Americans: An Ethnic Community.* New York: Twayne.

Said, E. W. (1978). *Orientalism.* New York: Vintage.

Simon, S. B., Harmin, M., & Raths, L. E. (1991). *Values and Teaching: Working with Values in the Classroom* (rev. ed.). Columbus, Ohio: Charles E. Merrill.

Rodriguez, C. (1991). *Puerto Ricans Born in the U.S.A.* (rev. ed.). Boulder, Colo.: Westview.

Shaftel, F. R. and Shaftel, G. (1982). *Role Playing in the Curriculum* (2nd ed.). Englewood Cliffs, N.J.: Prentice-Hall.

Slavin, R. E. (1995). Cooperative Learning and Intergroup Relations. In J. A. Banks & C. A. M. Banks (Eds.). *Handbook of Research on Multicultural Education* (pp. 628–634). New York: Macmillan.

Takaki, R. (1993). *A Different Mirror: A History of Multicultural America.* New York: Little Brown.

Takashima, S. (1971). *A Child in Prison Camp*. New York: William Morrow.

Tamura, E. H. (1994). *Americanization, Acculturation, and Ethnic Identity*. Urbana: University of Illinois Press.

Tan, A. (1992). *The Moon Lady*. Illustrated by G. Schields. New York: Macmillan.

Taylor, M. (1990). *The Road to Memphis*. New York: Puffin (Penguin) Books.

Terkel, S. (1992). *Race: How Blacks & Whites Think & Feel about the American Obsession*. New York: The New Press.

Thernstrom, S., Orlov, A., & Handlin, O. (Eds.). (1980). *Harvard Encyclopedia of American Ethnic Groups*. Cambridge: Harvard University Press.

Totten, H. L. & Brown, R. W. (1994). *Culturally Diverse Library Collections for Children*. New York: Neal-Schuman Publishers, Inc.

Uchida, Y. (1981). *A Jar of Dreams*. New York: Atheneum.

Uchida, Y. (1982). *Desert Exile: The Uprooting of a Japanese-American Family*. Seattle: University of Washington Press.

Uchida, Y. (1985). *The Best Bad Thing*. New York: Atheneum.

Uchida, Y. (1985). *The Happiest Ending*. New York: Atheneum.

Walker, A. (1991). *Finding the Greenstone*. New York: Harcourt.

Yep, L. (1993). *Dragon's Gate*. New York: HarperTrophy.

Yep, L. (1995). *Thief of Hearts*. New York: HarperCollins.

BIBLIOGRAPHY

Multiethnic References

Amott, T. L. & Matthaei, J. A. (1991). *Race, Gender & Work: A Multicultural Economic History of Women in the United States*. Boston: South End Press.

Fuchs, L. (1995). The American Civic Culture and an Inclusivist Immigration Policy. In J. A. Banks & C. A. M. Banks (Eds.). *Handbook of Research on Multicultural Education* (pp. 293–309). New York: Macmillan.

Rimers, D. M. (1992). *Still the Golden Door: The Third World Comes to America* (2nd ed). New York: Columbia University Press.

African Americans

Blackwell, J. E. (1985). *The Black Community: Diversity and Unity*. (2nd ed.). New York: Harper and Row.

Franklin, J. H. & Moss, A. A., Jr. (1994). *From Slavery to Freedom: A History of Black Americans* (7th ed.). New York: Knopf.

Harley, S. (1995). *The Timetable of African-American History: A Chronology of the Most Important People and Events in African American History*. New York: Simon & Schuster.

Hine, D. C. (Ed.) (1993). *Black Women in America: An Historical Encyclopedia* (2 vols.). Brooklyn, N.Y.: Carlson.
Hine, D. C., King, W., & Reed, L. (1995). (Eds.). *We Specialize in the Wholly Impossible: A Reader in Black Women's History.* Brooklyn, N.Y.: Carlson.

American Indians

Allen, P. G. (1992). *The Sacred Hoop: Recovering the Feminine in American Indian Traditions.* Boston: Beacon Press.
Josephy, A. M., Jr. (1991). *The Indian Heritage of America* (enlarged ed.). Boston: Houghton Mifflin.
Josephy, A. M., Jr. (Ed.). (1991). *America in 1492: The World of the Indian Peoples before the Arrival of Columbus.* New York: Knopf.
Snipp, C. M. (1995). American Indian Studies. In J. A. Banks & C. A. M. Banks (Eds.). *Handbook of Research on Multicultural Education* (pp. 245–264). New York: Macmillan.
Wright, R. (1992). *Stolen Continents: The "New World" through Indian Eyes.* Boston: Houghton Mifflin

Arab Americans

Hooglund, E. J. (1987). *Crossing the Waters: Arabic-Speaking Immigrants to the United States before 1940.* Washington, D.C.: Smithsonian Institution Press.
McCarus, E. (Ed.) (1994). *The Development of Arab-American Identity.* Ann Arbor: The University of Michigan Press.
Naff, A. (1985). *Becoming American: The Early Arab Immigrant Experience.* Carbondale: Southern Illinois University Press.

Asian Americans

Asian Women of California (Ed.) (1989). *Making Waves: An Anthology of Writings by and about Asian American Women.* Boston: Beacon Press.
Chan, S. (1991). *Asian Americans: An Interpretive History.* New York: Twayne.
Cordova, F. (1983). *Filipinos: Forgotten Asian Americans. 1773–1963.* Dubuque, Iowa: Kendall/Hunt Publishing Company.
Kitano, H. L. & Daniels, R. (1995). *Asian Americans: Emerging Minorities* (2nd ed.) Englewood Cliffs. N.J.: Prentice-Hall.
Nakano, M. (1990). *Japanese American Woman: Three Generations 1890–1990.* Berkeley, Calif.: Mina Press Publishing.
Okihiro, G. Y. (1994). *Margins and Mainstreams: Asians in American History and Culture.* Seattle: University of Washington Press.
Takaki, R. (1989). *Strangers from a Different Shore: A History of Asian Americans.* Boston: Little, Brown.
Yung, J. (1986). *Chinese Women of America: A Pictorial History.* Seattle: University of Washington Press.

Hispanic Americans

Gutiérrez, R. A. (1995). Historical and Social Science Research on Mexican Americans. In J. A. Banks & C. A. M. Banks (Eds.). *Handbook of Research on Multiculural Education* (pp. 223–244). New York: Macmillan.

Meier, M. S. & Ribera, F. (1993). *Mexican Americans/American Mexicans: From Conquistadors to Chicanos* (rev. ed.). New York: Hill and Wang.

Moore, J. & Pachon, H. (1985). *Hispanics in the United States*. Englewood Cliffs,z N.J.: Prentice-Hall.

National Association for Chicano Studies (Ed.) (1990). *Chicano Voices: Intersections of Class, Race and Gender.* Albuquerque: University of New Mexico Press.

Olson, J. S. & Olson, J. E. (1995). *Cuban Americans*. New York: Twayne.

Rebolledo, T. D. & Rivero, E. (Eds.). (1993). *Infinite Divisions: An Anthology of Chicana Literature*. Tucson: University of Arizona Press.

Rodriguez, C. E. (1991). *Puerto Ricans Born in the U.S.A.* (rev. ed.). Boulder, Colo.: Westview.

Rodriguez, C. E. (1995). Puerto Ricans in Historical and Social Science Research. In J. A. Banks & C. A. M. Banks (Eds.). *Handbook of Research on Multicultural Education* (pp. 223–244). New York: Macmillan.

European Americans

Berrol, S. C. (1995). *Growing up American: Immigrant Children in America: Then and Now.* New York: Twayne.

Dinnerstein, L. & Reimers, D. M. (1990). *Ethnic Americans: A History of Immigration* (3rd ed.). New York: HarperCollins.

Jones, M. A. (1992). *American Immigration* (2nd ed). Chicago: The University of Chicago Press.

Mangione, J. & Morreale, B. (1993). *La Storia: Five Centuries of the Italian American Experience*. New York: HarperCollins.

Pula, J. S. (1995). *Polish Americans: An Ethnic Community*. New York: Twayne.

Jewish Americans

Barnavi, E. (Ed.) (1992). *A Historical Atlas of the Jewish People: From the Time of the Patriarchs to the Present*. New York: Shocken Books.

Bletter, D. & Grinker, L. (1989). *The Invisible Thread: Portraits of Jewish American Women*. Philadelphia: Jewish Publication Society.

Gribetz, J. with Greenstein, E. L. & Stein, R. S. (1993). *The Timetables of Jewish History: Chronology of the Most Important People and Events in Jewish History.* New York: Simon & Schuster.

Hertzberg, A. (1990). *The Jews in America. Four Centuries of an Uneasy Encounter: A History.* New York: Simon & Schuster.

Sacor, H. M. (1992). *A History of the Jews in America*. New York: Vintage.

II

THE FIRST AMERICANS AND AFRICAN AMERICANS

CONCEPTS AND STRATEGIES

This part consists of content, concepts, teaching strategies, and materials for teaching about American Indians, Native Hawaiians, and African Americans. Although different in many ways, these groups share some important experiences. American Indians and Native Hawaiians are native to the land that is now the United States. African Americans were one of the first groups to come to America from a distant land. They were the only group to come in chains. Each of these groups has deep roots in America.

American Indians and Native Hawaiians are two of the nation's smallest ethnic groups (1990 population—1,878,000 and 211,000 respectively). African Americans are the nation's largest ethnic minority group (1992 population—31,635,000). African Americans comprised about 12.4% of the nation's population in 1992.

Despite the tremendous differences in the sizes of the populations of African Americans, Indians, and Native Hawaiians, the experiences of these groups have often been characterized by common concepts and themes, such as racism, discrimination, protest, and resistance. A study of these three ethnic groups will help students better understand the long journey toward freedom in the United States. It might also help them renew their commitment to justice and equality.

5
CHAPTER

AMERICAN INDIANS

CONCEPTS, STRATEGIES, AND MATERIALS

The earth was created by the assistance of the sun, and it should be left as it was.... The earth and myself are of one mind.

Chief Joseph, Nez Perce

Popular images about American Indians and Eskimos are widespread and often stereotypic. They contribute to students' misunderstandings of Indian and Eskimo cultures. Older Western movies shown on television contribute greatly to the stereotypic image of American Indians within U.S. society. Statements made in schools by educators, such as "Sit like an Indian," also contribute to the perpetuation of Indian stereotypes. Even though textbooks in the 1990s do not include the blatant stereotypes of the "hostile" Indian often found in textbooks in the past, they usually present history from a Western-centric point of view and perspective. Textbooks often call the Americas *The New World,* imply if not state that Columbus "discovered" America, and describe the migration of European Americans from the eastern to the western part of the United States as "The Westward Movement."

These approaches to the study of American history and culture are Eurocentric and mainstream-centric because they imply that American civilization did not exist until the Europeans first arrived in the late fifteenth century. They consequently deny the existence of the Native American cultures and civilizations that had existed in the Americas for centuries before the Europeans came.

Archaeologists estimate that human beings have lived in the Americas for at least 40,000 years. These peoples had established complex civilizations before the Europeans arrived in the fifteenth century. These cultures included elaborate irrigation works and massive artificial mounds crowned with temples. The Olmec in Mexico, the Chavin in Peru, and the civilizations of Teotihuacan, the Maya, the Toltecs, and Aztecs were important American civilizations before the Europeans arrived in the Americas (*Hammond Past Worlds*, 1988, p. 205).

A major goal of American Indian curriculum content should be to help students to view the development of the Americas—and of U.S. society in particular—from the point of view of the Native Americans. For example, the movement of the European Americans from the eastern to the western part of the United States was not, from the Indian point of view, a westward movement. The Lakota Sioux did not consider their homeland the west but the center of the universe. Students should be helped to understand key events, concepts, and issues from different ethnic and cultural perspectives. The "Westward Movement" had very different meanings for the migrating European Americans and for the Indians whose homelands were being invaded. To Indian people, it could more appropriately be called "An Age of Doom" or "The Great Invasion" rather than "The Westward Movement." By helping students to view concepts, events, and issues from diverse cultural and ethnic perspectives, we can help them become critical thinkers and more compassionate citizens of the nation-state. Content about American Indians can contribute greatly to these important and generic educational goals.

EARLY LIFE IN THE AMERICAS

When the European explorers arrived in the Western Hemisphere in 1492, it was populated by many different cultures and groups that became collectively known as "Indians" to Europeans. Columbus thought that he had reached India when he landed in San Salvador in 1492. This misnaming of the aboriginal peoples of the Americas by the Europeans foreshadowed the misunderstandings, distrust, and hostility that later developed between the two groups.

The early history of American Indians is still somewhat of a mystery to scientists. Archaeologists are trying to unravel their early history by digging up fossils that give clues to early human life in the Americas. Occasionally, landmark archaeological discoveries are made, enabling scientists to learn more about early people in the Western Hemisphere. In 1927, near Folsom, New Mexico, scientists found a point embedded between the ribs of a Pleistocene bison that early Americans used for hunting. This finding proved that men and women were in the Americas when Ice Age animals were roaming freely on this continent. Similar points were found at a dig near Clovis, New Mexico, in 1932. Scientists were able to date the points to 9200 B.C. by using Carbon 14 (Ceram, 1971).

AMERICAN INDIANS: HISTORICAL PERSPECTIVE

Important Dates	
1513	Juan Ponce de León landed on the Florida peninsula while on route from Puerto Rico. The relationship between Europeans and North American Indians began.
1565	The Spaniards established the St. Augustine colony in Florida, the first settlement organized by Europeans in present-day United States.
1637	Connecticut colonists killed more than 500 Indians when the Pequot tribe tried to stop the colonists from invading their territory. This event is known as the Pequot War.
1675–76	King Philip, a Wampanoag chief, led a coalition of Indian troops that nearly defeated the English colonists. However, his forces were eventually beaten and his body dismembered by the colonists.
1680	The Pueblos rebelled against the Spaniards and drove them from Pueblo territory. Many Spaniards were killed during the uprising.
1754–63	The French and Indian War occurred. It was one of a series of wars in which the French and the British struggled for control of the eastern part of North America. Each nation vied for Indian support.
1784	A group of Indians suffered a crushing defeat at Fallen Timbers in Ohio on August 20. In 1795, they were forced to sign a treaty that ceded large segments of their lands in the Northwest Territory to Whites.
1812	The War of 1812, a war between the United States and Britain, caused deep factions among the Indian tribes because of their different allegiances. The Indian allies of the British were severely punished by the United States when the war ended.
1824	The Bureau of Indian Affairs was established in the War Department.
1830	Congress passed a Removal Act that authorized the removal of Indians from east to west of the Mississippi and stated conditions under which removal could be legally undertaken.

Important Dates	
1831	The Supreme Court recognized Indian tribes as "domestic dependent nations" within the United States. In an 1832 decision, the Court declared that such nations had a right to self-government.
1838–39	The Cherokee were forcefully removed from Georgia to Indian Territory in present-day Oklahoma. Their poignant journey westward is recalled as the "Trail of Tears."
1864	The Colorado militia killed nearly 300 Cheyennes in a surprise attack at Sand Creek, after the Cheyenne leaders had negotiated an armistice. This incident is known as the Sand Creek Massacre.
1871	A congressional act prohibited the making of further treaties with Indian tribes.
1876	Sioux tribes, under the leadership of Sitting Bull, wiped out Custer's Seventh Cavalry at Little Big Horn. This was one of the last victories for Indian tribes.
1881	Helen Hunt Jackson's *A Century of Dishonor* was published. It was the first influential book to dramatize the plight of Indian peoples in the United States.
1886	The brave Apache warrior, Geronimo, surrendered to U.S. forces in September 1886. His surrender marked the defeat of the southwest tribes.
1887	Congress passed the Dawes Severalty Act, which was designed partially to terminate the Indian's special relationship with the U.S. government. It proved to be disastrous for Indians.
1890	Three hundred Sioux were killed at Wounded Knee Creek in South Dakota.
1924	The Snyder Act made American Indians citizens of the United States.
1928	The Meriam Survey recommended major changes in federal policy relate to Indian affairs. Many of its recommendations were implemented in subsequent years.
1934	The Wheeler-Howard Act made it possible for Indians to reestablish aspects of their traditional cultures, including tribal lands and governments.

Important Dates

1944	The National Congress of American Indians was organized by Indians.
1946	The Indian Claims Commission was established to hear cases related to possible compensations due Indians for loss of land and property.
1948	Indians were granted the right to vote in New Mexico and Arizona.
1954	Congressional acts terminated the relationship between the federal government and several Indian tribes, including the Klamath tribe in Oregon, the Menominee of Wisconsin, and the California Indians.
1969	*Custer Died for Your Sins: An Indian Manifesto* by Vine DeLoria, Jr., was published. This book represented a significant point in the Indian civil rights movement. N. Scott Momaday won the Pulitzer Prize for *House Made of Dawn*.
1970	President Richard M. Nixon made a statement advocating Indian self-determination.
1972	Congress restored the Menominee tribe of Wisconsin to federal-trust status.
1973	Members of the American Indian Movement and other Indians occupied Wounded Knee, South Dakota, to dramatize the Indian's condition in the United States.
1975	The Indian Self-Determination Act recognized the autonomy of Indian tribes and their special relationship with the federal government.
1978	The Indian Freedom of Religion Act was passed. This act granted Indians the right to practice their religious beliefs.
1979	The Supreme Court upheld the fishing rights claims of the Indian tribes of Washington state.
1980	The Passamaquoddy and Penobscot tribes of Maine received a settlement of their land claims after a long and difficult legal battle.

Important Dates	
1989	Native American tribal groups were successful in convincing the Smithsonian Institution to develop a policy that will allow it to return the remains of their ancestors to them. Native American tribes felt that the remains of their ancestors were being desecrated by the Smithsonian as well as by other museums.
1990	The Native American Graves Protection and Repatriation Act was enacted. It requires federal agencies to return human remains and other objects to tribes that request them.
1991	Native Americans were honored by the renaming of the Custer Battlefield to the Little Bighorn National Monument.

The Origins of American Indians

We do not know exactly when people first came to the Americas. However, archaeologists have ruled out the possibility that human beings evolved in the Western Hemisphere because no fossils of pre–Homo Sapiens have been found on the American continent (Josephy, 1991). No remains of the closest cousins of human beings, the great apes, have been found in the Americas, either. Despite these theories, however, many Indian groups believe that they were created by the Great Spirit in the Americas. Archaeologists believe that the ancestors of American Indians originally came from Asia. However, when they came is a topic of tremendous controversy. In the late 1960s, a few American archaeologists accepted dates before 13,000 B.C. In the early 1980s, some archaeologists put the date as far back as 100,000 years. In the 1990s, the dates accepted by archaeologists range from 16,000 to 40,000 years ago, with few accepting a date more than 40,000 years ago (*The World Atlas of Archeology,* 1985).

Most archaeologists use the Bering Strait theory to explain how people first reached the Western Hemisphere. The body of water separating Siberia and Alaska today is called the Bering Strait. Archaeologists believe that at various times in prehistory this water receded and a landmass bridged present-day Siberia and Alaska. This land bridge is called Beringia. The early ancestors of the Native Americans crossed this stretch of land while hunting animals and plants to eat. (See Figure 5-1.)

The Indian Population before the Europeans Came

There is as much controversy about the size of the Indian population when the Europeans arrived in the Americas in the fifteenth century as there is about when the Indians crossed Beringia to reach the Americas. The population esti-

Figure 5-1 THE BERING STRAIT LAND BRIDGE AND THE MIGRATION OF EARLY INDIANS

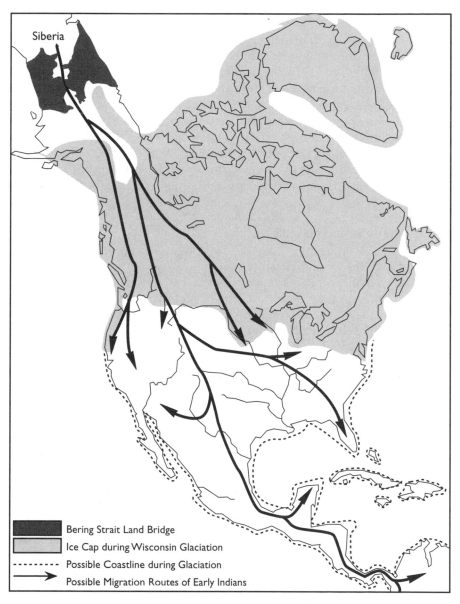

Siberia

Bering Strait Land Bridge

Ice Cap during Wisconsin Glaciation

Possible Coastline during Glaciation

Possible Migration Routes of Early Indians

SOURCE: From *Atlas of the North American Indian,* by Carl Waldman. Copyright © 1985 Carl Waldman. Reprinted with the permission of Facts on File, Inc., New York.

mates vary greatly. In 1924, Rivet estimated the Western hemisphere population to have been 40 to 50 million and the North American population to have been 2 to 3.5 million when the Europeans arrived. Mooney, in 1928, estimated the Indian North American pre-Columbian population to be 1,153,000. In 1939, Kroeber estimated the Western hemisphere population to be 8,400,000 and the North American continent population to be 900,000 (Stuart, 1987).

In the 1960s and 1970s researchers such as Dobyns (1976) and Denevan (1976) seriously challenged the estimates by Mooney (1928) and Kroeber (1934). They have given much higher estimates. Dobyns believes that the Americas were heavily populated when the Europeans arrived. In 1966, Dobyns estimated that the Western hemisphere population at contact was 90,043,000 and that the North American population was 9,800,000 (see Table 5-1) (Stuart, 1987). Dobyns and Denevan estimate that the population north of the Rio Grande was at least 10 million when the Europeans first came to the Americas.

The Diversity of Indian Cultures

Although the word *Indian* often connotes a stereotypic image in the popular mind, Indian peoples are quite diverse, both physically and culturally. Their skin color, height, hair texture, and facial features vary greatly.

It is not possible to determine exactly how many languages were spoken in the Americas before the Europeans came or to determine how many people spoke each language. Two frequently accepted estimates of the number of languages spoken are 1,800 and more than 2,000 (Harris & Levey, 1975). Anthropologists have tried with great difficulty to categorize Indian languages into six major language families.

How Indians survived also varied widely. Some groups like the tribes of the subarctic, did not practice agriculture, but obtained food by fishing and hunting. Agriculture was the basis of the sedentary communities and complex cultures of the southwest Indians.

Political institutions in Indian cultures were also quite diverse. Highly sophisticated confederations were common among the northeast tribes, such as the Creek Confederacy and the League of the Iroquois. These confederations contrasted strikingly with political life within the California tribes. These tribes usually had no formal political institutions, but were organized into small family units that were headed by men who had group responsibilities but little authority over others. Warring and raiding were important aspects of the Apache culture. However, the Hopi, who called themselves "the peaceful ones," were one of the most tranquil peoples on earth. Social class had little meaning among the southwest tribes, but it was extremely important in the northwest Pacific Coast cultures. Food, hunting methods, house types, clothing, tools, and religious ceremonies also varied greatly among and within various American Indian cultural groups (Underhill, 1971).

Table 5-1   TWENTIETH-CENTURY ESTIMATES OF THE
ABORIGINAL POPULATION OF NORTH AMERICA

North America	United States	Scholar (Date)
1,148,000	846,000	Mooney (1910)
1,148,000	—	Rivet (1924)
2–3,000,000	—	Sapper (1924)
1,153,000	849,000	Mooney (1928)
1,002,000	—	Wilcox (1931)
900,000	720,000	Kroeber (1939)
1,000,000	—	Rosenblat (1945)
1,000,000	—	Steward (1945)
2–2,500,000	—	Ashburn (1947)
1,001,000	—	Steward (1949)
2,240,000	—	Aschmann (1959)
1–2,000,000	—	Driver (1961)
9,8–12,240,000	—	Dobyns (1966)
3,500,000	2,500,000	Driver (1969)
2,171,000	—	Ubelaker (1976)
4,400,000	—	Denevan (1976)
—	1,845,000	Thornton (1981)
18,000,000[a]	—	Dobyns (1983)
7,000,000	5,000,000	Thornton (1987)
1,894,000	—	Ubelaker (1988)

[a]North of Mesoamerica

SOURCE: Reprinted from *Race, Discourse, and the Origin of the Americas,* by V. L. Hyatt and R. Nettleford (Washington, DC: Smithsonian Institution Press), page 94, by permission of the publisher. Copyright 1995.

Similarities in Indian Cultures

Although American Indian cultures are highly diverse, they are similar in many ways. Some of their similar characteristics, especially those related to core values, make up "Indianness" or what is uniquely "Indian." Indian cultures were and are based on a deep spirituality, which greatly influences all aspects of life. Because Indians see people existing within a spiritual world that includes all other living things, they see themselves living in harmony with all beings on earth. They view the universe as a harmonious whole, with every object and being having a sacred life: to separate human beings from nature is antithetical to the Great Spirit, for to the Great Spirit all is life.

The tribes of the northwest Pacific Coast believed in many spirits. They sought the protection of these spirits through various ceremonies and rituals.

Shamen, who played a key role in many Indian religions, helped them gain contact with the spiritual world.

The southwest tribes had a rich and elaborate year-round sequence of ceremonials including songs, dances, and poetry. American Indians often called on the help of the spirits in their daily lives. The Hopi performed dances to bring rain. The Apaches engaged in special dances and ceremonies to gain the support of the spirits before undertaking raids or going into war. Many Indian groups often sought contact with the spirits by going on a vision quest. Spiritual beliefs and ceremonies permeated every aspect of Indian life.

American Indians had a deep respect and reverence for the earth and for all other living things. They believed that people must not harm the earth and should regard it as sacred. Many Indian religious leaders were often shocked by the ways in which the White people's agriculture defiled the Mother Earth. Forbes (1973) has summarized these beliefs:

> The Earth our Mother is holy and should be treated as such... all forms of life are our brothers and sisters and have to be respected.... Life itself is a holy, sacred experience... we must live our lives as a religion, that is, with constant concern for spiritual relationships and values... we must live lives that bring forth both physical and spiritual 'beauty.' All life has the potentiality of bringing forth Beauty and Harmony, but [humans] in particular [have] also the ability to bring forth ugliness and disharmony. (pp. 208–209)

In their literature and speeches, American Indians often bemoaned how the Whites destroyed and defiled the earth, as in this passage by a Winto elder (cited in McLuhan, 1971):

> The White people plow up the ground, pull down the trees, kill everything. The tree says, 'Don't. I am sore. Don't hurt me.' But they chop it down and cut it up. The spirit of the land hates them. They blast our trees and stir it up to its depths.... How can the spirit of the earth like the White man?... Everywhere the White man has touched it, it is sore. (p. 15)

The Indian conception of the earth and their relationship to the land differed greatly from the Europeans' and was a source of conflict among the cultures. The Indians believed that people could use the earth as long as they treated it with respect, but they could not sell it anymore than they could sell the air or the sea. When, in exchange for gifts, American Indians gave Europeans permission to use their lands, many did not realize that from a European viewpoint they were also giving up their own rights to use the lands. The Europeans regarded the earth as a commodity that could be broken into parts and owned by individuals. To the American Indian, the earth was sacred and consequently could never be owned by human beings.

Indian people also had a deep respect for the rights and dignity of the individual. Decisions in Indian councils and confederacies were usually based on group consensus. Deliberations were often long and decisions of governing bodies slow because consensus had to be attained. The Creek Confederacy reached all of its decisions by consensus. However, each nation within the confederacy maintained its autonomy and was not bound to a decision with which it did not agree. The Europeans learned a great deal from the American Indians about representative government and the rights and dignity of the individual, which they incorporated into the major constitutional documents on which U.S. democracy is based.

Leaders of groups within the subarctic tribes had little authority over their followers. This was characteristic of Indian societies. Leaders were rarely deified as they were in Europe, the Middle East, and Asia. There were few hierarchical political organizations in the Americas. Leaders often had to earn the respect of others by becoming outstanding warriors, acquiring a special ability to communicate with the spirits, or learning to perform some other service the community needed and valued. Communities were usually democratic, with no kings or other kinds of rulers. However, there were important exceptions to these generalizations. The Inca Empire of Peru was one of the most totalitarian states that ever existed in human history.

Because of their feudalistic background, the Europeans looked for kings among the Indians and assumed that Indian chiefs had absolute authority over their tribes. The European settlers created tremendous problems by imposing their conceptions of the nation-state on Indian societies. They made treaties with chiefs and assumed that they were binding to their tribes. They did not understand that the chief's authority was usually limited by the tribal council. He had little power that the tribe did not grant him. This cultural conflict between the Europeans and Indian groups haunted their relationships for centuries.

Early Contact with Europeans

The Indians' earliest contacts with the Europeans were usually friendly and generally involved trade. The French, the English, and the Dutch exchanged European goods and tools for furs. This exchange of goods was initially beneficial for both groups. The furs greatly increased the Europeans' wealth; the European goods and tools made life easier for the Indians. Eventually, the Indians began to consider the European goods necessities rather than luxuries. What had begun as a mutually beneficial trade relationship was destined to cause disaster for the Indians.

Indians acquired rum, guns, gunpowder, horses, and other goods from the Europeans. Tribes that wanted European goods but had depleted the supply of fur-producing animals on their lands began to invade the territories of other tribes to obtain furs for trade. These invasions led to skirmishes and eventually to wars. European goods made intertribal warring more likely and possible. It was rather easy for the tribes that had European guns and gunpowder to defeat tribes lacking these supplies. Thus, the Europeans, through trade and other schemes (discussed later), initiated divide-and-conquer tactics among the Indian tribes in New England. Indian wars, raids, and attacks were greatly intensified by the presence of the Europeans.

The League of the Iroquois began an aggressive campaign to gain a monopoly of the European trade and to dominate competing tribes. The League had eliminated hundreds of Hurons and forced those remaining into captivity in 1649. The Iroquois were feared by tribes throughout New England. They eventually dominated the Delawares, the Nanticokes, and other groups of Algonkian-speaking tribes by 1680. The League became so powerful that the British regarded it as power to be reckoned with.

Indian and European Wars

From about 1540 to the 1790s, no one power was dominant in the Indian territory that had been invaded by the Europeans in the Northeast. The Swedes and the Dutch had been driven from the area before 1700. However, the French, Spanish, and English struggled for control of the region. The Indians also tried to maintain their power. The power struggle became more intricate and intense when the British colonies entered the contest. Until the American Revolution, the Indians were unable to tell which of the warlike European nations, if any, would become the dominant power. The Indians probably thought that a balance of power would eventually be established in the region, in which they would be a major participant.

The European wars and struggles for power deeply influenced Indian policy and political institutions. In each war with European people, the Indians had to decide which group, if any, they would support. Each of the powers competed for Indian alliance and support. Although the Indians often tried to maintain a policy of neutrality, this became increasingly difficult as the European nations aggressively vied for their support. The Creeks and the Cherokees fought on the side of the French, against the British, in the French and Indian War. The French were defeated, and their Indian allies were severely punished by the British for helping the enemy. The Indians were also weakened by their severe losses during the war.

The European wars caused deep factionalism within the Indian tribes and confederations. In the War of 1812, the various tribes became deeply divided over whether they should support the United Sates or the British. The treaties ending the American Revolution and the War of 1812 stunned and angered Britain's Indian allies. Neither treaty acknowledged the decisive roles the Indians had played in these wars. After the American Revolution, the British granted the colonists lands that were occupied by these Indian allies. The British had pitted Indian tribes against each other and then ignored these allies' self-interests when the fighting stopped. In time, the Indians began to see the futility of becoming involved in the European wars. They became increasingly committed to a policy of neutrality. Alexander McGillivray, the Creek diplomat, used the Europeans' tactics and pitted the colonists against the Spaniards by astutely negotiating.

The Decline of the League of the Iroquois

The League of the Iroquois was deeply affected by the European wars and was eventually destroyed by the factionalism caused by the wars. The League, the French, and the British were the three major powers in the Northeast in the first decades of the 1700s. Factionalism developed within the League over the positions it should take in the European wars. One of the nations, the Senecas, fought on the side of the French in the French and Indian War. The other nations supported the British. Even greater disunity developed within the League when the American Revolution began. Some of the nations supported the British; others were sympathetic to the colonists. Internal splits developed within several of the nations over this issue. The colonists looted and burned Iroquois villages after the Revolution and flaunted their newly gained power.

The fate of the Iroquois was later experienced by other tribes. The Iroquois had warred against other Indian tribes in order to obtain furs to trade and had fought as allies in the European wars. Their confederation was later destroyed because of splits caused by the European wars. The Indian nations did not realize that they had a common fate in the Northeast, and that the future of one Indian nation was intricately tied to the future of all Indian tribes. Culturally and politically, the Indians were separate and distinct groups. However, the Whites saw them as a group that had to be pushed west of the Mississippi and ultimately conquered or destroyed.

Treaties and Indian Removal

The relationship between Indians and European settlers had developed into a pattern by the time of the American Revolution. The initial contact usually involved trade, whereby Indians acquired tools and firearms and the Europeans obtained furs. These initial events usually pitted Indian tribes against each other as they competed for the European trade and for the lands containing fur-producing animals. When the furs had been depleted, the Europeans began an aggressive drive to obtain the lands the Indians occupied. The Indians often formed confederations and alliances to fight back the European invaders or extended the functions of existing confederations. Ironically, however, the Indians' involvement in the White people's wars usually disrupted these confederations. Indians adamantly resisted the attempts by the Whites to displace them. They fought defensive wars, such as the King Philip's War in 1675 and the Black Hawk War in 1832. Indian uprisings also occurred, like the Sioux uprising in 1862 and the Little Crow uprising in 1863.

Despite their aggressive and bold resistance, the Europeans were destined to win the struggle. The Whites retaliated with shocking massacres, like Sand Creek in 1864, biological warfare, and massive wars in which men, women, and children were killed and often dismembered and scalped. After Indian resistance was crushed, Whites legitimized the taking of Indian lands by convincing the Indian leaders to sign treaties. Indian chiefs were frequently offered gifts or other bribes to sign treaties. Once an Indian group had signed a treaty, the Whites schemed to remove them from their land. Often the Indians were forced west of the Mississippi into Indian Territory (present-day Oklahoma), land the Whites considered uninhabitable. If only a few Indians remained after the conquest, they were often absorbed by local tribes or forced onto reservations.

This cycle was repeated many times as the White settlers pushed westward. When Whites went farther west, Indians were forced to sign new treaties granting Whites the lands earlier treaties had assured them. Some Indian groups, like the Winnebagos, were forced to move as many as six times during a period of thirty years. No aspects of U.S. history are more poignant than the accounts of the making and breaking of Indian treaties by Whites and the forced removal of Indians across the United States. This prediction by a Cherokee newspaper describing how Whites would obtain Indian land in Texas highlights how treaties were often made (cited in Hagan, 1961):

> *A Commissioner will be sent down to negotiate, with a pocket full of money and his mouth full of lies. Some chiefs he will bribe, some he will flatter, and some he will make drunk: and the result will be . . . something that will be called a treaty.* (p. 99)

THE WESTWARD JOURNEYS

Some Indian tribes, realizing the futility of resistance, moved westward without force. Others, however, bitterly resisted removal and were removed by military troops. Generally, the tribes that had to be removed at gunpoint suffered the most. However, they all suffered greatly. The Winnebagos, who offered little resistance, were shifted from place to place between 1829 and 1866. About half of them perished during the perpetual sojourn. The Seminoles, who signed a removal treaty in 1832, violently resisted removal. Hostilities began in 1835 and continued for seven years. The United States lost nearly 1,500 men and spent more than $50 million in its attempts to crush the Seminoles' resistance. Most of the Seminoles were eventually forced to Indian Territory. However, several hundred remained in the Florida Everglades, where their descendants live today.

The Georgians began an aggressive drive to remove the Cherokees from their homeland when gold was discovered on Cherokee land in 1829. The Cherokees initiated a court battle against removal. In 1832, the Supreme Court ruled that the Cherokees had a right to remain on their land. However, this ruling by the high court did not halt the determined efforts of the Georgians and President Andrew Jackson to remove the Cherokees. Harassed and pressured, part of the tribe finally signed a removal treaty in 1835. Even though only a minority of the tribe's leaders signed the treaty, the Cherokees were forced to move to Indian Territory. During the long march from Georgia to Oklahoma in 1838 and 1839, almost one-fourth of the Cherokees died from starvation, diseases, and the perils of the journey. Their long westward journey is recalled as the "Trail of Tears." The Creeks were forced to sign a treaty in 1832, which gave the Whites rights to their lands east of the Mississippi. Nearly half of the Creeks perished during the migration to and during their early years in the West.

Like the White people's wars, removal caused deep factions within the various Indian tribes and nations. Some leaders felt that it was in their best interests to cooperate with the White authorities; others believed that removal should be resisted until the bitter end. These splits within the tribes intensified when the Indians arrived in the West and hastened the disintegration of their institutions that had begun before removal.

In retrospect, it is clear that Indian people either had to relocate or be exterminated. The federal government legitimized Indian removal with the Removal Act of 1830. This act legalized Indian removal and specified the conditions under which Indians could be removed legally. The act provided funds for removal and authorized an exchange of lands for displaced Indians. The act stipulated that the tribe's consent must be obtained. It made little difference in the actual removal of Indians. Local officials continued to use any possible tactics to convince Indians to sign treaties and to move westward.

Indians in the West

Much tension developed in the western territories when the eastern tribes reached their destinations. Many of the eastern tribes were forced to settle in territories occupied by the plains Indians. The plains tribes had acquired the White people's guns and horses and were tough fighters when the eastern tribes began to settle in their territories. When competition for the buffalo became acute, they fought and raided the eastern tribes. The U.S. government failed to provide the eastern tribes military protection as it had promised when they were forced to settle in the West.

The conquering and displacement of tribes that took place in the East later occurred west of the Mississippi. However, the conquest of the plains tribes and other western tribes took place in a shorter period of time. The powerful Sioux nations of the northern plains were defeated and forced onto reservations within twenty-seven years. The Comanche of the southern plains had been conquered by the White settlers by 1873. Writes Spicer (1969), "The other plains tribes presented about the same picture as the Comanche or the Sioux: a twenty or twenty-five year period of intensive warfare both with other tribes and the Americans, a period of unsettled and sometimes desperate conditions as they were forced on reservations and finally unhappy acceptance of the new way" (p. 87).

When the United States acquired most of the territory that now comprises the Southwest from Mexico in 1848 (see chapter 10 on Mexican Americans), the southwestern tribes quickly learned that their new conquerors were enemies, not friends. The Spaniards had never completely conquered the southwestern tribes: they had retained a great deal of their culture and many institutions. Indians such as the Pueblos and the Pimas had hoped that the United States would protect them from the Navajos and the Apaches. However, the new government's goals were to conquer all of the tribes and to place them on reservations. The California gold rush of 1849 hastened the defeat of the western tribes. A congressional act in 1871 that prohibited further treaties indicated that Indian resistance had been broken and that the Indians were now considered a conquered and defeated people. The act declared that in the future, "no Indian nation or tribe within...the United States shall be acknowledged or recognized as an independent nation, tribe, or power." (cited in Josephy, 1991, pp. 339–340). This act represented a major change in federal policy in Indian affairs and reversed the policy declared by the Supreme Court in 1831. The Court ruled in 1831 that the "Cherokees and other Indians were dependent domestic nations...definable political entities within the United States" (Spicer, 1969, p. 66). The 1871 Congressional act closed an important chapter in Indian history. When he surrendered in 1877, Chief Joseph of the Nez Perce said:

> Hear me, my chiefs, I am tired; my heart is sick and sad. From where the sun now stands, I will fight no more forever.

Messianic Movements: The Utopian Quests

Indians had been conquered by the late 1880s, and vigorous efforts to eradicate their cultures, values, and ways of life were already under way. Many were forced to live on reservations that were operated by superintendents and government agents who ruled the Indians with an iron hand and stifled all their efforts for self-initiative. Confined to reservations (some of which were fenced in), many were forced to farm, which they considered women's work. In their desperation, Indians turned to religious prophets who promised a return to the traditional ways and the extermination of Whites and their life-styles. Messianic leaders who heralded the end of White domination emerged within many of the eastern and western tribes.

As early as the 1760s, a prophet arose among the Delawares. He urged his followers to reject European goods and return to their old way of life. Tenskwatawa, a Shawnee, experienced a revelation in 1805 that told him that White Americans would be destroyed by a natural catastrophe. Tenskwatawa and his brother, Tecumseh, taught the Shawnees to hold firm to their lands and refuse to relinquish them to the Whites. Handsome Lake began preaching among the Senecas around 1800 after the League of the Iroquois had been broken up. He urged the Senecas to remain neutral in the White people's wars, not to indulge in the White vices, and to live by his moral code. Handsome Lake became important to those Senecas who were trying to resist cultural domination by the Whites.

As Whites began to conquer Indian tribes in the West, prophets who envisioned a utopian future emerged among the western tribes. In 1855, a prophet called Smohalla began preaching among the Wanapum Indians in the Oregon Territory. Like the eastern prophets, Smohalla preached that the White people would be eliminated and that their way of life was detrimental. He believed that the way the White people farmed harmed Mother Earth.

A Paiute prophet named Wovoka began having visions in 1885. He preached that a natural catastrophe would destroy White people and that the Indians' ancestors would return. The White authorities became alarmed about Wovoka's religion and its ritualistic "Ghost Dance." It spread rapidly among the Great Plains Indians and eventually reached the Lakota on the Pine Ridge Reservation in South Dakota. A frightened Indian agent called soldiers to the reservation in 1890. When a misunderstanding arose between the soldiers and Big Foot followers, the soldiers killed 300 Sioux at Wounded Knee Creek. This incident shocked the nation and wiped out the Ghost Dance among most Indian tribes.

AMERICAN INDIANS AND FEDERAL POLICY

When the Indians had been thoroughly subjugated and placed on reservations, White authorities began efforts to "civilize" them; civilize meant to make them as much like Whites as possible. The goal of federal policy was to assimilate the Indians quickly into the mainstream society. No attempt was made to give them a choice or to encourage them to retain elements of their cultures. Efforts were made to make Indians farmers and to give their children White people's education. Indian children were sent to boarding schools far away from home reservations so that the authority of their parents would be undermined. The schools were a dismal failure. When Indian children left them, they were frequently unable to function well either in their ethnic communities or within the mainstream society. What the schools tried to teach had almost no relevance to life on the reservations. The schools also failed to teach Indian children the White people's culture. The quality of the teachers and the curricula were very poor.

Policymakers felt that they had to break up the Indians' communally held tribal lands and make individual allotments to family heads in order to make Indians independent and successful farmers. That this would violate Indian cultures and traditions was not a major concern. In 1887 Congress passed the Dawes Severalty Act. Designed to make Indians independent and to terminate their special relationship with the federal government, the act was destined to have the opposite effect. The act authorized the president to break up tribal lands and to make individual allotments to family heads. Each family head was to receive 160 acres; minors, 80 acres each. "Surplus" land was to be sold on the open market. The government was to hold the land in trust for 25 years. Citizenship was to be granted to family heads when they received their allotments. Many tribes adamantly opposed the act from the beginning.

The results of the act were disastrous for Indians. Many Whites bought or leased lands from Indians at outrageously low prices or obtained land from them in extralegal ways. Some Whites persuaded their Indian friends to will them their lands. Indians who made such wills often turned up mysteriously dead shortly after finalizing the will. A 1906 Congressional act gave the federal government more authority to supervise the administration of the Dawes Act. However, schemes for obtaining the Indian land developed more rapidly than government policies to safeguard it. Many Indians became poverty stricken during the period in which the act was in effect. Indians lost about 90 million out of a total of 138 million acres of land between 1887 and 1932.

It was clear by the late 1920s that the Dawes Act had failed. It had not only resulted in the loss of millions of acres of tribal land but had also increased rather than decreased the role of the federal government in Indian affairs. The Meriam Report, published in 1928, recommended major reforms in federal Indian policy, including the abandoning of the allotment plan and the consolidation of Indian land for use by the tribes. John Collier, who became commissioner of Indian affairs in 1933, believed that tribal land should be reestablished, as well as Indian government and other aspects of Indian culture. In 1934 Congress passed an act sanctioning the new federal policy. Termination had failed; the government would now take a more active role in Indian affairs and urge Indians to reestablish aspects of their cultures. The Wheeler-Howard Act of 1934 brought a halt to the allotment of Indian lands, made it possible for tribes to acquire additional lands, and granted American Indians the right to local government based on their traditional cultures.

By the 1950s, advocates for the termination of the federal government's role in Indian tribal affairs were again dominant in the nation's capital. In

1953, the federal government stated its intent to abolish the federal role in tribal affairs and to treat Indians the same as other Americans in House Concurrent Resolution 108. During the 1950s, Congress passed several laws that gave the states additional responsibilities for Indian affairs. A 1954 termination bill ended the relationship between the federal government and the Klamath tribe in Oregon. The tribe and its reservation were abolished. However, the termination was disastrous for the Klamaths because they had not achieved economic independence when it began. The Menominee Reservation in Wisconsin was also terminated during the 1950s.

SELF-DETERMINATION AND THE CHALLENGE TO TERMINATION

Most Indians are strongly committed to their tribal groups and to the continuation of their special legal relationship with the federal government. They feel that only in this way can they, a relatively small group, acquire their political rights and justice. Indians believe that they are too few to exercise significant political power. Most Indian leaders remained strongly committed to self-determination and against termination during the period of the 1950s and 1960s, when a termination policy was pursued by the federal government. However, termination received a severe blow when President Richard Nixon stated his Indian policy in 1970. He said (cited in Spicer, 1980):

> *Self-determination among the Indian people can and must be encouraged without the threat of eventual termination.... This is the only way that self-determination can effectively be fostered. This, then, must be the goal of any new national policy toward the Indian people: to strengthen the Indians sense of autonomy without threatening the sense of community.... We must assure the Indian that he can assume control of his own life without being separated involuntarily from the tribal group. And we must make it clear that Indians can become independent of federal control without being cut off from federal concern and federal support. (p. 120)*

The challenge to termination and the support of Indian self-determination continued throughout the 1970s. According to the U.S. Commission on Civil Rights (1981), "The executive branch repudiated the policy of termination and successive administrations adopted a policy of Indian self-determination—a policy favoring Indian control over decision-making and promoting tribal interest" (p. 180). In 1975, the Indian Self-Determination Act made it clear that Indians could "control their relationships both among themselves and with non-Indian governments, organizations, and persons." The 1978 Indian Child Welfare Act provides for tribal jurisdiction and Indian community involvement in the adoption and foster placement of Indian children.

FISHING RIGHTS AND LAND CLAIMS

Tremendous controversies developed during the 1970s over both Indian fishing rights in the state of Washington and the land claims of Indian tribes in the states that originally made up the thirteen colonies. The fishing-rights controversy arose because of treaties signed by the federal government and Indians in the Washington Territory in the 1850s. The Indians gave up vast land claims in return for specific federal promises. One was a recognition of Indian fishing rights. The Indians were promised that they "could continue to fish where they always had fished, exclusively on reservation and in common with the citizens of the territory at the Indians' usual and accustomed grounds and stations off reservation" (U.S. Commission on Civil Rights, 1981, p. 180).

As the supply of fish grew smaller, the state of Washington began to regulate fishing in a way that favored non-Indian fishing and violated the Indians' treaty promises. Some Indians were jailed for fishing in ways that violated state law. However, these Indians felt that their fishing was legal because of the terms of the nineteenth century treaties. When the Indians took their cases to the courts, they won major legal victories. In 1974, Judge George Boldt ruled in a federal District Court that the Indians had separate rights to a significant share of the fish and that the state should protect their rights and not interfere with them. The Boldt decision evoked a storm of controversy among the non-Indians of Washington state and led to personal attacks on Judge George Boldt.

The non-Indian fishermen strongly rejected the Boldt decision and worked to get the case to the Supreme Court. They hoped that the high court would reverse the Boldt decision. The Supreme Court ruled on the controversial case on July 2, 1979. It upheld the decision made by Judge Boldt.

In 1790, the U.S. Congress enacted the Indian Trade and Intercourse Act, also known as the Nonintercourse Act of 1790. This act, which is still in effect, requires the federal government to supervise the transfer of Indian lands to non-Indians in states that formerly made up the original thirteen colonies. This act was designed to maintain friendly relationships between Whites and Indians. Most of the land in these states was transferred from Indians to non-Indians without the required federal supervision. During the 1970s, a number of eastern Indian tribes went to court to claim that their lands had been transferred illegally and to demand redress and compensation for the illegal transfer of their lands.

The Passamaquoddy and Penobscot tribes of Maine took legal actions to regain more than ten million acres of land in the state of Maine. Their claim made up one-half of the state and included land inhabited by 350,000 non-Indians. This property was valued at $25 million. After a long and difficult battle, these tribes received a settlement of their claim in 1980.

Other tribes that have made land claims with varying results include the Oneidas in New York state, the Mashpee tribe in Massachusetts, the Schaghiticoke tribe in Connecticut, and the Narrangansetts in Rhode Island. The Narragansetts received a rather rapid settlement of their claim. They made their claim in 1976 and received a settlement in 1978. Congress provided the funds to carry out the 1,800-acre settlement.

AMERICAN INDIANS TODAY

The Indian Population

Once known as the "vanishing Americans," the American Indian population has increased at every Census count since 1940. The Indian population in 1940 was 345,000. The first complete census of American Indians was conducted in 1890. There were 248,000 Indians counted that year. The biggest increase in the Indian population since 1890 occurred between the 1970 and the 1980 Censuses. The Indian population increased 42% during that ten-year period, from 793,000 to 1,364,000 (U.S. Bureau of the Census, 1988, 1993). A number of factors other than the increase in the number of births over deaths may have accounted for this dramatic increase in the Indian population. These factors may have included improvements in the way the Census Bureau counted people in 1980, the wider use of self-identification to obtain information about ethnic group membership, and the greater tendency for people to identify as Indian in 1980 than in 1970 (U.S. Bureau of the Census, 1988).

The 1990 Census identified about 500 American Indian tribes and bands (U.S. Bureau of the Census, 1993). These tribes and bands varied greatly in size. The Cherokee, the Navajo, the Chippewa, and the Sioux were the only tribes that included more than 100,000 people. About 16% of all Indians identified as Cherokee; about 12% identified as Navajo; and 6% each as Chippewa and Sioux. Figure 5-2 shows the ten largest American Indian tribes in 1990 and their populations. The four states with the largest Indian populations in 1990 were Oklahoma (252,000), California (242,000), Arizona (204,000), and New Mexico (134,000) (U.S. Bureau of the Census, 1993).

Indians in Urban Communities

American Indians have become increasingly urbanized since the 1950 Census. In 1950 about 56,000 Indians, or 16% of the total population, lived in urban areas and cities. That number had increased to 146,000, or 28% of the population, in 1960. In 1980, about 49% of Indians lived in urban areas (Snipp, 1991). This was a 4% increase from 1970. In 1990, 22.3% of Ameri-

Figure 5-2 TEN LARGEST INDIAN TRIBES: 1990

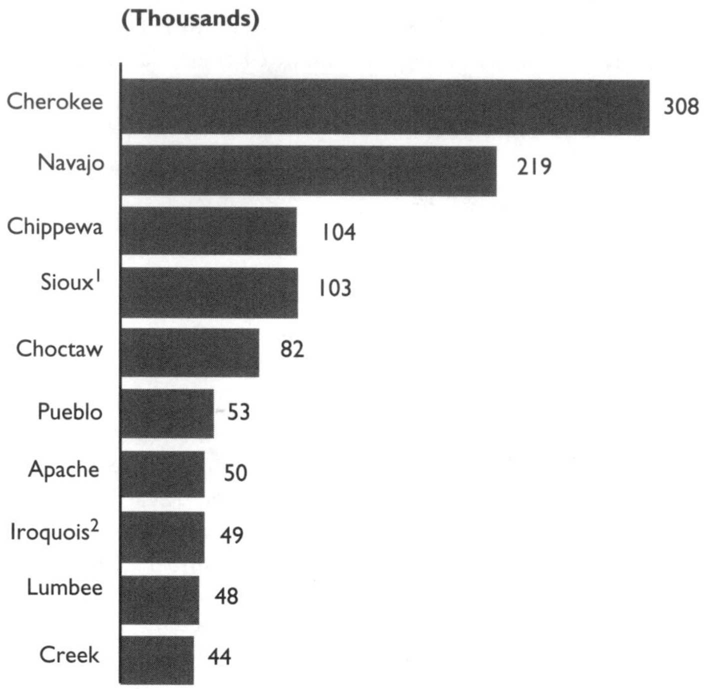

(Thousands)

Cherokee	308
Navajo	219
Chippewa	104
Sioux[1]	103
Choctaw	82
Pueblo	53
Apache	50
Iroquois[2]	49
Lumbee	48
Creek	44

[1]Any entry with the spelling "Siouan" was miscoded to Sioux in North Carolina.

[2]Reporting and/or processing problems have affected the data for this tribe.

SOURCE: U.S. Bureau of the Census (1993, September). *We, the First Americans.* Washington, D.C.: U.S. Government Printing Office, p. 2.

can Indians, Eskimos, and Aluets lived on reservations and trust lands; 10.2% lived on tribal jurisdiction statistical areas; and most (62.3%) lived in other parts of the United States (see Figure 5-3). About 60% lived in urban areas.

Even though about 62% of American Indians lived off reservations in 1990, many reports, statistical sources, and other kinds of informational sources focus on the minority of Indians who live on reservations. Detailed studies of urban Indians are scarce. Wax (1971) includes a chapter, "Indians in the Cities," in his dated but informative book, *Indian Americans: Unity and Diversity.* After a general discussion of Indians in cities, Wax discusses several case studies of urban Indian communities, including the Sioux in Rapid City, Iowa, the Tuscarora (a branch of the Iroquois) in New York state, and the Indians in Minneapolis.

Figure 5-3 AMERICAN INDIANS, ESKIMOS, AND ALEUTS BY TYPE OF AREAS: 1990

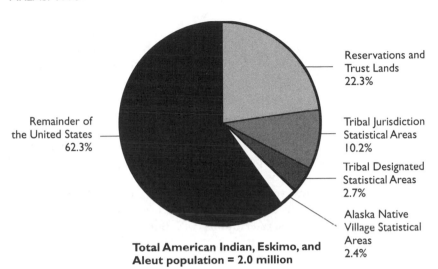

Reservations and
Trust Lands
22.3%

Tribal Jurisdiction
Statistical Areas
10.2%

Tribal Designated
Statistical Areas
2.7%

Alaska Native
Village Statistical
Areas
2.4%

Remainder of
the United States
62.3%

**Total American Indian, Eskimo, and
Aleut population = 2.0 million**

SOURCE: U.S. Bureau of the Census (1993, September). *We, the First Americans.* Washington, D.C.: U.S. Government Printing Office, p. 7.

Wax (1971), as well as other authors, such as Sorkin (1978) and Bolt (1987), point out that many Indians have a difficult time adjusting to life in urban communities. Often cut off from families and reservation benefits, they have trouble getting jobs, health and medical care, and good schooling for their children. Reservation Indians who migrate to urban areas tend to settle in towns and cities near reservations and to maintain contacts with their kin on the reservation. They frequently settle near reservations, such as in Gallup, New Mexico, Rapid City, South Dakota, and Ponca City, Oklahoma.

When teaching about Indians in the cities, you should not gloss over the enormous problems that urban Indians often have. However, you should remember that there is tremendous diversity within Indian urban communities. White, in a study summarized by Wax (1971), identified three social classes among Indians in his study of the Indians in Rapid City, South Dakota. He called one group "middle class mobiles." These individuals constituted what White called "the Mixed-blood elite." They were upwardly mobile and not highly identified with the full-blood Indians who lived on the reservation. He called another group "upper middle class White Indians." These individuals were descendants of upwardly mobile mixed-blood families. They occasionally identified with a female Indian ancestor. The final group of urban Indians that White identified were lower-class, rural, and reservation Indians who faced tremendous problems in the urban environment.

The Social, Economic, and Demographic Characteristics of American Indians

In 1990, the percentage of American Indians twenty-five years or older who had completed four years of high school or more was considerably below that of the general population, but much higher than the Indian percentage in 1980. In 1990, the Indian percentage was 65.5 compared to 75.2 for the total population. The Indian percentage in 1980 was 55.8. The median family income for American Indians in 1990 was 62% of the median family income for the total population—$21,750 compared to $35,225. The percentage of Indian families living below the poverty level in 1989 was substantially higher than the percentage for the total population—31%, compared to 13%. Slightly over half (51%) of the Indians who lived on reservations and trust lands in 1989 lived in poverty. However, there were vast differences in the poverty rates on different reservations. The lowest poverty rates were on the Hopi, Blackfeet, Zuni Pueblo, and Fort Apache reservations (U.S. Bureau of the Census, 1993).

Indians Face the Future

As we approach the final years of this century, American Indians are in a unique demographic, cultural, legal, and historical situation. In 1990, Indians numbered nearly 2 million. They are increasing rather than vanishing Americans. However, they are never likely to be a powerful political force because of their relatively small population in a nation that numbers more than 250 million people. Yet, they have treaty rights to land and a special relationship with the federal government that no other ethnic group has. Consequently, they are able to exercise considerable power within the courts. When they do, however, as with fishing rights and land claims, they often evoke considerable hostility among non-Indians.

By most measures, Indians are one of the nation's poorest and least educated ethnic groups. Yet they own lands that contain rich resources that are of enormous value to this nation (Dorris, 1981). The challenge that Indians face as we enter a new century is how to marshal their legal claims and resources in ways that will help them to attain the full benefits of U.S. citizenship.

TEACHING STRATEGIES

To illustrate how content related to Indians can be used to integrate the curriculum, exemplary strategies are identified for teaching these concepts at the grade levels indicated: *cultural traditions* (primary grades), *cultural diversity and similarity* (intermediate and upper grades), and *federal policy* (high school grades).

Primary Grades

CONCEPT: Cultural Traditions

Generalization: Cultural traditions such as potlatches help us to remember and celebrate our past, to express caring and kindness, and to fulfill obligations and expectations.

1. Ask the students to list some of the ways that we show kindness and caring to family members and to friends. Responses might include: (a) with warm and cordial greetings such as "good morning and "good bye"; (b) saying "thank you" and "excuse me"; (c) helping family members with chores; and (d) helping a friend who is in trouble. Write their responses on the board or butcher paper.

2. Tell the children that we have special days that we celebrate. On these special days we give gifts to family members and friends to show kindness and caring, to fulfill expectations, and to satisfy obligations. Ask the children to name some of the special days on which we give or receive gifts. Responses might include birthdays, Valentine's Day, weddings, Christmas, and Chanukah. List their responses on the board or butcher paper.

3. Ask the children to name the people to whom we usually give or from whom we usually receive gifts on these special days. Responses will probably include family members and friends. List their responses on the board or butcher paper.

4. Ask the children: "Why do we usually give or receive gifts on these special days to family members and friends and not to strangers or to people we do not know?" By using questions and discussion, help the students to develop and state the idea that "gift giving is a way of continuing our cultural traditions and expressing caring and kindness for family members and friends and of fulfilling obligations and expectations."

5. Tell the students that some American Indian and Eskimo groups have special occasions for giving gifts called *potlatches.* Explain that *potlatch* is from the Indian word *pat shotl,* which means giving (Tucker, 1995). Read or phrase in your own words the description of *potlatches* that Mark Tucker, a Yupik Eskimo from Emmonak, Alaska wrote in 1990:

> At a potlatch, one village invites another village to watch some dancing and to accept gifts.... Alaska native villages have sponsored this kind of potlatch as far back as anyone can remember. The Indians of the Northwest Coast also hold potlatches to celebrate the completion of a new totem pole or to celebrate the building of a new house by members of the clan. [Explain what a *totem pole* is to the students and show them pictures of some. Excellent photographs of totem poles are in Bruggmann & Gerber (1987), *Indians of the Northwest Coast*].

. . . Once a child attains a certain age, the parents and grandparents prepare a "first dance" [like a debut] for that child. The mother and grandmothers make such gifts as yarn gloves, socks, mittens, hot plate holders and aprons. The father and grandfathers make things like spears, spear throwers, harpoons, ice picks, fish traps and ulus.

. . . When the child is ready to dance, his family hands out these gifts to the family of the person whose name was handed down to the child. It is a Yup'ik custom that a newborn child is named after the last elder in the village to die. After the potlatch, the child is allowed to dance as many songs as he or she wants at any social event. (pp. 193–194)

6. Summarize the lesson by pointing out how that traditions of giving gifts within mainstream U.S. society are in some ways similar to traditions within American Indian and Eskimo groups to show caring and kindness and to fulfill obligations and expectations. *Potlatches* are also unique and different in many ways from giving traditions within mainstream society. However, stress similarities so that the students will understand the ways in which gift giving is a tradition shared by human groups. The students can learn about other important characteristics of *potlatches,* such as their relationship to social status and about their spiritual aspects, in later grades.

Intermediate and Upper Grades

CONCEPT: Cultural Diversity and Similarity

Generalization: Indian cultures used both different and similar means to satisfy common human needs and wants.

1. Ask the students to name some things they think all human beings need in order to survive and satisfy unique human wants. Their responses will probably include "food," "a place to live in," and "clothing." Probing questions might be necessary to bring out that people also have such needs as the need to explain unknown phenomena in the universe, for government, and for self-esteem.

2. List the student responses on the board and, with the class, group them into specific categories, such as food, shelter, clothing, government, family, religion, and economy.

3. Ask the students to name some institutions and means used in our society to meet the needs they have identified and categorized. Write their responses, in abbreviated form, on the board. Tell the class that in this unit they will be studying about how four earlier cultures in North America satisfied these same human needs in ways different from the ways in which we usually satisfy them today.

4. Before introducing the four cultures, develop, with the class, key questions related to each category. The students will use the questions as guides when studying the four cultures. Examples are as follows:

    a. Food
       (1) What kinds of foods did the people eat?
       (2) Were they primarily hunters and gatherers or farmers?
       (3) How was the food usually prepared? By whom?

    b. Government
       (1) Who or what group made major decisions and laws?
       (2) How were major decision makers chosen?
       (3) How were rules and laws enforced?

    c. Economy
       (1) What goods and services were produced?
       (2) How were they produced? By whom? For whom?
       (3) How were goods and services exchanged? Was some form of money used? Barter?

5. The students should record the key questions in their notebooks. They will use them as guides when examining the four cultures.

6. Introduce the four cultures the class will study. When selecting four Indian cultures for the unit, try to select cultures (1) that have both similarities and differences that the students will be able to see rather clearly, and (2) for which you have adequate and high-quality student books and resources. To assure cultural diversity, select the four groups from four different geographical areas, such as the Southeast, the Northwest, the Southwest, and California. This unit could be taught with as few as two groups. However, generalizations are more powerful when they are developed from a larger content sample. On the other hand, it is difficult for elementary students to study more than four cultures in one unit. In our example, we have chosen the Iroquois (a northeastern Indian group), the Haida (Northwest), the Hopi (Southwest), and the Pomo (California). These four groups clearly illustrate both the similarities and diversity that existed within Indian cultures.

7. Ask the students to construct a data retrieval chart (like the one illustrated in Table 5-2) that includes: (1) the categories and key questions they identified earlier, and (2) the names of the four groups. As they read and discuss each group, they should complete the blank spaces in the chart. When the chart is completed, ask the students key questions that will enable them to formulate this generalization: *Indian cultures used both different and similar means to satisfy common human needs and wants.*

8. Show the students the videotape *Weave of Time: The Story of a Navajo Family 1938–1986.* This film shows four generations of change in one Navajo family. The videotape covers nearly fifty years. Ask the students to compare the changes over the four generations in the Navajo family with changes over the generations in their own families.

Valuing Activity

    Speeches and selections that highlight traditional Indian values can evoke reflective value discussion and reasoning in the classroom. Rich and powerful

Table 5-2 DATA RETRIEVAL CHART FOR COMPARING
AND CONTRASTING FOUR CULTURES

Categories and Related Questions	Iroquois	Haida	Hopi	Pomo
Food (Questions)				
Shelter (Questions)				
Clothing (Questions)				
Government (Questions)				
Family (Questions)				
Religion (Questions)				
Economy (Questions)				

sources of Indian speeches and statements are found in *Great Documents in American Indian History,* edited by Wayne Moquin with Charles Van Doren (1973), and *Touch the Earth: A Self-Portrait of Indian Existence,* edited by T. C. McLuhan (1971). The following statement was made by Chief Standing Bear (1933), a Sioux born in 1868. The teacher can read this statement to the class and/or project it using an overhead or opaque projector. He or she can then ask the questions that follow the selection and discuss them with the class. The teacher should encourage the students to give reasons for their responses and to defend rationally their moral choices.

The Lakota Was a True Naturalist—A Lover of Nature

He loved the earth and all things of the earth, the attachment growing with age. The old people came literally to love the soil and they sat or reclined on the ground with a feeling of being close to a mothering power. It was good for the skin to touch the earth and the old people liked to remove their moccasins and walk with bare feet on the scared earth. Their [tipis] were built upon the earth and their altars were made of earth. The birds that flew in the air came to rest upon the earth and it was the final abiding place of all things that lived and grew. The soil was soothing, strengthening, cleansing, and healing.

That is why the old Indian still sits upon the earth instead of propping himself up and away from its life-giving forces. For him, to sit or lie upon the ground is to be able to think more deeply and to feel more keenly; he can see more clearly into the mysteries of life and come closer in kinship to other lives about him. . . . Kinship with all creatures of the earth, sky, and water was a real and active principle. For the animal and bird world there existed a brotherly feeling that kept the Lakota safe among them and so close did some of the Lakotas come to their feathered and furred friends that in true brotherhood they spoke a common tongue. The old Lakota was wise. He knew that a man's heart away from nature becomes hard; he knew that lack of respect for growing, living things soon led to lack of respect for humans too. So he kept his youth close to its softening influence. (pp. 192–197)

Questions

1. What are the main values of the Lakota (tribal name for the Sioux) that are revealed in this statement by Chief Standing Bear?
2. In what ways might these values of the Lakota have conflicted with the values of the Europeans who settled in North America?
3. What problems do you think developed between the Lakota and the Europeans because of their value differences? Why?
4. How do traditional Lakota values, as revealed in the statement by Chief Standing Bear, conflict with many modern-day American values?
5. Do you think it is possible for individuals who endorse traditional Lakota values, such as those revealed in Chief Standing Bear's statement, to function successfully within a highly modernized nation such as the United States? Why or why not? What conflicts might such individuals experience? How might they resolve them?
6. Do you think that traditional Lakota values, as revealed in the Chief's statement, could help strengthen a modernized nation such as the United States? Why or why not? If so, in what ways?
7. Which of the traditional Lakota values revealed in Chief Standing Bear's statement do you personally endorse? Which do you reject? Are you willing to act on those that you endorse? Why or why not?
8. When did you last act on the values in the statement that you endorse? When do you plan to act on them again?

High School Grades

CONCEPT: Federal Policy

Generalization: Most federal policy on Indian affairs was made without Indian input and usually sought Indian assimilation and the termination of federal-tribal relationships.

1. To gain an understanding of the legal relationship Indian tribes have with the federal government, the students should examine some of the Indian treaties made between the United States government and Indian tribes. These treaties were usually made when Indian tribes were forced to cede their territories and to relocate on reservations. They were granted reservation land in exchange for their land. Several such treaties are reprinted in chapter 2 of *Of Utmost Good Faith,* edited by Vine Deloria, Jr. (1971).

2. Shortly after Indians had been conquered and forced onto reservations in the late 1800s, efforts were begun by the federal government to terminate its special relationship with the tribes, to force them to give up most aspects of their cultures, and to force assimilation into the dominant culture. These goals of federal policy were implemented in the Dawes Severalty Act of 1887. Ask the students to research the arguments, both pro and con, that preceded the passage of the act.

    a. Although many White liberals favored the passage of the act, most Indian tribes opposed it. When the bill was being debated in Congress, representatives of the Five Civilized Tribes sent a strong message to Congress opposing its passage. Ask the class to read and discuss this statement, which is reprinted in *Of Utmost Good Faith,* edited by Vine Deloria, Jr. (1971).

    b. White allies of Indians strongly supported the passage of a bill, such as Dawes, that would break up tribal lands and allot them to individual household heads. They felt that such a bill would enable Indians to assimilate into the dominant culture. In 1884, the Indian Rights Association of Philadelphia, whose members were White friends of the Indian, issued a pamphlet strongly advocating the passage of an allotment bill. Ask the students to read and discuss excerpts from this pamphlet, reprinted in *The Indian and the White Man,* edited by Wilcombe Washburn (1964). The class should then compare the statement sent to Congress by the Five Civilized Tribes and the excerpt from the pamphlet. They should discuss the merits and weaknesses of the two positions.

3. Ask several students to role-play a debate between those who favored the Dawes bill and those who opposed it.

4. Ask the students to research these questions: "What effects did the Dawes Severalty Act have on Indian people?" "On White society?" "How do you think Indian life might be different today if the bill had failed in Congress?" "Why?" Two books— Alvin M. Josephy, Jr. (1991), *The Indian Heritage of America,* and Edward H. Spicer (1969), *A Short History of the Indian in the United States*—contain good discussions of the disastrous effects of the act on Indian tribes.

5. Because of the loss of millions of acres of tribal lands and the severe poverty of Indians, it was clear by the 1920s that the Dawes Act had been a colossal failure. John Collier, who became Commissioner of Indian Affairs in 1933, outlined a new federal policy for Indians. Ask the students to read and discuss his statement, "A New Deal for the Red Men," in Washburn (1964) and the federal act of 1934 that embodied the new federal policy, the Wheeler-Howard Act, in Deloria (1971).

6. Ask the class to research the effects the Wheeler-Howard Act has had on Indian life and on the larger society. They can share their research findings by using role-playing, debates, or group discussion techniques.

7. Heated arguments for the termination of federal-tribal relationship surfaced again in the 1950s. Ask the class to prepare research reports on these topics:

    a. The House Concurrent Resolution 108, 83rd Congress, 1st session, passed on August 1, 1953, called for the termination of the federal role in Indian affairs.

    b. How termination policy affected these tribes and the conditions of the termination policy in each case:
        (1) the Klamaths of Oregon
        (2) the Menominees of Wisconsin
        (3) the Alabamas and the Coushattas in the South

8. Ask the class to study the various debates on termination that took place in the 1960s and 1970s between Indians and federal officials. An interesting argument against termination by an Indian is Earl Old Person (Blackfoot). See "Testimony against Proposed Congressional Legislation, 1966," reprinted in *Great Documents in American Indian History,* edited by Moquin and Van Doren (1973).

9. To terminate this unit, ask the students to divide into three groups and pretend that they are three different reservation tribes that have legal relationships with the federal government. Each tribe must unanimously decide, in the Indian tradition, whether they will terminate or maintain their legal relationship with the federal government. When the role playing is over, the class should reassemble and discuss the decisions of each tribe and the process and arguments they experienced in reaching them.

REFERENCES

Bolt, C. (1987). *American Indian Policy and American Reform: Case Studies of the Campaign to Assimilate the American Indians.* London: Allen and Unwin.

Bruggmann, M. & Gerber, M. (1987). *Indians of the Northwest Coast.* New York: Facts on File Publications.

Ceram, C. W. (1971). *The First Americans: A Story of North American Archaeology.* New York: Mentor Books.

Chief Luther Standing Bear. (1933). *Land of the Spotted Eagle.* Boston: Houghton Mifflin.

Deloria, V., Jr. (Ed.). (1971). *Of Utmost Good Faith.* San Francisco: Straight Arrow Books.

Denevan, W. M. (1976). *The Native Population of the Americas in 1492.* Madison: The University of Wisconsin Press.

Dobyns, H. F. (1976). *Native American Demography: A Critical Bibliography.* Bloomington: Indiana University Press.

Dorris, M. A. (1981, Spring). The Grass Still Grows, the Rivers Still Flow: Contemporary Native Americans. *Daedalus 110,* 43–69.

Forbes, J. D. (1973). Teaching Native American Values and Cultures. In J. A. Banks, (Ed.). *Teaching Ethnic Studies: Concepts and Strategies* (pp. 201–225). Washington. D.C.: National Council for the Social Studies.

Hagan, W. T. (1961). *American Indians.* Chicago: The University of Chicago Press.

Hammond Past Worlds: The Times Atlas of Archaeology. (1988). Maplewood. N.J.: Hammond, Inc.

Harris, W. H. & Levey, J. S. (Eds.) (1975). *The New Columbia Encyclopaedia.* New York: Columbia University Press.

Josephy, A. M., Jr. (1991). *The Indian Heritage of America* (enlarged ed.). Boston: Houghton Mifflin.

Kroeber, A. L. (1934). Native American Population. *American Anthropologist, 36,* 1–25.

McLuhan, T. C. (Ed.). (1971). *Touch the Earth: A Self-Portrait of Indian Existence.* New York: Pocket Books.

Mooney, J. M. (1928). *The Aboriginal Population of America North of Mexico.* In J. R. Swanton (Ed.). Smithsonian Miscellaneous Collections (Vol. 80, no. 7). Washington, D.C.

Moquin, W. with Van Doren, C. (Eds.). (1973). *Great Documents in American Indian History.* New York: Praeger.

Snipp, C. M. (1991). *American Indians: The First of This Land.* New York: Russell Sage Foundation.

Sorkin, A. L. (1978). *The Urban American Indians.* Lexington, Mass.: D.C. Heath.

Spicer, E. (1980). American Indians: Federal Policy toward. In S. Thernstrom, A. Orlov, & O. Handlin (Eds.). *Harvard Encyclopedia of American Ethnic Groups* (pp. 114–122). Cambridge: Harvard University Press.

Spicer, E. H. (1969). *A Short History of the Indians in the United States.* New York: Van Nostrand Reinhold.

Stuart, P. (1987). *Nations within a Nation: Historical Statistics of American Indians.* New York: Greenwood Press.

Tucker, M. (1995). Contemporary Potlatches. In A. Hirschfelder (Ed.). *Native Heritage: Personal Accounts by American Indians 1790 to the Present* (pp. 193–194). New York: Macmillan.

U.S. Bureau of the Census. (1988, December). *We, the First Americans.* Washington, D.C.: U.S. Government Printing Office.

U.S. Bureau of the Census (1993, September). *We, the First Americans.* Washington, D.C.: U.S. Government Printing Office.

U.S. Commission on Civil Rights. (1981). *Indian Tribes: A Continuing Quest for Survival.* Washington, D.C.: The Commission.

Underhill, R. M. (1971). *Red Man's America* (rev. ed.). Chicago: The University of Chicago Press.

Washburn, W. E. (Ed.). (1964). *The Indian and the White Man.* New York: Doubleday.

Wax, M. L. (1971). *Indian Americans: Unity and Diversity.* Englewood Cliffs. N.J.: Prentice-Hall.

The World Atlas of Archaeology. (1985). New York: Portland House.

ANNOTATED BIBLIOGRAPHY

Books for Teachers

Especially Recommended

Champagne, D. (Ed.). (1994). *Native America: Portrait of the Peoples*. Detroit: Visible Ink.

> *This comprehensive book (786 pages) is one of the few books that treats Native Americans in today's society. It is divided by regions and includes contributions by twenty-seven authors.*

Deloria, V., Jr. (1995). *Red Earth, White Lies: Native Americans and the Myth of Scientific Facts*. New York: Scribner.

> *Deloria argues that Native oral history is more truthful than Western scientific facts in this provocative book that is destined to be controversial. It is a harsh critique of Western science.*

DeMallie, R. (Ed.). (1984). *The Sixth Grandfather: Black Elk's Teachings Given to John G. Neihardt*. Lincoln: University of Nebraska Press.

> *This version of the teachings of the Oglala holy man, Black Elk, has an extensive (74 page), useful, and informative introduction. Excellent for teaching the perspectives and points of view of an important Indian elder.*

Green, R. (1992). *Women in American Indian Society*. New York: Chelsea House.

> *An informative book that is also appropriate for middle and high school students.*

Harvey, K. D. & Harjo, L. D. (1994). *Indian Country: A History of Native People in America*. Golden, Colo.: North American Press.

> *This rich teaching resource includes historical informative on Native American groups as well as lesson plans and a comprehensive bibliography.*

Hirschfelder, A. (Ed.). (1995). *Native Heritage: Personal Accounts by American Indians 1790 to the Present*. New York: Macmillan.

> *This excellent collection of documents written or spoken by Native Americans is grouped into these categories: family, law and its resources, language, Native education, traditional storytelling, traditions, worship, and discrimination.*

Hyatt, V. L. & Nettleford, R. (Eds.). (1995). *Race, Discourse, and the Origin of the Americas*. Washington, D.C.: Smithsonian Institution Press.

> *This excellent scholarly book contains a group of seminal papers that present transformative views on racial groups and European contact in the Americas.*

Jaimes, M. A. (Ed.). (1992). *The State of Native America: Genocide, Colonization and Resistance*. Boston: South End Press.

> *This excellent edited collection includes chapters that focus on contemporary issues facing Native Americans, such as "The State of Native America," "Key Indian Laws and Cases," "Federal Indian Identification Policy," and "American Indian Women."*

Reddy, M. A. (Ed.). (1993). *Statistical Record of Native Americans*. Detroit: Gale Research.

A massive and comprehensive reference work that covers many different aspects of Native American life.

Snipp, C. M. (1995). American Indian Studies. In J. A. Banks & C. A. M. Banks (Eds.). *Handbook of Research on Multicultural Education* (pp. 245–264). New York: Macmillan.

This chapter is a comprehensive overview of the status of Native Americans today. It also discusses research trends in American Indian studies.

Stannard, D. E. (1992). *American Holocaust: Columbus and the Conquest of the New World*. New York: Oxford University Press.

Stannard describes the rich cultures that existed in the Americas before the Europeans came and the path of genocide that took place throughout the Americas. An important and revealing book.

Other References

Allen, P. G. (1992). *The Sacred Hoop: Recovering the Feminine in American Indian Traditions*. Boston: Beacon Press.

This influential book on the feminine in Native American cultures has now been reissued with a new preface.

Bataille, G. M. & Sands, K. M. (1984). *American Indian Women: Telling Their Lives*. Lincoln: University of Nebraska Press.

An informative and important book on the autobiographies of Native American women.

Coltelli, L. (1990). *Winged Words: American Indian Writers Speak*. Lincoln: University of Nebraska Press.

The author interviews distinguished Indian writers, including Paula Gunn Allen, Louise Erdrich, Michael Dorris, N. Scott Momaday, and Leslie Marmon Silko.

Dorris, M. (1994). *Paper Trail*. New York: Harper-Perennial.

A thoughtful collection of essays by the noted Native American scholar and writer.

Erdrich, L. (1994). *The Bingo Place*. New York: Harper/Collins.

A novel about Native Americans in the Midwest. It is the most recent of Erdrich's novels in the series with her well-known Love Medicine.

Forbes, J. D. (1993). *Africans and Native Americans: The Language of Race and the Evolution of Red-Black Peoples*. Urbana: University of Illinois Press.

This scholarly book discusses the biological relationship between African Americans and American Indians and how race was constructed in the Americas. This is an important book by a veteran Native American scholar.

Hirschfelder, A. & Kreipe de Montaño, M. (1993). *The Native American Almanac: A Portrait of Native America*. New York: Prentice-Hall General Reference.

Historical overviews of relations between Whites and Indians; Native Americans today; Supreme Court decisions; Treaties; Language; and Education and Religion are among the topics covered in this useful reference.

Josephy, A. M., Jr. (1991). *The Indian Heritage of America* (enlarged ed.). Boston: Houghton Mifflin.

An excellently written and comprehensive history that has stood the test of time.

Josephy, A. M., Jr. (Ed.). (1991). *America in 1492: The World of the Indian Peoples before the Arrival of Columbus.* New York: Knopf.

The chapters in this important book are scholarly and comprehensive.

Klein, L. F. & Ackerman, L. A. (1995). *Women and Power in Native North America.* Norman: University of Oklahoma Press.

A scholarly book that describes the role of women in ten culture areas of North America. An important and timely publication.

Lomawaima, K. T. (1994). *They Call It Prairie Light: The Story of Chilocco Indian School.* Lincoln: University of Nebraska Press.

A prize-winning historical study of an Indian school by a perceptive Native American scholar and educator.

Lomawaima, K. T. (1995). Educating Native Americans. In J. A. Banks & C. A. M. Banks (Eds.). *Handbook of Research on Multicultural Education* (pp. 331–347). New York: Macmillan.

An insightful, informative, and beautifully written chapter on effective ways to educate Native American students.

Mankiller, W. & Wallis, M. (1993). *Mankiller: A Chief and Her People.* New York: St. Martin's Press.

This autobiography by the Chief of the Cherokee Nation reveals her personal story as well as the history of her people.

Momaday, N. S. (1976). *The Names: A Memoir.* Tucson: University of Arizona Press.

A memoir by the distinguished author of House Made of Dawn, *winner of a Pulitzer Prize for literature.*

Nabokow, P. (Ed.). (1992). *Native American Testimony: A Chronicle of Indian-White Relations from Prophecy to the Present, 1492–1992.* New York: Penguin.

A history of Indian-White relations seen through the eyes of Native Americans.

Nash, G. B. (1992). *Red, White and Black: The Peoples of Early America* (3rd ed.). Englewood Cliffs: Prentice-Hall.

This informative book describes the historical interactions among Native Americans, African Americans, and European Americans in early North America.

Prucha, F. P. (1994). *American Indian Treaties: The History of a Political Anomaly.* Berkeley: University of California Press.

A scholarly and comprehensive book on Indian treaties that describes the important role they have played in U.S. history.

Riley, P. (Ed.). (1993). *Growing up Native American: An Anthology.* New York: Morrow.

This book consists of personal accounts of growing up by Native American writers.

Thompson, L. (1991). *To the American Indian: Reminiscences of a Yurok Woman.* Berkeley, Calif.: Heyday Books.

Originally written in 1916, an Indian women gives her perspectives on the changes in her traditional Yurok culture wrought by the coming of Whites. A rich resource for teaching about Indian perspectives on history.

Weatherford, J. (1991). *Native Roots: How the Indians Enrich America.* New York: Fawcett Columbine.

An informative and gracefully written book. Weatherford is also the author of Indian Givers: How the Indians of the Americas Transformed the World *(New York: Fawcett Columbine, 1988).*

Wright, R. (1992). *Stolen Continents: The "New World" through Indian Eyes.* Boston: Houghton Mifflin.

A Canadian writer tells the story of the Aztec, Maya, Inca, Cherokee, and Iroquois before and after the coming of the Europeans.

Books for Students

(Note: These designations are used throughout this book: **Primary, grades 1–3; Intermediate, 4–6; Middle School, 7–8; High School, 9–12**)

Adler, D. A. (1993). *A Picture Book of Sitting Bull.* New York: Holiday House.

A clearly written biography—enhanced with beautiful color illustrations—that tells the story of Sitting Bull, the Sioux leader. (Primary)

Andrews, E. (1992). *Indians of the Plains.* New York: Facts on File.

Focused on several Indian tribes, this book shares the history and culture of the people who traditionally inhabited the plains of North America. Several photographs help to capture the attention of young readers. (Intermediate)

Baylor, B. (1994). *The Table Where Rich People Sit.* Illustrated by P. Parnell. New York: Scribner's.

This is the story of a young girl whose family explains to her that wealth is more than money. She is taught to view sunsets, mountains, the feel of the wind, and the smell of the rain as aspects of wealth. (Primary)

Bruchac, J. (1993). *Flying with the Eagle, Racing the Great Bear: Stories from Native North America.* Mahwah, N.J.: BridgeWater Books.

A collection of sixteen short stories, this book's central coming-of-age theme features stories of young Native American boys stepping into manhood. (Intermediate)

Chief Dan George. (1989). *My Heart Soars.* Drawings by H. Hirnschall. Blaine, Wash.: Hancock House Publishers.

A powerful collection of sage statements and poems that is excellent for teaching. This collection cogently exemplifies the harmony that Native Americans have with all living things. (All levels)

Chief Jake Swamp. *Giving Thanks: A Native American Good Morning Message.* Illustrated by E. Printup, Jr. New York: Lee & Low Books.

The text of this strikingly illustrated book is based on the Iroquois Thanksgiving Address, a traditional message of peace and appreciation that honors the earth and all living beings. (All levels)

Dixon, A. (1992). *How Raven Brought Light to People.* New York: Margaret McElderry Books.

This book retells a Tlingit Indian legend that focuses on Raven and his magical powers. (Primary)

Dorris, M. (1992). *Morning Girl.* New York: Hyperion Books for Children.

This is the story of a twelve-year-old Taino girl who strives to understand why she and her brother Star Boy view the world so differently. (Intermediate)

Dove, M. (1981). *Cogewea: The Half-Blood.* Lincoln: University of Nebraska Press.

This is the story of Cogewea, a bi-racial girl who is caught between the worlds of Anglo ranchers and full-blood reservation Native Americans. She struggles to reconcile the perceived incompatibility of book learning and the folk wisdom of her Native American grandmother. (High School)

Dove, M. (1990). *Coyote Stories.* Lincoln: University of Nebraska Press.

This is a collection of Native American legends about the Animal People. Within these stories the reader learns why Skunks tail is black and white, why Spider has such long legs, and why Mosquito bites people. (All levels)

Dove, M. (1990). *Mourning Dove: A Salishan Autobiography.* Lincoln: University of Nebraska Press.

This is the autobiography of Mourning Dove, a Salish writer. She explores the complexities of tribal life through conversations, celebrations, and events. (High School)

Echo-Hawk, R. C. & Echo-Hawk, W. R. (1994). *Battlefields and Burial Grounds: The Indian Struggle to Protect Ancestral Graves.* Minneapolis: Lerner.

An informative book on an important topic. (Middle School/High School)

Fradin, D. B. (1992). *Hiawatha: Messenger of Peace.* New York: Margaret McElderry Books.

A biographical account of the Iroquois leader who helped to create the Iroquois Federation, this book helps young readers to gain insight into the Iroquois culture and the United States Constitution. (Intermediate)

Goble, P. (1992). *Love Flute.* New York: Bradbury Press.

With unique color illustrations and text, the author retells a Plains Indian love story that conveys the power and grace of the culture. (Primary)

Griese, A. (1995). *Anna's Athabaskan Summer.* Illustrated by C. Ragins. New York: Boyd Mills Press.

The story describes a summer in the life of a young girl who discovers its wonders and learns about the life cycle. (Primary)

Himler, R. (1993). *The Navajos: A First Americans Book.* New York: Holiday House.

With impressive illustrations and clear text, this book examines the Navajo culture and way of life. (Primary)

Himler, R. (1993). *The Sioux: A First Americans Book*. New York: Holiday House.

This book retells Sioux history with easy-to-read text and color illustrations. (Primary)

Hirschfelder, A. B. & Singer, B. R. (1992). *Rising Voices: Writings of Young Native Americans*. New York: Scribner's.

A captivating collection of essays and poems, this book explores Native American culture through the voices of young people. (High School)

Hoobler, D. & Hoobler, T. (1992). *The Trail on Which They Wept*. Morristown, N.J.: Silver Burdett Press.

From a young Cherokee girl's perspective, this book explores the Trail of Tears. It gives readers a personal view of this American tragedy. (Middle School)

Hoyt-Goldsmith, D. (1991). *Pueblo Storyteller*. New York: Holiday House.

Through the voice of ten year-old April, this book gives readers an insightful view of the Pueblo Indian culture. (Intermediate)

Hoyt-Goldsmith, D. (1993). *Cherokee Summer*. New York: Holiday House.

Through the eyes of a ten-year-old girl this book examines the Cherokee culture in the past and present. (Primary)

Hubbard, J. (1994). *Shooting Back from the Reservation*. New York: The New Press.

This is a book of photographs taken by Native American youth capturing their cultures. It provides positive photographic images of Native American life. (All Ages)

Jacobs, S. K. (1993). *The Boy Who Loved Morning*. Boston: Little, Brown.

This story offers striking color illustrations that help to tell the story of a young Native American boy and his maturation. (Intermediate)

James, B. (1994). *The Mud Family*. Illustrated by P. Morin. New York: G. P. Putnam's Sons.

This is the story of a young Anasazi girl named Sosi whose people depend on rainfall to live. After weeks without rain Sosi's family must find a new place to live. This creates a stressful household. (Intermediate)

Keams, G. (1995). *Grandmother Spider Brings the Sun*. Illustrated by J. Bernardin. Flagstaff: Northland Publishing.

This beautifully illustrated book tells the Cherokee creation story. (Primary)

Keegan, M. (1991). *Pueblo Boy: Growing Up in Two Worlds*. New York: Dutton.

This book explores the merging of two cultures as readers follow the experiences of a young Pueblo boy living in contemporary society. (Intermediate)

Kendall, R. (1992). *Eskimo Boy: Life in an Inupiaq Eskimo Village*. New York: Scholastic.

With many color photographs, this book introduces young readers to modern-day Eskimo culture as they meet the inhabitants of an Eskimo Village in Alaska. (Intermediate)

King, S. (1993). *Shannon: An Ojibway Dancer.* Minneapolis: Lerner.

> *A portrait of a young Ojibway girl who participates in both mainstream U.S. culture and her more traditional ethnic culture. (Primary)*

Klausner, J. (1993). *Sequoyah's Gift: A Portrait of the Cherokee Leader.* New York: HarperCollins.

> *A biography that examines the life of Cherokee leader Sequoyah, who dedicated his life to literacy by creating a system of writing for his native language. (Intermediate)*

Laan, N. V. (1993). *A Blackfoot Legend: Buffalo Dance.* Boston: Little, Brown and Company.

> *An intricate relationship between human beings and nature is explored through this book that tells the story of a bond between the Blackfoot people and the buffalo. (Primary)*

Lacapa, K. & Lacapa, M. (1994). *Less Than Half, More Than Whole.* Illustrated by M. Lacapa. Flagstaff: Northland Publishing.

> *This is an excellent book that can be used to explain racial identity to children. Tony realizes that he is neither a White like his friend Scott, nor 100% Indian like Will. Tony's realization that he is more than whole is comforting to children who have ever felt "different." (Primary)*

Lippard, L. R. (Ed.). (1992). *Partial Recall.* New York: The New Press.

> *This collection of essays and photographs deconstructs the images that have shaped our ideas about "Indianness." The authors describe the role that certain images have had in shaping the relationships between native and non-native people. (High School)*

Lipsyte, R. (1993). *Jim Thorpe: 20th-Century Jock.* New York: HarperCollins Publishers.

> *Young readers are introduced to the Native American athlete Jim Thorpe, who crossed many cultural barriers during his life.*

Liptak, K. (1991). *Indians of the Pacific Northwest.* New York: Facts On File.

> *An exploration of the Native American tribes that traditionally inhabited the Pacific Northwest, this book gives readers extensive information about and insight about these groups. (Intermediate)*

Littlechild, G. (1993). *This Land Is My Land.* San Francisco, Calif.: Children's Book Press.

> *The author uses texts and colorful paintings to describe his experiences growing up in Canada as a Plains Cree Indian. His experiences and perceptions are shared by many Indians throughout North America, especially the Plains Indians. (Middle School)*

Loewen, J. W. (1992). *The Truth about Columbus: A Subversively True Poster Book for a Dubiously Celebratory Occasion.* New York: The New Press.

> *This is an excellent resource for deconstructing the notion that Columbus "discovered" America. The author examines the words textbooks use to describe Columbus's voyages and indicate how they are misleading. (High School)*

Lyon, G. E. (1993). *Dreamplace*. New York: Orchard.

> *When tourists visit an ancient Pueblo village they are taken back to a time when the Anasazi lived. (Primary)*

Mayo, G. W. (1993). *Meet Tricky Coyote!* New York: Walker and Company.

> *Through the delightful character Coyote, young readers learn about life from his humorous adventures. (Primary).* Mayo has also written That Tricky Coyote! *(1993).*

Nez, R. T. as told to Wilder, K. (1995). *Forbidden Talent*. Illustrated by R. T. Nez. Flagstaff: Northland Publishing.

> *This is the story of a young Navajo boy named Ashkii who lives on the Navajo Reservation. Ashkii loves to make art but is forbidden to do so by his grandfather. He continues to paint in secret, and the reader learns his fate. (Intermediate)*

O'Dell, S. & Hall, E. (1992). *Thunder Rolling in the Mountains*. Boston: Houghton Mifflin.

> *A moving tale, this book tells about the historic defeat of the Nez Perce through Chief Joseph's young daughter. (High School)*

Oughton, J. (1992). *How the Stars Fell into the Sky*. Boston: Houghton Mifflin.

> *A beautifully illustrated book, it retells a Navajo folk tale that explains how stars came to be in the night sky. (Primary)*

Peters, R. M. (1992). *Clambake: A Wampanoag Tradition*. Minneapolis: Lerner.

> *With interesting text and illustrative color photographs, this book introduces readers to the unique Wampanoag tradition of clambakes. (Intermediate)*

Raczek, L. T. (1995) *The Night the Grandfathers Danced*. Illustrated by K. O. Ehling. Flagstaff: Northland Publishing.

> *Raczek tells the story of Autumn Eyetoo, an Ute Mountain Ute girl who prepares to dance in her first Bear Dance. This dance signaled the end of winter and was to be a highlight for autumn until she had no one with whom to dance. (Primary)*

Regguinti, G. (1992). *The Sacred Harvest: Ojibway Wild Rice Gathering*. Minneapolis: Lerner.

> *This book explores the Ojibway tradition of harvesting wild rice through young Glen Jackson's first harvest. (Middle School)*

Roessel, M. (1993). *Kinaaldá: A Navajo Girl Grows Up*. Minneapolis: Lerner.

> *This book describes a Navajo coming-of-age ceremony through thirteen-year-old Celinda. (Primary)*

Sattler, H. R. (1993). *The Earliest Americans*. New York: Clarion Books.

> *Readers learn about the prehistoric people of the Americas through thoroughly researched text and informative illustrations. (High School)*

Seymour, T. V. N. (1993). *The Gift of the Changing Woman*. New York: Henry Holt and Company.

An introduction to the Navajo coming-of-age ceremony for young women, with concise text and color illustrations. (Primary)

Spinka, P. K. (1992). *Mother's Blessing.* New York: Atheneum.

This book follows a young Chumash girl as she learns about the world. (High School)

Swentzell, R. (1992). *Children of Clay: A Family of Pueblo Potters.* Minneapolis: Lerner.

Readers are introduced to the Pueblo tradition of pottery through a young girl's family. Color photographs help to enhance this delightful book. (Intermediate)

Whitethorne, B. (1994). *Sunpainters: Eclipse of the Navajo Sun.* Illustrated by B. Whitethorne. Flagstaff: Northland Publishing.

Whitethorne tells a wonderful story about a young Navajo boy, Kii Leonard, who witnesses his first total solar eclipse. During this experience Kii learns how to show respect for Mother Earth, the Navajo Way. (Intermediate)

Williams, N. (Recorded by) (1995). *Patrick DesJarlait: Conversations with a Native American Artist.* Minneapolis: Runestone Press.

This beautiful book has striking illustrations and an informative text. (All levels)

Wolfson, E. (1993). *From the Earth to Beyond the Sky: Native American Medicine.* Boston: Houghton Mifflin.

In this fascinating book, readers are introduced to the wisdom and mystery of the traditional Native American world of medicine. (High School)

Wood, N. (1993). *Spirit Walker.* New York: Doubleday Books.

The beauty and grace of traditional Native American culture are revealed in this collection of poems. (High School)

Wunderli, S. (1992). *The Blue between the Clouds.* New York: Henry Holt and Company.

Set in the 1940s, this novel deals with the friendship and experiences of a young Navajo boy and his friend Matt. (High School)

Younkin, P. (1992). *Indians of the Arctic and Subarctic.* New York: Facts On File.

The cultures of the traditional inhabitants of the Americas' arctic and subarctic regions are explored in this thoroughly researched book. (High School)

6

NATIVE HAWAIIANS

CONCEPTS, STRATEGIES, AND MATERIALS

You must not think that this is anything like olden times, that you are the only chiefs and can leave things as they are. Smart people have arrived from the great countries that you have never seen. They know our people are few in number and living in a small country; they will eat us up.

David Malo, 1837

he experiences of Native Hawaiians parallel those of other indigenous peoples whose cultures and traditional life-styles were drastically altered by European contact. Like the American Indians, the numbers of Native Hawaiians were sharply reduced in the past two centuries. Their culture was initially modified and finally overwhelmed by European and American settlers.

Native Hawaiians often found it difficult to assume a viable role in a Hawaiian society in which Western practices were foreign to them. Values that, for centuries, had been hallmarks of Native Hawaiian culture were often counterproductive in a Hawaiian society run by foreigners. This conflict inevitably led to helplessness and despair for some of Hawaii's original inhabitants.

Yet, the culture of Hawaii has shown remarkable resiliency despite the great odds against its survival. The Hawaiian Renaissance of the 1970s indi-

This chapter was written by Carlos F. Diaz, Associate Professor of Education, Florida Atlantic University, Boca Raton, Florida. The bibliographies at the end of this chapter were revised by Virgie O. Chattergy, Professor of Education, University of Hawaii, Manoa.

cated that a new consciousness of what it means to be Hawaiian had developed. The Hawaiian independence movement of the 1980s and 1990s showed that, at least for some Hawaiians, there is dissatisfaction with the political status quo and their role in it. For some Native Hawaiians, the American dream has borne fruit. For most, it has been largely deferred. Students should be aware that, although small in number, Native Hawaiians have made unique and lasting contributions to the American saga.

In 1778, Captain James Cook's expedition landed on the islands that he named the Sandwich Islands, now called the state of Hawaii. There, Cook found nearly 300,000 people living in relative isolation. Since that time, Hawaiian history has been fraught with benevolent paternalism by Europeans and Americans, to the detriment of Native Hawaiians. This story is one of broken promises and exploitation of the Native Hawaiians by foreigners that, in some ways, is similar to the poignant plight of American Indians.

Until foreigners started coming to Hawaii, Native Hawaiians did not have a word for *race*. There were two groups, Hawaiians and strangers. They called themselves *kanakas* and referred to strangers as *haoles*. This total unimportance of race was to change with the coming of Europeans. The word *haole* acquired the meaning of White instead of stranger as Whites became more prevalent on the islands. The Hawaiian people were forced to deal with an alien White economic, social, and legal system that they did not understand.

NATIVE HAWAIIANS: HISTORICAL PERSPECTIVE

Important Dates	
1778	The beginning of European contact. Captain James Cook's expedition landed on the Hawaiian Islands.
1795	The rise to power of King Kamehameha I, who united the Hawaiian people under one ruler. This marked the beginning of the Kamehameha dynasty.
1820	The breaking of eating *kapu* by King Kamehameha II, which signaled the end of the ancient Hawaiian religion as a state religion. The first missionaries arrived in Hawaii from New England.
1835	King Kamehameha III granted an American firm the first long-term lease for a sugar plantation.
1845	The Great Mahele; all the land on the islands was divided among the king and 245 chiefs.

**Important
Dates**

1893	Queen Liliuokalani was overthrown in a bloodless revolution led by American planters. The Republic of Hawaii was established, with Sanford B. Dole as president. This government lasted until annexation by the United States.
1920	The Hawaiian Homes Commission was started to benefit the native Hawaiians. Very little of this land was used for its stated purpose. (By the 1930s, the commission was leasing half of its land to corporations or to non-Hawaiians.)
1954	For the first time since Hawaii became a territory, the Democratic party captured a majority in both houses of the legislature.
1959	Hawaii became the fiftieth state of the United States.
1974	George Ariyoshi was the first non-*haole* elected governor of Hawaii.
1975	The U.S. Congress passed a law recognizing Native Hawaiians as a Native American group.
1976	The voyage of the Hawaiian canoe Hokule'a from Hawaii to Tahiti reinforced pride in the Polynesian roots of Hawaiian culture. Daniel Akaka became the first Native Hawaiian member of the U.S. House of Representatives.
1977	The first edition of the newsletter *Native Hawaiian* was published, marking a growing Hawaiian consciousness movement.
1978	The Office of Hawaiian Affairs was established by the state government to help Native Hawaiians secure their rights.
1980	The Hawaiian tourist industry suffered its first decline since 1949. This fueled debate about diversification of the Hawaiian economy.
1984	Hawaii celebrated twenty-five years of statehood.
1986	John D. Waihee, the first Hawaiian governor of Hawaiian ancestry, took office. Hawaii's population was 1.06 million.
1993	President Clinton signs PL103-150 into law, officially apologizing to the Hawaiian people for the overthrow of the Hawaiian monarchy.

Important Dates	
1995	Seven hundred people demonstrate at the state capitol to pass a 600-million dollar settlement to allow faster development of Hawaiian homelands.

NATIVE HAWAIIANS: BEFORE EUROPEAN CONTACT

In the early subsistence economy of Hawaii, the survival of Hawaiians depended on a communal effort to reap the maximum benefits from the islands' scarce resources. The Hawaiians were an agricultural and fishing people with a complex socioreligious structure. The islands were governed by the *ali'i,* who were powerful chiefs. The power of these chiefs was legitimized by the priest, or *kahuna,* who interpreted the religious doctrine set forth in the *kapu.* The common people, or *maka'ainana,* were extremely devoted to their chiefs. The high chief, or *ali'inui,* was the supreme ruler over his territory and was expected to provide protection for his people. People had the freedom to move to the district of another chief, but rarely did so. Although sharing was a predominant practice, there was a considerable difference between the lifestyles of the chiefs and the common people.

There were two Hawaiian customs that would lead to inevitable conflict with *haoles* in the future. One was a system of sharing and bartering, in which products were exchanged from one island to another. The Hawaiians did not use currency, and therefore the accumulation of wealth in a market economy as we know it was unknown. The other custom was the notion that the land belonged to the gods, and, therefore, in a sense, belonged to everyone and could not be owned. The earliest visitors to the islands found the natives willing to share whatever they had. After all, that was the Hawaiian way.

EUROPEAN CONTACT

The propensity of Hawaiians to share eventually helped to seal their demise. Besides providing provisions for ships, Hawaiians were quite willing to share their women, and Whites were eager to become intimate with them. These casual contacts over a long period of time had a decimating effect on the islands' population. The venereal diseases introduced by European and American sailors found little natural resistance among the Hawaiians and, along with measles, cholera, and alcoholism, took a deadly toll.

An estimated 300,000 people inhabited the Hawaiian Islands at the time of European contact. By 1840, only abut 100,000 Hawaiians remained. Many Native Hawaiians were naturally alarmed at what was taking place due to contact with the *haoles*. According to David Malo (cited in Jacobs & Landau, 1971), a Native Hawaiian writer who espoused this viewpoint, "The ships of the White man have come and smart men have arrived from the great countries. . . . They know our people are few in number and living in a small country; they will eat us up" (p. 22). His prophecy came true eventually, but at that time it fell on deaf ears. When David Malo died, he was buried at his request in Lahaina, next to a school where he had received his education from missionaries.

The paternalism of *haoles* began with sea captains, who needed the islands as a place to replenish supplies and repair their ships. Often, chiefs were given a few metal items in return for supplies. As commercialism grew and the chiefs saw more European goods, there began to be a desire for these items. Sandalwood, which was plentiful on the islands, was in great demand for carving as well as for its aromatic qualities. It could be bought in Hawaii for 1 cent per pound and sold lucratively in Canton, China, for 34 cents per pound (Kent, 1983, p. 18). As the Yankee traders increased their demands for sandalwood, many chiefs forced their subjects to cut more of the mountain trees and haul the lumber down steep slopes. Some chiefs also became fervent consumers of Western goods and kept their subjects away from their own food-producing activities in order to satisfy the sandalwood trade and their own avarice. This continued until the slopes of Hawaii were nearly denuded of sandalwood trees. Today, they are scarce on the islands.

The ascension to power of King Kamehameha I marked the rise of the Kamehameha dynasty. According to Day (1968), "One of Kamehameha's greatest qualities was his ability to attract many White men to his service and retain their loyalty for years or even a lifetime" (p. 44). Even though Kamehameha was skillful in retaining power, this practice proved disastrous in the long run for his heirs, because often the *haole* advisers held their own interests ahead of the Hawaiian people they were supposed to help.

Kamehameha I is often regarded as one of the greatest Hawaiian monarchs because he conquered populations of other islands and unified the entire island chain under one rule. The weapons and technology he had obtained through contact with Westerners were of great assistance in this campaign.

After the death of Kamehameha I in 1819, he was succeeded by his son, Liholiho. During the reign of Liholiho (Kamehameha II), he was pressured into abolishing the *kapu* system of taboos. This had far-reaching effects on Hawaiian society. Although the *kapu* system was often oppressive and sometimes abused, its elimination began an erosion of Native Hawaiian culture with no satisfactory substitutes provided.

Besides the traders and the confidants of chiefs, another group entered the Hawaiian scene to lend its paternalistic hand. In 1820, the first groups of missionaries arrived in the islands from New England. Their goal was to Christianize the natives, but in most cases their influence far surpassed the religious realm. According to Jacobs and Landau (1971), "Under increased influence of the missionaries of the king, more haoles were given the right to lease land for commercial enterprises. But these men did not want merely to lease the land, they wanted to own it outright so they could sell or lease it to others" (p. 26).

A further blow to the survival of Hawaiian culture was dealt in 1848, when King Kamehameha III took the suggestions of his foreign advisors and decided to redistribute the land of the Hawaiian islands. This act by the king was known as the *Great Mahele*. Kent (1983) notes that under its provisions, "60% of the land was allocated to the crown and government, 29% to the 208 chiefs, and less than 1% to 11,000 commoners" (p. 31).

After the Great Mahele, there was a steady decline in subsistence farming among the Native Hawaiian people. Alien concepts such as land deeds and property taxes clashed with the traditional Hawaiian view that land was for the use and enjoyment of all the people. Slowly, even small plots of land owned by Native Hawaiians passed into the hands of the *haoles*. This loss of control over their land by Native Hawaiians somewhat parallels the saga of American Indians.

As the sandalwood trade faded, the Hawaiian economy began to rely more on supplying whaling ships with meat, vegetables, and water. Hawaii also became a convenient location to make any repairs needed by whaling vessels on their long voyages. With the income earned from these activities, Hawaii imported manufactured goods mainly from the United States. When whaling in the Pacific began to decline, the Hawaiian economy shifted to plantation agriculture.

During each of these phases, the Hawaiian economy was being controlled by forces thousands of miles away from the islands. The interests and needs of the Native Hawaiian population were inconsequential when compared to the potential for large profits.

The plantation system began to flourish in the latter part of the nineteenth century. Native Hawaiians worked in the cane fields as laborers but were not as productive as plantation owners had expected. The dawn-to-dusk labor in the cane fields and rigid production quotas were difficult adjustments for Native Hawaiians. Lacking a significant economic niche on their islands, and slowly losing political control, the Native Hawaiian population continued to decline.

From a population of 71,019 in 1853, the Hawaiian population, including those of mixed ancestry, dropped to 39,504 by 1896 (Lind, 1980). During this period, planters were importing field labor to the Hawaiian islands from nearly the entire world. The first major group was the Chinese, soon followed by the Japanese, Portuguese, Koreans, Puerto Ricans, and other nationalities.

The planters' strategy was to keep any one nationality of laborers from becoming too numerous and thus to thwart any type of labor organization. George H. Fairfield (cited in Takaki, 1983), manager of the Makee Sugar Company, stated the planters' strategy as follows: "Keep a variety of laborers, that is of different nationalities, and thus prevent any concerted action in case of strikes, for there are few, if any, cases of Japanese, Chinese, and Portuguese entering into a strike as a unit" (p. 24). Largely as a result of these methods, Hawaii's population was transformed into a multiethnic one.

As the plantation economy matured, a Big Five emerged among planters that would eventually dominate the Hawaiian economy for decades: Hackfield and Company (AMFAC), C. Brewer and Company, Theo Davis Company, Castle and Cooke, and Alexander and Baldwin.

The nature of the sugar and pineapple plantations of the nineteenth and early twentieth centuries required a large concentration of land and capital, as well as a disciplined work force. Such large-scale operations also required that the political climate of Hawaii be conducive to the interests of planters.

The practice of surrounding the Hawaiian monarch with *haole* advisors created a facade of political sovereignty by the latter part of the nineteenth century. In 1873, the Hawaiian throne was denied to Queen Emma by a group of planters who bribed, cajoled, and threatened electors into giving the crown to David Kalakaua. Pro-Emma supporters stormed the courthouse to register their outrage. This group was dispersed by U.S. Marines and British sailors whose assistance was requested by planter Charles Bishop to "quell the riotous mob" (Kent, 1983, p. 45).

In 1877, the planter oligarchy rewrote the Hawaiian constitution and presented it to King Kalakaua for his signature under a state of armed siege. The constitution the king signed became known as the bayonet constitution to Hawaiians. It made the king a ceremonial monarch, disenfranchised most Native Hawaiians through strict property requirements, excluded all Asians from voting by declaring them aliens, and gave the vote only to U.S. citizens. After this action, the remaining days of pretended sovereignty were numbered.

Annexation

To paint a picture of something other than imperialistic motives by the United States in annexing Hawaii would be doing a severe injustice to the facts. American military leaders saw Hawaii as a coaling station for the Pacific fleet. As Jacobs and Landau (1971) note, "The strength and influence of the pro-annexation Americans grew in Hawaii and on the mainland, where the concepts of expansion and 'manifest destiny' were attracting a growing number of adherents" (p. 29). The latter doctrine, having reached the Pacific shore, seemed to have had its sights set on Hawaii. The American planter oligarchy viewed annexation as an opportunity to guarantee in perpetuity the largest market for Hawaiian agricultural products. Expansionist, military, and economic motives worked to end the last vestiges of Hawaiian autonomy.

The first attempt at the deposition of the monarchy came on January 17, 1893. This coup was supported by U.S. troops (although not officially) and was led by Lorrin P. Thurston, a Honolulu publisher. U.S. minister John L. Stevens gave an order to disembark 162 troops, ostensibly to protect American life and property. The troops had the coercive effect of forcing the queen's resignation. Controversy has always surrounded the issue of whether Minister Stevens acted on his own or on direction from the U.S. government. Writes Imperatore (1992), "A review of Stevens' correspondence with the U.S. Secretary of State implies premeditation with the action simply awaiting opportunity" (p. 263).

Queen Liliuokalani ruled Hawaii from 1891 to 1893. Her overthrow was an event from which Hawaiians never recovered. The queen did not order her troops to battle the insurgents because the odds were overwhelmingly against her and she trusted the fairness of the United States. After losing her throne, the queen wrote a desperate plea to President Cleveland to have it restored. President Cleveland sent an emissary, James Blount, to investigate the overthrow of the queen. After receiving a report critical of the coup leaders, President Cleveland urged Sanford B. Dole and the conspirators to return the queen to her throne. Dole responded to Cleveland by telling him not to interfere in Hawaiian affairs (Imperatore, 1992).

The Republic of Hawaii was established, with Sanford B. Dole as its first and only president. Annexation by the United States was imminent. In 1898, under President William McKinley, the islands became part of the territorial possessions of the United States. Manifest Destiny had triumphed again. The *haoles* who had once come as guests had managed to usurp the entire kingdom. Richard Olney (cited in Wright, 1972), the secretary of state at that time, summarized the situation: "Hawaii is ours," he said, "But as I look back upon the first steps in this miserable business and as I contemplate the means used to complete the outrage, I am ashamed of the whole affair" (p. 21).

From Territory to State

Once Hawaii became a territory of the United States, its political and economic affairs were managed by forces on the mainland or by island elites responding to powerful people on the mainland. The territorial governorship of Hawaii was a powerful position. The governor was appointed by the president of the United States. This appointment was heavily influenced by the recommendation of the Hawaiian elite. The economy of the territory depended on favorable legislation from the U.S. Congress to subsidize Hawaiian sugar and other agricultural products. The opening of the Panama Canal made it much easier for Hawaiian products to reach markets on the east coast of the United States. Favorable subsidies and market shares from the U.S. Congress made Hawaii nearly totally reliant on sugar.

The Big Five corporations ran the economy of the islands through a variety of interlocking directorates and the vertical integration of business. To the average Native Hawaiian, this world of Merchant Street was alien and remote. The original inhabitants of Hawaii found themselves on the bottom rung of a plantation society with little hope of improving their situation.

Prince Jonah Kuhio Kalanianaole became the territorial delegate to the Congress by serving the interests of plantation owners. However, his frustrations would sometimes emerge, as they did in 1912, when he told a Hawaiian audience (cited in Kent, 1983), "Under the political conditions in the territory, a man doesn't own his soul" (p. 45).

Native Hawaiians' need for land was supposed to be reconciled in 1921 with the passage of the Hawaiian Rehabilitation Act. Under the auspices of the Hawaiian Homes Commission, 200,000 acres of land were to be distributed to landless Hawaiians for small-scale farming. Most of the land actually distributed was not suitable for farming. Eventually, it passed into the hands of large plantation interests (Parker, 1989). The large amount of acreage devoted to export crops like sugar and pineapples meant that the traditional small-scale farming of the Native Hawaiian was nearly a relic from the past. Hawaii had become a major importer of food from the mainland, although historically it had been self-sufficient in food. Once again, actions intended to improve living conditions for Native Americans resulted in benefits for other groups.

The plantation economy continued earning large profits with the support of the Republican party, which had dominated island politics for the first fifty years of the twentieth century. On some plantations, managers monitored the actions of their workers by hanging pencils by strings from the ceilings of the voting booths. By noting in which direction the string moved, party preference could be determined. Anyone voting for a Democrat would be fired (Shaplen, 1982).

After World War II, political leaders in Hawaii began to seriously discuss seeking statehood from the U.S. Congress. It was argued that becoming a state would guarantee the large U.S. market for Hawaiian products. Hawaiian leaders also believed that statehood would significantly increase the tourist industry and that many new construction and service jobs would be created.

While economic predictions turned out to be in general correct, Native Hawaiians did not share proportionately in the new prosperity. As Joseph Keoloha, Chairman of the State Office of Hawaiian Affairs, observed, "Statehood was the final act following the confiscation of our land and the overthrow of our Queen, and Native Hawaiians have mixed feelings about it" (Chrysler, 1984, p. 40).

NATIVE HAWAIIANS TODAY

Social Class and Politics

Present-day Hawaii is a polyglot of peoples with varied backgrounds. There are sizable communities of Chinese Americans and Japanese Americans. There is a Korean American population that originally came to work in the pineapple and sugar cane estates. Filipinos and Portuguese also came as agricultural workers. There are also a few thousand African Americans in Hawaii, as well as the still-powerful *haoles*. Americans of Japanese ancestry have been especially successful in the political arena. Chinese Americans have become business leaders in many areas.

Upward mobility by Asian Americans in Hawaii contrasts sharply with their status as primarily agricultural workers one or two generations ago. This change in status has caused some interethnic discords and ill feelings. Many Native Hawaiians who perceived the *haoles* as the holders of all-powerful positions often see Japanese Americans in their place. Other groups besides Hawaiians who find themselves disproportionately represented in the lower-economic classes realize the ethnic caste system of the big plantation era still exists in a modified form.

Dissatisfaction bred by this earlier caste system caused the major political movement of this century. Organizers tried to convince workers that their future would best be served by identifying politically with their working-class brethren regardless of their ethnic origin. This movement achieved its first major success in 1954, when the Democratic party broke the traditional Republican control in both houses of the territorial legislature. The man given a major share of the credit for this triumph was John A. Burns, who would play an important role in Hawaii's future politics by lobbying vigorously for statehood and by becoming governor.

The 1954 victory was viewed generally as the beginning of a progressive movement in island politics. By 1970, the Democrats were the solidly entrenched party, and John Burns was a candidate for a third term as governor. The main opposition within the Democratic party came from Tom Gill, who had been lieutenant governor under Burns. Gill charged that what may have started out as progressive political forces in 1954 had now become a power structure that was working together with the business and economic interests they originally opposed. The Gill campaign had a strong issue orientation capitalizing on respect for Hawaii's fragile environment. Governor Burns, with a network of loyal supporters on several islands, relied primarily on a media campaign and was successful in gaining a third term.

In 1974, George Ariyoshi became the first non-*haole* governor of Hawaii. He was later reelected to second and third terms of office. Governor Ariyoshi was followed by John D. Waihee in 1986. Governor Waihee became the first person of Hawaiian ancestry to hold this office and was reelected in

1990. Neither major political party in Hawaii has a homogeneous political base. To make a viable appeal to a diverse society, each party has had leaders who represent most of Hawaii's major ethnic groups.

The issues that are likely to dominate Hawaiian politics in the foreseeable future are land use, tourism, economic diversification, and the preservation of Hawaii's fragile natural environment. Today, 55% of all land in Hawaii is privately owned, and 95% of that land is held by 70-odd corporations or individuals (Shaplen, 1982). The zoning and distribution of land are likely to evoke strong feelings among many Hawaiians. Tourism is clearly Hawaii's largest source of income. In 1959, Hawaii had only about 243,000 visitors each year. By the mid-1990s, that number had reached nearly 7 million (Trask, 1992, p. 34). By the mid 1990s tourism had become a business worth nearly $11 billion annually (Hunter, 1994).

Some critics of the tourist-dependent economy note that visitors cannot be relied on as a stable source of income. There are many viewpoints but no clear consensus on exactly how to diversify Hawaii's economy. Agricultural land is too expensive for farming to ever gain its former prominence. Transportation and labor costs work against Hawaii's becoming a manufacturing center. Meanwhile, tourism remains the mainstay of the economy while Hawaiians attempt to reach a consensus on new directions for the islands' economic future.

Adapting Native Hawaiian Values

The Hawaiian spirit of *Aloha Aina* (love for the land) has had a resurgence in response to growing developments. A governor's conference in the early 1970s produced three possible scenarios for Hawaii's future: Hawaii unleashed, Hawaii primeval, and a balance between the two (Tabrah, 1980). The balanced approach was the option recommended.

The traditional value of *ohana* is a cooperative system of social relationships found within an extended family. A study in a Hawaiian community near Honolulu found that the spirit of *ohana* still permeates the lives of Native Hawaiians. This study noted the following (cited in Howard, 1974): "Our research continually affirmed that the overwhelming proportion of the people find gratification in their life-style. If wages were higher, most would continue to invest in a life-style similar to the one they are currently leading" (p. 226).

This value of *ohana* is sometimes counterproductive to Hawaiian children attending school where cooperation on academic work may be perceived as "cheating." Also, Hawaiian youngsters do not particularly relish the peer competition engendered in many school situations and consequently they often do not respond well to competitive tasks.

The Hawaiian value of *kokua* undergirds a traditional economic system based on cooperation with some element of competition. Under this system, one expression of *kokua* (cooperation) should be repaid with another expression of *kokua*. In this manner, the status of the individual is enhanced (Ogawa, 1978). As the trend toward development continues in a state with limited natural resources, the spirit of *kokua* might point the way toward an accommodation among competing groups.

Another Hawaiian value that could prove helpful in a multiethnic and growing society is *ho'oponopono*. Literally, this means "setting to right of wrongs" (Ogawa, 1978, p. 579). In early Hawaii, *ho'oponopono* meant that all people had an opportunity to speak out on a problem until a solution was reached that would be binding on all parties. This ancient tradition could possibly be adapted to modern Hawaii and become a valuable tool for building consensus on a difficult issue.

The Hawaiians Today and Tomorrow

Proper classification of Native Hawaiians is difficult because the overwhelming majority of them are part Hawaiian. Today, about 1% (approximately 10,000 people) of the Hawaiian population can be classified as pureblooded Hawaiian. Estimates vary as to the number of part-Hawaiians. In 1994, approximately 170,000 people claimed some Hawaiian ancestry. These figures contrast sharply with the estimated 300,000 Native Hawaiians on the islands when Captain Cook first visited in 1778.

Under current law, only people with 50% or more Hawaiian blood are entitled to land and to medical and legal benefits. Perhaps no more than 60,000 of the state's one million people can prove that pedigree (Egan, 1990, p. 29A). An issue in Hawaii is whether to lower the 50% requirement in order to qualify for any program designated for Native Hawaiians. Even if the current policy is followed, the matter of establishing Hawaiian lineage to meet the 50% requirement often leaves the Office of Hawaiian Affairs in a quandary.

The average Native Hawaiians fall far below their White counterparts in the area of economic prosperity. They generally live in communities whose facilities are substandard. They comprise a disproportionately high percentage of school dropouts and police arrests.

Native Hawaiians have generally not adapted to the competitive nature of the dominant society. They are oriented toward affiliation rather than competition. Friendship and family harmony are prized possessions not to be traded for economic status. Perhaps this reluctance to compete has been one way at their disposal to retain an ethnic identity in a society that rewards competition. Hawaiian school children seem to achieve much better when they are evaluated collectively rather than individually.

During the 1970s, there was a rise of Hawaiian nationalist groups whose primary purpose was to return lost economic and political power to people of Hawaiian ancestry. Along with those movements, there has been a revision in Hawaiian history that does not consider the whole era of Hawaiian monarchy to be a glorious age of benevolent rule. Among some of these Hawaiian nationalists, Kamehameha III is seen as a ruler who broke up the traditional system of land ownership and started the islands on their steady slide toward *haole* control. Queen Liliuokalani is seen as a great monarch who tried to retain power in the hands of Hawaiians while facing insurmountable odds.

This militancy is reflected in the formation of such groups as the *Kokua* and the Hawaiians. Membership in the *Kokua* is limited to non-*haoles*. This group espouses a Third World outlook. The Hawaiians limit their membership to people with at least some Hawaiian blood. Their ideology is more moderate than the *Kokua*. The existence of these two groups has had little impact on the economic status of most Native Hawaiians.

A manifestation of this militancy was the Free Kahoolawe movement in the mid-1970s. Kahoolawe, a small island owned by the military six miles off the coast of Maui, had been used for bombing practice since World War II. The movement began with an occupation of the island by a group of Hawaiians joined by people from nearly all segments of Hawaii's population. The goal of the Free Kahoolawe movement was the return of the island to state government jurisdiction and public access (Tabrah, 1980). In 1994, the Free Kahoolawe movement succeeded. The U.S. Navy returned Kahoolawe to the State of Hawaii. The Hawaiian legislature designated Kahoolawe as a cultural and educational preserve.

There can be little doubt that a true Hawaiian Renaissance occurred in the 1970s. This trend represented a sharp contrast to predictions that the Hawaiian culture was slowly being extinguished. The renaissance went beyond a renewal of interest in cultural activities. It resulted in a new economic and political consciousness, as well as increasing involvement with other Pacific Island peoples (Kanahele, 1982). How long this ethnic revitalization movement lasts remains an open question. It can be said, however, that the Hawaiian Renaissance arrived at a propitious time, when Native Hawaiian culture was being practiced less and less.

The issue of sovereignty for Native Hawaiians has received added attention in recent years. Dudley and Agard (1990) chronicle the history of the Hawaiian sovereignty movement and discuss various forms of possible Native Hawaiian sovereignty. Among the variations are: (a) the American Indian model, (b) a broader model of "nation within a nation" that American Indians enjoy, or (c) restoration of the Hawaiian nation.

The Hawaiian sovereignty question is much more than a philosophical issue. The Hawaiian Sovereignty Elections Council (appointed by the governor of Hawaii) is scheduled to hold a plebiscite in 1996. Any individual of Hawaiian ancestry who is eighteen years old or older can vote in the plebiscite. The question will be: "Shall the Hawaiian people elect delegates to propose a Native Hawaiian government?" If the majority votes yes, there will an election of delegates for a native Hawaiian constitutional convention.

As Native Hawaiians look to the twenty-first century, they are vitally concerned with the future of their islands' natural environment. High real estate prices in Hawaii promote vertical expansion of new dwellings, but the environment of the islands is particularly fragile. Foreign investment is playing an ever-increasing role in Hawaii's economy. Will absentee landlords be appropriately concerned with the environmental impact of development, particularly if such measures reduce profit margins? These quality-of-life issues are important to all Hawaiians and are particularly salient to Native Hawaiians, whose culture is inextricably tied to the land.

Hawaii is sometimes presented as the personification of the aloha spirit. This is a misrepresentation to some degree. Hawaii is more ethnically harmonious than some societies. However, it is not an ethnic or a racial paradise. The future of racial and ethnic distinctions in Hawaii is unclear. The Native Hawaiians' out-marriage rate is the highest of any group on the islands. Write Blaisdell and Mokuau (1994), "A consistent pattern since 1950, the rate for Native Hawaiian men marrying non-Native Hawaiians was the highest (56.5%) when compared with men of other ethnic backgrounds" (p. 55). In a strictly biological sense, it appears that the Native Hawaiian population is being slowly dissolved into other groups. Perhaps a more optimistic outlook is that the culture of the Native Hawaiian is, to some extent, enriching the lives of all of the inhabitants of these beautiful islands.

TEACHING STRATEGIES

The concept of expansion can be illustrated in many ways. The Native Hawaiians provide a classic case of the displacement of a native population because they were an obstacle to the expanding forces. Their story can be related to other native inhabitants who suffered a similar fate.

CONCEPT: Expansion

Generalization: As a nation expands to obtain territory, often the rights of the native population are not protected.

1. After giving the students sufficient background information about the Native Hawaiians, ask them to make a list of factors that apply to the Native Hawaiian and the American Indians. These factors can include both past and present situations. Afterwards, these points can be grouped, classified, and discussed.

2. Organize your students into small groups. Present them with this hypothetical situation. One person in the group would be chosen to supervise and control the finan-

cial affairs of all the members. What problems may develop with such an arrangement? A tape could be made of their reactions. Later, this tape could be replayed and compared to what occurred between American advisors and Hawaiian rulers.

3. Role-play the following situation, which occurred in Hawaii in 1845. The *haole* advisor to the King is trying to persuade him to grant some land to Mr. Farmer, a prospective planter. Kaeo opposes the entire proposition. After the role-play situation, ask the students the questions that follow. The role descriptions are as follows:

> **King Kamehameha III:** He is indecisive over what to say to the planter. Yet, he greatly respects the advice of his *haole* counsel, Mr. George Bennett.
>
> **George Bennett:** Advisor to the king and a good friend of Mr. Farmer, whose interests he protects. He has been a missionary for nearly twenty years.
>
> **Floyd S. Farmer:** Planter and business tycoon. He intends to start sugar plantations in Hawaii because of the predictably warm weather.
>
> **Kaeo:** A Native Hawaiian and a member of the king's court. He vehemently opposes the granting of any more land to *haoles*.

Questions

1. Did George Bennett succeed in persuading the king to grant the land to Mr. Farmer? If so, why? If not, why?

2. Was Kaeo successful in his opposition to the land deal? Why or why not?

3. Did Mr. Farmer tell the king his plans for using native labor? Why or why not?

4. Did the king decide to grant the land lease to Mr. Farmer? If he did, what were his reasons? If he did not, why not?

5. Did Mr. Bennett use his position as a missionary to help his argument? Why or why not?

CONCEPT: Adaptation

Generalization: When a native culture finds itself surrounded by a dominant culture, it becomes increasingly difficult to maintain the native culture.

1. Read the following story to the class and ask the questions that follow.

A Hawaiian Dilemma

The old ramshackle house had stood relatively unchanged since the family had obtained it more than forty years ago from the Hawaiian Homes Commission. Around it were the two acres of vegetables that had provided subsistence for the Panui family during that time. Mary Panui lived on the property along with her sons, George and Eddie. Mr. Panui had died five years before and since that time things had not been the same. One afternoon George was weeding one of the vegetable patches when Eddie returned from a day in town. Feeling that he deserved some help, George asked his brother. "Hey, aren't you going to help out around here?"

Eddie answered, "No, I have gotten a job in town with the tourist agency. I will drive the mainland *haoles* around during the day, and in the evenings I will dance at the luaus."

George couldn't believe his ears. After all of those years that their father had taught them to respect their Hawaiian heritage, his brother was suddenly changing. "Eddie, how can you do a thing like this?" George wondered. "It would have broken Dad's heart, and anyway, what will mother say?"

Eddie looked at his brother casually and said, "I have been weeding taro root all of my life and I'm tired of it. I know Dad would probably say that I'm putting our culture up for sale but it's the only way to get ahead!"

The two brothers entered the home where Mary Panui was cooking dinner and told her of their conversation. The old woman with the creased brow was also unhappy with what Eddie was considering. However, she could not deny that the vegetable gardens would never provide more than a subsistence living.

Seeing his mother caught up in the dilemma, George tried one last time, "Eddie, can you imagine yourself in one of those flowered shirts selling shell necklaces to the tourists? Where is your pride?"

Eddie thought for a moment and answered smugly, "Pride doesn't fill your wallet: when will you realize that?"

With that, George started out of the door but stopped short and told his brother, "I may never have much money to my name, but I'll never be a practicing Hawaiian!"

Questions

1. What would you have done if you had been Eddie Panui?

2. Do you feel Eddie's brother is justified in calling him a practicing (commercialized) Hawaiian?

3. Can you think of other ethnic groups in other settings that have had their culture commercialized? If so, how much was this trend sanctioned or resisted by the group?

REFERENCES

Blaisdell, K. & Mokuau, N. (1994). *Kanaka Maoli, Indigenous Hawaiians*. In U. Hasager & J. Friedman (Eds.). Hawaii: Return to Nationhood. Copenhagen, Denmark: International Work Group for Indigenous Affairs (Document NO. 75).

Chrysler, K. M. (1984, August 27). Hawaii: Youngest State Finds Its Place in the Sun. *U.S. News and World Report*, p. 40.

Day, A. G. (1968). *Hawaii and Its People*. New York: Meredith Press.

Dudley, M. K. & Agard, K. K. (1990). *A Call for Hawaiian Sovereignty*. Honolulu: Na Kane O Ka Malo Press.

Egan, T. (1990, January 20). Blood and Benefits: Hawaii to Vote on Ancestral Rights. *Miami Herald,* p. 29A.

Howard, A. (1974). *Ain't No Big Thing: Coping Strategies in a Hawaiian American Community.* Honolulu: The University Press of Hawaii.

Hunter, B. (Ed). (1994). *The Statesman's Year Book, 1994–1995* (131st ed.). New York: St. Martin's Press.

Imperatore, W. (1992, Nov/Dec). The Deposing of the Hawaiian Monarch: The Changing Narrative in Textbooks. *The Social Studies,* pp. 261–266.

Jacobs, P. & Landau, S. with Pell, E. (1971). *To Serve the Devil,* Vol. 2: *Colonials and Sojourners.* New York: Vintage.

Kanahele, G. (1982). *Hawaiian Renaissance.* Honolulu: Project Waiaha.

Kent, N. J. (1983). *Hawaii: Islands under the Influence.* New York: Monthly Review Press.

Lind, A. (1980). *Hawaii's People.* Honolulu: The University Press of Hawaii.

Miami Herald. (1994, June 3). Hawaii Grappling with Sovereignty Movement, p. 7A.

Ogawa, D. (1978). *Kodomo No Tame Ni.* Honolulu: The University Press of Hawaii.

Parker, L. S. (1989). *Native American Estate: The Struggle over Indian and Hawaiian Lands.* Honolulu: The University Press of Hawaii.

Shaplen, R. (1982, September 6). A Reporter at Large: Islands of Disenchantment. *New Yorker,* p. 85.

Tabrah, R. (1980). *Hawaii: A Bicentennial History.* New York: Norton.

Takaki, R. (1983). *Pau Hana: Plantation Life and Labor in Hawaii.* Honolulu: The University Press of Hawaii.

Trask, H. K. (1992). Racism against Native Hawaiians at the University of Hawaii. *Amerasian Journal 18* (3), pp. 33–50.

Wright, T. (1972). *The Disenchanted Isles.* New York: Dial Press.

ANNOTATED BIBLIOGRAPHY

Books for Teachers

Allen, H. (1982). *The Betrayal of Liliuokalani: Last Queen of Hawaii 1838–1917.* Glendale, Calif.: Arthur H. Clark Co.

> *A detailed biography of the Hawaiian queen whose reign was ended by the overthrow of the monarchy. It is instructive and reveals the intrigues and joys of courtly life and displays the drama of power as these unfold in the telling of her life story.*

Barratt, G. (1987). *The Russian Discovery of Hawaii.* Honolulu: Editions Limited.

> *Translated from Russian manuscripts, this English version of a historical and ethnographic record of eight of the men on an early Russian exploration to Hawaii is an addition to the many perspectives Europeans held of early Hawaii.*

Bell, R. (1984). *Last among Equals: Hawaiian Statehood and American Politics.* Honolulu: The University Press of Hawaii.

An incisive analysis of the struggle to gain equality and autonomy as a state. Useful reference for historians, as well as for any scholar studying the patterns of support and opposition generated by the process of becoming a state whose population was predominately non-White.

Bell, S. (1986). *Unforgettable True Stories of the Kingdom of Hawaii.* Van Nuys, Calif.: Delta Lithographic Co.

A personalized and episodic version of Hawaiians that began as a curiosity for the author and ended as an investigative search to understand some of the enigmas she came across while living in Hawaii. A worthwhile trip for the reader to discover Hawaii from both an insider and an outsider perspective.

Bingham, H. (1981). *A Residence of Twenty-One Years in the Sandwich Islands.* Rutland, Vt.: Charles E. Tuttle and Co.

This text is a reprint of a missionary's experiences in Hawaii in the early part of the nineteenth century. It is a valuable primary historical source.

Boggs, S. (1985). *Speaking, Relating and Learning: A Study of Hawaiian Children at Home and at School.* Norwood, N.J.: Ablex Publishing Corporation.

A scholarly study of those aspects of speaking and relating to others, peers or adults, by Hawaiian children within the context of the home and the school environments. The author addresses the relationship of school success or failure to the consequences resulting from the congruences or incongruencies between the manner and function of speech learned at home against those required and rewarded at school.

Bosserant, d. M. G. (1987). *A Tree in Bud: 1889–1893.* (A. L. Korn, Trans.). Honolulu: The University Press of Hawaii.

A period of Hawaiian history from the perspective of a French gentleman whose observations, although uniquely personal, draw the reader's participation so that you see what the author sees and feel what he feels as you relive life in the Island during those years.

Buck, E. (1993). *Paradise Remade: The Politics of Culture and History of Hawai'i.* Philadelphia: Temple University Press.

The author argues that the arrival of the White man altered the social relationships, fundamentals, and long-standing political and economic practices of the Hawaiian people. The book provides an alternative history, recounting social trends and events through the eyes of commoners. It focuses on nineteenth-century Hawaii just at the entrance of missionaries into the islands.

Charlot, J. (1983). *Chanting the Universe: Hawaiian Religious Culture.* Honolulu: Emphasis International Ltd.

A refreshing and excellent portrayal of the Hawaiian world view as expressed by the beauty and power of poets. The appeal is universal even as the reader is introduced to the basic concepts and sentiments underlying Hawaiian culture.

Coffman, T. (1973). *Catch a Wave.* Honolulu: The University Press of Hawaii.

This is a well-written study of Hawaiian politics, with a case study on the 1970 gubernatorial election.

Cooper, G. & Daws, G. (1985). *Land and Power in Hawaii: The Democratic Years.* Honolulu: Benchmark Books.

Research regarding the political developments in Hawaii during three decades, from the mid-1950s just prior to the Islands' becoming the 50th state and through the 1980s. Extensively researched, the authors relate economic and political power in an island environment, where land has a high premium.

Daws, G. (1976). *Shoal of Time.* Honolulu: University Press of Hawaii.

This is a complete interpretive history of Hawaii from European contact to statehood.

Day, G. A. (1984). *History Makers of Hawaii.* Honolulu: Mutual Publications of Hawaii.

This is a rich resource for anyone inquiring into the lives of individuals who have made an impact on the shaping of cosmopolitan Hawaii. It includes a chronology of significant events presented within the context of U.S. historical development.

Defries, E. (Ed). (1992). *Light upon the Mist: A Reflection of Wisdom for the Future Generations of Native Hawai'ians.* Honolulu: Mahina Productions.

Reflections of Akaiko Akana, an early tenth-century minister and author of an instructive book for young Hawaiians, is the focus of this book. His writings were meant to bring meaning and direction for living the Hawaiian Way. Akana believed that "the Hawai'ans were for sharing the true essence of aloha—love for everyone and everything. With the spirit of aloha, there is no race, color or class distinction." The authors believe that kana's message is applicable for Hawaiians today.

Dudley, M. K. (1991). *A Hawai'ian Nation: Man, Gods and Nature.* Honolulu: Na Kane O Ka Malo Press.

The author describes and outlines a philosophical framework of the world view of ancient Hawaiians. The study of the Hawaiian traditional system is analyzed using a collection of ancient chants and stories by early Hawaiian poets and writers.

du Plessix Gray, F. (1973). *Hawaii: The Sugar-Coated Fortress.* New York: Vintage Books.

This brief but excellent book was written with great empathy for Hawaii's underprivileged groups.

Forbes, D. W. (1992). *Treasures of Hawai'ian History.* Honolulu: The University of Hawaii Press.

The author, an art historian with expertise in Hawaiian history, catalogued items displayed in the Hawaiian Historical Society library collection in honor of the Society's centennial. Each item is described within its historical context. The catalogue contains more than seventy black-and-white and colored reproductions.

Fuchs, L. H. (1961). *Hawaii Pono*. New York: Harcourt, Brace and World.

> *Perhaps the most highly regarded book on the social history of Hawaii, it covers the period from annexation through statehood.*

Gallimore, R., Boggs, J., & Jordan, C. (1974). *Culture, Behavior and Education: A Study of Hawaiian Americans*. Beverly Hills, Calif.: Sage Publications.

> *This sociological study of the adaptation of the community of 'Aina Pumehena contains chapters on socialization, schools, and culture conflict.*

Hazama, D. (1986). *Okage Sama De: The Japanese in Hawaii, 1885–1985*. Honolulu: The Bess Press.

> *A historical account of the 100 years of the Japanese experience in Hawaii presented through personal anecdotes. The narrators capture the dilemma and tensions experienced by a generation of Japanese immigrants who bridged or tried to bridge the traditions of ethnic roots with present realities.*

Howard, A. (1974). *Ain't No Big Thing: Coping Strategies in a Hawaiian American Community*. Honolulu: The University Press of Hawaii.

> *This book is an excellent source on conflicts between traditional Hawaiian values and modern Hawaiian society written from a sociological perspective.*

Kanahele, G. (1986). *Ku Kanaka (Stand Tall): A Search for Hawaiian Values*. Honolulu: The University Press of Hawaii.

> *Kanahele has long been in the forefront of searching and expressing for himself and others the core values and traditions of the Hawaiian people. This book is a valuable first attempt to deal with a complex subject. Anyone interested in Hawaii and its people will find it informative and provocative.*

Kent, N. J. (1983). *Hawaii: Islands under the Influence*. New York: Monthly Review Press.

> *The author elaborates on the thesis that the Hawaiian Islands have been controlled by external forces from the period of the sandalwood trade under the Hawaiian monarchy to the tourism economy present today. This source provides a well-researched geopolitical perspective.*

Kimura, Y. (1988). *Issei: Japanese Immigrants in Hawaii*. Honolulu: University Press of Hawaii.

> *This sociohistorical account of the first generation of Japanese immigrants to Hawaii covers fifteen years of retelling, from 1970 to 1985. Each of the four parts focuses on a particular aspect of the Issei's experience. It is a comprehensive and informative presentation told primarily from the Issei's (first generation) point of view.*

Kittelson, D. J. (1985). *The Hawaiians: An Annotated Bibliography*. Honolulu: Social Science Research Institute, University of Hawaii, Series No. 7.

> *This comprehensive and useful guide to Hawaiian sources includes books, articles, and other publications. Indexed, with 384 pages.*

Kodama, N. M., Nishimoto, W., & Oshiro, C. H. (1984). *Hanahana: An Oral History Anthology of Hawaii's Working People.* Honolulu: Ethnic Studies Oral History, University of Hawaii.

A compilation of stories gleaned from documents and interviews depicting the lives of twelve working individuals. An informative account of part of Hawaii's social history.

Kyselka, W. (1987). *An Ocean in Mind.* Honolulu: University Press of Hawaii.

An unusual and challenging approach to presenting ideas about how we think and how we live. The author bases his explanation of these processes on the experiences of two navigators who were largely responsible for charting the successful voyage of the Hokulea. The Hokulea is a recreation of a traditional vessel that journeyed from Tahiti to the Hawaiian Islands and back.

Lind, A. W. (1980). *Hawaii's People.* Honolulu: The University Press of Hawaii.

This volume describes social patterns based on statistical evidence gathered about Hawaii's diverse population during the twentieth century. It is particularly useful for students of social trends.

Mitchell, D. K. (1972). *Resource Units in Hawaiian Culture.* Honolulu: The Kamehameha Schools.

This rich teaching resource includes a gold mine of information about Native Hawaiian culture and society.

Nordyke, E. C. (1989). *The Peopling of Hawaii.* (2nd ed.). Honolulu: The University Press of Hawaii.

This book contains important demographic data about Hawaii's multiethnic population.

Orozco, D. J. (Ed). (1989). *Hawai'ian Reflections.* Honolulu: Mauna Loa Publishing House.

Selected writings of three major literary figures and a famous journalist were edited and compiled in this book to present various perspectives of Hawaii as these authors experienced life in the islands. Collectively, they pay tribute to the "spirit" or essence of the islands prior and up to the early years of the twentieth century, when modernization changed the Island ways.

Parker, L. S. (1989). *Native American Estate: The Struggle over Indian and Hawaiian Lands.* Honolulu: The University Press of Hawaii.

This source is particularly useful for anyone interested in the process by which Native Hawaiians lost control of their lands. The author also discusses the Hawaiian Homes Commission and the long and difficult process of land restitution.

Pukui, M. K. (1983). *Olelo No'Eau: Hawaiian Proverbs and Poetical Sayings.* Honolulu: Bernice Pauahi Bishop Museum.

This book contains a rich source of Hawaiian sayings compiled, translated, and explained succinctly. The collection presents a wide variety of literary styles (metaphors, allegory, personifications, puns, etc.) and reflects the wisdom, beauty, and wit of cultural expressions not only of Hawaiians but also of all who wish to understand the human condition.

Roth, R. (Ed.). (1992). *The Price of Paradise*, Vols. I and II. Honolulu: Mutual Publishing; (1993).

> *Two volumes of essays about far-ranging topics written for the lay person but authored by individuals who are, by profession and experience, experts in the subject. Both volumes (Volume II bears the same title) address questions posed by the author. The various authors write in an informal manner and each essay is short, appealing, and readable for all ages.*

Shaplen, R. (1982, September 6). A Reporter at Large: Islands of Disenchantment. *New Yorker,* 50–91.

> *This article contains a thorough discussion of political and economic issues that have dominated Hawaii from the period of annexation to the present. This would also be a good overview for high school students who want a concise overview of the past ninety years in Hawaii.*

Stewart, F. (Ed.). (1987). *Passages to the Dream Shore*. Honolulu: The University Press of Hawaii.

> *An anthology of short stories written about contemporary Hawaii by people of all ages and from all walks of life. Each story contributes to the socially diverse patchwork quilt and unique evolution of the Islands through the writers' experiences.*

Tabrah, R. M. (1980). *Hawaii: A Bicentennial History*. New York: Norton.

> *This text about the history of Hawaii was written in conjunction with the U.S. bicentennial celebration. The last chapter provides useful information on contemporary Hawaii.*

Takaki, R. (1983). *Pau Hana: Plantation Life and Labor in Hawaii*. Honolulu: The University Press of Hawaii.

> *This work examines the experiences of plantation workers who came from many nations to work in the fields of Hawaii. The author also examines the world of corporate power and the formation of the Big Five in the sugar industry.*

Trask, H. K. (1993). *From a Native Daughter: Colonialism and Sovereignty in Hawai'i*. Monroe, Me.: Common Courage Press.

> *The book is a collection of speeches and essays by the author written at different times and for different audiences. The essays address issues and topics involving Hawaiian sovereignty, colonialism, Pacific Island women, and racism. An overriding appeal is the author's strong and clear voice, which leaves the readers thinking about these subjects after they have laid the book aside.*

Weinstein, M. (Ed.). (1982). *Social Process in Hawaii*. Vol. 29. Honolulu: The University Press of Hawaii.

> *The entire volume is useful for its contribution to our knowledge about the major ethnic groups in Hawaii. The overview of race and ethnic relations in Hawaii is recommended for any student of race relations.*

Wichinan, F. (1985). *Kauai Tales*. Honolulu: Bamboo Ridge Press.

> *A collection of eighteen stories on a variety of subjects about the island of Kauai. Some stories explain old trails and ancient roadways. Others describe mythical figures. All entertain and present tales of Kauai to amuse.*

Whittaker, E. (1986). *The Mainland Haole: The White Experience in Hawaii*. New York: Columbia University Press.

> *The only book that studies the haole or White population. This contribution will be welcomed by scholars in the social sciences.*

Books for Students

Bagamery, A. (1983, April 22). Extra! Capitalism Breaks Out in Hawaii! *Forbes 22*, 48–49.

> *This source discusses compromises being made between Hawaii's political and business interests to try to diversify the economy of the islands. (High School)*

Beamer, W. D. (1984). *Talking Story with Nona Beamer*. Honolulu: The Bess Press.

> *A collection of selected favorite stories of Hawaii told by a well-known and popular Hawaiian composer and choreographer. A unique feature is the author's original, easy-to-learn chants created to capture the essence of some of the stones. (Primary/Intermediate)*

Buffet, G. (1973). *Kahala: Where the Rainbow Ends*. Norfolk Island, Australia: Island Heritage Books.

> *A romantic Hawaiian folktale, this book explains the reason for the rainbow in Manoa Valley. (Intermediate)*

Chrysler, K. M. (1984, August 27). Hawaii: Youngest State Finds Its Place in the Sun. *U.S. News and World Report*, 39–40.

> *This brief, informative article on economic conditions in Hawaii includes an interview with Governor George Aanyoshi. (Middle School/High School)*

Cieply, M. (1983, January 31). East of Eden. *Forbes*, 34–36.

> *This article discusses land distribution in the Hawaiian Islands and the politics involved in changing zoning from agricultural to other uses. It also contains useful data on Hawaii's economy. (High School)*

Dunford, B. (1987). *The Hawai'ians of Old*. Honolulu: The Bess Press.

> *A revised edition of the author's earlier book on selected segments of Hawaiian life-styles. The book introduces various occupations of early Hawaiians, the islands themselves, and their flora and fauna. She details the varied ways in which early Hawaiians entertained themselves through sports, music, and talk stories about their mythical heroes. The glossary and reference list are useful additions to the book. (Middle School/High School)*

Galuteria, P. (1991). *Lunalilo*. Honolulu: Kamehameha Schools. Bernice Pauahi Bishop Estate.

> *The story about one of the seven monarchs who ruled Hawaii. It chronicles his birth, his life, and his short reign. The young king was very popular with his people, and the author captures this feeling in this book. (Intermediate)*

Gomes, B. (1984). *Maile and the Marvelous One*. Taiwan: Press Pacifica.

> *This imaginative and fanciful story is about a Hawaiian mongoose, Maile, who is teased for being a dreamer. She becomes the pride of the family when she meets*

and befriends the "Aumakua," the Marvelous One, protector of Hawaii's land and people. The Aumakua is disguised as a snake to test the mongoose's ability to trust. (Primary)

Guard, D. (1984). *Hale-Mano: A Legend of Hawaii.* Milbrae, Calif.: A Dawne-Leigh Book.

This charming Hawaiian legend is about Hale-Mano's adventures, foremost of which was winning the love of a princess. (Intermediate)

Kanahele, G. (1982). *Hawaiian Renaissance.* Honolulu: Project Waiaha.

This is the first in a series of essays dealing with traditional and modern Hawaiian values. Topics include perceptions of young Hawaiians about being Hawaiian, and it features Hawaiian values regarding courage and hospitality. (Intermediate)

Kane, H. K. (1987). *Pele.* Honolulu: The Kawainui Press.

Accompanied by attractive drawings and illustrations, this book presents various aspects of the mythology of Pele, the goddess of Hawaii's volcanoes. The book also provides some background information on the Island of Hawaii's formation and the Volcano National Park. (Primary/Intermediate)

Kikukawa, C. (1982). *Ka Mea Ho' Ala—The Awakener.* Honolulu: The Bess Press.

This biography is about Henry Obookiah, who lived around the turn of the nineteenth century. Spared from death several times in his young life, Obookiah, then called Opukaha'ia, sailed in his teens to the East Coast, and there, he was converted to Christianity. He was instrumental in starting a Christian mission in Hawaii. (Intermediate)

Lowe, R. H. (1993). *Lili'uokalani.* Honolulu: Kamehameha Schools. Bernice Pauahi Bishop Estate.

The story of the last reigning monarch, Queen Lili'uokalani, written for very young children. A chronology of major events is presented in simple language and story line for easy and fast reading. (Middle School)

MacKenzie, M. K. (Ed). (1991). *Native Hawai'ian Rights Handbook.* Honolulu: Native Hawai'ian Legal Corporation (distributed by the University Press of Hawaii).

A manual written to inform readers of fundamental issues relative to the sovereignty movement in Hawaii. The essays center on the rights of native Hawaiians to their land and water resources, federal programs, and Trusts. It is written in a straightforward manner, devoid of technical and legal language, and, with guidance, is readable at the high school level. (High School)

McBarnet, G. (1987). *Fountain of Fire.* Puunene, Hawaii: Ruwanga Trading.

A simple and charming story about a young girl who lives in a community threatened by volcanic eruptions. Easy to read and attractively presented with many pictures. The author gives his readers a feel for what life is like when a volcano erupts in Hawaii. (Primary)

Menton, L. & Tamura, E. (Eds). (1989). *A History of Hawai'i.* Honolulu: The University Press of Hawaii.

A textbook of Hawaiian history, spanning pre-colonial Hawaii to the present. The emphasis placed on highlighting issues of concern to the state and its people makes this a better than average, traditional text for high school students. (High School)

Perry, Y. N. (1994) *The Other Side of the Island*. Santa Barbara, Calif.: Daniel and Daniel Publishers.

A collection of short stories by the author who depicts local Hawaiian scenes with poignancy as she weaves story after story of people and events taking place in the islands. The book should appeal to young adults and families sympathetic to the Hawaiian life-style. (High School)

Salisbury, G. (1992). *Blue Skies of the Sea*. New York: Delacorte Press.

A collection of short stories that captures the ambiance of a fanciful life in Hawaii. Written by a descendant of early missionaries, the author scripts an adventuresome tale from the perspective of a fictionalized family whose members, no doubt, were inspired by his own. Delightful reading for high school students or young adults. (High School)

Stanley, F. (1991). *The Last Princess: The Story of Princess Ka'iulani of Hawai'i*. Illustrated by D. Stanley. New York: Four Winds Press.

A beautifully illustrated and informative biography of the princess who never ruled her kingdom.

Summers, C. C. (1988). *The Hawaiian Grass House in Bishop Museum*. Honolulu: Bishop Museum Press.

An informative description of the style of houses people in Hawaii built and lived in before the turn of the century. This replica of the hale pili or grass house is useful as a take-off point for comparing and contrasting the types of housing, materials used, and construction of dwellings and for drawing inferences on the skills and use of resources applicable to one's surroundings in a given time and place. (Intermediate)

Titcomb, M. (1983). *The Ancient Hawaiians: How They Clothed Themselves*. Honolulu: Hogarth Press.

A simple and easy-to-follow explanation of how the early Hawaiians made garments for themselves prior to the arrival of Whites. Numerous drawings show how tapa, the inner bark of a cloth plant, was prepared and treated with dye and made into loincloths for men and skirts for women. (Middle School/High School)

Tuen, C. S. (1988). *How Maui Slowed the Sun*. Honolulu: The University Press of Hawaii.

A delightfully retold story of the legend of Maui, the boy who forced the sun to slow down to help his people accomplish more with a longer day. This version is appealing to young children because the story line is simple, vocabulary is at their level and the colorful drawings accompanying the story are attractive. (Primary)

Veary, N. (1989). *Change We Must*. Honolulu: Water Margin Press.

Reflections of life in Hawaii through the eyes of the author who grew up in a Hawaii of another era, "a place that was extremely different from what we know today." It is a book that informs and inspires. (Primary)

Westervelt, W. D. (1987). *Myths and Legends of Hawaii: Ancient Lore Retold*. Honolulu: Mutual Publishing.

Selected folk tales from ancient Polynesian lore retold for the enjoyment of today's readers. (High School)

7

AFRICAN AMERICANS

CONCEPTS, STRATEGIES, AND MATERIALS

The ultimate measure of a person is not where they stand in moments of comfort and convenience, but where they stand at times of challenge and controversy.

Martin Luther King, Jr.

Africans have had a unique experience in the Americas. They came with the earliest European explorers and settlers and were gradually enslaved in the North American colonies in the 1600s. When the eighteenth century began, slavery was flourishing in North America. The African experience in the United States has strikingly revealed the gross discrepancies between American ideals and reality. Throughout their history, African Americans have called on America to make its dream a reality. Their cries have usually fallen on deaf ears. African American history and culture must be studied to enable students to understand and appreciate fully the great conflicts and dilemmas in American society and to develop a commitment to help make America's ideals a reality.

AFRICAN EXPLORERS IN AMERICA

Africans have been in America for many centuries. Inconclusive evidence suggests that they established a colony in Mexico long before Columbus's voyage in 1492. Africans were with the first Europeans who explored America. Afri-

AFRICAN AMERICANS: HISTORICAL PERSPECTIVE

Important Dates	
1565	Africans helped to establish a colony in St. Augustine, Florida.
1619	The first Africans arrived in the English North American colonies.
1808	The slave trade was legally ended, but illegal slave trading began.
1829	David Walker published his *Appeal,* in which he harshly denounced slavery and urged slaves to take up arms and rebel.
1831	Nat Turner led a slave revolt in which nearly 60 Whites were killed.
1850	The Fugitive Slave Act, which authorized the federal government to help capture runaway slaves, was enacted. It helped pave the way to the Civil War.
1857	The Supreme Court ruled in the *Dred Scott Decision* that slaves did not become free when they moved to free territory. It also held that African Americans were not and could not be citizens.
1861–62	Congress enacted several Confiscation Acts designed to prevent the Confederacy from using slaves in its war efforts.
1863	Many African Americans in New York City were attacked and killed by largely Irish mobs that were protesting the draft laws and expressing anti-Black feelings. On January 1, 1863, President Lincoln issued the Emancipation Proclamation, which freed slaves in those states fighting the Union.
1865	Slavery was legally abolished throughout the United States by the enactment of the Thirteenth Amendment to the Constitution.
1866	The Fourteenth Amendment, which made African Americans United States citizens, was enacted. The Civil Rights Act of 1866 was enacted. It extended the African American's civil liberties in several areas.
1870	The Fifteenth Amendment was enacted. It enabled many African Americans to vote.

**Important
Dates**

1876	In the disputed Hayes-Tilden election, Hayes's supporters promised that he would remove the remaining federal troops from the South. This bargain symbolized the extent to which northern Whites had abandoned the southern African Americans.
1896	In a historic decision, *Plessy v. Ferguson,* the Supreme Court ruled that "separate but equal" facilities were constitutional.
1905	W. E. B. Du Bois and a group of African American intellectuals organized the Niagara Movement to promote civil rights for African Americans.
1910	The National Association for the Advancement of Colored People (NAACP) was organized. It successfully fought for African American legal rights.
1911	The National Urban League was founded to help the Black urban migrant adjust to city life and find jobs.
1914	Marcus Garvey organized the Universal Negro Improvement Association. Garvey urged African Americans to return to Africa.
1917	One of the worst riots in U.S. history occurred in East St. Louis, Illinois. Thirty-nine African Americans were killed.
1919	A series of riots occurred in a number of cities during the "Red Summer" of 1919. One of the most serious occurred in Chicago, in which 38 people lost their lives.
1943	White violence directed at African Americans led to a serious riot in Detroit, in which 34 people were killed.
1954	In a landmark decision, *Brown v. Board of Education,* the Supreme Court ruled that school segregation was inher ently unequal.
1955	African Americans in Montgomery, Alabama, began a boycott of the city's buses that ended bus segregation there in 1956.
1957	Martin Luther King, Jr., and a group of Baptist ministers organized the Southern Christian Leadership Conference (SCLC). National guardsmen were required to help integrate Central High School in Little Rock, Arkansas.

Important Dates	
1960	On February 1, 1960, the sit-in movement, which desegregated public accommodation facilities throughout the South, began in Greensboro, North Carolina.
1961	The Congress of Racial Equality (CORE) led Freedom Rides throughout the South to desegregate interstate transportation.
1963	More than 200,000 people participated in a "March on Washington for Freedom and Jobs." In a Birmingham demonstration, led by Martin Luther King, Jr., civil rights demonstrators were violently attacked by the police.
1992	Carol Mosely Braun (Democrat, Ill.) became the first African American woman elected to the U.S. Senate.
1993	Toni Morrison was the first African American woman and the eighth woman to receive the Nobel Prize for Literature.

cans had been living in Europe for many years when European explorations to America began. The Moors, a North African people, invaded Europe in 711. They eventually conquered and ruled Spain. Other Africans were brought to Europe as slaves beginning in the 1400s. These Africans worked in private homes as servants, in banks and shipyards, and in mercantile establishments.

Diego el Negro was with Columbus on his last voyage to America in 1502. When Balboa arrived at the Pacific Ocean in 1513, his crew included a Black man, Nuflo de Olano. Africans explored present-day Kansas in 1541 with Coronado. Africans were also with many of the other early Spanish expeditions to the Americas. Estevanico, a Moor, is one of the most famous early Black explorers. Arriving in America in 1529, he explored present-day New Mexico and Arizona and paved the way for later Spanish explorations of the Southwest.

In addition to exploring America, Africans were among its first non-Indian settlers. Some of the settlers of the ill-fated South Carolina colony in 1526, San Miguel de Gauldape, were African. Africans helped to establish St. Augustine, Florida, in 1565, which is the oldest non-Indian settlement in the United States. A number of colonies were established by Africans and the French. These groups settled in the Mississippi Valley in the seventeenth century.

THE SLAVE TRADE

The Arabs invaded Africa and enslaved Africans long before Europeans arrived on the continent. The European nations became involved in the African slave trade when they started trading with Africa in the 1400s. In the mid-fifteenth century, European monarchs sent explorers to Africa to obtain such goods as skins and oils. Many of these explorers brought back these wares as well as African slaves and gold as gifts for their rulers. These gifts greatly pleased the European monarchs. As more and more Europeans explored Africa and brought Africans back to Europe, the slave trade gradually gained momentum. However, Black slavery never became widespread in Europe, but it grew by leaps and bounds when Europeans started settling in America in the 1600s. Europeans developed large plantations in the West Indies that grew crops such as sugar, indigo, cotton, and tobacco. Sugar production reigned supreme over all other crops. To produce increasing amounts of sugar, the Europeans brought thousands of Africans to the West Indies.

The slave trade became highly lucrative. European nations competed aggressively to monopolize it. At first, the Portuguese dominated the slave trade. Portugal was eventually challenged by the Dutch. Gradually, more and more nations gained a toehold in Africa. However, England was dominating the slave trade when it peaked in 1700. The European nations greatly benefited from the slave trade. They obtained many raw materials from Africa that helped them to attain high levels of industrial growth. The ships that left Europe carried small items to use for exchange with the Africans. While in Africa, they picked up wares such as gold, ivory, and dyewood as well as captives. The ships usually traveled from Africa to the West Indies, where the captives were sold and exchanged goods acquired. The goods were taken back to Europe. The journey from the West Coast of Africa to the West Indies was known as the "Middle Passage" because it was only part of a route that eventually led back to Europe.

When the slave trade in the West Indies began, European nations granted monopolies to a few favorite companies, such as the Dutch West India Company and the Royal African Company of England. Later, when these nations realized that they could make more money by allowing companies to compete, the monopoly system was abandoned. Before the monopolies ended in the late 1600s, the European colonists in North America were not able to obtain nearly as many Africans as they wanted. The major companies sold most of their Africans on the more profitable markets on the West Indian sugar plantations. However, the North American colonists were able to buy as many Africans as they wished when monopolies ended. The smaller companies were eager to trade with them.

Whereas the slave trade was profitable for European nations and contributed to their industrial growth and development, it was disastrous for the

West African nations. When the trade first began, African rulers sold captives and criminals. Most of the captives had been taken from other tribes during warfare. There was no concept of "Africans" among the diverse groups that lived in Africa in the seventeenth century. The peoples of Africa identified with their clans or tribal groups, not with the continent (Ladson-Billings, 1994). As the Europeans sought more and more Africans, these sources became inadequate. The African rulers were so fascinated with the trinkets, rum, firearms, and other items they received in exchange for captives that they started warring to obtain captives, using the firearms they received from Europeans. Warring became increasingly frequent and destructive as the Europeans' desire for captives soared. As warring increased, some groups had to sell captives to acquire the firearms they needed to protect themselves. These wars adversely affected African political stability. The slave trade also drained off many of Africa's strongest and most productive young men and women. The slave traders wanted only healthy captives who could survive the horrible middle passage and the backbreaking work on the plantations in America.

The Beginning of Bondage

The captive's life was terrifying, brutal, and shocking. Slave catchers, who were usually Africans, raided the interior of the West African coast looking for captives from other tribal groups. When Africans were caught, they were chained together and marched long distances, often hundreds of miles, to the European forts near the coast. Here they waited, sometimes for months, to be forced onto ships headed for America. The captives adamantly resisted bondage. Some of them escaped on the long march to the forts. Others jumped overboard once the ships were at sea. Mutinies occurred, both on the African shore and in mid-ocean. In 1753 a group of captives seized a ship bound for America, killed the White crew, and forced the ship back to Africa. In 1839, the *Amistad,* a slave ship, was brought into New London, Connecticut, by a group of Africans who had revolted against their captors. Cinque, the young African leader, and his followers were granted their freedom by the U.S. Supreme Court (Ladson-Billings, 1994).

Conditions on the slave ships were degrading and dehumanizing. The captured Africans were packed into the ships like sardines. They were chained together with iron ankle fetters. The space for each slave was so small that they were forced to lie down in the ship. Because of the crowded and filthy conditions on the ships, diseases were rampant and took many lives. Many Africans died from scurvy, dysentery, and smallpox. Sometimes everyone on a ship was blinded by ophthalmia. Africans who became very sick were dumped into the ocean because dead Africans were worthless on the American slave market. More than half of the Africans sometimes died during the journey.

Some historians estimate that one out of every eight captives died in the middle passage and never reached the Americas. This painful trip usually took from forty to sixty days.

Slavery in North America

The first Africans to arrive in the English North American colonies came in 1619 on a Dutch ship. These twenty Africans were not slaves but, like most of the Whites who came to the colonies during this period, were indentured servants. To pay for their passage to America, indentured servants agreed to work for their sponsors for a specified period of time. When they had completed their period of service, they became free. At first, the English colonists met their labor needs with indentured servants. Increasingly, the colonists began to feel that they were not obtaining enough workers with this system and that slavery had many more advantages. For one thing, indentured servitude was more expensive than slavery. The servants had to be provided certain goods and services, and eventually they became free. With slavery, the worker received few benefits and remained a servant for life. Also, the slaves' children would also be slaves. Clearly, slavery was a more profitable system than indentured servitude. The colonists deliberately decided to replace indentured servitude with African slavery for economic reasons.

Slavery existed in practice in most of the colonies long before it acquired legal status. The legal institutionalization of slavery was a gradual process. By 1630 in Virginia laws and legal cases were beginning to evolve that would culminate in the legalization of slavery. In that year, a court sentenced a White man to a whipping for having sex with an African woman. The Virginia House of Burgesses passed a law in 1643 limiting the years for White indentured servants but not for African servants. The House enacted a law in 1662 that declared that children would inherit their mother's status. This law reversed English common law, which held that children inherited their father's status. A 1667 law enacted by the House enabled Christians to be slaves. A law passed in Maryland in 1664 openly declared that Blacks and their children would be slaves in that colony. By the end of the seventeenth century, slavery existed in fact as well as in law in Colonial America.

American slavery was a unique institution in human history; it was designed to dehumanize Africans and to convince them that they were inferior and deserved the treatment they received. It was also designed to enable Whites to make maximum profits from African labor and to reinforce ideals of White supremacy. All of the laws, customs, and norms that developed around slavery reflected and reinforced its major goals. Slaves were regarded as property who should cater to the whims and wishes of their masters. A number of arguments and traditions emerged to justify slavery and to ensure its continuation. Because of their treatment of Blacks, and because of constant attempts by the captives to resist bondage, Whites developed a chronic fear of slave rebellions and retaliation. Sometimes, especially after a slave rebellion or when one was rumored, White fears of slave insurrections and uprisings became chronic, paranoid, and widespread. Consequently, the slave codes were made more severe and the institutions and norms supporting bondage were revitalized.

Attempts by Whites to deny the African captives humanity and to oppress them are reflected in the numerous slave codes enacted in colonies from New York to Georgia. These codes varied from colony to colony but tended to be most severe in the southern colonies. However, all of them were degrading and designed to reinforce bondage. In some colonies, slaves could not form groups without the presence of a White; they could not carry or own firearms, testify in court against a White person, or be taught to read or write. Some colonies prevented them from owning property or drinking liquor and did not recognize their marriages as legal. They were forbidden from leaving the plantation unless they had a special pass. Punishment for crimes was severe, although some planters did not welcome the death penalty because it deprived them of profitable workers. Slaves were subject to the death penalty for such crimes as rape, arson, and robbery.

Slaves worked in a wide variety of occupations, especially in the northern colonies. They worked as laborers and house servants in New England, and also as skilled artisans. Many skilled slaves in the North hired themselves out and saved enough money to buy their freedom. Few skilled slaves in the South were allowed to keep the money they earned hiring themselves out. Although slaves in the South worked in many different jobs, especially in the cities, where many were skilled artisans, most worked on the large plantations owned by a few rich members of the southern aristocracy. Life on these large plantations, which specialized in such crops as tobacco and cotton, was arduous and poignant. Often driven by a merciless overseer and a driver, the slaves worked from sunup to sundown. They usually lived in mud-floor shacks on the plantation that were cold in the winter and hot in the summer. Their food consisted mostly of hominy and fatback. Their clothing was limited. Men usually had little more than two shirts and two pairs of trousers.

Even though Whites tried to deny the slaves a human existence, Africans succeeded in developing a sense of community and a social life quite apart from the world of Whites. Slaves had stable marriages, even though they were not legally recognized by White society. These marriages usually occurred after long courtships. The family was important to the slaves. Family members taught their children how to survive the harsh White environment, as well as how never to submit totally to the whims of the master. Black fathers openly disapproved of the ways Whites treated their families. However, these men usually obeyed the master so that they could avoid severe punishment or death. Many slave families that had developed strong bonds of love and kinship were broken up when their master sold family members to different buyers or sold only some members of the family. Some slaves escaped to search for members of their families when they were sold.

Most African captives never totally submitted to slavery or accepted it. They resisted it in both covert and blatant ways. To avoid work, slaves would sometimes feign illness. They sometimes destroyed farm equipment deliberately or cut up the plants when they were hoeing crops. A few slaves maimed themselves to avoid work. Some domestic slaves put poison in their masters' foods and killed them. Other slaves escaped. The number of runaways increased greatly when the Civil War began and when the Emancipation Proclamation was issued in 1863. Many slaves were helped to the North and Canada by a loosely organized system known as the Underground Railroad. Free Blacks, many of whom were escaped slaves, made numerous trips to the South to help Blacks escape. Africans such as Harriet Tubman and Josiah Henson helped hundreds of slaves follow the North Star to freedom. Many slaves traveled by night and were helped by "conductors" of the Underground Railroad. Other slaves escaped alone. These lone and brave captives were determined to escape bondage at any cost.

African captives also resisted slavery by rebellion (Genovese, 1979). Even though most slave uprisings were unsuccessful, partly because of slave informers, historical records indicate that at least 250 occurred (Aptheker, 1987). One of the most ambitious slave uprisings was planned by Gabriel Prosser in 1800. Prosser and a group of about 1,000 slaves armed themselves and headed for Richmond, Virginia. A heavy rainstorm stopped the rebels, and the authorities in Richmond, who had been alerted, were armed and waiting for them. Gabriel Prosser and 30 of the other captives died at the end of a rope.

Denmark Vesey, a free Black in Charleston, South Carolina, planned an insurrection in 1822. The group he led armed themselves and were prepared to take Charleston's two arsenals. The revolt was crushed before it got started, and the participants were hanged. The most successful slave revolt of the antebellum period was led by Nat Turner in 1831. Turner was a highly imaginative African American preacher who felt that he was destined by God to free his people from bondage. Turner organized and armed a crew that killed about sixty Whites, including his master and family. The Turner rebels caught their victims by surprise. Whites crushed the rebellion after it had raged for forty-eight hours. When they were seized, Turner and nineteen other rebels were hanged.

The Abolitionists

The first societies organized to agitate for the abolition of slavery were formed during and after the American Revolution. The earliest was founded in

Philadelphia in 1775. The Quakers were the leading figures in this society. However, slavery was hotly debated among the Quakers. There were also Quakers in the South who owned slaves (Ladson-Billings, 1994). Other abolitionary societies were formed during this period. Most of the members of these early societies were propertied men who were sympathetic to the South. They spoke kindly of the South, were soft spoken, and felt that slave owners who freed their slaves should be compensated. They advocated a gradual abolition of slavery. Because of the tactics they used, many Southerners supported these societies. These abolitionists did not believe in or practice social equality. Women and African Americans were excluded from their organizations.

The abolitionary societies organized in the 1800s were much more militant and aggressive than the earlier ones. They harshly denounced slavery and slave owners and demanded an immediate end to slavery. These groups were unpopular in both the North and the South. They became known as militants and extremists. Both Whites and Blacks participated in these societies, although the Whites, who did not believe in racial equality, tried to keep the African Americans in the background. Frederick Douglass, Robert Purvis, and Sojourner Truth were some of the leading African American abolitionists (Quarles, 1969; Yee, 1992).

One of the most militant societies was the American Anti-Slavery Society, organized in 1833. Although this society vigorously denounced slavery, it kept Blacks in the background. In its early years, it had no African American lecturers. Most of the policy was made by Whites. Members of the society discouraged African Americans when they started editing their own newspapers and lecturing. They wanted only a few Blacks to be visible in the organization for symbolic purposes. The African American abolitionists harshly condemned the White abolitionists, accusing them of discriminating against Blacks in their businesses and their daily lives.

The African American abolitionists often went their separate ways (Quarles, 1969). They edited newspapers and gave moving speeches giving Black views of abolition. Despite objections from White abolitionists such as William Lloyd Garrison, Frederick Douglass edited and published a paper, the *North Star*. Black abolitionists also expressed their views in the series of conventions they held in the antebellum period. At the National Negro Convention in 1843 Henry Highland Garnet gave a controversial speech in which he urged slaves to rise up and fight for their freedom. He later worked with William G. Allen to edit a newspaper, *The National Watchman*. Sojourner Truth and Harriet Tubman were also important African American abolitionists. Truth worked with other abolitionists such as William Lloyd Garrison and Frederick Douglass. She also became active in the women's rights movement. Harriet Tubman was one of the most successful "conductors" on the Underground Railroad. She helped more than 300 captives to escape to freedom.

As was to be the case in later years, African American and White participants in Black liberation movements in the 1800s often had different goals
and aims, and they used different approaches. These divergent goals and methods inevitably led to conflict and hostility between these groups.

THE COLONIZATION MOVEMENT

In the early nineteenth century, an intense movement developed among Whites
to deport African Americans to another country. The motives of the advocates
of colonization varied. Some saw themselves as humanitarians and felt that
because of White racism African Americans would never be able to achieve
equality in the United States. They believed that Blacks would have a much
better chance in another nation. Other advocates of colonization were supporters of slavery and wanted to deport free Blacks because they felt that nonslave Blacks were a threat to slavery. Many southern Whites eagerly supported
the American Colonization Society, organized in 1816 by a group of eminent
White Americans.

Many influential Whites, such as Francis Scott Key and Henry Clay, supported colonization. A region in West Africa, named Liberia, was acquired by
American colonizationists in 1822. Despite the enthusiastic support for the
movement, it did not succeed. Fewer than 8,000 African Americans had immigrated to Liberia by 1852. Many of these were captives who had been granted
their freedom on the condition that they immigrate to Africa. The colonization
movement failed primarily because most African Americans were adamantly
against it. The American Colonization Society made its plans and solicited
support from eminent White Americans but ignored the feelings of African
Americans. African American leaders denounced the society, which often con-
doned racist practices, in loud terms. They argued that they would not leave
the United States because their parents had helped to build this nation and
because they had a right to live in this country by birthright. The free African
Americans who strongly opposed colonization saw it as an attempt by slave
owners to get rid of them and thus make slavery more safe and secure. These
leaders argued that their fate rested with the fate of their enchained brothers
and sisters.

A few African Americans who became disillusioned with the United
States began to advocate colonization. However, some of the leaders, such as
Martin Delany, strongly criticized the American Colonization Society. Delany
felt that the society's members were "arrogant hypocrites." He correctly perceived the White colonizationists' motives as being quite different from his.
African American colonizationists wanted to leave the United States because
they had become disillusioned and frustrated. Most White colonizationists

hoped to deport African Americans so that they could get rid of a racial group they did not want in the United States.

From time to time, small groups of despairing African Americans thought seriously about colonization and sometimes took concrete actions to realize their aspirations. Paul Cuffe took thirty-eight Blacks to Sierra Leone in 1815. In 1859, Martin D. Delany obtained a piece of land in Africa for an African American settlement. A Black colonization group, the African Civilization Society, was organized by a group of eminent African Americans in 1858. Despite these attempts, African American colonizationists had no more success than White colonizationists because most African Americans were determined to remain in the United States. Back-to-Africa advocates emerged later in the nineteenth and twentieth centuries, but their cries continued to fall on deaf ears. Marcus Garvey was a strong advocate of African colonization in the 1930s.

Nonslave African Americans

Not all African Americans were slaves, either in the North or South, during the antebellum period. Many African Americans in the North hired themselves out and earned their freedom. Some in New England sued for their freedom in courts and won it. Some bondsmen were awarded their freedom after service in the Revolutionary War. A few African Americans were descendants of Black indentured servants and thus were never slaves. In the South, some slave masters left wills freeing their slaves on their deaths. Often these slaves were their children or other blood relatives that resulted from forced sex with Black women captives. Some southern slaves were given their freedom after meritorious service to their communities. Others obtained their freedom by escaping. In both the North and the South, nonslave Blacks were harassed and demeaned and were often treated as if they were slaves. When Whites saw African Americans, they assumed that they were slaves. Nonslave Blacks had to prove that they were free. Free Blacks had to carry papers, which they usually had to purchase, that certified their freedom. However, they were often captured and enslaved whether they carried "free" papers or not.

Many of the legal limitations imposed on the slave also governed the nonslave African American. In many parts of the South, nonslave Blacks were forbidden from forming groups without the presence of a White, were prohibited from testifying against a White, and were not allowed to own a gun or a dog. In the North, they were denied the franchise and prohibited by law from migrating to such states as Illinois, Indiana, and Oregon. The free African American could settle in other old northwest states only after paying bonds up to a thousand dollars. Southerners regarded free African Americans as a nuisance and a threat to slavery. They blamed them for most of the slave rebellions and for encouraging slaves to escape. For these reasons, many southern Whites eagerly supported the move to deport free Blacks to Africa.

Nonslave northern Blacks played an extremely important role in African American life. They strongly protested the racism and discrimination Blacks experienced. The Negro Convention Movement served as an important protest forum. Black conventions were held from 1830 up to the beginning of the twentieth century. At most of them, the delegates issued cogent statements demanding an end to racism in various areas of American life. The colonization movement, discrimination in northern schools, and segregation in the church were targets of Black protest.

Free African Americans also organized significant institutions, including the numerous self-help and mutual-aid societies from which most of today's Black insurance companies grew. One of the earliest mutual-benefit societies, the African Union Society, was organized in Newport, Rhode Island, in 1780. Like many similar societies organized later, it helped its members when they were out of work, gave them decent burials, and set up an apprentice program that trained young Blacks to be skilled artisans. Other mutual-aid societies included the Masonic Order organized by Prince Hall in 1787 and the Grand United Order of Odd Fellows, established in 1843. These organizations were extremely important within the Black community.

African Americans also organized their own churches. African Americans were forced to sit in separate pews in White churches and were sometimes interrupted in the middle of prayers if they were seated in the "wrong" sections. These kinds of indignities led Blacks such as Richard Allen and Absalom Jones to organize independent Black churches. In 1794, two Black Methodist churches were founded in Philadelphia, St. Thomas Protestant Episcopal Church and the Bethel African Methodist Episcopal Church. African American Methodist churches soon spread to many other cities. African American Baptists also established independent churches. The Black church became an extremely important institution in African American life. It trained most Black protest leaders, opened schools for Black children, and gave Blacks practice in self-governance and increased their self-respect. The church and the fraternal orders, which were affiliated with the church, were the key institutions within Black America. Today, the African American church still performs many of its historic functions and remains an important institution.

THE CIVIL WAR AND RECONSTRUCTION

African Americans viewed the Civil War as the God-sent conflict that would emancipate them from bondage. However, they were virtually alone in this view. Most White Americans, including President Lincoln and the U.S. Congress, viewed the war as a conflict to preserve the Union. When news of the war spread, northern Blacks rushed to recruiting stations and tried to enlist in the armed forces. Their services were rejected. Leaders thought that the war would last only ninety days. The war dragged on for four long years. When it became evident that the war would last much longer than was originally thought, the Union, and later the Confederacy, reluctantly allowed African Americans to take up arms.

Congress and President Lincoln took a number of steps to weaken the Confederacy. They realized that the slaves were being used to help the Confederate forces to maintain their strength. Consequently, Congress enacted a number of laws that undermined the Confederacy. In 1861, Congress enacted legislation enabling it to free slaves who were used to help the Confederate forces. In the summer of 1862, Congress passed a bill that freed slaves who had escaped and authorized the president to use Black troops. President Lincoln also used his authority to weaken the Confederacy. On September 22, 1862, he announced that slaves in rebel states would be freed on January 1, 1863. Lincoln kept his promise and issued the Emancipation Proclamation freeing those slaves in rebel states on January 1, 1863. Although African Americans and abolitionists rejoiced when the Emancipation Proclamation was issued, legally it did no more than the act that was passed by Congress in 1862. The thousands of slaves in states not fighting the Union were not freed. However, the proclamation did give African Americans a moral uplift and motivated more captives to escape. However, captives had been escaping in large numbers ever since northern soldiers started coming to the South.

After four bitter years and the bloodiest war in U.S. history up to that time, General Lee surrendered at Appomattox on April 9, 1865, and the Civil War ended. On April 14, 1865, Lincoln was assassinated by John Wilkes Booth. Andrew Johnson became president. President Johnson, like Lincoln, favored a lenient plan for readmitting the southern states back into the Union. However, the Republican Congress wanted to gain a toehold in the South so that the Republican party could win future presidential elections. To obtain their objective, they franchised the newly freed African Americans so that they would develop an allegiance to the Republican party. In a series of acts, Congress gave Black men the right to vote and extended their civil rights, thereby endearing them to the Republicans. In 1865, it enacted the Thirteenth Amendment, which abolished slavery throughout the United States. Congress passed a Civil Rights Act in 1866 that made African Americans citizens and granted them certain legal rights. The Fourteenth Amendment, enacted in 1866, also recognized Blacks as citizens. The Reconstruction Act of 1867 divided the South into five military districts and required the Confederate states to enact constitutions that would be approved by Congress and to ratify the Fourteenth Amendment before they could be redacted into the Union. The South considered the Reconstruction Act especially galling.

Because they could now vote and run for public office, a number of African Americans held elected offices for brief periods during Reconstruction. Most of them held minor local offices. However, twenty-two served in the U.S. Congress, two as U.S. senators. Black elected officials were too few in number and their tenure too brief for them to play a leading role in shaping policy. However, the South established its most enlightened state constitutions during Reconstruction and enacted some of its most humane social legislation. For years after Reconstruction, southern apologists justified southern violence by arguing that the South was reacting to the former Black control of the southern states. However, African Americans never controlled any of the states' legal bodies and none were elected governors.

The Rise of White Supremacy

The Republicans' plan to grab the Black man's vote was successful. Blacks in large numbers voted for the Republican presidential candidate in the election of 1868. However, by 1876 the Republicans, who were dominated by northern industrial interests, had new interests and no longer needed the Black man to attain them. In fact, African Americans stood in their way. Northern industrialists were now interested in extending their trade in the South and consequently wanted to court the southern Whites. To appease southern Whites, northern Whites decided to leave the question of the Black person's fate up to the South. The handling of the Hayes-Tilden election in 1876 indicated the extent to which northern Whites had abandoned African Americans. In that disputed election, an Electoral Commission named the Republican candidate, Hayes, president. To placate the South, Hayes's supporters promised White southerners that when he became president, Hayes would remove all of the remaining federal troops from the South.

Hayes kept this promise when he became president. By the time that the last federal troops were removed from the South, southern Whites were reestablishing their control of state governments throughout the South and had aggressively begun their campaigns to make African Americans chattels even though slavery had been legally abolished. One of the first acts of the state legislatures was to disenfranchise African Americans. A motley collection of ingenious methods were used to keep Blacks from voting. The Democratic primary election, the grandfather clause, literacy tests, and the poll tax were among the many ways in which African Americans, and inadvertently some poor Whites, were prevented from voting.

Determined to "put Blacks in their place," violence against African Americans became rampant. The goals of this violence were to intimidate African Americans to keep them from voting and to reestablish the caste system that had existed before the Civil War. African Americans became victims of a rash of riots that swept throughout the South between 1866 and 1898. When African Americans tried to obtain the right to vote in New Orleans in 1866, a riot erupted in which forty-eight Blacks were killed. A riot broke out in Savannah, Georgia, in 1872 when Blacks tried to end segregation on the city's streetcars. Thirty African Americans were killed in a riot that erupted in Meridian, Mississippi, in 1871. Forty-six died in a Memphis riot in 1866. Even though Blacks were usually innocent victims in these riots, they struck back at Whites in the Charleston Riot of 1876.

The Ku Klux Klan was reorganized in 1915. It became a prime leader of anti-Black violence. The lynching of African Americans also became widespread. About 100 Blacks met their death each year at the end of a rope during these difficult years.

Southern state legislatures also enacted most of their Jim Crow laws during this period. Laws were passed requiring segregation in schools, parks, restaurants, theaters, and in almost all other public accommodation facilities. Tennessee passed a Jim Crow railroad car act in 1881. Most of the other southern and border states soon followed Tennessee's lead. In a series of cases, the Supreme Court upheld and legitimized the South's Jim Crow laws. In 1883 it ruled that the Civil Rights Act of 1875 was unconstitutional. In the *Plessy* v. *Ferguson* case of 1896, it upheld a Louisiana law that required segregation in railroad cars. The Court ruled that literacy tests and poll taxes required for voting were constitutional. It stripped the Fourteenth and Fifteenth Amendments of all their meaning as far as African Americans were concerned and encouraged White southerners to enact more racist laws.

Many African Americans expected to receive forty acres and a mule after the Civil War. However, most of the land confiscated from southern plantation owners was either given back to them or to other members of the southern aristocracy. Few African Americans were able to obtain land. Most of them became bound to the land and to White landowners in the sharecropping system. The sharecropper's life was similar to that of a slave's. In theory, a sharecropper received a share of the crop. However, Black sharecroppers, who had to buy their merchandise from their boss's store, were severely cheated. Each year when the crops were harvested, they found themselves further and further in debt and required to stay on the land until they paid their bill. The sharecropper's status was little better than that of a slave's and in some ways worse.

To make the system even more like slavery, southern state legislatures enacted a series of laws between 1865 and 1866 that became known as the Black Codes. These laws were similar to the old slave codes. In some states, Blacks could not testify in court against Whites, carry guns, or buy some types of property. African Americans who were unemployed could be arrested. Those who were unable to pay their fines were hired out. In some places, Black workers could not leave the farm without permission. By the beginning of the twentieth century, White southerners had totally succeeded in reestablishing White supremacy and reducing the African American to the status of peons. Black hopes born during the Civil War had been almost completely shattered. When the twentieth century opened, African Americans were deeply disillusioned and saw little hope for the future. They attempted to solve their problems by migrating North, still in search of the American Dream.

Migration and City Life

After the Civil War, large numbers of African Americans began to migrate to urban areas in the South and to settle in the Southwest (Lemann, 1991). Because of the widespread discrimination they faced in the United States, some African Americans established all-Black towns. Nearly thirty such towns were established near the turn of the century, including Mound Bayou, Mississippi, in 1887 and Langston, Oklahoma, in 1891. Many African Americans also wanted to make Oklahoma an all-Black state, but this idea never materialized.

Although many African Americans settled in the South and Southwest, most who migrated near the turn of the century settled in large cities in the Midwest and East (Adero, 1993). New York City's Black population doubled between 1900 and 1910. During the same period, Chicago's increased by more than 30%. African Americans migrated to northern cities in large numbers in the early 1900s because of the severe economic, political, and social conditions in the South. Southern states had stripped African Americans of most of their legal rights. Disastrous floods, the boll weevil, and the sharecropping system combined to make life on the southern plantations nearly intolerable. The beginning of World War I had nearly stopped immigration from southern and eastern Europe. Consequently, northern manufacturers badly needed laborers. Some of them sent agents to the South to lure Blacks to the North. Black newspapers such as the *Chicago Defender* described the North as a land of milk and honey and urged African Americans to leave the South. These forces led nearly one-half million southern Blacks to head for the North during and immediately after World War I. This mass migration to the North greatly disturbed southern Whites because it deprived them of a cheap source of labor. They tried to stop Blacks from going North, but their efforts were useless.

When the African Americans arrived in midwestern and eastern cities, they had a rude awakening. Life in these cities was extremely difficult. African Americans were the victims of White violence and experienced gross discrimination in housing and employment. Many Blacks who moved into White communities were beaten and their homes were bombed. Because of a variety of techniques used by real estate agents, Blacks were excluded from many neighborhoods. Consequently, the Black urban community grew by leaps and bounds because African Americans were forced to live in areas that were predominantly Black. Also, many Blacks preferred to live in communities that had established Black churches, clubs, and fraternal orders.

As African Americans competed with Whites for housing and jobs, conflict and tension developed between them. Whites were determined to keep Blacks from their jobs and out of their communities. White aggression and violence in the early 1900s led to some of the bloodiest riots that the United States had experienced. One of the worst riots occurred in East St. Louis in 1917. The riot was started when a group of Whites fired into a Black neighborhood and Blacks retaliated. Thirty-nine African Americans and nine Whites were killed. During the same year, riots also occurred in Philadelphia and Chester, Pennsylvania. More than 20 riots occurred in cities throughout the United States in 1919. The gifted writer James Weldon Johnson called that summer the "Red Summer" because of the blood that ran in city streets. The most tragic riot that summer occurred in Chicago. The riot started when a Black youth was drowned after being chased by a group of Whites at a segregated beach on Lake Michigan. The riot lasted for almost two weeks. When it ended, 38 people had been killed, 23 of them Black. More than 1,000 homes were destroyed and 537 people were injured. In 1919, riots also occurred in such cities as Washington, D.C., and Longview, Texas.

WORLD WAR I

As with other wars, African Americans enthusiastically supported World War I and were impressed with President Wilson's high-sounding rhetoric about fighting the war to "make the world safe for democracy." African Americans took Wilson seriously and joined the armed forces in massive numbers. However, it was not long before they realized that White Americans intended African Americans to be second-class citizens in the military. The discrimination that Black soldiers experienced during the war was blatant. When the United States first entered the war, no training camps were established for African American soldiers. Many Black professionals, like doctors, were made privates in the army. Most Black soldiers were given noncombatant assignments, although some fought on the battlefield. A tragic incident that occurred in Houston, Texas, in 1917 symbolized to African Americans more than anything else the status of the Black soldier. When a group of Black soldiers tried to board a segregated street car, a fight occurred in which twelve civilians died. Thirteen of the soldiers were sentenced to die, and fourteen were sent to prison for life. The fate of these soldiers shocked and dismayed the African American community.

ORGANIZATIONS

During these trying times a number of African American institutions and organizations emerged to help African Americans adjust to city life and to fight racism and discrimination in the courts. W. E. B. Du Bois, a militant spokesman for Black rights, and a group of Black intellectuals founded the Niagara Movement in 1905. The men in this movement issued a strong statement denouncing American racism. The Niagara Movement was short-lived. However, the National Association for the Advancement of Colored People (NAACP), organized in 1910, was an outgrowth of it. Although most of the officers of the NAACP were White, Black people strongly supported it. The NAACP concentrated on improving the African American's legal status. Under its leadership, the legal status of Blacks greatly improved. A group of social workers founded the National Urban League in 1911 to help Black migrants adjust to city life and to find employment. The Urban League worked against enormous odds because of job discrimination. However, it experienced some gains.

Whereas the NAACP and the National Urban League appealed greatly to middle-class and upwardly mobile African Americans, Marcus Garvey's Universal Negro Improvement Association (UNIA), organized in 1914, was a movement that strongly attracted the Black poor. Garvey preached Black pride and urged African Americans to return to Africa because they would never have equality in the United States. He also urged Blacks to establish businesses and to improve their own communities. The UNIA operated a number of businesses, including restaurants, grocery stores, and a hotel. Garvey was contemptuous of light-skinned and middle-class African Americans because he felt that they wanted to associate with Whites instead of other Blacks. The leading Black spokesmen and organizations were threatened by Garvey. Partly as a result of their efforts, he was jailed for irregularities in the handling of his Black Star Line. More than any other leader during this period, Garvey helped the lower-class African American to feel proud of being Black.

The Harlem Renaissance

During the 1920s and 1930s, African American artists, writers, and musicians produced some of their best work. Like their counterparts in the 1960s, they deliberately tried to reflect the African American cultural heritage in their works. They emphasized Black pride and strongly protested racism and discrimination. Gifted poets, such as Claude McKay and Countee Cullen, penned angry poems that reflected Black aspirations and frustrations. Other African American writers during this period, such as Langston Hughes, Jean Toomer, and Zora Neale Hurston, wrote outstanding novels. African American musicians further developed blues and jazz. These two types of music became recognized throughout the world.

WORLD WAR II AND THE YEARS AFTER

African Americans did not expect World War II to bring them any great gains. Their memories of World War I were still too vivid and poignant. However, the war created additional jobs in the large cities, and masses of southern Blacks migrated during and after the war years. Many Blacks migrated to the West Coast as well as to the North. More than 150,000 African Americans left the South each year between 1940 and 1950. Black city migrants encountered problems similar to those experienced by African Americans who had migrated in earlier decades. Segregation in housing was still increasing. Many manufacturers with government contracts to make war-related materials refused to hire Blacks or hired them only for the lowest-paying jobs. President Roosevelt refused to take action to stop job discrimination until A. Philip Randolph threatened to march on Washington with 100,000 African Americans. To prevent the march, Roosevelt issued an executive order that outlawed discrimination in defense-related jobs and set up a federal committee on fair employment.

Violence and riots also erupted in the cities. The most serious riot during this period occurred in Detroit in the summer of 1943. It lasted for more than thirty hours. When the riot was over, thirty-four people were dead, twenty-five of them Black. During the same summer, riots also occurred in Los Angeles and in the Harlem district of New York City. These riots, especially the one in Detroit, greatly alarmed U.S. politicians. Mayors in many cities formulated commissions to study the causes of the racial outbreaks and to recommend ways to eliminate their causes.

President Truman

President Harry S Truman, who won the presidential election in 1948 with heavy Black support, took a number of steps to improve race relations and helped to pave the way for the civil rights movement that reached its height in the 1960s. With the use of executive orders, he desegregated the armed forces and created a Committee on Civil Rights that investigated the condition of African Americans. The committee's publication, *To Secure These Rights,* recommended total integration in U.S. society. Truman also ordered industries doing business with the federal government to end discrimination. These measures were mainly symbolic and did not seriously affect the African American's status in the United States. However, they contributed significantly to setting an atmosphere of racial tolerance and to the rising expectations of African Americans.

The Supreme Court

More important than Truman's action in improving race relations during the 1940s and 1950s were the actions of the U.S. Supreme Court. During the decades after the Civil War, the Supreme Court had consistently made decisions that denied African Americans civil liberties and legitimized and legalized racist practices. It now began to rule in favor of civil rights. In a series of cases, most of which were led or supported by the NAACP, the Court ruled for greater civil liberties for African Americans, thus reversing its racist tradition. In 1946, the Court ruled against segregation in interstate commerce. It made a negative ruling regarding the restrictive covenants in 1948. In a number of cases related to African Americans attending segregated White universities in the southern and border states, it consistently ruled that Black Americans should be provided a higher education equal to that of Whites in their home states. These rulings forced many states to integrate their state universities. However, many of them created "instant" professional schools for African Americans. The landmark decision of this period was the *Brown v. Board of Education of Topeka* decision of 1954, which ruled that school segregation is inherently unequal. Perhaps more than any other single event, this decision by the high court helped pave the way for the civil rights movement of the 1960s and 1970s.

THE CIVIL RIGHTS MOVEMENT OF THE 1960S AND 1970S

In the 1960s, African Americans began a fight for their rights that was unprecedented in the nation's history. However, the civil rights movement of the 1960s was intimately related to the heritage of Black protest in America, marked by the slave rebellions and uprisings. Black Americans have always protested, and in ways consistent with the times in which they lived. David Walker, W. E. B. Du Bois, Ida B. Wells, and Ella Baker are a few of the many eminent African Americans who strongly protested against American racism through the years. Individuals like Martin Luther King, Jr., Stokely Carmichael, and Fannie Lou Hamer joined this long family of protest leaders in the 1960s. The Black protest in the 1960s was unique in our history because the times were different. Black protest tends to reflect the times in which it occurs.

During the late 1940s and 1950s, events that occurred to elevate Black people's hopes for a better life in the United States included the actions of President Truman, the *Brown* decision of 1954, and the Civil Rights Act of 1957. As African Americans saw more and more signs indicating that social, economic, and political conditions were improving, they became increasingly impatient with their caste status. Signs of the African American's second-class status were rampant throughout the South when the Montgomery bus boycott began in 1955. The boycott was conceptualized and planned by Jo Ann Gibson Robinson and the Women's Political Council, a group of civic-minded African American women in Montgomery. Robinson gives her accounts of these events in her memoir edited by Garrow (1987).

The boycott started when Rosa Parks, a Black seamstress, was jailed for refusing to move to the back of a city bus. Montgomery Blacks decided that they had taken enough and that they would fight the city's bus company until it eliminated segregation. They began a boycott of the bus line that did not end until a federal court outlawed racial segregation on Montgomery buses a year later. Martin Luther King, Jr., the young Black preacher who led the boycott, became the country's most influential civil rights leader and remained so until he was assassinated in 1968. Under his leadership and influence, the civil rights movement used direct-action and nonviolent tactics to protest racism and discrimination in housing, education, and politics and also in other areas.

The civil rights movement actually began when four African American students, who sat down at a segregated lunch counter at a Woolworth's store in Greensboro, North Carolina, on February 1, 1960, refused to leave when they were not served. They had launched the sit-in movement. Within a short time, the sit-in movement had spread throughout the South, and African American college students were desegregating lunch counters and other public accommodation facilities in many cities below the Mason-Dixon line. African American student activists formed the Student Nonviolent Coordinating Committee (SNCC) in 1960 to coordinate their protest activities.

The student protests stimulated other civil rights groups to become more active. The Congress of Racial Equality (CORE), which had been organized since 1942, sponsored a number of freedom rides to Alabama and Mississippi in 1961 to test interstate transportation laws. The CORE riders were the victims of much hostility and violence. Many of them were beaten and jailed, and some of the buses in which they rode were burned. In 1957, King and a group of Black ministers organized the Southern Christian Leadership Conference (SCLC). SCLC trained its volunteers to use civil disobedience tactics and led numerous mass demonstrations. In 1963, King led a demonstration in Birmingham to protest racism and discrimination. The demonstrators were the victims of blatant police violence that was viewed throughout the United States and the rest of the world on television. Mass demonstrations culminated in the summer of 1963, when more than 200,000 people participated in the March on Washington for Freedom and Jobs.

These demonstrations resulted in some small but significant legal gains for African Americans. The historic March on Washington helped to rally public opinion for support of the Civil Rights Act, which finally passed in 1964 after much filibustering in Congress. A voting rights act was enacted in 1965 after King led demonstrations in Selma, Alabama. As a result of this act, which authorized federal workers to oversee elections in the South, the number of African American voters increased sharply in some southern states and counties. However, the mass of African Americans remained poor and without political power. By 1965, many young African American leaders, such as Stokely Carmichael and H. Rap Brown, who had been staunch supporters of nonviolent resistance, began to raise serious questions about this approach and to urge for more militant action and different goals.

During a civil rights demonstration in 1966, Carmichael issued a call for "Black Power," and both the phrase and the ideas it signified spread throughout Black America like wildfire. Carmichael had coined a term that described a mood already pervasive within Black America. The concept of Black Power emerged during a time when the civil rights movement was losing momentum and when African Americans were becoming increasingly frustrated with the gains they had acquired using civil disobedience tactics. Black Power had different meanings for most Whites than for most African Americans. To most African Americans, it meant political power, pride in Blackness, Black control of schools and communities, and Black self-help organizations. To most Whites, the concept meant retaliatory violence and "Black racism." Malcolm X candidly articulated the concept to the Black masses. Black organizations such as the Black Panther party, which was organized in Oakland, California, in 1966, tried to implement the concept. The Panthers attempted to protect the Black community and organized free lunch programs for African American children. The Nation of Islam (Black Muslims) also reflected the concept in its businesses, farms, schools, and weekly newspaper.

Black frustrations, which reached new highs in the mid- and late 1960s, were manifested in a series of tragic race riots in U.S. cities. Unlike the earlier riots in which Whites attacked Blacks, these riots were different because they involved little contact between Whites and Blacks. Rather, urban Blacks directed their attacks toward the symbols of White society within their communities. They burned buildings owned by absentee landlords and looted stores run by merchants who they believed cheated them. The prestigious Kerner Commission, which was appointed by President Lyndon B. Johnson, concluded in 1968 that the riots were caused by the White racism that was endemic in American life. Riots occurred in cities from New York to Los Angeles. Two of the most serious occurred during the summer of 1967 in Newark and Detroit. Twenty-three people lost their lives in the Newark riot; forty-three died in the Detroit outbreak. As in all of the riots during the 1960s, most of the victims were African Americans killed by White law officials. The Kerner Commission concluded in its massive report on the rebellions, "Our nation is moving toward two societies, one White, one Black—separate and unequal" (*Report of the National Advisory Commission on Civil Disorders,* 1968, p. 1).

Women in the Civil Rights Movement

With a history of activism and opposition to oppression trailing them, Black women embraced their legacy of active resistance and worked toward ending racial oppression during the civil rights movement. Despite sexism throughout U.S. society and within the civil rights movement itself, many Black women participated in organizational segments of the movement. Others provided direct and indirect leadership in civil rights organizations.

Black women formed the foundation of the organizational segment of the civil rights movement (Payne, 1993). In many civil rights organizations, they coordinated activities and also mobilized groups. These groups were often composed of large numbers of Black women who participated in voter registration, boycotts, and demonstrations. These grass-roots activities, which took place throughout the South, enabled large numbers of African Americans to participate in and gain empowerment from the civil rights movement.

Although the civil rights movement worked against discrimination and exclusion, sexism existed within most of its organizations (Standley, 1993). Despite the small representation of women's leadership in some civil rights groups, a few women secured visible posts and others led groups indirectly. For example, Ella Baker helped to form and served as the chief advisor of the Student Nonviolent Coordinating Committee from 1960 to 1964. Fannie Lou Hamer was a co-founder of the Mississippi Democratic Freedom Party and ran as a candidate for Congress under the party's name. Septima Clark greatly influenced the civil rights movement through her role as the director of education and teaching for the Southern Christian Leadership Conference. She traveled throughout the South to educate African Americans in literacy and helped in voter registration.

Other women played significant roles in the civil rights movement through leadership in lesser-known organizations. Jo Ann Gibson Robinson and the other members of the Women's Political Council provided the organizational support for the Montgomery bus boycott (Garrow, 1987). Before the boycott they exposed the abuses against Blacks that occurred when they rode the city buses. In rural communities, women formed business cooperatives such as the Madison County Sewing Firm and the Hopedale Sewing Project. These small corporations provided jobs for women who had been fired for participating in civil rights activities (Crawford, 1993).

Black women's participation in civil rights activities placed in jeopardy not only their lives, but also the livelihood of their families. They could lose their jobs and homes and become victims of terrorist activities. Black women who participated in the civil rights movement faced serious personal, social, and political challenges, which they were willing to take.

TOWARD THE TWENTY-FIRST CENTURY

Several major trends can be identified in the social, economic, and political condition of African Americans since the civil rights movement of the 1960s. African Americans experienced significant economic gains relative to Whites during the 1960s (Jaynes & Williams, 1989). However, the economic condition of Blacks relative to Whites since the early 1970s has stagnated or deteriorated. In 1992, the median income for African American families was $21,161, compared to $38,909 for Whites and $23,901 for Hispanics (U.S. Bureau of the Census, 1994, p. 469). African American family median income was only 54% of White median family income. It was 88.5% of Hispanic family median income. In 1993, unemployment rates were substantially higher for Blacks than those for Whites. The rate was 12.9% for Blacks and 6% for Whites. The unemployment rate for young Black males, ages sixteen to nineteen, was 40.2% and 37.5% for Black females. The comparable percentages for Whites were 17.6% and 14.6%, respectively (U.S. Bureau of the Census, 1994, p. 403).

Another important index of the status of African Americans is the percentage of Black persons living below the poverty level compared to Whites. In 1992, about 10.6 million Blacks, or 33.3% of the population, were living below the official government poverty level. This figure compared to 24.5 million Whites, or 11.6 % of the White population, who lived below the poverty level. About 6.7 million Hispanics, or 29.3% of the population, lived below the poverty level in 1992 (U.S. Bureau of the Census, 1994, p. 475).

A number of factors have contributed to the stagnating or deteriorating conditions of African Americans since the 1970s. One important factor has been substantial changes in the economy. Most low-skilled workers were able to obtain well-paying jobs a generation ago. However, as the U.S. economy has become transformed, fewer low-skilled jobs are available. Increasingly, available jobs require technical skills and knowledge. Black workers are disproportionately concentrated among low-skilled workers. The movement of many jobs out of the central cities and into the suburbs, as well as racial discrimination, are additional factors that have slowed the economic progress of African Americans since the 1970s.

Conservative economic policies that favored the middle and upper classes rather than the poor shaped by the Reagan administration also slowed Black progress during the 1980s. The Reagan administration also took a number of legal steps to limit national affirmative action policies. A faltering national commitment to racial equality and to include people of color into the structure of the nation was also evident during the 1980s and 1990s (Carnoy, 1994). The nation's retreat on affirmative action during the mid 1990s was an important indication of its waning commitment to civil rights. Although affirmative action had enabled African Americans to make significant economic and social gains, its future was unclear by 1995. With the emergence of the majority Republican 121st Congress that year and a seemingly more conservative populous, further attempts at fostering equality for African Americans and other marginalized groups through affirmative action was severely challenged. Led by Governor Pete Wilson, the California Regents ended affirmative action in the state's college and universities in 1995. In June of that year, the decision of the Supreme Court in *Adarand Constructors* v. *Pena* to redefine and perhaps ultimately limit and/or end affirmative action in the federal government was perhaps a harbinger of affirmative action's ultimate demise.

The economic situation of Blacks since the 1970s has not been entirely bleak. A substantial number of African Americans have been able to enter the middle class as a result of opportunities and possibilities that resulted from the civil rights movement of the 1960s and 1970s (Cose, 1993). One of the most important developments in the social and economic situation of Blacks since the 1960s has been the development of substantial social class differences within the African American community and the increase of class differentiation (Wilson, 1978, 1987). Significant social class variation has existed within the African American community for many decades (Drake & Cayton, 1945).

However, class variation within the African American community has never been as steep, nor have African Americans ever been as separated as much in terms of neighborhoods and communities on a social class basis. New careers, opportunities, and possibilities opened up for African Americans as a result of the civil rights movement and affirmative actions policies that followed it. Many of the African Americans who had the education and other skills to take advantage of these opportunities are now functioning in mainstream institutions as physicians, college professors and administrators, business people, and corporation heads. Many of these individuals, like their White peers, have joined the exodus to the suburbs and are sending their children to predominantly White suburban public schools or to elite private schools (Banks, 1984). However, despite their social class mobility and high levels of acculturation, the Black middle class still experiences racism and discrimination, as works by Cose (1993) and Feagin and Sikes (1994) document.

Any accurate and sophisticated description of the status of African Americans on the threshold of the twenty-first century must describe not only the large percentage of Blacks who are members of the so-called underclass, but also the smaller and significant percentage of African Americans who have entered the middle and upper classes and who function in the mainstream society. Many of the children of the new middle class are not only unacquainted with poverty, but also have been socialized in mainstream middle- and upper-class communities. They have little first-hand experience with traditional African American culture.

African Americans from all cultures, social classes, and walks of life experience institutional racism and discrimination. A new wave of racism swept through predominantly White college campuses as well as through the wider society during the late 1980s and early 1990s. The shared experiences of African Americans reinforce their sense of identity and peoplehood. Also, most middle- and upper-class African Americans want their children to know and to feel comfortable with other Blacks and with Black culture. Consequently, a number of middle- and upper-class African Americans encourage their children to attend historically Black colleges such as Fisk, Spelman, Morehouse, Howard, and Hampton.

Little careful work has been done on social class variation within the African American community. Most articles and research on African Americans focus on the bulk of African Americans who are living below the poverty level. Blackwell (1985) has developed a typology that conceptualizes social class variation within the African American community (see Figure 7-1).

African Americans have made substantial gains in politics since the voting rights legislation that resulted from the civil rights movement of the 1960s and 1970s. Their progress in politics is a direct result of African Americans being able to vote and run freely for office. Elected African American officials increased from a few dozen in 1940 to more than 6,800 in 1988 (Jaynes & Williams, 1989). In 1990 there were 300 African American mayors, 10% of whom were mayors of cities with at least 400,000 people (Shearer, 1990). African Americans witnessed several significant election victories in 1988 and 1989, including the election of Douglas Wilder as governor of Virginia, the nation's first Black elected governor, and the election of the first African American mayor in New York City, David Dinkins. Norm Rice was elected mayor of Seattle in 1989 by a predominantly White electorate, with less than 10% African American voters. In 1992, Carol Mosley-Braun (Democrat, Illinois) became the first African American woman elected to the U.S. Senate.

As the turn of the century approached, African Americans were deeply troubled about the erosion of their social, economic, and educational status. However, a consensus was developing within the African American community that it must and could take the leadership for its own improvement and that it had the resources to do so. These resources have to be mobilized. African Americans have a significant middle class that functions in many of the nation's leading institutions, they have Black colleges with a distinguished

Figure 7-1 THE SOCIAL STRUCTURE OF THE BLACK
COMMUNITY

Solid lines denote relatively stable divisions between classes, whereas broken lines
indicate that demarcations between substrata are often blurred.

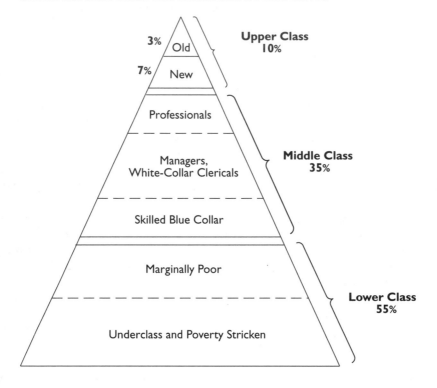

SOURCE: Table 4.1 on page 126 from *The Black Community: Diversity and Unity* by
James E. Blackwell. Copyright © by Harper & Row Publishers Inc. Reprinted by permission of HarperCollins, Inc.

record of academic excellence, and they have a strong tradition of self-help
that has built impressive institutions and businesses. As the twenty-first century approached, Blacks organized to help themselves and thought deeply
about their future—and their children's future—in America.

TEACHING STRATEGIES

To illustrate how content related to African Americans can be used to integrate
the curriculum, exemplary strategies are identified for teaching these concepts

at the grade levels indicated: *tradition* (primary grades), *Black protest* (intermediate and upper grades), and *separatism* (high school grades).

Primary Grades

CONCEPT: Tradition

Generalization: African American songs and music are an important part of their cultural traditions and are passed down from generation to generation.

1. Ask the students, "What special days do you celebrate in your families?" List their responses on the board or butcher paper. Answers might include birthdays, Christmas, Chinese New Year, Chanukah, the Fourth of July, and Thanksgiving.

2. Select several of their responses, such as birthdays, the Fourth of July, and Thanksgiving. Ask the children to give their ideas about why these special days are celebrated in their families. Ask them, "Which of the special days celebrated in your families are also celebrated (a) in other families? (b) in school? (c) throughout the nation? Ask: "Why are these special days also celebrated by these other groups?"

3. Help the students to develop and state the idea that we celebrate these special days because they help us to remember and to honor important events in our personal histories (birthdays), the histories of our families (family reunions), or in the history of our nation (Thanksgiving and the Fourth of July).

4. Explain that the celebration of these special days helps us to remember and to honor our heritages and traditions. Explain that traditions are important ideas, events, and memories that are handed down from one generation to the next. Say, "Not only do families and nations have traditions, but so do groups of Americans such as African Americans, Mexican Americans, Japanese Americans, and Jewish Americans.

5. Tell the students that an important part of the heritage and traditions of African Americans is the song "Lift Ev'ry Voice and Sing," written by James Weldon Johnson and set to music by his brother, J. Rosamond Johnson. Tell the class that the song is often referred to by African Americans as the "Black National Anthem." Remind them that our national anthem is "The Star-Spangled Banner" by Francis Scott Key. Ask the students, "Why do you think that 'Lift Ev'ry Voice and Sing' is sometimes referred to as the 'Black National Anthem'?"

6. Working with the music teacher in your school, introduce your students to "Lift Ev'ry Voice and Sing" by James Weldon Johnson. A beautifully illustrated version of the song makes up the book *Lift Ev'ry Voice and Sing* by Johnson (1995), with moving illustrations by Jan Spivey Gilchrist.

7. Before teaching the students to sing the song, teach the words to them as a poem. Discuss the meaning of each stanza in the song. After the students have discussed each stanza in the song, summarize the lesson by explaining that the song describes the history and struggle of African Americans in the United States and that it is an impor-

tant part of their traditions. Conclude the unit by teaching the students to sing "Lift Ev'ry Voice and Sing."

Intermediate and Upper Grades

CONCEPT: Black Protest

Generalization: African Americans have protested against racism and discrimination throughout their history in America. The forms of protest reflected the times in which they occurred.

1. Begin this unit by showing and discussing with the students Part I of the videotape series *Eyes on the Prize* (or a similar one). In the discussion, focus on the reasons Black protest emerged and the forms that it took during the years covered in this videotape, 1954 to 1956.

2. Tell the students the story of the slave mutinies that occurred both on the West African coast and in mid-ocean. Herbert Aptheker (1987), *American Negro Slave Revolts,* and Eugene D. Genevese (1979), *From Rebellion to Revolution: Afro-American Slave Revolts in the Making of the Modern World,* are well-researched and highly regarded sources of information on slave rebellions. Ask the students to act out, in role-play situations, the stories they have heard. After the role-play situations, ask them to hypothesize by responding to the following questions. Write their responses on the board.

    a. Why do you think the slaves were captured?
    b. Why do you think they started mutinies?
    c. Why didn't the mutinies end the slave trade?
    d. Do you think it was right for slaves to be captured? Why or why not?
    e. Do you think it was right for slaves to rebel? Why or why not?

After the students have responded to these questions, read to them, or ask them to read, selections on the slave trade so that they can test their hypotheses.

3. Ask three different groups of students to research the following three topics:

    a. The Gabriel Prosser revolt of 1800
    b. The Denmark Vesey revolt of 1822
    c. The Nat Turner revolt of 1831

To help them guide their research, ask the groups to focus on the following questions:

    a. Where did the revolt occur?
    b. Why did the revolt occur?
    c. Who led the revolt?
    d. Was the revolt successful? Why or why not?
    e. How were the rebels punished? Why were they punished?

Discuss the questions above with the entire class when the groups have presented their research. List the students' responses on the board. Through questioning, help the student see how the slave insurrections were both alike and different, and why of the three rebellions, only the Turner revolt was successful. After the class discussion, ask each group to plan and present to the class a dramatization showing the sequence of events in the rebellion they studied.

4. African Americans were active in the abolitionist movement and in the Underground Railroad, a loosely organized system that helped many slaves escape to the northern states and to Canada. Ask individual students to research the lives of and to "become," in a dramatization, the following people.

    a. David Walker
    b. Henry Highland Garnet
    c. Robert Purvis
    d. Sojourner Truth
    e. James Forten
    f. Frederick Douglass
    g. Harriet Tubman

When the dramatizations are presented, discuss the following questions with the class:

    a. Why did African American abolitionists oppose slavery? How did their views differ from those of White abolitionists? Why did White abolitionists discriminate against Black abolitionists? Excellent sources on the Black abolitionists are Shirley J. Yee (1992), *Black Women Abolitionists;* and Benjamin Quarles (1969), *Black Abolitonists.*
    b. What was the Underground Railroad? How did it help slaves escape? Who were some of the outstanding "conductors" on the railroad? What risks did captives take when they escaped? Why did they take them? If you had been a slave, would you have tried to escape? Why or why not?

5. Ask individual students or groups of students to research the following organizations and movements and to describe ways in which they protested racism and discrimination:

    a. The Negro Convention movement (1800s)
    b. The Niagara Movement (1905)
    c. The National Association for the Advancement of Colored People (1910)
    d. The National Urban League (1911)
    e. The Universal Negro Improvement Association (1914)
    f. The Black church in the 1800s

When their research is complete, the students should share it with the class. The class should discuss how these organizations and movements expressed discontent with the plight of African Americans, the actions they took to improve it, and the successes and failures they experienced and why.

6. Have the class role-play a civil rights conference in 1966 in which leaders of the organizations listed below debate the future directions of the movement. Each organizational representative should be thoroughly familiar with his or her organization's philosophical position in 1966. By that year. the civil rights movement was becoming increasingly radicalized, and deep factions had developed between the various organizations.

    a. Southern Christian Leadership Conference (SCLC)
    b. National Association for the Advancement of Colored People (NAACP)
    c. National Urban League
    d. Congress of Racial Equality (CORE)
    e. Student Nonviolent Coordinating Committee (SNCC)
    f. Black Panther party
    g. Revolutionary Action Movement (RAM)

7. Have the students role-play a meeting of the following people after a serious racial rebellion in a major city in 1967. These people have met to decide what can be done to eliminate the causes of city riots. Ask individual students to play specific roles. To structure this activity more tightly, write a role description for each character on a three-by-five-inch index card and give the cards to the student role-players.

Roles are as follows:

    a. The mayor of the city
    b. An SCLC spokesperson
    c. An NAACP spokesperson
    d. A National Urban League spokesperson
    e. A CORE spokesperson
    f. A SNCC spokesperson
    g. A Black Panther party spokesperson
    h. A RAM spokesperson
    i. A young person who has participated in a riot

8. To enable the students to summarize this unit and to derive the key generalizations stated above, have them complete the data retrieval chart in Table 7-1.

Valuing Activity

Read the following story to the class and ask the questions that follow.

Trying to Buy a Home in Lakewood Island

About a year ago, Joan and Henry Green, a young African American couple, moved from the West Coast to a large city in the Midwest. They moved because Henry finished his Ph.D. in chemistry and took a job at a big university in Midwestern City. Since they have been in Midwestern City, the Greens have rented an apartment in the central area of the city. However, they have decided that they want to buy a house. Their apartment has become too small for the many books and other things they have accumulated during the year. In addition to wanting

Table 7-1 BLACK PROTEST: DATA RETRIEVAL CHART

Form of Protest, Organization, or Movement	Goal of Protests	Ways of Protests	Results of Protests
Slave mutinies			
Slave rebellions (in USA)			
Black abolitionary movement			
Underground Railroad			
Niagara Movement			
NAACP			
National Urban League			
SCLC			
CORE			
SNCC			
Black Panther party			
RAM			

more space, they want a house so that they can receive breaks on their income tax, which they do not receive living in an apartment. The Greens also think that a house will be a good financial investment.

The Greens have decided to move into a suburban community. They want a new house and most of the houses within the city limits are rather old. They also feel that they can obtain a larger house for their money in the suburbs than in the city. They have looked at several suburban communities and have decided that they like Lakewood Island better than any of the others. Lakewood Island is an all-White community, which is comprised primarily of lower-middle-class and middle-class residents. There are a few wealthy families in Lakewood Island, but they are the exceptions rather than the rule.

Joan and Henry Green have become frustrated because of the problems they have experienced trying to buy a home in Lakewood Island. Before they go out to look at a house, they carefully study the newspaper ads. When they arrived at the first house in which they were interested, the owner told them that his house had just been sold. A week later they decided to work with a realtor. When they tried to close the deal on the next house they wanted, the realtor told them that the owner had raised the price $10,000 because he had had the house appraised since he had put it on the market and had discovered that his selling price was much too low. When the Greens tried to buy a third house in Lakewood Island, the owner told them that he had decided not to sell because he had not received the job in another city that he was almost sure that he would receive when he had put his house up for sale. He explained that the realtor had not removed the ad about his house from the newspaper even though he had told him that he had decided not to sell a week earlier. The realtor the owner had been working with had left the real estate company a few days ago. Henry is bitter and feels that he and his wife are victims of racism and discrimination. Joan believes that Henry is paranoid and that they have been the victims of a series of events that could have happened to anyone, regardless of their race.

Questions

1. Do you think that the Greens were discriminated against in Lakewood Island? Why or why not?
2. What should the Greens do? Why?
3. If you were the Greens, what would you do? Why?
4. What can the Greens do to determine if they are victims of discrimination?

High School Grades

CONCEPT: Separatism

Generalization: Black separatist movements emerge when African Americans experience acute discrimination and a heightened sense of racial pride.

1. Either through choice or force, Black separatism has always existed in America. Most of the social life of the slaves was confined to their communities. One of the earliest manifestations of Black separatism was the colonization movement led by African Americans. To begin this unit, ask several students to prepare and present research reports on the following topics:

    a. Martin R. Delany

    b. Paul Cuffe

    c. The African Colonization Society

When the reports are presented to the class, the following questions should be discussed:

    a. Why did colonization movements emerge among African Americans?

    b. Were these movements popular and successful? Why or why not?

    c. Why did back-to-Africa movements fail to appeal to most African Americans?

    d. If early Black-led colonization attempts had succeeded, how do you think the subsequent history of African Americans would have differed?

2. Because of discrimination and the need for group solidarity, a number of African American organizations emerged in the 1800s. Ask a group of students to prepare short papers on the following topics and present them to the class in a panel discussion on separate Black institutions in the 1800s.

    a. The Black church

    b. Black fraternal and self-help organizations

    c. Black businesses

    d. Black schools and colleges

    e. The Negro Convention Movement

Role-play a Negro Convention in the 1800s in which the participants draft a position statement detailing their major grievances about the plight of African Americans and a plan of action for social change. All of the delegates to the simulated convention must reach agreement on the position statement they prepare. The student roleplayers will need to be thoroughly familiar with the Negro Convention Movement and the various points of view that were presented in the series of Negro Conventions held in the 1800s.

3. The Niagara Movement was a Black protest organization organized in 1905 by W. E. B. Du Bois and a group of Black intellectuals. Ask a group of students to prepare a research report on this movement and present it to the class.

4. Most of the national civil rights organizations in the early 1900s were interracial. Ask the students to do required readings on the history and development of the NAACP and the National Urban League. When they have completed the readings, they should compare and contrast these two organizations with the Niagara Movement and earlier Black protest movements and organizations such as the Negro Convention Movement. Particular attention should be paid to (1) reasons the organizations emerged, (2) people who made major policy decisions and held key positions within them, (3) types of problems that arose within the organizations, (4) the major goals of the organizations, and (5) ways in which the organizations succeeded or failed and

why. While studying these organizations, the students should compare and contrast the ideas and actions of Booker T. Washington and W. E. B. Du Bois. To conclude this activity, ask two students to roleplay a debate between Washington and Du Bois on the kind of education needed by African Americans. Two excellent references for this last exercise are *Up from Slavery* by Booker T. Washington and *The Souls of Black Folk* by W. E. B. Du Bois.

5. Ask a group of students to prepare a panel discussion on the ideas and actions of Marcus Garvey and the Universal Negro Improvement Association. Ask them to focus on the following questions:

   a. What social, economic, and political conditions made Garvey's movement particularly appealing to low-income African Americans?
   b. How did Garvey's ideas help to improve low-income Blacks' feelings about themselves?
   c. Why was Garvey's back-to-Africa movement unsuccessful?
   d. Why did conflict develop between Garvey and other Black leaders?
   e. Why was Garvey ultimately crushed as a leader?
   f. What was the main significance of Garvey's movement? The classic biography of Garvey is *Black Moses* by E. D. Cronon. Another excellent book for this activity is *Marcus Garvey and the Vision of Africa* edited by John Henrik Clarke.

6. When the Black Revolt emerged in 1960, its major goal was to desegregate public accommodation facilities and other institutions. Action tactics and court battles achieved much desegregation. However, by 1965, many African Americans, especially young Black activists, were disillusioned with the attainments of the movement and realized that integration alone would not eliminate the African American's major social, economic, and political problems. These young activists felt that both the goals and tactics of the movement should be changed. They issued a call for Black Power.

Ask the entire class to read excerpts from *Black Power: The Politics of Liberation in America* by Stokely Carmichael and Charles V. Hamilton. Discuss each excerpt with the class. The following questions and exercises can help guide class discussion and student research.

   a. What did the concept "Black Power" mean? Did it mean the same things to African Americans and White Americans?
   b. Compare and contrast the goals of the Black Power movement and the goals of civil rights organizations like SCLC and the NAACP in the early 1960s.
   c. What kinds of economic, political, and social institutions were implied by the concept of Black Power?
   d. Compare and contrast the views of the following people:
      (1) David Walker
      (2) Martin R. Delany
      (3) Richard Allen
      (4) Prentice Hall
      (5) Paul Cuffe
      (6) Marcus Garvey

(7) W. E. B Du Bois
(8) Stokely Carmichael
(9) Malcolm X
(10) Angela Y. Davis
(11) Jesse Jackson
(12) Fannie Lou Hamer

7. Ask the students to research the Afrocentric movement in the 1990s and to state how it is similar to and different from early Black separatist movements. The ideas and work of Molefi K. Asante (1988) should be examined.

8. Conclude the unit by asking the students to present a dramatization that shows how Black separatism has developed and changed from the 1700s to the 1990s.

REFERENCES

Adero, M. (Ed.). (1993). *Up South: Stories, Studies and Letters of This Century's African-American Migrations.* New York: The New Press.

Aptheker, H. (1987). *American Negro Slave Revolts* (40th anniv. ed.). New York: International Publishers, Inc.

Asante, M. K. (1988). *Afrocentricity.* Trenton, N.J.: Africa World Press.

Banks, J. A. (1984). Black Youths in Predominantly White Suburbs: An Exploratory Study of Their Attitudes and Self-Concepts. *The Journal of Negro Education* 53,(1) 3–17.

Blackwell, J. A. (1985). *The Black Community: Diversity and Unity* (2nd ed.). New York: Harper and Row.

Carnoy, M. (1994). *Faded Dreams: The Politics and Economics of Race in America.* Oxford: Cambridge University Press.

Cose, E. (1993). *The Rage of a Privileged Class.* New York: HarperCollins.

Crawford, V. (1993). Beyond the Human Self: Grassroots Activists in the Mississippi Civil Rights Movement. In V. Crawford, J. A. Rouse, & B. Woods (Eds.). *Women in the Civil Rights Movement: Trailblazers & Torchbearers 1941–1965* (pp. 13–26). Bloomington: Indiana University Press.

Drake, St. C. & Cayton, H. R. (1945). *Black Metropolis: A Study of Negro Life in a Northern City.* New York: Harcourt.

Feagin, J. R. & Sikes, M. P. (1994). *Living with Racism: The Black Middle-Class Experience.* Boston: Beacon Press.

Garrow, D. (Ed.). (1987). *The Montgomery Bus Boycott and the Women Who Started It: The Memoir of Jo Ann Gibson Robinson.* Knoxville: University of Tennessee Press.

Genovese, E. D. (1979). *From Rebellion to Revolution: Afro-American Slave Revolts in the Making of the Modern World.* Baton Rouge: Louisiana State University Press.

Jaynes, G. D. & Williams, R. M., Jr. (1989). *A Common Destiny: Blacks and American Society.* Washington, D.C.: National Academy Press.

Johnson, J. W. (1995). *Lift Ev'ry Voice and Sing.* Illustrated by J. S. Gilchrist. New York: Scholastic.

Ladson-Billings, G. (1994). Review of *Teaching Strategies for Ethnic Studies,* 5th ed. Madison: University of Wisconsin, unpublished (prepared for 6th edition revision).

Lemann, N. (1991). *The Promised Land: The Great Black Migration and How It Changed America.* New York: Knopf.

Payne, C. (1993). Men Led, but Women Organized: Movement Participation of Women in the Mississippi Delta. In V. Crawford, J. A. Rouse, & B. Woods (Eds.). *Women in the Civil Rights Movement: Trailblazers & Torchbearers 1941–1965* (pp. 1–11). Bloomington: Indiana University Press.

Quarles, B. (1969). *Black Abolitionists.* New York: Oxford University Press.

Report of the National Advisory Commission on Civil Disorders. (1968). New York: Bantam Books.

Shearer, L. (1990, January 7). The Rise of Black Mayors. *Parade,* p. 14.

Standley, A. (1993). The Role of Black Women in the Civil Rights Movement. In V. Crawford, J. A. Rouse, & B. Woods (Eds.). *Women in the Civil Rights Movement: Trailblazers & Torchbearers 1941–1965* (pp. 183–202). Bloomington: Indiana University Press.

U.S. Bureau of the Census. (1994). *Statistical Abstract of the United States: 1994* (114th ed.). Washington, D.C.: U.S. Government Printing Office.

Wilson, W. J. (1978). *The Declining Significance of Race: Blacks and Changing American Institutions.* Chicago: The University of Chicago Press.

Wilson, W. J. (1987). *The Truly Disadvantaged: The Inner City, the Underclass, and Public Policy.* Chicago: The University of Chicago Press.

Yee, S. J. (1992). *Black Women Abolitionists: A Study in Activism, 1828–1960.* Knoxville: University of Tennessee Press.

ANNOTATED BIBLIOGRAPHY

Books for Teachers

Especially Recommended

Asante, M. K. & Mattson, M. T. (1992). *Historical and Cultural Atlas of African Americans.* New York: Macmillan.

A richly illustrated and fact-filled reference work. Many of the illustrations are in color.

Bennett, L. (1988). *Before the Mayflower: A History of Black Americans* (6th rev. ed.). New York: Penguin.

An excellent, popularly written history by a senior editor of Ebony *that includes an extensive chronology, a list of Black "firsts," and a comprehensive bibliography.*

Boyd, H. & Allen, R. L. (Eds.). (1995). *Brotherman: The Odyssey of Black Men in America—An Anthology.* New York: Ballantine Books.

Selections by Booker T. Washington, W. E. B. Du Bois, Marcus Garvey, Richard Wright, Langston Hughes, Malcolm X, and Henry Louis Gates are among those in this rich and inclusive anthology that provides diverse insights on the experiences of Black men in the United States.

Cantor, G. (1991). *Historic Black Landmarks: A Traveler's Guide.* Detroit: Visible Ink.

This excellent guide for field trips covers all regions in the United States.

Delpit, L. (1995). *Other People's Children: Cultural Conflict in the Classroom.* New York: New Day Press.

Sage advice and wisdom about teaching Black and other children in the margins by a compassionate and perceptive educator and researcher.

Franklin, J. H. & Moss, A. A., Jr. (1994). *From Slavery to Freedom: A History of Black Americans* (7th ed.). New York: Knopf.

This comprehensive history of African Americans is still regarded as the best. The senior author is one of the most highly regarded American historians in the United States.

Ham, D. N. (1993). *The African-American Mosaic: A Library of Congress Resource Guide for the Study of Black History and Culture.* Washington, D.C.: U.S. Government Printing Office.

A comprehensive and richly informative guide to Black historical resources.

Harley, S. (1995). *The Timetable of African-American History: A Chronology of the Most Important People and Events in African-American History.* New York: Simon & Schuster.

An excellent chronology and resource book. It includes photographs.

hooks, b. (1995). *Killing Rage: Ending Racism.* New York: Henry Holt.

A stimulating and perceptive collection of essays by the reknown feminist and public intellectual.

Hine, D. C. (Ed.). (1993). *Black Women in America: An Historical Encyclopedia* (2 vols.). Brooklyn, N.Y.: Carlson.

The definitive work on the experiences of African American women in the United States. An essential reference for school, college, and university libraries.

Hughes, L., Meltzer, M., Lincoln, C. E., & Spencer, J. M. (1995). *A Pictorial History of African Americans: From 1619 to the Present* (6th ed.). New York: Crown.

The history of African Americans told in more than 1,300 illustrations and with a text. The photographs are excellent for teaching purposes.

Logan, R. W. & Winston, M. R. (Eds.). (1982). *Dictionary of American Negro Biography.* New York: Norton.

Every school and college library should have this book. It contains a gold mine of information about the lives of African Americans who have shaped the nation's history.

Salzman, J., Smith, D. L., & West, C. (Eds.). (1996). *Encyclopedia of African-American Culture and History* (5 vols.). New York: Macmillan.

This outstanding, seminal, and comprehensive reference work covers all aspects of African American history and culture. This five-volume set is rich in biographies as well as in thematic essays on such topics as the Harlem Renaissance, intellectual life, and inventors. This encyclopedia should be in every school and university library.

Smith, J. C. (1994). *Black Firsts: 200 Years of Extraordinary Achievement.* Detroit: Visible Ink.

An excellent reference book with a comprehensive pull-out chronology with dates from 1919 to the present.

Smith, J. C. (Ed.). (1992). *Notable Black Women.* Detroit: Gale Research Inc.

A very informative and important reference work on African American women. Comprehensive and well-researched.

Other References

Beals, M. P. (1994). *Warriors Don't Cry: A Searing Memoir of the Battle to Integrate Little Rock's Central High School.* New York: Pocket Books.

A moving and poignant account of the desegregation of Little Rock's Central High School by one of the nine African American students who first enrolled.

Bernal, M. (1987, 1991). *Black Athena: The Afroasiatic Roots of Classical Civilization.* Vols. 1 & 2. New Brunswick, N.J.: Rutgers University Press.

In this comprehensive and seminal book, Bernal argues that classical Western civilization has deep roots in Afroasiatic cultures and that these influences have been ignored, denied, or suppressed since the eighteenth century, largely for racist reasons.

Billingsley, A. (1992). *Climbing Jacob's Ladder: The Enduring Legacy of African-American Families.* New York: Simon & Schuster.

In an examination of African American families, the author looks at these groups historically and also discusses contemporary dilemmas they face now.

Busby, M. (Ed.). (1992). *Daughters of Africa: An International Anthology of Words and Writings by Women of African Descent: From the Ancient Egyptian to the Present.* New York: Pantheon Books.

A collection of oral and written literature by women of African descent, this anthology provides readers with a heightened sense of the experiences of Black women throughout the world.

Christian, C. M. (1995). *Black Saga: The African American Experience.* Boston: Houghton Mifflin.

This comprehensive and well-researched chronology includes detailed information on the African American experience from "Before 1492" to "1994." It also includes photographs, maps, and an excellent bibliography for further reading. Also appropriate for high school students.

Fishkin, S. H. (1993). *Was Huck Black?: Mark Twain and African-American Voices.* New York: Oxford University Press.

This well-written and provocative book documents African American influences on Twain's famous characters and book.

Franklin, J. H. & McNeil, G. R. (Eds.). (1995). *African Americans and the Living Constitution.* Washington, D.C.: Smithsonian Institution Press.

This book consists of a collection of informative essays about African Americans and the U.S. Constitution.

Guy-Sheftall, B. (Ed.). (1995). *Words of Fire: An Anthology of African-American Feminist Thought.* New York: The New Press.

This richly textured and comprehensive anthology documents the experiences of African American women from 1831 to the present. Edited by a leading authority in Black women's studies, it also is appropriate for high school students.

Hale, J. E. (1994). *Unbank the Fire: Visions for the Education of African American Children.* New Haven: Yale University Press.

The author describes how teachers can build upon the cultural strengths of African American students to increase their academic achievement.

Hull, G. T., Scott, P. B., & Smith, B. (Eds.). (1982). *All the Women Are White, All the Men Are Black, But Some of Us Are Brave.* New York: The Feminist Press.

Making a significant contribution to Black women's studies, this book examines race and gender issues that Black women have faced historically and experience in contemporary times.

Hampton, H., Fayer, S., & Flynn, S. (Eds.). (1990). *Voices of Freedom: An Oral History of the Civil Rights Movement from the 1950s through the 1980s.* New York: Bantam.

This informative documentary history of the civil rights movement was designed to accompany the popular television series, Eyes on the Prize, Part II.

Hopson, D. P. & Hopson, D. S. (1990). *Different and Wonderful: Raising Black Children in a Race-Conscious Society.* New York: Prentice-Hall Press.

This book is a comprehensive guide for adults who want to raise positive and healthy Black children in contemporary America.

Hurston, Z. N. (1978). *Their Eyes Were Watching God.* Urbana: University of Illinois Press.

First published in 1937, this novel about the love between an African American man and woman is a classic.

James, S. M. & Busia, A. P. A. (Eds.). (1993). *Theorizing Black Feminisms: The Visionary Pragmatism of Black Women.* New York: Routledge.

Through presenting essays from diverse disciplines concerning Black feminism, this book makes a significant contribution to Black women's studies.

Jenkins, A. H. (1995). *Psychology and African Americans: A Humanistic Approach* (2nd ed.). Boston: Allyn and Bacon.

The author examines issues that concern contemporary African Americans from a humanistic psychological point of view.

Jones, M. L. (1993). *The Color of Culture*. Seattle: IMPACT Communications.

Moving and entertaining poems by a gifted poet and educator.

Mullane, D. (Ed.). (1993). *Crossing the Danger Water: Three Hundred Years of African-American Writing*. New York: Doubleday.

This book consists of a comprehensive collection of African American writing from both contemporary and historical authors (769 pages).

Ladson-Billings, G. (1994). *The Dreamkeepers: Successful Teachers of African American Children*. San Francisco: Jossey-Bass.

A well-written and insightful book that describes effective teachers of African American students.

Loewenberg, B. J. & Bogin, R. (Eds.). (1976). *Black Women in Nineteenth-Century American Life*. University Park: The Pennsylvania State University Press.

A collection of writings by and brief biographies of nineteenth century Black American women. This book examines the activism and resistance to racial and sexual oppression by Black women.

Mills, K. (1993). *This Little Light of Mine: The Life of Fannie Lou Hamer*. New York: Penguin.

An excellently written biography of an important but often neglected civil rights leader.

Rampersad, A. & Roessel, D. (Eds.). (1994). *The Collected Poems of Langston Hughes*. New York: Knopf.

This comprehensive volume has 708 pages. It includes old favorites and many less-well-known poems by the eminent poet.

Morrison, T. (1987). *Beloved*. New York: Knopf.

The author received a Pulitzer Prize for this outstanding novel about an escaped slave who has risked death in order to free herself from a living death.

Sterling, D. (Ed.). (1984). *We Are Your Sisters: Black Women in the Nineteenth Century*. New York: Norton.

This book contains a comprehensive collection of writings by Black women living in the nineteenth century.

Turner, E. H. (Ed.). (1993). *Jacob Lawrence: The Migration Series*. Washington, D.C.: The Rappahannock Press.

Captivating color illustrations and black-and-white photographs, along with a text, tell the story of the making and meaning of Lawrence's Migration Series.

Walker, A. (1984). *In Search of Our Mothers' Gardens: Womanist Prose*. New York: Harcourt.

An inspiring and brilliant collection of essays by one of the nation's most gifted and honored writers.

Watkins, M. (1994). *On the Real Side: Laughing, Lying, and Signifying*. New York: Simon & Schuster.

A comprehensive and well-researched book on African American humor.

Yee, S. J. (1992). *Black Women Abolitionists: A Study in Activism, 1828–1860.* Knoxville: The University of Tennessee Press.

This informative book examines the activism and work of Black women abolitionists in the nineteenth century.

Books for Students

Adler, D. A. (1993). *A Picture Book of Frederick Douglass.* New York: Holiday House. 1993.

This book introduces young readers to the civil rights leader with a clearly written text and appealing color illustrations. (Primary)

Adler, D. A. (1993). *A Picture Book of Rosa Parks.* New York: Holiday House.

A brief introduction to civil rights leader Rosa Parks enhanced with color illustrations. (Primary)

Adoff, A. & Pinkney, J. (1991). *In for Winter, Out for Spring.* San Diego: Harcourt.

This book chronicles the changing seasons and a young girl's growth. (Primary)

Allison, D. W. (1992). *This Is the Key to the Kingdom.* Boston: Little, Brown.

This story delights young children with its fantastical illustrations and a magical plot about a little girl who enters a mystical kingdom. (Primary)

Ashe-Moutoussamy, J. (1993). *Daddy and Me: A Photo Story of Arthur Ashe and His Daughter, Camera.* New York: Knopf.

This story poignantly examines AIDS by describing the relationship of the late tennis superstar Arthur Ashe and his young daughter. (Primary)

Barrett, M. B. (1994). *Sing to the Stars.* Boston: Little, Brown.

This book captures the attention of readers with beautiful color illustrations and a young boy who learns the value of music. (Primary)

Belton, S. (1993). *From Miss Ida's Porch.* New York: Four Winds Press.

In this story two young protagonists learn about the past through a caring neighbor's storytelling. (Primary)

Bullock, S. (1993). *Free at Last: A History of the Civil Rights Movement and Those Who Died in the Struggle.* New York: Oxford University Press.

This well-written history of the movement is profusely illustrated with excellent teaching photographs.

Bunting, E (1992). *Summer Wheels.* San Diego: Harcourt, 1992.

Every morning Lawrence and Brady borrow bikes from the neighborhood bicycle man, but their usual routine changes when a new boy gets a bike. (Primary)

Doctor, B. A. (1992). *Malcolm X for Beginners*. New York: Writers and Readers Publishers.

Telling illustrations and a powerful text make this book a wonderful introduction to the noted civil rights leader. (Intermediate)

Feelings, T. (1995). *The Middle Passage: White Ships/Black Cargo*. New York: Dial Books.

The moving and touching photographs in this book provide powerful insights into the journey of the captured Africans to the Americas. Contains a personal statement by the author/artist and an introduction by John Henrik Clarke. (All levels)

Gardner, R. & Shortelle, D. (1993). *The Forgotten Players: The Story of Black Baseball in America*. New York: Walker and Company.

This book provides a history of American baseball from an African American perspective. (High School)

Gillerlain, G. (1995). *The Reverend Thomas's False Teeth*. Illustrated by D. Schtzer. Mahwah, N.J.: Bridgewater Books.

Creative story about the Reverend Thomas's dinner at Gracie's house. On his way he looses his teeth in the Chesapeake Bay. Only Gracie is able to retrieve them. (Primary)

Greenberg, K. E. (1992). *Magic Johnson: Champion with a Cause*. Minneapolis: Lerner.

This biography touches readers with its moving history of the HIV-positive basketball star Magic Johnson. (Intermediate)

Greenfield, E. (1991). *Night on Neighborhood Street*. New York: Penguin Books.

Childhood is explored and celebrated in this touching selection of poems. (Primary)

Hamilton, V. (1992). *Drylongso*. San Diego: Harcourt Brace.

Drought plagues a family's farm, but after Drylongso blows in with a dust storm relief soon comes.

Hamilton, V. (1993). *Many Thousand Gone: African Americans from Slavery to Freedom*. New York: Knopf.

With a poignant text, this book traces slavery from its beginnings to the Emancipation Proclamation through several individual profiles. (Intermediate)

Haskins, J. (1993). *The March on Washington*. New York: HarperCollins.

This book describes the historical context of the landmark march.

Hayden, R. C. (1992). *Eleven African American Doctors*. Frederick, Md.: Twenty-First Century Books.

The lives of several African American doctors and their contributions to medicine. (High School). The author has also published, with the same publisher, Nine African American Inventors (1992); and Seven African American Scientists (1992).

Henry, S. & Taitz, E. (1992). *Coretta Scott King: Keeper of the Dream*. Hillside, N.J.: Enslow Publishers, Inc.

A biography of Coretta Scott King that includes information on her childhood and civil rights work in the past and present. (High School)

Hoffman, M. & Binch, C. (1995). *Boundless Grace*. New York: Dial Books

This is the sequel to Amazing Grace *(Dial, 1991). Grace is reunited with her father, of whom she has only dim memories. (Primary)*

Hoobler, D. R. & Hoobler, T. (1995). *The African American Family Album*. New York: Oxford University Press.

The African American experience is described in captivating and involving photographs, documents, and text.

Hopkinson, D. (1993). *Sweet Clara and the Freedom Quilt*. New York: Knopf.

A young girl's resourcefulness and creativity help to lead African American slaves to freedom. (Primary)

Hoyt-Goldsmith, D. (1993). *Celebrating Kwanzaa*. New York: Holiday House.

Through the eyes of a young woman, this book teaches readers about the African American holiday Kwanzaa with informative text and color pictures. (Primary)

Jackson, G. N. (1993). *Elijah McCoy, Inventor*. Cleveland: Modern Curriculum Press.

Young readers are introduced to the African American inventor Elijah McCoy. (Primary)

Johnson, D. (1993). *Now Let Me Fly: The Story of a Slave Family*. New York: Macmillan.

A young African child is kidnapped and sold into slavery in this informative story. (Primary)

Katz, W. L. (Ed.). (1995). *Eyewitness: A Living Documentary of the African-American Contribution to American History* (rev. ed.). New York: Simon & Schuster.

A rich collection of documents of African American history. (High School)

Katz, W. L. & Franklin, P. A. (1993). *Proudly Red and Black: Stories of African and Native Americans*. New York: Atheneum.

Through several biographies, this book tells the often untold stories of Americans of African and Native American ancestry. (Intermediate)

Kranz, R. (1992). *The Biographical Dictionary of Black Americans*. New York: Facts on File.

Names of famous African Americans are arranged alphabetically in this handy reference. (Middle School/High School)

Lyons, M. E. (1992). *Letters from a Slave Girl: The Story of Harriet Jacobs*. New York: Scribner's.

A young girl poignantly reveals the daily life of a slave through her journal. (Intermediate). The author has also published with Scribner's Starting Home: The Story of Horace Pippin, Painter *(1993) and* Stitching Stars: The Story Quilts of Harriet Powers *(1993).*

McKissack, P. & McKissack, F. (1992). *Madam C. J. Walker: Self-Made Millionaire.* Hillside, N.J.: Enslow Publishers.

> *This book examines the life of the first African American woman self-made millionaire. She made her fortune by founding a cosmetics company. (Primary). McKissack & McKissack have written many other excellent books for young children including* Christmas in the Big House, Christmas in the Quarters *(1994; Scholastic);* Red-Tail Angels: The Story of the Tuskegee Airmen of World War II *(1995; Scholastic); and* Rebels against Slavery *(Scholastic, 1996).*

McPherson, J. M. (1991). *Marching toward Freedom. Blacks in the Civil War, 1861–1865.* New York: Facts on File.

> *A powerful and informative history of the role that African Americans played in the Civil War. (High School)*

Medearis, A. S. (1993). *Come This Far to Freedom: A History of African Americans.* New York: Atheneum.

> *A revealing history of Blacks in America that includes an informative text, several biographies, and an extensive timeline. (Intermediate)*

Miller, R. (1992). *Reflections of a Black Cowboy.* Morristown, N.J.: Silver Burdett Press.

> *Children learn about new heroes of the wild West from the author's look at four African American cowboys. (Intermediate)*

Miller, W. (1994). *Zora Hurston and the Chinaberry Tree.* New York: Lee & Low Books.

> *A beautiful story inspired by the life of the famous writer. (Primary)*

Myers, W. D. (1993). *Brown Angels: An Album of Pictures and Verse.* New York: HarperCollins.

> *Filled with adorable photographs and charming poetry, this book celebrates African American children living near the turn of the century. (Primary)*

Parks, R. with Haskins, J. (1992). *Rosa Parks: My Story.* New York: Dial.

> *In this interesting and informative book, Rosa Parks gives her own version of her arrest that triggered the Montgomery Bus boycott.*

Porter, A. P. (1992). *Jump at de Sun: The Story of Zora Neale Hurston.* Minneapolis: Carolrhoda Books.

> *An informative biography of one of America's foremost literary figures. (Intermediate)*

Prather, R. (1992). *Fish and Bones.* New York: HarperCollins.

> *When a community bank is robbed young Bones tries to find the thief. He finds more than he expected. (Intermediate)*

Scheader, C. (1990). *Shirley Chisholm, Teacher and Congresswoman.* Hillside, N.J.: Enslow Publishers.

Students learn about overcoming barriers and triumph through this clearly written biography of former African American Congresswoman Shirley Chisholm. (High School)

Schick, E. (1993). *I Have Another Language: The Language Is Dance*. Louisville, Ky.: American Printing House for the Blind.

Young readers experience the joy in communicating through dance from the protagonist who prepares for her first dance performance. (Primary)

Stolz, M. (1991). *Go Fish*. New York: HarperCollins.

A special relationship between a grandfather and grandson is revealed when the two share a fishing trip. (Primary)

Strickland, D. S. & Strickland, M. R. (1994). *Families: Poems Celebrating the African American Experience*. New York: Wordsong/Boyds Mills Press.

Beautiful poems selected by the famous educator and her son. Captivating illustrations.

Thomas, J. C. (1993). *Brown Honey in Broomwheat Tea*. New York: HarperCollins.

This beautiful collection of poems explores African American culture and family. (Primary)

Thomas, J. C. (1992). *When the Nightingale Sings*. New York: HarperCollins.

This Cindarella-like story focuses on a young African American girl who dreams of leaving her mean caretaker. (Intermediate)

Turner, R. M. (1993). *Faith Ringgold*. Boston: Little, Brown.

This biography looks at an African American woman quilter known for her culturally rich works of art. (High school)

Walker, A. (1991). *Finding the Greenstone*. San Diego: Harcourt Brace.

In Johnny's town everyone keeps green stones that glow brightly when their hearts are filled with goodness and warmth. One day Johnny's cold actions cause him to lose his stone and he finds it only after rediscovering love. (Intermediate)

Woodson, J. (1991). *The Dear One*. New York: Delcorte Press.

A special friendship develops when Feni's pregnant working-class cousin comes to live in her middle-class home. (Intermediate)

EUROPEAN AMERICANS

CONCEPTS AND STRATEGIES

P art III consists of content, concepts, teaching strategies, and materials for teaching about European Americans. Most Americans are of European origin and descent. In 1990, the White population of European ancestry in the United States numbered about 191.5 million people and comprised about 76% of the nation's population. However, the percentage of the nation's population of European ancestry had declined significantly since 1900, when it comprised 87.7% of the population. Demographers predict that the percentage of European Americans in the U.S. population will continue to decline in future years. It is predicted that they will make up about 66% of the general population by the turn of the century and 54.5% of the school-age population by 2020.

White Americans of European descent are increasing at a slower rate than are other ancestry groups. Hispanic Americans increased by about 50% between 1980 and 1990, but the White population increased by about only 2%. This difference resulted primarily because a disproportionate number of Whites were middle class (and therefore have fewer children) and because

Europeans comprised only 11% of the immigrants to the United States between 1981 and 1986. Even though they are becoming a smaller percentage of the nation's population, Americans of European origin and descent still comprise the overwhelming majority of the nation's population and have the most influence on its culture, values, and ethos. A study of the sojourn of European immigrants across the Atlantic and of their journey in America is essential to a sound multicultural curriculum.

CHAPTER 8

EUROPEAN ETHNIC GROUPS

CONCEPTS, STRATEGIES, AND MATERIALS

The poorest, the most miserable came here because they had no future over there. To them, the streets of America were paved in gold. They had what the Finns called kuum, *the American fever.*

Andy Johnson, an immigrant
From Studs Terkel, *American Dreams: Lost and Found*

Between 1820 and 1992, about 59,795,158 legal immigrants entered the United States. Most of them (37,400,991, or about 63%) were Europeans who belonged to many different religious, political, and cultural groups (U.S. Department of Justice, 1993). The making of one society from so many different ethnic and nationality groups is one of the most amazing chapters in human history. Yet, social scientists, and therefore classroom teachers, have largely ignored the role of ethnicity in U.S. history and modern society. U.S. social scientists have been preoccupied with theories of assimilation and the melting pot concept. Nevertheless, scholars in the United States have given more attention to ethnicity as a variable in American life since the ethnic protest movements in the 1960s. However, a significant gap exists between scholarship and the school curriculum. The European ethnic experience is infrequently taught in the schools.

European ethnic groups should be included in a sound multicultural curriculum because the processes of acculturation and assimilation, which they have experienced and which many European ethnic groups are still experiencing, must be considered when students formulate concepts and generalizations about ethnicity and race in U.S. society. European Americans, like other Americans, often experienced ethnic rage, changed their names, and denied their ethnic heritages to gain social and economic mobility and to realize the American dream.

It is also important for students to study European ethnic groups because individuals of European origin comprise the bulk of the nation's population (about 73.6% in 1990) and Europeans continue to make up a significant proportion of the immigrants to the United States. Between 1981 and 1992, more than ten million (10,139,300) immigrants entered the United States. Of these, about 9.5% (968,200) were Europeans. Even though 9.5% is a significant drop in the percentage of European immigrants that settled in the United States in the decades prior to 1968, the number of European immigrants settling in the United States is still sizable.

The European immigrants who have entered the United States since 1981 are diverse in national origins and cultures. Table 8-1 shows the number of European immigrants that entered the United States from selected nations between 1989 and 1992. As this table indicates, a large number of immigrants came from the Soviet Union and Poland. The challenge to Communism that Poland experienced in the late 1980s and in 1990 and the second revolution that Russia experienced in 1990—in which the old political order crumbled— may have been factors that pushed immigrants from Poland and the various nations within the former Soviet Union (Bateman & Egan, 1993). Significant numbers of immigrants also came from the United Kingdom, Ireland, Germany, and Portugal between 1989 and 1992.

Table 8-2 shows the number of immigrants that entered the United States between 1981 and 1992 from three other predominantly White nations: Can-

Table 8-1   EUROPEAN IMMIGRANTS TO THE UNITED STATES FROM SELECTED NATIONS: 1989–1992

Country of Birth	Number
Soviet Union*	43,614
Poland	25,504
United Kingdom	19,973
Ireland	12,226
Germany	9,888
Portugal	2,748

*The 1992 figure includes immigration from each of the new republics.
SOURCE: U.S. Department of Justice (1993, October). *1992 Statistical Yearbook of the Immigration and Naturalization Service*. Washington, D.C.: U.S. Government Printing Office, p. 30.

Table 8-2 EUROPEAN IMMIGRANTS FROM CANADA, AUSTRALIA, AND NEW ZEALAND, 1981–1992

Country of Birth	Number
Canada	147,900
Australia	17,800
New Zealand	7,769*

*This figure is for 1982 to 1992.
SOURCE: U.S. Department of Justice (1993, October). *1992 Statistical Yearbook of the Immigration and Naturalization Service.* Washington, D.C.: U.S. Government Printing Office, p. 30; and U.S. Bureau of the Census (1994), *Statistical Abstract of the United States* (114th ed.). Washington, D.C.: U.S. Government Printing Office.

ada, Australia, and New Zealand. During these years, the United Kingdom and Canada were the sources of the largest numbers of White immigrants that entered the United States, 176,000 and 147,900 respectively (U.S. Bureau of the Census, 1994). Table 8-3 shows the percentage distribution of European (non-Hispanic) ancestry groups with a population of one million or more in 1990.

SPANIARDS IN THE AMERICAS

Spain was the first European nation to establish permanent settlements in the Americas. Spanish ships arrived in the Americas in 1492 under the leadership of Christopher Columbus. In 1496, Columbus and his brother Bartholomew founded the city of Santo Domingo on the island of Hispaniola. Santo Domingo was the first permanent continuing European settlement in the Americas. A number of Spanish explorers, including Coronado, Cortez, Cabeza de Vaca, and Ponce de Leon, followed Columbus. These and other Spaniards explored and settled in the Americas. In 1526, San Miguel de Gualdape, a Spanish colony in South Carolina, was established by Lucas Vasquez de Ayllon. Another Spaniard named Pedro Menendez de Aviles founded the oldest permanent city in the United States, St. Augustine, Florida, in 1565. These early Spaniards influenced the language, religion, and other cultural aspects of the Americas.

Even though their influence in the Americas was great, few Spaniards came to the Americas. It has been estimated that no more than 300,000 Spaniards came to the Americas during the entire three colonial centuries. Many of these people stayed only a short time. Many of the Spaniards who remained in

Table 8-3 PERCENT DISTRIBUTION OF EUROPEAN (NON-HISPANIC) ANCESTRY GROUPS WITH ONE MILLION OR MORE (1990)

Region	Total (1,000)	Percentage distribution				
		Total	Northeast	Midwest	South	West
German	57 947	100.0	17.1	38.8	25.2	18.8
Irish	38 736	100.0	24.3	24.9	33.4	17.4
English	32 652	100.0	18.0	22.3	34.8	24.8
Italian	14 665	100.0	51.1	16.6	16.9	15.4
French[1]	10 321	100.0	25.6	25.6	28.7	20.1
Polish	9 366	100.0	37.4	37.0	14.5	11.1
Dutch	6 227	100.0	16.4	34.1	18.6	20.9
Scotch-Irish	5 618	100.0	13.7	19.2	46.6	20.5
Scottish	5 394	100.0	20.2	21.0	32.8	26.0
Swedish	4 681	100.0	14.3	39.7	14.3	31.6
Norwegian	3 869	100.0	6.2	51.7	9.5	32.5
Russian[2]	2 953	100.0	43.8	16.0	18.5	21.7
Welsh	2 034	100.0	22.0	24.2	26.8	27.0
Slovak	1 883	100.0	40.3	34.4	14.5	10.8
Danish	1 635	100.0	8.9	34.0	11.9	45.2
Hungarian	1 582	100.0	35.7	31.9	16.5	15.9
Czech	1 296	100.0	10.0	51.8	22.5	15.8
Portuguese	1 153	100.0	48.9	2.6	7.9	40.6
British	1 119	100.0	16.8	17.5	39.3	26.3
Greek	1 110	100.0	37.2	23.0	21.1	18.6
Swiss	1 045	100.0	16.3	36.2	17.4	30.1

Note: Includes persons who reported two ancestry groups. Persons who reported a second ancestry group may be included in more than one category.
[1]Excludes French Basque.
[2]Includes persons who reported as "Russian," "Cossack," "Black Russian," "Red Russian," "Rossiya," and "Muscovite."
SOURCE: U.S. Bureau of the Census (1992). *1990 Census of Population, Supplementary Reports, Detailed Ancestry Groups for States, 1990 CP-S-1-2.* Washington, D.C.: U.S. Government Printing Office, p. (Abstract) III-4.

America fathered children with Indian women. These unions produced a new ethnic group in the Americas, the *mestizos* (see chapter 10 on Mexican Americans). Today, the number of Spanish-born Americans is still small. Between 1981 and 1992, about 19,200 people immigrated to the United States from Spain (U.S. Bureau of the Census, 1994).

EUROPEAN ETHNIC GROUPS: HISTORICAL PERSPECTIVES

Important Dates	
1565	Pedro Menéndez Avilés founded St. Augustine, Florida, on the site of an Indian village.
1607	English immigrants established their first permanent American colony at Jamestown, Virginia.
1620	The Pilgrims came to America from England on the *Mayflower* and established a settlement at Plymouth, Massachusetts.
1623	The Dutch West India Company settled New Netherland as a trading post.
1683	The first German immigrants to North America settled in Pennsylvania.
1718	The Scots-Irish began immigrating to the American colonies in large numbers.
1729	The Pennsylvania Colony increased the head taxes charged to entering immigrants to discourage further foreign settlement.
1798	A Federalist-dominated Congress enacted the Alien and Sedition Acts to crush the Republican party and harass aliens.
1803	The British Passenger Act was enacted to discourage immigration.
1825	Great Britain repealed laws that prohibited immigration. The first group of Norwegian immigrants arrived in the United States.
1845–49	A series of potato blights in Ireland caused thousands of its citizens to immigrate to the United States.
1855	The antiforeign Know-Nothing movement reached its zenith and had a number of political successes in the 1855 elections. The movement rapidly declined after 1855. Castle Garden immigrant depot opened in New York.
1863	The Irish working-classes expressed discontent with the Civil War and hostility toward urban Blacks in the New York draft riots, which lasted for four days.

Important Dates

1882	A congressional immigration act established a head tax of 50¢ and excluded lunatics, convicts, idiots, and people likely to become public charges.
1883–85	An economic depression escalated nativistic feelings in the United States.
1885	The Foran Act outlawed the immigration of contract laborers.
1886	The Haymarket Affair in Chicago significantly increased fear of foreign "radicals" and stimulated the growth of nativistic sentiments in the United States. The Statue of Liberty was dedicated as nativism soared in the United States.
1891	Eleven Italian Americans were lynched in New Orleans during the height of American nativism after being accused of murdering a police superintendent.
1892	Ellis Island opened and replaced Castle Garden as the main port of entry for European immigrants.
1894	The Immigration Restriction League was organized in Boston by intellectuals to promote the passage of a bill that would require entering immigrants to pass a literacy test. The passage of the bill was urged to restrict immigration from southern and eastern Europe.
1899	William Z. Ripley *The Races of Europe* was published. Ripley divided European people into three major racial groups, thus giving the nativists intellectual justifications for their movement.
1901–10	Almost 9 million immigrants entered the United States, most of whom came from southern and eastern Europe. This mass immigration intensified significantly the activities of nativistic groups.
1907	A congressional act extended the classes of immigrants excluded from the United States. Victims of tuberculosis and individuals who had committed certain kinds of crimes were added to the list.
1911	The Dillingham Commission, formed in 1907, issued its forty-one volume report in which it strongly recommended a literacy test for entering immigrants and made a marked distinction between the "old" and "new" immigrants.

**Important
Dates**

1916	Madison Grant, a well-known naturalist, published *The Passing of the Great Race in America*. This popular book gave the nativists more ammunition.
1916–19	The movement to Americanize aliens was widespread and intense.
1917	A comprehensive immigration bill was enacted that established the literacy test for entering immigrants, added to the classes of those excluded, and increased the head tax from $4 to $8. This act was a major victory for the nativists.
1919–20	During the height of antiradical attitudes in America, hundreds of alien radicals were captured and deported in a movement led by A. Mitchell Palmer.
1921	The Johnson Act signaled a turning point in American history. It set up a nationality quota system and imposed the first numerical limits on European immigration to the United States.
1924	The Johnson-Reed Act established extreme quotas on immigration and blatantly discriminated against southern and eastern European and non-White nations.
1927	Two Italian radicals, Nicola Sacco and Bartolomeo Vanzetti, were executed during a period of extreme antiradical sentiment in America. Their execution set off a wave of reactions throughout the Western world.
1952	The McCarran-Walter Act, which allegedly removed radical barriers to immigration, essentially continued the policy established in 1924 and was in some ways more restrictive.
1954	The closing of Ellis Island marked the end of mass European immigration to the United States.
1965	A new immigration act, which became effective in 1968, abolished the national origins quota system and liberalized significantly U.S. immigration policy.
1984	Presidential and vice-presidential candidates of both major political parties appeared at the National Italian American Foundation dinner, indicating the continued importance of ethnicity to U.S. politicians.
1986	The Centennial of the Statue of Liberty was commemorated.

Important Dates	
1990	The Immigration Act of 1990 made some significant changes in immigration law. It set immigration to 675,000 annually (beginning in 1995) to consist of these categories: 480,000 family-sponsored; 140,000 employment-based; and 55,000 "diversity immigrants." Ellis Island National Immigration Museum opened to honor the nation's immigrants.
1991	After disorder and fighting, the Communist USSR fell, leaving its former republics to create democracy in the chaotic aftermath.

MORE EUROPEANS COME TO AMERICA

Europeans began settling in America in significant numbers in the 1600s. The economic, social, and political conditions existing in Europe caused many of its inhabitants to cross the Atlantic searching for a new home. The main causes of the waves of immigrations were the drastic economic and social changes occurring in Europe. Serfdom had been the basis of European society for centuries. Most people were peasants who earned their living by farming. Throughout Europe, the old relationships between peasants and the land were changed and the peasants suffered severely. The land owned by the village was divided into individual plots. With each succeeding generation, the land was further divided. Eventually, the plots of land became so small that younger sons were unable to make a living. Some peasants suffered when land holdings were consolidated by the landlords.

The peasants became landless or feared the loss of land and their place in the social order. They were attached to the land. Without it, they were unable to make a living or maintain a sense of being. The tremendous population growth Europe experienced in the seventeenth and eighteenth centuries increased the peasants' problems. Famine and crop failures also caused many people to immigrate.

The early settlers were a diverse group, although most of them were peasants. Many were unable to pay for their passage and became indentured servants in order to make the journey. However, merchants, artisans, professionals, and laborers comprised a small but significant part of the immigrants during the entire colonial period. Vagrants and convicts, who were unwanted by European nations, were also among the first settlers.

Although the bulk of the first European immigrants came to North America primarily for economic reasons, some came for religious and political reasons. Most European nations had established churches associated with the state. Religious dissenters who wanted to practice other religions sometimes immigrated to America. The Separatists who arrived in the colonies in 1620 on the Mayflower were seeking a place where they could freely practice their religion. The Jewish immigrants who settled in North America during the colonial period also were seeking religious and political freedom.

Once the European immigrations were under way, the movement itself produced forces that stimulated it. The letters settlers sent back to friends and relatives in Europe extolling the opportunities in America were a cogent factor that pulled more Europeans to America (Kamphoefner, Helbich, & Sommer, 1991). Guidebooks about wages and living conditions in America were distributed in Europe by travel and shipping agents. These books helped to motivate thousands of Europeans to immigrate.

The rise of the industrial revolution and scientific farming in the nineteenth century also stimulated European immigration to America. The development of industry put many artisans out of work. Modern farming methods displaced many farmers. These displaced workers tried to solve their problems by immigrating to America. Ship companies eager to get passengers and U.S. states and railroad companies that wanted to settle sparsely populated areas in the nation recruited European immigrants. European governments either discouraged or legally prohibited immigration in the 1600s and 1700s. However, these obstacles to immigration were largely removed in the nineteenth century. This, too, encouraged Europeans to immigrate. The development of more efficient and inexpensive ocean transportation also stimulated European immigration in the nineteenth century.

Although all of these factors contributed to European immigration to America, it was the search for a chance to earn a better living that caused most European immigrants to come to the United States. The tide of immigration rose and fell with economic conditions in the United States. When times were good, the immigrants came in great numbers. When depression set in, immigration dropped significantly. During some brief periods, the number of immigrants returning to Europe actually exceeded the number that arrived. Historians estimate that about one-third of the immigrants returned to Europe (Vecoli & Sinke, 1991). The key role that economic factors played in the European immigrations to North America make them similar to other mass movements to the United States from such nations as Canada, Mexico, the Philippines, China, and Japan.

Although some religious and political dissenters came to America so that they could freely practice their beliefs, this aspect of European immigration has been greatly exaggerated and oversimplified in textbooks and in the popular mind. Most came mainly for economic reasons. Most who were religious and political dissenters also hoped to improve their economic lot. The widespread belief that most of the first European settlers in America loved freedom and liberty has also been grossly exaggerated. The Puritans and other religious dissenters who settled in North America were not liberty-loving people but were doctrinaire groups who believed that their religions were the only true and valid ones. They were as intolerant of religious differences as those who protected the official churches in Europe (Jones, 1960). Their aim was to find a place where they could practice *their* religions freely and not to build a nation in which all religions would be tolerated.

Religious freedom and toleration developed in North America not because of the goals and wishes of the early colonists, but because the motley collection of religious groups that came to America competed for and won the right to practice their beliefs. The same is true about American democracy and the colonists. The colonists were Europeans in mind and spirit. They tried hard to establish European institutions and beliefs on American soil. They were not liberty-loving citizens who had a deep belief in democracy. Quite the contrary was true. They were the products of a hierarchical and class-structured society and had internalized these beliefs (Jones, 1992). That they failed to establish a highly stratified society in America was not because they did not try. Rather, a form of democracy emerged in the United States in part because the social and economic conditions that developed in North America made it impossible to establish a new Europe and fostered the development of a more open society. The ideas of the Enlightenment—which found a fertile ground in the British colonies—combined with the unique social, economic, and political conditions in the United States to produce American democracy.

The Passage to America

Especially in the seventeenth century, the journey from the peasants' European homes to the American port cities was hard and hazardous (Handlin, 1951). The peasants made the decision to come to America only after much thought. Often, only the threat of starvation or the loss of status compelled them to attempt the difficult journey. The trip was also expensive, especially during the first immigrations. Thus, even after they made the decision to come to America, they often had to save money for a long time before they could begin the trip.

The immigrants' first step in the journey to America was taking a long trip, usually by foot, to a European city that had a seaport from which ships sailed to America. Not everyone who started out was able to complete this stage of the journey. Many of those who made it to the European port cities were tired and battered. Once they arrived in the port city, the peasants had to wait for weeks and sometimes months before the ship departed for America. The ship captains waited until the ships were full of goods and human cargo before they sailed for North America because the fuller ship was more profitable. During the long wait, the peasants became restless and tired. Some were not able to board the ship when it was finally ready to depart. As each day went by during the long wait for the American departure, the food the peasants had stored for the journey steadily dwindled. Renting a room at the European port city also took a large part of the meager funds they had saved for the trip.

Finally, the day came when the ship headed for America. The peasants' joy at the departure was to be short-lived. The conditions on the ships were depressing and harsh. To maximize his profits, the ship captain packed the people like sardines. Each family was assigned an extremely small space on the ship. The family spent most of its time in these dark, crowded compartments. Diseases were rampant on the vessels and took many lives. Dysentery, cholera, yellow fever, and smallpox were some of the more common ship diseases. The journey was long, often more than a month. Many families barely had enough food to last throughout the journey. Eventually, European nations passed laws requiring shipowners to provide a certain amount of food for the trip. However, ship captains who wanted to profit thought of many ingenious ways to evade these weakly enforced laws.

The Atlantic journey, especially before the time of the steamship, was a tremendous shock to the European immigrants. The family disruption that continued when they reached America began on the ship. Almost wholly dependent on the ship's crew, the father was unable to exercise his traditional role as leader and master of the family. The mother could not function in her traditional role, either. When food was getting scarce, she had to try to keep the family fed. These transatlantic conditions severely strained family relationships.

The immigrants who survived the journey eventually landed at an American port city. The landing was eagerly awaited and celebrated. However, the immigrants still had some hurdles to overcome. They had to be checked and questioned by American immigration officials before they could travel freely in America. Wrong answers to questions or poor health could mean further questioning by officials and boards, a stay in a hospital, or even a trip back to Europe. In the earliest years, the inspection focused on physical health and ability to work. Gradually, questions related to the immigrant's morals and political beliefs were added. In 1917, Congress enacted a law requiring immigrants to demonstrate literacy in some language before they could enter the United States.

Many of the immigrants were broken, both financially and physically, when they arrived at American seaport cities. Some were the sole survivors in their families. Broken and lonely, some found asylum in poorhouses. Many immigrants who had planned to settle elsewhere never left the port cities in which their vessels landed. Thousands who had planned to settle elsewhere stayed in cities like Milwaukee, Chicago, and St. Louis. Some of the first settlers found work on construction projects in cities. Later, railroad construction provided work for immigrants. When the industrial revolution began, factory work became available. In all these lines of work, the immigrants were paid low wages and were outrageously exploited by their employers. Many of the immigrants settled in urban areas. However, a large percentage of the nineteenth-century immigrants settled on farms and became successful farmers. Many Germans, Scandinavians, Dutch, and Belgians settled in farm areas in the Midwest and successfully farmed (Vecoli, 1994).

The Urban Ghetto

Most European immigrants settled in cities, like most migrants from rural areas today. They had neither the means nor the desire to settle in rural areas. Like their modern counterparts, the new immigrants settled in blighted and dilapidated areas that became ethnic ghettos. Irishtowns, Germantowns, and Little Italys developed in most of the cities in the Northeast and Midwest. Ethnic organizations, like schools, newspapers, and churches, emerged within these communities. The immigrants, especially the more recent arrivals, usually lived in rundown housing near the business and manufacturing districts that had been vacated by suburban-bound, upwardly mobile residents when the manufacturing district sprawled outward into their communities.

When the upwardly mobile left the inner city, their old mansions were converted into multiple-family dwellings for the immigrants. The multiple-dwelling units became a source of quick profit for the owners. Little was done to make these dwellings comfortable. Profit, not comfort, was what the slum landlord sought. When these neighborhoods were deserted by the old residents, they were also forsaken by the street cleaners and sanitation crews. The smells from the garbage were pungent. The immigrants' habit of throwing garbage out of the window and keeping animals in their backyards made these communities even more unpleasant. High-rise apartments went up in some of the ethnic communities. Most of these buildings were crowded and uncomfortable. Many did not have interior plumbing or central heating. Some of the earliest ones had no toilets. There were only two toilets on each floor in some later apartment buildings. To help pay the rent, some families took in lodgers.

The immigrants looked forward to the day when their income would permit them to leave the ghetto and join the exodus to the suburbs. For most ethnic groups, this day eventually came. However, as one ethnic group vacated the ghetto, another group replaced it. In New York City, Italians took over old

Irish neighborhoods. Jews from Russia and Poland occupied districts where the Germans had lived. After World War II, many of the urban areas that had been occupied by European ethnic groups received a large number of African Americans from the South, Mexican Americans from the Southwest, and migrants from Puerto Rico.

Immigrant Political Action

The participation of the immigrants in the urban political machines, though significant, was not the total of their importance in the U.S. political process. Early in U.S. political history, when the number of immigrants in U.S. cities became substantial, and their votes had the power to sway or determine election outcomes, politicians became increasingly sensitive to the concerns and wishes of immigrant groups. Even politicians like Theodore Roosevelt and Woodrow Wilson, who felt rather negatively about the "new" immigrants, were forced on occasion to say positive things about them publicly. However, it was difficult for President Wilson to convince the southern and eastern European immigrants that he had had a change of heart.

Nevertheless, the major political parties began to vie aggressively for immigrant support and to include references to immigrants in their political platforms that reflected the specialized concerns of ethnic groups in the United States. These groups had many special concerns and aspirations, usually related to U.S. foreign policy and the ways in which the United States was treating their "Mother" countries. Although many European immigrants did not have much of a sense of nationality when they arrived in the United States, intense nationalist movements developed among them. According to Jones (1960), "There was a tendency among Irish political refugees as well as German Forty-eighters, to look upon themselves as exiles and to use the United States simply as a base for promoting European causes.... [These movements] afforded a means of group identification and self-assertion" (pp. 141–142).

Although the actions of these political refugees were probably extreme, most European immigrant groups did continue to see themselves as Europeans. The immigrants formed many groups to campaign aggressively for European causes and to sway U.S. foreign policy. In World War I, German Americans criticized Wilson's actions toward Germany and the Irish Americans became bitter because of Wilson's pro-British actions. The Irish voted strongly against Wilson in the subsequent election. The militant actions by some European American groups, especially German Americans, caused many Americans to question seriously their loyalties to the United States. However, even though some of these movements were radical and aggressively nationalistic, the most radical ones were unable to attract mass support because of the deep conservatism of most immigrants.

Anglo-Saxon Cultural Dominance

The early European settlements were highly ethnically mixed. English, Scots-Irish, Germans, French Huguenots, Africans, and Jews were among the earlier colonists. Writes Bailey (1961), "The population of the thirteen colonies, though basically Anglo-Saxon, was perhaps the most mixed that could be found anywhere in the world. Counting [Africans], nearly 40% was of non-English origin, although New England boasted more native born and persons of English blood than the other sections. Of the 56 signers of the Declaration of Independence in 1776, 18 were non-English, and 8 of these had been born outside the colonies" (p. 67).

Ethnic conflict also developed early in the colonies. The English were dominant during the first years of colonial settlement. Consequently, they shaped the basic social and political institutions of Colonial America. The English cultural dominance of the colonies was challenged by the subsequent groups, but it remained the dominant social and political force in American life. Because of English political and cultural dominance, Anglo-Saxon culture became the ideal by which all subsequent ethnic groups were judged and by which levels of assimilation and acculturation were judged. To become *acculturated* became synonymous with acquiring Anglo-Saxon Protestant lifestyles, values, and language. The English language was dominant in almost every American colony by 1775.

Early in American colonial life, non-English groups began to be evaluated negatively. The New England colonies, which were predominantly English, took steps to bar the settlements of Roman Catholics. The French Huguenots became the focal point of English hostility. Later, the Scots-Irish and the German immigrants were the victims of English antagonism. An English mob prevented a group of Irish immigrants from landing in Boston in 1729. Several years later, another mob destroyed a new Scots-Irish Presbyterian church in Worcester, Mass. The attitude that English culture and institutions were superior to all others profoundly shaped American life and was extremely significant in the nativistic movements that emerged after the Civil War. However, when the southern and eastern European immigrants began their mass exodus to the United States in the late 1800s, public opinion leaders extended the supposedly superior traits of the English to all northern and western European "races." (In the nineteenth century, Europeans were considered to belong to several races, such as the Teutonic, the Alpine, and the Mediterranean. The races of northern and western Europe were considered superior to the races in southern, central, and eastern Europe.) This extension was necessary to enable the old immigrants to band together to condemn the new immigrants. However, race assumed a new meaning when the southern and eastern European groups attained acceptable levels of assimilation in the twentieth century. All White races became one. Racial hostilities could now focus on non-White ethnic groups, such as African Americans, Asian Americans, Mexican Americans, and American Indians. Whites of southern and eastern European descent joined former adverse White ethnic groups to exclude people of color from full participation in U.S. life.

THE SOUTHERN AND EASTERN EUROPEAN IMMIGRANTS

Before 1892, most European immigrants who came to America were from northern and western European nations, such as England, Germany, France, and Scandinavia. Northern and western Europeans exceeded the number of immigrants from other parts of Europe up to the last decades of the nineteenth century. However, by 1896, a major change had taken place in the source of European immigrants to the United States. Most European immigrants to America now came from southern, eastern, and central Europe. Austria-Hungary, Italy, and Russia sent the largest number of new immigrants. However, substantial numbers also came from such countries as Greece, Romania, Bulgaria, and Finland. Fifteen million European immigrants arrived in the United States between 1890 and 1914. Most of them came from southern and eastern Europe.

When immigrants from southern and eastern Europe began coming to the United States in significant numbers, a number of arguments evolved that were designed to distinguish them from immigrants who had come earlier from the northern and western parts of Europe. The southern and eastern immigrants became known as the "new" immigrants; the earlier immigrants were referred to as the "old" immigrants. The mass media, intellectuals, and politicians perpetuated the myth that the new immigrants were inferior to the older ones, that they caused major problems in the cities, and that steamship companies and U.S. industries eager for unskilled labor were the main causes of the new traffic. The Dillingham Commission, which was formed to investigate immigration in 1907, concluded that there was a fundamental difference in both the character and the causes of the new and old immigrations.

Repetition of this myth became evidence of its validity. It was eagerly embraced by writers, historians, and policymakers and significantly influenced the racist immigration legislation enacted in the 1920s. The nativistic movements reached their zenith in the 1920s and chose the southern and eastern European immigrants as their chief targets. Only the Asian immigrants in California were more harshly criticized. The distinctions made between the old and the new immigrants were artificial and based on inaccurate information and false assumptions. The southern and eastern European immigrants came to the United States for the same reasons that the earlier immigrants had come: to improve their economic conditions and to seek religious and political freedom. Steamship lines and U.S. industries played no greater role in stimulating immigration from southern and eastern Europe than they had played in stimulating immigration from other parts of Europe. In both cases, their influence was rather meager and has been grossly exaggerated.

The types of new immigrants who came from southern and eastern Europe, like the older immigrants, were highly diverse. Some southern and eastern Europeans came to the United States for temporary work, not because of something unique about them, but because the new steamship lines had so greatly reduced the length of the Atlantic trip that it was practical and possible to come to the United States for seasonal work.

Southern and eastern European immigrants were judged as being innately inferior to older Americans partly because they started coming to the United States when the notion that the United States should be an asylum for the oppressed peoples of Europe was beginning to wane. When the Statue of Liberty was dedicated in New York City in 1886, many Americans had lost faith in the poetic words penned by Emma Lazarus about Europe's "huddled masses." They had also begun to question the melting pot theory and to raise serious questions about whether Europeans could be as readily assimilated as they had originally believed. The doubts about the new immigrants were not caused by their inability to be assimilated, but by the conditions and conceptions of foreigners emerging within American life. Thus, the rush of southern and eastern European immigrants to the United States was poorly timed. The internal conditions in the United States were giving birth to distinctly antiforeign attitudes. A scapegoat was needed to blame for urban blight, political corruption in the cities, and economic recession. The new immigrants were vulnerable and convenient targets. Consequently, they were judged intellectually and culturally inferior to the old immigrants and declared unassimilable. That they were an inferior "race" became widely accepted both in the intellectual community and in the popular mind.

Nativistic Movements

As early as 1727, nativistic feelings toward the Germans in Pennsylvania ran high. (*Nativism* was a movement designed to restrict immigration to America and to protect the interests of the native-born. It was an extreme form of nationalism and ethnocentrism.) To discourage further foreign settlement in the colony, Pennsylvania passed a statute in 1729 increasing the head tax on foreigners, allegedly to prevent persons likely to become public charges from entering the colony. Other antiforeign legislation emerged in the eighteenth century. In 1798, Congress—dominated by the Federalists—passed the Alien and Sedition Acts to crush the Republican party by destroying its large base of immigrant support. These acts were also designed to silence criticism of the Federalists and to harass European immigrants. The Alien and Sedition Acts lengthened the time required to become a U.S. citizen from five to fourteen years and gave the president almost unlimited control over the behavior of immigrants. They virtually nullified the freedoms of speech and the press.

Nativistic sentiments continued to ebb and flow during the eighteenth and nineteenth centuries, although their most violent expressions did not arise until the late nineteenth and early twentieth centuries (Bennett, 1988). Nativism reached its zenith in the 1920s, culminating with the passage of the Johnson-Reed Act in 1924. The Know-Nothing movement, which emerged in the 1840s and reached its climax in 1855, was one of the most successful nativistic movements in the nineteenth century. The various secret organizations constituting this movement, such as the Order of United Americans and the Order of the Star-Spangled Banner, were strongly anti-Catholic and agitated for an extension of the period required for an immigrant to become a U.S. citizen and for the election of only "Americans" to political office. The movement, which became less secretive in 1855 and openly called itself the American Party, enjoyed tremendous political successes in a number of states in the 1855 elections. However, the Know-Nothing movement died as quickly as it had emerged. Conflict over slavery within the American Party severely strained and weakened it. Nativistic sentiments in the United States in the 1850s were not strong enough to sustain the Know-Nothing movement.

By the late 1800s, anti-Chinese agitation on the West Coast was virulent, and race ideologies emerged to justify it (Takaki, 1993). The concept of the inferiority and superiority of various races became rampant in the West. In 1882, Congress passed the Chinese Exclusion Act, the first immigration bill specifically designed to exclude a particular race. Although many Americans viewed the case of the Chinese as separate from European immigration, the anti-Chinese act gave impetus to antiforeign attitudes throughout U.S. society. Three months after the anti-Chinese bill was passed, Congress enacted a bill further restricting the classes of Europeans who could enter the United States. Convicts, idiots, and lunatics, as well as those who might become public charges, were excluded.

Nativism grew more and more intense as the fear soared of a Catholic takeover of the federal government and of foreign radicals. The big jump in the number of southern and eastern European immigrants entering the United States in the 1900s added fuel to the fire. Cries of "100% Americanism" and "America for Americans" became widespread. Agitations for antiforeign legislation became intense, especially legislation that would exclude foreign "radicals" and require immigrants to pass a literacy test.

Congress, responding to pressure in 1885, passed the Foran Act, which prohibited the importation of contract labor from Europe. Violence also erupted during these turbulent times. Italians and Jews were frequently the victims of violent and outrageous acts. Eleven Italians were murdered in a mass lynching in New Orleans in 1891, when they were accused of killing a police superintendent. Riots directed at Jews in Chicago increased public paranoia about foreign "radicals." Congress further extended the classes of immigrants excluded from the United States in 1907. Imbeciles and victims of tuberculosis were now added to the list.

Nativistic movements, which were directed against most Irish Catholics and German radicals in the 1850s, began to focus increasingly on southern and eastern European immigrants, as masses of them arrived in U.S. cities. The intellectual community legitimized the racist myths about the innate inferiority of southern and eastern Europeans (Tucker, 1994). William Z. Ripley was one of the leading intellectual nativists. His book, *The Races of Europe*, published in 1899, divided Whites into three major races: the Teutonic, the Northern blondes; the Alpine, the central race of stocky roundheads; and the Mediterranean, dark and slender longheads (Higham, 1972). The Teutonic was the superior race. Ripley warned against a racial mixture that would pollute the superior race with southern and eastern European racial groups.

Madison Grant (1916), a well-known naturalist, also argued for racial purity in his popular book, *The Passing of the Great Race in America*, published in 1916. Ripley and Grant, as well as other intellectuals and writers in the early twentieth century, provided the nativists with the scientific and intellectual justifications for their movements and issued a ringing plea for restrictive legislation (Higham, 1972; Smedley, 1993). As in other periods of mass hysteria in America, social and physical scientists justified and legitimized prevailing social attitudes and myths (Tucker, 1994).

When the twentieth century opened, nativist sentiments and attitudes had gained tremendous momentum in U.S. life. They did not subside until they culminated in the extreme restrictive legislation enacted in the 1920s. The Dillingham Commission, which issued its report in 1911, noted that the new European immigrants were essentially different from the old and strongly recommended the passage of a bill that would require immigrants to pass a literacy test. Agitation for a literacy test bill became intense, but the advocates of the bill faced repeated opposition in Congress and from President Wilson. As the United States prepared to enter World War I, nativism—directed especially at German Americans—became intense. Patriotic groups demanded that all aspects of German culture, including music and the names of streets and schools, be eradicated in the United States. Although most German Americans were loyal citizens during this period, they were often the victims of harassment. However, the abuses they endured were less severe than those suffered by Japanese Americans during World War II (see chapter 13).

Just before the United States entered World War I, the literacy bill advocates finally mustered enough congressional votes to override a second Wilson veto, and the literacy bill was passed on February 5, 1917. Adult immigrants now had to be able to read a passage in some language before they could enter the United States. The bill was comprehensive. It codified existing legislation and added vagrants, chronic alcoholics, and psychopaths to the list of excluded aliens. The head tax was increased from $4 to $8 (Higham, 1972). Although nativists celebrated their victory, they began immediately to plan strategies to restrict further immigration to the United States.

Campaigns to "Americanize" aliens already in the United States became a national passion during World War I. When the war ended, Congress was pressured again to enact restrictive legislation. The law requiring immigrants to pass a literacy test did not halt immigration as the nativists had thought. In fact, it reduced it very little. Consequently, nativists pushed for a quota system to restrict immigration. Antiforeign groups and organizations experienced tremendous growth in memberships. The Ku Klux Klan grew enormously in the South and Midwest. It had more than 2 1/2 million members by 1923. The phenomenal growth of the Klan was symptomatic of pervasive antiforeign attitudes in U.S. life.

Eventually, the nativistic forces gained congressional victories. The Johnson Act, enacted in 1921, marked a turning point in the history of American immigration. The Johnson Act established a nationality quota system and imposed the first numerical limits on immigration from European nations. The quota system was based on the various nationality groups in the United States. The most important immigration bill of this period was enacted in 1924—the Johnson-Reed Act. The quotas this act set were severe and blatantly discriminated against southern and eastern European and non-White nations. It stopped Asian immigration completely. After 1927, the act allowed only 150,000 Europeans to enter the United States each year, and they were "parceled out in ratio to the distribution of national origins in the White population of the United States in 1920." Because Europeans from the North and West represented the largest percentages of Whites in the United States in 1920, the authors of the Johnson-Reed Act had thought of an ingenious way to limit severely the number of immigrants from southern and eastern Europe, while assuring that a significant number were allowed to enter from the North and West. Nativism had triumphed, and an important chapter in U.S. history had been closed.

Subsequent Immigration Acts

There was little change in U.S. immigration policy from 1924 until the outbreak of World War II. A number of Europeans were displaced by the events of World War II and sought asylum as refugees in the United States. After much debate, a Displaced Persons Act was passed in 1948, which permitted about 400,000 refugees to enter the United States during a four-year period. The McCarran-Walter Act, passed in 1952, allegedly to remove racial barriers to immigration, essentially continued the policy established in 1924 and was in some ways more restrictive. In 1953, Congress passed a temporary measure, the Refugee Relief Act, to enable refugees from Communist nations to settle in the United States. However, major reform in U.S. immigration policy was not made until 1965. President John F. Kennedy strongly urged Congress to pass an enlightened immigration act. After much discussion and vigorous debate, the bill finally became a reality during the Johnson administration on July 1, 1968. This act abolished the national origins quota system and allowed 170,000 persons to enter the United States each year from the Eastern Hemisphere and 120,000 from the Western Hemisphere. Technical skill and family ties, rather than country of origin, became the major criteria for admitting immigrants to the United States. This bill was a major victory for liberal-thinking Americans and is a tribute to the ideals that many Americans profess.

Congress enacted a comprehensive immigration bill, the Immigration Reform and Control Act, on November 6, 1986 (U.S. Department of Justice, 1993). This act allowed aliens who had been in the United States illegally since January 1, 1982, to attain temporary and then permanent resident status. It also established sanctions for employers who knowingly hired illegal aliens. The Immigration Act of 1990 initiated a major overhaul of immigration law. It increased immigration to a flexible limit of 675,000 annually, beginning in 1995. The 675,000 level was to consist of 480,000 family-sponsored immigrants, 140,000 employment-based immigrants, and 55,000 "diversity immigrants" (U.S. Department of Justice, 1993, p. A-1-20).

EUROPEAN ETHNIC GROUPS IN U.S. SOCIETY

The mass settlement of Europeans in North America was one of the most unique phenomena in human history. Almost 60 million immigrants (59,795,158) entered the United States between 1820 and 1992 (U.S. Department of Justice, 1993). Most came from Europe. The European immigrants represented many religious, political, and cultural groups. Yet the United States, by forcing the immigrants to acquire the culture of the dominant society, was able to prevent the Balkanization of America and to establish a unified society. The immigrants paid a heavy price for cultural assimilation and acculturation. Nevertheless, a rather culturally homogeneous society emerged, although ethnicity is still a viable but complex force in U.S. life.

When European immigrants arrived on America's shores, their thoughts, feelings, aspirations, and attitudes were decidedly European. Many immigrants aggressively tried to structure European institutions in the United States. They tried to maintain their religious life by building churches similar to those in Europe. They established parochial schools, ethnic newspapers, ethnic theaters, and self-help organizations in their attempts to hold onto the old order. Some groups such as the German Americans created ethnic colonies, where their European cultures and ethnic kinships could flourish. Despite the concerted efforts by the immigrants to establish European institutions in the United States, these attempts were by and large destined to fail. Forces within American life worked against them and eventually eroded or greatly modified most European cultures in the United States.

The public schools, the U.S. press, and U.S. political institutions played key roles in mitigating the attempts to establish and maintain European institutions on U.S. soil. By the beginning of the nineteenth century, the English dominated most U.S. institutions, such as the schools, the courts, and the popular press. The immigrants and their children often found it necessary to acquire Anglo-Saxon cultural traits before they were allowed to participate fully in U.S. society. School teachers demeaned foreign languages; employers often preferred to hire assimilated immigrants. European Americans, especially the second generation, often responded to these cogent forces by becoming ashamed of their ethnic cultures, deliberately denying them, such as by Anglicizing or changing their surnames, and actively seeking to assimilate. Many second- and third-generation immigrants became—in mores, values, and outlook—similar to Anglo-Saxon Protestants. These immigrants paid a tremendous psychological price for denying their cultures, languages, and identities. However, as Greenbaum (1974) has perceptively written, the larger society shamed the immigrants into abandoning their ethnic cultures, but held out to them the hope of economic and structural inclusion into the mainstream society. White ethnic groups, unlike people of color, were able to attain full inclusion into the mainstream society once they were culturally identical to Anglo-Saxon Protestants and experienced social class mobility.

THE NEW ETHNICITY

During the 1950s, social scientists expected most ethnic characteristics eventually to disappear in the United States and a modernized shared culture to evolve. In this common national culture, social class would persist but factors such as race and ethnicity would be largely unimportant.

Glazer and Moynihan, in their 1963 pathbreaking book, *Beyond the Melting Pot* (1970), presented one of the first theoretical arguments that the melting pot conception of the United States was inaccurate and incomplete. They argued that ethnicity in New York was important and that it would continue to be important for both politics and culture. Significantly, they included case studies of the persistence of ethnicity among three White ethnic groups: the Jews, Italians, and Irish of New York City. They described how ethnicity persisted among these groups in politics and family structure.

During the 1960s, the civil rights movement emerged. This movement made ethnicity more legitimate. African Americans made claims on the federal government and other institutions because of the historic discrimination they experienced in the United States. The Black civil rights movement stimulated ethnic revitalization movements among other ethnic groups, such as American Indians and Mexican Americans, and among White ethnic groups, such as Jews, Poles, Italians, and Greeks. Southern, eastern, and central European ethnic groups were the most active participants in the White ethnic revitalization movements that emerged in the early 1970s.

These ethnic groups, through leaders and organizations, began to articulate ways in which they had been victims of ethnic stereotypes and discrimination, and how their histories and cultures had been omitted from history books and the school curriculum. They argued that, like Blacks, Indians, and Mexican Americans, they needed public policies that would enable them to acquire more equity and cultural democracy. Michael Novak (1971), an articulate theologian and humanist, became the most prolific speaker and writer for what he called the "unmeltable ethnics." His book, *The Rise of the Unmeltable Ethnics,* published in 1971, signaled the birth of the "new pluralism" among White ethnic groups.

In this widely reviewed and quoted book, Novak identified the "unmeltable ethnics" (Poles, Italians, Greeks, and Slavs), tried to explain how they were both different from and culturally alienated from Anglo-Saxon Protestants, and described how they were victims of discrimination, cultural arrogance, and the intellectual community. In moving prose, Novak also described how he and other Slavs were forced to deny their cultural identities. He wrote (1971), "The estrangement I have come to feel derives not only from a lack of family history. Early in life, I was made to feel a slight uneasiness when I said my name. . . . Liberal education tends to separate children from parents, from their roots, from their history, in the cause of a universal and superior religion" (pp. 64, 69).

Novak (1971) urged opinion leaders and politicians to recognize and respect the cultures of the White ethnics and predicted that they would be a powerful political force during the 1970s. He called the 1970s "the decade of the White ethnics." While Novak was arguing for the civil rights of White ethnics and attempting to mobilize them politically, researchers such as Andrew M. Greeley and William C. McCready (1974) were studying the extent to which ethnicity had survived among White ethnic groups, including the Irish Americans. In an article published in 1974, they described significant differences among the Anglo-Saxons, the Irish, and the Italians on personality variables, political participation, and attitudes toward sexuality and drinking. Publications that focused on the new ethnicity of White ethnic groups also emerged. *Ethnicity,* a journal published between 1974 and 1982, included a number of articles describing the cultural differences among White ethnic groups.

The ethnic revitalization movements among White ethnic groups during the 1970s evoked considerable controversy. Some scholars argued that the

White ethnic movement was not genuine but was a racist political movement designed to divert attention from the legitimate needs of ethnic groups of color, such as African Americans and Mexican Americans. Other critics argued that the movement was a "me-too," contrived movement. Critics of the new ethnic movements included scholars such as Orlando Patterson (1977), a Harvard sociologist, and distinguished historian Arthur Mann. Wrote Mann (1979), "The White ethnic revival was the product of a seriously divisive movement in history. Like previous revivals in America and elsewhere, secular as well as religious, the 1960s–1970s movement rested on the belief that the only way out for a troubled people lay in the return to a previous but languishing heritage" (pp. 41–42). Two anthropologists, Stein and Hill (1977), published a book-length work on the White ethnic movement in which they harshly criticized it. They wrote, "The New Ethnicity, then, is both a symptomatic expression of a disintegrated life and an attempt to cope with this sense of personal disintegration through regression to an earlier stage in individual development (p. 9)."

Scholars and civil rights leaders who defended the White ethnic movement argued that it was a genuine movement that had emerged in response to cultural assaults, discrimination, and epithets used to describe White ethnics by the liberal press. White ethnic leaders argued that those who dismissed the new pluralism as a "racist movement" had completely misunderstood its nature and complexity and were using a code word to dismiss it summarily.

WHITE ETHNIC GROUPS TODAY: INTO THE TWILIGHT OF ETHNICITY?

Most of the fervor of the ethnic revival movement of the 1970s has disappeared. Most European Americans, as they were in the 1970s, were continuing down the road toward assimilation into the mainstream society. The ethnic movement among White ethnic groups during the 1970s involved primarily ethnic leaders and intellectuals and not the common man and woman. As Alba (1985) indicates, the fact that ethnic leaders and intellectuals were able to articulate their rage and concerns in the mainstream media and intellectual community indicated that White ethnic groups had attained a significant level of structural inclusion into the mainstream society.

A lasting legacy of the White ethnic movement, and of the ethnic movements in the 1970s, is that ethnicity is more legitimate in the United States today than it was before the 1970s. Many Poles, Italians, and Yugoslavs no longer feel that they need to change their names or to become completely alienated from their ethnic culture in order to realize the American dream and attain economic and social mobility. Many social, political, and scholarly organizations are working to secure visibility and rights for European ethnic groups, including organizations such as the Illinois Consultation on Ethnicity in Education and the American Italian Historical Association. While many members of White ethnic groups are becoming more assimilated into the mainstream society, continuing immigration from Europe infuses some European ethnic groups, such as Greeks and Italians, with heavy doses of ethnic culture each year. Even though groups like Greeks and Italians may have entered the twilight of ethnicity, as Alba (1985) claims, new infusions of immigrants and various political and social events continue to renew ethnicity in the United States.

TEACHING STRATEGIES

To illustrate how content related to European Americans can be used to integrate the curriculum, exemplary strategies are identified for teaching these concepts at the grade levels indicated: *cultural contributions* (primary grades), *immigration* (intermediate and upper grades), and *nativism* (high school grades).

Primary Grades

CONCEPT: Cultural Contributions

Generalization: Our ancestors came from many different nations and belonged to many ethnic groups. All of these groups made outstanding contributions to American life.

1. To collect the information needed for this unit, duplicate the following letter and give each child one to take home. Tell the pupils to ask their parents to complete the form and return it to you the next day.

Name of Child _____

Ethnic Groups

English _____	Jewish _____
Scottish _____	(Specify nation)
Welsh _____	African American _____
German _____	American Indian _____
Irish _____	Mexican American _____
Italian _____	Asian American _____
Polish _____	(Specify group) _____
Russian _____	Puerto Rican _____
	Other(s) (Please specify) _____

Dear Parents:

   To help our students understand and appreciate the contributions all ethnic groups have made to American life, we are studying about ethnic groups and their role in America. I want to make sure that we study the ethnic heritages of all of my students. To do this, I need your help. Would you please study the list above and place an "X" by the group indicating your child's ethnic heritage. If your child has a mixed heritage, such as "English" and "Russian," please check both of these. However, please try to limit your checks to three by checking only the main strains in your child's ethnic heritage. The list above is based on the categories used by the U.S. Bureau of the Census. They represent the largest ethnic groups in the United States. However, many American ethnic groups are not included. If your child's ethnic heritage is not listed, please check "Other" and fill in the name(s) of your child's ethnic group(s), such as "Spanish" or "French."

   Please send this form back to me tomorrow morning. Thank you very much for your cooperation. I am sure that your response will help us to have a much better unit.

Sincerely,

Ms. Rosa Rivera
Third Grade Teacher

   2. When you have received the forms back from the parents, make a table, showing the ethnic groups represented in your class. Put the table on butcher paper and list the children's names under the appropriate ethnic categories. Your table might look like Table 8-4.

   3. Discuss the table with the students, noting that our ancestors came from many different nations. Using a primary globe, locate and write the names of some of the nations and continents from which the children's ancestors came, such as Great Britain, Africa, and Germany. Discuss these nations and continents with the students.

Table 8-4 OUR ETHNIC HERITAGES

English	Irish	Italian	German	African American	Polish
Susie	Cathy	Roy	*Pete	Jack	Linda
John	*Pete	Pat	Ray	Sam	Terry

*Pete has both Irish and German ancestors. Some of the children might be listed under several categories.

4. Using the photographs in a book such as *Ellis Island: An Illustrated History of the Immigrant Experience* by Ivan Chermayeff, Fred Wasserman, and Mary J. Shapiro (1991), tell the students the story of the great immigrations from Europe. Point out some of the reasons the immigrants came, how they came, and how they settled in the United States. The special case of the African Americans, as well as immigrants from other nations of color, should also be discussed.

5. Make another table on butcher paper listing the major ethnic groups represented in your class and other major U.S. ethnic groups. Under each major group, list some famous Americans and the fields in which they have made outstanding contributions to American life. Your table might look like Table 8-5.

Many books contain information about the ethnic backgrounds of famous Americans (see the annotated bibliographies in this chapter and in other chapters in Parts II through V of this book). Several series on ethnic groups that include books about famous Americans within those groups are listed and annotated in chapter 15 (pages 538–539).

6. After you have completed the Famous Ethnic Americans table, making sure that all the children's ethnic heritages are represented, discuss the table with the students and help them to formulate, in their own words, the following generalization: *Our ancestors came from many different lands and groups, and all these groups made many outstanding contributions to American life.*

Make sure that each child knows at least one famous person who belongs to his or her ethnic group. This exercise must be modified in classrooms in which there is only one ethnic group. Use some famous Americans from the students' own ethnic group, but also select heroes and heroines from at least five or six other ethnic groups not represented in your classroom.

Intermediate and Upper Grades

CONCEPT: Immigration

Generalization: Europeans immigrated to the United States for various economic, political, and social reasons. Their experiences in the United States were both similar and different.

Table 8-5 FAMOUS ETHNIC AMERICANS

English	Italian	African American	Polish
George Washington, *President*	Joe DiMaggio, *Baseball player*	Benjamin Banneker, *Scientist*	Helena Modjeska, *Actress*
Benjamin Franklin, *Scientist*	Frank Sinatra, *Singer*	Martin L. King, *Civil rights leader*	Edmund S. Muskie, *U.S. Senator*

1. To help the students gain the needed content background to study American immigration, assign appropriate readings that will enable them to answer the following questions about the first or old immigrants to America:

   a. What European nations did the first immigrants to America come from during the colonial period?
   b. Why did they come?
   c. Was America like they expected? If so, in what ways? If not, why not? Explain.

2. After the students have completed their reading assignments, discuss the three questions above with the class. During the discussion, list on the board the reasons that various groups immigrated to the United States. When the reasons have been listed, group them, with the class, into three or four categories, such as "economic," "political," and "social" reasons.

3. Ask the students to read about the new immigrants who came to the United States from Europe in the late 1800s and early 1900s. These immigrants came primarily from southern and eastern Europe and included Ukrainians, Russian Jews, Poles, Italians, Greeks, and many other groups. The students should discuss the same three questions about these immigrants that they had discussed after reading about the old immigrants.

4. After the students have read and discussed the old and new immigrants, they should compare and contrast these groups. The following questions can be used to guide discussion:

   a. Did the old and new immigrants come to the United States for similar or different reasons? Explain.
   b. How did the new immigrants differ from the old? Why?
   c. How did American life differ at the times when the old and new immigrants came to America? How did this difference affect the adjustment of the newly arrived immigrants?
   d. Both the old and the new immigrants experienced problems on the trip across the Atlantic. How were these problems similar and different?
   e. How were the problems of settlement and finding jobs in America similar and different for the two groups of immigrants?
   f. Ethnic conflict developed early during the settlement of European nationality groups in America. What problems of prejudice and discrimination were experienced by the various groups? Which groups of immigrants were discriminated against the most? The least? Why?

The students can summarize this phase of the unit by making a data retrieval chart to summarize and compare information about major ethnic groups representing old and new immigrants, similar to Table 8-6.

5. To help the students gain a feeling for the harshness of the journey across the Atlantic that the immigrants experienced, read aloud to them chapter 2, "The Crossing," in Oscar Handlin (1951), *The Uprooted*. The class can develop a dramatization of the passage as described in Handlin and present it in a school assembly. The entire class should be involved in writing and presenting the dramatization.

Table 8-6 GENERALIZING ABOUT THE OLD AND NEW EUROPEAN IMMIGRANTS

	Old Immigrants			New Immigrants Southern and Eastern		
	English	Irish	Germans	Italians	Jews	Poles
Reasons for immigrating						
Kinds of people in group						
Problems on Atlantic journey						
Problems of settlement						
Prejudice and discrimination experienced						
Immigration laws in European country of origin						
Relationships *within* the nationality group						

6. European immigrants in the United States often wrote to their friends and relatives in Europe describing the wonders of America and occasionally their problems. These two books contain letters that Germans and Norwegian immigrants wrote home: Walter D. Kamphoefner, Wolfgang Helbich, and Ulrike Sommer (1991), *News from the Land of Freedom: Immigrants Write Home;* Solveig Zempel (1990), *In Their Own Words: Letters from Norwegian Immigrants.*

Read and discuss selected letters from these two books (or similar ones) with the class. Ask the students to pretend that they are new European immigrants in the United States in the 1800s. They should write to a friend or relative in Europe telling about their experiences. This activity can be correlated with the language arts.

7. Have the students role-play the situation below, which involves a poor Italian farmer and an agent of a steamship company who tries to persuade the farmer to immigrate to the United States. After the role-playing situation, ask the students the questions that follow.

Mr. Pareto, a Poor Italian Farmer in Southern Italy in the 1800s

Mr. Pareto is in his thirties. He is a hard worker and is close to his family, which includes his wife, eight children, and both of his parents. For the past three years, Mr. Pareto has been unable to feed and clothe his family well because of severe crop failures. He has heard about the greatness of America and has often thought about going there. However, he knows that his father feels he should stay in Italy so that he can depend on him in his old age. He also realizes that if he goes to America he will have to leave his wife and children in Italy.

Mr. Rossi, an Agent for a Steamship Company That Makes Trips to America

Mr. Rossi tries to persuade Italian men to immigrate to America. The more men that he can persuade to go to America on his company's steamship line, the more money he makes. He goes up to Mr. Pareto at the village market and tells him about the wonders of America and why he should go there. He tells him that he can obtain a job quickly in America and become a wealthy man. He knows that if Mr. Pareto goes to America he will not be able to carry his family. However, Mr. Rossi tells Mr. Pareto that he will be able to send for his family within two or three months after he arrives in America.

Questions

1. Did Mr. Rossi persuade Mr. Pareto to go to America? Why or why not?
2. If Mr. Pareto goes to America, what do you think will happen to his family?
3. If Mr. Pareto stays in Italy, how do you think he will take care of his family?
4. How do you think his wife, parents, and children will react if Mr. Pareto goes to America? Why?
5. What else can Mr. Pareto do besides stay in his Italian village or immigrate to America?

6. If you were Mr. Pareto, would you immigrate to America? Why or why not? Explain.
7. Conclude this unit by viewing and discussing a videotape about European immigration.

Valuing Activity

Many European immigrants, especially those from southern and eastern Europe, changed their names and adopted Anglo-American culture characteristics so that they could assimilate more quickly into the dominant society and experience rapid social, economic, and political mobility. Other immigrants, however, even though they were the victims of affronts by the larger society, tried to hold onto their names and ethnic culture characteristics in America. In the following selection, written in 1939, a Polish American tells why he did not want to change his name. Read the selection to your students and ask them the questions that follow the selection.

I Was Ashamed of My Name

Twenty-odd years ago I was ashamed of my Polish name and heritage. To the boys in the neighborhood I was the lone "dirty Polack." This rankled, burned, and developed in me a bitter sense of inferiority. There was no Poland...I was no Polack! I was American! I didn't want to be a Polack! I would not go to a Polish school! If my parents spoke to me in Polish, I would answer in English. I dreamed of going West, changing my name to Edward R. Edwards, and being American. The end of the war and the Versailles Treaty brought some consolation. Now there was a Poland! True, we didn't hear much about it, but we knew it was there. We had found peace.

In high school, a teacher who had trouble with my name started calling me Scott. Others followed suit. I tried to convince people my name wasn't Scott but Kostyra. Some refused to accept the more difficult name. Mail came to my home for me addressed to Scott. My parents soundly berated me, because they considered the pseudonym an insult to them. I was in a quandary. (*Polish American Review*, 1939)

Questions

1. What problems did Kostyra face?
2. Why do you think it was difficult for his family to accept a new name for him?
3. Why was Kostyra ashamed of his Polish name?
4. Why do you think some Americans refused to call Kostyra by his Polish name?
5. Do you feel that an individual should change his or her name under any circumstances? Why or why not? If so, under what circumstances?

6. What are some things that Kostyra could have done to solve his problems? What were probable consequences of each course of action?
7. What do you think Kostyra should have done? Why?
8. If you had been Kostyra, what would you have done? Why?
9. Have you ever been in a situation similar to the one that Kostyra was in? If so, what did you do? Why?

High School Grades

CONCEPT: Nativism

Generalization: Negative feelings toward immigrant groups emerged early in colonial America. However, American nativism did not become widespread until the late nineteenth and early twentieth centuries. It eventually led to a virtual halt to European immigration.

1. Ask the students to read chapter 2, "Ethnic Discord and the Growth of American Nationality," in Maldwyn Allen Jones (1992), *American Immigration*; and chapter 1, "A Colonial Heritage," in David H. Bennett (1988), *The Party of Fear: From Nativist Movements to the New Right in American History*, and be able to discuss the following questions when they have finished the reading:

    a. Antiforeign attitudes were present in the early American colonies. What groups were the main victims of these negative feelings?

    b. What forms did nativism take in colonial America? What acts and laws were passed in colonial America that reflected antiforeign attitudes?

When the students have completed these readings, discuss the above questions with the class. They will discover that the Irish, French, Huguenots, Catholics, and Germans were the main targets of early antiforeign attitudes in America. Record their responses to the questions above, in summary form, on the board.

2. Ask individual students or groups of students to prepare reports on the following topics and present them to the class.

- The Know-Nothing movement in the 1850s
- The Chinese Exclusion Act of 1882
- The Immigration Act of 1882, which excluded certain classes of European immigrants
- The Immigration Restriction League, formed in 1894
- The Foran Act of 1885
- The Haymarket Affair, 1886
- The Lynching of eleven Italians in New Orleans, 1891
- William Z. Ripley's *The Races of Europe*, published in 1899
- The Dillingham Commission, which issued its report in 1911
- The 1917 Immigration Act
- Madison Grant, *The Passing of the Great Race in America*, published in 1916

- The Johnson Act of 1921
- The Johnson-Reed Act of 1924
- The McCarran-Walter Act of 1952
- The Immigration Act of 1965
- The Immigration Reform and Control Act of 1986
- The Immigration Act of 1990

The books by Jones (1992) and Bennett (1988), cited above, are two excellent sources for information about the above topics. When the students are sharing their reports, help them identify some causes of nativistic movements. These causes should be noted on the board and in the students' notebooks. They include anti-Catholic attitudes, fear of foreign "radicals," economic recession and depression, the mass of new immigrants that arrived in the United States in the late 1800s and early 1900s, the belief that aliens were taking jobs away from American citizens, and the popularity of beliefs about the innate inferiority of southern and eastern European immigrants perpetuated by such writers as William Z. Ripley and the well-known naturalist, Madison Grant.

3. Heated debates took place in Congress, as well as in other public forums, about the passage of a bill that would require immigrants to pass a reading test before they could enter the United States. Two opposing views of the literacy test are found in chapter 8 of Oscar Handlin (1959), *Immigration as a Factor in American History.* Samuel Gompers defends the test and President Woodrow Wilson opposes it. Read these two accounts to the class. Ask the students to role-play a session of Congress in 1917 in which the bill is discussed. Different students should argue for and against the bill. After the speeches on the floor, the students should vote for or against the bill. After the voting, they should discuss why their final vote was similar to or different from the Congressional vote in 1917.

4. Anthropologists and physical scientists divided Whites into various races in the 1800s (Tucker, 1994). William Z. Ripley (1899) and Madison Grant (1916) popularized these views and argued that southern and eastern European immigrants were innately inferior to immigrants from the northern and western parts of Europe. Ask the class to compare the views of these writers with the racial views of contemporary scientists such as Richard J. Herrnstein and Charles Murray (1994). Excellent critiques of the views of Herrnstein and Murray are found in *The Bell Curve Debate: History, Documents, Opinions,* edited by Russell Jacoby and Naomi Galauberman (1995).

5. Social and physical scientists blamed the new immigrants for political corruption, urban blight, crime, and large welfare rolls. Ask the students to study writings about the immigrants during the 1800s and to compare these writings with writings today about ethnic minorities such as African Americans, Mexican Americans, and Puerto Ricans. The class can discuss the ways in which the old and new criticisms are alike and different and why they are alike and different. Oscar Handlin (1959), *The Uprooted*; Maldwyn A. Jones (1992), *American Immigration*; and David H. Bennett (1988), *The Party of Fear: From Nativist Movements to the New Right,* contain information and references that will help students to carry out this activity.

6. The Johnson-Reed Act of 1924 marked the end of an era in the history of American immigration because it put a virtual end to immigration and discriminated blatantly against southern and eastern European immigrants and non-White nations.

Duplicate a copy of this act for the class and ask them to discuss its legal, moral, and political implications. The students can then compare the Johnson-Reed Act with these acts: the McCarran-Walter Act of 1952, the Immigration Act of 1965, the Immigration Reform and Control Act of 1986, and the Immigration Act of 1990.

Students can also compare nativism near the turn of the century directed against southern, central, and eastern European immigrants with the nativism that is directed against Asians and Hispanics today. For example, a number of states with large Hispanic populations have passed referenda that make English the official state language. In 1994 California voters passed Proposition 187, an initiative that denies undocumented workers and their children schooling and nonemergency medical care. You can conclude this unit by asking the students to write a five- to ten-page paper on "Nativism as a Factor in American Society: Today and Yesterday." This activity can be correlated with English or the language arts.

REFERENCES

Alba, R. D. (1985). *Italian Americans: Into the Twilight of Ethnicity.* Englewood Cliffs, N.J.: Prentice-Hall.

Bailey, T. A. (1961). *The American Pageant: A History of the Republic* (2nd ed.). Boston: D.C. Heath.

Bateman, G. & Egan, V. (1993). *Encyclopedia of World Geography.* New York: Barnes & Noble.

Bennett, D. H. (1988). *The Party of Fear: From Nativist Movements to the New Right in American History.* Chapel Hill: The University of North Carolina Press.

Chermayeff, I., Wasserman, F., & Shapiro, M. J. (1991). *Ellis Island: An Illustrated History of the Immigrant Experience.* New York: Macmillan.

Glazer, N. & Moynihan, D. P. (1970). *Beyond the Melting Pot: The Negroes, Puerto Ricans, Jews, Italians, and Irish of New York City* (2nd ed.). Cambridge: The M.I.T. Press.

Grant, M. (1916). *The Passing of the Great Race.* New York: Charles Scribner's Sons.

Greeley, A. M. & McCready, W. C. (1974, April). Does Ethnicity Matter? *Ethnicity 1,* 91–108.

Greenbaum, W. (1974, August). America in Search of a New Ideal: An Essay on the Rise of Pluralism. *Harvard Educational Review 44,* 411–440.

Handlin, O. (Ed.). (1951). *The Uprooted: The Epic Story of the Great Migrations That Made the American People.* New York: Grosset and Dunlap.

Handlin, O. (Ed.). (1959). *Immigration as a Factor in American History.* Englewood Cliffs, N.J.: Prentice-Hall.

Herrnstein, R. J. & Murray, C. (1994). *The Bell Curve: Intelligence and Class Structure in American Life.* New York: The Free Press.

Higham, J. (1972). *Strangers in the Land: Patterns of American Nativism 1860–1925.* New York: Atheneum.

Jacoby, R. & Glauberman, N. (Eds.). (1995). *The Bell Curve: History, Documents, Opinions.* New York: Times Books/Random House.

Jones, M. A. (1960). *American Immigration.* Chicago: The University of Chicago Press.

Jones, M. A. (1992). *American Immigration* (2nd ed.). Chicago: The University of Chicago Press.

Kamphoefner, W. D., Helbich, W., & Sommer, U. (Eds.). (1991). *News from the Land of Freedom: Immigrants Write Home.* Ithaca, N.Y.: Cornell University Press.

Mann, A. (1979). *The One and the Many: Reflections on the American Identity.* Chicago: The University of Chicago Press.

Novak, M. (1971). *The Rise of the Unmeltable Ethnics: Politics and Culture in the Seventies.* New York: Macmillan.

Patterson, O. (1977). *Ethnic Chauvinism: The Reactionary Impulse.* New York: Stein and Day.

Polish American Review. (1939, July).

Ripley, W. Z. (1899). *The Races of Europe: A Sociological Study.* New York: D. Appleton & Company.

Smedley, A. (1993). *Race in North America: Origin and Evolution of a Worldview.* Boulder, Colo.: Westview Press.

Stein, H. F. & Hill, R. F. (1977). *The Ethnic Imperative: Examining the New White Ethnic Movement.* University Park: The Pennsylvania State University Press.

Takaki, R. (1993). *A Different Mirror: A History of Multicultural America.* New York: Little, Brown.

Tucker, W. H. (1994). *The Science and Politics of Racial Research.* Urbana: University of Illinois Press.

U.S. Bureau of the Census. (1994). *Statistical Abstract of the United States* (114th ed.). Washington, D.C.: U.S. Government Printing Office.

U.S. Department of Justice. (1993, October). *Statistical Yearbook of the Immigration and Naturalization Service.* Washington, D.C.: U.S. Government Printing Office.

Vecoli, R. J. (1994). *Review of Teaching Strategies for Ethnic Studies* (5th ed.). (Comments prepared for author's revision of text for this 6th edition).

Vecoli, R. J. & Sinke, S. (Eds.). (1991). *A Century of European Migrations 1830–1930.* Urbana: University of Illinois Press.

Zempel, S. (Ed.). (1990). *In Their Own Words: Letters from Norwegian Immigrants.* Minneapolis: University of Minnesota Press.

ANNOTATED BIBLIOGRAPHY

Books for Teachers

Especially Recommended

Alba, R. (1990). *Ethnic Identity: The Transformation of White America.* New Haven, Conn.: Yale University Press.

In this informative, thoughtful, and provocative book, Alba uses data from in-depth interviews with more than 500 people to examine the impact of ethnicity on the lives of White ethnics. He argues that ethnic specific characteristics, such as those of Polish American and Italian American origin, are increasingly less important. However, a new collective White ethnic identity and group has emerged, which he calls "European Americans."

Bennett, D. H. (1988). *The Party of Fear: From Nativist Movements to the New Right in American History.* Chapel Hill: The University of North Carolina Press.

This is a sweeping and comprehensive history of nativism and anti-democratic groups in American society. The most comprehensive book on the topic since the publication of John Higham's Strangers in the Land: Patterns of American Nativism 1860–1925, *first published in 1963.*

Berrol, S. C. (1995). *Growing up American: Immigrant Children in America Then and Now.* New York: Twayne Publishers.

The author describes the life of European immigrants form the 1700s to today.

Daniels, R. (1990). *Coming to America: A History of Immigration and Ethnicity in American Life.* New York: Harper/Collins.

This excellent history by a veteran immigration historian weaves the history of White ethnic groups with that of ethnic groups of color. An excellent source that can be used with advanced high school students.

Fuchs, L. (1995). The American Civic Culture and an Inclusivist Immigration Policy. In J. A. Banks & C. A. M. Banks (Eds.). *Handbook of Research on Multicultural Education* (pp. 293–309). New York: Macmillan.

This chapter provides an overview of American immigration policy and its inclusivist characteristics.

Jones, M. A. (1992). *American Immigration* (2nd ed.). Chicago: The University of Chicago Press.

This excellently written and influential history of American immigration by a British historian has been updated to include immigration history from 1960 to 1991. This well-written book can be used with advanced high school students.

Kamphoefner, W. D., Helbich, W., & Sommer, U. (Eds.). (1991). *News from the Land of Freedom: Immigrants Write Home.* Ithaca, N.Y.: Cornell University Press.

This book consists of 350 letters arranged in 20 different categories that German immigrants wrote home. These letters are excellent and rich teaching resources.

Nugent, W. (1995). *Crossings: The Great Translantic Migrations, 1870–1914.* Bloomington: Indiana University Press.

The author examines the period of immigration from Europe from 1870 to 1914 in a well-written and informative history. He discusses immigrations from Europe to Argentina, Brazil, Canada, and the United States.

Seller, M. S. (Ed.). (1994). *Immigrant Women* (2nd ed., rev.). New York: State University of New York Press.

This rich and informative resource includes memories, diaries, oral history, and fiction.

Vecoli, R. J. & Sinke, S. (Eds.). (1991). *A Century of European Migrations 1830–1930.* Urbana: University of Illinois Press.

A comprehensive and informative collection of historical papers.

Other References

Alba, R. D. (1985). *Italian Americans: Into the Twilight of Ethnicity.* Englewood Cliffs, N.J.: Prentice-Hall.

This sociological and historical study of the experiences of Italians in the United States is written from an assimilationist perspective. The author emphasizes how European ethnic groups, including the Italians, are becoming part of the U.S. mainstream and consequently entering the "twilight" of ethnicity.

Alfonsi, F. P. (1989). *Dictionary of Italian-American Poets.* New York: Peter Lang.

This reference book contains 1,000 Italian American poets, including a short biography of each, a list of his or her books, and available published criticisms that have been given of each book.

Anderson, P. J. (Ed.). (1995). *Scandinavian Immigrants and Education in North America.* Chicago: Swedish-American Historical Society.

A historical study that focuses on education.

Archdeacon, T. J. (1983). *Becoming American: An Ethnic History.* New York: The Free Press.

This carefully researched and readable history contains informative chapters on the "old" and "new" European immigrants to the United States.

Baiamonte, J. (1990). *Immigrants in Rural Society: A Study of Italians of Tangiipahoa Parish, Louisiana.* New York: Garland.

Reprint edition of a study of Italians in a rural community in the South.

Barolini, H. (Ed.). (1985). *The Dream Book: An Anthology of Writings by Italian American Women.* New York: Schocken Books.

This collection of writings by Italian American women includes one play, prose and poetry, oral history, and fiction. This book also includes an informative introductory essay by the editor.

Barton, H. A. (1994). *A Folk Divided: Homeland Swedes and Swedish Americans, 1840–1940.* Carbondale: Southern Illinois University Press.

This book reports the results of a longitudinal study of how Swedes in Europe and the United States experienced both strong attachments and alienation and conflict.

Brown, B. A. (1990). *The Assimilation Experience of Five American White Ethnic Novelists of the Twentieth Century.* New York: Garland Publishing.

A reprint edition of an informative literary study.

Brown, M. E. (1995). *Communities, Churches, and Children: Italian Immigrants and the Archdiocese of New York, 1880–1950.* New York: Center for Migration Studies.

An informative study of Italian immigrants in New York City.

Bukowczyk, J. J. (1987). *And My Children Did Know Me: A History of Polish Americans.* Bloomington: Indiana University Press.

An informative and scholarly history of Poles in the United States.

Capozzoli, M. J. (1990). *Three Generations of Italian American Women in Nassau County 1925–1981.* New York: Garland Publishing.

A historical regional study of Italian American women in a county in New York state.

Diner, H. (1983). *Erin's Daughters in America.* Baltimore: The Johns Hopkins University Press.

A scholarly treatment of the Irish experience in the United States.

Dolan, J. (1985). *The American Catholic Experience.* Garden City, N.Y.: Doubleday and Company.

An informative treatment of the sojourn of Catholics in the United States.

Greene, V. R. (1987). *American Immigrant Leaders 1800–1910: Marginality and Identity.* Baltimore: The Johns Hopkins University Press.

A scholarly and comparative study of leadership in these U.S. ethnic groups: the Irish, the Germans, the Norwegians and the Swedes, the Jews, the Poles, and the Italians. The author formulates generalizations about ethnic leadership in the United States.

Grimes, R. R. (1996). *How Shall We Sing in a Foreign Land: Music of Irish-Catholic Immigrants in the Antebellum United States.* Notre Dame, Ind.: University of Notre Dame.

An informative historical study of the music of Irish Catholic immigrants.

Handlin, O. (1973). *The Uprooted: The Epic Story of the Great Migrations That Made the American People* (rev. ed.). New York: Grosset and Dunlap.

In this landmark book, the author chronicles the story of European immigrants to the United States from their peasant life in Europe to the nativistic movements in the late nineteenth and early twentieth centuries. It was the recipient of the Pulitzer Prize in history in 1952.

Handlin, O. (1991). *Boston's Immigrants* (50th anniv. ed.). Cambridge: Harvard University Press.

A reprint edition of a classic study.

Higham, J. (1972). *Strangers in the Land: Patterns of American Nativism 1860–1925.* New York: Atheneum.

This is a perceptive and pioneering study of nativistic movements in U.S. society in the late nineteenth and early twentieth centuries. In this interpretive work, the author views economic events as major determinants of nativistic forces. This highly readable and copiously documented book contains a useful bibliographic essay.

Kivisto, P. (Ed.). (1989). *The Ethnic Enigma: The Salience of Ethnicity for European-Origin Ethnic Groups*. Philadelphia: The Balch Institute Press.

This book, which consists of case studies of various European-origin ethnic groups in the United States, contains an excellent theoretical overview essay on ethnicity in America by the editor.

Kuropas, M. B. (1991). *The Ukrainian Americans 1884–1954*. Toronto: University of Toronto Press.

A massive, detailed, and well-written history of the Ukrainian experience in the United States by an author who has a studied the subject for many years.

Lieberson, S. & Waters, M. C. (1988). *From Many Strands: Ethnic and Racial Groups in Contemporary America*. New York: Russell Sage Foundation.

One of the volumes in "The Population of the United States in the 1980s" monograph series, this volume includes rich data on White ethnic groups from the 1980 Census. "The Ethnic and Racial Composition of the United States," "Economic Attainment," and "Intermarriage" are three of the chapters.

Mangione, J. & Morreale, B. (1993). *La Storia: Five Centuries of the Italian American Experience*. New York: HarperCollins.

A well-written, comprehensive, and informative history of the Italian Americans. It can be used with high school students.

Miller, K. A. (1985). *Emigrants and Exiles: Ireland and the Irish Exodus to North America*. New York: Oxford University Press.

This is a scholarly and important study of Ireland and the exodus of Irish immigrants to North America.

Moskos, C., Jr. (1980). *Greek Americans: Struggles for Success*. Englewood Cliffs, N.J.: Prentice-Hall.

This sociological study of Greek Americans is an informative introductory source.

Muller, T. E. (1993). *Immigrants and the American City*. New York: New York University Press.

A scholarly study of immigrants in the American city.

Pacyga, D. (1991). *Polish Immigrants and Industrial Chicago: Workers on the South Side, 1880–1922*. Columbus: Ohio State University Press.

A scholarly historical study of an ethnic group that is very important in the history of Chicago.

Portes, A. & Rumbaut, R. G. (1990). *Immigrant America: A Portrait*. Berkeley: University of California Press.

Why immigrants came to America, who they were, making it in America, and from immigrants to ethnics are some of the topics discussed in this scholarly book.

Pula, J. S. (1995). *Polish Americans: An Ethnic Community*. New York: Twayne Publishers.

An informative synthesis of the history of Polish Americans.

Rasmussen, J. E. (1993). *New Land, New Lives: Scandinavian Immigrants to the Pacific Northwest.* Seattle: University of Washington Press.

An historical study of Scandinavian immigrants in a region in which they settled in large numbers.

Swander, M. (1995). *Out of This World: A Woman's Life among the Amish.* New York: Viking.

A non-Amish woman describes her life among her Amish neighbors in Iowa.

Swierenga, R. P. (Ed.). (1985). *The Dutch in America: Immigration, Settlement, and Cultural Change.* New Brunswick. N.J.: Rutgers University Press.

The scholarly chapters in this book discuss diverse aspects of the Dutch experience in the United States, such as "Dutch Literary Culture in America 1850–1950" and "The Reformed Churches and Acculturation."

Thernstrom, S., Orlov, A., & Handlin, O. (Eds.). (1980). *Harvard Encyclopedia of American Ethnic Groups.* Cambridge: Harvard University Press.

This comprehensive and scholarly reference book includes historical and sociological survey discussions of more than 100 ethnic groups, including Italians, Poles, Greeks, Czechs, and Danes in the United States. Although dated, this reference is still useful for studying the history of ethnic groups in the United States prior to 1980.

Tomasi, L. F. (Ed.). (1985). *Italian Americans: New Perspectives in Italian Immigration and Ethnicity.* New York: Center for Migration Studies.

This book contains some excellent and scholarly papers on the Italian American experience, such as "Italian Americans and the Media: An Agenda for a More Positive Image," by Joseph Giordano; "Italian Americans in Contemporary America," by Humbert S. Nelli; and "The Search for an Italian American Identity: Continuity and Change," by Rudolph J. Vecoli.

Books for Students

Bartone, E. (1993). *Peppe the Lamplighter.* New York: Lothrop, Lee & Shepard.

A story about an Italian American boy who takes a job lighting the gas street lamps. The illustrations are striking and powerful. (Primary)

Chermayeff, I., Wasserman, F., & Shapiro, M. J. (1991). *Ellis Island: An Illustrated History of the Immigrant Experience.* New York: Macmillan.

This is an excellent and attractive teaching resource that includes photographs, many in color, of people, artifacts, and documents. (All levels)

Conlon-McKenna, M. (1991). *Wildflower Girl.* New York: Holiday House.

The story of a thirteen-year-old girl in America who came from Ireland. (Middle School)

di Franco, P. (1988). *The Italian American Experience.* New York: Tom Doherty.

This book includes an interesting historical overview of Italian Americans. (Middle School)

Eubank, N. (1986). *The Russians in America.* Minneapolis: Lerner.

This book includes an overview of the Russian experience in the United States and profiles of Russian Americans who have made important contributions to American society. (Intermediate/Middle School)

Fisher, L. E. (1985). *The Statue of Liberty.* New York: Holiday House.

An interesting account of the building of the Statue of Liberty and its history as a beacon of freedom. (Intermediate)

Fisher, L. E. (1986). *Ellis Island: Gateway to the New World.* New York: Holiday House.

This well-written book is illustrated with powerful black-and-white photographs. (Intermediate)

Franck, I. M. & Brownstone, D. M. (1988). *America's Ethnic Heritage: The Scandinavian-American Heritage.* New York: Facts on File.

This book provides an overview of Scandinavian immigrants from the mid-seventeenth century until 1920. It chronicles their experiences as they traveled from their European homeland to the United States and their experiences in the United States. Finnish settlements in Alaska, Danish Mormons in Utah, and Scandinavian settlements in the Midwest are described. The authors also discuss Scandinavian religious beliefs and occupations of early Scandinavian immigrants. Another book by Franck is The German-American Heritage *(Facts on File, 1988). (Middle School)*

Grossman, R. P. (1993). *Italians in America.* Minneapolis: Lerner Publications.

This book describes the experiences of Italians in the United States. It is illustrated with photographs. (Intermediate)

Harvey, B. (1987). *Immigrant Girl: Becky of Eldridge Street.* Illustraed by D. K. Ray. New York: Holiday House.

The story of a Russian immigrant girl who moves to New York's Lower East Side in 1910. (Intermediate)

Helgadottir, G. (1989). *Flumbra: An Icelandic Folktale.* Minneapolis: Lerner.

This beautifully illustrated book tells a poignant tale that explains why some natural catastrophes occur. (Primary/Intermediate)

Hoobler, D. & Hoobler, T. (1994). *The Italian Family Album.* New York: Oxford University Press.

This rich and appealing book contains captivating period photographs as well as diaries, letters, interviews, and other period sources. Other titles in The American family series on European Americans include The German Family Album *(1995), and* The Irish Family Album *(1995). Each of the titles in* The American Family Album *series is similar in reading level, design, and appearance. (Middle School and up)*

Howell, T. (1989). *Peter and the North Wind.* New York: Scholastic.

This Norwegian folk tale is written in simple vocabulary for beginning readers and is illustrated with full-color paintings. (Primary)

Kherdian, D. (1989). *The Road from Home: The Story of an Armenian Girl.* New York: Viking.

This Newbery Honor Book tells a young girl's story of survival and courage during 1915, when Armenians were attacked by Turkish forces. (High School)

Kuropas, M. B. (1985). *The Ukranians in America.* Minneapolis: Lerner.

This book contains a survey of Ukranian immigration to the United States and the contributions Ukranians have made to American life. (Intermediate/Middle School)

Lavallee, B. (1989). *The Snow Child.* New York: Scholastic.

This Russian folktale describes how a girl built out of snow comes to life. (Primary)

Levine, E. (1994). *If Your Name Was Changed at Ellis Island.* New York: Scholastic.

Students will find this illustrated book interesting and informative. (Primary)

Levinson, R. (1985). *Watch the Stars Come Out.* Illustrated by Diane Goode. New York: Dutton.

This beautifully illustrated book tells the story of a long journey to the United States. A little girl and her brother are going alone to join their parents during the time of the great migrations. (Primary)

McGill, A. (1988). *The Swedish Americans.* New York: Chelsea House.

This book discusses the history, culture, and religion of the Swedish Americans. (Intermediate and up)

Magnus, E. (1989). *The Boy and the Devil.* Minneapolis: Lerner.

This Norwegian folktale tells the story of a boy who was able to capture the devil by tricking him. Another book by Magnus is Old Lars *(Lerner, 1985). (Primary)*

Maestro, B. (1995). *Coming to America: The Story of Immigration.* Illustrated by S. Ryan. New York: Scholastic.

This book tells the story of immigrating to the United States.

Mayberry, J. (1991). *Eastern Europeans.* New York: Franklin Watts.

This informative book on Eastern Europeans is illustrated. (Intermediate)

Montaufier, P. (1989). *One Summer at Grandmother's House.* Minneapolis: Lerner.

Full-color paintings illustrate this delightful story about a summer in the 1950s when the author went to visit her grandmother in the Alsace region of France. (Intermediate)

Murphy, J. (1993). *Across America on an Emigrant Train.* New York: Clarion Books.

This book describes the journey that a young writer from Scotland makes in 1979 to find the woman he loves in the United States. (Middle School/High School).

Parnell, H. (1988). *Cooking the German Way.* Minneapolis: Lerner.

This book is part of a series of cookbooks that include easy-to-cook recipes from various countries. In addition to recipes and menus, the cookbooks include infor-

mation about the history and culture of people in the country. *Other books in the series include* Cooking the English Way, Cooking the French Way, Cooking the Greek Way, Cooking the Hungarian Way, Cooking the Italian Way, Cooking the Norwegian Way, Cooking the Polish Way, *and* Cooking the Russian Way.

Pellegrimi, A. (1986). *An Immigrant Quest: American Dream*. San Francisco: North Point Press.

An immigrant who becomes a college professor chronicles his journey from Italy to the Pacific Northwest and his life in the United States. (High School)

Petersen, P. L. (1987). *The Danes in America*. Minneapolis: Lerner.

The Danish American way of life and the contributions of the Danes to their new country are discussed in this book. (Intermediate/Middle School)

Reeves, P. (1991). *Ellis Island: Gateway to the American Dream*. New York: Dorset Press.

An illustrated resource that most students will find appealing and interesting. (Intermediate and up)

Shiefman, V. (1993). *Good-Bye to the Trees*. New York: Atheneum.

A thirteen-year-old Russian girl leaves home to go to Chelsea, Massachusetts. This novel describes her adventures in the United States. (Middle School)

Tenzythoff, G. J. (1985). *The Dutch in America*. Minneapolis: Lerner.

An overview of Dutch immigration to the United States and the contributions of the Dutch to various areas of American life are included in this book. (Intermediate/Middle School)

Watson, M. (1995). *The Butterfly Seeds*. New York: Tambourine Books.

Jake's excitement about moving to the United States is overshowded by the sadness of leaving his grandfather. He lands at Ellis Island. (Primary).

9

JEWISH AMERICANS

CONCEPTS, STRATEGIES, AND MATERIALS

The twentieth-century ideals of America have been the ideals of the Jew for more than twenty centuries.

Louis D. Brandeis

About 5.5 million Jewish Americans live in the United States, comprising about 2.2% of its population (Kosmin, et al., 1991, p. 5). They constitute a religious, cultural, and ethnic minority group that originated in the land that is today Israel. They are a diverse group, living in each of the fifty states, with about 55% in the Northeast and Midwest and 45% in the South and West. The population movement has generally been from the Northeast and Midwest to the South and West (Kosmin, et al., 1991).

Jewish Americans have been an integral part of American history since the days of Columbus, and they have contributed significantly in the arts and sciences, medicine, education, law, and other fields. American culture has been enriched by the works of Jewish novelists, playwrights, and critics who write from a Jewish perspective and on Jewish themes.

Yet the role of Jews in American history clearly transcends a mere listing of their contributions. Their presence is intimately intertwined with many fun-

---

This chapter is contributed by Jerome L. Ruderman, Department Head, Social Studies, Frankford High School, Philadelphia, Pennsylvania. Mr. Ruderman's books include *Jews in American History: A Teacher's Guide* (1974), *Heritage: Civilization and the Jews, Resource File* (1984), and *The American Experience: An Educational Guide for Teachers and Librarians* (1988).

JEWISH AMERICANS: HISTORICAL PERSPECTIVE

Important Dates	
1492	The Jews were expelled from Spain. Jews accompanied Columbus on his first voyage to America.
1654	Twenty-three Jewish immigrants from Brazil arrived in New Amsterdam. They established the first Jewish settlement in North America.
1730	The first synagogue in North America was completed in New Amsterdam.
1740	An act of Parliament exempted Jews from saying the words, "on the true faith of a Christian," in the naturalization oath, enabling them to become citizens in English colonies.
1774	Francis Salvador was elected to the South Carolina Provincial Congress. He was the only Jewish delegate to any representative assembly in colonial times.
1786	The Virginia Statute of Religious Freedom was passed. It guaranteed religious equality to Jews in Virginia and became a model for other colonies.
1787	The Constitution of the United States barred religious tests for federal office.
1791	The First Amendment of the Bill of Rights prohibited congressional establishment of religion in the United States.
1809	Jacob Henry, a Jew, was allowed to retain his seat in the North Carolina House of Commons despite a state law limiting office holding to Protestants.
1815	The Congress of Vienna nullified the rights of German Jews, causing thousands to immigrate to the United States.
1826	The Maryland "Jew Bill" was passed. It ended religious tests against Jews in Maryland.
1848	The Revolution of 1848 in Europe caused many German Jews to come to America as political refugees.
1862	Rabbis were permitted to serve as U.S. military chaplains. General Ulysses S. Grant issued General Order No. 11, which expelled Jews as a class from the Department of the Tennessee.

Important Dates

1868	The Fourteenth Amendment was adopted. Subsequent court decisions broadened it to guarantee religious equality in the states.
1877	Joseph Seligman, a Jewish manufacturer, and his family were excluded from a resort hotel, foreshadowing the pattern anti-Semitism was to take in the United States.
1881–82	Discriminatory legislation and *pogroms* (government-sponsored attacks) against Russia's Jews spurred wholesale immigration to America.
1885	The Pittsburgh Platform was enunciated by Reform Jews. It stated their principles and beliefs.
1886	The Jewish Theological Seminary was founded by leaders of Conservative Judaism.
1914	Louis D. Brandeis became the leader of the American Zionist movement.
1915	Leo Frank, a Jew, was lynched in Georgia, a result of anti-Semitic hatred.
1924	The Johnson-Reed National Origins Quota Act drastically curtailed Jewish immigration to the United States.
1930–40	Anti-Semitism, stimulated by Nazi propaganda, reached alarming levels in the United States.
1939–46	Six million Jews were killed by the Nazis during World War II.
1948	President Harry S Truman recognized the State of Israel immediately after its establishment.
1967	Jewish Americans strongly supported Israel during the Six Day War.
1973	Jewish Americans contributed huge sums of money to Israel when the Yom Kippur War broke out.
1976	Jews throughout the world took pride in the heroic Israeli commando raid on Entebbe airfield in Uganda. This action freed hostages held by Palestinian terrorists.
1979	Egypt's President Anwar el-Sadat and Israel's Premier Menachim Begin signed a peace treaty, together with President Carter, in a White House ceremony a few months after a thirteen-day conference at Camp David.

Important Dates	
1981	Pressure generated by the New Right and Christian Right troubled many Jewish Americans as the "moral majority" and similar groups challenged the concept of separation of church and state.
1982	Many Jewish Americans were privately critical of Israel's military thrust into Lebanon to end PLO terrorism, which thus reflected a shift from unquestioned support to criticism of the Begin government.
1985	American Jews were shocked by President Reagan's visit to a military cemetery in Bitburg, Germany, which contains the graves of forty-seven members of the Waffen SS (Hitler's elite armed guard).
1993	Israel signed a peace agreement with the Palestine Liberation Organization (PLO). The United States Holocaust museum was opened in Washington, D.C. Ruth Bader Ginsberg was appointed to the United States Supreme Court.
1994	Israel and Jordan signed a peace agreement.

damental themes and concepts that have characterized American history, such as religious freedom, the achievement of civic equality, and the struggle of a group to maintain its ethnic identity while assimilating into the U.S. mainstream.

HISTORICAL ROOTS

Jewish history, from Biblical times to the settlement of the first Jews in America, is a vast, complicated story, woven into nearly 4,000 years of Western civilization. In the year 70 A.D., conquering Romans crushed the Jewish state in Palestine, driving most, but not all, of its inhabitants into exile. Many fled to Babylonia, where they established a community that soon outshone Palestine as a center of Jewish life. By the ninth century, the hub of the Jewish world had shifted to Spain, where cooperative attitudes of the Moors encouraged a golden age of Jewish scholarship, literature, and science. This lasted until the thirteenth century, when Christian brutality against Jews replaced the tolerant

Moorish rule. Entire Jewish communities were decimated, and countless numbers of Jews were forced or frightened into the Catholic church. Many professed Christianity but secretly adhered to Judaism. They were derisively referred to by the Spanish as *Marranos* (pigs). In 1492, the Spanish monarchs expelled the entire Jewish community. Nearly 150,000 Jews left Spain. A few made their way to America, where they laid the foundations of the Jewish community in America, which in time was to become the largest Jewish population in the world. Today approximately 31% of the world's Jews live in the United States, compared with 22% in Israel (Famighetti, 1993; Kosmin et al., 1991).

The earliest Jews *(Marranos)* to reach America arrived with Christopher Columbus in 1492. By the sixteenth century, *Marranos* were prominent in Portuguese Brazil, particularly in the city of Recife. In 1630 that city fell to the liberal Dutch, and Marranos joyfully abandoned the mask of Christianity. In 1654, when the Portuguese reconquered the city, they gave Jews the choice of baptism or exile. Most chose exile. Twenty-three of them found their way to the Dutch colony of New Amsterdam. Since then, Jewish immigration to the United States has been nearly continuous.

The Colonies

In New Amsterdam, Governor Peter Stuyvesant wished to expel the Jews, but the Dutch West India Company disagreed. He was ordered to permit them to remain as long as they did not become a burden on the colony. However, Stuyvesant confined them to homes in a narrow street that came to be known as "Jews' Alley." He denied them equality with other people in New Amsterdam, even refusing them permission to build a synagogue. The Jews, nonetheless, formed a congregation (1656) and worshipped in private homes. With the transfer of power to the British in 1664 their status gradually improved. A synagogue was permitted; it was completed in 1730. Ten years later, Parliament exempted Jews from saying the words, "upon the true faith of a Christian" in the oath required for naturalization in the English colonies.

Jews were welcomed in other colonies such as Rhode Island, Pennsylvania, Georgia, and South Carolina. There, under the enlightened leadership of men like Roger Williams, William Penn, James Oglethorpe, and John Locke, Jewish communities were established. But even in these colonies, Jewish participation in civic life was limited. Throughout the entire colonial period only one Jew, Francis Salvador of South Carolina, was elected (1774) to a representative congress or assembly. Nonetheless, Jews slowly gained the rights of domicile, trade, and religious organization. Where restrictions against them existed, they were usually ignored.

In some colonies, however, Jews were barred altogether. No Jewish community developed in Massachusetts, for example, until after the American Revolution. Virginia and Maryland, too, were unfriendly to Jews. Maryland was actually one of the last states to lift restrictions against Jews (1826).

Biblical Influence

Ironically, though few Jews lived in New England, Jewish influence there was pervasive and penetrating. The Puritan theocracy was modeled after that of ancient Israel, its early legal codes were patterned after the Law of Moses, and daily life and religious practices were influenced by the Hebrew Bible and the Judaic tradition. In New England, as was true throughout the colonies, there was considerable interest in the Hebrew language. Intelligent laymen studied it and frequently assembled collections of Hebraica. At Harvard and Yale, proficiency in Hebrew was required for graduation. In the eighteenth century the New England clergy, often in the forefront of the drive for independence, frequently referred to the democratic principles in the Hebrew Bible, as did political pamphleteers like Thomas Paine. In their hands it became a political, as well as a religious, text.

THE AMERICAN REVOLUTION

At the outbreak of the Revolution, Jewish Americans numbered about 2,000 of a total population of 2 million. Many were merchants and traders. Others were doctors, manual laborers, candlemakers, watchmakers, shoemakers, silversmiths, wigmakers, bakers, or butchers. Like other colonists, Jews participated in a wide range of professions and occupations. The notion of Jews as a homogeneous population was as erroneous then as it is today.

When fighting broke out, most Jews participated in the struggle for independence, even those of the merchant-shipowner class, whose commercial interests were in England. A few Jews were loyalists, but the majority participated as enlisted men and officers in the American army. Bernard Gratz of Philadelphia and other Jewish merchants signed nonimportation agreements. Aaron Lopez of Newport donated much of his personal fortune to the Continental cause. He and other shipowners outfitted their vessels with cannons and dispatched them against British ships. In Philadelphia, Haym Salomon was undoubtedly the most competent bill broker in America. As Broker to the Office of Finance, he sold bills of exchange and government notes for the highest possible prices and the lowest commissions. His son and the sons and grandsons of numerous Jews of the Revolutionary period served in the War of 1812.

Uriah Phillips Levy is perhaps the best known of these men. He ultimately reached the rank of Commodore in the U.S. Navy, despite a lifetime struggle to overcome anti-Semitism. Levy is best remembered for his crusade to end corporal punishment in the navy and for preserving Thomas Jefferson's home, Monticello, as a national shrine.

A result of the Revolution was that the colonists were no longer subjects of a king, but enfranchised citizens of their own country. Important as that was for the colonists in general, it was even more important for the Jews because it legitimized the rights and privileges they had won. It was the first time in the history of Western civilization that they had been a legitimate part of the body politic, no longer excluded from the civic life of the community because of their religion. This transformation was eloquently expressed in 1790 by George Washington in a letter to the Jews of Newport, Rhode Island, in which he wrote, "happily the government of the United States, which gives to bigotry no sanction, to persecution no assistance, requires only that they who live under its protection should demean themselves as good citizens."

Equality in the States

Constitutional guarantees of freedom of religion implicit in the Revolution were not automatically or universally guaranteed by the federal Constitution. Its protections were limited to suffrage and office-holding at the federal level. The states were as free as ever to impose religious tests that, in some cases, remained on the statute books long after the adoption of the Constitution. In Pennsylvania, state office-holding was limited to Christians; in New Jersey and North Carolina, it was restricted to Protestants. Not until the adoption of the Fourteenth Amendment in 1868 was a significant attempt made to limit the power of the states in this regard. Even then, it was many years before the Supreme Court wrote interpretations of the Fourteenth Amendment supporting the rights of religious minorities in the states. Thus, the struggle for full equality was thrown back to the states. In Virginia, Jefferson and Madison led the way with the Virginia Statute of Religious Freedom in 1786. By 1790, New York, Georgia, Pennsylvania, and South Carolina, states with established Jewish communities, had passed similar laws. Others tarried well into the nineteenth century.

In North Carolina in 1809, Jacob Henry, a Jew, was reelected to the state House of Commons. He was challenged on the grounds that his election violated a state requirement that all public officials be Protestant and accept the divine authority of the Christian Bible. After a spirited defense, he was permitted to retain his seat, but only by a legal subterfuge. The law itself was not changed regarding Jewish Americans until 1868, when the North Carolina state constitution, which also enfranchised Blacks, was adopted by a Reconstruction government.

Similarly, the Maryland Constitution of 1776 required "a declaration of belief in the Christian religion" in order to hold state office. A protracted struggle by Maryland Jews, with the aid of a gentile, Thomas Kennedy, who was a member of the state legislature, resulted in the Maryland "Jew Bill" in 1826. It provided that any citizen could qualify for any public office by declaring "his belief in a future state of rewards and punishments." Though still a religious test of sorts, it was not specifically aimed at Jews. By the end of the Jacksonian period, the few religious disabilities that remained were largely unenforced and a friendly attitude toward Jewish Americans prevailed.

GERMAN-JEWISH IMMIGRATION

Though German Jews had predominated in the colonies since 1728, the years from 1820 to 1880 are considered the period of German-Jewish immigration. During those sixty years, about 200,000 Jews came to the United States from Germany and neighboring countries, where for centuries Jews had been vulnerable to recurring outbursts of mass hysteria and violence by the surrounding Christian population. Often confined to ghettos and forbidden to enter many skilled trades and farming, Jews had developed a close-knit society that emphasized study of the Bible and frequently turned to trade and commerce. In the eighteenth century, the Enlightenment and the reforms of Napoleon battered down their civic disabilities, and the Jews entered the secular worlds of France and Germany. However, their emancipation was short-lived. In 1815, the Congress of Vienna sought to nullify their newly won rights, causing thousands to depart for America. They were actually part of an exodus of about 5 million Germans who sought political freedom and economic opportunity in the United States. After the Revolution of 1848, the number who came as political refugees increased.

The German immigrants spread out across the country, though most settled in the Ohio and Mississippi valleys. Many of them, Christians as well as Jews, turned to peddling, an occupation that required no training and little capital and that served the needs of rural and frontier America. From these humble beginnings, some peddlers managed to accumulate enough capital to acquire a cart, then a horse and wagon, and finally a small store, which in some cases evolved into modern department stores. Some stores founded by Jewish peddlers are Bamberger's, Bloomingdale's, Filene's, Magnin's, Gimbel's, and Macy's (a dry goods business that Isidor and Nathan Straus turned into a giant department store). Other Jewish immigrants remained in the growing cities of the East and were frequently engaged in tailoring or shoemaking or dealt in secondhand clothing or dry goods.

A small number of Jews went West and became part of the saga of the frontier as buffalo hunters, ranchers, newspaper men, mayors (Galveston, Texas, had a Jewish mayor in 1850), miners, explorers, traders, artists, and photographers. Solomon Nunes Carvalho was a prominent Jewish artist and photographer. He traveled with John Charles Fremont. Levi Strauss manufactured strong, copper-riveted denim trousers (Levi's) for the gold miners in California. By the mid-1850s, San Francisco had about 4,000 Jews.

The German-Jewish community in the nineteenth century was characterized by the multitude and variety of voluntary, self-help organizations that it established to meet a variety of social and political needs. A "Hebrew Benevolent Society" usually served many purposes in small communities. In larger cities, specific societies met specific needs, such as care of orphans or the poor. Five Jewish fraternal orders were born. The best known was B'nai B'rith in 1843. The Young Men's Hebrew Association (YMHA) was established at this time, as were a number of Jewish hospitals that provided kosher food to Jewish patients and training for Jewish medical students. During the Civil War, they admitted so many non-Jewish casualties that they became nonsectarian and have remained so to the present day.

Early attempts at Jewish schools met with little success. As public schools became popular, Jewish students attended them during the day and Jewish religious schools in the late afternoon or on Saturday or Sunday morning. This is still the most common form of Jewish education in the United States.

In 1843, the Reverend Isaac Leeser of Philadelphia founded a monthly publication, *The Occident*. Other Jewish periodicals appeared; the most important was that of Rabbi Isaac Mayer Wise, an outstanding Jewish leader and the father of Reform Judaism in America.

Reform Judaism

Most German Jews established their own congregations rather than join the existing Spanish congregations whose ritual and liturgy differed somewhat from their own. Consequently, between 1850 and 1870 the number of congregations in the United States rose from 37 to 189.

Among the new congregations, demands were soon heard for shorter religious services, elimination of Sabbath observance, the use of English rather than Hebrew for prayer, modified dietary laws, and elimination of many traditional restrictions that had been part of Jewish tradition for centuries. Their demands were answered by the Reform movement, which, having begun in Germany, found fertile ground in America. Its leader, Rabbi Isaac Mayer Wise, preached that Judaism must adapt to the American environment or it would die. Notwithstanding the bitter opposition of traditionalists, who felt it wrong to tamper with sacred law and tradition, the new movement had become so much a part of Jewish life in America by 1885 that a panel of Reform rabbis met in Pittsburgh to codify their principles and beliefs. While adhering to the moral teachings of Judaism, the "Pittsburgh Platform" rejected traditional practices "not adapted to the views and habits of modern civilization."

THE CIVIL WAR

Before and during the Civil War, Judaism took no common position on the question of slavery. Then, as now, individual Jews and congregations were entirely free of hierarchical control. Pronouncements by individuals, even rabbis, represented no more than their personal opinions, which varied from those of fanatical abolitionists like Michael Heilprin of Philadelphia to champions of slavery like Judah P. Benjamin, Secretary of State in the Confederate government and an intimate and influential adviser of Jefferson Davis.

Jewish merchants, whatever their inclination, played only a minimal role in the Atlantic slave trade. In the seventeenth century they were excluded from the Spanish and Portuguese colonies and banned from the French West Indies, areas of major slave trade activity. In the next century, when the slave trade was dominated by England, France, and Holland, Jewish names are virtually absent from the records. In general, geography determined the allegiance of American Jews, whose attitudes toward slavery reflected the culture in which they lived. Many Southern Jews, sensitive to proslavery pressures and concerned about anti-Semitism, prudently accepted the status quo. Others, steeped in the traditions of the South, embraced the Confederate cause promptly and enthusiastically. But Jews were not major slaveholders. Over 90% of the American slave population was concentrated in plantation districts where Jews were a rarity. Those who did hold slaves generally lived in cities and owned small numbers of domestic servants. In the North, many Jews were recent immigrants from Germany whose experience with persecution usually pitted them against slavery. When the fighting broke out, Jews in the North and South flocked to their respective colors. More than 6,000 Jewish soldiers and officers served in the Union forces, and several thousand Jews fought for the Confederacy, including 24 known staff officers.

Of greater significance than the number of Jewish participants in the war was the growth of anti-Semitism during this period. Though anti-Semitism had been present in American society since 1654, when the first Jews arrived in New Amsterdam, it was not until the Civil War that it became a national issue. The first incident occurred early in the war as Jewish soldiers in the Union army sought to have rabbis ordained as military chaplains. A furor of protest ensued as certain Protestant groups objected. In December 1861, the Reverend Arnold Fischel visited President Lincoln, who rectified the injustice.

But anti-Semitism would not be stilled. In December 1862, Ulysses S. Grant issued General Order No. 11. It expelled "the Jews, as a class" from the Department of the Tennessee without trial or hearing (the Department of the Tennessee was the district controlled by Grant's armies). Violators would be jailed until they could be deported as prisoners. Jews sent letters and telegrams to Jewish leaders all over the country. Cesar Kaskel, one of those deported, visited President Lincoln in Washington to protest. Lincoln was sympathetic. He directed Grant to cancel the infamous order.

The press of the country was divided. Newspapers supporting the administration generally defended Grant. Some printed anti-Jewish invective previously unheard in America. The *New York Times* condemned the order as "one of the deepest sensations of the war." Jewish Americans were stunned when the Senate and House of Representatives failed to pass resolutions castigating Grant's action. Partisan arguments in both houses obscured the moral and legal aspects of the matter. Grant never apologized for the order, but as president he displayed no antagonism toward Jewish Americans. Rather, he supported Jewish causes on a number of occasions and appointed Jews to public office.

In the Confederacy, verbal attacks against Jews were widespread. Jews were frequently accused of speculating in all manner of merchandise, thereby causing the horrendous wartime inflation that paralyzed the South. A Jewish stereotype became the Confederacy's scapegoat, whereas the real causes of inflation, insufficient industrial base, heavy wartime demands on industry, and a successful Union blockade, were ignored.

Postwar Anti-Semitism

The years following the Civil War witnessed the emergence of the chief forms of anti-Semitism that Jewish Americans have had to contend with: discrimination in certain professions and occupations and exclusion from certain residential areas, social clubs, fashionable resorts, private schools, and universities, particularly medical schools. Such anti-Semitic discrimination became more striking in the 1920s, 1930s, and 1940s.

As early as 1867, attempts by a number of insurance companies to deny Jews fire insurance became a public issue. Ten years later, Joseph Seligman, an eminent Jewish clothing manufacturer and his family, were excluded from a fashionable hotel in Saratoga, New York. At about the same time, the president of the Long Island Railroad declared, "We do not like Jews as a class." These incidents and the pattern of discrimination they foreshadowed must be viewed against a background of the improved social and economic status of Jews in America. By 1877, most Jews had left the ranks of the working class. But their rapid rise from humble origins made them abhorrent to high society. Moreover, thousands of eastern European Jews began immigrating to the United States after 1880. Their foreignness undoubtedly stimulated nativist tendencies and added to the determination of the White Anglo-Saxon Protestants in the country to exclude all Jews from their ranks.

Although anti-Semitism has never been an instrument of governmental policy in the United States, as has been the case in Europe, and though violence has never been a serious problem for Jewish Americans—even Grant's order produced no physical violence against them—the pattern of bigotry and hatred that characterized the post–Civil War years did lead to the Georgia lynching in 1915 of a Jew named Leo Frank.

Conservative and Orthodox Judaism

By 1885, Reform Judaism had deviated drastically from received Jewish tradition. Even before that year, traditionalists, alarmed at its growing strength, had organized a countermovement that became known as Conservative Judaism. By 1886, it was strong enough to found the Jewish Theological Seminary in New York City. Though it made some concessions to the modern world, Conservative Judaism remained faithful to the core of Jewish law and ancestral traditions.

The early organizational efforts of Conservative Judaism were unimpressive, but with the arrival of one-half million Orthodox eastern-European Jews by the end of the century, its prospects improved greatly. To many of the American-born children of the Orthodox, the Conservative movement offered an attractive compromise between their middle-class desire for social integration and their attachment to traditional Jewish culture. In 1901, Jewish philanthropists financed the reorganization of the Jewish Theological Seminary, which soon began graduating American-trained rabbis to satisfy the flourishing Conservative movement.

But it was Orthodox Judaism that benefited most from the immigration of eastern European Jews. By 1900, most of the 850 congregations in the United States were Orthodox. Two years later, the Union of Orthodox Rabbis was organized to "place Orthodox Judaism in America on a firm basis." One of the educational institutions it supported became the nucleus of Yeshiva University.

Despite the growth of both the Reform and Conservative movements, Orthodox Judaism has maintained a significant place in the American Jewish community. Its numbers were augmented after World War I with the influx of thousands of Orthodox Jews from eastern Europe, many of whom settled in New York City.

THE NEW IMMIGRATION

Between 1881 and 1924, more than 2 million Jews left eastern Europe because of anti-Jewish legislation and *pogroms* (government-sponsored attacks) against them. In some years, they came to the United States at the rate of more than 100,000 per year. The vast majority, as was true of other immigrant groups, settled in the northeastern states, particularly in the port cities of New

York, Boston, Philadelphia, and Baltimore. Others crowded into the great cities of the Midwest. The Jews moved into densely populated ethnic neighborhoods such as New York's Lower East Side, South Philadelphia, or Chicago's West Side. Data from 1908 to 1924 indicate that only 5% of Jews arriving in the United States returned to Europe, compared to 33% of the general immigration (Thernstrom, Orlov, & Handlin, 1980). Many found work in the new ready-to-wear clothing industry. They were attracted to it, not because of an inherent proclivity for tailoring, but because of the constant demand for cheap labor and the fact that many had had garment experience in Europe. Working conditions were deplorable. The highly competitive contract system and the sweatshops it generated regularly exploited the workers. The sweatshops were dark, airless, unsanitary firetraps in which whole families often worked to meet production quotas. Tuberculosis and other diseases were rampant. Laborers worked from 4:00 A.M. to 10:00 P.M. Men earned $6 to $10 a week; women and children much less.

Such conditions led to the formation in 1888 of the United Hebrew Trades in New York. It was the first organization to introduce Jewish immigrants to the trade union movement. After the turn of the century, Jewish clothing workers organized the powerful International Ladies' Garment Workers Union and the Amalgamated Clothing Workers of America. In 1911, a tragic fire at the Triangle Shirtwaist Factory in New York City underscored the need for better working conditions in the industry. Over the years, the International and the Amalgamated improved conditions and benefits and broke new ground in employer-employee relations. Since the end of World War I there has been a steady exodus of Jewish workers from the garment industry, but the legacy of the once largely Jewish unions remains an important chapter in the history of American labor.

Yiddish

Yiddish was the daily language of most of the eastern European Jews. Hebrew, the holy tongue, was reserved for prayer and study of the Bible. Though both use the Hebrew alphabet and are written from right to left, they are not the same. Yiddish is similar to German; Hebrew is a Semitic language.

Daily newspapers in Yiddish appeared in several U.S. cities, most notably in New York. They taught the immigrants American history and civics in the language they understood best. Many read Yiddish fiction in America. The stories of Sholom Aleichem, one of the better known Yiddish writers, inspired the hit Broadway musical *Fiddler on the Roof*. Yiddish theater, too, flourished and attained a high literary and dramatic level, producing a host of Yiddish dramatists. But the flowering of Yiddish was a phenomenon of the immigrant generation. By midtwentieth century, it had fallen into disuse. Gifted writers like Waldo Frank, Ben Hecht, Ludwig Lewisohn, Michael Gold, and Abraham Cahan wrote about the Yiddish experience in English. The stories of one contemporary Yiddish writer, Isaac Bashevis Singer, are enjoyed in their English translations. Singer was awarded the Nobel Prize for Literature in 1978.

Courses in Yiddish are offered in universities and adult education programs today in an attempt to preserve and revitalize Yiddish culture. The National Yiddish Book Center, founded in 1980, oversees the recovery, collection, and cataloguing of Yiddish books from around the world that would otherwise be thrown away. The center, which has collected 1.2 million books, has instituted a Yiddish library development program, Yiddish musical projects, and most recently a series of public radio broadcasts of Yiddish stories in English translation (Garnick, 1994).

THE INTERWAR PERIOD

Following World War I, America's traditional hospitality toward immigrants suddenly changed. Undoubtedly, anti-Semitic factors account in part for the series of restrictive immigration laws that, by 1924, virtually stopped Jewish immigration. In that year, the Johnson-Reed National Origins Quota Act blatantly curtailed immigration from eastern Europe, where most Jews lived, from southern Europe, and from non-White countries. Its system of national quotas remained in effect until 1965.

The prosperity of the war years enabled many Jewish Americans to move to newer, middle-class neighborhoods, foreshadowing a later exodus to the suburbs. The less affluent, often more religious Jews tended to remain in older neighborhoods, where eastern European orthodoxy survived in its purest forms. Kosher restaurants flourished, late afternoon Jewish schools, Yiddish publications, and Orthodox synagogues were abundant. In the newer neighborhoods, indifference, even skepticism, toward Jewish ritual was a common attitude. It seemed to foreshadow the demise of Judaism in America; yet that is not what happened. Instead, most Jewish Americans felt an overriding desire to preserve their Jewish cultural identity and pass it on to their children. This can be seen in their high rate of endogamous marriage and in the growth of congregations and Jewish schools in the newer Jewish neighborhoods during these years.

By 1940, Jewish Americans had transformed themselves from a working-class to a middle-class community of commercial, white-collar, and professional people who established an excellent record of achievement in the sciences, medicine, and other fields of endeavor.

For many Jews, education was a calculated means of social and economic improvement. But a more likely explanation of their drive for education is to be found in Jewish culture itself, which places a high priority on knowledge and learning for its own sake. Education was part of the value system that the Jewish immigrants brought with them, as well as part of the value system that sustained generations of pious Jews in their perpetual study of the Bible.

During these years, anti-Semitism assumed an ominous hue. The Ku Klux Klan reappeared. It burned fiery crosses in front of synagogues and smashed store windows of Jewish merchants. By 1925, it had more than four million members. In 1920, Henry Ford reprinted *The Protocols of the Elders of Zion* in his weekly newspaper, *The Dearborn Independent*. It was a clumsy fabrication, originally published in 1904 in Russia, purporting to be the minutes of a secret meeting of Jewish leaders in Prague in the last years of the nineteenth century, who plotted the overthrow of the world. Many Americans were prepared to believe it. During the Great Depression, Jewish bankers were accused of controlling world finance. A *Fortune Magazine* survey in 1936 proved conclusively that Jews played, at best, a minimal role in national and international banking, yet the myth persisted. Later, in the 1930s, as the influence of Nazism was increasingly felt in the United States, and attempts to prove that Jews were biologically inferior were imported, anti-Jewish propaganda intensified. Hatemongers like Father Charles E. Coughlin, the Detroit "radio priest," revived the myth of a Jewish take-over of the world. But they made little headway in the United States, and with the end of World War II, when the full dimensions of the Nazi holocaust were revealed, anti-Semitism ebbed to its lowest level in years. A 1981 public opinion poll showed anti-Semitism in the United States had declined significantly and that stereotyping of Jews by non-Jews was at an all-time low (Yankelovich, Skelly, & White, 1981).

ZIONISM

The two most important events in the history of the Jewish people since their dispersion 2,000 years ago have been the Nazi holocaust and the creation of the State of Israel in 1948. Modern political Zionism, as the proposal for the return of the Jewish people to Zion (Palestine) is known, is considered to have begun in 1897, when Theodore Herzl convened the first Zionist Congress in Basel, Switzerland. The Zionist movement in the United States drew its greatest support from the eastern European Jewish immigrants. A major factor in its growth was the emergence of Louis D. Brandeis as its leader, a role he held at the time of his appointment as associate justice of the U.S. Supreme Court in 1916. Yet, it was the Nazi holocaust that brought the Zionist goal to fruition (Linenthal, 1995).

Six million of Europe's Jews and five million other people were killed by the Nazis in World War II (Berenbaum, 1993). The majority were systematically murdered in specially built death camps. The commander of Auschwitz estimated that two and one-half million victims were executed at that camp alone, and another one-half million died there of starvation and disease. Had it not been for America's restrictive immigration laws during these years, many lives could have been saved. Only a pitifully small number of Jewish refugees reached the United States in the 1930s. The best known was Albert Einstein. Ships carrying refugees from Germany were actually turned away from U.S. shores and sent back to the Nazi crematoria. The consistent refusal of the United States and other Western nations to accept Jewish refugees led to the near fanatical determination of Zionists the world over to reestablish a homeland in Palestine as a haven for persecuted Jews from any land. It also accounts for the passionate support of contemporary Jews for Israel. After the war, when the culpability of the Western nations in not accepting more refugees became evident, the general public endorsed the Zionist program. When the State of Israel was proclaimed, President Harry S Truman recognized the new nation immediately. Though few Jewish Americans have moved to Israel, their emotional attachment to their homeland remains undiminished, as witnessed by their large outpouring of support during the Six Day War in 1967 and the Yom Kippur War in 1973. Nonetheless, Jewish Americans had mixed feelings about Israel's military push into Lebanon in 1982 to end PLO terrorism and were unwilling blindly to support the Begin government. Though many were uncomfortable with Israel's response to the intifada (Palestinian uprising on the West Bank), there was no broad-based decline in pro-Israel feeling.

JEWISH AMERICANS TODAY

Today, Jewish Americans are enjoying another golden age. Yet, as notable as their gains have been, there are a few important qualifications to be made. A sizable Jewish working class population still exists in a number of U.S. cities, where substantial numbers of Jews still live in poverty. A 1990 study showed that 14% of multiperson Jewish households had annual incomes below $20,000 and 19% of one-person households earned less than $12,500 (Kosmin et al., 1991, p. 19).

Until the early 1970s few Jews occupied positions of genuine power in the country's largest corporations. However, a 1982 study found no evidence of gross anti-Semitism, and another study, in the mid-1980s, also found no significant climate of corporate discrimination against Jewish executives (Klausner, 1989, pp. 33–39, 55).

The changed corporate environment for Jewish Americans was dramatically symbolized by the appointment in 1973 of Irving Shapiro, the Yiddish-speaking son of a poor Lithuanian Jewish immigrant, as chairman and chief executive officer of E. I. du Pont de Nemours and Company.

Postwar prosperity and the end of educational quotas and social barriers after World War II opened up opportunities for Jews, who entered the academic world in disproportionate numbers. The percentage of Jewish students and Jewish teachers in colleges and in graduate and professional schools is much higher than that of the general population. Seventy-one percent of Jewish men are college graduates, compared with 25% of American men generally, and 57% of Jewish women are college graduates, compared with 19% of all American women (Kosmin, 1992, p. 31).

Another symbol of Jewish acceptance in contemporary America was the explosive growth in Jewish-studies programs in colleges and universities in the 1980s. By 1985 more than 300 offered courses in Judaic studies, at least 40 had Jewish studies majors, and 27 offered graduate degrees. This was true even in institutions with relatively small Jewish enrollment (Silberman, 1985, pp. 226–227).

Further evidence of the assimilation of Jews is seen in their number in Congress. Today there are ten Jewish Senators. In 1963 there were only two and thirty-three Jewish members of the House of Representatives. While Jewish Congressmen in the past tended to represent the largely Jewish districts in New York, the forty-three Jewish members of the 103rd Congress represent diverse communities all over the United States, where the Jewish population is often minuscule. States like Vermont (0.9% Jewish population) and New Mexico (0.4%) have elected Jews to represent them (Hoffman, 1993).

Politically, American Jews tend to be more liberal than the general population. Despite the shift in the early 1970s, when the U.S. political center moved to the right, carrying many Jews with it, the center of the Jewish political spectrum remained left of the national center. Today nearly two out of three Jews consider themselves liberal rather than conservative (Kosmin, et al., 1991, p. 31).

Although the reasons for their liberal attitudes are unclear, the commitment of Jews to the reformist tradition, no doubt, has deep roots in their religious, economic, and political history and is related to their own struggle for equality and security from persecution. It may also be a concomitant aspect of a highly educated people as much concerned with values as with economic interest.

The generation of Jews that came of age after World War II was in the forefront of the civil rights movement and active in liberal and radical politics. Students, professors, and rabbis were especially prominent in the demonstrations, marches, sit-ins, and voter-registration campaigns of the 1960s.

Today, Jewish Americans are unquestionably more secure in U.S. society and more willing to demonstrate, protest, and lobby in their own self-interest than ever before. Nonetheless, disturbing manifestations of bigotry and anti-Semitism by such organizations as the revived Ku Klux Klan and the American Nazi Party are cause for anxiety, as are signs of a worldwide increase in anti-Semitism. Of particular concern is the outbreak of anti-Semitism in segments of the Black community.

Friction between Blacks and Jews emerged in the mid-1980s and erupted into violence in 1991, when Blacks rioted in Crown Heights, an orthodox Jewish community in Brooklyn, after a Jewish motorist struck and killed a Black youngster. Tension heightened in the autumn of 1993, when Khalid Abdul Muhammad, a top aide to Nation of Islam leader Louis Farrakhan, delivered an anti-Semitic speech at Kean College in New Jersey. Though the golden age of Black-Jewish cooperation seemed over, well-meaning Blacks and Jews sought to quiet the angry voices and repair the damage to Black-Jewish relations.

Since the 1960s, the number of Jews allowed to leave the Soviet Union and settle in the United States or Israel has fluctuated greatly. It has varied from a high of 51,000 in 1979 to as few as 1,000 in 1984. Then, under *glasnost*, the number spurted to more than 30,000 in 1989 (A Troublesome Exodus, 1989). However, under the Reagan and Bush administrations, the Immigration and Naturalization Service began to deny many Soviet Jewish emigres status as political refugees, greatly reducing the numbers coming to this country and vastly increasing the numbers relocating in Israel.

There are also major changes in the Jewish family. Only 14% of Jews live in a traditional household consisting of a Jewish married couple with children, and over 19% of Jewish Americans live alone. Thirteen percent of households consist of an interfaith couple with children, which is the fastest growing group. The rate of out marriage in 1990 was 52%, up from 31% in 1974, which seems to threaten the survival of Judaism in America (Kosmin et al., 1991). Fears of its demise, however, are premature. The Jewish community remains an important ethnic and religious group in U.S. society, reflecting a wide diversity of social class, religious commitment, political outlook, and economic status.

TEACHING STRATEGIES

To illustrate how content related to Jewish Americans can be used to integrate the curriculum, exemplary strategies are identified for teaching these concepts at the grade levels indicated: *values* (primary grades), *anti-Semitism* (intermediate and upper grades), and *identity* (high school grades).

Primary Grades

CONCEPT: Values

Generalization: The values of Jewish Americans, like those of other ethnic minority groups, are often reflected in their literature.

1. The obligation to help the poor and needy is one dominant value of Judaism. The Bible and rabbinic literature teach that charity is not a favor to the poor but something to which they have a right and the donor an obligation. It is a duty usually equated with righteousness or justice. Ask the class: Which is better, to give charity or to receive it? Ask students to explain their answers and to give examples from their own experience.

2. A great Jewish philosopher, Maimonides, listed eight increasingly virtuous ways of giving charity. People are to give as follows:

    a. But grudgingly.
    b. Less than is fitting, but willingly.
    c. Only after being asked to.
    d. Before being asked to.
    e. In such a way that the giver does not know to whom he or she is giving.
    f. In such a way that the one who receives does not know who has given to him or her.
    g. In such a way that neither the giver nor the one who receives knows the identity of the other.
    h. The highest form of charity is to help the poor become self-supporting by lending them money, taking them into partnership, or giving them work, for in this way there is no loss of self-respect.

3. Put Maimonides's eight steps on the chalkboard in scrambled order (or reproduce as a handout). Ask the class to arrange them in the proper order, from least to most virtuous. Ask students to explain the order of their lists. Then show the eight steps according to Maimonides. Discuss and ask for student examples of charity at each level.

4. Tell the class that Jewish stories, like those of other people, often reflect the ideas that they think are important, that is, their values. "If Not Still Higher," a story by Isaac L. Peretz, deals with charity. It is in *The Case against the Wind and Other Stories* by I. L. Peretz (New York: Macmillan, 1975). Read or tell the story to the class and ask the questions that follow.

If Not Still Higher

The Rabbi of Nemirov disappeared every morning during High Holy Days Selichoth prayers (prayers asking for forgiveness). Some people thought he went to heaven each morning. One day a Jew from Lithuania came to town. He laughed and assured the people that no one could go to heaven while still alive. But he decided to find out for himself where the rabbi went.

    Early the next morning he followed the rabbi to a nearby forest. The rabbi was dressed as a workman. He saw the rabbi chop down a small tree, cut it into sticks, make a bundle of them, and sling them over his shoulder. He then walked to a broken-down hut where a sick, old woman lived.

    "Who is it?" called the woman.

    "Vassili," answered the disguised rabbi, "I have wood for sale for only six cents." He entered the house without waiting for an answer. The Lithuanian stole in behind him.

"How can a poor widow afford even six cents?" asked the old woman.

"I trust you," replied the rabbi.

"And who will light the fire?" lamented the widow. "I am too weak to get up."

"I will," said the rabbi.

As he lit the fire, the rabbi recited the Selichoth prayers. The Lithuanian watched in silence. From that moment on, he became a follower of the Rabbi of Nemirov. Later, when the people would say their rabbi flew to heaven during Selichoth prayers, he would add quietly, "If not still higher!"

Questions

1. What puzzled the people of Nemirov?
2. Where did they think their rabbi went each morning during Selichoth prayers? What does this tell about their opinion of him?
3. Was it right for the Lithuanian to follow the rabbi the next day?
4. What did the Lithuanian find out? How did it influence him? Why?
5. What does the title of the story mean?
6. Why didn't the Rabbi of Nemirov give the old woman the wood for nothing? At which level of Maimonides's list does the rabbi's deed belong? Explain.
7. What important Jewish idea does the story bring out?

Intermediate and Upper Grades

CONCEPT: Anti-Semitism

Generalization: Anti-Semitism has been and remains a serious concern of most Jewish Americans.

1. Read the following letter to the class. It was written to the editor of the Jewish *Daily Forward* in 1932. It is reprinted from *A Bintel Brief,* edited by Isaac Metzker (Garden City, N.Y.: Doubleday, 1971). After reading, ask the questions that follow.

Dear Editor,

I am an immigrant from Russia, my wife is American-born, and we are both free thinkers. We have two grown children, a son and a daughter, who know they are Jews but never saw any signs of religion or holidays in our home. Even *Yom Kippur* is just another day to us. For the last twenty years we've lived among Christians and we socialize with them. Our children also go around with Gentiles.

Some time ago a Christian girl began to come to our house, seemingly to visit our daughter, but it was no secret to us that she was after our twenty-three-year-old son, with whom she was friendly. We said nothing about it, because we wouldn't have minded having her for a daughter-in-law.

Once the girl invited our son to a party at her house where all the other guests were Gentiles. They were all having a good time until one of the guests, whether in jest or earnest, began to make fun of Jews. I don't know what happened there, but I am sure they didn't mean to hurt my son, because none of them, not even his girlfriend, knew that he is Jewish. But he was insulted and told the girl so. Then he told her that he is Jewish and this was a surprise to her.

My son left the party immediately and from that day on he is changed. He began to ask questions about religion, debated with me about things that formerly hadn't interested him. He wanted to know where I was born, how many Jews there are in the world, why the religious don't eat pork, where the hatred of Jews came from, and on and on. He was not satisfied with my short answers but began to read books looking for more information. My son also berated me for not giving him a Jewish upbringing.

His Gentile girlfriend came to beg him to forgive her. She cried and explained that it was not her fault, but he didn't want to have anything to do with her because, it seems, he was deeply insulted. His head was filled with one thought, Jewishness. He found Jewish friends, he was drawn into a Zionist club and they worked on him so that he has come to me with a suggestion that I give up the business and we all go to Palestine. And since he sees that I am not about to go, he's getting ready to go alone.

At first we took it as a joke, but we see now that he's taking it very seriously. Well, my going is out of the question. I am not that crazy. But what can be done about him? I'm willing to give in to his whim. I'm sure that in Palestine he'll sober up and realize that not everyone who is Jewish must live in Palestine. My wife is carrying on terribly; what do I mean, allowing my son to travel to a wild country [where there is conflict between Arabs and Jews]? She says we should not give him the money for the trip. But our son says he will find a way to reach the Jewish Homeland.

My wife and I are very anxious to hear your opinion.

Respectfully, A Reader

SOURCE: Excerpt from *A Bintel Brief* by Isaac Metzker. Copyright © 1971. Reprinted by permission.

Questions

1. How would you advise the writer of the letter? (The editor replied: "Your son is a very sensitive and thinking person. Since he is an adult you must let him go his way and do what he wants to do.")
2. Did the son overreact to the anti-Jewish insult? Explain. How else might he have reacted? How would you react if someone insulted you because of your race, religion, or ethnic group?
3. Where and how do people learn anti-Semitism (or any kind of prejudice)? What can you do to help combat it?

4. If someone in your family made anti-Semitic jokes with which you disagreed, what could you do? What would you do?

2. Ask students to prepare a short report accounting for Jewish survival after centuries of persecution in Europe. Ask them to find out what Jews did to survive (e.g., developed strong Jewish communities and families, became *Marranos,* emigrated, etc.).

3. Write to any of the following Jewish organizations to learn how they combat anti-Semitism in the United States. (Consult your telephone directory for local offices.)

American Jewish Committee, 165 East 56th Street, New York, NY 10022

American Jewish Congress, 15 East 84th Street, New York, NY 10028

Anti-Defamation League of B'nai B'rith, 823 United Nations Plaza, New York, NY 10017

Council of Jewish Federations, 730 Broadway, New York, NY 10003

National Conference of Christians and Jews, 71 Fifth Avenue, Suite 1100, New York, NY 10003

National Jewish Community Relations Advisory Council, 443 Park Avenue South, New York, NY 10016

4. Assign reports on any of the following topics:
   a. The Leo Frank case in 1915 (a rare case of a Jewish lynching in the United States).
   b. The revived Ku Klux Klan of the 1920s.
   c. The revived Ku Klux Klan and American Nazi Party today.
   d. Grant's Order No. 11, during the Civil War.
   e. *The Protocols of the Elders of Zion.*
   f. Nazi-inspired hate organizations in the United States during the 1930s (e.g., The German-American Bund, The Silver Shirts, The Order of '76).
   g. Father Charles E. Coughlin, the Detroit radio priest.

5. Have students read an appropriate book on the Holocaust. (Refer to the student bibliography of this chapter.) After reading, discuss with the class how anti-Semitism led to the Nazi holocaust. Ask: Could a Holocaust happen in the United States? Is it likely to happen? What is the difference between the two questions? Could it happen to a minority group other than Jews? Why or why not?

6. Ask students to compare anti-Semitism to racism and other forms of discrimination and prejudice in the United States. Ask what can be done to combat them.

7. Assign research reports about anti-Semitism in the United States in any of the following periods:
   a. Colonial
   b. 1776–1860
   c. 1860–1924
   d. 1924–1948
   e. 1948–1980
   f. The present.

Valuing Activity

Read the following story to the class and ask the questions that follow.

Mr. Cohen and the Christmas Tree

Mr. and Mrs. Cohen live in Chicago, where Mr. Cohen owns a small business. The Jewish religion is an important part of their family life. They are members of a synagogue and attend religious services every week. They observe Jewish holidays and customs, and Mrs. Cohen keeps a traditional Kosher home and lights Sabbath candles every Friday evening. Their only son is a college professor. His wife is Jewish but she is from a nonreligious background. They do not follow the Jewish religion closely. They have two children, a girl, eight, and a son, four. They live in a suburb not far from Mr. and Mrs. Cohen.

Last Christmas the Cohens were in their son's neighborhood and dropped in for a surprise visit. When they entered the living room they saw their son trimming a Christmas tree and his two children helping him. Mr. Cohen was furious. His two grandchildren greeted him with "Merry Christmas."

Mr. Cohen did not answer. He did not even take off his coat. He looked at his son and said, "Jews do not have Christmas trees." He took his wife by the arm and they turned to leave. Their son and daughter-in-law begged them to stay, but Mr. Cohen would not change his mind. Mrs. Cohen was confused. She felt her place was with her husband and returned home with him.

Mr. Cohen's son says he had the Christmas tree only for the sake of his children, so they would not feel different from their non-Jewish friends. He assured his father the Christmas tree had nothing to do with religion. He did not consider it wrong having a Christmas tree and felt his father had no right to be angry about it.

Mr. Cohen says his grandchildren are different from Christian children and should feel the difference. He argues that Jews and Gentiles should observe national American holidays, but Christmas is the most important religious holiday of the Christians, and Jews have nothing to do with it. They should not have Christmas trees.

He refuses to visit his son's home and Mrs. Cohen cannot convince him to change his mind.

Questions

1. Who is right, Mr. Cohen or his son?
2. Do you think Mr. Cohen is being unfair to his wife, his son, his daughter-in-law, his grandchildren?
3. What alternatives are open to Mr. Cohen? To his son?
4. Do you think Mr. Cohen's son should be concerned that his children feel that they are different from other children?
5. Do you think Christians should send or expect to receive Christmas cards from their Jewish friends? Justify your answer.

High School Grades

CONCEPT: Identity

Generalization: Jewish Americans have become highly assimilated in U.S. society, yet many maintain a strong Jewish identity that they are anxious to preserve and transmit to their children.

1. Jewish Americans are frequently referred to as "American Jews." This reversal of noun and adjective is generally not true of other ethnic minority groups. Ask students to explain the difference and tell its significance. Have students ask a sample of Jewish Americans which term they prefer. Have them report their findings to the class.

2. Ask the class: "Are the Jews a nation, an ethnic group, a religious minority, a people, a race, all of these, some of these, or none of these?" (The answer is, "some of these." Jews are not a race.) Tell the class that the government of Israel in 1958 established a special committee to provide an answer to the perplexing question, "Who is a Jew?" The results were inconclusive. Have students conduct a survey of their own to see if they can provide an answer. Ask if other ethnic minority groups have trouble defining themselves. Why? Why not?

3. Have students read and report on a book about Jews by a Jewish American author. Reports should tell how the individuals or families they read about reconcile their desire to become Americanized with the desire to preserve their Jewish heritage. A list of some Jewish authors follow:

Sholom Aleichem	Chaim Potok
Mary Antin	Leo Rosten
Sholom Asch	Henry Roth
Saul Bellow	Irwin Shaw
Abraham Cahan	Leon Uris
Edna Ferber	Ellie Wiesel
Alfred Kazin	Herman Wouk
Ludwig Lewisohn	Israel Zangwill
Bernard Malamud	

4. Jews, like other ethnic minorities, have been concerned with maintaining their identity in America. One way they have done this is by establishing numerous Jewish institutions and organizations. Have the students complete the chart in Table 9-1 by listing parallel institutions of other ethnic minority groups in column 2 and similarities and differences in column 3.

5. Since 1948, Jewish Americans have become passionate supporters of Israel, despite the fact that few of them or their immediate ancestors were born there or plan to live there. Assign essays comparing Jewish attitudes toward Israel with those of another ethnic minority group to its country of origin. What similarities and differences exist? How do students account for them?

6. The rate of intermarriage for Jewish Americans has increased dramatically in recent years. Ask students to conduct an informal survey among their friends and fam-

Table 9-1 SIMILARITIES AND DIFFERENCES IN JEWISH
AND NON-JEWISH ORGANIZATIONS

1. Jewish Institutions	2. Non-Jewish Institutions	3. Similarities, Differences
YMHA		
Jewish Social Centers		
Synagogues		
Jewish Hospitals		
Yiddish Theater		
Yiddish Press		
Jewish Publication Society		
Fraternal Organizations		
Fund-Raising Organizations		

ilies to determine if this is true of other ethnic and religious groups. Then discuss or debate the pros and cons of intermarriage.

7. Read the letter quoted earlier from *A Bintel Brief* to the class (or distribute as a handout) and ask the following questions:

a. Does the family described in this letter maintain a strong Jewish identity? Do they attempt to preserve and transmit it to their children? What evidence can you find in this letter to support your answer?

b. Should the son have been angry with his father for failing to give him a Jewish upbringing? Should parents teach their children to think of themselves as members of their particular ethnic group?

c. Why does the son join a Zionist club and want to go to Palestine? How will this solve his problem?

d. In what ways could the son satisfy his need to identify as a Jew without moving to Palestine?

8. Have students contact an office of the Allied Jewish Appeal of the Federation of Jewish Charities to learn through what institutions Jewish Americans financially support their own community and Israel. Have them report their findings to the class.

9. If possible, visit an observant Jewish home on a Friday evening or on a Jewish holiday. Or invite a rabbi to speak to the class. Try to learn what customs, traditions, and values have helped the Jewish family to withstand many of the disruptive influences of history and of contemporary life.

REFERENCES

Berenbaum, M. (1993). *The World Must Know: The History of the Holocaust as Told in the United States Holocaust Memorical Museum.* Boston: Little, Brown.

Famighetti, R. (Ed.). (1993). *The World Book Almanac and Book of Facts, 1994.* Mahwah, N.J.: Funk & Wagnalls.

Garnick, D. (1994, July 14). One Mentsh's Dream. *The Jerusalem Report,* pp. 34–35.

Hoffman, M. (1993, February). More Jews in Congress: Doesn't It Make a Difference? *Moment,* pp. 32–39.

Klausner, S. Z. (1989, September). Anti-Semitism in the Executive Suite, Yesterday, Today and Tomorrow. *Moment,* pp. 33–39, 55.

Kosmin, B. (1992, August). The Permeable Boundaries of Being Jewish in America. *Moment,* pp. 30–33, 51.

Kosmin, B., Goldstein, S., Waksberg, J., Lerer, N., Keysar, A., & Scheckner, J. (1991). *Highlights of the CJF 1990 National Jewish Population Survey.* New York: Council of Jewish Federations.

Linenthal, E. T. (1995). *Preserving Memory: The Struggle to Create America's Holocaust Museum.* New York: Viking.

Silberman, C. E. (1985). *A Certain People.* New York: Summit Books.

Thernstrom, S., Orlov, A., & Handlin, O. (Eds.). (1980). *Harvard Encyclopedia of American Ethnic Groups.* Cambridge: Harvard University Press.

A Troublesome Exodus. (1989, September 25). *Newsweek,* p. 52.

Yankelovich, Skelly, and White (an opinion research company). "Anti-Semitism in the United States," prepared for the American Jewish Committee, mimeograph, 1981, in a study cited in M. Himmelfarb & D. Singer (Eds.). *American Jewish Year Book* (Vol. 83, pp, 67, 98). New York: American Jewish Committee; and Philadelphia: Jewish Publication Publication Society.

ANNOTATED BIBLIOGRAPHY

Books For Teachers

Especially Recommended

Dinnerstein, L. (1994) *Anti-Semitism in America.* New York: Oxford University Press.

A study of anti-Semitism from its origins in European Christianity to the present. Dinnerstein argues that anti-Semitism is waning, notwithstanding its increase in the Black community.

Feingold, H. L., (Ed.). (1992) *The Jewish People in America.* Baltimore: The Johns Hopkins University Press.

A five-volume set sponsored by the American Jewish Historical Society. Chronicles Jewish life in the United States from colonial times to the present.

Fischel J. & Pinsker, S. (Eds.). (1992). *Jewish-American History and Culture: An Encyclopedia*. New York: Garland.

A one-volume encyclopedia of American Jewish life. Emphasis is on the impact Jews have had on American life and culture.

Johnson, P. (1987). *A History of the Jews*. New York: Harper & Row.

Perhaps the best examination of Judaism and Jewish history in the English language by a non-Jew.

Lipset, S. M. & Raab, E. (1995). *Jews and the New American Scene*. Cambridge: Harvard University Press.

This important book relies heavily on statistical data. The authors are concerned about the future of American Judaism as Jews are increasingly absorbed by the universalism of U.S. society.

Sachar, H. M. (1992). *A History of the Jews in America*. New York: Knopf.

This is a major work covering the Jews in America from their arrival in 1654 to the present.

Singer, D. (Ed.). (1995). *American Jewish Yearbook* (Vol. 95). New York: American Jewish Committee; and Philadelphia: Jewish Publication Society.

This annual yearbook, in continuous publication since 1889, is an excellent source of information about the American Jewish community. Yearly editions include a compendium of issues of concern to Jews and directories of national and community Jewish organizations, welfare funds, community councils, and other vital information.

Telushkin, J. (1991). *Jewish Literacy:* New York: William Morrow.

In 346 short entries, Rabbi Telushkin tells the most important things to know about the Jewish religion, essential trends, concepts, personalities, and culture.

Other References

Birmingham, S. (1984). *"The Rest of Us": The Rise of America's Eastern European Jews*. Boston: Little, Brown.

This book tells the story of the eastern European Jews who came to North America between 1882 and 1915 and their role in American business and society.

Bletter, D. & Grinker, L. (1989). *The Invisible Thread: Portraits of Jewish American Women*. Philadelphia: Jewish Publication Society.

Through interviews and stunning photographs the authors provide intimate portraits of Jewish women that shatter stereotypes of the Jewish mother and the Jewish American princess.

Cohen, N. W. (1984). *Encounter with Emancipation: The German Jews in the United States, 1830–1914*. Philadelphia: Jewish Publication Society.

This well-documented study portrays the Americanization of the Jews who came to this country in the nineteenth century and, as the author maintains, set the stage for the great wave of eastern European Jewish immigrants who came later.

Dawidowicz, L. S. (1984). *On Equal Terms: Jews in America 1881–1981*. New York: Holt, Rinehart and Winston.

This book gives an overview of American Jewish history from the beginning of the Jewish mass migrations from eastern Europe in 1881 to the present.

Dershowitz, A. M. (1991) *Chutzpah*. Boston: Little, Brown.

The author, a well-known lawyer, reflects on his origins as an Orthodox Jew in Brooklyn and his generation of Jews coming of age in America. He argues that Jews are as fully American as the descendants of the Mayflower.

Einstein, S. J. & Kukoff, L. (1989). *Every Person's Guide to Judaism*. New York: Union of American Hebrew Congregations.

An introduction to Judaism as a civilization. It is organized into four sections: "The Cycle of the Year," "The Cycle of Life," "Aspects of Faith," and "Contemporary Jewish Life."

Frazier, N. (1992). *Jewish Museums of North America: A Guide to Collections, Artifacts, and Memorabilia*. New York: Wiley.

A guide to collections of Judaica in the United States and Canada. Gives address, telephone number, and hours of each museum as well as a brief essay about its history and collections. Includes some museums that are not exclusively Jewish but that feature Jewish works.

Geffen, R. M. (Ed.). (1993). *Celebration & Renewal: Rites of Passage in Judaism*. Philadelphia: Jewish Publication Society.

Topics in this book include birth, parenting, conversion to Judaism, marriage, midlife, divorce, sickness, aging, death, and mourning.

Hertzberg, A. (1989). *The Jews in America: Four Centuries of an Uneasy Encounter: A History*. New York: Simon & Schuster.

A survey of the Jewish experience in America. Topics include the erosion of Jewishness, the problematic relationship between Jews and Blacks, Jews and the state of Israel, and the invention of the so-called Jewish mother.

Karp, A. J. (1985). *Haven and Home: A History of the Jews in America*. New York: Schocken Books.

Explores the Jewish experience from colonial times to the present day. Includes a variety of source documents.

Kertzer, M. N., Revised by Hoffman, L. A. (1993). *What Is a Jew?* New York: Macmillan.

A guide to the beliefs, traditions, and practices of Judaism. Excellent for both Jew and non-Jew. Answers more than 100 commonly asked questions.

Landau, R. S. (1994). *The Nazi Holocaust*. Chicago: Ivan R. Dee.

The author asks key questions about the Holocaust, such as, "How was it possible for a civilized society to produce such barbarity?" or "Was the Holocaust a unique phenomenon?" He then looks for answers and the lessons inferred from them.

Libo, K. & Howe, I. (Eds.). (1984). *We Lived There, Too: A Documentary History of Pioneer Jews and the Westward Movement of America, 1630–1930.* New York: St. Martin's Press.

This is a story of pioneer Jews told in their own words and pictures.

Pogrebin, L. C. (1991). *Deborah, Golda, and Me: Being Female and Jewish in America.* New York: Crown Publishers.

This is the personal story of the author's disillusionment with traditional, male-dominated Judaism, her embrace of feminism, and her struggle to reconcile her Jewish and female identities. She deals with a wide range of contemporary issues.

Silberman, C. E. (1985). *A Certain People: American Jews and Their Lives Today.* New York: Summit Books.

In this examination of American Jewish life the author repudiates the prophets of doom and decline and maintains that contemporary society offers Jews and other ethnic groups opportunities heretofore undreamed of.

Wyman, D. S. (1984). *The Abandonment of the Jews: America and the Holocaust 1941–1945.* New York: Pantheon Books.

This is a documented account of the degree to which all segments of the U.S. population failed to do even the minimum to save some of the 6 million Jewish victims of the Nazi holocaust.

Books for Students

Barrie, B. (1990). *Lone Star.* New York: Delacourt.

This is the story of ten-year-old Jane, who does not understand why her Orthodox Jewish grandfather objects to her having a Christmas tree. Understanding comes when she learns of the Nazi murder of European Jews. (Intermediate/Middle School)

Bresnick-Perry, R. Illustrated by M. Reisberg. (1992) *Leaving for America.* San Francisco: Children's Book Press.

The humorous story of the author's migration to the United States at age seven. Brightly colored illustrations complement the tone of the story. (Primary)

Brooks, J. (1990). *Naked in Winter.* New York: Watts/Orchard/Jackson.

The story of a teenage Jewish boy in Chicago in the late forties who has problems with girls. His guilt comes partially from the pain in his Jewish immigrant home. (Middle School/High School).

Bukiet, M. (1995) *While the Messsiah Tarries.* New York: Harcourt.

Nine short stories of American Jews who search for answers and for their faith. Reminiscent of Isaac Bashevis Singer. (High School)

Bush, L. (1986). *Rooftop Secrets and Other Stories of Anti-Semitism.* New York: Union of American Hebrew Congregations.

Each of the eight short stories in this book describes a Jewish child's bout with anti-Semitism, from the Spanish Inquisition to modern times. (Middle School)

Butwin, F. (1991). *The Jews in America*. Minneapolis: Lerner.

This informative book is part of the Lerner In America *Series. (Middle School/ High School)*

Chaikin, M. (1989). *Feathers in the Wind*. New York: Harper and Row.

This is a thoughtfully written chapter in a boy's development. Black-and-white drawings mirror the Orthodox Jewish milieu in which the author roots her story. (Intermediate)

Cohen, B. (1994). *Make a Wish, Molly*. New York: Doubleday.

When Molly is invited to a classmate's birthday party during Passover she must decide whether to eat birthday cake or respect the Passover restrictions against regular baked goods. An excellent book to read aloud. (Primary)

Cohen, B. (1989). *Tell Us Your Secret*. New York: Bantam Books.

An involving story of second-generation survivor guilt set in the context of high school philosophizing about religion, writing, and self-determination. (Middle School)

Dolan, E. F. (1985). *Anti-Semitism*. New York: Franklin Watts.

This book is as much a general history of the Jewish people as it is a history of anti-Semitism. (Middle School)

Epstein, J. (1991). *The Goldin Boys*. New York: Norton.

Nine charming short stories set in Chicago. Epstein's characters have a uniquely Jewish way of thinking and speaking. (High School)

Fluek, T. & Finkler, L. (1994). *Passover: As I Remember It*. New York: Knopf.

A nostalgic portrait of Passover in a tiny Polish village sixty years ago. Gives an excellent picture of a bygone way of life. (Primary/Intermediate)

Frank, A., Edited by O. H. Frank & M. Pressler, Translated by S. Massotty. (1995). *The Diary of a Young Girl: The Definitive Edition*. New York: Doubleday.

This new edition of The Diary of Anne Frank *restores passages that previously had been deleted. The new translation is far superior to earlier versions. (High School)*

Greene, P. (1993). *The Sabbath Garden*. New York: Dutton/Lodestar.

This is the story of conflict between a teenager and an elderly Orthodox Jew. Set in Manhattan's Lower East Side. Lots of action. (Middle School/High School)

Haas, G. (1995). *Tracking the Holocaust*. Minneapolis: Runestone Press (Lerner).

The author uses eight stories of survivors, including her own, to describe the Holocaust.

Hesse, K. (1992) *Letters from Rifka*. New York: Holt.

In letters to her cousin back "home" in Russia, twelve-year-old Rifka describes her journey through Europe to the United States in 1919. (Intermediate/Middle School)

Hoobler, D. & Hoobler, T. (1995). *The Jewish Family Album*. New York: Oxford University Press.

An informative and excellent resource containing an exciting text that includes original documents and selections from diaries, letters, and other memorabilia. (Middle School/High School)

Jaffe, N. (1993). *The Uninvited Guest and Other Jewish Holiday Tales*. Illustrated by Elivia. New York: Scholastic.

This book tells seven Jewish holiday tales, one each for Shabbat (Sabbath), Rosh Hashanah, Yom Kippur, Hanukkah, Sukkot, Passover, and Purim. Bright, colorful artwork enhances the book. Includes a glossary with pronunciation guide and also a bibliography. (Intermediate)

Kane, A. (1995) *Rabbi, Rabbi*. New York: St. Martin's.

A warm, moving story of a young man groomed by his Orthodox Jewish parents to be a rabbi, and Rebecca, a young woman he meets at a Catskill resort. Tension develops when Rebecca wants to become a rabbi, contrary to Orthodox law. Jewish faith and practice are beautifully portrayed. (High School)

Koltach, A. (1992). *The Jewish Child's First Book of Why*. Illustrated by H. Araten. Middle Village, N.Y.: Jonathan David Publishers.

A question-and-answer book about the spirit and history of Jewish holidays. The art work is colorful and very contemporary. (Primary)

Lehrman, R. (1992). *The Store That Mama Built*. New York: Macmillan.

This story is about a close-knit, Russian Jewish immigrant family in Steeltown, Pennsylvania, in 1917, struggling to assimilate into the mainstream society, yet retaining its ethnic and religious traditions. The story deals with ethnic prejudice and includes racial epithets, which may be disturbing to some readers. (Intermediate)

Levine, P. (1992). *Ellis Island to Ebbets Field: Sport and the American Jewish Experience*. New York: Oxford University Press.

The first real history of sport in Jewish American life. Covers basketball, baseball, boxing, track and field, and tennis. Challenges stereotypes that Jews were uninterested in sports. (High School)

Levitin, S. (1993). *Journey to America*. New York: Atheneum.

A reissue of Levitin's 1970 novel about a Jewish family that flees Hitler's Germany in 1938. After Papa sails to the United States, Mama and her three daughters wait in Switzerland until he can send for them. (Intermediate)

McPherson, S. S. (1995). *Ordinary Genius: The Story of Albert Einstein*. Minneapolis: Carolrhoda Books.

The story of one of the most noted Jewish immigrants to the United States.

Mamet, D. (1995) *Passover*. New York: St. Martin's.

A short, dazzling story told by a grandmother to her young granddaughter of how family members once survived a pogrom. Deals with contemporary anti-Semitism. Illustrated with beautiful woodcuts by D. McCurdy. (High School)

Nixon, J. (1992). *Land of Hope*. New York: Bantam/Starfire.

The story of fifteen-year-old Rebekah Levinsky, who immigrates with her family to New York. The author gives a realistic picture of the harshness of immigrant life in the early 1900s and the promise offered by free public education. (Middle School)

Perl, L. (1994). *Isaac Bashevis Singer: The Life of a Storyteller*. Philadelphia: Jewish Publication Society.

A sensitive account of the great Yiddish writer, first in Poland and later as an immigrant in the United States. The author captures Singer's personality and his passion for the Yiddish language and culture. (Intermediate)

Polacco, P. (1992). *Mrs. Katz and Tush*. New York: Bantam/Little Rooster.

This picture book tells the story of Mrs. Katz, a lonely, old Jewish widow who lives in a multicultural neighborhood. She is helped by those around her, especially an African American boy who brings her a kitten to love. (Primary).

Ray, K. (1994). *To Cross a Line*. New York: Orchard/Richard Jackson.

The thrilling story of a teenager's struggle for survival during the early days of the Nazi Holocaust, based on the experience of the author's father, who escaped Hitler's Germany in 1938. (Middle)

Roth, H. (1994). *Mercy of a Rude Stream*, Vol. I, *A Star Shines over Mt. Morris Park*. New York: St. Martin's Press.

Roth's first novel since Call It Sleep *(1934). Autobiographical, this is the story of young Ira Stigman growing up in an Irish neighborhood in New York City. Deals with anti-Semitism, racism, and Ira's awareness of sex. Many Yiddish expressions. Includes a Yiddish glossary. (High School)*

Roth, H. (1995). *A Diving Rock on the Hudson: Mercy of a Rude Stream*. Vol. II. New York: St. Martin's.

The second in a projected six-volume fictional autobiography by the author of Call It Sleep. *It is the continuing story of Ira Stigman, an immigrant Jewish youngster growing up in an Irish ghetto in Harlem, and of Ira Stigman, the old man, struggling to write the story of his youth sixty years earlier. (High School)*

Roth-Hanno, R. (1993). *Safe Harbors*. Portland, Ore.: Four Winds.

This autobiographical novel is a sequel to Touch Wood *(1988), which was about the author's experiences as a Jewish child hidden in a convent. This intriguing story is about her coming of age in New York City after the war, her disillusionment with traditional Judaism, and her discovery of reform Judaism. (Middle School/High School)*

Schotter, R. Illustrated by M. Hafner (1995). *Passover Magic*. Boston: Little, Brown.

A delightful book about a warm, charming family as it prepares for the Passover seder. Bright watercolors enhance this family portrait. (Primary)

Schuman, M. (1994). *Ellie Wiesel: Voice from the Holocaust*. New York: Enslow.

A biography of the Nobel Laureate who survived a Nazi death camp. Includes excerpts from Weisel's writings, photographs, a short bibliography, and list of videos. (Middle)

Sherman, E. (1990). *Independence Avenue*. Philadelphia: Jewish Publication Society.

The engrossing story of a fourteen-year-old Jewish immigrant who travels to Galveston, Texas, in 1907 and later to Kansas City. Told within the context of the Galveston Movement, which brought about 10,000 Jewish immigrants to the United States between 1907 and 1914. (Intermediate/Middle)

Shiefman, V. (1993) *Good-Bye to the Trees*. New York: Atheneum.

The story of a young Fagel Fratrizsky's courage and determination to reunite her family after immigrating to Boston in 1907. Based on the story of Shiefman's grandmother. (Middle School).

Siskind, L. (1992). *The Hopscotch Tree*. New York: Bantam/ Skylark.

Fifth-grader Edith Gold copes with a vicious anti-Semitic bully in her new school in Los Angeles in the 1960s. (Intermediate)

Weiss, N. (1992). *The First Night of Hanukkah*. New York: Putnam/Grosset & Dunlap.

Uncle Dan tells Molly the story of the Jews who defied their ruler by refusing to worship more than one God. Easy to read. (Primary)

Wolff, F. (1989). *Pink Slippers, Bat Mitzvah Blues*. Philadelphia: Jewish Publication Society.

This realistic novel captures the dilemmas and agonies of a busy, concerned eighth grader following her Bat Mitzvah. (Middle School)

Wood, E. T. & Jankowski, S. M. (1995). *Karski: How One Man Tried to Stop the Holocaust*. New York: John Wiley.

The dramatic story of a debonair Polish diplomat who left Poland in 1942 and publicized Hitler's treatment of Poland's Jews. (High School)

PART IV

HISPANIC AMERICANS

CONCEPTS AND STRATEGIES

P art IV consists of content, concepts, teaching strategies, and materials for teaching about three major Hispanic groups in the United States: Mexican Americans, Puerto Ricans, and Cuban Americans. Hispanics are one of the nation's fastest growing ethnic groups. The number of Hispanics in the United States grew from 14.6 million in 1980 to more than 22.4 million in 1990, a 53% increase. Mexican Americans are the largest Hispanic group in the United States, and this group is growing faster than are Cubans or Puerto Ricans. Between 1980 and 1990, Mexican Americans increased about 54%, compared to a 30% increase of Cubans and a 35.4% increase of Puerto Ricans. The Hispanic population is growing about five times faster than the rest of the U.S. population. The rapid growth of Hispanics is due primarily to massive immigration and to a high birthrate.

CENTRAL AND SOUTH AMERICANS

A substantial number of immigrants from Central and South America have entered the United States since 1970. Between 1981 and 1991, 627,400 Central American and 591,100 South American immigrants settled in the United States (U.S. Bureau of the Census, 1994). A significant number of these immigrants have come from El Salvador, Guatemala, Colombia, Guyana, and Ecuador. Central and South Americans made up 10.7% of the Hispanic population

329

of the United States in 1990 (U.S. Bureau of the Census, 1993a) (see Figure A). It is misleading, however, to conceptualize these diverse groups of immigrants as one people because they have wide cultural, racial, and ethnic differences.

DEMOGRAPHIC CHARACTERISTICS OF HISPANICS

The Hispanic population, compared to the rest of the U.S. population, is young. The median age of Hispanics in 1992 was 25.8, compared to 33.4 for

Figure A   HISPANIC POPULATION BY TYPE OF ORIGIN: 1990 (IN PERCENT)

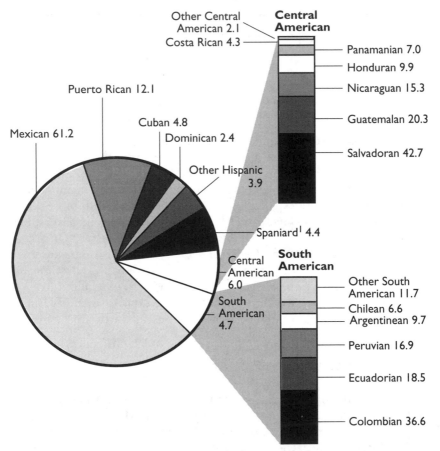

Other Central American 2.1
Costa Rican 4.3
Central American
Panamanian 7.0
Honduran 9.9
Nicaraguan 15.3
Guatemalan 20.3
Salvadoran 42.7

Puerto Rican 12.1
Cuban 4.8
Dominican 2.4
Mexican 61.2
Other Hispanic 3.9
Spaniard[1] 4.4
Central American 6.0
South American 4.7

South American
Other South American 11.7
Chilean 6.6
Argentinean 9.7
Peruvian 16.9
Ecuadorian 18.5
Colombian 36.6

[1]Includes those who reported "Spanish."

SOURCE: U.S. Bureau of the Census (1993). *We, the Hispanics.* Washington, D.C.: U.S. Government Printing Office, p. 4.

the non-Hispanic population (U.S. Bureau of the Census, 1994). The Hispanic population is also highly concentrated in the Southwestern United States. In 1990, nearly nine of every ten Hispanics lived in just ten states. California, Texas, New York, and Florida had the largest Hispanic populations (U.S. Bureau of the Census, 1993a). About half of all Hispanics (54%) lived in just two states, California and Texas. Figure B shows the Hispanic population for selected states in 1990.

Hispanics continue to lag behind the rest of the population in educational and income status. In 1993, 53.1% of Hispanics 25 years or older had completed four years of high school or more, compared to 70.4% for Blacks and 81.5% for Whites (the categories Hispanic and White overlap. Persons of Hispanic origin may be of any race) (U.S. Bureau of the Census, 1994). In 1993, 9% percent of Hispanics, compared to 12.2% for Blacks and 22.6% for Whites, had completed four or more years of college. Hispanics, as well as other students of color, are becoming a larger proportion of the nation's school-age population. Hispanics were 9.3% of the nation's school-age population (0 to 17-year-olds) in 1982. In 1990, they made up 12% of the children in the nation below the age of 18 (U.S. Bureau of the Census, 1993b). Demographers predict that they will make up about 25.3% of the nation's school-age population by the year 2020 (Pallas, Natriello, & McDill, 1989).

In 1992, about 29% of Hispanic persons were living below the poverty level, compared with 14.5% for the total population, 11.6% for Whites, and 33.3% for African Americans. The poverty rates for different Hispanic groups

Figure B   HISPANIC POPULATION FOR SELECTED STATES: 1990 (PERCENT DISTRIBUTION)

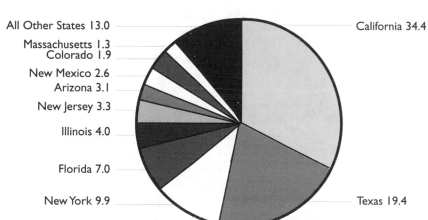

All Other States 13.0 — California 34.4
Massachusetts 1.3
Colorado 1.9
New Mexico 2.6
Arizona 3.1
New Jersey 3.3
Illinois 4.0
Florida 7.0
New York 9.9 — Texas 19.4

SOURCE: U.S. Bureau of the Census (1993). *We, the Hispanics.* Washington, D.C.: U.S. Government Printing Office, p. 3.

varied. The percentage rate (for persons) was 18.1% for Cubans, 30.1% for Mexican Americans, and 36.5% for Puerto Ricans (U.S. Bureau of the Census, 1994).

DIVERSITY WITHIN HISPANICS

It is misleading to consider Hispanics as one ethnic group. Even though the various Hispanic groups share a past influenced significantly by Spain and the Spanish language, there are tremendous historical, racial, and cultural differences among and within them. Most Mexican Americans are mestizos, whereas some Cubans and Puerto Ricans are Black. Some Mexican Americans are native to the United States; others, as well as some other Hispanics, arrived in the United States quite recently. Language is probably the most important factor that binds the various Hispanic groups. In 1990, about 78 percent of Hispanics spoke a language other than English at home. Spanish was spoken by most of the Hispanic non-English speakers (U.S. Bureau of the Census, 1993a).The multicultural curriculum should help students understand the ways in which the various Hispanic groups are both alike and different.

REFERENCES

Pallas, A. M., Natriello, G., & McDill, E. L. (1989). The Changing Nature of the Disadvantaged Population: Current Dimensions and Future Trends. *Educational Researcher, 18* (5), 6–22.

U.S. Bureau of the Census. (1993a). *We, the American Hispanics.* Washington, D.C.: U.S. Government Printing Office.

U.S. Bureau of the Census. (1993b). *We, the American Children.* Washington, D.C.: U.S. Government Printing Office.

U.S. Bureau of the Census. (1994). *Statistical Abstract of the United States: 1994* (114th ed.). Washington, D.C.: U.S. Government Printing Office.

ANNOTATED BIBLIOGRAPHY

Augenbraun, H. & Stavans, I. (Eds.). (1993). *Growing Up Latino: Memories and Stories.* Boston: Houghton Mifflin.

This anthology includes a comprehensive collection of Latino writing that can be used to enrich lessons and units.

Bean, F. D. & Tienda, M. (1987). *The Hispanic Population of the United States.* New York: Russell Sage Foundation.

A comprehensive sociological analysis of the Hispanic population based on the 1980 Census.

Castillo-Speed, L. (Ed.). (1995). *Latina: Women's Voices from the Borderlands*. New York: Touchstone.

Memorable and powerful fiction as well as nonfiction are included in this useful anthology.

de la Garza, R. O. (Ed.). (1992). *Latino Voices: Mexican, Puerto Rican & Cuban Perspectives on American Politics*. Boulder, Colo.: Westview.

A scholarly collection of informative papers.

Kanellos, N. (Ed.). (1993). *The Hispanic Alamanac: A Reference Work on Hispanics in the United States*. Detroit: Gale Research.

This comprehensive work (780 pages) includes historical overviews; significant historical documents in U.S. history; literature; media; music; and theatre, as well as many other topics. An excellent resource for teachers and researchers. A more popular and condensed version of this book is described below.

Kanellos, N. (1994). *The Hispanic Almanac: From Columbus to Corporate America*. Detroit: Visible Ink.

History, business, media, labor, politics, media, art, literature, theater, film, music, and sports are among the topics covered in this useful reference. Suitable for use by high school students.

Kanellos, N. & Esteva-Fabregat, C. (General Eds.). (1993–1994). *Handbook of Hispanic Cultures in the United States* (4 vols.). Houston: Arte Público/University of Houston.

This landmark and seminal publication includes four volumes, each with a separate editor. Each volume and editor follows: T. Weaver, Anthropology; A. Jiménez, History; F. Lomelí, Literature and Art; F. Padilla, Sociology. A highly recommended reference.

Moore, J. & Pinderhughes, R. (Eds.). (1993). *In the Barrios: Latinos and the Underclass Debate*. New York: Russell Sage Foundation.

An excellent collection of scholarly and informative essays that focus on an important and controversial topic.

Pachon, H. & DeSipio, L. (1994). *New Americans by Choice: Political Perspectives of Latino Immigrants*. Boulder, Colo.: Westview.

A well-researched, informative, and scholarly volume.

Padilla. A. (Ed.). (1995). *Hispanic Psychology*. Newbury Park, Calif.: Sage.

A scholarly collection of articles reprinted from the Hispanic Journal of Behavioral Sciences *edited by the journal's founding editor.*

Reddy, M. A. (Ed.). (1993). *Statistical Record of Hispanic Americans*. Detroit: Gale Research.

A massive (1172 pages) reference work that includes chapters on demographics, family, education, culture, health and health care, social and economic conditions, business and industry, government and politics, and law and law enforcement.

Shorris, E. (1992). *Latinos: Biography of the People.* New York: Norton.

A comprehensive book written for a popular audience. It can be used with high school students.

Stavans, I. (1995). *The Hispanic Condition: Reflections on Culture and Identity in America.* New York: HarperCollins.

This profile of Hispanics in the United States by a Mexican immigrant who teaches at Amherst College is thoughtful and informative.

Telgen, D. & Kamp, J. (Eds.). (1993). *Notable Hispanic American Women* (1st ed.). Detroit: Gale Research.

This valuable reference work includes biographical sketches of Hispanic women from various ethnic groups, occupations, and professions.

Unterburger, A. L., Delgado, J. L., & Peck, T. W. (Eds.). (1994). *Who's Who Among Hispanic Americans* (3rd ed.). Detroit: Gale Research.

This book includes brief educational and professional backgrounds of noted contemporary Hispanics in the United States.

CHAPTER 10

MEXICAN AMERICANS

CONCEPTS, STRATEGIES, AND MATERIALS

It would be a disservice to portray the future in idealistic terms. Hope is important, but the falsification of reality can immobilize a community.

Rodolfo Acuña

Mexican Americans are the second largest ethnic group of color in the United States. (African Americans are the largest group.) They are also the largest Hispanic group. Mexican Americans comprised about 61.2% of the Hispanics in 1990. They are increasing at a much faster rate than are the other two major Hispanic groups, Puerto Ricans and Cubans. There were about 13,496,000 Mexican American living in the United States in 1990 (U.S. Bureau of the Census, 1994), up from about 8,740,439 in 1990. The Mexican population increased about 54% during that ten-year period.

The rapid growth in the Mexican American population results primarily from a higher birthrate, compared to other ethnic and racial groups, and a significant and continuing immigration from Mexico. Between 1981 and 1992, 2,813,300 legal immigrants arrived in the United States from Mexico (U.S. Bureau of the Census, 1994a). A large, but unknown, number of undocumented Mexican aliens in the United States are not reflected in these Census figures. There is little agreement on how many undocumented Mexican aliens are living in the United States. It is also difficult to determine the extent to which the Immigration Reform and Control Act of 1986, designed to reduce the number of undocumented immigrants who enter the United State each year, has been successful. The act imposes severe penalties on employers who

335

knowingly hire illegal aliens. Under the conditions of this act, employers are required to ask job applicants for proof of citizenship.

The Mexican American population is highly concentrated in the West and Southwest, particularly in California and Texas. In 1990, about 72% of all Mexican Americans lived in California and Texas; 43% lived in California, and 29% lived in Texas. Illinois and Arizona had the next largest concentrations of Mexican Americans, each about 6%. In 1990, about 81.2% of Mexican Americans lived in the following four states: California, Texas, Illinois, and Arizona (see Table 10-1).

Even though Mexican Americans are highly concentrated in California, the Southwest, and Illinois, pockets of them are found throughout the United States, including the South and the Northwest. More than 63,000 lived in Oklahoma in 1990. Washington state, in the Northwest, had (in 1990) the

Table 10-1 POPULATION OF MEXICAN AMERICANS IN SELECTED STATES (1990)

State	Population
California	6,119,000
Texas	3,891,000
Illinois	624,000
Arizona	616,000
New Mexico	329,000
Colorado	283,000
Florida	162,000
Washington	156,000
Michigan	138,000
New York	93,000
Oregon	86,000
Nevada	85,000
Kansas	76,000
Indiana	67,000
Oklahoma	63,000
Ohio	58,000
Wisconsin	58,000
Utah	57,000
Georgia	49,000
Idaho	43,000
Missouri	38,000
Louisiana	24,000

SOURCE: Based on data in the U.S. Census, 1990.

eighth largest population of Mexican Americans—156,000. Mexican Americans are also becoming increasingly urbanized. Significant numbers are concentrated in large cities, such as Los Angeles, Chicago, Milwaukee, and Detroit.

Mexican Americans were in the land that is now the United States before all other American groups, except the American Indians, Aleuts, Eskimos, and Native Hawaiians. Their ancestors had settled in the region that is now the southwestern United States before Jamestown was settled by the English colonists in 1607. They became an ethnic minority when Texas was annexed by the United States in 1845. More of their territory was conquered by the United States during the Mexican American War, which lasted from 1846 to 1848. Their property, civic, and cultural rights were guaranteed by the Treaty of Guadalupe Hidalgo, the treaty ending the war in 1848. In the decades after 1848, the Treaty was blatantly disregarded, and Mexican Americans were made second-class citizens by Anglo-Americans who migrated and settled in the Southwest. There were about 80,000 Mexicans living in the territory Mexico ceded to the United States in 1848. Most modern Mexican American communities were formed by Mexican immigrants who came to the United States after 1910. The study of the conquest and subjugation of Mexican Americans and their resistance, which greatly intensified in the 1960s, is necessary to understand the nature of U.S. society and the genesis of the ethnic conflict and tensions in American life.

MEXICAN AMERICANS: HISTORICAL PERSPECTIVE

Important Dates	
1519	Hernán Cortés, the Spanish conquistador, and a group of Spaniards arrived in the region that is now Mexico.
1521	Cortés, with the support of thousands of Indian allies, seized the Aztec capital city, Tenochtitlán, and the empire fell.
1598	Juan de Oñate established the first Spanish settlement in what is today New Mexico. The Spanish colonial period began.
1718	New Spain founded the mission and presidio of San Antonio.
1769	Fray Junípero Serra and Gaspar de Portolá established the mission and presidio of San Diego, the first in Upper California.

Important Dates

1810	On September 16, 1810, Father Miguel Hidalgo sounded a battle cry known as the *El Grito de Dolores,* which signaled the beginning of the Mexican revolutionary era that eventually resulted in Mexican independence from Spain in 1821.
1836	Mexico's President Santa Anna and his troops defeated the rebelling Texans at the Alamo. Six weeks later, Santa Anna was defeated by Sam Houston and his Texan troops at San Jacinto. Texas declared itself independent and formed the Lone Star Republic.
1845	The United States annexed Texas, which had declared itself independent from Mexico in 1836. This was one key event leading to the Mexican-American War.
1846	On May 13, 1846, the United States declared war on Mexico and the Mexican-American War began.
1848	The United States and Mexico signed the Treaty of Guadalupe Hidalgo, which ended the Mexican-American War. Mexico lost nearly one-third of its territory, and the United States acquired most of the territory that comprises the southwestern states.
1853	James Gadsden, representing the United States, purchased from Mexico 45,532 square miles of additional land, which was rich in copper, and opened a railroad route.
1859	Juan N. Cortina, who became a U.S. citizen under the provisions of the Treaty of Guadalupe Hidalgo, led a series of rebellions against Anglo-Americans in the Lower Rio Grande Valley of South Texas.
1862	On May 5, 1862, French forces that had invaded Mexico were defeated at Puebla by Mexican forces led by Ignacio Zaragosa, a Texas Mexican. May 5 (*Cinco de Mayo*) is an important holiday observed by Mexican Americans.
1877	The El Paso Salt War occurred, in which Mexicans organized and rebelled against Anglos because of a dispute over rights to salt beds.
1910	A revolution starting in Mexico caused thousands of Mexicans to immigrate to the United States looking for jobs and to escape political turmoil and persecution.
1924	Congress established the Border Patrol to monitor traffic across the Mexican-U.S. border. This border had previously been primarily open.

Important Dates

1929	The League of United Latin American Citizens was formed in Harlingen, Texas. Like other earlier Mexican-American civil rights organizations, the League stressed U.S. citizenship and assimilation.
1929–35	Thousands of Mexican immigrants and their families were repatriated to Mexico, most without legal proceedings.
1942	The United States and Mexico made an agreement that authorized Mexicans to work temporarily in the United States. This project is known as the *bracero* program.
1943	The anti-Mexican "zoot-suit" riots occurred in Los Angeles during the summer.
1954	The U.S. Immigration and Naturalization Service began "Operation Wetback," a massive program to deport illegal Mexican immigrants to Mexico.
1965	A grape strike led by César Chávez and the United Farm Workers Association began in Delano, California, a town in the San Joaquin Valley. Rodolfo "Corky" Gonzales formed the Crusades for Justice in Denver. This important civil rights organization epitomized the Chicano movement that emerged in the 1960s. The U.S. Congress passed an immigration act limiting the number of Mexican immigrants to the United States to 20,000 annually.
1970	La Raza Unida party was organized by José Angel Gutiérrez in Crystal City, Texas.
1976	Jerry Apodaca and Raul Castro were elected governors of New Mexico and Arizona, respectively.
1979	Luis Valdez' play, *Zoot Suit,* was the first Mexican American play produced on Broadway.
1982	Toney Anaya was elected governor of New Mexico.
1986	The Immigration Reform and Control Act of 1986 was passed. Designed to control the entry of undocumented (illegal) immigrants to the United States, it imposed severe penalties on employers who knowingly hired illegal immigrants.
1992	President Bill Clinton named Henry G. Cisneros Secretary of the Department of Housing and Urban Development. President Clinton named Federico Peña Secretary of Transportation.

THE SPANISH CONQUEST

More than 25 million Indians were living in the Western Hemisphere when the Spanish conquistadores arrived in 1517. There were a wide variety of Indian cultures and groups in the region that is now Mexico. The Mayas and the Aztecs developed some of the most complex societies in the region. Mayan domestication and cultivation of corn significantly influenced agriculture in the Americas. A powerful military state and the most impressive contemporary cities were built by the Aztecs. Tenochtitlan, their capital city, has been called "the most modern city in the world" at the time of the Spanish conquest (Forbes, n.d., p. 3).

Hernan Cortés, a Spanish explorer, led an expedition into Mexico in 1519. Before he reached the Aztec capital, he gained military help from other Indian civilizations by negotiating and conquering. After a two-year intermittent struggle with the Aztecs, Cortés finally seized Tenochtitlan on August 13, 1521, and the Aztec empire fell. Despite the Aztecs' military strength, the Spaniards were able to defeat them because they were helped by other Indian nations and had horses and superior firearms. Although the Spaniards were eventually successful in their conquest of much of the land stretching from southern South America to most of what is today the southwestern United States, this task was not easily accomplished. The Indians living in these areas fought hard to maintain their power and started many rebellions after the Spanish conquest. The Spaniards defeated most Indian groups only gradually and with the loss of many of their men.

The Spanish Settlements

The Spanish settlements in Mexico and what is today the southwestern United States differed in several significant ways from the English colonies in the eastern parts of North America. Because of a number of complex reasons, more settlers from England than from Spain immigrated to the Americas. This was in part because at the time of the conquest, Spain had a small population compared to other nations in Europe (Jiménez, 1994). It had, for example, about half the population of France. It is estimated that only about 300,000 Spaniards came to the Americas during three centuries of settlement (McWilliams, 1968). More English than Spanish colonists brought their wives, although a severe shortage of women was also a problem in the original English colonies. In 1619 the London Company sent 100 women who were willing to marry colonists to Virginia. Each man who married one of these women had to pay 54 kilograms (120 pounds) of the best tobacco. The serious shortage of women in the Spanish colonies was not dealt with as successfully as in Virginia. Writes Jiménez (1994):

It is apparent that between 1493 and 1519 women represented less than 6 percent of all emigrants [to new Spain]. In the next twenty years they hardly surpassed this percentage. More favorable conditions in the colonies and the pressure exercised by the laws to encourage the emigration of women and the marriage of the conquistadors and settlers increased these ratios in the following years. (p. 79)

The unique characteristics of the Spanish settlers significantly influenced the physical and cultural development of the new "race" that was formed in the Americas. Because few women came to the colonies from Spain, most of the Spanish men had Indian concubines or wives. The offspring of these ethnically mixed unions were known as *mestizos*. The biological and cultural heritage of the Mexican American includes African strains although it is primarily Spanish-Indian. When they came to the Americas, the Spaniards had had long contact with a group of Africans called Moors. Moors came with the conquistadores to the Americas. Estevanico is perhaps the most famous. Nearly 200,000 African slaves were also brought to Mexico. They were so thoroughly mixed with the Spaniards and Indians by 1900 that they were no longer distinguishable as a separate racial group (Franklin & Moss, 1994). The Mexican's biological heritage is more Indian than Spanish. Although the Spaniards imposed their culture and religion on the Indian nations, many Indian culture elements survived and highly influenced the development of Mexican culture. Thus, both the physical traits and culture of the Mexicans are primarily blends of Spanish and Indian influences. McWilliams wrote (1968) "To attempt to unravel any single strand from this pattern and label it 'Spanish' is to do a serious injustice to the Mexican and Indians . . . through whom . . . Spanish cultural influences survived (p. 34).

The Texas Revolt

At the beginning of the nineteenth century, Mexico was in a perpetual state of political turmoil. Greatly concerned about the declining population in Texas, the Spanish and later the Mexican government encouraged Anglo-Americans to settle there by making empresario land grants. The Spanish government gave an empresario grant to Moses Austin in 1821. His son Stephen received a reconfirmation of the original grant from the Mexican government in 1823. Because Texas was geographically close to the United States, it attracted a large number of Anglo immigrants. They were interested in Texas's rich resources and open territory. Most Anglo settlers in Texas failed to keep the terms of their land-grant agreements with the Mexican government, such as becoming loyal citizens and Catholics, learning Spanish, and giving up their slaves. They were not interested in Mexican culture but wanted to establish Anglo institutions in the Mexican province and to control it.

Texas Mexicans were angry about President Santa Anna's attempts to centralize his power over the northern Mexican territories. The Anglo immigrants in Texas added fuel to the fire because of their disdain for the Mexican government. By permitting and encouraging U.S. citizens to settle in sparsely inhabited Texas, Mexico had inadvertently set the stage for revolt in the province and its eventual loss to the United States.

By the time Mexico realized that Anglo-Mexicans were gaining control in Texas and took steps to undermine their power, antigovernment forces in Texas had already been firmly established. The Mexican government attempted to undermine Anglo power in Texas by abolishing slavery in 1829, by restricting Anglo immigration into Texas, and by enforcing customs regulations at the Texas-U.S. border. These actions greatly angered the Texas Anglo-Mexicans and evoked attacks against the central government. Mexican federal troops arrived in Texas in 1835 after Texas proclaimed itself "conditionally independent." These troops were badly defeated. In 1836, President Santa Anna led several thousand Mexican troops into Texas. His army killed 187 Texans at a Franciscan mission in San Antonio called the Alamo. The Mexican army had another victory at Goliad, but they were crushed at San Jacinto on April 21 by Sam Houston and his Texas troops shouting "Remember the Alamo!" After this victory, Texas sought world recognition of its independence and started the chain of events that eventually led to its annexation by the United States in 1845.

THE MEXICAN AMERICAN WAR

When the Mexican government took serious steps to halt Anglo immigration to the Southwest, the United States had begun, in the name of Manifest Destiny, an aggressive campaign to annex all of Mexico's northern territories. The United States began a military conquest when negotiations failed and then angered Mexico by annexing Texas in 1845. The United States declared war on Mexico in 1846, when a boundary dispute developed between the two nations. The United States defeated Mexico within two years and occupied California and New Mexico by the end of 1846. Mexico's northern provinces had little allegiance to the nation's capital. Anglo settlers who had a strong toehold in Mexican provinces such as California and New Mexico actively sought Mexico's defeat. Mexico was also greatly weakened by internal strife and its inability to rally internal support for the war.

The Treaty of Guadalupe Hidalgo

After Mexico was defeated by the United States, representatives of the two nations signed a treaty on February 2, 1848, in the Mexican village of

Guadalupe Hidalgo. The United States forced Mexico to surrender its claim to Texas, which the United States had annexed in 1845, and to cede about one-third of its territory to the United States. This chunk of land included most of the territory now comprising the states of the U.S. Southwest, including Arizona, California, New Mexico, Utah, Nevada, and a section of Colorado. The United States paid Mexico $15 million for this large piece of land.

All Mexicans who remained in this newly acquired territory received the right to become U.S. citizens. Only about 3,000 of the nearly 80,000 people living in the area chose to leave their homes and move to the Mexican side of the border. The treaty guaranteed Mexican Americans "all the rights of citizens of the United States...[and] the free enjoyment of...Liberty and property" (The Treaty of Guadalupe Hidalgo, 1971). "By this treaty the United States gained not only an immense new territory but also a large group of new citizens. Although they were left in their same geographic and cultural setting, these new citizens were now exposed to unfamiliar legal, political, and social institutions.... Guaranteed full protection of property rights, they soon became enmeshed in a web of confusing Anglo laws which required proof of ownership unfamiliar to them" (Meier & Rivera, 1972, p. 71).

After the Conquest: Oppression and Conflict

After 1848, forces were set in motion that were destined to make the Mexicans in the United States a conquered, powerless, and alienated ethnic minority. Although they were guaranteed property and citizenship rights by the Treaty of Guadalupe Hidalgo, it was only a matter of time before Anglo-Americans, through a series of legal and financial maneuvers, had obtained control in all of the southwestern territories and reduced the native Mexicans to the status of second-class citizens.

The pattern of conquest differed somewhat in the various southwestern territories. Before the Anglos came to New Mexico, a rigid class structure existed that sharply divided the rich and the poor. The Anglos in New Mexico pitted the rich against the poor in order to gain control of the territory. Anglo dominance emerged more gradually in New Mexico than in California and Texas. A mass of Anglos immigrated to California during the gold rush of 1849 and in subsequent years. Mexicans were completely outnumbered. Anglos thoroughly dominated northern California by 1851, but domination of southern California was somewhat delayed because most Anglo immigrants first settled in the northern part of the territory. However, they eventually settled in the south and within a few years expanded their dominance over the entire state. There were more than 30,000 Anglos and only 5,000 native Mexicans in Texas as early as 1834. Anglos had controlled Texas since it became independent as the Lone Star Republic in 1836. This dominance continued after U.S. annexation in 1845.

The Anglo-Americans were able to obtain most of the land owned by the Mexicans by imposing a series of legal and financial restraints. Land boundaries in Mexico had been rather loosely and casually defined. Many Mexicans had to appear in Anglo courts to defend their rights to the land they owned. Often they did not have the legal papers proving ownership of their land, and Mexican legal papers did not conform to superimposed U.S. law. In many cases they had to sell their land to pay taxes imposed by the new government or exorbitant fees to Anglo lawyers to argue their cases in court. Legal battles over land titles often dragged out in the courts for years and became expensive. Tactics such as these and the Congressional Land Act of 1851, which required U.S.-recognized proof of land ownership, had the ultimate effect of making the Mexican largely landless and poverty stricken.

Rioting, lynchings, burnings, vigilante action, and other forms of violence were directed at the country's "newest aliens" during this period of turmoil and Hispanic defeat in the Southwest. Moore (with Pachon, 1976) contends that "No other part of the United States saw such prolonged intergroup violence as did the Border States from 1848 to 1925" (p. 36). Many Anglo outlaws and social misfits settled in the Southwest during this period. They declared open season on Mexicans and often attacked them just for fun. There was little or no law enforcement in many parts of the Southwest during this period. In 1850, California passed a Foreign Miner's Tax that was designed to drive Mexicans out of the mines.

The Mexican Revolution of 1910 contributed to this atmosphere of hostility and violence. Banditry and filibustering (filibustering is pursuing military activity in a foreign nation for adventure) occurred on both sides of the border. Mexican-Anglo hostility reached new highs. Mexicans considered Anglo-Americans "gringos," and Anglos called Mexicans "greasers." By the turn of the century, the Mexicans had been conquered and made foreigners within their homeland. Culturally, politically, and economically they were second-class citizens. Mexican Americans faced the beginning of the twentieth century suffering from a crushing second defeat in the Southwest.

NORTH FROM MEXICO

Early Immigrants

During the early development of agriculture in the Southwest, agribusinessmen depended on a large and cheap labor supply. This labor need was met in the late 1800s by the Chinese immigrants and later by immigrants from Japan and the Philippines (see chapter 13). The expansion of irrigated farming in the Southwest at the turn of the century coincided with the Mexican Revolution of 1910. Many Mexicans were displaced by the Revolution. They came north to the U.S. Southwest seeking job opportunities. They found jobs in truck farming, in cotton and sugar beet fields, in mines, in industry, and on the railroads. Hundreds of Mexican immigrants worked on the construction of railroad lines that crossed the West. Many Mexican American communities in the Southwest grew up around railroad campsites.

There was no legal agreement between Mexico and the United States that protected the rights of these immigrants. Consequently, they were often exploited blatantly by their employers. They were paid the lowest wages, given the worst jobs, and forced to live in the crudest shacks. Many became migrant workers who followed the crops. The mass of Mexican immigrants to the Southwest depressed wages so drastically that many native Mexican Americans migrated to midwestern cities, such as Detroit, Gary, and Chicago, to obtain higher wages. The large number of Mexican immigrants who came to the Southwest between 1910 and 1930 laid the foundations for most modern Mexican American communities.

Many Anglo groups in the Southwest became alarmed by the large numbers of Mexicans who were entering the United States in the 1920s. Between 1920 and 1929, 498,900 Mexican immigrants entered the United States. Vigorous efforts were made to halt their immigration. Although the legal attempts to stop their immigration failed because of the powerful opposition from agribusinessmen who wanted them for cheap labor, other efforts were successful. The U.S.-Mexican border had historically been an open border, with Mexicans and U.S. citizens crossing it at will. The Border Patrol was established in 1924 by Congress to control traffic across the border.

When the Great Depression hit in 1929, and many Mexicans, like other Americans, lost their jobs and found it necessary to obtain welfare to survive, loud cries were heard against the Mexicans. Mexicans were regarded as "foreigners" who did not deserve welfare benefits. As with other non-White immigrants who came before them, attempts were made to deport the Mexicans when their labor was no longer needed. Jobs became increasingly scarce as the dust bowl White immigrants fled to the Southwest to compete for the few available jobs. The U.S. Immigration Service, as well as state, county, and local governments, began an aggressive drive to repatriate immigrants.

In the eagerness to rid the United States of Mexicans in order to cut back on welfare rolls, many Mexican American citizens were "encouraged" or forced to go to Mexico. The civil rights of U.S. citizens of Mexican descent were violated seriously in this unfortunate repatriation movement. More than 64,000 Mexican aliens were returned to Mexico between 1930 and 1934 without the benefits of legal proceedings. The Mexican population in the United States declined from 639,000 to 377,000 from 1930 to 1940 (Moore with Pachon, 1976, p. 42).

The Bracero Program

When World War II began, a new demand for unskilled labor developed in the United States. Agribusiness leaders spoke vigorously about their desperate need for Mexican labor. Partly as a gesture to help with the war effort, Mexico agreed to a seasonal work program with the United States. The two nations signed an agreement in July 1942, which enabled Mexican citizens to work in the United States during work seasons. They were to return to Mexico when the work season ended. Unlike the earlier Mexican immigrants, these workers came under an agreement that guaranteed them specific conditions relating to such problems as wages, working conditions, transportation, and worker rights.

Although these contract stipulations helped reduce some of the extreme conditions experienced by earlier Mexican immigrants, their wages and living conditions were often depressing. The bracero program formally ended in December 1947. When it terminated, the number of undocumented immigrants crossing the U.S.-Mexican border soared. Smuggling undocumented immigrants across the border became a highly profitable business in which many "men snatchers" engaged and profited (McWilliams, 1968, pp. 178–179).

In 1954, the U.S. Immigration and Naturalization Service began a massive drive known as Operation Wetback to deport undocumented immigrants to Mexico. Operation Wetback grossly violated the civil rights of many Mexicans, as had the repatriation project in the 1930s. Hundreds of Mexican American citizens were arrested and harassed. They were threatened and forced to produce proof of their citizenship. Only a few of the thousands of Mexicans deported had formal hearings. Operation Wetback successfully attained its goal but alienated and outraged many Mexican American citizens. When the project ended, more than a million people had been deported to Mexico.

In 1951, the United States and Mexico jointly accepted a Migratory Labor Agreement known as Public Law 78. This agreement set forth conditions for a new bracero program. It contained conditions similar to the earlier bracero agreement. Public Law 78 was extended for various periods until it ended in December 1964. In 1965, the United States Congress passed a new immigration act, which became effective in 1968, that limited the annual immigration from Western Hemisphere nations to 120,000. Each nation, including Mexico, was given an annual quota of 20,000. This new act solved, at least for the time, problems concerning the number of Mexican nationals that could legally enter the United States.

Because of the chronic economic and population problems in Mexico, large numbers of undocumented Mexican immigrants enter the United States each year. The U.S. Census indicated that more about 22,354,00 million Hispanics lived in the United States in 1990 (U.S. Bureau of the Census, 1994a). However, the actual number of Hispanics who lived in the United States in

1990 was much higher than this figure because of the large numbers of undocumented immigrants that enter the United States from Mexico each year. The largest foreign-born group in the United States are Mexican Americans. In 1990, more than one in five of the people in the United States who were foreign born were of Mexican origin (U.S. Bureau of the Census, 1993b).

VIOLENCE AND RACE RIOTS

In the 1940s, anti-Mexican feelings and stereotypes were rampant in the Southwest. The stereotypes, which depicted the Mexican American as criminal and violent, were perpetuated by the established Anglo press, especially the newspapers. The anti-Mexican press propaganda inflamed racial feelings and antagonisms toward the Mexican Americans. Anti-Mexican racism was the basic cause of the case of the Sleepy Lagoon and the zoot-suit riots that occurred in Los Angeles in the summer of 1943.

The Sleepy Lagoon Case

A young Mexican American, José Diaz, died mysteriously on August 2, 1942, apparently from a fractured skull. Without seriously seeking the facts of the case, the Los Angeles police immediately arrested twenty-four young men who were thought to be members of a Mexican gang accused of killing Diaz. All of them were charged with murder. A gravel pit, which became a central focus in the case, was dubbed "The Sleepy Lagoon" by a Los Angeles reporter. When seventeen of the twenty-four youths were convicted, the Sleepy Lagoon Defense Committee was organized. The committee, headed by journalist Carey McWilliams, successfully appealed the case. The case was dismissed because of insufficient evidence when the district court of appeals reversed the convictions on October 4, 1944.

The Zoot-Suit Riots

On June 3, 1943, eleven sailors were allegedly attacked by a group of boys in a predominantly Mexican neighborhood in Los Angeles. After this incident, the Los Angeles police conducted a raid that inflamed the community but failed to find the attackers. This incident kicked off a chain reaction resulting in one of the most serious series of race riots that has occurred in the United States. Encouraged by the actions of the police and the pervasive anti-Mexican attitudes in Los Angeles, about 200 sailors began to attack violently Mexican American youths on the night of June 4.

The police responded by arresting the victims of the attacks and keeping their hands off the sailors. The Los Angeles press played its usual role in the conflict; it warned that the dangerous zoot-suiters would retaliate the next night. Some Mexican American youths were referred to as "zoot-suiters" because of their style of dress during the 1940s. The press succeeded in alarming the public and in stirring up anti-Mexican feelings. On the night of June 7, hundreds of Anglos went into the streets and began a massive attack on Mexican American youths. Many zoot-suiters were beaten and stripped naked in the streets. This ruckus continued until military authorities intervened late on the night of June 7. Other riots occurred in cities as far away as Philadelphia, Chicago, and Detroit in the summer of 1943.

THE CHICANO MOVEMENT

Prior to the civil rights movement of the 1960s, *Chicano* was a term used to refer to lower-class Mexican immigrants from rural areas and small towns. The term was viewed negatively by the middle class and elite Mexican Americans but not by the lower-class people who used it. During the 1960s, leaders of the Mexican American protest and civil rights movement used the term in a positive way to describe their new quest for political, social, economic, cultural, and educational equality. The term *Chicano* was also used to link Mexican American political activists and intellectuals to their Mexican Indian heritage. In the past, their Spanish heritage was usually emphasized. The Chicano movement was broad in scope: it had economic, educational, religious, and cultural goals. The push for bilingual education in the schools was one of its major goals. Including more Mexican American priests and other church officials in the Catholic church hierarchy was another.

The Chicano movement was also political. Its leaders saw political clout as one of the best ways to attain the other goals of the movement. Its leaders, who often differed on tactics, had a variety of goals. Many believed that Chicanos would be able to overcome oppression in the United States only when they had political power and control over the institutions, such as schools and courts, that influenced their lives and destinies.

It is inaccurate to interpret the Chicano movement as a protest force that suddenly arose in the 1960s, or to refer to Chicanos as the "awakening minority." Often this was done in the 1960s. To understand the Chicano movement fully, we must view it as an important link in the long chain of resistance activities in which Chicanos have been involved since 1848. The movement cannot be viewed in isolation. As historian Rodolfo Acuña (1972) pointed out in the 1970s, "Men like Juan Patron and J. J. Herrerra were the precursors of today's breed of rebels or insurrectionists. In understanding them... and others of their kind, we shall better understand the present, and the words of Reis Lopez Tijerina will take on more significant meaning" (p. 77).

Early Resistance to Anglo Dominance

Mexican Americans have resisted Anglo oppression and colonization since Anglo-Americans conquered and occupied the Southwest. Chicanos such as Juan N. Cortina, Juan Jose Herrerra, and Juan Patron led organized resistance efforts in the 1800s. Cortina issued a "declaration of grievances" and urged Mexican Americans to "exterminate" their oppressors. Many Mexicans responded to the revolutionary calls issued by Cortina, Herrerra, and Patron (Acuña, 1988). Mexican American organizations, such as Las Gorras Blancas, fought Anglo leaders who were illegally taking land owned by Mexican Americans in New Mexico.

Unions and Strikes

In the first decades of the twentieth century, most Mexican Americans worked in agriculture, although many worked in mines, industry, and on the railroads. Farm workers were highly exploited by rich and powerful agribusinessmen. Mexican American workers aggressively opposed their conditions and organized unions and strikes, thus shattering the myth that they were docile workers. The period from 1900 to 1940 was characterized by active Chicano involvement in strikes and union organization. In 1927 the Confederacion de Uniones Obreras Mexicanas was organized in California. This union organized a strike in 1928 in the Imperial Valley. Farm owners and law officials, who formed coalitions, responded violently to the strike. They broke it up by deporting some strikers to Mexico and assaulting and intimidating others.

This pattern was used extensively by farm owners to crush strikes by Mexican Americans. However, strikes and union activities continued in the midst of these oppressive tactics. Meier and Rivera (1972) summarize this period: "Although Mexican Americans gained much labor union experience from 1900 to 1940, their organizations achieved only limited success. Some gains were made in wages and working conditions; however, the hopes and aspirations of Mexican-American workers continued to be frustrated by repression and discrimination" (p. 184).

Civil Rights Organizations

A number of civic, service, and political organizations have been organized since the late nineteenth century to promote the civil rights and interests of Mexican Americans. One of the first was a mutual aid organization formed in Arizona in 1894, the Alianza Hispano-Americana. These early societies restricted membership to individuals of Mexican descent who were citizens of the United States. They were made up primarily of the middle- and upper-classes and promoted assimilation by urging their members to become loyal U.S. citizens. Cuellar (Moore with Cuellar, 1970) argues that these organizations pursued a "politics of adaptation," rather than aggressively pushing for their political rights. They included the Order of the Sons of America, organized in San Antonio in 1921, and the League of United Latin-American Citizens, formed in Corpus Christi, Texas, in 1929.

Mexican Americans became more politicized in the post–World War II period. The organizations emerging during these years reflected acute political awareness and skill. The Community Service Organization, which was formed in Los Angeles in 1947, stressed political involvement and broad political participation. It organized a number of successful voter registration drives. The American G.I. Forum, founded in 1948, the Mexican American Political Association organized in 1959, and the Political Association of Spanish-Speaking Organizations, formed in 1960, stressed political involvement. These organizations were direct predecessors of the Chicano movement that emerged in the 1960s.

THE MILITANT CHICANO MOVEMENT

Mexican Americans' protest activities, which had been going on historically, were intensified in the 1960s and 1970s and became collectively known as the "Chicano movement" (Meier & Ribera, 1993). In addition to being more intense than earlier Mexican American movements, the Chicano movement had other unique characteristics. It was more militant and often used forms of direct confrontation. It included a large range of individuals among its ranks, such as intellectuals, students, and community activists. Its goals were more ambitious than the goals of traditional Mexican American civil rights groups. It sometimes demanded Chicano control of institutions within the Mexican American community. Some of its leaders argued that Chicanos in the United States were a colonized people who had been culturally and politically oppressed. They demanded redress of these grievances.

Chicano leaders also gave more attention to their mixed Mexican heritage than did earlier leaders. Their unique heritage, they argued, was to be celebrated and not denied, as was often done in the past by Mexican Americans who insisted on being viewed as "Spanish" instead of "Mexican." Much emphasis was placed on Mexican culture, values, foods, and especially on the speaking of Spanish. They demanded the right to speak Spanish in all U.S. institutions, such as the school and church. Some Chicano leaders argued that "revolution" was necessary to liberate them.

Of the many local Chicano civil rights leaders, four young men epitomized the movement in the public vision. They were Cesar Chávez, Reies

Lopez Tijerina, Rodolfo "Corkey" Gonzales, and José Angel Gutierrez. Chávez headed the United Farm Workers Organizing Committee, unionized farm workers, and successfully led the famous Delano grape strike in 1965, as well as many subsequent farm strikes. Tijerina demanded that Anglos in New Mexico return the lands they had taken from Mexican Americans in the 1800s. He formed the Federal Alliance of Free Cities in 1963 to push for the return of New Mexico lands to Chicanos or compensation to Chicanos for the loss of these lands. An important and militant civil rights group, the Crusade for Justice, was organized in Denver in 1965 by Gonzales. The crusade initiated successful projects related to improved education, better housing, and the elimination of police brutality in the Mexican American community. As a result of the activities of the political party, La Raza Unida, which was organized in 1970 by Gutierrez, Chicanos exercised unprecedented political power in Crystal City, Texas, in the 1970s, which spread throughout the lower Rio Grande Valley. These four charismatic leaders embodied the hopes and aspirations of millions of Mexican Americans.

MEXICAN AMERICANS TODAY

Mexican Americans, like African Americans and other people of color, made important educational and economic gains during the 1960s. However, many of these gains faded during the 1970s and 1980s. This loss during the 1970s and 1980s was caused by a number of factors, including the conservative national policies during the Reagan years and important changes in the U.S. economy. In previous decades, when industrial manufacturing was an important part of the U.S. economy, groups with few skills that were highly concentrated in the lower and working classes—such as Mexican Americans and African Americans—could move to large cities and obtain manufacturing jobs that paid well. There has been a substantial decrease in such jobs in the United States during the last twenty years as the United States and other major Western nations have increasingly become societies characterized by high technology and service occupations. These developments in the economy have had a disproportionately negative influence on job availability for groups heavily concentrated in the lower rungs of the economic and educational ladder, such as Mexican Americans, Puerto Ricans in the United States, and African Americans (Gregory & Sanjek, 1994; Wilson, 1987).

At the beginning of the 1990s, and despite some progress in education and income status, Mexican Americans lagged behind Whites and the U.S. total population. In 1993, 46.2% of Mexican Americans twenty-five years old and over had completed four years of high school. This compared to 59.8% for Puerto Ricans, 53.1% for all Hispanics, 81.5% for Whites, and 80.2% for the total U.S. population (U.S. Bureau of the Census, 1994b, p. 157). About

5.9% of Mexican Americans twenty-five years old and over had completed four years or more of college in 1993. This compared to 8% for Puerto Ricans, 16.5% for Cuban Americans, 9% for all Hispanics, 12.2% for African Americans, 22.6% for Whites, and 21.9% for the total U.S. population.

The median family income for Mexican Americans in 1993 was $23,714, compared to $20,301 for Puerto Ricans, $31,015 for Cuban Americans, $23,912 for all Hispanics, $21,161 for African Americans, $38,909 for Whites, and $31,241 for the total U.S. population. The percentage of Mexican American persons living below the official poverty level was considerably above the percentage for Whites and that for the total population in 1993. The percentages were 29.3 for Mexican Americans, 36.5 for Puerto Ricans, 29.3 for all Hispanics, 33.3% for African Americans, 11.6% for Whites, and 15.1 for the total population (U.S. Bureau of the Census, 1994b).

By the late 1980s, the militant Chicano movement of the 1960s had been transformed into more pragmatic forms of political organization. The various Hispanic groups, such as Mexican Americans, Puerto Ricans, and Cubans, were working cooperatively to form political, cultural, and business organizations to push for their collective rights and to improve the economic and educational status of U.S. Hispanics. These organizations included the National Association of Latino Elected and Appointed Officials, the Congressional Hispanic Caucus (comprised of Hispanics in the U.S. Congress), the National Hispanic Chamber of Commerce, the League of United Latin American citizens, and the Hispanic Policy Development Project, an organization that gathers data and analyzes public policy related to U.S. Hispanic groups. Many Mexican American organizations also remained viable, such as the Mexican-American Legal Defense and Education Fund. This organization was making tremendous strides in size, scope, and influence.

Mexican Americans were also reaping benefits in local and state elections and were becoming more conscious of their potential political clout. In 1984, Eligio de la Garza (Texas), Manual Lujan, Jr. (New Mexico), and Matthew G. Martinez (California) were among the eleven Hispanics in the U.S. House of Representatives. Mexican American mayors of large cities included Henry G. Cisneros in San Antonio and Federico Pena in Denver. Toney Anaya was governor of New Mexico. Mexican Americans continued to make visible political gains during the Clinton administration in the 1990s, epitomized by the appointment by Clinton of Henry G. Cisneros as secretary of Housing and Urban Development in his administration.

In 1993, there were 19 Hispanics in the U.S. House of Representatives; none were in the Senate (Reddy, 1993). All were members of the Congressional Hispanic Caucus, formed in 1976. This is a bipartisan group that works to improve conditions for all Hispanics. Mexican Americans in the House in 1992 included Henry G. González (Democrat, Texas), Matthew G. Martínez (Democrat, California), and Ed Lopez Paster (Democrat, Arizona) (Kanellos, 1994).

Despite the political gains they had made by the 1980s and 1990s, Mexican American leaders realized that their ethnic group had more potential political power than it was realizing. The nine states in which Hispanics are concentrated (California, Texas, New York, Florida, Illinois, New Jersey, New Mexico, Arizona, and Colorado) have 193 electoral votes, which is 71% of the 270 needed to put a presidential candidate in the White House. Yet, several factors worked against Mexican Americans realizing their potential political strength, including the low voter turnout rate among them and the fact that a significant percentage of Mexican Americans are not U.S. citizens.

The Mexican American population is becoming increasingly urbanized, although it is less urban than other Hispanic groups. More than 75% of Mexican Americans lived in metropolitan areas in 1960. By 1980, that number had increased about 10%, and about four of every five Mexican Americans lived in metropolitan areas (Bean & Tienda, 1987, p. 86). In 1990, about 89% of Mexican Americans lived in urban areas.

Large populations of Mexican Americans are concentrated in such cities as Los Angeles, Houston, Dallas, Denver, and Chicago. The Mexican American population, like the African American population, has also become more economically stratified since the 1970s. There have always been middle-class Mexican Americans. However, a new group of middle-class Hispanics developed as a result of the economic and educational opportunities they experienced during the civil rights movement of the 1960s and 1970s (Acuña, 1988).

This new middle-class group of Mexican Americans are professionals and business people. They frequently work in mainstream White institutions and live in predominantly White middle-class communities; consequently, they have little contact with the Hispanic barrio or with lower- and working-class Mexican American communities. The children of this new middle class often have little knowledge of the traditional Mexican American culture in the United States. Acuña (1988) has pointed out that these new middle-class professionals and business people often have an identity with and use the term *Hispanic* to refer to themselves. These new middle-class Hispanics, according to Acuña (1988), are often more interested in business development than social action and see business leaders, rather than social activists, as the important movers and shakers in the Mexican American community.

During the 1980s, which some media writers called "The Decade of the Hispanic," the emphasis in the Mexican American community was often on educational and economic development rather than on the kind of strident social action that characterized the civil rights movement of the 1960s and 1970s. Both Presidents Reagan and Bush appointed successful and visible Mexican Americans to important federal positions. President Reagan appointed a university president, Dr. Lauro F. Cavazos, to be Secretary of the Department of Education. Cavazos was the first Hispanic appointed to a Cabinet post. Bush kept him in that position when he was took office in 1989. In

1983, Reagan made history again when he appointed Linda Chavez to the U.S. Commission on Civil Rights. Both Bush and Carter also appointed a number of Hispanics to important positions in their administrations.

Nativism in the 1990s: New Xenophobia

The so-called Decade of the Hispanics was not without its stresses and strains, emergent xenophobia (fear of foreigners), and subtle and sometimes blatant racism. The new xenophobia, nativism, and sometimes racism have been triggered by several factors, including the large influx of legal Asian and Latin American immigrants to the United States, the nation's inability to control the large but undetermined number of undocumented or illegal immigrants (some estimates put the figure at 200,000 annually), the radical changes in the U.S. economy discussed above, and the escalating class schism in U.S. society.

Nativistic sentiments and proposals surfaced during the years of heated discussion that finally resulted in the passage of the Immigration Reform and Control Act of 1986. The act is designed to curb the rapid flow of undocumented (illegal) immigrants who enter the United States each year. It severely penalizes employers who knowingly hire undocumented workers. The enacted bill was a difficult compromise. Some of the voices heard during the strident debates over the proposed bill were decidedly anti-Hispanic in tone. The English-Only movement, which came to the forefront during the 1980s, sometimes articulates chilling language that is reminiscent of the nativistic movements at the turn of the last century. A major goal of this movement is to get enacted in as many states as possible referenda that make English the "official language." What these referenda exactly mean in a legal sense is ambiguous. However, important purposes are to halt the growth of bilingual education programs and to send the message to native speakers of languages other than English, such as Spanish, that the only language accepted in the United States is English.

The English-Only movement is fostered by U.S. English, a political action group that has a deep pocket and the endorsement of some influential Americans. The English-Only movement initially targeted states with large Hispanic populations for the passage of English-Only referenda. One of its major successes was the November 1986 passage of Proposition 63 in California. U.S. English knew that the stakes were high in California. It spent more than $700,000 to get Proposition 63 passed there (Crawford, 1989). By the beginning of 1990, U.S. English had been instrumental in getting English-Only referenda enacted in sixteen states, including Arizona, Colorado, and Florida.

California continued to be an influential center of nativistic activities and movements throughout the 1990s, perhaps because of its high concentration of Spanish-speaking and other immigrants. In 1990, nearly one-third of the nation's immigrants lived in California. About half of the foreign-born lived in just two states, California and New York (U.S. Bureau of the Census, 1993b). In 1994 anti-immigrant feelings surfaced and were sometimes encouraged by politicians. This trend was epitomized by the passage of Proposition 187 in California, which was dubbed by its supporters the "Save Our Children" proposition. This initiative denies undocumented workers and their children schooling and nonemergency medical care (*Encyclopaedia Britannica*, 1995). California Governor Pete Wilson endorsed Proposition 187 and made it a key issue in his reelection campaign. Proposition 187 faced a legal challenge immediately after its passage.

Mexican Americans face several important challenges in the years ahead, including the need to increase the educational status of its youth, to close the income gap between Mexican Americans and the total U.S. population, and to work with other Hispanic groups to influence political elections and national policy. There are encouraging signs that the Mexican American community will face these challenges creatively.

TEACHING STRATEGIES

To illustrate how content about Mexican Americans can be used to integrate the curriculum, three key concepts have been identified and exemplary strategies are given for teaching them. Strategies are presented for teaching *stereotypes, immigration,* and *social protest* for the primary, intermediate and upper, and high school grades respectively.

Primary Grades

CONCEPT: Stereotypes

Generalization: People have many stereotypes about what makes a person an American. These stereotypes often cause hurt and harm.

1. Read the following story to the class and ask the questions that follow:

Child from Another Land

Manuel and Maria Gonzales are descendants of Indian, Mexican, and Spanish people who have lived in the state of New Mexico for at least a century. The Gonzaleses are proud to be Americans but are just as proud of their Mexican American heritage. In their upper-middle-class community in the Southwest, their eight-year-old son, Ramon, went to a public elementary school that had a 20% Mexican American population. Ramon felt at home at the school and was sorry when he learned that his father, an engineer, was moving to the Midwest to accept an important job at a well-known computer company. Mrs. Gonzales, a high school English teacher, was also able to get a job in the Midwest city to which the family was moving.

Manuel and Maria were excited about the move to the Midwest because of the opportunity it offered Manuel. Ramon was very sorry to leave his friends and the only home and community he had ever known. He had decided, however, that he would try to make the best of the move. Ramon was the only Mexican American child in the third grade in his new school. There were only five Mexican American children in the entire school. During the first several days in his new school, Ramon fared okay but felt awkward when the teacher had trouble pronouncing his name and several children asked him, "What country are you from?"

Questions

1. How do you think Ramon felt about leaving his friends?
2. How do you think he felt in his new school? Why did he feel that way? Have you ever felt that way?
3. How do you think Ramon felt when the teacher had trouble pronouncing his name?
4. Why did the children ask Ramon, "What country are you from?"
5. Why do you think the children thought Ramon was from another country?

2. Introduce the concept *stereotype* to the students. Tell the students that a stereotype is a rigid and simplified way of thinking about a group of people and that it often causes harm to individuals and groups. Explain to the students how stereotypes lead to prejudice and discrimination. Ask them to list some of the stereotypes of different groups they may have, such as stereotypes about boys, girls, rich people, poor people, and fat people.

3. Explain to the students that the children thought that Ramon was from a different country because he was a person of color who had a Spanish name. Explain that the children had a stereotypic notion of what an American is. Tell the students that Americans are of all racial, ethnic, and cultural origins. Given them several examples. Also, show them pictures of African Americans, Mexican Americans, and Asian Americans. Summarize the lesson by asking the children to list the hurt and harm that stereotypes cause.

Intermediate and Upper Grades

CONCEPT: Immigration

Generalization: Social, economic, and political conditions have influenced Mexican immigration to the United States. Mexican immigrants in the United States have been the victims of racism, deportation, and labor exploitation.

1. Tell the students that about one million Mexican immigrants came to the United States between 1910 and 1930. Ask them to state hypotheses to explain why so many Mexicans immigrated to the United States during this period. List their responses on the board. When the students have finished stating their hypotheses, ask them to group their hypotheses into several categories, using symbols such as "×" and "+" to indicate statements that should be grouped together. When the statements have been grouped, ask the students to label the groups. The hypotheses might be grouped into such broad categories as "social reasons," "political reasons," and "economic reasons." These categories need not be mutually exclusive. In this initial exercise, you will be teaching your students how to hypothesize and conceptualize, which involves three major steps: listing, grouping, and labeling. (See James A. Banks, with Ambrose A. Clegg, Jr. (1990), *Teaching Strategies for the Social Studies: Inquiry, Valuing and Decision-Making*, 4th ed. [White Plains, N.Y.: Longman, Inc., 1990], p. 95.)

2. When the first exercise is completed, the students should record their hypotheses and categories in their notebooks. They will need to refer to them later in this exercise when they are tested. The students should now collect and study data to test their hypotheses. Their readings should include information on the Mexican Revolution of 1910 and the tremendous need for agricultural labor that had developed in the Southwest by the turn of the century. The Mexican Revolution caused many displaced Mexican peasants to come to the United States looking for jobs after 1910. The wealthy farmers in the Southwest wanted a large and cheap labor supply.

3. Students should investigate the conditions of the early Mexican immigrants to the United States. Most became migrant workers who followed the seasonal crops. Many of their dreams were shattered in the United States. Their problems are vividly and poignantly revealed in Manuel Gamio (1971), *The Life Story of the Mexican Immigrant*. Ask four students to read and dramatize to the class the accounts by these migratory laborers: Gumersindo Valdez, Juan Berzunzolo, Elias Garza, and Nivardo del Rio. Accounts by these writers are found on pages 141–159 of the Gamio book.

4. When the Great Depression struck in 1929, a movement began to deport Mexican immigrants to Mexico. Ask a student to prepare a class presentation giving the views of the U.S. Immigration Service and another to prepare a report revealing how different segments of the Mexican American community felt about this massive repatriation movement. The class should discuss the problem after these two presentations have been given.

5. Beginning in 1942, Mexican immigrants entered the United States under the terms of an agreement between the United States and Mexico. Ask the students to pretend that it is January 1942, and that the *bracero* bill is being debated in the U.S. Congress. Ask different members of the class to play the roles of various kinds of people in the Mexican American community (old settlers, new immigrants, etc.), southwest agribusinessmen, and representatives of major unions in the United States. Ask the students playing the assigned roles to argue for or against the bill before the simulated Congress. The class should vote to decide the fate of the *bracero* bill of 1942 after they have heard the arguments. The class should then compare the results of their vote with the bill passed by Congress in 1942.

6. Ask several students in the class to make reports on Public Law 78, the Migratory Labor Agreement, and Operation Wetback, which began in 1954. Conduct a class discussion on the legal, social, and moral implications of these two activities that were implemented by the U.S. government. Particular attention should be given to how they affected U.S. citizens of Mexican descent.

7. During the debates and discussion on the passage of the Immigration Reform and Control Act of 1986, many problems of undocumented immigrants to the United States were revealed. Ask the students to research the debates that took place when the proposed act was being discussed, to describe the main goals of the act, and to determine the extent to which the act has been successful.

8. Because of the economic problems in Mexico today, a large number of people (both documented and undocumented) are entering the United States from Mexico. In 1992, 213,000 legal Mexican immigrants entered the United States. A large but unknown number of undocumented immigrants also enter the United States each year.

Ask the students to investigate the economic conditions in Mexico today that cause large numbers of Mexicans to leave their nation and head for the United States. Unlike the past, most of these immigrants settle in large U.S. cities, such as Los Angeles, Dallas, and Houston. Ask the students to find out what kinds of jobs these immigrants obtain in U.S. cities, the problems they encounter, and their general status in U.S. society.

9. Summarize the unit by asking the students to take out the hypotheses they formulated at the beginning of this unit and evaluate them, using the information they have collected and evaluated. They should determine which hypotheses can remain as they were originally stated, which ones must be modified, and which ones must be totally rejected on the basis of the evidence collected.

10. Culminate the unit by showing and discussing a videotape or film on the experiences of Mexican Americans. See Appendix B for the descriptions and annotations of videotapes and films. In the discussion, focus on social, economic, and political conditions that have influenced Mexican immigration to the United States.

Valuing Activity

Read the following story to the class and ask the questions that follow.

The Sanchez Family and the Grape Strike

Mr. and Mrs. Sanchez and their seven children came from Mexico to live in California four years ago. Mr. Sanchez had been told by relatives who had been to the United States that he could make money very quickly if he came to California. When Mr. Sanchez arrived in California, he found that it was hard to make a living working in the fields. Since the Sanchez family has been living in California, the family has had to move many times in order to follow the crops and find work. The family has traveled as far as Texas and Michigan to work in the fields.

The work in the fields is very hard. Everyone in the family, except little Carlos, works in the fields so that the family can make enough money. Even Mrs.

Sanchez, who used to stay at home and take care of the home when they lived in Mexico, now must work in the fields. The pay for the work is low. Mr. and Mrs. Sanchez find that they become further and further in debt each year.

The Sanchez family is now living in the San Joaquin Valley in California. The family went to live there to work in the grape fields. For a while everything there was okay. Recently, a lot of things have been happening in the valley that Mr. and Mrs. Sanchez do not fully understand. Most of the field workers have said that they will not go to work next week because the Mexican American Union, led by Juan Gonzalez, who is popular with the workers, has called a strike. The union is demanding that the owners of the grape fields pay the workers more money and give them better worker benefits. The workers who belong to the union are threatening to attack any worker who tries to go to work while the strike is on.

Mr. Sanchez is not a member of the union. He wants very much to go to work next week. He has many bills to pay and needs money for food and clothing. The family simply cannot get by with the small amount of money that the union has promised to give Mr. Sanchez if he joins it and refuses to work next week. Mr. Sanchez also realizes that if the grapes are not picked within the next two weeks, they will rot. He has heard that these strikes sometimes last for months. His boss told him that if he wants to go to work next Monday morning—the day the strike is to begin—he will protect him from the unionized workers. Mrs. Sanchez thinks that Mr. Sanchez should support the strike so that he can make higher wages in the future.

Questions

1. Do you think that Mr. Sanchez and his family will go to work in the fields next Monday? Why or why not?
2. If Mr. Sanchez does go to work, what do you think will happen to him and his family?
3. If Mr. Sanchez does not go to work in the grape fields next Monday, what do you think he might do to earn money?
4. What do you think Mr. Sanchez should do? Why?
5. What would you do if you were (a) Mr. Sanchez (b) Mrs. Sanchez (c) the children? Why?
6. Tell whether you agree or disagree with this statement and why: "The head of a family should never let his or her spouse and children do without the food and clothing they need."

High School Grades

CONCEPT: Social Protest

Generalization: Since the Anglo-American conquest of the Southwest, Mexican Americans have used a variety of means to resist oppression and discrimination. This resistance intensified and assumed new characteristics in the 1960s and 1970s.

1. The teacher can begin this unit by having the students read and dramatize the epic poem of the Chicano movement, *I Am Joaquin/Yo Soy Joaquin*, by Rodolfo Gonzales (1972). This poem is a powerful statement of the history and culture of Chicanos, with emphasis on their oppression and struggle for freedom. Among the many references made in the poem related to social protest are Father Miguel Hidalgo and *El Grito de Dolores of 1810*, Cinco de Mayo, the Treaty of Guadalupe Hidalgo, and the Anglo conquest of the Southwest in the 1800s. This poem will stimulate many questions students can pursue during this study of Chicano resistance to oppression. The teacher may also want to show the film based on the poem *I Am Joaquin.*

2. References are frequently made to the Treaty of Guadalupe Hidalgo by Chicano leaders. After students have studied the events that led to the treaty, have them examine the treaty in detail and give their interpretations of it. They should compare their interpretations of the treaty with interpretations given by contemporary Chicano leaders. The complete text of the treaty is found in *A Documentary History of Mexican Americans,* edited by Moquin with Van Doren (1972).

3. Ask a group of students to prepare and present to the class a dramatization portraying the positions and statements of early Mexican American militant leaders, such as Juan Patron, J. J. Herrerra, and Juan N. Cortina.

4. Some of the earliest Chicano resistance activities were unionization and strikes. Ask a group of students to prepare short reports on the various strikes and union activities during the period from 1900 to 1940. The strike in the California Imperial Valley in 1928 should be highlighted.

5. The earliest Mexican American civil rights organizations pursued what Cuellar (Moore with Cuellar, 1970) has called a "politics of adaptation." Mexican American civil rights organizations became more politicized in the post–World War II period. Militant Chicano organizations emerged in the 1960s. Ask the students to research the goals, tactics, and strategies used by the following Mexican American civil rights groups. They will discover the trends described above.

  a. Order of the Sons of America (formed in 1921)
  b. League of United Latin-American Citizens (1929)
  c. The Community Service Organization (1947)
  d. The American G.I. Forum (1948)
  e. Federal Alliance of Free Cities (1963)
  f. Crusade for Justice (1965)

6. Ask the class to research the following questions: How was the Chicano movement similar to other Mexican American protest movements? How were its goals and strategies different? When did the movement emerge? What problems did it help to solve? What had happened to the movement by the late 1980s? Why? In what ways was the Chicano movement similar to, and different from, civil rights movements that emerged within other ethnic minority communities in the 1960s? What long-term effects do you think the Chicano movement has had and is having on U.S. society?

7. The union activity led by Cesar Chávez during the 1960s and 1970s was an integral part of the Chicano movement. You may begin a study of these events by reading to the class the brilliant and poignant letter that Chávez wrote to E. L. Barr, Jr., president of the California Grape and Tree Fruit League, reprinted in Fusco and Horwitz, *La Causa: The California Grape Strike*. The moving photographs in this book will evoke many questions and comments about the strike. The students can also read the excellently written book on the strike by John Gregory Dunne, *Delano: The Story of the California Grape Strike*.

8. After the students have read and discussed accounts and interpretations of Mexican American resistance and the Chicano movement, ask them to write and present a dramatization on "Mexican American Resistance to Oppression in the United States, 1848 to the Present."

REFERENCES

Acuña, R. (1972). *Occupied America: The Chicano's Struggle toward Liberation*. San Francisco: Canfield Press.

Acuña, R. (1988). *Occupied America: The Chicano's Struggle toward Liberation* (3rd ed.). New York: Harper and Row.

Banks, J. A. with Clegg, A. A., Jr. (1990). *Teaching Strategies for the Social Studies: Inquiry, Valuing and Decision-Making* (4th ed.). White Plains, N.Y.: Longman.

Bean, F. D. & Tienda, M. (1987). *The Hispanic Population of the United States*. New New York: Russell Sage.

Crawford, J. (1989). *Bilingual Education: History, Politics, Theory and Practice*. Trenton, N.J.: Crane Publishing Company.

Encyclopaedia Britannica. (1995). *1995 Book of the Year*. Chicago: Author.

Forbes, J. D. (n.d.). *Mexican-Americans: A Handbook for Educators*. Washington, D.C.: U.S. Government Printing Office.

Franklin, J. H. & Moss, A. A., Jr. (1994). *From Slavery to Freedom: A History of Negro Americans* (7th ed.). New York: Knopf.

Gamio, M. (1971). *The Life Story of the Mexican Immigrant*. New York: Dover Publications.

Gonzales, R. (1972). *I Am Joaquin/Yo Soy Joaquin*. New York: Bantam.

Gregory, S. & Sanjek, R. (Eds.). (1994). *Race*. New Brunswick, N.J.: Rutgers University Press.

Jiménez, A. (1994). The Spanish Colonial Model. In A. Jiménez, (Ed). *Handbook of Hispanic Cultures in the United States: History* (pp. 66–95). Houston: Arte Público/ University of Houston.

Kanellos, N. (1994). *The Hispanic Almanac: From Columbus to Corporate America*. Detroit: Gale Research.

McWilliams, C. (1968). *North from Mexico: The Spanish-Speaking People of the United States*. New York: Greenwood Press.

Meier, M. S. & Ribera, F. (1993). *Mexican Americans/American Mexicans: From Conquistadors to Chicanos*. New York: Hill & Wang.

Meier, M. S. & Rivera, F. (1972). *The Chicanos: A History of Mexican Americans.* New York: Hill and Wang.

Moore, J. W. with Cuellar, A. (1970). *Mexican Americans.* Englewood Cliffs, N.J.: Prentice-Hall.

Moore, J. W. with Pachon, H. (1976). *Mexican-Americans* (2nd ed.). Englewood Cliffs, N.J.: Prentice-Hall.

Reddy, M. A. (Ed.). (1993). *Statistical Record of Hispanic Americans.* Detroit: Gale Research.

The Treaty of Guadalupe Hidalgo. In W. Moquin with C. Van Doren (Eds.). (1971). *A Documentary History of Mexican Americans* (pp. 241–249). New York: Bantam.

U.S. Bureau of the Census. (1993a). *We, the American Hispanics.* Washington, D.C.: U.S. Government Printing Office.

U.S. Bureau of the Census. (1993b). *We, the Foreign Born.* Washington, D.C.: U.S. Government Printing Office.

U.S. Bureau of the Census. (1994a). *Statistical Abstract of the United States: 1994* (114th ed.). Washington, D.C.: U.S. Government Printing Office.

U.S. Bureau of the Census. (1994b, December). Current Population Reports Special Studies, Series P–23, No. 188, *How We're Changing.* Washington, D.C.: U.S. Government Printing Office.

Wilson, W. J. (1987). *The Truly Disadvantaged: The Inner City, the Underclass, and Public Policy.* Chicago: The University of Chicago Press.

ANNOTATED BIBLIOGRAPHY

Books for Teachers

Especially Recommended

Acuña, R. (1988). *Occupied America: A History of Chicanos* (3rd ed.). New York: Harper and Row.

> *This comprehensive and readable history of Mexican Americans presents different and refreshing perspectives on their experiences in the United States.*

Cortés, C. E. (1980). Mexicans. In S. Thernstrom, A. Orlov, & O. Handlin (Eds.). *Harvard Encyclopedia of American Ethnic Groups* (pp. 696–720). Cambridge: Harvard University Press.

> *An excellent historical overview of Mexican American history from the Spanish settlements to about 1980 by a veteran historian and multicultural educator.*

Fuentes, C. (1992). *The Buried Mirror: Reflections on Spain and the New World.* New York: Houghton Mifflin.

> *A veteran writer chronicles the events that led to the creation in New Spain of a new people. This book contains striking illustrations, many in color.*

Garcia, E. E. (1995). Educating Mexican American Students: Past Treatment and Recent Developments in Theory, Research, Policy, and Practice. In J. A. Banks & C. A. M. Banks (Eds.). *Handbook of Research on Multicultural Education* (pp. 372–387). New York: Macmillan.

An informative chapter by a veteran Mexican American educator.

Gutiérrez, R. A. (1991). *When Jesus Came, the Corn Mothers Went Away: Marriage, Sexuality, and Power in New Mexico, 1500–1846.* Stanford, Calif.: Stanford University Press.

A monumental and seminal historical study of marriage, sexuality, and power in New Mexico by a leading Mexican American historian.

Gutiérrez, R. A. (1995). Historical and Social Science Research on Mexican Americans. In J. A. Banks & C. A. M. Banks (Eds.). *Handbook of Research on Multicultural Education* (pps. 203–222). New York: Macmillan.

A beautifully written and perceptive overview of research trends and issues in research on Mexican Americans by the MacArthur-fellowship author.

Martinez, O. J. (1994). *Border People: Life and Society in the U.S.-Mexico Borderlands.* Tucson: University of Arizona Press.

This book focuses on the life of the border population and provides typologies and a wealth of oral history.

Meier, M. & Ribera, F. (1992). *Mexican Americans/American Mexicans: From Conquistadors to Chicanos.* New York: Hill & Wang Incorporated.

This historical analysis covers Mexican history in three phases: prior to the arrival of Columbus and up to the arrival of the conquistadors; the period of Mexican Independence through the Mexican American War and the Treaty of Guadalupe Hidalgo; and the period since 1848 to the present.

Other References

Alarcon, N. (Ed.). (1993). *Chicana Critical Issues.* Berkeley: Third Woman Press.

This is a collection of articles written by Chicana scholars that covers a wide array of topics from Chicana feminism to Chicanas in literature.

Anaya, R. (1995). *Zia Summer.* New York: Avon.

The first mystery novel by the famed author of Bless Me Ultima, *the popular novel.*

Anaya, R. and Lomeli, F. A. (1991). *Aztlan: Essays on the Chicano Homeland.* Albuquerque: University of New Mexico Press.

This collection of essays describes the development and importance of the concept of Aztlan to Chicanos and the Chicano movement.

Buss, F. L. (Ed.). (1993). *Forged under the Sun/Forjada bajo el sol.* Ann Arbor: The University of Michigan Press.

The autobiography of María Elena Lucas, an activist for migrant workers, told in her own words. This powerful autobiography has an extensive and informative introduction written by the editor.

Castillo, A. (1992). *Massacre of the Dreamers: Essays on Xicanisma.* Albuquerque: University New Mexico Press.

This is a compilation of essays by Chicanas about the Mexi-Amerindian female experiences on both sides of the border.

Cordova, T., Cantu, N., Cardena, G., Garcia, J., & Sierra, C. M. (Eds.). (1993). *Chicana Voices: Intersections of Class, Race and Gender.* Albuquerque: University of New Mexico Press.

This is a collection of papers presented at the National Association of Chicano Studies annual conference in 1984. The papers represent Chicana scholarship from a variety of disciplines. Topics discussed include Chicanas in literature, Chicana feminism, and Chicanas in the workplace.

Delgado-Caitan, C. & Trueba, H. (1991). *Crossing Cultural Borders.* New York: The Falmer Press.

This is an ethnographic study of the education of Hispanic children in a town in California. It focuses on Mexican American and Mexican immigrant families and their children.

Garcia, M. T. (1991) *Mexican Americans: Leadership, Ideology and Identity.* New Haven: Yale University Press.

This critical and scholarly account of the 'Mexican American Era' covers the period from 1930 to 1960 when many Mexican American political and social organizations began. Women's participation in political action is not covered as extensively, but is infused throughout.

Garcia, M. T. (1994). *Memories of Chicano History: The Life and Narrative of Bert Corona.* Berkeley: University of California Press.

This important biography of a Chicano labor leader was written by a distinguished Mexican American historian.

Griswold del Castillo, R. & Hidalgo, M. (Eds.). (1992). *Chicano Social and Political History in the Nineteenth Century.* Encino, Calif.: Floricanto Press.

This anthology contains essays that provide a variety of interpretations of the Mexican American experience in the "formative" years of the 19th century.

Gutiérrez, D. G. (1995). *Walls and Mirrors: Mexican Americans, Mexican Immigrants, and the Politics of Ethnicity.* Berkeley: University of California Press.

The author analyzes the relationship between native-born Mexican Americans and Mexican immigrants and the history of Mexican American political activism.

Gutiérrez-Jones, C. (1995). *Rethinking the Borderlands between Chicano Culture and Legal Discourse.* Berkeley: University of California Press.

The author argues that Chicano history "has been consistently shaped by racially biased, combative legal interactions." An informative and important scholarly book.

Herrera-Sobek, M. (1993). *Northbound: The Mexican Immigrant Experience in Ballad and Song.* Bloomington: Indiana University Press.

An excellent resource for enriching the curriculum with ballads and songs. The author describes their historical and social contexts.

Lopez, T. A. (Ed.). (1993). *Growing up Chicano.* New York: Avon Books.

This useful anthology includes twenty selections by Chicano and Chicana writers.

Navarrette, R. (1993). *A Darker Shade of Crimson: Odyssey of a Harvard Chicano.* New York: Bantam Books.

This is an autobiographical account of the experiences of a Mexican American male student in one of the nation's most prestigious institutions of higher education.

Ornelas, M. (Ed.). (1991). *Between the Conquests: Readings in Early Chicano History.* Dubuque, Iowa: Kendall/Hunt.

This is an historical account of the two major events in Chicano history: the Spanish conquest of Mexico in the early sixteenth century and the U.S. victory over Mexico in the middle of the nineteenth century.

Ornelas, M. R. (Ed.). (1993). *Beyond 1848: Readings in the Modern Chicano Historical Experience.* Dubuque, Iowa: Kendall/Hunt.

This collection of articles examines the ramifications of the Treaty of Guadalupe Hidalgo and the rise of the Chicano movement.

Padilla, G. M. (1993). *My History, Not Yours: The Formation of Mexican American Autobiography.* Madison: University of Wisconsin Press.

A collection of autobiographies written by Mexican Americans during the nineteenth and early twentieth centuries.

Sanchez, G. J. (1993). *Becoming Mexican American: Ethnicity, Culture and Identity in Chicano Los Angeles, 1900–1945.* New York: Oxford University Press.

A seminal historical study that focuses on Mexican immigrants to Los Angeles from 1900 to 1945. Recipient of the Robert G. Athearn Award from the Western Historical Association.

Skerry, P. (1993). *Mexican Americans: The Ambivalent Minority.* Cambridge: Harvard University Press.

A popular treatment of Mexican Americans—viewed form the "outside."

Thomas, H. (1993). *Conquest: Montezuma, Cortés, and the Fall of Old Mexico.* New York: Simon & Schuster.

A massive (812 pages) popular account of these important historical events. Selected by the editors of the New York Times Book Review *as an "Editor's Choice" of the year.*

Trejo, A. D. & Avendano, F. (Eds.). (1979). *The Chicanos: As We See Ourselves.* Tucson: University of Arizona Press.

A compilation of articles from different fields of the social sciences written by Mexican Americans.

de la Torre, A. & Pesquera, B. M. (Eds.). (1993). *Building with Our Hands: New Directions in Chicano Studies*. Berkeley: University of California Press.

A scholarly and informative collection of articles make up this important book.

Trueba, H. T. et al. (1993). *Healing Multicultural America: Mexican American Immigrants Rise to Power in Rural California*. Washington D.C.: Falmer Press.

This is an ethnographic study focusing on the social and cultural context of education. It focuses on a small town in California populated primarily by Mexican Americans.

Urrea, L. A. (1993). *Across the Wire: Life and Hard Times on the Mexican Border*. New York: Doubleday.

This book is a collection of writings about life in the various border barrios. It starkly depicts the experiences of Mexican immigrants lives on the border between the United States and Mexico.

Villarino, J. & Ramirez, A. (Eds.). (1992). *Chicano Border: Culture and Folklore*. San Diego: Marin Publications.

A reader for college students and nonspecialists in the field of Chicano studies.

Books for Students

Ada, A. F. (1993). *My Name Is María Isabel*. New York: Atheneum.

A young girl encounters cultural obstacles in school because of her traditional Hispanic name. (Intermediate)

Anzaldúa, G. (1993). *Friends from the Other Side/Amigos Del Otro Lado*. San Francisco: Children's Book Press.

Prietita, a young Mexican American girl, befriends a recent undocumented immigrant boy from neighboring Mexico. Written in both English and Spanish, this book captures the obstacles and experiences of life near the border. (Intermediate)

Atkin, B. S. (1993). *Voices from the Field: Children of Migrant Farmworkers Tell Their Stories*. New York: Little, Brown and Company.

Through first-person accounts, photographs, and poems, this book captures the lives of today's Hispanic migrant children. (Primary)

Brimner, L. D. (1992). *A Migrant Family*. Minneapolis: Lerner.

With several telling black-and-white photographs and powerful text, this book brings to life the experiences of a Mexican American migrant family. (Intermediate)

Cisneros, S. (1991). *House on Mango Street*. New York: Vintage Books.

Stories of a Mexican American girl growing up in a Chicago barrio, told in a series of vignettes. (Middle School/High School)

Codye, C. (1990). *Vilma Martinez.* Chatham, N.J.: Raintree/Steck-Vaughn.

Part of the Hispanic Stories series, this is a biography of a prominent civil rights lawyer. (Primary/Intermediate)

Covault, R. M. (1994). *Pablo and Pimienta/Pablo y Pimienta.* Illustrated by F. Mora. Flagstaff, Ariz.: Northland.

Pablo is excited about going to the watermelon fields of Arizona. Along the bumpy ride Carlos and his canvas cover are thrown out of the truck. Pablo spends the night with a coyote he befriended. They begin the trek to Arizona, and the reader finds out if he makes it or not. This book is in English and Spanish, which makes it an excellent bilingual resource. (Middle School)

DeRuiz, D. C. (1993). *La Causa: The Migrant Farm Workers' Story.* Chatham, N.J.: Raintree/Steck-Vaughn.

This is an account of the work of Cesar Chávez and Delores Huerta to organize migrant farm workers. (All Ages)

Emberley, R. (1993). *Let's Go: A Book in Two languages/Vamos: Un Libro en Dos Lenguas.* Boston: Little, Brown.

Younger readers are introduced to two languages with this book written in both Spanish and English. Simple phrases and basic words are written next to colorful pictures, allowing students to learn easily. (Primary)

Emberley, R. (1990). *My House: A Book Written in Two languages/Mi Casa: Un Libro en Dos Lenguas.* Boston: Little, Brown.

Written in Spanish and English, students learn the words for a house and its contents. With bold illustrations, younger readers have fun learning a new language. (Primary)

Goodwin, D. (1991). *Cesar Chávez: La Esperanza Para el Pueblo.* New York: Fawcett Columbine.

This is a biography of the famous advocate for migrant farm worker rights.

Hammond, A. (1993). *The Home We Have Made.* New York: Crown Publishers.

A homeless youngster finds a parade in the nighttime sky and sets out for an adventure to find a home. This story is enhanced with striking colorful images and is written in both Spanish and English. (Intermediate)

Herrera, J. F. (1995). *Calling the Doves/El Canto de las Palomas.* San Francisco, Calif.: Children's Book Press.

The author reminisces about his childhood in California with his mother and father, who were farm workers. His perceptions of his experieinces provide a rich opportunity to teach about environmental perceptions. The book is written in both English and Spanish. (Middle School)

Hoobler, D. T. (1994). *The Mexican American Family Album.* New York: Oxford University Press.

An excellent resource that documents the journey of Mexicans from Mexico to the United States. (Middle School/High School)

Jimenez, C. M. (1993). *The Mexican American Heritage.* Berkeley, Calif.: TQS Publications.

This is a comprehensive look at Mexican culture dating back to before the arrival of the Spaniards to the present. (Middle School/High School)

Kanellos, N. (Ed.). (1993). *Short Fiction by Hispanic Writers of the United States.* Houston: Arte Publico Press.

This is a collection of short stories by Hispanic American writers. (Middle School/High School)

Lomas Garza, C. (1991). *A Piece of My Heart/Padacito de mi Corazón: The Art of Carmen Lomas Garza.* New York: The New Press.

This beautiful book includes striking color photographs as well as a text describing the art of Carmen Lomas Garza, a noted Chicana artist.

Lopez, Tiffany (Ed.). (1993). *Growing Up Chicana/o.* New York: Morrow.

An anthology of writings by Mexican American authors. (Middle School/High School)

Martin, P. P. (1992). *Songs My Mother Sang to Me: An Oral History of Mexican American Women.* Tucson: University of Arizona Press.

Mexican American women from Arizona are interviewed, and histories of social life, folklore, and customs are discussed. (High School)

Mora, P. (1992). *A Birthday Basket For Tía.* New York: Macmillan.

A young girl celebrates her great-aunt's birthday by collecting memories that exemplify their special relationship. (Primary)

Rodriguez, L. J. (1994). *Always Running: La Vida Loca: Gang Days in L.A.* New York: Simon & Schuster Trade.

This is the autobiographical account of a former Mexican American gang member growing up in Los Angeles. (High School)

Samora, J. (1993). *A History of Mexican American People* (rev. ed). Notre Dame, Ind.: University of Notre Dame Press.

A historical review of the roles that Mexican Americans have had in U.S. history. (Middle School/High School)

Soto, G. (1990). *Baseball in April and Other Stories.* San Diego: Harcourt Brace.

This is a collection of stories about the everyday experiences of working class/ poor, Mexican American young people growing up in Fresno, California. (Intermediate/Middle School)

Soto, G. (1992). *Neighborhood Odes.* San Diego: Harcourt Brace Jovanovich.

With a collection of telling poems, the author brings a Mexican American neighborhood to life. (Intermediate)

Stevens, J. R. (1995). *Carlos and the Cornfield/Carlos y la milpa de maiz.* Illustrated by J. Arnold. Flagstaff, Ariz.: Northland Publishing.

A sequel to Carlos and the Squash Plant/Carlos y la planta de calabaza. *In this story Carlos learns about the rewards of hard work and listening. This book is in English and Spanish. (Intermediate)*

Westridge Young Writer's Workshop. (1992). *Kids Explore America's Hispanic Heritage.* Santa Fe, N.M.: John Muir Publications.

This book chronicles Hispanic American culture through the eyes of its student authors. (Intermediate)

Zapater, B. M. (1992). *FIESTA!* Cleveland, Oh.: Modern Curriculum Press.

A young boy prepares for the Fiesta de Santiago while learning the history of the Latin American tradition of fiestas in honor of different saints. (Intermediate)

CHAPTER 11

PUERTO RICANS IN THE UNITED STATES

CONCEPTS, STRATEGIES, AND MATERIALS

Colonialism has always played an important role in the Puerto Rican experience. Puerto Rico and the United States are connected through colonial ties, and this gives the [Puerto Rican] migration a unique character.

Sonia Nieto

Puerto Ricans are the second largest Hispanic group in the United States. Their 1990 population, about 2,278,000, is about 12.1% of the total population of documented Hispanics living in the United States (U.S. Bureau of the Census, 1994). The Puerto Rican population increased about 34.4% between 1980 and 1990 (U.S. Bureau of the Census, 1993). This rate of growth was considerably greater than the rate of increase for the total U.S. population and for Whites but below the rate of growth for the total Hispanic population (about 53%). The 35.4% population increase experienced by Puerto Ricans between 1980 and 1990 was due primarily to a high birthrate rather than to migration. Puerto Rican migration to the United States peaked in 1953, with about 75,000 net arrivals. Since that time net migration between Puerto Rico and the United States has ebbed and flowed with economic conditions in the two nations (see Figure 11-1) (Rodriguez, 1991).

The Puerto Rican population on the U.S. mainland is growing faster than the population in Puerto Rico. In 1990, Puerto Rico's population was about 3,522,037, compared to a mainland Puerto Rican population of about

Figure 11-1 MIGRATION FROM PUERTO RICO TO THE UNITED STATES, 1920–1986

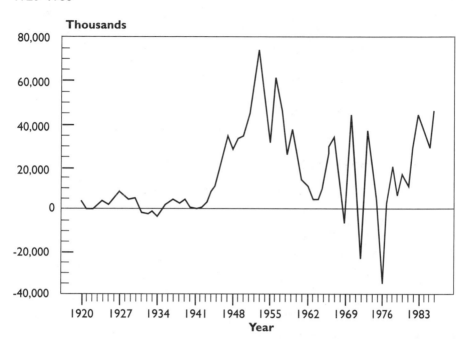

SOURCE: Figure 1.1 from *Puerto Ricans Born in the U.S.A.* by Clara E. Rodriguez. Copyright © 1991 by Westview Press. Reprinted by permission of Westview Press.

2,278,000. The island's population increased about 10% between 1980 and 1990, whereas the Puerto Rican population on the mainland increased about 35.4% (U.S. Bureau of the Census, 1993). Not all of the people who lived on the island, however, were of Puerto Rican descent. Puerto Rico has a sizable immigrant population, including many Cubans. Some population experts predict that if the current disproportionate rate of population growth on the island and the mainland continues, the number of Puerto Ricans on the U.S. mainland will equal if not exceed the number on the island by the turn of the century.

Content about Puerto Ricans should be included in the mainstream curriculum because they are an integral part of U.S. society. Knowledge of their experiences on the mainland can help students master important social science concepts, such as *migration, cultural diversity, racism,* and *colonialism.*

When studying about Puerto Ricans on the U.S. mainland, students can compare and contrast their experiences with those of other migrant and immigrant groups. In some ways, Puerto Rican migration is similar to the movement of other groups to the United States. Puerto Ricans are culturally uprooted, like European immigrants were, when they migrate to the United States. However, their migration is also unique in U.S. history. When large numbers of Puerto Ricans began to migrate to the U.S. mainland, automation had greatly decreased the need for manual labor in the United States. Puerto Ricans are U.S. citizens when they set foot on U.S. soil. Their migration is the first "airborne migration" in U.S. history. Puerto Ricans bring racial attitudes to this country that are considerably different from those they find here. The study of the complex nature of the Puerto Rican migration and experience on the mainland provides students with excellent opportunities to formulate generalizations that are essential components of a sound multicultural curriculum.

THE ISLAND BACKGROUND

Puerto Rico

Puerto Rico, called San Juan Baptista by Christopher Columbus, is a beautiful, small tropical island in the Caribbean Sea. The island, which sits on the top of a large underwater mountain, is smaller than the state of Connecticut. It is about 35 miles wide, 100 miles long, and is made up of slightly more than 3,400 square miles. Puerto Rico, which has become one of the favorite vacation places for U.S. tourists, has one of the highest population densities in the world, 1,039.2 persons per square mile in 1994. In 1994, about 3,653,000 people lived on this attractive island (*Encyclopaedia Britannica,* 1995).

Puerto Rico's history is just as interesting as its terrain and demography. During the last four centuries, its fate has been determined by two faraway nations that ruled it the way absentee landlords govern a slum. Spain ruled the country from the sixteenth century up to the Spanish-American War in 1898. In 1898, the United States took control. It governed Puerto Rico awkwardly and ambiguously. Although the Commonwealth of Puerto Rico has existed since July 1952, Puerto Rico's relationship with the United States is still shaky and unclear. Puerto Rico, which is neither a state nor an independent nation, continues to suffer from the burden of colonialism. Puerto Rico's ambiguous colonialist status is likely to continue for some years to come, especially as cries for independence keep emerging in Puerto Rico, even if they are voiced only by a determined, forceful few. In a plebiscite held in 1993, Puerto Rico's current Commonwealth status won by a slim margin.

Since 1917, Puerto Ricans have been U.S. citizens. In the period between the two world wars, they started migrating to the mainland in large numbers, mainly to New York City. In 1990, about 39% of all Puerto Ricans lived on the U.S. mainland. About half of the mainland Puerto Ricans were born in the United States. The number of Puerto Ricans in the United States mainland is significant and increases at every Census count. The Puerto Rican mainland population grew from 900,000 in 1960 to about 2,278,000 in 1990.

PUERTO RICANS IN THE UNITED STATES: HISTORICAL PERSPECTIVE

Important Dates	
1493	Columbus landed on the island of Boriquén, November 19, 1493. Boriquén was the home of the Taíno (or Arawak) Indians, the native inhabitants of Puerto Rico.
1508	Juan Ponce de León became the governor of Puerto Rico.
1511	The Taino Indians unsuccessfully rebelled against the Spanish system of forced labor.
1513	African slaves were introduced on Puerto Rican plantations.
1868	*El Grito De Lares*: a group of Puerto Rican revolutionaries called for independence and planned an unsuccessful revolt.
1873	Slavery was abolished in Puerto Rico.
1898	Spain ceded Puerto Rico to the United States under the terms of the Treaty of Paris, the treaty that formally ended the Spanish-American War.
1900	Under the terms of the Foraker Act, the United States established a government in Puerto Rico in which the president of the United States appointed the governor and the Executive Council. The House of Delegates and the resident commissioner were to be elected by popular vote.
1910	The U.S. Census indicated that there were 1,513 native Puerto Ricans living in the United States.
1917	The Jones Act was passed by the U.S. Congress. It made Puerto Ricans U.S. citizens and subject to the U.S. draft. The act also provided for the popular election of both houses of the Puerto Rican legislature.
1920	11,811 persons born in Puerto Rico were living in the United States. That number increased to 58,200 in 1935.
1937	Twenty people were killed in a tragedy known as the "Ponce Massacre" on Palm Sunday.
1947	The U.S. Congress amended the Jones Act of 1917. Puerto Ricans were granted the right to elect their own governor. The governor was given the right to make most of the appointments for high public offices.
1948	Luis Muñoz Marin became the first elected governor of Puerto Rico. He was governor of Puerto Rico until 1964.

Important Dates	
1952	On July 25, Governor Luis Muñoz Marin led the inaugural ceremonies establishing the Commonwealth of Puerto Rico, or the Associated Free State.
1961	ASPIRA of America (now the ASPIRA Association, Inc.) was founded.
1965	With the passage of the Civil Rights Act of 1965, Puerto Ricans in the United States were no longer required to pass an English literacy test to vote in the state of New York.
1967	In a plebiscite, Puerto Ricans voted to maintain the Commonwealth status. Statehood and independence were the second and third choices, respectively.
1970	Herman Badillo was elected to the U.S. House of Representatives. He was the first mainland Puerto Rican elected to Congress.
1971	Cuban representatives to the United Nations proposed a resolution to have U.S. colonialism in Puerto Rico debated during a meeting of the United Nations Trusteeship Council.
1972	The United Nations Decolonization Committee declared that Puerto Rico is a colony of the United States.
1974	The legal case, *ASPIRA of New York, Inc. et al. v. Board of Education of the City of New York, Inc. et al.*, ended when the two parties reached an agreement, legally termed a "consent decree." The Board of Education agreed to provide bilingual instruction for Puerto Rican students.
1992	The New Progressive Party, which supports statehood, won the governorship.
1993	In a plebiscite, Puerto Ricans voted by a narrow margin to maintain the Commonwealth status. Statehood was a close second. Independence received only 4.4% of the vote.

The Taino Indians

Puerto Ricans have three major racial heritages—Indian, African, and Spanish. The island was inhabited by a group of Indians called the Tainos when the Spanish came in the fifteenth century. Because they left no written records, little is known about the Tainos, except what archaeologists have been able to detect from potsherds and skulls (Rouse, 1992). Some social scientists believe that there were about 40,000 Tainos on the island when the Spanish came and that they had straight black hair and copper-colored skin (Babin, 1971). Their culture was based on farming, hunting, and raising animals. Religion was also an important part of the Taino culture. The Spaniards caught the Indians by surprise and totally without the kinds of weapons they needed to fight men who fought with swords (Wagenheim, 1975).

The Coming of the Spaniards

In search of a new route to India, Columbus arrived in the Americas in 1492. When he came back to the Americas in 1493, he landed on the island of Boriquen, home of the Taino Indians. Columbus's arrival on the island foreshadowed the Spanish takeover. When Juan Ponce de Leon was made governor of the island in 1508, the Spanish occupation of Puerto Rico was well underway. From the time of the arrival of the Spanish conquistadors, life for the native Indians became increasingly more difficult. Eventually, they were almost totally exterminated. The Spanish set up a kind of forced labor, known as the *encomienda* system. Under this system, each Spanish colonizer was given a group of Indians to work for him. The Spanish colonizer was supposed to "teach" the Indians Spanish "culture" in return for their work.

At first, the Indians did not fight back. They thought the Spaniards were immortal. Eventually, a group of Taino Indians decided to find out if the Spanish were actually immortal. They tried to drown a young Spaniard and succeeded. Once they discovered that the Spaniards died like other men, they started fighting back. A number of Indian rebellions occurred in various parts of the island. Many Spaniards were killed in these skirmishes. The Tainos also ran away from the Spanish settlements. The conquistadors searched for them, often with little success. So many Indians were killed by the Spaniards and their diseases, and so many escaped from the island, that by 1777 they had all but disappeared from Puerto Rico.

Spanish Rule

By the late nineteenth century, Puerto Rico was one of the most neglected colonies in the Western Hemisphere. For nearly 400 years, Spain had ruled the colony from across the Atlantic like an absentee landlord and had woefully neglected it. Puerto Rico's last series of Spanish governors were incompetent and autocratic. They ineptly governed the island with an oppressive, heavy hand. When Spain and the United States entered the Spanish-American War in 1898, Spain's 400-year neglect of her small Caribbean colony was painfully visible. The masses of the people were peons, and the country's wealth was concentrated in the hands of the small upper class. No middle class existed. Most of the people were illiterate, and 92% of the children were not in school. Contagious diseases were widespread. Public health facilities were almost totally absent. Nearly 80% of the draftable Puerto Rican males failed the physical test given by the U.S. military during World War I.

Spain's neglect and mistreatment of Puerto Rico had led to an aggressive movement for home rule by the 1800s. In 1868, the famous Lares Revolt occurred. A group of independence advocates took the city of Lares and proclaimed it the "Republic of Puerto Rico." The revolt failed, but the agitation for home rule continued, even though it was often sporadic and poorly organized. Eventually the movement bore fruit. On November 28, 1897, Puerto Rico was granted autonomy by Spain. This proved to be one of the shortest and most meaningless political changes in history. Barely before the new Puerto Rican government could begin to function, U.S. troops landed on the island.

The Spanish-American War

Spain declared war on the United States on April 24, 1898. A truce was signed on August 12 of that same year. Spain was a pushover for the United States. The two nations formally ended the war with the Treaty of Paris, signed on December 10, 1898. At the meeting, the United States reigned supreme. Spain ceded the Philippines and Puerto Rico to the United States and gave up rights to Cuba. The United States also acquired American Guam.

As had been the case for 400 years, nobody asked Puerto Rico about its political future. Its fate was determined by the United States and Spain. After the meeting, Puerto Rico lost the little autonomy that Spain had granted it in 1897 and became a United States possession. Puerto Rican independence leaders were shocked and dismayed. They had thought that their neighbor from the North had come to free them from colonialism. It was a rude awakening to discover that the United States, the "citadel of freedom and democracy," would also subjugate Puerto Rico just as Spain had done.

UNITED STATES RULE

When the U.S. government took control of Puerto Rico in 1898, it had little experience in governing colonies. In fact, "self-determination of nations" had been one of the main ideas voiced by the U.S. government. However, with the emergence of the doctrine of Manifest Destiny, the United States began to go after foreign lands rather aggressively. It acquired nearly one-third of Mexico's territory in 1848 and increasingly saw how important Caribbean possessions would be to it, both financially and militarily. When the United States entered the Spanish-American War, it hoped to acquire a toehold in the Caribbean Sea. By defeating Spain and gaining Puerto Rico, the U.S. government was better able to make claims to supremacy in the Western hemisphere and show the world that it was a powerful military force.

The U.S. relationship with Puerto Rico was awkward and ambiguous during the first two years of U.S. rule. Military governors from the United States ran the island. This type of government did not prove satisfactory. Congress attempted to establish a more workable relationship with Puerto Rico in 1900. That year it passed the Foraker Act. Under the terms of this act, Puerto Rico became "the People of Puerto Rico." Puerto Ricans were not U.S. citizens nor was the nation independent. The governor and the Executive Council (the Upper House) were to be appointed by the president of the United States. The House of Delegates (the Lower House) and the resident commissioner were to be chosen by popular election. The resident commissioner's job was to present the island's views on issues in the U.S. House of Representatives, although he would be unable to vote. Any action taken by the elected House of Delegates could be vetoed by the U.S. Congress. The Circuit Court of Boston was named the high court for the island. Puerto Rican leaders were shocked by this arrangement, which they interpreted as a slap in the face. They had hoped that when the United States took over the island, its people would be able to decide their own political destiny with a plebiscite. The Foraker Act shattered their hopes.

The Struggle for Self-Governance

Cries for independence were heard throughout Puerto Rico during the sixteen years that the Foraker Act was in effect. Anti-U.S. feelings continued to grow and spread on the island. The island's factional parties shared the belief that Puerto Rico had been betrayed by the United States. As anti-American feelings escalated, the president and the Congress decided that action had to be taken. The then-resident commissioner in Washington, Muñoz Rivera, wanted to poll Puerto Rico's citizens to determine what they felt should be the political status of the island. Muñoz's arguments were ignored. Congress decided to deal with the problem by making Puerto Ricans U.S. citizens with the Jones Act in 1917. This act only further alienated the Puerto Ricans who wanted self-governance on the island. The act not only "forced" citizenship on Puerto Ricans, but it also made them obligated to serve in the U.S. armed forces. Many Puerto Ricans resented the "forced" U.S. citizenship and the fact that they had no voice in the matter. They could resist U.S. citizenship, but resistance meant that they would lose many benefits and become aliens within their homeland. Because of the Jones Act, 140,000 Puerto Ricans fought in World War I.

The Nationalist Party

The Nationalist party, the radical party that strongly advocated the independence of Puerto Rico, emerged out of the forces that opposed how the United States was handling Puerto Rico's affairs. The party leaders felt, with some justification, that the major Puerto Rican parties were too sympathetic to U.S. interests and that party members could not deal with the United States effectively by using traditional means such as the ballot and appealing to the U.S. conscience. Pedro Albizu Campos emerged as the militant leader of the party. A graduate of Harvard, Albizu knew U.S. politics well. The party became a target of the Puerto Rican and U.S. governments, who considered it extreme and dangerous.

At a parade sponsored by the Nationalist party on Palm Sunday, March 21, 1937, a shot fired into a crowd resulted in a massacre in the streets of Ponce. When the Nationalists' initial request for a parade permit to march in San Juan was denied, they decided to move the parade to Ponce. The mayor of Ponce granted the parade request because the Nationalists agreed to keep the march peaceful. Despite a last-minute attempt by Governor Blanton Winship to prevent the parade, the Nationalists marched. The marchers did not carry arms, but the police were heavily armed. In the ruckus that occurred after the shot was fired, 20 people lost their lives and more than 100 were wounded. A inquiry by the Brookings Institution revealed that the police instigated the gunfire and were excessively brutal (Nieto, 1995). This infamous event in Puerto Rican history is known as the "Ponce Massacre." It symbolizes the independence struggle in Puerto Rico.

Luis Muñoz Marin: Governor of Puerto Rico, 1948–1964

Between 1900 and 1946, Puerto Rico was headed by a series of fifteen U.S. governors appointed by the president of the United States. With only a few exceptions, they were unimpressive men. They differed little from the Spaniards who had ruled Puerto Rico prior to 1898. Medical, educational, and economic conditions on the island reflected poor leadership. By 1940, conditions in Puerto Rico were not substantially different from conditions in 1898. Persistent expressions of dissatisfaction with the governors by Puerto Rican leaders led the United States to grant Puerto Rico the opportunity to elect its own governor in 1947. In 1948, Senator Luis Muñoz Marin was elected governor of Puerto Rico. He was the first elected governor in Puerto Rico's history.

THE COMMONWEALTH OF PUERTO RICO

Muñoz was destined to change decisively the course of Puerto Rican history. More changes occurred in Puerto Rico during his sixteen years as governor than had taken place during the previous four centuries of Spanish rule. Without question, Muñoz's influence on the island was unprecedented. Like any political leader who gets things done and shapes history, he was a charismatic and controversial figure.

Once in office, Muñoz took a position on the polemical status question. He favored what later became known as the Commonwealth or the *Estado Libre Asociado* (Free Associated State). With this status, Puerto Rico would maintain a tie with the United States, but would have a degree of governmental autonomy. Muñoz fought hard to make the Commonwealth a reality. The people approved it in a plebiscite on June 4, 1951. Muñoz led an inauguration ceremony for the Commonwealth of Puerto Rico on July 25, 1952.

The Commonwealth did not solve the status question, and the controversy continued. Both statehood and independence advocates opposed the new status. Many people refused to go to the polls, claiming that the plebiscite was a hoax because the voters were presented with only two choices. They had to vote either to maintain the status quo or to initiate the proposed Commonwealth. Thus, the meaning of the plebiscite was bitterly debated. To this day, the status question is still one of the hottest political issues on the island. It tends to dominate and overshadow other issues.

Urbanization and Operation Bootstrap

Muñoz also set Puerto Rico on a new economic course. He felt that income from the island's three main cash crops—sugar, tobacco, and coffee—was inadequate to support Puerto Rico. Muñoz wanted to industrialize the island by luring U.S. manufacturers to set up plants in Puerto Rico. He formed "Operation Bootstrap" to attract U.S. industry to Puerto Rico. He offered generous benefits, such as lower wages and tax exemptions for up to ten years. Many U.S. companies set up plants in Puerto Rico under this program. Like most changes that Muñoz implemented, the program was both successful and controversial. The changes that Operation Bootstrap stimulated in Puerto Rico were truly amazing. By 1971, the program had recruited 2,000 plants and millions of dollars in investments. Income from manufacturing was more than three times that from agriculture, although agriculture was still important in the island's economy. The island's per capita income jumped from $188 a year in 1940 to $1,234 a year in 1969.

The Operation Bootstrap reforms and modernization of Puerto Rico that occurred during the 1940s, 1950s, and 1960s were mixed blessings. Urbanization brought the usual problems in housing and created a new poverty class: the urban poor. Although Operation Bootstrap was designed to help solve the problem of unemployment, it actually increased it. Industrialization displaced small farmers, who migrated to the cities and became unemployed. Many Puerto Ricans left the island and migrated to the U.S. mainland to look for work. Migration from the island to the United States peaked during the 1950s, at a time when Operation Bootstrap was booming.

The Puerto Rican economy remains precarious. The island has a high level of unemployment. Even when Operation Bootstrap was booming, the large numbers of Puerto Ricans who migrated to the United States each year helped maintain a healthy economy on the island. Urbanization has pulled many families to the cities looking for work and has created city slums, housing congestion, and other problems associated with urban growth. The percentage of persons living below the poverty level in Puerto Rico is considerably above the percentage for Puerto Ricans on the U.S. mainland. In 1990, 58.9% of persons on the Island compared to about 35.5% on the U.S. mainland lived below the poverty level (U.S. Bureau of the Census, Current Population Reports, 1990; U.S. Bureau of the Census, 1994).

Although urbanization created a middle class in Puerto Rico and bedroom suburban communities, Muñoz's critics correctly note that Operation Bootstrap brought the greatest benefits to the upper class and to U.S. industrialists. U.S. companies take the bulk of the money they earn on the island back to the United States. Many of them are now deserting Puerto Rico for nations in Asia where they can find cheaper labor. Urbanization in Puerto Rico, like so many other developments, has done little to change the living conditions of the poor, except perhaps to show them how to live poor "urban" rather than poor "rural" style. Despite the mixed blessings of the Muñoz reforms, his sixteen-year reign made a tremendous difference in Puerto Rico's present and future.

LIFE ON THE MAINLAND

The Migration

After the United States gained control of Puerto Rico, the stage was set for the mass movement of islanders to the U.S. mainland. A few Puerto Ricans, such as cigar makers and merchant seamen, had settled in New York before the 1920s; but Puerto Ricans did not begin to migrate to the United States in significant numbers until the 1920s and 1930s. When Mills, Senior, and Goldsen (1967) published their pioneering study in 1950, most Puerto Ricans in New York City had come during the years between the two great world wars. The number of Puerto Ricans migrating to the United States decreased considerably during World War II because of the closing of transportation routes between New York and Puerto Rico.

After the war, the number of Puerto Ricans migrating to the United States increased. In 1945, only 22,737 Puerto Ricans came to the United States. That number increased to 101,115 in 1947. Puerto Rican migration to the United States has always reflected economic trends. A significant number of migrants usually return to the island when the mainland economy is depressed. During the Great Depression of the 1930s, the net migration back to the island reached 8,694 people in a four-year period (Mills, Senior, & Goldsen, 1967). *Net migration* is the difference between the number of Puerto Ricans who enter the United States and the number who leave within a specific time period. It can be a positive (+) or a negative (–) figure. When the U.S. economy is booming, Puerto Rican migration usually increases and return migration decreases considerably.

Rodriguez (1991) describes three major periods of Puerto Rican migration to and from the U.S. mainland. The first significant number of migrants arrived between 1900 and 1945. Most of these migrants settled in New York City. The second period of migration took place between 1946 and 1964. During this period, the largest number of migrants from Puerto Rico settled in the U.S. mainland. Rodriguez (1991) calls the third period of Puerto Rican migration, from 1965 to the present, "the revolving-door migration." During this period, migration to the mainland has varied with economic developments on the island and the mainland. Migrants have also dispersed to other regions in the United States, such as New Jersey, Illinois, and California.

The lack of legal barriers is a major factor in Puerto Rican migration to and from the U.S. mainland. The Jones Act of 1917 made Puerto Ricans U.S. citizens. As U.S. citizens, they can move freely from the island to the mainland and within various parts of the United States. Their migration to the United States is not limited by restrictive quotas, as is the case in Mexico and in the various Asian nations. Many Puerto Ricans take advantage of their freedom of movement and migrate to the United States. Although the movement of Puerto Ricans to the mainland has many of the sociological characteristics of an immigration, Puerto Ricans are technically migrants rather than immigrants because they are citizens of the United States.

Easy and inexpensive transportation to the mainland also facilitates Puerto Rican migration. In the 1930s, Puerto Ricans could make a boat trip from San Juan to New York City in the relatively short period of three and a half days, and for as low as $40 (Chenault, 1938). After World War II, plane transportation from the island became more available and inexpensive. During this period, a migrant could fly from San Juan to New York City for as low as $35 (Mills, Senior, & Goldsen, 1967). Today, transportation from the island is more convenient and still inexpensive. Whereas the flight from San Juan to New York City took eight bumpy hours in the 1940s, the trip could be made as quickly as three hours and for as low as $206.00 in 1995. Convenient and inexpensive transportation has not only stimulated migration from the island to the mainland but has also helped make Puerto Ricans transients between the island and the United States. Many Puerto Ricans in New York return to the island to visit relatives, to vacation, or to take care of business for short periods.

The "Americanization" of Puerto Rico since 1898 and economic factors have played major roles in motivating Puerto Ricans to migrate to the United States. Since Puerto Rico became an American colony, U.S. culture and institutions have profoundly influenced Puerto Rican culture and life-styles. Americans forced the teaching of English in Puerto Rican schools for years and introduced textbooks that venerated George Washington and Abraham Lincoln rather than Puerto Rican leaders (Negron de Montilla, 1975). These books also described the United States as the neighbor to the North in which "democracy and freedom" flourished. American stores such as J. C. Penney and Sears dot the streets in San Juan as they do in Chicago.

During the period of high migration to the U.S. mainland in the 1950s, many Puerto Ricans who returned to the island told their relatives and friends about the "great" new life in New York City. The availability of jobs in New York City during periods of intensive migration and the higher pay Puerto Ricans could earn in New York, compared to San Juan, lured many Puerto Ricans from the island to the mainland.

Since the great period of migration to the U.S. mainland from Puerto Rico between 1946 and 1964, migration to and from the U.S. mainland has followed economic trends. When economic times are good on the mainland, the number of migrants from Puerto Rico increases. However, migrants tend to return to the island during economic hard times on the mainland. In 1953, migration from Puerto Rico to the mainland peaked at 74,000. Since the mid-1960s, migration from Puerto Rico to the mainland has been fluctuating. A deep drop occurred around 1976 (see Figure 11-1).

The population increase in the Puerto Rican mainland community today results primarily from new births rather than from migration. Migration still occurs. However, much of it consists of unemployed individuals who circulate from the island to the mainland and back again. These migrants often cannot find jobs on the island or the mainland.

Although the migration of Puerto Ricans from the island to the mainland is similar in many ways to other movements of peoples to the United States, it is unique in several ways. As Fitzpatrick notes, it was the first "airborne migration" in U.S. history (Fitzpatrick, 1987, p. 20). Puerto Ricans, unlike many of the earlier immigrants, are also U.S. citizens when they arrive in the United States. Puerto Ricans bring attitudes toward race that are different from and more complex than those in the United States. They also started migrating to the United States at a time when automation had eliminated most of the jobs requiring unskilled laborers. Most of these factors, along with the racism and discrimination they experience in the United States, have increased rather than mitigated their problems in the United States.

The Family

The family, which is important in traditional Puerto Rican culture, is experiencing tremendous changes on the island. Cultures are not static in modernized societies; they are dynamic and changing. As Puerto Rico becomes increasingly urbanized, many of its traditional rural values—including those related to the family—are changing. While the Puerto Rican family and its values are changing on the island, the family faces even more conflicts and problems when it moves to the U.S. mainland. It becomes part of a U.S. mainstream culture that is often unaware of and unsympathetic to traditional Puerto Rican values related to family and community. The racism and discrimination that the Puerto Rican family experiences in the United States also create adjustment problems.

The serious economic problems that faced the Puerto Rican community by the mid-1990s affected the family. In 1993, about 32.5% of Puerto Rican families were living below the official government poverty level (U.S. Bureau of the Census, 1994). This percentage was greater than that of all other Hispanics and also greater than that of African Americans and Whites. A deep sense of family remains within the Puerto Rican community despite the economic problems it faces.

A number of values are still strongly held within Puerto Rican families, including respect for the elderly and for parents, and extremely strong bonds within the family, particularly with the mother (Sanchez-Ayendez, 1988). The family, rather than the individual, tends to be the main identification focus. The extended family is important, and all family members tend to feel obligated to care for and be responsible for one another. The protection of children, especially girls, is very important to the family. This protection is often viewed as overprotection by people outside the culture. These traditional values of Puerto Rican families are being challenged by modernization, by urbanization, and by the levels of assimilation occurring among the current generation of Puerto Ricans in the United States. However, they still have a great deal of tenacity in the Puerto Rican community.

Despite the problems that they face in the United States, many Puerto Rican migrants remain in the United States. A few return to the island for many different reasons, including the lack of a job, alienation, discrimination, and longing for their homeland, family, and friends. Most Puerto Ricans who remain in the United States retain important aspects of their culture but re-create and change their culture in ways that reflect their participation within U.S. society. How Puerto Ricans use language illustrates this process of cultural adaptation and change. While learning English, most Puerto Ricans also continue to speak Spanish. In 1990, about 41.4% of Puerto Ricans reported that they "speak Spanish, do not speak English very well"; 58.6% reported that they "speak Spanish, speak English very well" (U.S. Bureau of the Census, 1993, p. 7).

The Issue of Race and Racism among Puerto Ricans

Although racism exists in both Puerto Rico and the U.S. mainland, race is highly complex in Puerto Rico, and social race has different meanings in the two cultures. Scholars such as Zenon Cruz (1975) and Betances (1972) believe that social scientists have exaggerated the differences between racism in the United States and in Puerto Rico. These two researchers believe that most social scientists have underestimated the extent to which Blacks are victimized by racism in Puerto Rico. They believe that racism is an important part of Puerto Rican society. Although Zenon and Betances provide a needed perspective on race relations in Puerto Rico, social-class status in Puerto Rico interacts with race in complex ways. Upper-class Whites tend to exclude both poor Whites and poor Blacks from their social gathering. However, poor Whites and poor Blacks tend to mix more freely in Puerto Rico than in the United States. Even though Whites tend to marry other Whites in Puerto Rico, racial intermarriage occurs more often in Puerto Rico than in the United States.

The primary identity for most Puerto Ricans is culture rather than race, whereas race has primacy in the United States. Most Puerto Ricans tend to think of themselves first as Puerto Rican and secondarily as *blanco, negro, trigueño,* or *indio.* Writes Rodriguez (1991), "Perhaps the primary point of contrast was that, in Puerto Rico, racial identification was subordinate to cultural identification, while in the United States, racial identification, to a large extent, determined cultural identification" (p. 52).

Puerto Ricans on the U.S. mainland are forced to fit into one of two racial categories: Black or White. These categories are often less meaningful in the Puerto Rican community. Puerto Ricans, both on the island and on the mainland, recognize and use a number of different racial categories, such as *blanco* (Whites), *prieto* (dark-skinned), *negro* (Blacks), and *trigueño* (tan) (Wagenheim, 1975). Other words they use to make color distinctions among themselves are *indio, grifo,* and *de color* (Padilla, 1958). When determining an individual's color, Puerto Ricans consider hair color and texture as well as skin color. Also, an individual's color classification is determined primarily by his or her physical traits rather than by the color of parents or relatives. Within one family there can be individuals who are considered *blanco, negro,* and *trigueño.* Also, the social status of individuals can be important factors in their racial classifications. In general, the higher an individual's social status, the less likely he or she will be considered *negro.*

The different ways in which color is recognized and treated on the mainland cause problems for the Puerto Rican migrant, especially for those who are intermediate in skin color. In their community, they are neither Black nor White; but they are often considered Black by outsiders. This causes the intermediate individual to feel alienated from both the White and Black communities in the United States. A study by Mills, Senior, and Goldsen (1967) indicated that Puerto Rican migrants who were intermediate in color experienced more adjustment problems in the United States than did individuals who were clearly identified as either Black or White.

THE PUERTO RICAN MAINLAND COMMUNITY

When they first started migrating to the United States, most Puerto Ricans settled in New York City. However, the percentage of Puerto Rican migrants settling in New York City has steadily decreased in recent decades; the percentage settling in other mainland cities and states has increased. In 1940, 88% of the Puerto Rican population in the United States lived in New York City. By 1960, that number had declined to 69%. In 1990, 52% of Puerto Ricans lived outside New York state.

While 61% of Puerto Ricans in the United States lived in the states of New York and New Jersey in 1990, many lived in other parts of the nation. A considerable number of Puerto Ricans (23%) lived in Illinois, Florida, and California. In 1990, most Puerto Ricans (99.7%) were concentrated in these eight states: New York, New Jersey, Florida, Massachusetts, Pennsylvania, Connecticut, Illinois, and California. Pockets of them also lived in many other states, including Texas (43,000), Georgia (17,000), and Washington state (9,000) (see Table 11-1).

Pockets of Puerto Ricans in U.S. cities constitute ethnic neighborhoods. The Puerto Rican community is usually a poor community, with the characteristics of people who are poor. In 1994, Puerto Ricans had the lowest median family income of the major Hispanic groups and the largest percentage of persons below the poverty level (U.S. Bureau of the Census, 1994). The median family income was $20,301 for Puerto Ricans, compared to $23,714 for Mexicans, and $31,015 for Cuban Americans. In 1993, about 35.5% of Puerto Ricans lived below the poverty level, compared to 29.3% of Mexican Americans, 18.1% of Cubans, 33.2% of African Americans, and 11.6% of Whites.

The educational status of Puerto Ricans was also comparatively low in 1987. Even though the percentage of Puerto Rican persons twenty-five years old and over who had completed four years of high school was above the percentage for Mexican Americans, 59.8% compared to 46.2%, it was below the percentage for African Americans (70.4%), Whites (81.5%), and the total population, 80.2% (U.S. Bureau of the Census, 1994) (see Table 11-2).

The sound of Spanish, *bodegas,* travel agencies, and Pentecostal storefront churches are familiar sounds and sights in most Puerto Rican mainland neighborhoods. Although Puerto Rican mainland culture is decidedly different from Puerto Rican culture, certain parts of the old culture are retained on the mainland. Hispanos, as many Puerto Ricans call themselves, usually speak Spanish at home and English when talking with outsiders. To obtain the foods to prepare favorite ethnic dishes, such as rice and beans, fried plaintains, or dried codfish, the family may shop at the *bodegas,* the little corner grocery

Table 11-1 PUERTO RICAN POPULATION
IN SELECTED STATES (1990)

State	Population
New York	1,087,000
New Jersey	320,000
Florida	247,000
Massachusetts	151,000
Pennsylvania	149,000
Connecticut	147,000
Illinois	146,000
California	126,000
Ohio	46,000
Texas	43,000
Hawaii	26,000
Virginia	24,000
Michigan	19,000
Wisconsin	19,000
Maryland	18,000
Georgia	17,000
Indiana	14,000
Washington	9,000
Arizona	8,000
Colorado	7,000
Louisiana	6,000

SOURCE: Based on data in the U.S. Census, 1990.

store usually run by Puerto Ricans. Increasingly, however, supermarkets are carrying Puerto Rican foods and other goods. Herbs and plants needed to cure illnesses or to fight the "evil" can be bought at the *botanicas*. Tickets for an air trip back home can be bought at the local travel agency, perhaps on easy terms. The Pentecostal Church, a fast-growing institution in the Puerto Rican mainland community, serves the spiritual needs of the migrants. The Puerto Rican community, with its *bodegas, botanicas,* and Pentecostal churches, helps to ease the cultural shock for the migrants and helps them to develop roots in their new land.

THE FUTURE

On most major indices, such as occupational status, education, and income, Puerto Ricans fall far behind the general U.S. population and most other Hispanic groups. Yet, the future of the Puerto Rican community can be shaped by

Table 11-2 SELECTED EDUCATIONAL AND INCOME CHARACTERISTICS OF PUERTO RICANS COMPARED TO SELECT GROUPS, 1993

	Puerto Ricans	Mexican Americans	Cubans	All Hispanics	African Americans	Whites	Total Population
Percentage 25 years or older who have completed 4 years of high school or more	59.8	46.2	62.1	53.1	70.4	81.5	80.2
Percentage 25 years or older who have completed 4 years or more of college	8.0	5.9	16.5	9.0	12.2	22.6	21.9
Median family income	$20,301	$23,714	$31,015	$23,912	$21,161	$38,909	$31,241
Percent of persons below poverty level	36.5	29.3	18.1	29.3	33.3	11.6	15.1

SOURCE: U.S. Bureau of the Census (1994). *Statistical Abstract of the United States* (114th ed). Washington, D.C.: U.S. Government Printing Office.

educational, political, and social action. Puerto Ricans in the United States are a young and growing population—they had the youngest median age, 20. 7, of any Hispanic group in 1980. There are signs that the Puerto Rican community is becoming more politically and legally active than it has been in the past. By the mid-1990s, the New York Puerto Rican community was playing an increasingly important role in local, state, and national elections.

A number of Puerto Rican educational and civic organizations are working to strengthen the Puerto Rican community. One of the most important is The ASPIRA Association, Inc., an organization founded in 1961 to promote educational achievement and leadership development among youths. Today, it is an important, active, and effective organization within the Puerto Rican community (The ASPIRA Association, Inc., n.d.). Other important Puerto Rican organizations include the National Puerto Rican Coalition, which coordinates a group of organizations and works to improve the social and economic conditions of Puerto Ricans in the United States; and the Puerto Rican Legal Defense and Educational Fund, which litigates for Hispanics who live in the Northeast. The National Congress for Puerto Rican Rights (NCPRR) works to obtain "civil and human rights for Puerto Ricans."

The future of Puerto Ricans in the United States will be heavily influenced by political, economic, and social developments on the island. These two communities are integrally bound. Many Puerto Ricans see Puerto Ricans on the island and those on the mainland as one divided nation. Consequently, the status question that haunts the island cogently influences the ideologies, debates, and visions of mainland Puerto Ricans.

TEACHING STRATEGIES

To illustrate how content related to the Puerto Rican experience can be incorporated into a conceptual curriculum, I have identified three key concepts related to the Puerto Rican experience and sample strategies for teaching them. Strategies are presented for teaching *cultural conflict, racial categories,* and *colonialism* in the primary, intermediate and upper, and high school grades, respectively.

Primary Grades

CONCEPT: Cultural Conflict

Generalization: The Puerto Rican migrant family in the United States experiences many conflicts and problems because it encounters new norms, values, and roles on the mainland that conflict with those in Puerto Rico.

1. Read the following case study to the students and ask the questions that follow. During the discussion of the story, help the children to state the generalization in their own words.

The Ramos Family

Mr. and Mrs. Ramos and their two children, Maria, age three, and Carlos, age seven, live in New York City in an area called El Barrio. The Ramos family moved to New York two years ago from San Juan, Puerto Rico. When the family lived in San Juan, Mr. Ramos worked in a factory. Mrs. Ramos stayed at home and took care of the children and house.

Both Mr. and Mrs. Ramos were happy living in San Juan until some of their relatives moved from San Juan to New York City. First, Mrs. Ramos's two sisters, whom she liked very much, moved to New York. Later, Mr. Ramos's brother moved to New York. They missed their relatives very much. They wanted to be able to see them more often. Mr. and Mrs. Ramos decided to go to New York to pay their relatives a visit.

When Mr. and Mrs. Ramos arrived in New York to visit, their relatives were very glad to see them. Mrs. Ramos kissed her two sisters. She told them about all the news back home. Her sisters told her about New York City. They liked it very much. Mrs. Ramos became very excited about New York City as she listened to her sisters talk about it. Mr. Ramos and his brother were also glad to see each other. Mr. Ramos told his brother how the family was doing in San Juan. Mr. Ramos's brother told him about how good things were in New York. He told Mr. Ramos that he could make twice as much money in New York as he made in San Juan! Mr. and Mrs. Ramos enjoyed New York City for two weeks. When they left, they had decided that they would move to New York City as soon as they got back home.

When the Ramos family got to New York again, things were not as nice as they thought they would be. The family was not as happy as it had been in San Juan. They had to live with Mr. Ramos's brother for two months because they could not find a nice apartment right away. When they did find one, it cost much more than they had paid for rent in San Juan. Mr. Ramos looked a long time before he could find a job. To help the family pay its bills, Mrs. Ramos got a job in a garment factory. Mrs. Ramos was the only person in the family working. She began to make more and more decisions for everyone in the family.

Mr. Ramos spent most of each day looking for a job. He spoke good Spanish but many companies would not hire him because he spoke little English. Since Mrs. Ramos was working and Mr. Ramos was job hunting, Carlos and Maria had to spend a lot of time without either parent. Sometimes they would get into trouble with the neighborhood children.

Carlos became sad when he started to school. He was a top student in Puerto Rico. However, he did poorly in school in New York. He could not read English well. He fell further and further behind in school each week. The teacher called him "Charlie" instead of "Carlos." The children teased him because he spoke "funny." Carlos tried hard to speak English, even at home. His parents wanted him to speak Spanish at home so that they could understand him.

After looking for three months, Mr. Ramos found a job in a hotel. The family then moved into their own apartment. Things got better then. Mr. Ramos wanted Mrs. Ramos to quit her job and stay at home with the children. Mrs. Ramos wanted to keep working because she felt that it took more money to live in New York than in San Juan. Sometimes the family wished that they had stayed in San Juan.

The Ramos family has now been in New York City for two years. They are much happier now, but they still miss their friends and relatives in San Juan. Mr. Ramos understands why Mrs. Ramos wants to work. Carlos is speaking better English and getting better grades in school. The family is planning to visit Puerto Rico during the Christmas season. Carlos is counting the days until Christmas!

Questions

1. Why did the Ramos family move from San Juan to New York City?
2. Was New York City like the family expected it to be? Why or why not?
3. What problems did each of the family members have in New York City that he or she did not have in San Juan?
4. Which family member faced the greatest problems in New York? Why?
5. Which family member faced the fewest problems in New York? Why?
6. What problems do you think the family faced in New York City that are not brought out in the story? Why?
7. How do you think the family will feel about New York a year from now? Do you think that the family will move back to Puerto Rico? Why or why not?

Intermediate and Upper Grades

CONCEPT: Racial Categories

Generalization: Racial categories differ in Puerto Rico and on the U.S. mainland. These differing racial categories make the experience of Puerto Rican migrants to the mainland more difficult.

1. Find old copies of magazines such as *Ebony, Hispanic, Essence, Black Enterprise,* and *Life.* Locate pictures of people who look (a) obviously European American, (b) obviously African American, and (c) like fair-skinned African Americans. Mount these pictures on cardboard.

2. Show the students three of the pictures, one that will fit into each of the categories described above. Ask the students to name the "race" of the person in each picture. They will most likely say that one of the pictured persons is "White," and that the other two are "Black" or "African American." Ask: "Why do we use only two categories to classify the people in these pictures?" With the use of careful questions, explain that in the United States any person, regardless of his or her physical appearance, is considered "Black" or "African American" if he or she has any *known* African ancestry.

3. Show the class mounted pictures of (a) a fair-skinned African American male adult, (b) a fair-skinned African American female adult, (c) a dark-skinned African American male child, (d) a female child who looks Caucasian.

4. Ask the students to name the "race" of each of the pictured persons. After discussing their responses, tell the class that the pictures represent a Puerto Rican family that recently moved from San Juan to New York City. In the pictures are mom, dad, brother, and sister. Point out that even though we may call the parents and the son "Black," Puerto Ricans have words to describe each color. Introduce these words. They would call the parents *trigueño,* the son *Negro* or *de color,* and the daughter *blanca.* Tell the students that in Puerto Rico "color" has a special meaning that is different from its meaning in the United States. Ask the students what race would the different family members belong to in the United States and why. Through questioning, bring out that all of them would be considered "Black" or "African American" and why.

5. Ask: "Now that the family is in New York City, what kinds of racial problems might they encounter?" "Why?" Through questioning, reveal that mother and father will be considered "Black" on the mainland even though they were intermediates *(trigueños)* in Puerto Rico. Discuss with the class the kinds of identity and social problems that the couple will face on the mainland and how they might cope with them. Ask the class the following questions:

   a. How do you think mother and father will feel when mainland Whites call them "Black" or "African American"?
   b. How do you think they will feel when African Americans call them "Black"? Do you think they will identify with the Black struggle for civil rights? Why or why not?
   c. Do you think they will want to be called "White" or "Black"? Why? What problems might they encounter when seeking to obtain their preferred racial identification? Why? How might they go about solving them?

6. With these and other questions, bring out the generalization that Puerto Rican migrants to the mainland who are intermediate in color have serious racial and adjustment problems because they are neither White nor Black in Puerto Rico but are forced to be "Black" on the mainland. Ask the class these valuing questions: Do you think that it is right to consider intermediates on the mainland "Blacks"? Why or why not? Do you think they should be considered "White"? Why or why not? If you were an intermediate Puerto Rican on the mainland, would you want to be considered "White" or "Black"? Why? When asking such valuing questions, accept all responses and maintain an open classroom atmosphere. Ask the class these questions:

   a. What special identity and racial problems might the son have in his family? In school? In the community? Why? How might he deal with them?
   b. What special racial and identity problems might the daughter have in the family? In school? In the community? Why? How might she deal with them?

Read the following case study to the class and ask the questions that follow.

Mr. Diaz and Mr. Seda on the Mainland

Mr. Diaz looks Caucasian. In Puerto Rico he and Mr. Seda, who is *de color,* were close friends. They both now live in New York City. When they first came to New York City, they would visit each other often, as they had done in Puerto Rico. Eventually Mr. Diaz started visiting Mr. Seda less and less and would often act unfriendly when Mr. Seda came to visit him, especially when his White friends were over. Mr. Diaz's White friends would always give Mr. Seda strange looks when he came over. Mr. Diaz began to understand that in New York City he was expected to mix socially with Whites only. Now, Mr. Diaz never visits Mr. Seda, and Mr. Seda goes to Mr. Diaz's house very seldom. When he does, he stays only a short time. The last time that Mr. Seda visited Mr. Diaz's home, Mr. Diaz left in the middle of the visit with a White American friend. He told Mr. Seda that he and his White American friend had to go out and take care of some important business.

Questions

1. What is the main problem in this case study?
2. What kind of relationship did Mr. Diaz and Mr. Seda have in Puerto Rico?
3. Why did their relationship change when they moved to the mainland?
4. If you were Mr. Diaz, would you act as he acted when he moved to the mainland? Why or why not?
5. If you were Mr. Seda, would you act as he acted when he moved to New York City? Why or why not?

Valuing Activity

Ask the students independently to complete these open-ended sentences. After they have completed them, discuss their responses and summarize the lesson by highlighting the generalization about the racial problems Puerto Rican migrants experience on the U.S. mainland.

1. Mr. Diaz should _____
2. Mr. Seda should _____
3. Mr. Diaz values _____ more than _____
4. Mr. Seda value _____ more than _____
5. If I were Mr. Diaz, I would _____
6. If I were Mr. Seda. I would _____

High School Grades

CONCEPT: Colonialism

Generalizations: Since the late fifteenth century, Puerto Rico has been controlled by foreign powers. This has caused rebellions, political ambiguity, and instability on the island.

1. Give the students a copy of the questions below and ask them to read a selection about the Taino Indians prior to 1493. One source is Irving Rouse (1992), *The Tainos: Rise and Decline of the People Who Greeted Columbus*. Tell them to be able to

respond to these questions when they have finished their reading. After the students have completed the reading assignment, discuss the questions.

  a. How did the Tainos obtain food?
  b. What kind of political system did they have?
  c. What kind of religion did they have?
  d. What was a typical day like for (1) a Taino adult female, (2) a Taino adult male, (3) Taino children?
  e. What kinds of relationships did the Tainos have with other American Indian groups?
  f. What kinds of weapons did the Tainos use when they were at war with other Indian tribes?

2. Divide the class into research groups and ask them to prepare and give short reports on each of the following topics. They should be encouraged to present their reports to the class in the form of debates, simulations, and role-play situations, and with the use of visual aids such as charts and graphs.

  a. Columbus's trip to North America and his relationship with the native populations.
  b. The establishment of Spanish domination in Puerto Rico in the 1500s.
  c. The *encomienda* system of forced labor that the Spanish established in Puerto Rico during the early years of domination.
  d. Ways in which the Tainos resisted Spanish colonization by rebelling and running away.
  e. Spanish domination in Puerto Rico in the 1600s, 1700s, and 1800s.
  f. *Grito de Lares* of 1868.
  g. The political, economic, and social status of Puerto Rico in 1898.
  h. The Spanish-American War (causes and effects).
  i. The American takeover of Puerto Rico in 1898.
  j. The Treaty of Paris, 1898.

After the students have a basic understanding of Puerto Rican history up to 1898, they can then become involved in activities like those below to gain a better understanding of the island's political and economic status today.

3. Ask the students to pretend that they are members of the U.S. Congress in 1898. Spain has just ceded Puerto Rico to the United States. Their job is to decide on specific political and economic policies for their new territory. They must develop a plan for governing the island and have it approved by majority vote. After this exercise is completed, ask the students to compare their plan with the plan the United States used to govern Puerto Rico during the first two years of U.S. rule and with the plan delineated in the Foraker Act of 1900. Ask the students to discuss the similarities and differences in the three plans and possible reasons for them.

4. Ask the students to research the positions advocated by the following political parties regarding the political status of Puerto Rico:

  a. The Independence party (Independence)
  b. The New Progressive party (Statehood)
  c. The popular party (Commonwealth)

After this research, ask three students to role-play an advocate of each status position. The advocate of each position should argue his or her position in front of the class. The three speakers will debate the status question and answer questions posed by the class. After the debate and discussion, each class member will vote for one of the three following positions: (1) the Commonwealth, (2) statehood, or (3) independence. After the voting, conduct a class discussion in which the class will compare their choice with the choice made by the citizens of Puerto Rico in a plebiscite held in 1993. (See the chronology at the beginning of this chapter.) The students should discuss the reasons for the similarities and differences in their choice and the choice made by Puerto Rican citizens.

5. Ask a group of students to role-play a discussion between the individuals named below about what should be the future of Puerto Rico. Conduct a class discussion about the roleplay situation when it ends.

a. Pedro Albizu Campos
b. Luis Muñoz Marin
c. Luis A. Ferré
d. Rafael Hernandez Colon
e. A U.S. businessperson who is president of a company that owns several factories in Puerto Rico
f. A southern U.S. senator
g. A U.S. congressional representative from the Midwest

6. Since the Spanish colonized Puerto Rico in the sixteenth century, there have been uprisings and rebellions against oppression on the island. Ask the students to prepare a short research paper on forms of resistance to oppression in Puerto Rico since the sixteenth century. Make sure that they note resistance as exemplified by (1) the Taino Indians, (2) the Lares Rebellion of 1868, (3) the Nationalist party, and (4) the university student uprisings in Puerto Rico in the 1960s. After the students have completed and discussed their papers, ask them to write and present a dramatization about "The Struggle for Home Rule in Puerto Rico." They can invite another class or their parents and friends to attend the presentation.

REFERENCES

The ASPIRA Association, Inc. (n.d.). *The ASPIRA Story, 1961–1991*. Washington, D.C.: Author.

Babin, M. T. (1971). *The Puerto Ricans' Spirit*. (B. Luby, Trans.). New York: Collier Books.

Betances, S. (1972, Winter;1973, Spring). The Prejudice of Having No Prejudice in Puerto Rico. Part 1, *The Rican*, 41–52; Part II, *The Rican*, 22–37.

Chenault, L. R. (1938). *The Puerto Rican Migrant in New York City*. New York: Columbia University Press.

Encyclopeaedia Britannica (1995). 1995 Book of the Year. Chicago: Author.

Fitzpatrick, J. P. (1987). *Puerto Rican Americans: The Meaning of Migration to the Mainland* (2nd ed.). Englewood Cliffs, N.J.: Prentice-Hall.

Mills, C. W., Senior, C., & Goldsen, R. K. (1967). *The Puerto Rican Journey: New York's Newest Migrants.* New York: Russel and Russel.

Negron de Montilla, A. (1975). *Americanization in Puerto Rico and the Public School System 1901–1920.* Rio Piedras: University of Puerto Rico Press.

Nieto, S. (1995). Unpublished review of J. A. Banks, *Teaching Strategies for Ethnic Studies* (5th ed.). Boston: Allyn and Bacon, 1991.

Padilla, E. (1958). *Up from Puerto Rico.* New York: Columbia University Press.

Rodriguez, C. E. (1991). *Puerto Ricans Born in the U.S.A.* Boulder, Colo.: Westview.

Rouse, I. (1992). *The Tainos: Rise and Decline of the People Who Greeted Columbus.* New Haven: Yale University Press.

Sanchez-Ayendez, M. (1988). The Puerto Rican American Family. In C. H. Mindel, R. W. Haberstein, & R. Wright Jr. (Eds). *Ethnic Families in America: Patterns and Variations* (pp.173–195) (3rd ed.). New York: Elsevier.

U.S. Bureau of the Census. (1990). *Current Population Reports, Population Characteristics, P23–183.* Washington, D.C.: U.S. Government Printing Office.

U.S. Bureau of the Census. (1993). *We, the American Hispanics.* Washington, D.C.: U.S. Government Printing Office.

U.S. Bureau of the Census. (1994). *Statistical Abstract of the United States: 1994* (114th ed.). Washington, D.C.: U.S. Government Printing Office.

Wagenheim, K. (1975). *Puerto Rico: A Profile* (2nd ed.). New York: Praeger.

Zenon Cruz, I. (1975). *Narcisco Descubre Su Trasero.* Homacao, Puerto Rico: Editorial Furidi.

ANNOTATED BIBLIOGRAPHY

Books for Teachers

Especially Recommended

Aparicio, F. R. (1993). From Ethnicity to Multiculturalism: An Historical Overview of Puerto Rican Literature in the United States. In F. Lomelí (Ed.). *Handbook of Hispanic Cultures in the United States: Literature and Art* (pp. 19–39). Houston: Arte Público Press.

An excellent overview of literature written by Puerto Ricans in the United States. It includes a comprehensive bibliography and photographs of writers.

Fitzpatrick, J. P. (1987). *Puerto Rican Americans: The Meaning of Migration to the Mainland* (2nd ed.). Englewood Cliffs, N.J.: Prentice-Hall.

This sociological survey of Puerto Ricans focuses on their experiences in New York City. Chapters are included on the dynamics of migration, the island background, the Puerto Rican community in New York City, the Puerto Rican family, and Puerto Ricans and the schools of New York City.

Nieto, S. (1995). A History of the Education of Puerto Ricans in U.S. Mainland Schools: "Losers," "Outsiders," or "Leaders"? In J. A. Banks & C. A. M. Banks (Eds.). *Handbook of Research on Multicultural Education* (pp. 388–411). New York: Macmillan.

This comprehensive chapter provides a brief history of Puerto Ricans in the United States, a discussion of themes in their education, and a review of selected studies and reports on the education of Puerto Ricans.

Rodriguez, C. E. (1991). *Puerto Ricans Born in the USA*. Boulder, Colo.: Westview Press.

This is an excellent, readable, and informative introduction to the experiences of Puerto Ricans in the United States. It has an excellent chapter on race, "The Rainbow People," as well as informative chapters on "The Political-Economic Context," "Housing and the South Bronx," and "Educational Dynamics." The book focuses on the Puerto Ricans in New York City.

Rodriguez, C. E. (1995). Puerto Ricans in Historical and Social Science Research. In J. A. Banks & C. A. M. Banks (Eds.). *Handbook of Research on Multicultural Education* (pp. 223–244). New York: Macmillan.

The author provides an historical overview of the depiction of Puerto Ricans in historical and social science research. She critically describes how social scientists such as Oscar Lewis constructed the "cultural of poverty" concept to describe Puerto Ricans and other groups of color. The chapter concludes with suggestions for multicultural teaching.

Sánchez Korrol, V. (1994). In Their Own Right: A History of Puerto Ricans in the U.S.A. In A. Jiménez (Ed.). *Handbook of Hispanic Cultures in the United States: History* (pp. 281–301). Houston: Arte Público Press.

An excellent, comprehensive and brief history of Puerto Ricans in the United States that can be used with high school students. It contains interesting photographs.

Other References

Acosta-Belen (Ed.) (1986). *The Puerto Rican Woman: Perspectives on Culture, History and Society* (2nd ed.). New York: Praeger.

This collection of scholarly papers focuses on the historical, socioeconomic, and cultural factors that have influenced the role of women in Puerto Rican society.

Acosta-Belen, E. & Sanchez Korrol, V. (Eds.). (1993). *The Way It Was and Other Writings*. Houston: Arte Público Press.

Work by Jesus Colon from the 1920s to the 1960s are included in this book.

Algarín, M. & Holman, B. (Eds.). (1994). *Aloud: Voices from the Nuyorican Poets Cafe*. New York: Henry Holt.

A comprehensive collection of Nuyorican poetry.

Baver, S. L. (1983). *The Political Economy of Colonialism: The State and Industrialization in Puerto Rico*. Westport, Conn.: Praeger.

A scholarly treatment of an important topic for understanding historical and economic developments in Puerto Rico.

Biddle, G. (1992). *Alphabet City.* Berkeley: University of California Press.

This book describes, with powerful black-and-white photographs and text, a Puerto Rican Lower East Side neighborhood in New York City that is being slowly gentrified.

Carrion, A. M. (1984). *Puerto Rico: A Political and Cultural History.* New York: Norton.

This is a comprehensive history of Puerto Rico. A good history of Puerto Rico is needed to fully understand the experiences of Puerto Ricans in the United States because of the ways in which the experiences of mainland Puerto Ricans are connected to the island.

Flores, J. (1993). *Divided Borders: Essays on Puerto Rican Identity.* Houston: Arte Público Press.

A collection of essays on history, literature, and culture by a noted writer on Puerto Rican and Caribbean culture in the United States.

Gallardo, E. (1990). *Simpson Street and Other Plays.* Houston: Arte Público Press.

This anthology contains three plays: Waltz on a Merry-Go-Round, Simpson Street, *and* Women without Men.

Hidalgo, N. M., Bright, J. A., Siu, S.-F., Swap, S. M., & Epstein, J. L. (1995). Research on Families, Schools, and Communities: A Multicultural Perspective. In J. A. Banks & C. A. M. Banks (Eds.). *Handbook of Research on Multicultural Education* (pp. 498–542). New York: Macmillan.

This chapter includes an excellent section that describes the Puerto Rican family and school involvement.

Lewis, G. K. (1963). *Puerto Rico: Freedom and Power in the Caribbean.* New York: Monthly Review Press.

This classic history of Puerto Rico is written from a refreshingly perceptive and sympathetic point of view. It is a dated but valuable resource.

Meléndez, E. & Meléndez, E. (Eds.). (1993). *Colonial Dilemma: Critical Perspectives on Contemporary Puerto Rico.* Boston: South End Press.

A collection of papers that were original published in Radical America.

Nieto, S. (1992). We Have Stories to Tell: A Case Study of Puerto Ricans in Children's Books. In V. J. Harris (Ed.). *Teaching Multicultural Literature in Grades K–8* (pp.171–201). Norwood, Mass.: Christopher-Gordon.

This chapter describes the history of the image of Puerto Ricans in children's books, themes in recent books, and the use of literature in the curriculum. The bibliography at the end of the chapter critically reviews selected books.

Ortiz, A. (1994). Historical Vignettes of Puerto Rican Women Workers in New York City, 1895–1990. In F. Padilla (Ed.). *Handbook of Hispanic Cultures in the United States: Sociology* (pp. 219–238). Houston: Arte Público Press.

An excellent source for integrating content about Puerto Rican women into the curriculum. It includes a helpful bibliography.

Padilla, F. M. (1985). *Latino Ethnic Consciousness: The Case of Mexican Americans and Puerto Ricans in Chicago.* Notre Dame, Ind.: University of Notre Dame Press.

This book provides a careful and scholarly treatment of the topic.

Padilla, F. (1987). *Puerto Rican Chicago.* Notre Dame, Ind.: University of Notre Dame Press.

An informative and comprehensive study of the Puerto Rican community in Chicago. It is a welcomed addition to the literature on Puerto Ricans, most of which focuses on their experiences in New York City.

Padilla, F. M. & Santiago, L. (1993). *Outside the Wall: A Puerto Rican Woman's Struggle.* New Brunswick, N.J.: Rutgers University Press.

The story of a Puerto Rican American woman who is struggling to maintain her marriage to a husband who has been in prison for ten years. Padilla, a social scientist, helps Lourdes Santiago tell her story.

Sanchez-Korrol, V. E. (1983). *From Colonia to Community: The History of Puerto Ricans in New York, 1917–1948.* Westport, Conn.: Greenwood Press.

This is an important and informative study of early Puerto Rican migrants to New York City.

Santiago, E. (1993). *When I Was Puerto Rican.* New York: Vintage.

The writer's story begins in rural Puerto Rico and continues to New York City, where she experiences conflicts with culture and language.

Torre, C. A. (Ed.). (1994). *The Commuter Nation: Perspectives on Puerto Rican Migration.* Río Piedras, Puerto Rico: Editorial De La Universidad De Puerto Rico.

A scholarly and informative collection of papers that includes scholarly findings, statistical information, and explanations about Puerto Rican migration. Highly recommended.

Torres, A. (1995). *Between Melting Pot and Mosaic: African Americans and Puerto Ricans in the New York Political Economy.* Philadelphia: Temple University Press.

Chapters in this scholarly book include "Class, Race, and the Reproduction of Inequality," "African Americans and Puerto Ricans in New York," and "Native Minorities, Immigrant Minorities."

Turner, F. (Ed.). (1991). *Puerto Rican Writers at Home in the USA: An Anthology.* Seattle: Open Hand Publishing.

A well-organized, comprehensive and highly recommended anthology.

Wagenheim, K. with Jiménez de Wagenheim, O. (Ed.). (1993). *Puerto Ricans: A Documentary History.* New York: Markus Wiener Publishers.

An informative collection of primary resources and documents that can be used to enrich lessons and units.

Books for Students

Aliotta, J. J. (1995). *The Puerto Ricans* (2nd ed.). New York: Chelsea House.

An informational book in Chelsea House's "Immigrant Experience" series. (Middle School)

Bernier-Grand, C. T. (1995). *Poet of Puerto Rico: Don Luis Muñoz Marin.* Chicago: Orchard Books.

An illustrated book about the famous Puerto Rican leader. (Primary)

Delacre, L. (1989). *Arroz Con Leche: Popular Songs and Rhymes from Latin America.* New York: Scholastic.

Children's songs and rhymes as well as beautiful illustrations from Puerto Rico are highlights of this book. (Intermediate)

Delacre, L. (1990). *Las Navidades: Popular Christmas Songs from Latin America.* New York: Scholastic.

Twelve Christmas songs from Spanish-speaking countries are contained in this book. (All levels)

Delacre, L. (1993). *Vejigante/Masquerader.* New York: Scholastic.

A bilingual book that tells the story of a boy who makes a costume for the carnival celebration in Ponce. (Primary)

Fradin, D. B. & Fradin, J. B. (1995). *Puerto Rico.* Danbury, Conn.: Children's Press.

A short (sixty-four page) illustrated book that describes Puerto Rico. (Intermediate)

Johnson, J. (1995). *Puerto Rico.* Minneapolis: Lerner.

A brief (seventy-two page) history of Puerto Rico that is illustrated with interesting photographs. Available in both English and Spanish editions. (Intermediate)

Larsen, R. J. (1989). *The Puerto Ricans in America.* Minneapolis: Lerner.

A historical overview of Puerto Rico and Puerto Rican migration to the mainland is included in this readable book. (Intermediate/Middle School)

Mohr, N. (1986). *Going Home.* New York: Dial.

This sequel to Felita *focuses on the dilemmas faced by a Nuyorican girl who returns to Puerto Rico. (Middle School). Other books by Nicholasa Mohr include* Nilda *(1973),* El Bronx Remembered *(1975),* Felita *(1979), and* In Nueva York *(1977).*

Mohr, N. (1993). *All for the Better: A Story of El Barrio.* Illustrated by R. Gutierrez. Austin, Tex.: Raintree Steck-Vaughn.

An interesting and well-crafted biography of a New York community activist. (Primary)

Mohr, N. & Martorell, A. (1995). *The Song of el Coqui and Other Tales of Puerto Rico.* New York: Viking.

This collection of stories reveals the rich ancestral traditions of Puerto Rican culture. (All levels)

Nieves, E. R. (1994). *Juan Bobo: Four Folktales from Puerto Rico.* New York: Harper Collins.

Four classic folktales are retold in this illustrated book. (Primary)

Nodar, C. S. (1992). *Abuelita's Paradise.* Illustrated by D. Paterson. Morton Grove, Ill.: Albert Whitman & Co.

A girl warmly remembers stories her grandmother told as she rocks in her rocking chair that she inherited. (Intermediate)

Ortiz Cofer, J. (1987). *Terms of Survival: Poems by Judith Ortiz Cofer.* Houston: Arte Público Press.

These poems can be used to enrich lessons in the language arts and social studies. (Middle School/High School)

Ortiz Cofer, J. (1990). *Silent Dancing: A Partial Remembrance of a Puerto Rican Childhood.* Houston: Arte Público Press.

The personal story of a writer and artist who was born in Puerto Rico and spent her childhood shuttling between the island and New Jersey. (High School)

Ortiz Cofer, J. (1995). *An Island Like You: Stories of the Barrio.* New York: Orchard Books.

An interesting collection of stories that can be used to enrich the curriculum. (Middle School/High School)

Peña, S. C. (1987). *Kikirikí Stories and Poems in English and Spanish for Children.* Houston: Arte Público Press.

This is a series of short stories, poems, and riddles. (Primary)

Peña, S. C. (1986). *Tun-ta-ca-tun: More Stories and Poems in English and Spanish for Children.* Houston: Arte Público Press.

This is an anthology of stories about the Latino experience in the United States. (High School)

Pico, F. (1994). *The Red Comb.* Illustrated by M. A. Ordonez. Mahwah, N.J.: Bridge-Water Books.

A picture book set during slavery in Puerto Rico about a young woman who escapes slavery. (Primary)

Pitre, F. (1993). *Juan Bobo and the Pig.* Illustrated by C. Hale. New York: Dutton.

A pig is dressed up in this retelling of a story by Juan Bobo. (All levels)

Press, P. (1995). *Puerto Rican Americans.* Benchmark, N.Y.: Benchmark Books.

An informational book in the "Cultures in America Series." (Intermediate)

Rappoport, K. (1993). *Bobby Bonilla.* New York: Walker and Company.

A profile of the major league baseball player. (Intermediate)

Tashlik, P. (Ed.). (1994). *Hispanic, Female and Young: An Anthology.* Houston: Piñata Books.

The voices of a group of Latina teenagers at a public alternative school in New York City's El Barrio make up this interesting book. (High School)

Wagenheim, K. (1978). *Cuentos: An Anthology of Short Stories from Puerto Rico.* New York: Schocken.

A rich collection of short stories in both Spanish and English. (Middle School)

CHAPTER 12

CUBAN AMERICANS

CONCEPTS, STRATEGIES, AND MATERIALS

If in things concerning my country I should be given a choice above all others . . . this would be the good I would choose: I should want the cornerstone of our Republic to be the devotion of Cubans to the dignity of humankind.

José Marti

This chapter discusses the background and experience of one of the newer major groups of Hispanics in the United States. Cubans have lived in small communities in New York, Tampa, and Key West, Florida, since the latter part of the nineteenth century. Large numbers did not immigrate to the United States until after Fidel Castro assumed power in the revolution that occurred in 1959.

It would be difficult to appreciate the Cuban experience in the United States without fully understanding the political situation that prompted Cubans to emigrate. The intense feelings toward the forces that caused Cubans to leave their homeland often surface as they adjust to life in the United States.

Yet, the experiences of immigrant and refugee groups like Cubans, Jews, and Vietnamese indicate how the United States has often been a beacon of hope for many uprooted groups and has sometimes been the only possibility for the realization of their dreams and aspirations. This chapter illustrates that the

This chapter is contributed by Carlos F. Diaz, Associate Professor of Education, Florida, Atlantic University, Boca Raton, Florida.

American dream is much more than an abstraction for a people who have left one homeland but gained another. The influx of Cubans on the American scene has provided another major element among the diverse Spanish-speaking ethnic groups in the United States, such as Mexican Americans and Puerto Ricans.

CUBAN IMMIGRANTS TO THE UNITED STATES

Since the 1960s, Cubans have been one of the largest groups immigrating to the United States. Of the foreign nationals entering the United States from Spanish-speaking nations, they have been the second largest immigrant group, exceeded only by Mexicans. The number of Cubans immigrating to the United States between 1971 and 1980 (276,800) was 28% larger than the number that settled in the United States between 1951 and 1960 (78,300) (U.S. Bureau

CUBAN AMERICANS: HISTORICAL PERSPECTIVE

Important Dates	
1959	Fidel Castro took over the reins of power in Cuba from the government of dictator Fulgencio Batista.
1961	Diplomatic relations between the United States and Cuba were severed. The Cuban exile brigade 2500 landed at the Bay of Pigs on the southern coast of Cuba, in an ill-fated attempt to overthrow the Castro regime.
1962	Commercial air flights between the United States and Cuba were ended. Immigration to the United States became strictly clandestine. The Cuban missile crisis prompted President Kennedy to blockade Cuba. The Soviet Union eventually withdrew the missiles from Cuban soil.
1965	Beginning of the Cuban Refugee Airlift program. Flights from Cuba to Miami, Florida, were sponsored by the U.S. government.
1973	Termination of the Cuban Refugee Airlift program. Immigration to the United States returned to a clandestine status or took place through a third country, such as Spain or Mexico.

Important Dates

1977	Diplomatic interest sections were established by the U.S. and Cuban governments in embassies of third countries. Cuba used the Czechoslovakian embassy in Washington and the United States used the Swiss embassy in Havana. This moved was strongly opposed by most Cuban Americans.
	Fidel Castro allowed U.S. citizens and their Cuban dependents living in Cuba who wished to leave to depart Cuba.
1980	125,000 Cubans arrived in the United States via a boatlift from Mariel. Reaction in the United States ranged from welcome to open hostility.
1984	The Immigration and Naturalization Service ruled that Cubans who entered the United States via Mariel with the classification of "entrant" would be permitted to apply for permanent resident status under the Cuban Refugee Readjustment Act of 1966.
1985	In response to Radio Martí broadcasts beamed at Cuba, Fidel Castro stopped familial visits of Cuban Americans and abrogated the agreement with the United States to repatriate Mariel Cubans who were being held in American jails.
	Xavier Suarez was elected mayor of Miami, Florida. He was the first Cuban American to be elected to that office.
1987	Mariel refugee inmates imprisoned in Atlanta, Georgia, and Oakdale, Louisiana, rioted and took hostages on learning they might be deported. Riots ended after the U.S. government set up a review process for anyone facing deportation.
1988	The Cuban American National Foundation began a program with the U.S. immigration's approval to reunite Cubans in third countries with relatives in the United States. The foundation paid all travel and relocation costs.
1989	Rep. Ileana Ros-Lehtinen became the first Cuban-born member of the U.S. Congress in a special election to replace the late Rep. Claude Pepper.
	Florida followed the precedent set in California, Illinois, and other states and voted 84% to 16% to amend the state constitution declaring English the state's official language. Cuban Americans largely opposed this measure.

**Important
Dates**

1994   Fidel Castro announced that he would not stop Cubans
        attempting to flee the island. A massive rafting exodus fol-
        lowed, with the U.S. Coast Guard interdicting Cubans and
        sending them to camps at the Guantanamo naval base.

1995   Cuba and the United States negotiated an agreement that
        would slowly bring refugees from Guantanamo and Panama
        to the U.S. Future entry visas for Cubans were set at 20,000
        per year.

of the Census, 1985). After the 125,000 entrants from the Mariel boatlift in 1980, Cuban immigration declined during the remainder of the decade. Immigration from Cuba has been a sporadic process since 1959. In 1994, the Castro government temporarily suspended enforcement of Cuban law forbidding Cuban citizens from leaving national territory by "illegal means." This temporary window of opportunity resulted in tens of thousands of *balseros* (rafters) openly launching their rafts in an effort to reach Florida or at least a U.S. Coast Guard cutter. This window was closed after negotiations between the Clinton administration and the Castro government established that Cuba would again enforce its law forbidding illegal exit and the United States would fill all or most of its allotment of 28,000 visas for legal Cuban entrants.

Cuban Americans are a group with low visibility because their relocation has occurred almost exclusively in a few large urban areas. In 1994, they numbered slightly more than 1 million, or about 5% of the Hispanic population of the United States. The largest Cuban American community is in the greater Miami, Florida, area and it includes more than 500,000 people. Other large concentrations are found in the New York City metropolitan area and in the greater Los Angeles area (see Table 12-1).

The Cubans' brief history on U.S. soil shares some common elements with older and more established immigrant groups. Yet, many unique differences distinguish their exodus. Most Cubans have migrated to the United States since the Castro revolution of 1959. Those who came did so primarily because they felt threatened by the political situation they experienced in Cuba. This contrasts with most other American immigrants who came to the United States searching mainly for economic promise.

Another characteristic of the Cuban influx is that those who left the island in search of a political haven are not a representative sample of the Cuban population at large. A demographic study by Fagen, Brody, and O'Leary (1968) indicated that "a disproportionate number of refugees come from the

Table 12-1 CUBAN AMERICAN POPULATION
IN SELECTED STATES (1990)

State	Population
Florida	674,000
New Jersey	85,000
New York	74,000
California	72,000
Illinois	18,000
Texas	18,000
Louisiana	9,000
Georgia	8,000
Massachusetts	8,000
Connecticut	6,000
Nevada	6,000
Maryland	6,000
Virginia	6,000
Michigan	5,000
North Carolina	4,000
Ohio	4,000
Alabama	2,000
South Carolina	2,000
Indiana	2,000

SOURCE: Based on data in the U.S. Census, 1990.

middle-and upper-strata of pre-revolutionary society" (p. 16). People in the lower socioeconomic strata who opposed the revolution had fewer resources at their disposal to turn their dissatisfaction into some viable action.

The middle and upper strata of Cuban society were most heavily represented in the first wave of immigration during the early 1960s. As time progressed, Cuban immigrants became a more representative sample of the Cuban population. However, the total number of Cuban immigrants in the United States still contains a higher proportion of business and professional persons than are present in the Cuban population.

This over-representation of the Cuban upper class among immigrants can be partly explained by the fact the people in this class felt particularly threatened by government-made changes that eroded their economic position. Most Cuban Americans were never part of the elite in their homeland so their departure cannot be attributed to a loss of great wealth. They left their native land primarily because of their genuine opposition to the political system and for reasons of family reunification.

Another group that is over-represented in the Cuban American population is older people. Barriers to their exit from the island have been considerably fewer than those faced by younger Cubans. Another factor contributing to this demographic trend is that many Cuban families sent for their parents or grandparents after they had gained an economic foothold in the United States.

The ethnic composition of Cuban Americans is also disproportionate to the Cuban population. According to Pérez (1980), "Black Cubans were probably less likely to emigrate because of their perception that race relations in the United States are less satisfactory than they are in socialist Cuba" (p. 257). Even though Black Cubans are underrepresented among immigrants, their numbers increased significantly after the Mariel influx in 1980. Caucasians and Chinese Cubans are found in greater proportions among Cubans in the United States than in the Cuban population. In prerevolutionary Cuba, Caucasian and Chinese Cubans were more prevalent in the middle and upper economic strata of society. Conversely, Black Cubans were more likely to be present in the lower economic class. Most Cuban Americans, regardless of racial and ethnic background, share an opposition to the Castro regime in Cuba. Among those who immigrated as adults, it is difficult to describe the depth and emotional nature of their sentiments. The desire for political as well as economic stability has shaped the Cuban migration to the United States.

The Cuban immigrant has generally accepted and lived by the predominant American ethos that hard work will ultimately be rewarded. Considering the deprived economic conditions that most started with, the results have been notable. Their accomplishments have caused some observers to tout them as a "model minority," much like their Japanese American counterparts. Yet the success of Cubans should not be construed to obscure the general plight of Spanish-speaking Americans. For most, this success has not occurred without hardship. Their accomplishments do not mean that Cuban Americans do not have problems. Their median income still lags behind the national average. To attain their median income, a disproportionate number of working wives are found in Cuban American households. Also, the cohesive nature of the Cuban family has sometimes suffered because of economic pressures.

The assimilation of Cubans has occurred at different levels among people living in various locations in the United States. Like other immigrant groups, assimilation has been less for the older segment of the population and for Cubans living in cities with large Cuban communities. The continuum of assimilation ranges from the almost perfectly integrated to those who have failed to accept the permanence of their U.S. surroundings.

LIFE IN CUBA

On January 1, 1959, the city of Havana, Cuba, rocked with the effects of a drastic change. The regime of dictator Fulgencio Batista had been deposed by *la Revolucion,* led by a bearded young rebel named Fidel Castro. His triumphal entry into the capital city was seen by nearly everyone as the coming of a new messiah. His popularity was more than that of a political figure; he had all the markings of a charismatic leader.

Promises of economic prosperity and of uniting the Cuban people were among the many Fidel Castro made. The synthesis of the Cuban revolution took place in a slow, deliberate series of steps, to the delight of some and the disillusionment of others. The Agrarian Reform confiscated large holdings of land in private hands. This land became government property. Farmers became government employees.

As the course of the revolution drifted politically left, a marked polarization of Cuban society began to occur. A person either supported the revolution or was thought of as a *gusano* (worm). The latter was a parasite to progress and the revolution was better off without him or her. True to the Cuban sense of humor, the expression *abrir los ajos* (see the light) marked a person who took exception to revolutionary policies. These political divisions permeated the family unit and caused bitter disagreements among relatives who advocated the revolution and those who opposed it. Many of these rifts remain today. The Cuban revolution affected everyone, regardless of his or her place in society. Fundamental changes reached the economic, political, social, and religious sectors of Cuban life.

The educational system in Cuba was affected fundamentally by the revolution. The number of schools in rural areas was increased in a campaign to end *analfabetismo* (illiteracy). Also, new high schools were located primarily in rural areas. Many urban students had to board at school in order to obtain a secondary education. In the public schools, instruction in the humanities and the natural and physical sciences was fraught with political socialization, which placed a premium on loyalty to the revolution. Along with expanding education in the rural areas, the Cuban government increased the number of health facilities. Clinics are more readily available to farmers than in prerevolutionary times.

The Cuban economy today deemphasizes consumer goods in favor of products for export. As a result of this emphasis, as well as of production lags, rationing is fairly common. The following ration limits were obtained by interviewing an exile and were in effect in 1994 (author's interview with Cuban family recently arrived in the United States, April 23, 1994):

Rice	5 pounds per month
Beans	6 ounces per month
Coffee	6 ounces per month
Meat	Not available through the rationing process
Eggs	5 eggs per month
Sugar	3 ½ pounds per month
Bread	¾ pounds per day
Soap	½ bar available every 3–4 months (if available)

For Children

0–2 years of age	15 small jars of baby food per month
1–7 years of age	1 liter of milk per day
7–12 years of age	½ liter of milk per day

Clandestine Market

1 pound of rice	45 pesos
1 pound of pork	50 pesos
1 bar of soap	60 pesos
1 liter of milk	25 pesos
1 liter of gasoline	25 pesos

Since the collapse of the Soviet empire, most of the favorable trading or bartering agreements Cuba had with former communist nations have collapsed. New goods must be purchased with hard currency, which the Cuban peso is not. Daily life in Cuba, particularly the procurement of sufficient food, has become increasingly difficult when compared to circumstances on the island prior to 1992.

It was ironic that in the world's leading sugar-producing nation Cubans were rationed to 3.5 pounds per month in 1995 (author's personal letter from Cuba, Sept. 4, 1995). It should be noted that even though quantities are very limited, prices on the official market are inexpensive. For years, Cubans have resorted to an illicit clandestine market system in which food has sold at five to ten times the price of rationed items. The Cuban government has sporadically allowed farmers to sell certain (though not all) food products on the open market. However, as the earlier example of clandestine market prices indicates, it is difficult for average Cubans to supplement their basic diets significantly.

In addition to the rationing, Cubans must plan on spending a fair amount of time waiting to buy their food items. It is not an uncommon occurrence for the shopper to spend two hours or more per day making food purchases. Whenever something extra can be obtained, people do so for friends or relatives. Any outing from the home is a potential shopping trip. Because the availability of products is often sporadic, the shopping bag (*jaba*) is a constant companion.

Socioeconomic mobility in Cuba is accomplished by a mixture of individual talent, effort and loyalty. The last of these factors creates some wrenching psychological dilemmas for certain individuals. To hold most of the managerial and many professional positions, the person must be a card-carrying *militante* (militant). Some people hold this status out of conviction for communist or revolutionary beliefs and others because the card is an asset for upward mobility in society. These people must be particularly careful of their associations. Participating in religious activity would be grounds for the revocation of the militant status.

A constant dilemma for the militants of convenience is whether their activities or associations will help or hinder their image as militants. For this reason, some children have been baptized without the knowledge of one parent. It is also assumed that people with militant status will be prepared to serve on any international mission that may be assigned. This is also true for people studying any one of the professions, particularly those in the health fields. These missions may last two or three years, and some couples are separated for that long.

Other adaptations to revolutionary society include having every salary in the nation specified by the government. The money derived from working is not sufficient to purchase most foodstuffs or consumer goods. It must be accompanied by a ration coupon permitting the purchase of specific items.

Salary laws require workers to meet a production quota of either goods or services. If this quota is not reached, the worker's salary is reduced by a proportional amount. In addition to a worker's obligatory job, there is volunteer labor available on Sundays or holidays. This volunteer work may consist of cleaning details, construction projects, or harvesting sugar cane, as well as many other tasks. Workers who want to purchase a major item such as a refrigerator often accumulate many hours of volunteer labor.

Leaving the country entails many sacrifices. Invariably, relatives are left behind. This point is particularly significant when one realizes the close-knit nature of the Cuban extended family, which makes it difficult for members to break from the family unit.

Forfeiture of all possessions is another factor to consider. Everything a person has worked for in a lifetime finds its way into government hands. Also, there is the prospect of starting over in a strange environment. For most immigrants, this happens without command of the English language. Despite all these difficulties, however, more than a million Cubans have felt compelled to leave their homeland.

Opinions about the Castro regime vary within Cuba. Supporters point out that the Cuban government has vastly expanded health care and education. Cubans on the island who are strong supporters of the Castro government and its philosophy cite wide gaps in living standards between the elite and common persons in other Latin American nations. These issues, however valid, are not salient with the Cuban American population. For most of them, the ills perpetrated by the Castro government outweigh any of its positive measures.

In the early 1960s, the United States accepted as a political refugee any Cuban who could reach its shores. In 1966, the Cuban Readjustment Act gave Cuban refugees the status of parolees and allowed a change to permanent resident status after two years in the United States. This law also gave Cubans special immigration status so their number would not be limited or counted against the limits allowed for other nations in the Americas.

This remained U.S. policy until the Refugee Act of 1980 removed special immigration status for Cuban immigrants. In order to accommodate the influx of Cubans in 1980, President Carter created a special immigration category of entrants. People who held this entrant status remained as temporary residents of the United States until late 1984, when the Immigration and Naturalization Service decided to allow them to apply for permanent residency status. Today, Cubans no longer hold officially favored immigration status.

DEPARTURE

Prohias and Casal (1973) have identified the following three stages in the migration of Cubans to the United States:

> They are as follows: A first stage, *between January 1959 and October 1962, when commercial flights between Cuba and the United States were available; (b) a* second stage, *between October 1962 and December 1965, with a corresponding slowdown of the migration rate as Cubans had to resort to unconventional means (small boats, rafts, etc.) or flights through third countries to come to the United States; a* third stage, *with daily airflights between Varadero and Miami throughout most of the period. (p. 257)*

The third stage, known as the Cuban Refugee Airlift, was terminated in January 1973. From 1973 to 1980, Cubans reverted to the unconventional means of the second stage. In 1980, a temporary policy change by the Cuban government produced a fourth stage, resulting in a wave of 125,000 Cubans coming by sea from Mariel to Key West, Florida. At the conclusion of this boatlift in May 1980, Cubans reverted to stage-two methods.

In 1988, the Cuban American National Foundation received permission from the U.S. Immigration and Naturalization Service to sponsor Cubans living outside of Cuba. This effort was to reunify them with relatives living in the United States. The visas granted to these individuals stipulated that their relocation would occur at no cost to the national, state, or local government.

The trauma of leaving Cuba varied greatly with the particular experience. Leaving by commercial airline in 1960 was fairly conventional. However, escaping in a small boat meant jeopardizing one's life. Also, the date of departure determined how much difficulty an exile would encounter in leaving the island. In general, the longer a family waited before making the decision to leave, the more obstacles it would have to face before it could secure permission to exit. In the early 1960s, many families sent their children out of Cuba via Catholic or other religious relief agencies in the hope that the parents could follow later. This effort was called Operation Peter Pan. Most of these families have been reunited; others are still waiting.

Many Americans have heard of Cubans reaching U.S. shores in small boats or rafts, but little publicity is given to the fact that many never made it after encountering a patrol boat or drifting away in the Gulf Stream current. Table 12-2 describes estimates of Cuban arrivals in the United States between 1959 and 1980.

THE MARIEL IMMIGRANTS OF 1980

In April 1980, more than 10,000 Cubans sought political asylum in the Peruvian embassy in Havana. The Cuban government's initial response was to allow them permission to leave Cuba via Peru or other willing Latin American nations, such as Costa Rica. Within days, that policy was changed to allow the exit of those people, as well as others who had sought to immigrate, directly to the United States. The Cuban American community in the United States saw this temporary respite in Cuban immigration policy as an opportunity to reunite themselves with relatives whom they had been trying to join for years.

A small port city on the northern coast of Cuba, Mariel, became the staging area for people waiting for transportation to the United States. On May 5, 1980, President Carter stated that the United States would receive the refugees "with an open heart and open arms." Nine days later, a presidential order forbade boats going to Cuba to pick up refugees. By then, hundreds of boats were on their way to or waiting in Mariel. Many Cuban American families spent their savings or pooled their earnings to pay for passage on a boat for relatives in Cuba.

The hundreds of boats that had crossed the Straits of Florida found a chaotic situation at the port of Mariel. Most boats had to anchor and wait, sometimes for weeks, until the government indicated that a group of people was ready for loading. Boat captains brought lists of people they came to transport, but often the lists were ignored or only one or two people on the list would be permitted to leave.

Meanwhile, food and supplies began to run low on board these vessels. Provisions had to be purchased from the Cuban government at three to six times their price in the United States. As time passed, tempers began to flare in the Mariel harbor.

People who had declared a willingness to leave via Mariel were gathered from all parts of Cuba. In some instances, people departing were publicly humiliated by zealous supporters of the revolution. Some people who declared a desire to leave through Mariel were not able to do so for logistical or other reasons. Their declaration caused them to lose their jobs, and many could not find other jobs.

The return crossing of the Straits of Florida was often a perilous ordeal. As a rule, boats were loaded beyond their capacity. Some captains objected to

Table 12-2 ESTIMATES OF CUBAN ARRIVALS, 1959–1980

Immigration Stages	Manner of Transportation	Estimate 1	Estimate 2
First Stage			
Early departures (Castro's takeover January 1, 1959– October 22, 1962)	Commercial flights from Havana	248,070[a]	153,534[b]
Second Stage			
Postmissile crisis (October 22, 1962– September 28, 1965)	No direct transportation; small boats, and rafts; escapees	55,916[a]	29,962[b]
Third Stage			
Freedom flights (family reunification projects September 28, 1965– April 6, 1973)	U.S. airlift	297,318[a]	268,040[b]
Fourth Stage			
Third country arrivals (April 6, 1973– September 1978)	Commercial flights from Spain, Mexico, and Jamaica	38,903[a] (January 1972/ December 1974)	17,899[b]
Fifth Stage			
Ex-political prisoners, family, and other arrivals (October 1978–April 1980)	Flights from Cuba; small boats and rafts	10,000	21,839[b]
Sixth Stage			
Mariel boatlift (April 22, 1980– September 27, 1980)	Boatlift to Key West from Mariel Harbor	124,789[c]	124,789[c]
Totals		774,996	616,063

SOURCE: C. B. McCoy & D. H. Gonzalez, In J. Szaponznik et al., eds., *Coping with Adolescent Refugees* (Praeger, an imprint of Greenwood Publishing Group, Inc., Westport, CT, 1985), p. 25. Reprinted with permission.
[a]Juan Clark, 1975
[b]Cuban Refugee Program Registration
[c]Office of Refugee Resettlement Records Cuban-Haitian Task Force

this, as well as to carrying people for whom they had not come. When the Cuban authorities insisted on both points, boat captains faced the dilemma of violating these directives or violating U.S. directives to stop the boatlift when they returned to Florida. More than fifty people died during these crossings. Some drowned when boats capsized in heavy seas, and others succumbed to carbon monoxide fumes in the holds of overloaded vessels. A frequently repeated ritual was of Cuban refugees kissing the ground after arriving in Key West, Florida.

As the flood of refugees continued, they were housed in a variety of temporary holding centers, including the Orange Bowl in Miami, Florida. People with immediate relatives were the most likely to be released quickly. Others without relatives waited patiently for relocation in other parts of the United States. As the numbers of refugees increased, a backlash of public opinion began. A Gallup poll conducted nationally in late May 1980 found that 59% of respondents felt that Cuban emigration was bad for the United States (Alpen, 1980). In the Miami area, a similar survey conducted by the *Miami Herald* in May 1980 found that 68% of the non-Latin White population and 57% of the African American population surveyed felt that the new wave of Cuban refugees would have a negative influence on the local community (Morin, 1980, p. 1).

The Cuban community in Miami raised more than $2 million in cash and other assistance to help accommodate the new arrivals. Nevertheless, the size of the influx made it necessary to relocate many Cubans in holding centers outside southern Florida. As Cuban refugees were relocated on military bases in predominantly rural areas of Arkansas, Pennsylvania, Wisconsin, and Florida, residents of those areas vehemently protested the Cuban presence.

The characteristics of the Cubans who emigrated via the Mariel boatlift showed that there was a higher proportion of Black Cubans, single males, and blue-collar workers than among previous groups of Cuban immigrants. Much has been written about the undesirable or criminal element that came to the United States during the boatlift. The Cuban government seized the opportunity to rid itself of people who had committed serious crimes or suffered mental or physical problems; but people in these categories constituted fewer than 5% of the 125,000 entrants. Also, the fact that a person had spent time in a Cuban jail could be due either to criminal or political activity. Consequently, not all criminals would have had that label if they had been living in the United States. Most of the Mariel Cubans originally detained were eventually released. In 1992 about 1,200 Mariel Cubans had remained in jail since their arrival in the United States (Barberis, 1982). The bulk of these prisoners have been detained at the Atlanta Federal Penitentiary.

Most Cubans who came via the 1980 boatlift were of humbler origins than their predecessors but just as determined to improve themselves. A few gave the term *Marielito* a pejorative connotation. Unfortunately, that connotation has sometimes tainted the majority of Mariel Cubans who have worked hard and respected the law. Today, more than a decade after their arrival, the evidence indicates that Mariel Cubans have generally adjusted well to U.S. society.

THE CUBAN RAFTERS OF 1994

While Cubans have been risking their lives trying to cross the straits of Florida in makeshift rafts for decades, some unusual events occurred in the summer of 1994. The sequence began with a small Cuban vessel that was hijacked by a group of Cubans seeking to come to Florida. In the process, a Cuban military officer was killed. The vessel eventually made its way to Florida.

The Castro government protested that the United States was harboring hijackers and should return the group to Cuba. When the United States refused to do so, Fidel Castro retaliated by refusing to stop any Cubans who tried to leave the nation by sea. Tens of thousands of Cubans took to the ocean mostly in makeshift rafts. The United States Coast Guard was rescuing thousands every day at the peak of this exodus.

President Clinton issued a proclamation that Cubans leaving in rafts would no longer be granted entrant status to the United States. The last vestiges of the Cuban Refugee Readjustment Act of 1966 had been nullified. Cuban rafters were confined in a camp at the military base in Guantanamo, Cuba. Some Cubans were transferred to a camp in Panama.

After negotiations between Cuban and United States authorities in New York, the Cuban government agreed to enforce Cuban law prohibiting exit from the country without documentation. The United States agreed to give all or nearly all of the 28,000 yearly visas to Cubans promised under an earlier accord negotiated in 1984. (An average of 2,000 to 3,000 visas per year had been granted from 1984 to 1994). The fate of those Cubans detained in Guantanamo and Panama was resolved by an accord reached in 1995 between the United States and Cuba. Cubans in the Guantanamo and Panama camps would be slowly resettled in the United States, beginning with children and those who had close family relationships in the United States. Cubans in Cuba were to apply for U.S. entry visas. The United States promised to issue at least 20,000 per year.

ADAPTATION TO LIFE IN THE UNITED STATES

Most immigrants to the United States have come with the unwavering conviction of making this country their permanent home. Many Cubans arrived here with the thought of returning to their homeland as soon as the political climate changed. Although grateful to the United States for their asylum, their ultimate plans were not in this country. Thus, they did not feel the immediate need to assimilate into the mainstream culture. With the passing of time, only the most optimistic clung exclusively to this viewpoint. Because the Castro regime showed strong signs of longevity, exiles tried to adapt to their new environment.

The adaptation of Cubans to American life has often been difficult. This process has been more extensive in areas where the Cuban population is small. In a city like Miami, with its large Cuban community, it is possible to live without crossing the boundaries of the ethnic neighborhood. Assimilation is not imperative in this situation. One major change has been to forsake the more leisurely mood of the Cuban life-style. According to the *New York Times* (1971), "Conversion to the pace of American life has threatened to disrupt the traditional Cuban way of life. The initial cultural shock was compounded by the dizzying social changes underway in this country that perplexed most Americans."

The high percentage of Cuban American working wives has had a significant social, as well as economic, impact on the Cuban community. Richmond (1980) found that "Resources of the wife, particularly as they compared favorably to the resources possessed by her husband, were found to be an additional influence in the absorption of a more egalitarian ideology" (p. 115). The traditional dominant role of the husband in the Cuban household has undergone some modification, particularly in locations where families live in a largely non-Cuban community.

One problem encountered by Cuban parents was having their children adhere to Cuban values, norms, and customs. These permitted less freedom than their American peers enjoyed. This gap was felt more acutely by daughters in Cuban families than sons, since traditionally girls have been more closely supervised by parents.

The custom of having someone chaperone a date has caused conflicts in many Cuban American families. Girls who had to abide by this custom often felt that they were at a disadvantage in their peer group. This situation does not differ significantly from those faced by other immigrant groups as their children drifted away from traditional customs. With the passage of time, fewer and fewer families still insist on a chaperone and have substituted other methods of supervision that are more prevalent in the United States.

Where Cubans resettled in large numbers, they were received in a variety of ways. A former Cuban lawyer related his impression in the following manner: "There are many people in Miami who still resent the Cubans settling here," he said, "but for the most part, since we have been the most successful immigrants in American history, Americans find it hard to look down their noses at us because we arrived here loaded with American characteristics. We are just too outgoing and enterprising and hard-working for them to stay mad at us" (*New York Times*, 1971, p. 4).

The reactions experienced by Cuban immigrants depended on the time and location of their immigration. People who were relocated to cities and towns with low Hispanic populations experienced little negative reaction. The influx of a few families is probably noticed little in most communities. Among Cubans who settled in areas like Miami, Florida, initial opposition to their arrival came from people in unskilled and blue-collar jobs. These new arrivals were perceived as an economic threat. People with higher socioeconomic positions were relatively unconcerned and often praised the hard-working émigrés.

With time and command of English, Cubans began to climb the socioeconomic ladder. They began to assert themselves economically and, to a lesser extent, politically. In 1969, Dade County (Miami) had 3,449 Hispanic businesses. By 1977, that figure became 8,248, and in 1985 it had grown to 15,000. The Hispanic (mostly Cuban) population of Dade County had an annual income in 1985 of $6.7 billion (Oppenheimer, 1985). In the 1990s, the economic output of the Dade County Hispanic business community exceeded that of Hispanic businesses in Los Angeles, which has more than double the Hispanic population of Miami.

When Cubans started to become a potent economic force in Miami and in other cities where their numbers were significant, they encountered difficulties from segments of the community that traditionally held most of the economic and political influence and wanted no change. Many of these people had been relatively unconcerned a decade or two before. Today, they realize that Cuban Americans are a viable economic entity and a competitive force. Competition is not always welcomed.

Like many immigrant groups, Cuban Americans have formed their own organizations to promote common interests. Groups such as the Latin American Chamber of Commerce were formed in Miami and claim the greatest membership among Cuban American business people. While a time may come when members of this association may join the Greater Miami Chamber of Commerce in large numbers, the Latin chamber is expected to continue in the foreseeable future.

The median income of Cuban Americans ($32,417) is higher than that of Puerto Ricans or Mexican Americans, but they rank slightly below the median income ($35,225) for the entire nation (U.S. Department of Commerce, 1993). Higher Cuban median income (compared to Puerto Ricans and Mexican Americans) is partly explained by an unusually high percentage of Cuban American women in the workforce.

In 1980, the entrance of thousands of Mariel Cubans into the U.S. work force in predominantly low-skill jobs temporarily decreased Cuban American median income. However, their economic status increased sharply within ten years. According to Olson and Olson (1995), Mariel Cubans "were proving to be as successful in learning English, finding jobs and building businesses as the earlier generation of Cuban immigrations after only 10 years in the United States" (Olson & Olson, 1995, p. 91).

When they tried to pursue their former occupations in the United States, many Cubans ran into difficulties. The main obstacle to white-collar employment was mastery of the English language, which most did not have. In the professional fields, degrees earned in Cuba were often not recognized, and individuals frequently returned to college if they wanted to obtain work related to their former professions in Cuba. Even though many Cubans have regained their former occupational status and some have even surpassed it, a slight loss of occupational status remains.

The typical newly arrived exile family received some assistance from the Cuban Refugee program while it existed. Afterwards, Cubans took whatever employment was immediately available, anticipating that their preferred work could be obtained later. When the concentration of Cubans in the Miami area became substantial, the government started a resettlement program. This program offered jobs and one month's free rent to immigrants who agreed to move outside Florida. In recent years, some Cubans who had been relocated trickled back into the South Florida area after they had achieved a financial foothold.

Many Cubans arriving via the 1980 boatlift had a more difficult time, especially single males with no family in the United States. Many waited months behind camp fences looking for an organization or person to sponsor their release. As time passed, frustration grew and even erupted into hostility at some camps. Even after being released in the care of a sponsor, some Mariel Cubans found it difficult to adjust to a competitive capitalist society with opportunities but few guarantees. After decades of working in a socialist economic system, some were unaccustomed to or unsure of work patterns and habits in the United States. Others adapted quickly and easily.

A rift sometimes developed between the older, established Cuban immigrant and the Mariel émigré. The former sometimes felt that the latter were insufficiently driven to succeed or grateful for the assistance received. This situation is similar to the relationship that had developed in the latter part of the nineteenth century between the established German American Jews and the new arrivals from Eastern Europe.

Mariel refugees have had a more difficult time adjusting to U.S. life than their predecessors for a variety of reasons. They arrived in the midst of a recessionary economic cycle, which made obtaining the first jobs more difficult. On average, they possessed fewer marketable skills than did their predecessors. A year after their arrival, 45,000 Mariel entrants were living below the official poverty line and committing suicide at a rate seven times the U.S. average (Kelly, 1981). Despite difficult economic conditions and homesickness at first, both rates diminished significantly in the years that followed.

The children who entered via Mariel also had to make major adjustments, as did the school systems that were to receive them. Writes Silva (1985), "In absolute numbers, the Dade County Public Schools faced integrating a school population larger than 95% of the school districts in the United States" (p. 23). The Dade County schools enrolled more than 11,500 Cuban refugee children in the 1980–1981 school year. Students were divided between two entrant facilities established exclusively for Mariel students, and the remaining students attended special programs in schools designated as entrant centers, as well as neighborhood schools.

Along with the new language and curriculum, some students had to learn a new value system. Self-discipline was sometimes lacking, along with a concept of private property. Authority was equated with people one does not trust and taking someone else's property synonymous with "need," not "bad" (Silva, 1985). With time and the patience of teachers, these students have usually adjusted to the new value system and most have progressed well. It is difficult to measure their degree of academic or social integration because Mariel students were not identified beyond their initial period of adjustment.

Mariel Cubans often cite a lack of closeness and spirituality about life in the United States. Many centered their lives in Cuba around these qualities, which helped them endure hardships and privations. They see themselves as distinct from the older émigrés, some of whom they view as living in a frozen Cuban culture. This frozen culture is based solely on Cuban values, beliefs, and attitudes and all aspects of contemporary life are compared to this Cuban cultural baseline. These people exist as a subculture within a subculture. It will be interesting to see the degree to which Mariel Cubans will exhibit some of the characteristics of the older Cuban immigrants as time passes.

The process of assimilation has been most difficult for the elderly Cuban population. They represent an unusually high percentage of the exile population because older people faced fewer restrictions in trying to leave the island. This elderly population faces the usual problems of the aged, compounded by an environment to which many cannot adapt. For those whose families have strayed from traditional Cuban customs regarding the aged, they miss being the center of the family. Elderly persons living alone are found in larger than expected numbers in the Cuban American community. Many of the Cuban elderly who live in an extended family household provide the crucial day-care function that allows many Cuban women to join the labor force.

As might be expected, the Cuban American elderly are the least culturally assimilated segment of the Cuban community in the United States. Most speak minimal or no English and are thus limited from taking part in many facets of American life. Their children and grandchildren are often their link to the non-Cuban community. Some, though not most, of these people belong to what has been described as the frozen culture.

News from relatives in Cuba keeps Cuban Americans of all ages aware of life in their former country. They feel deeply the difficulties and privations that loved ones may be experiencing, and they do whatever they can to help ameliorate the circumstances. In 1979, the Cuban government decided to allow familial visits. Tens of thousands of Cubans in the United States returned to the island with suitcases bulging with clothes, food, and gifts for relatives.

These visitors were described by the Cuban population as belonging to the community. The stories of their lives in the United States were sometimes exaggerated toward more affluence than truly existed, but it became evident to Cubans in Cuba that most visitors were not suffering the way the Cuban government had claimed. These visits brought badly needed foreign exchange to Cuba; therefore, they were allowed to continue for quite some time. In 1994, President Clinton forbade these visits in all but the most critical cases. This measure, along with significant reductions in cash transfers to persons in Cuba, was intended to limit access to dollars for the Cuban government. By increasing economic pressure, the intent of this policy is to promote democratic change in Cuba.

Politically, Cuban Americans have been in general more conservative than most recently arrived immigrants. However, this conservatism should not be equated unequivocally with American conservatism. Cuban Americans are conservative on foreign policy issues, especially if those issues concern nations with communist governments. They tend to be considerably more moderate on domestic social issues.

In the Miami metropolitan area, Cubans are becoming an increasing portion of the electorate through naturalization. In the fall of 1981, Raul Martinez was elected mayor of Hialeah, Florida, thus becoming the first Cuban American mayor of a large U.S. city. Until 1982, no Cuban American had been elected to the state legislature of Florida, even though Cuban Americans comprised approximately one-half of Miami's Dade County. In 1982, Florida changed from multimember to single-member legislative districts, and a number of Cuban Americans were elected to serve in the state house of representatives. The mid- and late 1980s saw Xavier Suarez elected mayor of Miami and Cuban Americans also elected to the Florida state senate. In 1989, Ileana Ros-Lehtinen was elected to the U.S. House of Representatives, becoming the first Cuban American member of Congress. She was joined by two fellow Cuban Americans; Lincoln Diaz-Balart of Miami and Robert Menendez of Union City, New Jersey, were elected respectively in 1991 and 1993. As more Cuban Americans become naturalized citizens and turn their attention to U.S. politics, their political participation and influence should grow proportionately.

THE SECOND GENERATION

The Cuban American community now has a significant population that immigrated to the Untied States when they were young children or were born in the Untied States. This second generation represents a unique group of English-dominant bilingual persons who function well in both the Cuban American community and within mainstream society. They range approximately from age twenty to forty and are found in nearly every walk of life.

They are sometimes referred to as YUCAS (young upwardly mobile Cuban Americans). The term has a double meaning because the yucca is a starchy root that Cubans frequently eat. The perspectives of this second generation are neither those of their parents nor of their American peers. One American-born young woman in her early twenties commented, "The Cubans consider me an American and the Americans consider me a Cuban." Another American-born young man observed, "I didn't realize how Cuban I was until I left South Florida for Boston to attend college." Many of these young people understand the anachronisms in Cuban American culture but are respectful of the persons who hold them.

Cuba is not a personal experience or memory for most of these people. They know of Cuba only from their parents' accounts, which typically grow fonder with each telling. It thus is understandable that most do not hold as strong an attachment for a place and a way of life that appears mythical.

Most of this second generation is fundamentally pragmatic. They are generally less politicized and conservative than their parents, but they still see themselves as culturally distinct. Their identity as Cuban Americans does not generally include thinking of themselves as minority group members. They sometimes are surprised when they interact with other young Hispanics who identify with minority group status.

As a rule, the YUCAs see the perpetuation of the Spanish language through their own children as a desirable goal even if some of their own command of Spanish grammar is rudimentary. A study by Garcia and Diaz (1992) of language use among Hispanic (mostly Cuban American) high school seniors in Miami confirmed that most of the youth spoke English in formal and informal settings; Spanish predominated in familial settings. The one exception to this pattern was that English was used more than Spanish as the preferred language among siblings. The continued use of English among siblings suggests that the family setting is no longer the sole province of the Spanish language. Time will tell whether this generation of Cuban Americans will be able to pass on significant amounts of Spanish to its children.

This group understands and respects the sacrifices and hardships that their parents faced as a consequence of immigration. However, they are generally not preoccupied with nostalgia. They seek the best in both cultures in order to carve out their own unique identity in U.S. society.

CUBAN AMERICANS TODAY

Cuban Americans represent an ethnic group that, while making economic, social, and cultural contributions to the United States, also seek to maintain their cultural identity. In general, Cubans have adapted relatively well to American life.

As Prohias and Casal (1973) note, "A cursory reading of the studies surveyed seems to indicate that Cubans have adjusted well to life in the United States and that, after the initial influx which caught Miami by surprise, they have not been a social problem. Early studies found Cubans to be low in all indices of social disorganization or maladjustment" (p. 6). Their statement suggests that the process of acculturation is slowly occurring. As in the case of the Japanese Americans, the amount of cultural assimilation has exceeded the degree of structural assimilation. Where large Cuban settlements occur, a great deal of the social and civic life still revolves around the ethnic community. In Miami, theaters show films in Spanish; the city has Latin civic clubs and a Latin Chamber of Commerce. Miami has become a de facto bilingual city.

This Latinization of Miami, while a boon to economic development with Latin America, has created a discernible backlash among a significant portion of the non-Latin community. In 1980, voters in Dade County (Miami) approved a local "anti-bilingual ordinance" barring the expenditure of county taxes to use or promote any language other than English. The same community owes much, if not most, of its economic viability to Latin American tourists and trade.

In 1989, Florida voters amended the state constitution to make English the state's official language. This amendment was overwhelmingly approved by an 84% vote of the electorate. Cuban Americans usually agree with other Hispanic groups that these efforts are lightly veiled attempts to limit the viability and options of Hispanic Americans. Cuban Americans, like their Mexican American and Puerto Rican counterparts, believe that it is imperative that people who choose to live in the United States should learn to speak English (Diaz, 1984). It would be almost impossible to find an individual in the Cuban community who does not want his or her children taught English. However, many Cuban Americans regard English-only legislation as emblematic of coerced assimilation. Some feel that any pressure to assimilate implies they are not acceptable as they are.

Another language-related issue with significant support among Cuban Americans is bilingual education. Most feel that bilingual education is a necessary bridge for limited and non-English-speaking students to succeed in U.S. classrooms. Elimination of these programs would not find support among most Hispanics in this nation, including Cuban Americans. Concluded Baratz-Snowden, Rock, Pollack, and Wilder (1988), "Cuban Americans see learning of the non-English language as one of the three most important things that a child should learn at school" (p. 47).

The average Cuban immigrant has gone through a great psychological transition, the severity of which is strongly related to age at the time of leaving. Much trauma was involved. Many former professional men in Cuba had to begin in middle age as unskilled workers. This change required some mature adjustment in order to cope.

It would be conjecture to estimate how many Cubans would return to their native land if the Castro regime were replaced by a government more acceptable to them. Many have established roots in the United States that cannot be severed. Others would find the lure of a free Cuba irresistible, even though they might be well established in the United States.

Even though most Cubans are opposed to any thaw in relations between the governments of Cuba and the United States, a growing number favor accommodation, particularly if it can help bring families together. The intellectual and academic Cuban American community tends to be more favorable to a less rigid policy toward Cuba than do blue-collar Cubans.

Some intellectuals in the Cuban American community are speculating on what influence the 1989 fall of Soviet and Eastern European communist regimes will have on Cuba. Cuba's former benefactor, Russia, is going through an internal restructuring process favoring greater openness and payment for its products in convertible currency. Meanwhile, the Castro government has maintained an orthodox communist posture. These changes have resulted in Cuba suffering through the most difficult economic period in the nearly four decades of the Castro government. Even by Cuban standards, the challenge of feeding and caring for families has never been greater.

Today, Cuban Americans are the third largest Spanish-speaking group in the United States; Mexican Americans and Puerto Ricans rank first and second. The Cuban experience indicates that they have been a viable and beneficial addition to U.S. society. This pattern can be expected to continue.

TEACHING STRATEGIES

CONCEPT: Immigration

Generalization: Many Cuban immigrants found themselves unable and/or unwilling to live with the Castro government and chose to leave their homeland instead.

1. Divide your class into small groups and instruct them as follows: Your family is forced to move to a country in which the language and customs are alien. Each of you is allowed to take only a small amount of clothes. All of your possessions are left behind and forfeited, since you cannot return. Describe what your life might be like where you are going. What clothing would you take with you? Why? How well do you think your family would fare? What adjustments would all of you have to make? The students' reactions can be taped or written. The taping would provide more spontaneous responses. Afterwards, compare and discuss reactions among groups.

2. After sufficient background information is presented, ask each student to write an essay titled, "If I Had Been a Cuban in 1959, What Would I Have Done?"

3. Organize a debate in which one side takes the position that deposing the Castro regime is feasible and the other feels it is impossible.

4. Read the following story to the class and ask the questions that follow.

The Pina Family

Ernesto Pina was a fisherman who lived in Cardenas, on the north coast of Cuba. He and his wife, Iliana, had never been wealthy, but fishing had always provided for the necessities of life. Ernesto always seemed to be able to return with fish of one type or another.

They had been happy to see the tyrant Batista deposed by the Castro revolution. Ernesto felt that Fidel Castro had the interests of the "little man" like himself at heart. One day when he returned to the fishery to sell his catch, Ernesto was informed that part of it would go to the government. Officials said that his fish would be exported and goods received in return would help the revolution. Ernesto did not want to be considered greedy, but he needed his entire catch to support his family. At the risk of being caught, he would hide some fish and sell them privately to his friends.

The family's only son, Jose, was sixteen and had been forced to join the militia. Neither parent liked this, but it could not be helped.

One night Ernesto and Iliana were talking and she suggested going to the United States. Yet both knew that they could not depart legally, because Jose was of military age. Obviously, they could not leave their only son behind. So the three decided to try to escape in the fishing boat one night. They knew they would be shot in the water if discovered, but decided to take the risk anyway.

The eventful night came, and the Pina family slipped away from the harbor. Ernesto was sailing the craft because he did not want the noise of the engine to be heard. He had been quite careful to wait for the proper tide and a moonless night. After a short time, they heard an engine; the sound kept coming closer. It was the shore patrol! He lowered the sail quickly and they hid in the bottom of the boat. The patrol boat passed within fifty yards but had not spotted them. They had been saved by the darkness!

When morning came, Ernesto started his small engine because the breeze had faded. He hoped for the best because he did not have much gasoline. After two days at sea he was beginning to worry. His family was sunburned, he was out of gasoline, and he had not yet spotted the Florida coast. Yet, they kept their faith. They were lucky to be seen by a U.S. Coast Guard cutter, which towed them into port. As the three stepped off the boat onto American soil, they each said a prayer for having been so fortunate.

Questions

1. If you had been one of the Pina family and found yourself in their circumstances, would you have taken the risk they did? Why or why not?
2. What problems did Mr. Pina encounter that made him decide to leave Cuba?
3. Why didn't the Pina family attempt to leave Cuba by legal means?
4. What kind of future do you foresee for the Pina family in the United States?
5. Have each student (either in writing or orally) describe the circumstances of a political situation in the United States that would cause him or her to escape to a foreign nation, which would involve risking his or her life.

CONCEPT: Intergenerational Conflict

Generalization: The second generation of any immigrant group is going to absorb from the larger society values, beliefs, and priorities that are sometimes at odds with their parents' beliefs.

Read the following story to the class and ask the questions that follow.

The Rodriguez Family

Carlos Rodriguez is a young, successful professional person working in the Miami branch of a major American corporation. His wife, Maria, teaches in the public schools; their daughters, Gloria and Cecilia, are ages three and four.

Both Carlos and Maria's parents live within a twenty-minute drive. Maria's parents provide the much-needed day-care for their granddaughters, and Carlos's parents are happy to substitute if needed. Most other family members who left Cuba are also living in the greater Miami area; family gatherings are frequent and well attended.

One day Carlos tells his wife of a possible promotion, which would involve moving to Minneapolis. Carlos can choose to accept the promotion or can stay in his current job.

Carlos and Maria informed their parents before deciding. As expected, both sets of parents were opposed to the family's moving. They pointed out that Carlos's and Maria's combined income enabled them to live comfortably and that in Minneapolis, the girls would be cared for by strangers and their contact with their grandparents would be limited. Maria's father also remarked that some things are more important than higher positions and more money, such as family.

Questions

1. What is the value system that is prompting the objections from the Rodriguez's grandparents?
2. How do the grandparents' values compare with the predominant values in U.S. society regarding advancement and mobility?
3. When you think of the term *family,* do you think of it as a nuclear or an extended family?
4. If you think Carlos and Maria should remain in Miami, give at least three reasons.
5. If you think the Rodriguez family should move to Minneapolis, give at least three reasons.

CONCEPT: Nativism

Generalization: A new group of immigrants arriving in the United States is likely to encounter rejection from some segments of the population.

The following is an example of letters to the editor that appeared in South Florida newspapers in response to the 1980 Mariel boatlift. Read the sample letter to the students and ask the questions that follow.

South Florida Saturated

As a citizen of South Florida for the past ten years, I strongly object to the masses of Cuban refugees being dumped on our shores. I am also distressed at the lack of response by national and state elected officials to stop this alien infusion.

We are having sluggish economic times and adequate housing is scarce for American citizens. How can we continue to be "nice guys" and accept more Cubans and Haitians. We already have enough!

We, the tax paying public of Florida, are being forced to subsidize these unwanted refugees that should either stay in their own country or go elsewhere. Included among these refugees are Castro's gifts of criminals, insane, and other undesirables.

I also understand that Cubans are training military groups on Florida soil. Why can't we prosecute these people? Meanwhile, many of our own Americans around the country need the assistance being given to these people we don't want.

Why can't we take care of our own first and forget about the headaches of other nations?

Name withheld by request

Questions

1. What facts does the letter's author use to substantiate his or her positions?
2. Compare the positions in the letter with the idea that the United States is the land of immigrants.
3. Do you agree or disagree with the author's positions? Which ones? Explain the reasons for your responses.
4. As a comparative exercise where library facilities permit, ask students to look for letters to the editor in major newspapers concerning immigration around 1910. Afterwards, ask the students to compare reactions to immigration in 1910 to the letter above.

REFERENCES

Alpen, D. (1980, May 26). Carter and the Cuban Influx. *Newsweek,* p. 25.

Baratz-Snowden, J., Rock, D., Pollack, J., & Wilder, G. (1988). *Parent Preference Study.* Princeton, N.J.: Educational Testing Service.

Barberis, M. (1982). Hispanic America. (Editorial Research Reports), *Congressional Quarterly.* Washington, D.C.: U.S. Government Printing Office.

Diaz, W. (1984). *Hispanics: Challenges and Opportunities.* New York: Ford Foundation.

Fagen, R. R., Brody, R. A., & O'Leary, T. J. (1968). *Cubans in Exile.* Stanford, Calif.: Stanford University Press.

Garcia, R. L. & Diaz, C. F. (1992). The Status and Use of Spanish and English among Hispanic Youth in Dade County (Miami) Florida. *Language and Education 6,* (1), 13–22.

Kelly, J. (1981, May 18). Closing the Golden Door. *Time,* p. 27.

Morin, R. (1980, May 11). Dade Fears Refugee Wave, Poll Shows. *Miami Herald,* p. 1.

New York Times. (1971, April 16). p. 4.

Olson, J. S. & Olson, J. E. (1995). *Cuban Americans: From Trauma to Triumph.* New York: Twayne Publishers.

Oppenheimer, A. (1985, August 25). Dade's Latins Feel a Separate Economy. *Miami Herald,* p. 1.

Pérez, L. (1980). Cubans. In S. Thernstrom, A. Orlov, & O. Handlin (Eds.). *Harvard Encyclopedia of American Ethnic Groups* (pp. 256–261). Cambridge: Harvard University Press.

Prohias, R. J. & Casal, L. (1973). *The Cuban Minority in the U.S. Cuban Minority Planning Study.* Boca Raton: Florida Atlantic University.

Richmond, M. L. (1980). *Immigrant Adaptation and Family Structure among Cubans in Miami, Florida.* New York: Arno Press.

Silva, H. (1985). *The Children of Mariel: Cuban Refugee Children in South Florida Schools.* Washington, D.C.: The Cuban American National Foundation.

U.S. Bureau of the Census. (1985). *Statistical Abstract of the United States, 1985* (105th ed.). Washington, D.C.: U.S. Government Printing Office.

U.S. Department of Commerce. (1993). *We, the American Hispanics,* Washington, D.C.: U.S. Government Printing Office.

ANNOTATED BIBLIOGRAPHY

Books for Teachers

Especially Recommended

Boswell, T. D. & Curtis, J. R. (1984). *The Cuban-American Experience: Culture, Images and Perspectives.* Totowa, N.J.: Rowman and Allanheld.

This is a useful source for understanding the cultural adjustments Cuban immigrants have made in the United States.

García, M. C. (1994). Cuban Women in the United States. In A. Jiménez (Ed.). *Handbook of Hispanic Cultures in the United States* (pp. 203–217). Houston: Arte Público Press.

An informative and comprehensive overview of the experiences of Cuban American women.

Olson, J. S. & Olson, J. E. (1995). *Cuban Americans: From Trauma to Triumph.* New York: Twayne Publishers.

This book provides a comprehensive discussion of Cuba and the migration and settlement of Cuban Americans in the United States. It includes chapters on the Mariel Cubans and on the status of Cuban Americans in 1995.

Poyo, G. E. & Díaz-Miranda, M. (1994). Cubans in the United States. In A. Jiménez (Ed.). *Handbook of Hispanic Cultures in the United States* (pp. 301–320). Houston: Arte Público Press.

Cuban immigration, Cuban communities in the United States, and Cuban women and Cubans of color are among the topics in this informative historical overview of the Cuban American saga. Includes a helpful bibliography.

Other References

Alpern, D. et al. (1980, May 26). Carter and the Cuban Influx. *Newsweek,* pp. 22–31.

This article concerns immigration policy during the 1980 Mariel boatlift.

Casal, L. & Hernandez, A. (1975, July). Cubans in the U.S.: A Survey of the Literature. *Cuban Studies 5,* 25–51.

The authors provide an annotated bibliography and a well-documented summary of information on Cuban Americans organized by topics.

Cortés, C. E. (Ed.). (1980). *Cuban Exiles in the United States.* New York: Arno Press.

A series of articles written in the early 1970s that discuss mostly the occupational adaptation of Cubans in the United States.

Fagan, R. R., Brody, R. A., & O'Leary, T. J. (1968). *Cubans in Exile.* Stanford, Calif.: Stanford University Press.

This is a major published source on Cubans in Miami, Florida, and their reasons for leaving Cuba. It is complete with demographic information on the Cuban exodus.

Fox, G. E. (1979). *Working-Class Émigrés from Cuba.* Palo Alto, Calif.: R. E. Research Associates.

This sociological study examines the attitudes of recently arrived blue-collar Cubans in the Chicago area toward many aspects of life in Cuba.

Gallagher, P. (1980). *The Cuban Exile: A Socio-Political Analysis.* New York: Arno Press.

This source is a 1974 doctoral dissertation reprint. It concerns the political adaptation of the Cuban immigrant and describes Cuban political attitudes on a range of issues.

Hernandez, A. (Ed.). (1980). *The Cuban Minority in the U.S.* (Vol. 2). New York: Arno Press.

This is a continuation of the 1973 Prohias study concentrating on educational and occupational mobility and the needs and problems of Cuban American youth and the elderly population.

Jaffe, A. J., Cullen, R., & Boswell, T. (1980). *The Changing Demography of Spanish Americans.* New York: Academic Press.

This source covers all Hispanic groups in the United States; it also contains an excellent chapter on the education, demographics, and other variables of the Cuban American population.

Kelly, J. (1981, May 18). Closing the Golden Door. *Time*, pp. 24–27.

> *This article discusses efforts to stem the tide of immigration. It contains an interesting excerpt on Cubans who have been imprisoned since they arrived on the Mariel boatlift in 1980.*

Linehan, E. J. (1973, July). Cuba's Exiles Bring New Life to Miami. *National Geographic 144*, 68–95.

> *This is an excellent article with many photographs. This would be a good source for students to peruse.*

Mackey, W. R. & Beebe, V. N. (1977). *Bilingual Schools for a Bicultural Community.* Rowley, Mass.: Newburg House.

> *This work examines a variety of models used in bilingual education in Miami to accommodate students arriving from Cuba.*

Masud-Piloto, R. (1988). *With Open Arms: Cuban Migration to the United States.* Totowa, N.J.: Rowman and Littlefield.

> *This book focuses on the Cuban migration from 1959 to 1980. The author suggests that humanitarian concerns of either the United States or Cuba had little to do with migration. Rather, refugees became the prime weapon in the political war between the two nations.*

Mindel, C. H., Habenstein, R. W., & Wright, R., Jr. (Eds.). (1988). *Ethnic Families in America: Patterns and Variations* (3rd ed.). New York: Elsevier.

> *The chapter on the Cuban American family contributed by Jose Szapocznik and Roberto Hernandez contains an insightful section explaining the West African and Iberian influences on the Cuban character and family life.*

Oppenheimer, A. (1985, August 25). Dade's Latins Feel a Separate Economy. *Miami Herald*, p. 1.

> *This newspaper article provides valuable statistics to document the size and importance of the Latin (mostly Cuban) component of the economy in Miami, Florida.*

Pérez, L. (1980). Cubans. In S. Thernstrom, A. Orlov, & O. Handlin (Eds.). *Harvard Encyclopedia of American Ethnic Groups* (pp. 256–261). Cambridge: Harvard University Press.

> *This is an excellent but dated synopsis of the status of Cubans in the United States. However, this source does not contain information on the Mariel boatlift.*

Poyo, G. E. (1989). *With All and for the Good of All: The Emergence of Popular Nationalism in the Cuban Communities of the United States, 1848–1898.* Durham, N.C.: Duke University Press.

> *An excellent source for teachers interested in examining the long-established Cuban communities in the United States. The author examines the connection between these communities and the struggle for independence in Cuba.*

Prohias, R. J. & Casal, L. (1980). *The Cuban Minority in the U.S.* (Vol. 1). New York: Arno Press.

> *A comprehensive study on Cubans in the United States. This publication is based on a study completed in 1973. The demographic data relate to circumstances in the early 1970s.*

Richmond, M. L. (1980). *Immigrant Adaptation and Family Structure among Cubans in Miami, Florida.* New York: Arno Press.

This reprint of a 1974 doctoral dissertation provides the reader with considerable information on how the immigration experience affected the Cuban family.

Rieff, D. (1993). *The Exile: Cuba in the Heart of Miami.* New York: Simon & Schuster.

This source chronicles the Cuban American experience in great detail and is best suited for advanced high school students with some background in the topic. (High School)

Rogg, E. M. (1974). *The Assimilation of Cuban Exiles: The Role of Community and Class.* New York: Aberdeen Press.

This study is based primarily on interviews with 250 Cuban heads of households in western New York and New Jersey.

Rohter, L. (1980, May 26). What Today's Cuba Is Like. *Newsweek,* pp. 32–34.

This useful article could serve as a primer to acquaint the reader with conditions inside Castro's Cuba.

Silva, H. (1985). *The Children of Mariel: Cuban Refugee Children in South Florida Schools.* Washington, D.C.: The Cuban American National Foundation.

This report examines the programs established by the Miami (Dade Country) school system to cope with an immediate influx of more than 15,000 non-English-speaking students. Statistics abound to document funding and the nature of the academic programs offered through 1982.

Szapocznik, J., Cohen, R., & Hernandez, R. (Eds.). (1985) *Coping with Adolescent Refugees: The Mariel Boatlift.* New York: Praeger.

This source emphasizes the psychological adaptation of young Mariel refugees, particularly during the interment camps. A mental health perspective is taken in this work.

Thompson, E. H. (1977, April). Can Cuban Culture Last through the Next Generation? *Miami Magazine,* pp. 25–27, 54–57.

An informative source on the level of cultural retention among Cuban youths in South Florida. It discusses value conflicts between assimilated Cuban youths and their more traditional parents.

Valdivieso, R. & Davis, C. (1988). *U.S. Hispanics: Challenging Issues for the 1990's.* Washington, D.C.: Population Reference Bureau.

This source analyzes trends affecting the Hispanic community now and in the future. Cuban Americans are contrasted with other Hispanic groups in such areas as education, income, political trends, and use of the Spanish language.

Weyr, T. (1988). *Hispanic U.S.A.* New York: Harper and Row,.

This source contains information about Cuban American immigration, education, politics, and economic position interwoven among similar data concerning other Hispanic groups.

Books for Students

Arnold, S. M. (1993). *Alicia Alonso: First Lady of the Ballet.* New York: Walker and Company.

> *This carefully researched biography introduces readers to the Cuban ballerina Alicia Alonso. (High School)*

Curtin, M. (1974). *Cubanitos in a New Land: Cuban Children of Miami,* Hialeah, Fla.: Miami Press.

> *This is a collection of seven stories written at about a fifth-grade reading level. (Intermediate)*

Gernard, R. (1988) *The Cuban Americans.* New York: Chelsea House Pulishers.

> *This book is written in an easy-to-read manner and is well illustrated. It provides a brief foundation of Cuban history and a panoramic view of Cuban Americans in the United States. (Intermediate/High school)*

Haskins, J. (1982). *The New Americans: Cuban Boat People.* Hillside. N.J.: Enslow Publishers.

> *The author analyzes the reasons for the Mariel boatlift of 1980. The entrance and initial adaptation of these refugees are examined. Specific cases illustrate this experience, which gives the work a particularly human quality. (Junior High/ High School)*

Hoobler, D. & Hoobler, T. (1995). *The Cuban American Family Album.* New York: Oxford University Press.

> *This informative, interesting, and well-illustrated book includes photographs and other primary resources. (Intermediate and up)*

Méndez, A. (1994). *Cubans in America.* Minneapolis: Lerner.

> *This informative book describes the historical background of Cuban Americans in Cuba as well as their experiences in the United States. Well illustrated with black-and-white photographs. (Intermediate and Up)*

Philipson, L. & Llerena, R. (1980). *Freedom Flights.* New York: Random House.

> *This text is composed of a series of vignettes on how twenty different Cubans left Cuba. Some of the stories are tragic and poignant. (High School)*

Vázauez, A. M. & Casas, R. E. (1987). *Cuba: Enchantment of the World.* Chicago: Children's Press.

> *A brief history of Cuba from pre-Columbian to contemporary times. Besides the historical chronology, this source contains sections on sports, the arts, folklore, and Cuban customs. (Intermediate)*

PART V

ASIAN AMERICANS AND ARAB AMERICANS

CONCEPTS AND STRATEGIES

This part consists of content, concepts, teaching strategies and materials for teaching about Asian Americans and Arab Americans. Although different in many ways, these groups also share similarities. First, each term—*Asian American* and *Arab American*—describes a wide diversity of groups that differ in many significant ways. The Japanese are very different from the Hmong, just as the Iranians and the Lebanese differ in important ways. Second, Edward Said (1978) describes how the Europeans constructed the idea of *Orientalism* to refer to peoples in Asia as well as in the Middle East. Writes Said, "Taking the late eighteenth century as a very roughly defined starting point Orientalism can be discussed and analyzed as the corporate institution for dealing with the Orient—dealing with it by making statements about it, authorizing views of it, describing it, by teaching it, settling it, ruling over it: in short, Orientalism as a Western style for dominating, restructuring, and having authority over the Orient" (p. 3). He continues, "In brief, because of Orientalism the Orient was not (and is not) a free subject of thought and action" (p. 3).

When teaching about Asian Americans and Arab Americans, teachers can use Said's concept of Orientalism to help students examine the ways in which this concept was used historically and is being used today to construct ideas of the Japanese, the Chinese, the Iranians, and the Lebanese as "different." By having students examine and deconstruct images of Asian Americans and Arab Americans that are widespread within the popular media and the wider society, teachers can help students to understand the ways in which the concept of Orientalism still functions in Western societies and why its destructive power needs to be questioned and replaced with transformative, multicultural knowledge.

REFERENCE

Said, E. (1978). *Orientalism.* New York: Vintage Books.

CHAPTER 13

ASIAN AMERICANS

CONCEPTS, STRATEGIES, AND MATERIALS

In America, Asian immigrants and their offspring have been actors in history. . . . Their dreams and hopes unfurled here before the wind, all of them—from the first Chinese miners sailing through the Golden Gate to the last Vietnamese boat people flying into Los Angeles International Airport—have been making history in America.

Ronald Takaki

This chapter consists of content, concepts, teaching strategies, and materials for teaching about three of the oldest Asian groups in the United States—the Chinese Americans, Japanese Americans, and Filipino Americans.

Asian Americans, one of the most diverse and interesting ethnic groups in the United States, are rarely studied in the elementary and high school grades. When discussed in textbooks and in the popular media, they are often used to illustrate how an ethnic group of color can succeed in the United States. Because of their tremendous educational, occupational, and economic success, Asian Americans are often called the *model minority* in the popular media. It is true that some Asian American groups are better educated, have a higher occupational status, and earn more money than other Americans, including White Americans. However, the model minority concept is problematic for several reasons.

PROBLEMS WITH THE MODEL MINORITY CONCEPT

A focus on the economic success of Asian Americans results in several problems. It obscures the tremendous economic diversity within Asian American communities and the problems Asians have. When we look only at the group characteristics of Chinese Americans, for example, the serious economic problems of the new immigrants are overlooked. In 1990, about 42% of the Chinese immigrants had menial service, low-skilled, and blue-collar jobs. About 52% had managerial and technical jobs (U.S. Bureau of the Census, 1993a). Takaki (1989) has called the unskilled Chinese immigrant workers "a colonized labor force" (1989, p. 425). Many Chinese immigrant women work as seamstresses in San Francisco and in New York for long hours at very low wages. The model minority concept also obscures the stories of successful members of other ethnic groups, such as upwardly mobile African Americans and Hispanics. Finally, when overly emphasized, the model minority argument can divert attention from the racism that Asian Americans and other people of color in the United States still experience (Takaki, 1989). Daniels (1988) states that diverting attention from racism was one intent of William Petersen (1966), the writer who first used the concept of *the model minority* in a *New York Times Magazine* article.

RAPID INCREASES IN THE ASIAN AMERICAN POPULATION

Asian Americans, in percentage terms, increased faster than any other U.S. ethnic group between 1980 and 1990. The number of Asians in the United States increased from 3,466,847 in 1980 to 6,908,638 in 1990, a 99% increase, compared to a 53% increase for Hispanics and a 7% increase for the non-Hispanic population (U.S. Bureau of the Census, 1993b). The number of Asians immigrating to the United States has increased substantially since the Immigration Reform Act became effective in 1968. Five Asian nations—Vietnam, the Philippines, Mainland China, India, and Korea—were among the top fifteen nations from which immigrants came to the United States in 1992 (U.S. Immigration and Naturalization Service, 1993). The number of immigrants entering the United States from Vietnam (77,735) was exceeded only by Mexico (213,802). Immigrants of Asian origin from these five nations were among the largest groups entering the United States between 1981 and 1992 (U.S. Bureau of the Census, 1993b) (see Table 13-1).

The United States now has a sizable population of Vietnamese Americans (615,000 in 1990). After U.S. participation in the Vietnam War ended (1973) and Communists took control of that nation (1975), thousands of Vietnamese refugees rushed to the United States. Only 226 Vietnamese immigrated to the United States in 1965, but more than 87,000 came to the United States in

Table 13-1 ASIAN IMMIGRANTS TO THE UNITED STATES (1961–1992)

Country of Birth	1961–1970	1971–1980	1981–1992	Total
Cambodia [Kampuchea]	1,200	8,400	122,500	132,100
China	96,700	202,500	490,300	789,500
Hong Kong	25,600	47,500	83,900	157,000
India	31,200	176,800	343,600	551,600
Japan	38,500	47,900	59,200	145,600
Korea	35,800	272,000	360,700	668,500
Laos	100	22,600	164,300	187,000
Pakistan	4,900	31,200	91,900	128,000
Philippines	101,500	360,200	619,900	1,081,600
Thailand	5,000	44,100	78,900	128,000
Vietnam	4,600	179,700	534,400	718,700

SOURCE: U.S. Bureau of the Census. (1994). *Statistical Abstract of the United States.* (114th ed.). Washington, D.C.: U.S. Government Printing Office.

1978. Between 1981 and 1992, 534,400 Vietnamese immigrants settled in the United States (see Table 13-1).

The number of Chinese immigrants settling in the United States from China and Hong Kong has also increased substantially since 1965. In 1965, for example, 4,769 immigrants from China settled in the United States. Between 1981 and 1992, however, 490,300 immigrants entered the United States from China and 83,900 from Hong Kong (see Table 13-1) (U.S. Bureau of the Census, 1994).

KOREAN AMERICANS

The number of Koreans and Asian Indian immigrants to the United States has also increased tremendously since the Immigration Act of 1965 became effective in 1968. The Korean American population increased from 10,000 in 1960 to about one-half million in 1985 (Takaki, 1989). The first Koreans who came to the United States arrived in 1885. Later, between 1890 and 1905, 64 Korean students came to study in the United States (Kim, 1980). A significant number of Koreans were recruited to work in the sugar plantations in Hawaii in the early 1900s. However, few Korean immigrants settled in the United States until the 1970s. Only 6,231 Koreans immigrated to the United States between 1951 and 1960 and 34,526 between 1961 and 1970 (U.S. Immigration and Naturalization Services, 1985). However, 360,700 immigrated to the United States between 1981 and 1992.

Korean Americans are one of the fastest growing ethnic groups in the United States today. Koreans are one of the largest immigrant groups settling in the United States. Like the new immigrants from the Philippines, many of the new Korean immigrants are college-educated professionals. In 1990, immigrants from Korea had one of the highest percentage of its population that had a bachelor's degree or higher, 34.4%, compared to 23.1% for immigrants from the United Kingdom, 19.1% for immigrants from Germany, and 43% for immigrants from the Philippines (U.S. Bureau of the Census, 1993a).

ASIAN INDIAN AND PAKISTANI IMMIGRANTS

Only a small number of immigrants from India settled in the United States prior to 1965. A total of about 130,000 came during the period between 1820 and 1976 (Takaki, 1989). Most of the immigrants who came during the nineteenth century were professionals, adventurers, merchants, and monks (Jensen, 1980). A few thousand agricultural workers came to California between 1904 and 1923. Only 1,973 immigrants from India came to the United States between 1951 and 1960; 31,200 immigrated to United States between 1961 and 1979 (U.S. Immigration and Naturalization Services, 1985).

Since 1971, immigrants from India have been entering the United States in substantial numbers. About 343,600 Indian immigrants settled in the United States between 1981 and 1992. A significant number of immigrants to the United States from Pakistan have also entered the United States since 1960. About 91,900 Pakistani immigrants settled in the United States between 1981 and 1992.

There were about 815,000 Asian Indians living in the United States in 1990. Large numbers were concentrated in Northeastern states including New Hampshire (79,440) and Massachusetts (23,845). However, they were spread throughout the United States: for example, 159,973 lived in California, and 20,848 lived in Ohio (U.S. Bureau of the Census, 1993b). These Asian Indians are English speaking and are a highly educated group. Among the immigrants are a large number of engineers, scientists, physicians, dentists, and other professionals. Like the new Filipino immigrants, they are settling in the United States primarily because of the paucity of professional job opportunities in their native land.

SOUTHEAST ASIAN AMERICANS

The Southeast Asians who have settled in the United States have come from three contiguous nations—Vietnam, Kampuchea (Cambodia), and Laos. The Europeans referred to this area as *Indochina* because it had been historically influenced by India and China. The Southeast Asians Americans consist of Vietnamese, Laotian, Cambodian (Kumpucheans), Hmong, and ethnic Chinese refugees who fled to the United States in the aftermath of the Vietnamese War. In the decade before 1975, only about 20,000 Vietnamese immigrated to the United States (Wright, 1989). It is not known how many immigrants came from Laos and Kampuchea (Cambodia) during this period. The first refugees from Southeast Asia fled to the United States in 1975. Their journey to the United States was directly related to the ending of the Vietnam War and the resulting communist governments in Vietnam, Laos, and Kampuchea.

The Southeast Asians, like the Cuban refugees from 1959 to 1962, sought refuge in the United States when communist governments came to power in their homelands. A large number of Southeast Asian refugees were resettled in the United States between mid-May 1975 and December 31, 1978. This was one of the largest emergency resettlement programs in the nation's history.

The number of Vietnamese, Laotians, and Kampucheans in the United States grew significantly between 1981 and 1992. Vietnam was one of the ten nations that sent the most legal immigrants to the United States during this period. Nearly one million (821,200) immigrants from Vietnam, Laos, and Kampuchea settled in the United States between 1981 and 1992 (see Table 13-1). Most of these immigrants (65%) came from Vietnam.

The Vietnamese population in the United States is one of the nation's fasting growing populations. There were about 245,025 Vietnamese living in the United States in 1970 and 615,000 in 1990, a 60% increase within this twenty-year period. A number of developments have contributed to the rapid growth in the Indochinese population in the United States. Indochinese refugees continued to come to the United States from refugee camps in Southeast Asia between 1981 and 1989. Many Vietnamese, including Amerasian children (children of American fathers and Vietnamese mothers) and their close relatives have been permitted to immigrate to the United States by federal policies designed to facilitate family reunification. About 10,000 Amerasian children were scheduled for resettlement in the United States in 1989.

The Southeast Asians came to the United States for many different reasons. Singular political, economic, or personal concerns motivated some of the refugees to leave their homelands. Others were motivated by many factors. Many of the Southeast Asian refugees had been directly touched by the trauma of the Vietnam War (1954–1975) or its aftermath. The Southeast Asians left their nations as refugees and are now in the process of becoming Americans.

ASIAN AMERICANS: A DIVERSE GROUP

Asian Americans are one of the most highly diversified ethnic groups in the United States. They vary greatly in both cultural and physical characteristics.

The attitudes, values, and ethnic institutions often differ within Japanese American, Chinese American, Filipino American, and Asian Indian communities. However, the first waves of Chinese, Japanese, and Filipino immigrants had some parallel experiences in the United States. For example, their immigration began when there was a need for cheap labor, but they were harassed and demeaned, and eventually immigration laws were passed to exclude them. After the Chinese Exclusion Act was passed in 1882, there was still a desire for cheap laborers in Hawaii and California. Consequently, Japanese immigrants began arriving in California in significant numbers in the 1890s. When the Gentlemen's Agreement of 1908 and the Immigration Act of 1924 halted Japanese immigration, California farmers imported Filipinos from Hawaii and the Philippines to work in the fields. Anti-Filipino forces emerged on the West Coast and culminated in 1934, when Congress limited Filipino immigration to fifty people per year. This quota constituted, in effect, the virtual exclusion of Filipino immigrants.

Because of their tremendous diversity, similarities, and unique experiences in the United States, the study of Asian Americans can help students increase their ethnic literacy and develop a respect for cultural differences. Figure 13-1 shows the percentage distribution of the Asian American population for selected groups in 1990. Tables 13-2 and 13-3 show selected characteristics and the 1990 U.S. population of Asian Americans groups.

THE CHINESE, JAPANESE, AND FILIPINO AMERICANS: OVERVIEW

This section of this chapter discusses content, concepts, strategies, and materials for teaching about three Asian American groups that live in the United States: the Chinese Americans, Japanese Americans, and Filipino Americans. These groups have important similarities, as well as differences. Each group came to the United States seeking the American dream, satisfied important labor needs, and became victims of an anti-Asian movement designed to prevent their further immigration to the United States. Chinese Americans, Japanese Americans, and Filipino Americans have also experienced tremendous economic, educational, and social mobility and success in U.S. society.

The number of Chinese, Japanese, and Filipino immigrants that settled in the United States between 1951 and 1960 was small compared to the number from Europe. However, the number of immigrants to the United States from China and the Philippines has increased enormously since the Immigration Reform Act of 1965 became effective in 1968. The number of Japanese immigrating to the United States since 1968 has remained moderate. Between 1951 and 1960, 19,300 immigrants from the Philippines and 25,200 from China and Hong Kong settled in the United States. Between 1981 and 1992 the num-

Figure 13-1 ASIAN AMERICAN POPULATION FOR SELECTED GROUPS: 1990 (PERCENT DISTRIBUTION)

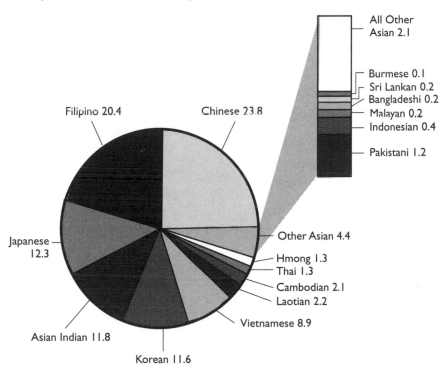

All Other
Asian 2.1

Burmese 0.1
Sri Lankan 0.2
Bangladeshi 0.2
Malayan 0.2
Indonesian 0.4

Pakistani 1.2

Filipino 20.4

Chinese 23.8

Japanese 12.3

Other Asian 4.4

Hmong 1.3
Thai 1.3
Cambodian 2.1
Laotian 2.2

Vietnamese 8.9

Asian Indian 11.8

Korean 11.6

SOURCE: U.S. Bureau of the Census (1993). *We, the American Asians.* Washington, D.C.: U.S. Government Printing Office.

bers were 619,900 from the Philippines, 83,900 from Hong Kong, and 490,300 from China (see Table 13-1).

As a result of the increasing number of immigrants from China, Hong Kong, and the Philippines, as well as from other Asian nations, the Japanese are becoming an increasingly smaller percentage of the Asian American population. In 1970, Japanese Americans were the largest Asian American group, followed by the Chinese and the Filipinos. By 1990, however, the Japanese were the third largest Asian American group, exceeded in size by both the Chinese, the largest group, and the Filipinos, the second largest group (see Table 13-3).

The story of the Chinese, Japanese, and Filipinos in the United States has been largely one of success, if we measure success by the educational, income, and occupational levels these groups have attained. They have attained tremendous educational, income, and occupational success even though they

Table 13-2 SELECTED CHARACTERISTICS OF THE JAPANESE, CHINESE, AND FILIPINO POPULATIONS, 1980 AND 1990

	Chinese	Japanese	Filipino	Non-Spanish Whites	African Americans	All Persons
Population 1980	812,178	716,331	781,894	180,602,838	26,091,857	226,545,805
Population 1990	1,645,000	848,000	1,407,000	190,802,000	30,316,000	255,082,000
Median Household Income 1990	$36,259	$41,626	$43,780	$32,960**	$21,232**	$29,943***
Median Family Income 1990	$41,316	$51,550	$46,698	$36,915***	$22,430	$35,225
Percentage of High School Graduates 1990	73.6%	87.5%	82.6%	79.8%	68.5%	75.2%
Percent with Bachelor's Degree or Higher	35%	28.2%	41.6%	21.5%	11.4%	20.3%

*1989 figure
**1993 figure
***SOURCE: U.S. Bureau of the Census, Current Population Reports, Series P-60, No. 174. (1991). *Money Income of Households, Families, and Persons in the United States: 1990.* Washington, D.C.: U.S. Government Printing Office.
SOURCE: U.S. Bureau of the Census (1994), *Statistical Abstract of the United States* (114th ed.). Washington, D.C.: U.S. Government Printing Office.

Table 13-3 RESIDENT POPULATION
OF ASIAN AMERICANS IN 1990

Group	Population
Chinese	1,645,000
Filipino	1,407,000
Japanese	848,000
Asian Indian	815,000
Korean	799,000
Vietnamese	615,000
Laotian	149,000
Cambodian [Kampuchean]	147,000
Thai	91,000
Hmong	90,000
Pakistani	81,000

SOURCE: U.S. Bureau of the Census (1994). *Statistical Abstract of the United States 1994.* Washington, D.C.: U.S. Government Printing Office, p. 30.

have historically been the victims of racism and discrimination and are often the victims of subtle discrimination today. The stories of the Chinese, Japanese, and Filipinos in the United States can help students understand how the American dream can be pursued and attained. However, when these groups are studied, the problems that Asian Americans still face in U.S. society, such as cultural conflict, identity, and attaining a balance between their ethnic cultures and the mainstream culture, should not be glossed over. The poverty that exists in Asian American communities, especially in urban ethnic communities where newly arrived immigrants settle in large numbers, should also be studied.

When studying about Asians in the United States, students should examine and analyze the new wave of racism that has been directed against Asian Americans, as well as against other ethnic groups of color. This new wave of racism, which emerged in the 1980s, has been expressed in a number of ways, including ugly racial incidents on college campuses. The rising number of Asian students at some of the nation's most prestigious colleges and universities has evoked comments that some Asians have interpreted as a call for restrictive quotas. In 1989, Asian Americans made up about 16% of the students at Stanford, about 25% at the University of California at Berkeley, and about 11% at Harvard (Takaki, 1989).

Many Americans, particularly unemployed auto workers, blame Japan for the stiff competition from Japanese car manufacturers. This hostility has sometimes been directed at Japanese Americans because some Americans do not distinguish Japanese nationals and Japanese Americans. This hostility has taken diverse forms, including bumper stickers that read, "Unemployment— Made in Japan" and statements such as "Auto unemployment is an economic Pearl Harbor" (Daniels, 1988, p. 342). The most odious incident was the June 19, 1982, beating death in a Detroit suburb of Vincent Chin by an unemployed auto worker, Ronald Ebens, and his stepson. Ebens thought Chin was a Japanese American. Despite their success—and sometimes because of it— Asian Americans are still victims of racism and discrimination. Some Americans still consider Asian Americans "strangers from a different shore" (Takaki, 1989).

CHINESE AMERICANS

The Immigration

When the news reached the Guandong Province in southeast China that there was a "Golden Mountain" across the Pacific, a number of young men violated both Chinese law and tradition and headed for the promised land. The decision to leave China for a foreign land was a serious one because it was illegal to immigrate and violators could be severely punished. Also, Confucian doctrine, which was an integral part of Chinese life during this period, taught that a young man should value his family above all else and thus should not leave it. However, both the promises of the land of the Mountain of Gold and the severe living conditions in the Toishan district in Guandong, from which most of the first Chinese immigrants hailed, helped push the young immigrants across the Pacific.

Political upheaval, famine, local warfare, excessive taxes, a severely depressed economy, and a rugged terrain in Toishan that was inimical to farming motivated young Chinese males to seek better opportunities in an unknown land where, according to a pervasive myth, one could easily strike gold and return to China a rich man. Most of the Chinese who headed for California were young married men. They were self-proclaimed "sojourners" who intended to earn their fortunes in the United States and return to their families in China. Because of tradition and the rough voyage across the Pacific, their families were left behind.

The journey across the Pacific was rugged and hazardous. On their arrival in California, the Chinese immigrants experienced a rude awakening. Although White Americans expressed little overt hostility toward the Chinese when they first started immigrating to the West Coast in substantial numbers in the 1850s, they considered them exotic, strange people. Whites thought that the Chinese were strange because of their traditional Chinese clothing, language, queue hairstyle (which Whites called pigtails), and skin color. Almost

CHINESE AMERICANS: HISTORICAL PERSPECTIVE

Important Dates	
1850	The U.S. Census showed 450 Chinese immigrants in the United States. This number increased to 34,933 in 1860. The California legislature passed a discriminatory Foreign Miner's Tax, which forced Chinese immigrants to pay a highly disproportionate share of the state taxes.
1859	Authorities in the Guangdong Province legalized the recruitment of Chinese laborers.
1882	The Chinese Exclusion Act was enacted by Congress. It stopped the immigration of Chinese laborers for 10 years.
1974	The U.S. Supreme Court ruled on *Lau* v. *Nichols* that the San Francisco Unified School District was denying Chinese American students who did not speak English "a meaningful opportunity to participate in the public educational program." This ruling by the high court established a legal basis for bilingual educational programs. Such programs were later established in various parts of the nation.
1980	The U.S. Census indicated that the Chinese were one of the largest groups that immigrated to the United States between 1970 and 1980. The percentage of Chinese in the United States increased 88% between 1970 and 1980, compared to 11% for the total population and 6% for Whites.
1982	Vincent Chin was beaten to death in a Detroit suburb by an unemployed auto worker and his stepson. Ronald Ebens, the unemployed auto worker, thought Chin was of Japanese descent.
1992	More than 49,000 immigrants from China and Hong Kong entered the United States, which made the Chinese the second largest Asian group immigrating to the United States. The Filipinos were the largest immigrating Asian group.

from the beginning, the Chinese were the victims of curiosity and racism. Writes Melendy (1972), "From almost the first moment the Chinese landed in San Francisco in the 1850s, they were subjected to harsh treatment. The aim was to exclude them from the United States because of basically *racist* fears and beliefs" (p. 20) [emphasis added].

Labor

In addition to receiving a curious and strange welcome from Californians, the Chinese immigrants found that the mines in which they had to dig for gold had already been thoroughly gone over by White gold diggers. They had to dig for the scraps. However, some Chinese immigrants managed to secure respectable sums of money by remining White claims.

When Congress decided to build a railroad linking the Missouri River to the Pacific Coast in 1862, the Central Pacific issued a call for men to build the western portion of the railroad. Because of the back-breaking work involved in building a railroad over the rugged Western terrain, few Whites would take the work. But the Chinese took up the challenge and almost single-handedly built the Pacific portion of the transcontinental railroad. While the nation celebrated the completion of the railroad on May 10, 1869, 25,000 laborers, most of them Chinese, lost their jobs.

It was not easy for the Chinese immigrants to save money because of the large debts they had incurred when they arranged to come to California. Most of them came to the United States through a credit-ticket system, which was similar to the indenture system used to bring many European immigrants to North America. In this system, a moneyless Chinese man could borrow money from a relative or fellow villager to pay for his passage to California. Chinese organizations, such as the Hui Kuan or Landsmanner, collected the money from the immigrant and sent it to the individuals from whom it was borrowed.

The leaders of the Hui Kuan also provided the immigrants with a place to eat and sleep on their arrival in San Francisco and sent groups of them to work in the mines. Before the worker received his wages, the amount he owed for his passage was deducted. Because of the credit-ticket system, some immigrants ended up worse off financially than they had been before they came to California. Some found that their return to China was indefinitely delayed. What at first promised to be a nation of gold turned out, for many, to be a land of disillusionment and shattered dreams. Writes Melendy (1972), "The Chinese existed at a poverty level, receiving low wages for their work. Even so, they gained materially a bit more than they had in China. The dream of coming to the Golden Mountain to make a fortune and return home still seemed possible to most. For many, however, this was the impossible dream" (p. 20).

Despite the difficulties the Chinese immigrants experienced, many were able to find enough work in a wide range of occupations that most Whites found unpalatable, such as domestic work, work on railroads, and intensive farming, to save enough money to return to China to visit their families and to father children, hopefully sons. The immigrants who returned to China usually told about the promises of California but said little about its difficulties. Also, the home folks were impressed with what seemed like sizable sums of money the sojourners brought back to China. As the news about the Mountain of Gold spread, and immigrants returned home with money or sent money home to their families, the number of Chinese immigrating to California rose tremendously.

Anti-Chinese Agitation

According to the 1860 census, there were 34,933 Chinese in the United States. By 1880, that number had risen to 105,465. Although the increase was sizable, there were still few Chinese immigrating to the United States compared to the number of European immigrants. Between 1820 and 1930, 38 million immigrants entered the United States, mostly from Europe. However, many Whites became alarmed at the number of Chinese entering the United States, and a vicious movement developed to keep them out. Although leaders of the anti-Chinese movement claimed that the Chinese could not be assimilated and that they competed unfairly with Whites on the labor market, racism was one of the main forces behind the anti-Chinese movement. As Saxton (cited in Melendy, 1972) has pointed out, "The Chinese inherited the long-standing hostility of Whites against people of color, particularly Blacks. White Californians, conditioned to the notion that Blacks were inferior persons and servile workers, easily transferred these perceptions to the Chinese" (p. 18).

Led by Dennis Kearney and the California Workingmen's party, "The Chinese Must Go" became the rallying cry of the anti-Chinese movement. Leaders of all types joined in the movement to push the Chinese out of the West. Labor leaders were among the most staunch anti-Chinese advocates. Politicians jumped on the bandwagon in order to gain votes. As the hostility against the Chinese mounted, they became increasingly defenseless. Unlike the Japanese, they did not have a strong nation that could threaten the balance of world power when its citizens in the United States were ill treated.

The anti-Chinese movement spread as the Chinese moved to such states as Washington, Oregon, Colorado, and Wyoming. Anti-Chinese activities took the form of racist newspaper stories; violent attacks against defenseless men, women, and children; and highly discriminatory laws aimed particularly at the Chinese, such as the Queues Ordinance, the Laundry Ordinance, and the 1876 Cubic Air Law. One of the most blatantly discriminatory laws was the Foreign Miner's Tax passed by the California legislature in 1850. Applied most effectively against the Chinese, it forced them to pay a highly disproportionate share of the taxes collected under the law. Taxes paid by the Chinese largely financed the California state and county governments during this period (Chun-Hoon, 1973). The movement to ban the immigration of Chinese culminated with the passage of the Immigration Act of 1882. This bill stopped the immigration of Chinese laborers for a period of ten years. A victory for the anti-Chinese leaders, it was followed by a series of similar bills that drastically reduced Chinese immigration for decades. The number of Chinese entering the United States dwindled from 39,579 in 1882 to 472 in 1893.

Violence and Riots

Violence directed against the Chinese was widespread in the late 1880s. An anti-Chinese riot occurred in San Francisco as early as 1869. A White mob in Los Angeles attacked a Chinese community in 1871. When the conflict ended, nineteen Chinese Americans had been killed and their community was in shambles. Another anti-Chinese riot exploded in Denver, Colorado, in 1880. One Chinese was killed and most of the homes in the Chinese community were wrecked during the riot. A serious anti-Chinese riot occurred in Rock Springs, Wyoming, in 1885. Twenty-eight Chinese were killed, fifteen were wounded, and many were driven from their homes. The property destroyed was estimated at $150,000. Most of the White aggressors in these riots went unpunished partly because testimony against a White person by a Chinese was inadmissible in the courts.

Chinatowns

The Chinese responded to this violence by moving farther eastward, to the Northeast (where they also became the victims of violence), and by retreating into ethnic communities in urban areas. Writes Lyman (1970), "By the end of the nineteenth century, the California Chinese had, for the most part, died off, returned to China, moved eastward or settled into the ghettos of American cities referred to as 'Chinatowns'" (p. 14).

Despite its outer glitter, life in Chinatown was and is tough and depressing. Since most of the male immigrants did not bring their wives to California and were unable to marry Caucasians because of miscegenation laws, Chinatown was made up primarily of desperate and lonely men who sought their recreation in the form of prostitution, gambling, and opium smoking. Because of the high population of lonely and virile men, and the scarcity of females, prostitution loomed large in Chinatown in the 1800s. It was controlled by the Chinese secret societies that paid off police officials so that they could "safely" practice their business. Competition between the various Chinese societies for power, women, and money was keen, and violence between them often erupted. These conflicts were sensationalized by the White press and were popularized as "tong wars." Such stories made good copy and were eagerly sought by many journalists. These news stories played into the hands of the anti-Chinese racists and were fully exploited.

Prostitution, tong wars, gambling, and opium smoking are largely things of the past in Chinatown. However, powerful antiquated Chinese organizations that care little about the masses still exercise considerable power. Poverty, squalor, and disease are rampant in some Chinese urban communities. San Francisco's Chinatown has one of the highest population densities in the nation. Many women in San Francisco's Chinatown work in the garment industry for very low wages. Housing and education in San Francisco's Chinatown are among the worst in the nation. The power elite in Chinatown, which profits from the misery of the masses, has helped obscure its outrageous conditions and publicized its glitter. Chinatown has been described as a "gilded ghetto whose tinseled streets and brightly lit shops barely camouflage a pocket of poverty in the metropolis" (Lyman, 1970, p. 8).

Chinese Americans Today

Chinatown served as a port of entry for most of the earlier immigrants; it provided them with a sense of security, ties with the old world culture, and a partial escape from discrimination. Many Chinese Americans who are descendants of these earlier immigrants have experienced upward social and economic mobility and are leaving Chinatown. They have joined the exodus to the suburbs (Horton, 1995). However, the American Chinatowns are still viable and important communities. The newly upwardly mobile Chinese Americans who are moving to suburban communities are being replaced in Chinatown by new waves of immigrants from China and Hong Kong. In 1990, 69.3% of the Chinese Americans were foreign-born, compared to 32.4% of the Japanese (U.S. Bureau of the Census, 1993a). In his anthropological study of New York's Chinatown, Wong (1982) identifies four groups that live there: (1) old overseas Chinese, (2) American-born Chinese and naturalized Chinese Americans, (3) jump-ship sailors and refugees, and (4) disenchanted/disenfranchised youths (Wong, 1982). The refugees from Southeast Asia face tremendous economic hardships and work long hours each day, sometimes from eighteen to twenty hours.

The new immigrants who have entered the United States since the Immigration Reform Act of 1965 have been bipolar in their social class backgrounds. In 1990, about 42% of Chinese Americans were menial service, low-skilled, and blue-collar workers. About 52% were managerial and technical workers (U.S. Bureau of the Census, 1993b). Even though the economic and educational levels of the total Chinese population are high, a large group of the new immigrants have low-paying jobs that are highly concentrated in restaurants and textile work. The bipolar nature of the Chinese community is also reflected in where they live. Many of the lower-level workers live in Chinatown, whereas many of the professional and upper-status workers live in suburban communities. Monterey Park, California, a suburban community of Los Angeles that had a population of 61,000 in 1988, had 50% Chinese residents. It had become "America's first suburban Chinatown" (Takaki, 1989, p. 425; Horton, 1995).

The social, educational, and economic characteristics of the total population of Chinese Americans in 1990 were impressive. Most Chinese Americans (about 73.6%) who were twenty-five years or older were high school graduates, compared to 79.8% for Whites, and 75.2% for all persons (U.S. Bureau of the Census, 1993b). The median family income of Chinese Americans in 1990 was $41,316, compared to $35,225 for all persons. Chinese Americans were also highly concentrated in managerial, professional, and technical jobs in 1990: 35.8% of them held managerial and professional specialty jobs, compared to 26.4% for all persons. In addition, 31.2% of them held technical, sales, and administrative support occupations in 1990, compared to 31.7% for all persons. On most leading indicators of success in 1990, the Chinese in the United States exceeded the general population (U.S. Bureau of the Census, 1993b).

Because of the educational, occupational, and economic success of Chinese Americans, many of them have moved out of Chinatown to other areas within the city. They are still primarily urban and metropolitan dwellers. Most lived in metropolitan areas in 1990. Almost all poor Chinese, aged bachelors, and most recent immigrants live in Chinatown. Other groups, however, also live there. Although many Chinese Americans have joined the larger society, the Chinatowns of the nation are still viable communities that satisfy important human and cultural needs. Even the highly assimilated Chinese American occasionally returns to Chinatown on the weekend for a good ethnic meal or to buy certain Chinese products unavailable in predominantly White communities.

The Chinese community has experienced an influx of immigrants since the passage of the Immigration Act of 1965, which gave a liberal quota of 170,000 to people who lived in Eastern Hemisphere nations. A chain migration has developed. Once they are in the United States and have become citizens, many Chinese send for relatives under the provisions of the immigrant act that allow families to join other family members. The process multiplies. Between 1970 and 1980, the Chinese population in the United States increased 88%, while the White population increased 6%. In 1965, only 4,769 Chinese immigrants entered the United States, whereas 65,600 persons born in China (Mainland and Taiwan) and Hong Kong immigrated to the United States in 1992. The Chinese American population in 1990 was 1,645,000, which made them the largest Asian American group. They made up 23.8% of the Asian American population (see Figure 13-1).

Despite the tremendous increase in the Chinese American population since 1965, Asians still comprised only a small percentage of the U.S. population of more than 250 million in 1990. However, the Asian population in the United States grew more rapidly than any other ethnic group between 1980 and 1990 (99% increase). The rapid growth of the Chinese population in the United States is likely to have a number of important consequences. One possible consequence is that U.S. foreign policy will focus more on Asia.

JAPANESE AMERICANS

The Immigration

Because of overpopulation, depressed farming conditions, and political turmoil in Japan in the late 1800s, its citizens began immigrating to Hawaii and the U.S. mainland in search of better economic opportunities. The arrival of 148 Japanese contract laborers in Hawaii in 1868 to work on the plantations violated Japanese law. Japanese immigrants did not arrive in the United States and Hawaii in significant numbers until the Japanese government, because of internal problems, legalized immigration in 1886. There were 55 people of Japanese ancestry in the United States in 1870; 2,039 in 1890; and 111,010 in 1920 (Lyman, 1970). The largest number of Japanese immigrants arrived in the United States between 1891 and 1924; about 200,000 came during this period (Kitano, 1976).

JAPANESE AMERICANS: HISTORICAL PERSPECTIVE

Important Dates	
1868	One hundred forty-eight Japanese contract laborers arrived in Hawaii.
1869	The unsuccessful Wakamatsu Colony, made up of Japanese immigrants, was established in California.
1906	The San Francisco Board of Education ordered all Asian children to attend a segregated Oriental school.
1907–08	The United States and Japan made the Gentlemen's Agreement, which was designed to reduce the number of Japanese immigrants entering the United States.
1913	The California legislature passed a land bill making it difficult for Japanese immigrants to lease land.
1924	An immigration bill was passed by Congress that stopped Asian immigration to the United States.
1930	The Japanese American Citizenship League was founded.
1941	Japan attacked Pearl Harbor on December 7.

Important Dates

1942	On February 19, President Franklin D. Roosevelt issued Executive Order 9066, which authorized the internment of Japanese Americans who lived on the West Coast.
1946	The last internment camp was closed.
1948	The Japanese American Evacuation Claims Act, signed by President Harry S Truman, authorized some compensation for the financial losses incurred by the Japanese Americans during the internment. The U.S. government eventually compensated the Japanese Americans for property loss at the rate of about 10¢ per dollar.
1952	The McCarran-Walter Immigration Act was passed by Congress. It ended the total exclusion of Asian immigrants, which had begun with the passage of the Immigration Act of 1924. Asian Americans were granted naturalization rights.
1972	Statistics indicated that 47% of the Japanese Americans living in Los Angeles were married to non-Japanese spouses.
1986	A U.S. Court of Appeals reinstated the claim that the U.S. Government illegally took property from a group of Japanese interned during World War II. This case made it possible for claims by survivors to be heard in court.
1988	The American Civil Liberties bill was passed by Congress and signed by President Reagan. It provided an apology for the internment of Japanese Americans during World War II and a $20,000 payment for each survivor of the internment.

After the anti-Chinese forces had successfully stopped Chinese immigration, epitomized by the Chinese Exclusion Act of 1882, there was still a need for seasonal farm laborers in the developing West. The Japanese immigrants filled the labor void in agriculture and in other areas that had been created by the cessation of Chinese immigration. Why Whites on the West Coast halted the immigration of one group of Asians and then encouraged the coming of another is a curious and complex historical event. However, it was only a matter of time before the anti-Asian forces, already mobilized, began to attack aggressively the Japanese Americans as they had earlier attacked the Chinese.

Most of the first Japanese immigrants were young men, some of whom were married. They hoped to earn a small fortune in the United States and return to Japan. Like the Chinese, however, most of them remained in North America. There were many similarities in the experiences of Japanese and Chinese immigrants to the United States. However, there were some significant differences that profoundly influenced the development of the Chinese American and Japanese American communities. Organizations emerged within the Little Tokyos of America, as in early Chinatown, to help the new immigrant secure lodging, food, and jobs.

There were also few women among the first Japanese immigrants. Like the Chinese, the men had to share the women who were available. However, the man-woman ratio never became as imbalanced within the Japanese American community as it became in the Chinese community because the Japanese immigrants were able to marry Japanese women, despite the exclusion laws that were directed against Japanese immigrants. Although the men were in the United States and the women in Japan, marriages were arranged with photographs. The wives would later join their husbands, whom they had never seen, in the United States. These women became known as "picture brides." (The picture bride custom was similar in some ways to the "tobacco bride" custom that was practiced in the Jamestown colony. The Virginia Company sent 90 European women to Virginia in the spring of 1620. Each man who married one of the women had to pay 120 pounds of the best tobacco to help pay for his bride's transportation costs from Europe. In later years, the company continued to send more "maids" to Virginia to marry the lonely male colonists.)

Although the picture-bride marriage practice was opposed vigorously by anti-Japanese groups, it was consistent with Japanese custom and continued until outlawed in Japan in 1920. Many parents of second-generation Japanese Americans (*Nisei*) were married in a "picture" ceremony. (Japanese Americans use specific terms to designate each generation: *Issei, Nisei, Sansei,* and *Yonsei* refer to the first, second, third, and fourth generations, respectively.) These marriages worked amazingly well, partly because traditionally romantic love had not been a major factor in Japanese marriages. Rather, marriages were more the joining of two families rather than two individuals. This Japanese adage expresses cogently this attitude toward marriage: "Those who come together in passion stay together in tears."

Although most of the Issei men were much older than their picture brides, the fact that they were able to marry helped the Japanese to establish strong families in the United States. Some writers consider the Japanese family the most significant factor in the social and economic mobility of Japanese Americans. Strong families developed early in the Japanese American community, partly because of the picture-bride custom. Because of exclusion laws that prohibited the immigration of Chinese females, family life in the Chinese American community developed slowly. A large and assertive second generation of Japanese Americans emerged because the Issei were able to establish families in the United States. Such a generation did not develop among the

Chinese for several decades because of their lack of family life. There were few Chinese women available and Chinese men were unable to marry Whites. The Chinese community, because of exclusion laws, was made up primarily of destitute, lonely, aging, and exploited men for several decades.

When they arrived on the West Coast, the Japanese immigrants worked in a variety of fields, including agriculture, the railroads, domestic work, gardening, small businesses, and industry. Because of job discrimination, they worked mainly in self-employment types of occupations. Consequently, they made their greatest impact in such fields as agriculture, gardening, and small business. Of all these areas, their accomplishments in agriculture, and especially truck farming, were the most impressive. Much of the land they were able to farm was considered unarable and largely useless by most White farmers. With a great deal of ingenuity and the use of intensive farming techniques, the Japanese began to dominate certain areas of California truck farming. They produced 90% of the state's peppers, strawberries, celery, and snap beans in 1941. In the same year, they raised a large percentage of California's cucumbers, tomatoes, cabbage, carrots, lettuce, and onions (Melendy, 1972).

The Japanese immigrants were often praised for their industry and eagerness when they first arrived in California. However, their tremendous success in agriculture eventually alarmed and frightened farmers. They no longer saw the Japanese merely as ambitious workers and servants, but rather as tough competitors in the marketplace. To halt their success and to drive them out of California, White farmers and labor leaders inflamed anti-Asian feelings and warned of a new "Yellow Peril."

Some familiar faces and organizations, such as Dennis Kearney and the California newspapers, renewed their anti-Asian tactics. Anti-Japanese attitudes were pervasive on the West Coast. Almost every institution was affected. In 1906, the San Francisco Board of Education ordered all Asian American children, including the Japanese, to attend the segregated Oriental school. Japan was upset by this order and considered it a gross insult. Because of Japan's growing military strength, President Theodore Roosevelt thought the order might cause a serious conflict with Japan. Consequently, he intervened and persuaded the school board to rescind it.

To help mitigate the pervasive anti-Japanese feelings on the West Coast, the United States and Japan worked out an agreement designed to reduce drastically the immigration of Japanese laborers to the United States. This agreement, which became known as the Gentlemen's Agreement, was completed in 1908. Japan agreed to halt the immigration of laborers to the United States; the United States agreed to end discrimination against the Japanese. After this agreement, the number of Japanese entering the United States was reduced drastically. However, the anti-Japanese movements continued unabated. The most extremist groups wanted nothing less than total exclusion of the Japanese.

"The Japs Must Go!" became the rallying cry of the anti-Japanese movements. Racist headlines in the press, attacks on Japanese businesses, and other forms of violence occurred. The anti-Japanese forces won a major victory when the California legislature passed the Alien Land Bill in 1913. Japanese immigrants were considered "aliens ineligible for citizenship." This bill, designed to drive the Japanese out of farming, prohibited the Issei from leasing land for more than three years. Although the Japanese found this law devastating, they were able, to some extent, to circumvent it. Consequently, it did not have the impact its architects had hoped. Many Issei used their children's names to secure land or obtained land with the help of White friends. In 1920, the California legislature passed a more severe law, which was destined to have the effects the legislators had hoped the 1913 law would have. This law prevented the Issei from leasing land and prohibited them from using their children's names to lease land they could not legally lease themselves. This law served as the prototype for laws later passed in such states as Arizona, New Mexico, Oregon, Utah, and Wyoming.

Even though the Alien Land Law of 1920 successfully reduced the number of Japanese Americans in agriculture, the anti-Japanese movement continued in full force. The groups comprising this movement wanted a total victory, which they viewed as a complete halt of Japanese immigration to the United States and the removal of the Japanese from California. They claimed that despite the Gentlemen's Agreement, the picture brides were swelling the Japanese population in the United States and that the Japanese were having an alarming number of children. The phobia of these groups was totally unfounded. The proportion of Japanese immigrants in the United States has always been small. From 1915 to 1924, when the movement to exclude Japanese immigrants was intense, 85,197 Japanese immigrants entered the United States, which comprised only 2.16% of all immigrants who came to the United States during this period (Petersen, 1971). A total of 45,533,116 immigrants came to the United States between 1820 and 1971; only 370,033 of these were Japanese. In 1920, there were only 111,010 Japanese immigrants in the United States. Thus, it was clearly fiction, politics, economic competition, and racism rather than the large number of Japanese immigrants that caused alarm about the "swelling" Japanese population in the United States.

The anti-Japanese forces experienced a long-awaited victory when the Immigration Act of 1924 was passed. This act fixed quotas for European countries on the basis of the percentages of their immigrants living in the United States and prohibited the immigration of aliens ineligible for citizenship. The act, in effect, stopped Asian immigration. Writes Kitano (1976), "The 1924 immigration act was a major victory for racists, nativists, and exclusionists, and there is little doubt that it was resented by an insulted and bewildered Japan, which having understood that she was to become an important member of the family of nations, did not now understand this slap in the face" (p. 28).

The Internment

On December 7, 1941, Japan attacked Pearl Harbor. Hysteria emerged on the West Coast as the anti-Japanese groups spread rumors about the so-called fifth column and espionage activities among the Japanese (Daniels, 1971). Some Whites argued that all Japanese Americans were still loyal to their mother country; others claimed that you could not tell a "good Jap" from a "bad Jap." Rumors, which spread like wildfire, suggested that the United States was in danger of being attacked by a fleet of Japanese soldiers and that Japanese Americans were helping to plan the attack. A tremendous fear of what came to be known as the Yellow Peril haunted the Pacific Coast. Daniels notes that the fear of conquest by Japan was irrational and racist (Daniels, 1971, p. 29). The press reinforced and perpetuated the fear by printing highly fictionalized and sensationalized news stories about the Japanese "threat."

It is significant to note that White California farmers and politicians played key roles in creating and perpetuating myths about the Yellow Peril. The farmers had long wanted to drive the Japanese out of California; politicians used the issue to gain votes and to divert attention from real political and social issues. It is also worth noting that we know of no sabotage activities in which Japanese Americans were involved during the war. In his perceptive study of the internment, Daniels (1971) argues that the decision to remove the Japanese from the West Coast was a political rather than military decision. Military officials knew during the war that the Japanese on the West Coast were not a security risk. However, because anti-Japanese groups in California urged the removal of the Japanese, it was politically expedient to intern them.

The uproar on the West Coast and the fear that spread throughout other parts of the nation resulted in the issuance of Executive Order No. 9066 by President Franklin D. Roosevelt on February 19, 1942. This order authorized the secretary of war to declare military areas "from which any or all persons may be excluded, and with respect to which, the right of any person to enter, remain in, or leave shall be subject to whatever restrictions the Secretary of War...may impose in his discretion." Although mention of the Japanese Americans by name is notably absent from the document, the order was clearly aimed at them. It authorized the secretary of war to remove Japanese Americans from the West Coast (declared a "military area") and to set up federal concentration camps to which they would be forcibly removed.

The Japanese were first sent to assembly centers, which served as temporary living quarters. Later, a total of 110,000 Japanese Americans (two-thirds of whom were citizens of the United States) were located in these ten concentration camps: Tule Lake and Manzanar in interior California, Minidoka in Idaho, Topaz in Utah, Poston and Gila River in Arizona, Heart Mountain in Wyoming, Granada in Colorado, and Rohwer and Jerome in Arkansas. Most of the camps were located in desolate and barren areas that had hot weather in the summer and cold weather in the winter. They were fenced in with barbed wire and guarded by soldiers.

The internment had some adverse effects on the culture and life of the Japanese Americans. Because of the wide differences in the cultures of Japan and the United States, the Issei and Nisei had been less able to understand each other than most other immigrants and their children. The camp experience increased their alienation. The position of the Issei was further undermined in the camps because often their children, who were U.S. citizens, were able to obtain responsible jobs for which the Issei did not qualify. This was a severe blow to the self-image and confidence of the Issei male, since for centuries the oldest Japanese male had been the undisputed head of the household.

Other events undermined the strength and cogency of the Japanese family, which traditionally had been the pivotal force within the Japanese community. The female often made as much money as the male, and the family had to eat in a communal dining room. The father was unable to exercise his usual authority because of these types of situations. Consequently, family solidarity was lessened in the camps.

Widespread conflict developed within the camps over the question of loyalty. The Nisei often questioned the loyalty of the Issei. Japanese nationals accused the leaders of the Japanese American Citizenship League, who cooperated with the War Relocation Authority, of participating in the oppression of the Japanese. In their eagerness to prove their loyalty to the U.S. government, some Japanese helped federal authorities to conduct witch hunts for "suspected" Japanese. The internment showed how a dehumanizing experience could demoralize a group, which had traditionally had high group solidarity and trust, and cause mistrust and suspicion within it.

Japanese Americans Today

The U.S. Japanese population has never been very large. Japanese immigration was halted by the Immigration Act of 1924 and did not resume until the ban on Asian immigration was lifted when the McCarran-Walter Act was passed in 1952. Although this act set a quota of only 185 Japanese immigrants per year, Asian immigrants were no longer totally excluded.

Compared to the other Asian immigrant groups, few Japanese have immigrated to the United States since the passage of the Immigration Reform

Act of 1965. This is because of the highly developed nature of the economy of Japan and its ability to provide jobs for large numbers of technical and professional workers. Most of the immigrants who come to the United States from nations such as the Philippines, Korea, and India—and many of those from China and Hong Kong—are professional workers who are not able to find jobs consistent with their educations in their native lands. This is not the case in Japan. Between 1981 and 1992, 59,200 immigrants came to the United States from Japan, compared to 619,900 from the Philippines, 490,300 from China, 83,900 from Hong Kong, 534,400 from Vietnam, 343,600 from India, and 122,100 from Cambodia (see Table 13-1).

As a result of its small immigrating population, Japanese Americans are becoming one of the smallest of the Asian American groups and have one of the smallest foreign-born populations. In 1990, most Japanese Americans (about 67.6%) were U.S.-born citizens (U.S. Bureau of the Census, 1993a).

The Japanese American population was 848,000 in 1990 (see Table 13-3). They were the third largest Asian American ethnic group and made up 12.3% of the Asians in the United States. However, their population was close to that of Asian Indians (815,000) and to Koreans (799,000). Because they have a relatively low immigration rate, Japanese Americans had the lowest level of foreign-born among its population than any other group of Asian Americans in 1990 (32.4%). Japanese Americans are highly culturally assimilated. This is indicated by their high rate of out-marriage with other groups (Kitano & Daniels, 1995). In 1989, the out-marriage rate for Japanese Americans living in Los Angeles County was 51.9%. It was 58.3% for women and 41.7% for men (see Table 13-4).

The Japanese Americans have been termed the so-called model American ethnic minority because of their success in education, social-class mobility, and low levels of crime, mental illness, and other social deviances. In 1990, the Japanese median family income was $51,500 compared to $35,225 for all Americans (U.S. Bureau of the Census, 1993b). The Japanese also had high educational achievement in 1990; 87.5% of Japanese, twenty-five years or older, were high school graduates or higher, compared to 75.2% for all persons in the United States. The Japanese were also highly concentrated in managerial, professional, and technical occupations in 1990 (employed persons age sixteen and older); 37% of the Japanese had managerial and professional specialty occupations, compared to 26.4% for all persons. In addition, 34.4% of the Japanese had technical, sales, and administrative support occupations, compared to 31.7% for all persons (U.S. Bureau of the Census, 1993b).

Writes Petersen (1971), "By almost any criterion of good citizenship that we choose, not only are Japanese Americans better than any other segment of American society, including native Whites of native parents, but they have realized this remarkable progress by their own almost unaided effort. . . . Every

Table 13-4 OUT-MARRIAGE RATES FOR CHINESE, FILIPINOS, JAPANESE, KOREANS, AND VIETNAMESE IN LOS ANGELES COUNTY, 1975–1989

Ethnicity	Year	Marriages	Out-Marriages Number	Out-Marriages Percentage	Percentage Out-Marrying by Gender Women	Percentage Out-Marrying by Gender Men
Chinese	1989	1,836	622	33.9	63.0	37.0
	1984	1,881	564	30.0	56.6	43.4
	1979	716	295	41.2	56.3	43.7
	1977	650	323	49.7	56.3	43.7
	1975	596	250	44.0	62.2	37.8
Filipinos	1989	1,384	565	40.8	74.2	25.8
Japanese	1989	1,134	588	51.9	58.3	41.7
	1984	1,404	719	51.2	60.2	39.8
	1979	764	463	60.6	52.7	47.3
	1977	756	477	63.1	60.6	39.4
	1975	664	364	54.8	53.6	46.4
Koreans	1989	1,372	151	11.0	74.8	25.2
	1984	543	47	8.7	78.6	21.4
	1979	334	92	27.6	79.6	20.4
	1977	232	79	34.1	73.4	26.6
	1975	250	65	26.0	63.1	36.9
Vietnamese	1989	555	147	26.5	54.4	45.6
	1984	560	34	6.0	74.7	25.3

SOURCE: Los Angeles County Marriage License Bureau. H. H. L. Kitano & R. Daniels, *Asian Americans: Emerging Minorities*, 2/e, © 1995, p. 187. Reprinted by permission of Prentice-Hall, Upper Saddle River, New Jersey.

attempt to hamper the progress of Japanese Americans, in short, has resulted in enhancing their determination to succeed" (pp. 4–5).

Breaking Silence and the Future of the Japanese in U.S. Society

The silence that many Japanese Americans had kept about their internment during World War II was broken during the hearings before the Commission on Wartime Relocation and Internment of Civilians (CWRIC). Congress created the Commission "to determine whether a wrong was committed against those American citizens and permanent residents relocated and/or interned as a result of Executive Order Numbered 9066 and other associated acts of the Federal Government, and to recommend appropriate remedies."

The Commission held twenty days of hearings and took testimony from more than 750 witnesses between July and December 1981 (Report of the Commission on Wartime Relocation and Internment of Civilians, 1982). Many people who spoke before the Commission were Japanese Americans who had been interned. They told about their experiences in poignant and moving language.

In December 1982 the Commission issued its report, *Personal Justice Denied* (Report of the Commission on Wartime Relocation and Internment of Civilians, 1982). The report condemned the internment and in June 1983 recommended that Congress allow $1.5 billion to provide personal redress to the Japanese who were interned during the war years. The Commission stated in its report:

> *The promulgation of Executive Order 9066 was not justified by military necessity and the decisions which followed from it—detention, ending detention and ending exclusion—were not driven by analysis of military conditions. The broad historical causes which shaped these decisions were race prejudice, war hysteria and a failure of political leadership. Widespread ignorance of Japanese Americans contributed to a policy conceived in haste and executed in an atmosphere of fear and anger at Japan. A grave injustice was done to American citizens and resident aliens of Japanese ancestry who, without individual review or any probative evidence against them, were excluded, removed and detained by the United States during World War II. (p. 18)*

It was a long road of debate and controversy, both within and outside of Congress, between the Commission's recommendation of redress for internees in June 1983 and the enactment of the American Civil Liberties bill by Congress in August 1988. The bill offered the Japanese Americans an apology for their internment and provided a payment of $20,000 for each internee. The payments, which were scheduled to begin in 1990, were to be made over a ten-year period, were to go to older persons first, and could be made to survivors' descendants in the event of the survivor's death. Because the payments were to be made over a ten-year period, many internees would die before the total payment was made. President Ronald Reagan praised the Japanese who served in World War II when he signed the bill and said that the nation was gravely wrong when it interned the Japanese Americans.

The success of the Japanese in U.S. society is indisputable. However, the future of Japanese culture, values, and behaviors in the United States is uncertain. Their success is probably a result largely of traditional Japanese values, attitudes, and beliefs. With a high out-marriage rate and a relatively low rate of immigration, cultural and structural assimilation into the mainstream society may erode the most important values that have taken the Japanese down the road to success. However, a more hopeful possibility is that as they become structurally integrated into the mainstream society, they will enrich it with traditional Japanese values and remain to some extent culturally Japanese as they become full participants in U.S. society.

FILIPINO AMERICANS

Early Filipino Settlement in the United States and Hawaii

Filipinos came to Hawaii and the United States in the first decades of the twentieth century seeking work and better opportunities. An early community of Filipinos in Louisiana has been documented by Espina (1988). Espina's (1988) research cites October 18, 1587, as the earliest known date when Filipino sailors aboard a Spanish galleon landed in what is known today as Morro Bay, San Luis Obispo County, California. Eventually, these sailors—"Manila-men"—jumped ship to escape Spanish domination and around 1763 founded the first permanent Filipino settlement in the bayous of Louisiana. These men developed a dried shrimp industry in their Louisiana settlement.

FILIPINO AMERICANS: HISTORICAL PERSPECTIVE

Important Dates	
1587	Filipino sailors landed in Morro Bay, San Luis Obispo County, California. They were among the first Asians to cross the Pacific Ocean for the North American continent because of the Manila galleon trade between Mexico and the Philippines.
1763	The first permanent Asian settlements in the continental U.S. were Filipino villages in the bayous of Louisiana. Filipino sailors escaped from Spanish colonizers.
1898	Filipinos fought Spanish rule, established the Malolos Congress, and elected Emilio Aguinaldo as the first Philippine president. The United States refuted Philippine claim to independence and purchased the islands for $20 million under the terms of the Treaty of Paris that ended the Spanish-American War.
1899–1901	Filipinos fought for independence from the United States in the Filipino-American War.

Important Dates	
1902	The Organic Act of July 1902 recognized the Philippines as an unincorporated territory of the United States.
1906	More than 200 Filipino contract laborers, *Sakadas,* were brought to Hawaii by the Hawaiian Sugar Planters Association.
1911	The Filipino Federation of Labor was founded in Hawaii.
1929	An anti-Filipino riot occurred in Exeter, California, in which more than 200 Filipinos were assaulted.
1930	Fermin Tobera, who later became a Filipino martyr, was killed in an anti-Filipino riot in Watsonville, California.
1934	Congress passed the Tydings-McDuffie Act. This act promised the Philippines independence in 10 years and limited Filipino immigration to the United States to 50 per year.
1935	President Franklin D. Roosevelt signed the Repatriation Act on July 11. This act offered free transportation to Filipinos who would return to the Philippines. The 2,190 who took advantage were unable to return to the U.S. except under the quota system.
1940	Under the terms of the Nationality Act of 1940, Filipino immigrants to the United States could become citizens through naturalization. U.S. citizenship was extended to other categories of Filipino Americans on July 2, 1946.
1941	Japan attacked the Philippines.
1946	On July 4, 1946, the Philippines becomes independent.
1965	Larry Itliong organized Filipino farm laborers.
1965	The Immigration Reform Act of 1965 opened the door for an influx of Philippine professionals to the United States. More than 32,000 Filipinos immigrated to the United States in 1974.
1990	The Immigration Act of 1990, Section 405, gave Filipino servicemen who were trained in the Philippines and who fought for the United States during World War II between 1939 and 1946 the opportunity to apply for U.S. citizenship.
1992	More than 61,000 Filipino immigrants entered the United States, making them the largest national group to enter the United States that year except the Mexicans.

Significant numbers of Filipinos did not settle in the United States and Hawaii until the turn of the century. Most Filipino immigrants were categorized as *pensionados* or *sakadas,* although some were neither. *Pensionados* were government-sponsored students who returned to the Philippines to apply the knowledge they acquired in the United States. *Sakadas* were contracted laborers who were recruited to work in the sugar fields of Hawaii for three years and either returned to the Philippines, remained in Hawaii, or ventured to the mainland. *Sakadas* were cheap and exploited field hands lured by the promises of a better life in America.

The Philippine revolution against Spanish domination began in 1896. By 1898, Spain and the United States were fighting the Spanish-American War. With the bulk of Spain's military forces concentrated in the Caribbean, its weakened position in the Philippines led the United States to seek control of the Philippines. The refusal of the United States to accept the Filipinos' claim to independence in 1898 launched the Filipino-American War. By 1902, the United States assumed guardianship over the Philippines, thus establishing Filipinos as nationals.

The Immigration

The magnet that pulled Filipinos to Hawaii and the United States came primarily from without rather than from within. Immigration from the Philippines during the 333 years that the islands were ruled by Spain was virtually nil. However, when the United States acquired the Philippines after the Spanish-American War in 1898, it was only a matter of time before farmers in Hawaii and the United States would successfully lure Filipinos away from the islands to work as cheap and exploited field hands. Recruiting and transportation agents lured Filipinos away from their homeland with high-pressure propaganda about the promises of Hawaii and the United States. Because of chronic unemployment and widespread poverty in the islands, thousands of Filipinos left their native land in search of the dream.

Since Chinese immigration had come to an abrupt end in 1882, Japanese immigrants had been the main source of cheap labor for plantation owners in Hawaii and big farmers on the U.S. West Coast. However, the Gentlemen's Agreement of 1907–1908 substantially reduced Japanese immigration, and the Immigration Act of 1924 virtually stopped it. When Japanese immigration ended, a new source of cheap labor was desired by farmers in Hawaii and in the United States. The United States had recently annexed both Puerto Rico and the Philippines. Each nation was regarded as a promising source of cheap labor. However, the attempt to start large-scale immigration from Puerto Rico failed, and the farmers turned to the Philippines, where they had considerable success. The powerful Hawaiian Sugar Planters Association became so alarmed when the Gentlemen's Agreement restricted Japanese immigration in 1907–1908 that it brought more than 200 Filipino workers to Hawaii that year. The association wanted to make sure that when Japanese immigration stopped, there would be a new source of labor just as abundant and cheap.

Filipino immigration to Hawaii continued and escalated after 1907. However, until the 1920s, most of the Filipino immigrants remained in Hawaii and did not come to the U.S. mainland. In 1920, there were only 5,603 Filipinos in the United States. However, from 1923, when Filipino immigration to the United States gained momentum, until it reached its peak in 1929, large-scale immigration to the mainland occurred. In 1929 alone 5,795 Filipinos entered California. Between 1907 and 1910, about 150,000 immigrants left the Philippines and headed for Hawaii or the United States.

Although the highly glorified and exaggerated tales spread by recruiting and transportation agents were the magnet that pulled hundreds of Filipinos from their homeland, the letters and money sent back home by immigrants, as well as the desire to get rich quickly, helped to motivate them to leave the poverty-stricken islands.

Filipino immigrants in the United States had some unique group characteristics that were destined to make their lives on the West Coast harsh and poignant. As the third wave of Asian immigrants, they were victims of the accumulated anti-Asian racism. They were also a young group. According to McWilliams (1943), they were the youngest group of immigrants in U.S. history. They ranged in age from about sixteen to thirty; most, 84.3%, were under thirty. The immigrants were predominantly male. Few Filipino women immigrated because female immigration violated tradition. Also, most of the immigrants were sojourners who hoped to return to the Philippines after attaining the riches of America. Like the other Asian sojourners, the longer they stayed in the United States, the more the hope waned that they would ever be able to return home.

The sex ratio was imbalanced, as it was in early Chinese American communities. In 1930, there was 1 woman for every 143 men. The Filipinos immigrated from a country that was a U.S. colony in which the American myth of "all men are created equal" was taught in the schools. Thus, unlike the other Asian groups, they came to the United States expecting to be treated like equals. Their acceptance of this myth made their adjustment in the United States more difficult.

Work

Like other Asian immigrants, the Filipinos came to Hawaii and the United States to do work the Whites disdained and refused to do. They were hired, usually under a contract system, to pick asparagus and lettuce and to do other kinds of "stoop" field work. In addition to farming, the Filipinos, especially after World War II, worked as domestics. They cooked, washed dishes, and worked as house servants. Some worked in the fishing industry and in canneries.

The Filipino Community

Unlike the Japanese and Chinese, the Filipinos were unable to develop tightly knit ethnic communities. The Little Manila districts in cities such as Los Angeles and San Francisco were primarily entertainment centers and stopping places for the field hands between seasons. The Filipinos could not establish highly cohesive communities because their jobs kept them moving and because, like the Chinese immigrants, they were unable to have much of a family life because of the small number of Filipino females.

The types of entertainment and recreation that emerged within Filipino American communities reflected the sociological makeup of young, unmarried males searching for meaning in life within a hostile and racist atmosphere. Prostitution, cockfighting, and gambling were favorite pastimes for the lonely, alienated men. The Filipino-owned dance halls, in which White girls danced and sold or gave other favors to the immigrants, were popular and a source of widespread tension between Filipinos and White men. Whites passed laws prohibiting Filipinos from marrying White women. However, these laws had little effect on biological drives and mutual attraction between White women and Filipino men. Stockton, California, was dubbed the Manila of the United States because so many Filipinos settled there. It was the site of much conflict and tension between Filipinos and Whites. Although there were few tightly organized Filipino communities, a strong sense of group solidarity and sense of peoplehood emerged among Filipinos. Strong nationalism, as the gifted Filipino American writer Carlos Bulosan epitomized (San Juan, 1972), was widespread among Filipinos in the United States.

Anti-Filipino Agitation

As the third wave of Asian immigrants to the West Coast, Filipinos inherited all of the anti-Asian prejudice and racism that had accumulated since the Chinese started immigrating to the United States in the 1850s. When Filipino immigration reached significant levels in the 1920s, familiar anti-Asian screams about the Yellow Peril were again heard. These anti-Asian movements were, again, led by organized labor and patriotic organizations such as the American Federation of Labor and the Native Sons of the Golden West. The arguments were identical to those that had been made against the Chinese and Japanese; the victims were different but the victimizers were the same. Labor groups claimed that Filipinos were "unfair competition"; patriotic groups argued that they were unassimilable and would pollute the "pure" White race. One exclusionist warned (cited in Divine, 1957, p. 70), "This mongrel stream is small, but when it is considered how rapidly it multiplies and grows it is clear that the tide must be stemmed before it gets beyond control."

Labor and nativistic groups had succeeded in halting Chinese and Japanese immigration by urging Congress to pass exclusion laws. However, the Filipinos presented a different problem. They could not be excluded as "aliens" under the provisions of the Immigration Act of 1924 because of their peculiar and ambiguous legal status. Because the United States had annexed the Philippines in 1898, its citizens were not aliens. However, unlike Puerto Ricans, they were not citizens of the United States either. Filipinos were "nationals" or "wards" of the United States. Consequently, they could not be excluded with the immigration laws that applied to foreign nations. Representative Richard Welch of California nevertheless fought hard to get an outright exclusion act through Congress in 1928. The attempt failed, but Welch succeeded in rallying widespread support for the anti-Filipino cause.

The failure of the Welch bill convinced the leaders of the exclusion movement that they had to try another strategy. The desire for independence within the Philippines had become intense by the late 1920s. The Philippines' independence movement gave the exclusionists new hope for a cause that had become an obsession: to exclude and deport Filipinos. They jumped on the independence bandwagon. If the Philippines became independent, they correctly reasoned, its citizens could be excluded under the provisions of existing immigration laws. The passage of the Tydings-McDuffie Act on March 24, 1934, was a significant victory for the exclusionists.

In addition to promising the Philippines independence, the Tydings-McDuffie Act limited Filipino immigration to the United States to 50 people per year. This act, as was the intention of its architects, virtually excluded Filipino immigration to the United States. Even this bill did not totally satisfy the exclusionists. They not only wanted Filipino immigration stopped, but they also wanted Filipinos deported. They pushed the so-called Repatriation Act through Congress. President Franklin D. Roosevelt signed the act on July 11, 1935. Under the terms of the act, any Filipino could obtain free transportation back to the Philippines. However, there was an insidious catch to this inducement. Once they returned, they could not reenter the United States. Few Filipinos were seduced by this act. Only about 2,000 returned to the Philippines under its provisions.

Riots and Anti-Filipino Violence

Both before and after the Filipino exclusion and deportation acts, anti-Filipino Whites carried out a vicious and active campaign of violence against Filipinos in the western states. One of the first anti-Filipino riots broke out in Yakima, Washington, on September 19, 1928. Some of the most serious riots occurred in California, where most Filipino immigrants first settled. On October 24, 1929, Whites attacked and assaulted more than 200 Filipinos and did considerable property damage in Exeter, California. Fermin Tobera, a lettuce picker, was killed in a riot that occurred in Watsonville, California, in January 1930. Tobera's murder greatly disturbed his native homeland, and a National Humiliation Day was declared in Manila. Some Filipinos felt that Tobera had been ruthlessly slain by a "mob of blood-thirsty Americans" (Wallovits, 1966, p. 124). Three people were shot in a riot that occurred near Salinas, California, in August 1934. An anti-Filipino riot occurred as late as June 1939 in Lake County, California. Writes McWilliams (1943), "No reparations or indemnities were ever made for these repeated outrages; nor were the culprits ever punished" (p. 240).

Filipino Americans Today

Between 1981 and 1992, Filipinos were the second largest group immigrating to the United States; they were exceeded only by immigrants from Mexico. The number of Filipinos entering the United States increased from 3,130 in 1965 to 61,000 in 1992. The Filipino population in the United States increased 80% in the decade between 1980 and 1990, while the White population increased by 6%. In 1990, there were about 1,407,000 Filipinos living in the United States. Of these, 52% lived in California and 12% lived in Hawaii. The next highest concentrations lived in Illinois (5%), New York (4%), and Washington state (3%). Most Filipinos lived in urban areas in 1990.

Most Filipinos who came to the United States in the 1920s were unskilled laborers. The Immigration Act of 1965 not only significantly increased the number of Filipino immigrants to the United States but also changed the characteristics of the immigrants. The majority of the immigrants now entering the United States from the Philippines are professional, technical, and kindred workers. These immigrants come to the United States to seek jobs that are more consistent with their training than those they can obtain in the Philippines. A significant number of them are specialists in the health professions. Professional and technical workers from the Philippines have encountered some difficulties obtaining licenses to practice their crafts in the United States and have experienced language problems and discrimination. Sometimes doctors, dentists, and pharmacists must take lower-level jobs out of their fields until they can obtain the licenses needed to practice their professions in the United States. Many Filipinos who eventually practice their professions in the United States have obtained additional training in U.S. schools.

The significant number of professionally trained Filipinos who have immigrated to the United States since the Immigration Act of 1965 was enacted has changed substantially the social and demographic characteristics of the Filipino Americans. In 1990, 66.4% of Filipinos in the United States were foreign-born. In terms of numbers, there were more foreign-born Americans of Filipino origin than of any other group other than Mexicans. There were 913,000 foreign-born Filipinos and 4,298,000 Mexicans. However, the Filipinos did not have the highest percentage of foreign-born persons among the Asian Americans; 79.9% percent of the Vietnamese were foreign-born and 79.4% of the Loatians were foreign-born (U.S. Bureau of the Census, 1993a).

Before 1970, Filipinos were heavily concentrated in the lower strata of the population on most indices, such as education, income, and job status. However, data from both the 1980 and 1990 U.S. Censuses indicate that the group characteristics of Filipino Americans—based on several criteria related to education, income, and job status—do not differ significantly from the Japanese, Chinese, and other Asian groups in the United States (see Table 13-1). Like the Chinese and Japanese, Filipinos are ahead of the general population on most of these indices. In 1990, the median family income for Filipinos was $46,698, compared to $35,225 for all persons in the United States. The percentage of Filipino high school graduates, twenty-five years or older, was 82.6%, compared to 75.2% for all persons in the United States (U.S. Bureau of the Census, 1993b).

Kim's (1978) study of Filipinos in Chicago indicates why the median family income of Asian families might be higher than that of White families. In many Asian families, both parents are highly trained and have professional jobs. Kim describes the typical Filipino in her study as follows:

> In broad terms, the Chicago Pilipino [sic] respondent can be categorized as young, well-educated, and fairly well-off financially: he [or she] is in his early thirties, has finished college, and may have a graduate or professional degree. Unlike most of the other groups in the study, it does not matter in this area whether the Pilipino respondent is male or female. In either case, the educational level and job level—skilled, white-collar, or professional—will probably be about the same. The Pilipino female will also be just about as likely as her male counterpart to have a full-time job, or to hold more than one job. (p. 172)

A study of the Chinese, Japanese, and Filipinos in the United States will help students to understand how these groups resisted racism and discrimination and attained success in U.S. society. However, their success was attained and is maintained by hard work, tenacity, and the will to overcome. Despite their success in U.S. society, Asians are still the victims of racism and discrimination—both subtle and blatant. Violent incidents against Asian Americans received national attention in 1985. A *New York Times* article was entitled "Violent Incidents against Asian-Americans Seen as Part of Racist Pattern" (Butterfield, 1985). Part of the violence may have its roots in the U.S. response to competition from the Japanese; some Americans blur the distinction between Japanese Americans and foreign Japanese. The violence may be partly a response to the significant number of Asian immigrants now entering the

United States. Regardless of the cause of this new wave of anti-Asian violence, it reminds us that racism is an integral part of U.S. society that can victimize any racial or ethnic group, no matter how successful.

TEACHING STRATEGIES

Concepts such as *immigration, discrimination,* and *cultural diversity* are highlighted in the historical overviews. This part of the chapter illustrates strategies for teaching three concepts, *similarities and differences, immigration,* and *discrimination.* An infinite variety of strategies can be used to teach each of these concepts. However, these activities are illustrative and can serve as a guide to teacher planning. Although each concept can and should be taught at all grade levels, we discuss strategies for teaching similarities and differences in the primary grades, immigration in intermediate and upper grades, and discrimination in the high school grades.

Primary Grades

CONCEPT: Names (Similarities and Differences)

Generalization: We all have names. However, our different names often give other people clues about our different origins, cultures, and experiences.

Introduction

Similarities and *differences* are two concepts that can be effectively taught in the primary grades. These concepts can be understood by young children when they are taught with concrete examples. A unit on names can help primary grade children learn that even though we all have names (a similarity), our names often give other people clues about our different origins, experiences, and cultural backgrounds. It is appropriate to help children better understand the nature and origins of names when they are studying Asian Americans because teachers and students often find some Asian names, such as Vietnamese names, difficult to pronounce and understand.

1. Begin this unit by telling the class that the people who live in our nation, the United States (point it out to the children on a primary globe), came from many different nations and lands. Ask the students: "Can you name some of the nations from which the people in the United States came?" Record accurate responses on the board or butcher paper.

Using a primary globe, show the students some of the nations and continents from which immigrants to the United States came. Ask the students if any of them have ever traveled to any of these nations and continents. If any of them have, ask them to tell briefly about their trips.

Say to the class: "The ancestors of American Indians came to what is now the United States thousands of years ago. The ancestors of many Jews and Italians came to the United States almost 100 years ago. Other Americans, such as many Cubans and Vietnamese, have lived in the United States for fewer than 50 years. People from different parts of the world have many different ways of living, often believe different things, eat different kinds of food, and have different religions. Often people from various nations keep some of their differences after they have lived in the United States for many years. People in various nations often have different kinds of names. Many Americans, whose ancestors came from many different nations or who came from different nations themselves, have names that sound and look different from the names of other groups. These different kinds of names give us clues about the homelands of their ancestors or about their homelands, and about their ways of life and beliefs."

Write the following names on the board or butcher paper:

Susan Schmidt

Juan Rivera Sanchez

Jennifer Kim

Patrick O'Shea

Ito Matsuda

Wing Chu

Katherine Ann Shilenski

Hoang Hy Vinh

Say to the class: "Here are the names of eight of the children in Mrs. Gonzales's third-grade class in a school in Los Angeles. Do their names give us any clues about where their ancestors came from, about what foods they might eat, and about which holidays they might celebrate?"

After giving the students an opportunity to state their ideas about what the children's names reveal about them, tell them a little about each of the eight students in Mrs. Gonzales's class. A brief description of each student follows.

Susan Schmidt. Susan's ancestors came to the United States from Germany in the 1820s. However, Susan says she is a *complete* American. She has no German characteristics that she knows about.

Ask the class: "Why do you think Susan has an American, rather than a German, given name? Why does she consider herself completely American rather than part German? Do any of you have German names? If so, do you feel totally American or part German? Why?"

Juan Rivera Sanchez. Juan was born in Mexico and moved to Los Angeles last year. Unlike Susan's name, Juan's name includes both his father's surname (Rivera), and his mother's maiden surname (Sanchez). This is a common practice in Spanish-speaking nations. In Mexico, it is correct to call Juan, "Mr. Rivera."

Ask the class: "Why do you think that in Spanish-speaking nations children's names often include both their father's surname and their mother's surname before marriage? If your name included both of your parents' surnames (and not just your father's), how would your name be written? If you don't know your mother's surname before she married, ask a parent tonight and be prepared to share your name written with your father's surname and your mother's surname before she married." (*Note:* Some of the children's mothers might use their maiden surnames, rather than the surnames of their spouses. Some of them may also be single parents who have never used any other surname.)

Jennifer Kim. Jennifer's grandparents came to the United States during the Korean War in 1952. Jennifer does not speak Korean but enjoys Korean foods. She also likes to visit her relatives who speak Korean and talk about what life was like in Korea.

Ask the class: "Why do you think Jennifer has an American, rather than a Korean, given name? Do you think Jennifer feels like a total American, or part Korean and part American? Why do you think she feels this way?"

Patrick O'Shea. Patrick's great-grandparents came to the United States from Ireland. He thinks of himself as both Irish and American—as an "Irish American."

Ask the class: "Why do you think Patrick feels more Irish than Susan feels German?"

Ito Matsuda. Ito was born in Japan and came to the United States when he was two years old. Ito speaks Japanese and English. He feels that he is both Japanese and American. At home, the Matsuda family usually eats Japanese, rather than American, food. Most of the time the Matsudas speak Japanese, rather than English, when talking to each other.

Ask the class: "Why do you think Ito is more Japanese than Jennifer is Korean?"

Wing Chu. Wing's family moved from China to the United States last year. Wing is still learning to speak English. Most of his family's friends are Chinese. He lives in a Chinese neighborhood.

Ask the class: "Do you think Wing feels Chinese and American, or Chinese? Why do you think he feels this way?"

Katherine Ann Shilenski. Katherine's grandparents came to the United States from Poland before her parents were born. Katherine does not speak Polish. She knows only a little about the Polish culture. She has often heard her parents talk about the problems of the people in Poland. Katherine is interested in learning more about the culture and language of her ancestors. She hopes to visit Poland someday.

Ask the class: "Why do you think Katherine feels more Polish than Susan feels German?"

Hoang Hy Vinh. Vinh came to the United States with his parents from Vietnam three years ago. Vinh's name is different in one important way from the names of his classmates. His surname (Hoang) is written first, his middle name (Hy) next, and his first or given name last (Vinh). Because of respect for him and his ancestors, the people in Vietnam would not address Vinh by his surname (Binh, 1975). Rather, they would call him "Vinh" or "Mr. Vinh." Point out to the class how Susan's, Jennifer's, Juan's, and Patrick's names, and most of their names, are written differently from Vinh's. Ask the students to write their names in the Vietnamese way and read them aloud.

Ask the class: "What problems do you think Vinh's teachers and classmates might have with his name? How do you think these problems make Vinh feel? If you moved to Vietnam and went to school, what do you think the teachers and students would call you? Why? How do you think this would make you feel?"

2. Tell the students to ask their parents to tell them the national origins of their surnames. End this unit by making a chart on butcher paper (or on the board) that shows each student's surname and the nation from which it came. Ask the children to tell as much as they can about the nations from which their surnames came, and whether their families eat foods, celebrate holidays, or have customs related to those nations. Second- and third-grade students can do research on these nations using a source such as *Britannica Junior.*

Note: Some children in your class might not be able to find out the nations from which their surnames came. It is difficult, for example, for many African Americans to find out the national origins of their surnames. In these cases, label their names *American* on the class chart and ask these students to tell what *American* customs their families practice.

Intermediate and Upper Grades

CONCEPT: Immigration

Generalization: Asian Americans immigrated to the United States to improve their economic conditions and to fulfill labor needs in Hawaii and in the continental United States.

1. Read to the class accounts that describe the early immigrations of Chinese, Japanese, and Filipinos to the United States (see bibliography at the end of this chapter for appropriate references).

Students should be able to answer the following questions when they have finished the readings:

    a. What economic, social, and political problems did the Chinese, Japanese, and Filipinos have in China, Japan, and the Philippines?

    b. What were the labor needs on the West Coast of the United States?

    c. Why did the immigrants leave China, Japan, and the Philippines?

    d. Was the United States what they expected? Why or why not?

2. Carefully study the historical summary on Filipino Americans in this chapter and read Chapter 9, "Dollar a Day, Dime a Dance: The Forgotten Filipinos," in Ronald Takaki (1989), *Strangers from a Different Shore: A History of Asian Americans*. Boston: Little, Brown. Prepare a two-page ditto summarizing the economic, social, and political conditions of the early Filipino immigrants who went to Hawaii and the United States. Assign this ditto to the students as a third reading.

3. After the students have read and discussed each of the three readings, have them complete Table 13-5.

4. When the students have completed the chart, have them summarize and generalize about why many Chinese, Japanese, and Filipinos immigrated to Hawaii and the United States, and about the labor needs they satisfied there.

5. Have the students role-play the situation below, which involves a representative of the Hawaiian Farmers Association trying to persuade a Filipino worker to go to Hawaii to work on a sugar plantation in 1910. After the role-play situation, ask the students the questions that follow. The role descriptions follow:

Mr. Howard Smith, the Hawaiian Sugar Planters Association Representative

Mr. Smith has been hired to recruit workers for the association. He realizes that his job depends on his success in recruiting workers. He also realizes that if he truthfully explains the situation in Hawaii, he will obtain few workers. He therefore decides to paint a rosy picture of the work on the sugar plantation in Hawaii. He explains to Mr. Ilanos that the contract is for three years and that the association will pay his transportation from the Philippines to Hawaii.

Table 13-5 DATA RETRIEVAL CHART ON ASIAN AMERICAN IMMIGRANTS

	Chinese Immigrants	Japanese Immigrants	Filipino Immigrants
Economic situation in homeland when immigration began			
Political situation in homeland when immigration began			
Social conditions in homeland when immigration began			
Labor needs on U.S. mainland when immigration began			
Labor needs in Hawaii when immigration began			

Mr. Jose Ilanos, a Filipino Who Lives in the Philippines

Mr. Ilanos is a young man with a wife and two children. He is a hard worker. However, in the last few years he has not been able to make enough money to support his family. He has heard about Mr. Smith and is interested in talking to him. However, his wife does not want him to leave the Philippines. Moreover, he has heard from friends that the work in Hawaii is hard and that the pay is rather low.

Questions

1. Did Mr. Smith succeed in persuading Mr. Ilanos to go to Hawaii to work? Why or why not?
2. If Mr. Ilanos decides to go to Hawaii, do you think that Mrs. Ilanos would go with him? Why or why not?
3. If Mr. Ilanos decides to go to Hawaii, what do you think will happen to him? Why? Do you think he might eventually immigrate to the United States? Why or why not?
4. If Mr. Ilanos decides to remain in the Philippines, what do you think will happen to him? Why?
5. Were there any other options open to Mr. Ilanos besides keeping his same job or going to Hawaii to work on the sugar plantations? If there were, what were they? If there were not, why?
6. If you were Mr. Ilanos would you have accepted a contract from Mr. Smith? Why or why not?

Valuing Activity

Read the following story to the class and ask the questions that follow.

Father and Son

Mr. Robert Morimoto is a second-generation Japanese American who lives in an upper-middle-class, predominantly White suburban community near Los Angeles. He is a successful businessman. Mr. Morimoto is proud to be an American and believes that even though our country has problems, any person, regardless of his or her race, can make it in the United States if he or she really tries. Mr. Morimoto does not like to talk about the years that he spent in the Heart Mountain federal concentration camp in Wyoming during World War II. The internment, he feels, is a thing of the past. Japanese Americans should not dwell on it too much today. Mr. Morimoto is impatient with those Sansei who talk about the internment all of the time. He feels that they have had it easy and do not have much right to criticize their country the way that they do.

Mr. Morimoto and his son have many fights because of their different beliefs. Henry is a student at a local university and is president of the Asian American Student Association on campus. Henry believes that the United States is a racist nation that oppresses all people of color, including the Japanese Americans. He often talks about the internment and harshly criticizes Japanese Americans like his father who try to "sweep it under the rug." Henry believes that all Third World people (by which he means all non-Whites) should join together to fight oppression and racism in America. When they had their last verbal fight, Henry told his father that even though he was successful in business, he had no political power in America, and was Yellow on the outside but was White on the inside. Mr. Morimoto became very upset with Henry. He told Henry that he would either have to start treating him with respect or move out of his house.

Questions

1. Why do you think Mr. Morimoto feels the way he does?
2. Why do you think Henry feels the way he does?
3. Do you think that Henry is treating Mr. Morimoto fairly?
4. Do you think that Mr. Morimoto is treating Henry fairly?
5. If you were Henry, what would you do? Why?
6. If you were Mr. Morimoto, what would you do? Why?

High School Grades

CONCEPT: Discrimination

Generalization: Asian Americans have been the victims of widespread prejudice and highly discriminatory immigration and migration laws.

Initiate this unit by showing the students a videotape about the internment such as *The Japanese Internment Cases*. This videotape tells the story of three Japanese American men who resisted the military order to be interned. After viewing the videotape, ask the students to write one-sentence reactions to it. Divide the class into groups of three to five to discuss their written reactions to the videotape. Each group should be asked to develop a written reaction, to be shared later with the entire class, on which all group members can agree.

1. Ask individual students or small groups of students to prepare short research reports on the following topics and present them to the class.

    a. The California Foreign Miner's Tax of 1850.

    b. Anti-Chinese riots that occurred in the 1800s.

    c. The Chinese Exclusion Act of 1882.

    d. Anti-Asian groups that developed on the West Coast in the late 1800s and continued through the 1930s, such as the Native Sons of the Golden West.

    e. The California Alien Land Laws that prohibited Japanese immigrants from owning or leasing land.

    f. The internment of Japanese Americans.

    g. The Immigration Act of 1924.

    h. Anti-Filipino riots that occurred in the 1920s and 1930s.

    i. The Tydings-McDuffie Act of 1934.

    j. The Repatriation Act of July 11, 1935.

2. When students share their reports, have them list on a master chart (a) ways in which all of the laws and actions were similar, (b) ways in which they were different, and (c) ways in which they discriminated against Asian Americans. Through the use of higher-level questions, help the students derive the key generalization stated previously.

3. Have your students role-play a session of Congress in which the Chinese Exclusion Act of 1882 is debated. The entire class can participate. However, assign several specific students to lead the debates. For example, ask one student to play the role of a California senator who is anxious to be reelected, and thus is strongly in favor of the act. Ask another student to argue against the act. Before the role-playing begins, read and discuss the act with the class. It is reprinted in Alexander Yamato, Soo-Young Chin, Wendy L. Ng, and Joel Franks (Eds.) (1993). *Asian Americans in the United States* (Vol. 1). Dubuque, Iowa: Kendall/Hunt Publishing, pp. 235–240.

When the main speakers start debating, the other class members can participate both by asking them questions and by arguing on the floor. When the discussion of the act is complete, the students should then vote on it. After the voting, the role-playing should be discussed, as well as the actual historical events. The students should discuss why their voting results were similar to or different from that of Congress in 1882 and why. In this activity, try to help the students to create the political and social atmosphere of the late 1800s. One way this can be done is to ask each student to pretend that he or she is a senator from a specific state with a particular mandate from his or her constituency.

4. Ask a group of students to do research and complete Table 13-6. After the students have completed the table, ask them to (a) write a generalization about the percentage of Asian immigrants that came to the United States between 1861 and 1960 and the total number of immigrants that came to the United States during this period; and (b) discuss, using the completed chart, whether White Americans on the West Coast had valid reasons to fear what was called the Yellow Peril. Ask them to discuss "If Whites on the West Coast had no valid reasons to fear a Yellow Peril, why do you think that Asian Americans were the victims of so much hostility and harassment?"

5. Ask the students to read a book on the internment. Recommended books are as follows:

- Yoshiko Uchida (1984). *Desert Exile: The Uprooting of a Japanese-American Family.* Seattle: University of Washington Press.
- Charles Kikuchi (1993). *The Kikuchi Diary: Chronicle from an American Concentration Camp.* Edited by John Modell. Urbana: University of Illinois Press.
- Deborah Gesensway and Mindy Roseman (1987). *Beyond Words: Images from America's Concentration Camps.* Ithaca, N.Y.: Cornell University Press. (Powerful art by artists who were interned.)

6. After they have read a book on the subject, ask them to do the following:

Table 13-6 ASIAN IMMIGRANTS IN THE UNITED STATES

Period	Number	Percentage of all Immigrants
1861–1880		
1881–1900		
1900–1914		
1914–1925		
1925–1940		
1940–1960		
1960–1970		
1970–1980		
1980–1990		

    a. Compare the interpretation of the internment in the book read with the interpretation in a high school American history textbook or some other source.

    b. Discuss why they think the internment occurred.

    c. Discuss the role of the Japanese American Citizenship League during the internment.

    d. Discuss the roles of the following men in the internment:

        (1) President Franklin D. Roosevelt

        (2) Secretary of War Henry L. Stimson

        (3) Lieutenant General John L. DeWitt

        (4) Assistant Secretary of War John J. McCloy

        (5) Colonel Karl R. Bendetsen

        (6) Major General Allen W. Gullion

    7. Role-play a meeting of the men listed above discussing whether the Japanese should be interned during World War II.

    8. Discuss the moral implications of the internment, that is: Should the internment have occurred? Why or why not? Who was responsible for the internment? What does the internment teach us about our society? Do you believe that an ethnic minority group cold be interned today? Why or why not? Why were the Japanese interned and not the Germans?

    9. Ask the students to review the hearing and testimony made before the Commission on Wartime Relocation and Internment of Civilians and to identify the factors

that resulted in the passage of the American Civil Liberties bill in 1988. The hearing and testimony are summarized in Report of the Commission on Wartime Relocation and Internment of Civilians (1982), *Personal Justice Denied.*

10. To summarize this activity, ask the students to write an *essay* on "The Meaning of the Internment—Then and Now."

11. Asian American authors, like other American writers, often express their reactions to and experiences with prejudice and discrimination in their writings. Literary works by Asian Americans can provide students with insights that cannot be gained from factual sources. To help your students understand better the reactions of Asian Americans to discrimination, have the class read and discuss selections from the following books:

    a. John Okada, *No-No Boy.* This is a powerful and well-crafted novel about a Japanese American who refused to fight in World War II.

    b. Carlos Bulosan, *America Is in the Heart.* This is a poignant, beautiful, and revealing book. It can serve as an excellent springboard for a discussion about anti-Filipino discrimination in the United States.

    c. Frank Chin et al., eds. *Aiiieeeee: An Anthology of Asian-American Writers.* This anthology includes stories, poetry, and excerpts from novels.

    d. Asian Women of California, *Making Waves: An Anthology of Writings by and about Asian Women.* Part 6 of this *excellent* anthology is called "Thunderstorms: Injustice." The readings provide first-hand accounts of the injustice experienced by Asian American women.

    e. Mine Okubo, *Citizen 13660.* An individual who was interned poignantly describes her experiences.

REFERENCES

Binh, D. T. (1975). *A Handbook for Teachers of Vietnamese Students: Hints for Dealing with Cultural Differences in Schools.* Arlington, Va.: Center for Applied Linguistics.

Butterfield, F. (1985, August 31). Violent Incidents against Asian-Americans Seen as Part of Racist Pattern. *New York Times* I, p. 8.

Chun-Hoon, L. K. Y. (1973). Teaching the Asian American Experience. In J. A. Banks (Ed.). *Teaching Ethnic Studies: Concepts and Strategies* (pp. 119–147). Washington, D.C.: National Council for the Social Studies.

Daniels, R. (1971). *Concentration Camps USA: Japanese Americans and World War II.* New York: Holt.

Daniels, R. (1988). *Asian America: Chinese and Japanese in the United States since 1850.* Seattle: University of Washington Press.

Divine, R. A. (1957). *American Immigration Policy, 1924–1952.* New Haven, Conn.: Yale University Press.

Espina, E. (1988). *Filipinos in Louisiana.* New Orleans: A. F. Laborde & Sons.

Horton, J. (1995). *The Politics of Diversity: Immigration, Resistance, and Change in Monterey Park, California.* Philadelphia: Temple University Press.

Jensen, R. (1980). East Indians. In S. Thernstrom, A. Orlov, & O. Handlin (Eds.). *Harvard Encyclopedia of American Ethnic Groups* (pp. 296–301). Cambridge: Harvard University Press.

Kim, B. C. (1978). *The Asian Americans: Changing Patterns, Changing Needs.* Montclair, N.J.: Association of Korean Christian Scholars in North America, Inc. [AKCS]

Kim, H. (1980). Koreans. In S. Thernstrom, A. Orlov, & O. Handlin (Eds.). *Harvard Encyclopedia of American Ethnic Groups* (pp. 601–606). Cambridge: Harvard University Press.

Kitano, H. H. L. (1976). *Japanese Americans: The Evolution of a Subculture* (2nd ed.). Englewood Cliffs, N.J.: Prentice-Hall.

Kitano, H. H. L. & Daniels, R. (1995). *Asian Americans: Emerging Minorities* (2nd ed).. Englewood Cliffs, N.J.: Prentice-Hall.

Lyman, S. M. (1970). *The Asian in the West.* Reno: Desert Research Institute.

McWilliams, C. (1943). *Brothers under the Skin.* Boston: Little, Brown.

Melendy, H. B. (1972). *The Oriental Americans.* New York: Hippocrene Books.

Petersen, W. (1966, January 6). Success Story, Japanese Style. *New York Times Magazine,* pp. 20 ff.

Petersen, W. (1971). *Japanese Americans.* New York: Random House.

Report of the Commission on Wartime Relocation and Internment of Civilians. (1982, December). *Personal Justice Denied.* Washington, D.C.: U.S. Government Printing Office.

San Juan, E., Jr. (1972). *Carlos Bulosan and the Imagination of the Class Struggle.* Quezon City: Philippines Press.

Takaki, R. (1989). *Strangers from a Different Shore: A History of Asian Americans.* Boston: Little, Brown.

U.S. Bureau of the Census. (1993a). *We, the American Foreign Born.* Washington, D.C.: U.S. Government Printing Office.

U.S. Bureau of the Census. (1993b). *We, the American Asians.* Washington, D.C.: U.S. Government Printing Office.

U.S. Bureau of the Census. (1994). *Statistical Abstract of the United States 1994* (114th ed). Washington, D.C.: U.S. Government Printing Office.

U.S. Immigration and Naturalization Service. (1985). *Statistical Yearbook of the Immigration and Naturalization Service, 1984.* Washington, D.C.: U.S. Government Printing Office.

U.S. Immigration and Naturalization Service. (1993). *Statistical Yearbook of the Immigration and Naturalization Service, 1992.* Washington, D.C.: U.S. Government Printing Office.

Wallovits, S. E. (1966). *The Filipinos in California.* Unpublished master's thesis, University of Southern California.

Wong, B. P. (1982). *Chinatown: Economic Adaptation and Ethnic Identity in Chinatown.* New York: Holt.

Wright, J. W. (Ed.). (1989). *The Universal Almanac 1990.* Kansas City: Andrews and McMeel.

ANNOTATED BIBLIOGRAPHY

Books for Teachers

Multiethnic

Aguilar-San Juan, K. (Ed.). (1994). *The State of Asian America: Activism and Resistance in the 1990s.* Boston: South End Press.

> *More than twenty writers contributed to this simulating and thoughtful collection of essays that focus on contemporary Asian American activism. Perceptive radical perspectives are provided on issues such as Asian Americans in the media, issues of identity, and feminism.*

Amerasia Journal. Published by the Asian American Studies Center, 3232 Campbell Hall, University of California, Los Angeles, CA 90024.

> *This scholarly journal publishes papers that deal with the experiences of Asians in the United States in both the past and present.*

Asian Women United of California. (Eds.). (1989). *Making Waves: An Anthology of Writings by and about Asian American Women.* Boston: Beacon Press.

> *This rich collection of works by and about Asian American women includes an informative introductory essay, "General Introduction: A Woman-Centered Perspective on Asian American History." The documents in this book are a rich teaching resource.*

Chan, S. (1991). *Asian Americans: An Interpretive History.* Boston: Twayne Publishers.

> *A perceptive, scholarly, and well-written history by a noted scholar in Asian American studies.*

Daniels, R. (1988). *Asian America: Chinese and Japanese in the United States since 1850.* Seattle: University of Washington Press.

> *This excellent and well-researched history of the Chinese and Japanese in the United States was written by a veteran scholar who has made many distinguished contributions to the scholarship on Asian Americans. It contains an excellent and comprehensive bibliography.*

Fu, D. (1995). *"My Trouble Is My English": Asian Students and the American Dream.* Portsmouth, N.H.: Heinemann.

> *This ethnographic study examines the learning experiences of four Laotian students in a secondary school. The author's findings have implications for teaching all Asian immigrant students.*

Gall, S. B & Gall, T. L. (Ed.). (1993). *Statistical Record of Asian Americans.* Detroit: Gale Research.

> *A massive (796 pages) statistical volume on Asian Americans that covers a myriad of topics and resources.*

Geok-Lin Lim, S. & Ling, A. (Eds.). (1992). *Reading the Literature of Asian America.* Philadelphia: Temple University Press.

> *An important and informative collection of essays.*

Hamamoto, D. Y. (1994). *Monitored Peril: Asian Americans and the Politics of TV Representation.* Minneapolis: University of Minnesota Press.

A scholarly study of the representation of Asian Americans in the media. The author examines selected television programs from the 1950s to the present.

Hing, B. O. (1993). *Making and Remaking Asian America through Immigration Policy 1850–1990.* Stanford, Calif.: Stanford University Press.

A scholarly treatment of an important topic.

Hongo, G. (Ed.). (1993). *The Open Boat: Poems from Asia America.* New York: Doubleday Anchor.

A valuable and comprehensive collection that is an excellent teaching resource.

Hongo, G. (Ed.). (1995). *Under Western Eyes: Personal Essays from Asian America.* New York: Doubleday.

Fifteen Asian American voices address difficult social and political issues in this anthology.

Houston, V. H. (Ed.). (1993). *The Politics of Life: Four Plays by Asian American Women.* Philadelphia: Temple University Press.

An important collection for teaching the language arts and the social studies.

Kitano, H. H. L. & Daniels, R. (1995). *Asian Americans: Emerging Minorities* (2nd. ed.). Englewood Cliffs, N.J.: Prentice-Hall.

This book consists of easy-to-read, brief historical overviews of the major Asian groups in the United States, including the Chinese, Japanese, Filipinos, Asian Indians, Koreans, Pacific Islanders, and Southeast Asians.

Min, P. G. (Ed.). (1995). *Asian Americans: Contemporary Trends and Issues.* Thousands Oaks, Calif.: Sage Publications.

This book consists of a comprehensive collection of scholarly articles on the diverse Asian Americans groups. It is an excellent and informative resource.

Nakanishi, D. (1995). Asian Pacific Americans and Colleges and Universities. In J. A. Banks & C. A. M. Banks (Eds.). *Handbook of Research on Multicultural Education* (pp. 683–695). New York: Macmillan.

Complex issues related to Asian Americans and higher education, such as whether universities have hidden quotas for Asian American students, are analyzed and documented in this comprehensive overview of the issues.

Nakanishi, D. & Nishida, T. Y. (Eds.). (1995). *The Asian American Educational Experience.* New York: Routledge.

An excellent comprehensive and informative collection of articles about educational issues, problems, and possibilities facing Asian Americans.

Ng, W. L., Soo-Young, C., Moy, J. S., & Okihiro, G. Y. (Eds.). (1995). *Reviewing Asian America: Locating Diversity.* Pullman: Washington State University Press.

This is a valuable collection of scholarly essays.

Okihiro, G. Y. (1994). *Margins and Mainstreams: Asians in American History and Culture.* Seattle: University of Washington Press.

In this perceptive and lucid history, the author argues that the nation's people of color, because of their resistance to oppression and push for freedom, have kept American democratic ideals alive.

Pang, V. O. (1995). Asian Pacific American Students: A Diverse and Complex Population. In J. A. Banks & C. A. M. Banks (Eds.). *Handbook of Research on Multicultural Education* (pp. 412–424). New York: Macmillan.

A veteran teacher educator reviews the research about and gives helpful information for teaching Asian American students.

Takaki, R. (1989). *Strangers from a Different Shore: A History of Asian Americans.* Boston: Little, Brown.

This is the best general history of Asians in the United States. Written by a veteran scholar in ethnic studies, it is comprehensive in the groups included and is extremely well written. The author interlaces stories of people with major historical events in describing the saga of the Asians in the United States.

Uba, L. (1994). *Asian Americans: Personality, Patterns, Identity and Mental Health.* New York: The Guilford Press.

A comprehensive and scholarly review of research on Asian Americans.

Watanabe, S. & Bruchac, C. (Eds.). (1990). *Home to Stay: Asian American Women's Fiction.* Greenfield Center, N.Y.: The Greenfield Review Press. (P.O. Box 308, 2 Middle Grove Road, Greenfield Center, NY 12833)

Well-known as well as less well known writers are included in this anthology. Writings by Maxine Hong Kingston and Amy Tan are represented.

Wei, W. (1993). *The Asian American Movement.* Philadelphia: Temple University Press.

A scholarly analysis of the rise and development of the Asian American movement. This movement was the major force for the development of Asian American studies programs and courses and for new scholarship on Asian Americans.

Wong, Sau-Ling C. (1993). *Reading Asian American Literature: From Necessity to Extravagance.* Princeton, N.J.: Princeton University Press.

An important and informative scholarly work on Asian American literature.

Yamato, A., Chin, S.-Y., Ng, W. L., & Franks, J. (Eds.). (1993). *Asian Americans in the United States* (Vols. 1 & 2). Dubuque, Ia.: Kendall-Hunt.

This excellent two-volume documentary history includes original sources written by both Asians and non-Asians that deal with the experiences of Asian Americans in the United States.

Chinese Americans

Chen, H.-S. (1992). *Chinatown No More: Taiwan Immigrants in Contemporary New York:* Ithaca, N.Y.: Cornell University Press.

An informative and important scholarly study.

Hom, M. K. (1987). *Songs of Gold Mountain: Cantonese Rhymes from San Francisco Chinatown.* Berkeley: University of California Press.

A seventy-page, detailed introduction is provided to these historically revealing songs. They are in both English and Cantonese.

Horton, J. (1995). *The Politics of Diversity: Immigration, Resistance, and Change in Monterey Park, California.* Philadelphia: Temple University Press.

A scholarly study of the "Chinese Beverly Hills," Monterey Park, a Los Angeles suburb. An important study of a Chinese American suburban community.

McClain, C. J. (1994). *In Search of Equality: The Chinese Struggle against Discrimination in Nineteenth-Century America.* Berkeley: University of California Press.

An important scholarly study of the Chinese efforts to fight government-sponsored discrimination.

See, L. (1995). *On Gold Mountain: The One-Hundred Year Odyssey of a Chinese-American Family.* New York: St. Martin's Press.

The author constructs the story of her family, and in the process, that of the Chinese in America. When she was a child she spent summers in Los Angeles's Chinatown, where she heard the stories of her family.

Tsai, S. H. (1986). *The Chinese Experience in America.* Bloomington: Indiana University Press.

A scholarly chronological history of the Chinese in the United States that includes a chapter on "Contemporary Chinese-American Society." Among the topics discussed are Chinese immigrants since 1965 and Chinese women in a changing American society.

Yung, J. (1986). *Chinese Women in American Society: A Pictorial History.* Seattle: University of Washington Press.

This informative pictorial history reveals, through photographs and an interesting text, the sojourn of Chinese women in the United States from 1834 to the 1980s.

Zhou, M. (1992). *Chinatown: The Socioeconomic Potential of an Urban Experience.* Philadelphia: Temple University Press.

This significant scholarly study provides important insights on the Chinese American experience.

Japanese Americans

Chang, T. (1991). *"I Can Never Forget": Men of the 100th/442nd.* Honolulu: Sigi Productions, Inc.

An illustrated history of the decorated Japanese American military unit that served bravely in World War II.

Daniels, R. (1993). *Prisoners without Trial: Japanese Americans in World War II.* New York: Hill and Wang.

A leading historian of the subject provides a perceptive synthesis of the most recent scholarship on the internment of Japanese Americans.

Fugita, S. S. & O'Brien, D. J. (1991). *Japanese American Ethnicity: The Persistence of Community.* Seattle: University of Washington Press.

The author examines why the Japanese Americans have maintained their ethnicity even though they have attained high levels of economic and educational success.

Gesensway, D. & Roseman, M. (1987). *Beyond Words: Images from America's Concentration Camps*. Ithaca, N.Y.: Cornell University Press.

This powerful and interesting book contains a text with the words of artists who were interned as well as their paintings. Highly recommended.

Glenn, E. N. (1986). *Issei, Nisei, War Bride: Three Generations of Japanese American Women in Domestic Service*. Philadelphia: Temple University Press.

This book is divided into three parts: roots, work, and family.

Hatamiya, L. T. (1993). *Righting a Wrong: Japanese Americans and the Passage of the Civil Liberties Act of 1988*. Stanford, Calif.: Stanford University Press.

This study examines the political and institutional factors that led to the passage of the Civil Liberties Act of 1988.

Kikuchi, C. (1993). *The Kikuchi Diary: Chronicle from an American Concentration Camp*. J. Modell (Ed.). Urbana: University of Illinois Press.

This view from the inside of an internment camp is an excellent and rich teaching resource.

Kimura, Y. (1988). *Issei: Japanese Immigrants in Hawaii*. Honolulu: University Press of Hawaii.

A scholarly historical study of the Issei in Hawaii.

Nakano, M. (1990). *Japanese American Women: Three Generations*. Berkeley, Calif.: Mina Press Publishing.

A historical account of the Issei women and their daughters and granddaughters.

O'Brien, D. J. & Fugita, S. S. (1991). *The Japanese American Experience*. Bloomington: Indiana University Press.

A concise and informative history of the Japanese American experience.

Takaki, R. (1995). *Hiroshima: Why America Dropped the Atomic Bomb*. New York: Little, Brown.

An eminent historian of the Asian American and American experience provides new insights and perspectives on the bombing of Hiroshima. He states that racism was a major cause.

Takezawa, Y. I. (1995). *Breaking the Silence: Redress and Japanese Americans Ethnicity*. Ithaca, N.Y.: Cornell University Press.

This study examines how the internment and the movement for redress affected Japanese Americans.

Tamura, L. (1993). *The Hood River Issei: An Oral History of Japanese Settlers in Oregon's Hood River Valley*. Urbana: University of Illinois Press.

An important scholarly historical study. It is richly textured and informative.

Tamura, E. H. (1994). *Americanization, Acculturation, and Ethnic Identity: The Nisei Generation in Hawaii.* Urbana: University of Illinois Press.

An informative scholarly study of the struggles and triumphs of the Nisei in Hawaii.

Taylor, S. C. (1993). *Jewel of the Desert: Japanese American Internment at Topaz.* Berkeley: University of California Press.

A scholarly study of the Japanese Americans who were interned at Topaz.

Filipino Americans

Agoncillo, T. (1975). *A Short History of the Philippines.* New York: New American Library.

An honest account of Philippine history.

Brainard, C. (1991). *Philippine Women in America.* Quezon City (Philippines): New Day Publishers.

An informative account of the experience of Filipino women in the United States.

Bulosan, C. (1973). *America Is in the Heart.* Seattle: University of Washington Press.

This is a powerful and extremely well written personal history by one of the most talented modern American writers.

Carino, B. V. (1990). *The New Filipino Immigrants to the U.S.* Honolulu: East West Population Institute.

Contains information that teachers will find helpful for teaching about the experiences of Filipinos in the United States.

Castilla, G. S. (1995). *Struggles from Both Shores.* Kirkland, Wash.: PaperWorks. (P.O. Box 2851, Kirkland, WA 98083-2851)

A collection of essays by a perceptive journalist that deals with issues both in the Philippines and the United States.

Cordova, F. (1983). *Filipinos: Forgotten Asian Americans.* Dubuque, Ia.: Kendall/ Hunt.

This interesting and informative book on the Filipino saga in the United States is based on oral history interviews and includes a gold mine of photographs that can be used to teach effectively about Filipinos in the United States.

De Castro, S. (1994). Identity in Action: A Filipino American's Perspective. In K. Aguilar-San Juan (Ed.). *The State of Asian America: Activism and Resistance in the 1990s* (pp. 295–320). Boston: South End Press.

A simulating and thoughtful essay.

Espina, M. (1988). *Filipinos in Louisiana.* New Orleans: A. F. Laborde & Sons.

A pioneering book that traces the early Filipino presence in Louisiana.

Filipinas Magazine. Published by Filipinas Publishing, Inc., 655 Sutter St., Suite 333, San Francisco, CA 94102.

A readable magazine that presents both the Philippine and Filipino American perspective on social, cultural, economic, and political issues.

Karnow, S. (1989). *In Our Image: America's Empire in the Philippines.* New York: Ballantine Books.

Written in a story-like manner, this book provides insight into the complex relationship and historical connection between the United States and the Philippines.

Rafael, V. L. (Ed.). (1995). *Discrepant Histories: Translocal Essays on Filipino Cultures.* Philadelphia: Temple University Press.

This collection includes an essay on "Filipinos in the United States and Their Literature of Exile."

Reed, R., Kaus, D., & Parker, D. (Eds.). (1993) *Finding Your Filipino American Roots: A Guide to Researching Your Ethnic American Culture Heritage.* San Jose, Calif.: RNA Publishers.

A useful guide for doing family history projects.

San Juan, E., Jr. (Ed.). (1983). *If You Want to Know What We Are: A Carlos Bulosan Reader.* Minneapolis: West End Press.

Essays, poetry, and short stories by the noted author are included in this anthology.

San Juan, E., Jr. (Ed.). (1995). *On Becoming Filipino: Selected Writings on Carlos Bulosan.* Philadelphia: Temple University Press.

Stories, essays, poems and correspondence are included in this anthology.

Books for Students

Multiethnic

Chiu, C. (1996). *Lives of Notable Asian Americans: Literature and Education.* New York: Chelsea House.

This book is illustrated with photographs. It is part of the "Asian American Experience" Series. (Intermediate and Up)

Hong, M. (Ed.). (1993). *Growing Up Asian American.* New York: William Morrow.

Thirty-two classic stories by new and established writers. (High School)

Lee, J. F. J. (1991). *Asian Americans: Oral Histories of First to Fourth Generation Americans from China, the Philippines, Japan, India, the Pacific Islands, Vietnam and Cambodia.* New York: The New Press.

These oral histories are a rich and informative source. (High School)

Morey, J. N. & Dunn, W. (1992). *Famous Asian Americans.* New York: Cobblehill Books.

This book examines the lives and contributions of fourteen Asian Americans from different ethnic groups. (Middle School and Up)

Chinese Americans

Chin, K. (1995). *Sam and the Lucky Money*. Illustrated by C. Van Wright & Y. Hu. New York: Lee & Low Books.

This is the story of a young boy who receives lucky money in red envelopes to celebrate the Chinese New Year. When he goes shopping in Chinatown he realizes he does not have enough money, but a stranger teaches him to appreciate his gift. (Primary)

Chin-Lee, C. (1993). *Almond Cookies and Dragon Well Tea*. Illustrated by Y. S. Tang. Chicago: Polychrome Books.

Erica, a young White girl, visits her friend Nancy's house. Nancy is Chinese American. Erica learns a lot about Chinese culture during her visit. (Primary)

Hoobler, D. & Hoobler, T. (1994). *The Chinese American Family Album*. New York: Oxford University Press.

An excellent, involving, and well-illustrated book. (Middle School/High School)

Namioka, L. (1995). *Yang the Third and Her Impossible Family*. Illustrated by K. de Kiefte. New York: Little, Brown.

This is the story of a Chinese American teenager trying to be "American." She changes her name to Mary and does other things to be accepted as "American," yet she feels that her family will not cooperate. (Intermediate)

Nunes, S. M. (1995). *The Last Dragon*. Illustrated by C. K. Soentpiet. New York: Clarion.

A young boy sees a dragon in the Lung Fung Trading Co. and wants to bring it to life because his aunt states that it looks tired. With his aunt's help he is successful and turns his summer in Chinatown into an exciting one. (Primary).

Waters, K. & Slovenz-Low, M. (1990). *Lion Dancer: Ernie Wan's Chinese New Year*. New York: Scholastic.

This book describes six-year-old Ernie Wan's life as he prepares for his first Lion's Dance performance. (Primary)

Yep, L. (1991). *The Lost Garden*. Englewood Cliffs, N.J.: Julian Messner.

The author examines his life as a Chinese American boy. (High School)

Yep, L. (1993). *Dragon's Gate*. New York: Harper.

A Chinese immigrant in San Francisco's Chinatown and fellow immigrants board a machine that changes his life. A thrilling adventure story. Winner of the Newbery Medal for 1994. (Middle School)

Yep, L. (1995). *Later, Gator*. New York: Hyperion Books for Children.

A humorous and charming story about two brothers growing up in Chinatown. (Intermediate)

Yep, L. (1995). *Thief of Hearts*. New York: HarperCollins.

A sequel to the author's popular Child of the Owl. *A story about Stacy, a Chinese American girl, who is torn between her Chinese and American cultures.*

Japanese Americans

Hamanaka, S. (1990). *The Journey: Japanese Americans, Racism and Renewal.* New York: Orchard Books.

The author painted a five-panel mural showing her family in the United States during the internment. The picture is a bleak one. However, the last panel depicts hope. (Intermediate and Up)

Hobbler, D. & Hoobler, T. (1995). *The Japanese American Family Album.* New York: Oxford University Press.

A well-illustrated, informative, and captivating book. (Middle School/High School)

Japanese American Curriculum Project. (1985). *The Japanese American Journey.* San Mateo, Calif.: AACP.

Historical and biographical essays are included in this excellent resource book for students in grade 5 through 8. It also includes three well-crafted short stories. (Intermediate/Middle School)

Kitano, H. H. L. (1995). *The Japanese Americans* (2nd ed.). New York: Chelsa House.

One of the books in "The Immigrant Experience Series." (Intermediate/Middle)

Leathers, N. L. (1991). *The Japanese in America.* Minneapolis: Lerner.

An informative historical account of the Japanese experience in the United States. Illustrated with photographs. (Intermediate)

Kessler, L. (1994). *Stubborn Twig: Three Generations in the Life of a Japanese American Family.* New York: Plume (Penguin Group).

The story of three generations of one Japanese American family is told in this book. (High School)

Minatoya, L. Y. (1992). *Talking to High Monks in the Snow: An Asian American Odyssey.* New York: HarperCollins.

This is the autobiographical account of a Japanese American woman and her quest for ethnic identity. (High School)

Mura, D. (1991). *Turning Japanese: Memoirs of a Sansei.* New York: Atlantic Monthly Press.

This is the author's account of his first trip to Japan as an adult. (High School)

Smith, P. (1995). *Democracy on Trial: The Japanese American Evacuation and Relocation in World War II.* New York: Simon & Schuster.

A veteran and widely published historian describes the events and people involved in the internment of the Japanese during World War II. Thorough, comprehensive, and sobering. (Advanced High School)

Uchida, Y. (1982). *Desert Exile: The Uprooting of a Japanese American Family.* Seattle: University of Washington Press.

A well-known writer tells the personal story of the internment of her family during World War II in this moving and powerful book. (High School)

Uchida, Y. (1985). *The Happiest Ending.* New York: Atheneum.

Rinko Tsujimura learns a valuable lesson when she rejects arranged marriages and tries to bring two people together who she thinks would make the perfect couple. (Intermediate). Other books by Uchida include The Best Bad Thing *(Atheneum, 1983);* A Jar of Dreams *(Atheneum, 1982); and* Journey to Topaz *(Atheneum, 1985).*

Uchida, Y. (1993). *The Magic Purse.* Illustrated by K. Narahashi. New York: Margaret McEldery Books.

A folktale from Japan about a poor farmer who wins a fortune because he is kind and courageous. (Primary)

Uchida, Y. (1994). *The Wise Old Woman.* Illustrated by M. Spingett. New York: Margaret McEldery Books.

A folktale from Japan about a cruel young lord who orders that everyone over age seventy be taken to the mountains and left to die. (Primary)

Westridge Young Writers Workshop. (1994). *Kids Explore America's Japanese American Heritage.* Santa Fe, N.M.: John Muir Publications.

Written by children, this book describes various aspects of the Japanese American experience including recipes, family stories, and biographies. (Intermediate)

Yep, L. (1995). *Hiroshima: A Novella.* New York: Scholastic.

Twelve-year-old Sachi and her older sister Riko are walking through the streets when the Enola Gay *drops a bomb. Sachi will never see her sister again. Based on a true-life account of survivors of the Hiroshima bombing. A powerful book that should be used with care. (Middle School and Up)*

Filipino Americans

Bandon, A. (1993). *Filipino Americans.* Morristown, N.J.: Silver Burdett Press.

An engaging book for young adults about Filipinos immigrating to the United States. (Middle School)

Brainard, C. M. (Ed.). (1993). *Fiction by Filipinos in America.* Quezon City: New Day Publishers.

A comprehensive literary collection by twenty-three Filipino American authors. (High School)

Daniels, R. (1990). *Filipino Americans.* New York: Franklin Watts.

A sixty-four-page illustrated book by an eminent historian. (Upper)

Espiritu, Y. L. (1995). *Filipino American Lives.* Philadelphia: Temple University Press.

An informative collection of firs-person narratives. Pre- and post-1965 immigrants share their sojourns in the United States. (High School)

Stern, J. (1989). *The Filipino Americans*. New York: Chelsea House.

This 110-page history of the Filipinos in the United States is illustrated with color and black-and-white photographs. (Middle School and Up)

Stern, J. (1990). *The Filipino Americans*. New York: Chelsea House.

An illustrated history of Filipino Americans for young readers. (Intermediate)

Takaki, R. (1994). *In the Heart of Filipino America: Immigrants from the Pacific Isles.* New York: Chelsea House.

An informative and well-illustrated history. (Intermediate and Up)

ARAB AMERICANS

CONCEPTS AND MATERIALS

Acquire Knowledge. It enables its possessor to distinguish right from wrong; it lights the way to heaven, it is our friend in the desert, our society in solitude, our compassion when friendless; it guides us to happiness; it sustains us in misery; it is an ornament amongst friends, and an armor against enemies.

Prophet Muhammad, Hadith (Adapted from *Al-Ghazaly Minaret Newsletter*)

With the exception of Arab Americans themselves, the typical citizen of the United States has been exposed to little information that provides humanistic and realistic insight into the identity of the Arab peoples. Shaped by a lack of multicultural education and a prejudicial, uninstructed film industry and print and television media, American perceptions about Arabs range from the overly romanticized to the harmfully negative. Quoting from W. Thesiger's *Arabian Sands*, Salah (1979) provides an example of a romantic image of Arabs, based on the desert bedouin: "I shall always remember how often I was humbled by those illiterate herdsmen, who possessed, in so much greater than I, generosity and courage, endurance, patience, and light-hearted gallantry. Among no other people have I felt the same sense of personal inferiority" (p. xiii). Although Thesiger's description captures a

This chapter was written by Patty Adeed and G. Pritchy Smith and is reprinted with permission of the publisher from: Carl A. Grant (Ed.) (1995). *Educating for Diversity: An Anthology of Multicultural Voices* (pp. 191–207). Boston: Allyn and Bacon.

The Annotated Bibliography at the end of this chapter was prepared by James A. Banks.

measure of the bedouins' nobility, it is also an image (like some of the romanticized images in such films as *Lawrence of Arabia*) that leaves uninformed Americans with incomplete and inaccurate perceptions about Arabs. Apart from their potential for being offensive and sometimes insulting, romantic images of Arabs, however, do seem somewhat harmful, and fewer in number, than the many negative images of Arabs that abound in the larger U.S. society.

Many Americans narrowly stereotype Arabs as greedy billionaires, corrupt sheiks, terrorists, desert nomads, camel-riding chieftains, slave traders, oil blackmailers, sex maniacs, harem girls, enslaved maidens, belly dancers, and veiled women. Arabs are often described as barbaric, uncultured, uneducated, committed to a religion dedicated to war, quick to torture and behead, and responsible for the conflict with Israel. Shaheen (1984) cited Shelly Slade's 1980 poll, for example, to illustrate that the American public perceives Arabs as "anti-American," "anti-Christian," "cunning," and "war-like," while having little or no knowledge of the Arab peoples' rich heritage and accomplishments. Unfortunately, the 1990s have brought little change in the way Arabs are perceived or depicted. Inspired by romanticism or prejudice, the Arab caricature in the United States continues to be dehumanizing and continues to deprive the Arab Americans of deserved respect and ethnic pride.

Despite—indeed, perhaps because of—the continuation of negative Arab images, a countertrend to dispel misconceptions about Arabs arose during the 1980s and continues today. This trend to combat defamation of both Arabs and Arab Americans has been regularly influenced by a number of factors. Increasing numbers and visibility of Arab immigrants, and the rapidly expanding economic and political relations between the United States and the Arab World, for example, have sparked a much-delayed interest in Arab Americans and their counterparts abroad. Educated immigrants, as well as foreign students in colleges and universities, have played an important part in the political and cultural revival of the Arab American communities and the revitalization of the doctrines and traditions of Islam. Furthermore, the Iran hostage situation, the war between Iraq and Iran, Suddam Hussein's invasion of Kuwait, the Israeli Palestinian conflict, the Russian occupation of Afghanistan, civil wars in Lebanon between Christians and Muslims, oil boycotts, and the control of the major natural resources of the area have magnified the need for the American educational system to present accurate information about Middle Eastern cultures.

WHO ARE THE ARAB AMERICANS?

Arab Americans are citizens or residents of the United States who are immigrants or descendants of immigrants who came to the United States primarily from the countries that constitute the present Arab World—Syria, Lebanon,

Jordan, Saudi Arabia, Iraq, Kuwait, Egypt, Libya, Algeria, Tunisia, Morocco, Oman, Yemen, Bahrain, Qatar, United Arab Emirates, and the newly declared Palestinian state. Thus, Arab Americans are extremely diverse with regard to their country of origin, the beginning of their family ancestry in America, and their religion. A study by Zogby (1990) indicates, however, that most Arabic-speaking Americans are descendants of Lebanese immigrants, and that 90 percent are Arab Christians.

Many Arab Americans trace their family ancestry in America to the 1890–1940 wave of Arab immigrants who were primarily from Lebanon and Syria. Others trace the family beginnings in America to the early post–World War II wave of Arab immigrants who were predominantly Muslim and hailed from various independent Arab states. Other Arab Americans trace their ancestry to the wave of Palestinian immigration that followed the Palestinian Israeli wars. Still others trace their Arab American ancestry to none of these well-known waves of immigration.

Because Islam is the predominant religion of the larger Middle East and the smaller geographical region known as the present Arab World, many uninformed, non–Arab Americans erroneously consider the term *Arab* to be synonymous with *Muslim;* but these are not interchangeable terms. In the present Arab World, an Arab is a person whose native tongue is Arabic and who lives by Arab cultural traditions and values. A Muslim is an adherent of the religion Islam and may or may not be Arab. Thus, whereas all Arab Americans do possess Arab ancestry and heritage, they nevertheless reflect considerable religious diversity among their numbers.

Religious diversity is characteristic of both the Arab World and the Arab American population. Although it is true that Islam is the religion of the majority of Arabs in the Arab countries, as Shabbas and Al-Qazzaz (1989) noted, many Americans are often surprised to learn that of the 190 million Arabs living in Arab countries (including North Africa), nearly 14 million are Christians and 10,000 are Jews. Arab Christians comprise the Catholic, Orthodox (Greek and Roman), and Protestant sects and believe in the *dual* nature of Christ. Other Arab Christians are loyal to either the Assyrian Church of the East, the Coptic Orthodox, the Syrian Orthodox, or the Armenian Orthodox, and believe in the *singular* nature of Christ. The Greek Orthodox who do not recognize papal supremacy are also known as United or Eastern Rite Catholics. The vast majority of Arab Americans are Christians, whereas the preponderance of Arabs in the Arab World countries are Muslims. It is significant to note, however, that Arab Muslims are increasing in number among recent immigrant populations. It is also significant to note that Islam is (after Christianity) the second largest religious group in the United States. In fact it is estimated that the United States has 6 million Muslims who worship in approximately 800 mosques throughout the country. Some of these 6 million people are Arab Americans, but the majority are Muslims of non-Arab ancestry with their origins in such countries as Indonesia, Pakistan, India, Bangladesh, Russia, China, Malaysia, Iran, Turkey, Afghanistan, and numerous nations on the African continent.

Arab Americans live throughout the United States, but Zogby (1990) noted that the Northeast remains the geographical location where most Arab Americans reside. The Detroit-Dearborn area boasts the largest Arab American community, with approximately 250,000. Michigan (Arab population of 250,000), New York (Arab population of 250,000), and California (Arab population of 350,000) feature the largest and perhaps the most visible Arab American communities. Massachusetts has one of the largest percentages of Lebanese, and Rhode Island has one of the highest percentages of Syrians.

To understand and appreciate the Arab American, one must remember that Western civilization owes a large measure of its heritage to the Arab World of the past. One must also remember that people of Arab descent have made modern contributions in almost every field of endeavor. In truth, the impact of the Arab American's presence has never been greater, and the reality of what is observed does not fit the stereotypes harbored by many Americans. Most Americans should, for example, readily recognize the names of Arab Americans such as John Sununu, former White House Chief of Staff; George Mitchell, U.S. Senate Majority Leader; Doug Flutie, former professional football player; Rony Seikaly, professional basketball player; Abe Gibron, Chicago Bears coach; Casey Kasem, Paula Abdul, and Paul Anka, music entertainers; Marlo Thomas and Jamie Farr, television entertainers; the late Danny Thomas, entertainer and founder of St. Jude's Hospital (recognized for research on and treatment of children afflicted with cancer and leukemia); Helen Thomas, senior White House correspondent and United Press International journalist; Najeeb Halaby, former head of the Federal Aviation Administration, holder of the aviation record for the first transcontinental solo jet flight across the United States, journalist, and father of Lisa Halaby, Queen Noor of Jordan; Vance Bourjaily, prominent novelist and author of *The Man Who Knew Kennedy;* Jim Haggar, founder and CEO of Haggar Slacks and Co.; Emile Khouri, creator of the Disneyland architectural conception; Dr. Michael DeBakey, pioneer heart surgeon and inventor of the heart-lung bypass pump; Candy Lightner, founder of Mothers Against Drunk Drivers (MADD); Christine McAuliffe, first teacher in space and one of the seven crew members who died aboard the shuttle *Challenger;* and Ralph Nader, consumer advocate.

For years, Arabs were ignored by Americans. In the fall of 1973, however, when Arab states cut back oil production while at the same time the Organization of Petroleum Exporting Countries (OPEC) raised oil prices sharply, Americans for the first time had great reason to think about the Arab World and the millions of Arab Americans, both American born and foreign born. As the U.S. economy suffered and worldwide panic evolved, it was realized by many that a bridge between Americans, Arab Americans, and the Arab World was essential. Subsequent events of international significance, particularly the U.S. military action against Iraq in 1991, brought this realization into greater focus. The American people began a struggle to recognize and understand their newest, and one of their fastest-growing, ethnic groups. Establishment of Arab organizations to preserve Old World traditions and combat negative stereotyping and gross misconceptions grew in number. These groups established positive roles through which to help build an ethnic identity for Arab Americans and laid a foundation for a bridge of acceptance, understanding, and respect between Americans, Arab Americans, and the peoples of the Arab World.

The following sections seek to further answer the question: Who are Arab Americans? Understanding Arab Americans requires an examination of their unique heritage of history and culture, both ancient and modern. The discussion in the first section centers on the Arab World and includes a discussion of the modern Arab World with emphasis on education, social life, and the effects of modernization on selected Arab traditions. The second section discusses Arab immigration to the United States. This section also presents the effects of acculturation and assimilation on people of Arab descent in America. The final section features educational implications.

THE MODERN ARAB WORLD: AN ERA OF POLITICAL, ECONOMIC, EDUCATIONAL, AND SOCIAL CHANGES

The nineteenth and twentieth centuries brought new changes that impacted the Arab World's political and economic status, educational systems, and social life. Political and economic changes were influenced greatly by foreign interference and the internal dynamics of the evolving, present-day Middle East countries. In the midnineteenth century, European colonial powers began to gain economic power in the Middle East and undermine the control and the power of the Ottoman Empire. The impact of the West, in fact, influenced all of Syria, and most notably Mount Lebanon. The positive focus by the European powers on the Christian sects eventually led to an even more pronounced division between the Muslims and Christians.

By the end of World War I, Arab agitation for independence broke out in a revolt against the Turks. In 1918, France and Britain designated boundaries of political control over Arab lands, thus ending the rule of the Ottoman Empire and adding yet another piece to the mosaic of the Arab culture. During the ensuing period of European rule, the Arab World was faced with requests for the reform of Islamic law. Some of these reforms centered on equality for both Muslims and non-Muslims, both males and females. Many modernistic attempts to reformulate the interpretations of Islam were being addressed in ways that would make it responsive and acceptable to modern life. Later, numerous Arab sectors resisted the European domination and again began their struggles for independence.

In 1948, lasting and devastating effects of the Jewish holocaust influenced the British to play a key role in the creation of a Jewish state in Palestine, causing the exile of thousands of Arab Palestinians from their homeland. When people view the Arabs as the source of conflict between the Israelis and Palestinians, it is wise to reflect back on their history of religious tolerance and to remember that the Israelis exiled the Palestinians from a homeland where Jews and Arabs (many of whom were Christians rather than Muslims) were already living and sharing. The final conquest of Jerusalem by the Israelis in 1967 caused again the exile of thousands of Palestinians and further confused feelings of allegiance by many for both the Israelis *and* the Palestinians. The Palestinians and the Israelis have *both* suffered great human losses; and to the outsiders, both often seem guilty of wrongdoing and killing one another. In their historical quest for the right to a homeland, each continues to express perceived legitimate grievances through methods deemed illegitimate by the other. Presently, no solution seems plausible for either the Israelis or the Palestinians, and the possibility of an international state to be recognized as a holy place for Judaism, Christianity, and Islam has not been eagerly received by most Israelis and Arabs.

Since World War II, the modern Arab World has experienced many other changes. The desire for Arab nationalism, social justice, acquisition of education, and closer unity has been prevalent throughout the Arab countries. Economic growth has been rapid due to oil resources. Resentment toward colonial policies, and a growing sense of national solidarity, have led to widespread appeals for Arab independence—the latter followed by revolts, riots, and wars. The death of Egyptian President al-Nasir weakened the illusions of independence but also gave birth to many Arab organizations that helped the Arab countries to grow closer; it generated a kind of solidarity, a feeling that there *was* such a thing as an Arab nation in the making.

With the end of British and French political dominance, the influence of the United States increased but carried with it both benefits and costs—particularly during the Suez conflict in 1956, the peace talks between Egypt and Israel in 1978, and various military conflicts in more recent times. The Arab World continues to find itself limited with respect to military power and to experience disunity due to separate interests and economic dependence. Yet, despite the various elements of this disunity, it remains strong in cultural ties. The bottom line seems to be that the individual Arab countries practice differing, vacillating relationships with the United States and European countries, due at least in part to the fact that individuals within Arab countries perceive the United States and European countries differently.

SOCIAL LIFE: FAMILY, HONOR, AND THE ROLE OF WOMEN

The roots of modern Arab family life are found in the Old World traditions. Old World Arabs cherished strong family ties and group loyalty. The family constituted the basic social and economic unit of production and was the center of social organization through which persons and groups inherited their religion, social class, and cultural identities in all three Arab patterns of living (bedouin, rural, and urban), and in particular among tribesmen, peasants, and urban poor. Family bound its members in work and in leisure; everyone worked to preserve its status, honor, and welfare. It provided economic and emotional support to its members in exchange for allegiance. Family was the source of unity among the immediate and extended family members, to the extent that the family's survival was placed above individual needs. Family honor represented a sense of pride for the Arab people—the essence of their identity. The reputation of the family was preserved by behaving properly and maintaining family honor. As Naff (1985) has noted, a strong sense of family honor and loyalty was at the core of Arab life. Combined with the competitive spirit of individualistic behavior, family honor could lead to clannishness, jealousy, factionalism, and volatile emotionalism. Combined with generosity, compassion, and warmth, family honor and pride underlie Arab hospitality. Naff wrote, "When the Arab's pride and honor are engaged, tables often groan under the weight of ostentatious quantities of food and, in a duel of etiquette, servings are pressed on the guest" (p. 50).

During the twentieth century, the Arab World has undergone changes with regard to the roles of the women and the structure of the family. But even with the reformation of Islamic laws, social customs that have been deeply rooted in the core of the Arabic culture have been slow to change, especially the social customs that preserved the domination of the male, the early marriage of girls, and arranged marriages.

From the ancient beginnings of Islam, relationships between the genders have always been complex and often misunderstood. As Najda (1975) asserted, the *Koran* and the teachings of Muhammad afforded great respect for women and assigned them equality with men rather than relegation to secondary roles. Islam afforded women the same rights as men with respect to the "Five Pillars of Faith," and their rights to possess property, keep their name after marriage, retain guardianship over their minor children, undertake professions, sue in court, and individually tailor a marriage. In the main, however, throughout the Arab World the social order remained male-oriented with respect to rights, inheritance, and power. Thus, females were expected to yield their own interests and goals to the male members of the family. The male child was a symbol of the father's masculinity and the continuance of his lineage—the birth of a son was greatly celebrated, whereas the birth of a daughter was received in silence.

The Arab woman's sexuality was intertwined with the honor of the Arab family and was the responsibility of all the male kin to protect. Describing this male duty, Kayal and Kayal (1975) wrote, "A man of honor sees that his daughter and other females of his lineage do not act wantonly toward men, or that the sons do not misbehave toward daughters of other men" (p. 117). To protect family honor, Muslim women endured strict limitations on freedom and independence to ensure their chastity and respectability. Restrictions ranged from periods of isolation to the complete veiling of the body and hair to prohibit communication and stares of nonfamily males. Many young Arab women were wed to older men to protect their moral and economic position. Even differences in age were not viewed as undesirable, but couples who crossed the *religious* barriers invited harsh penalties. Marriages were arranged, and dowries were received from the bridegroom as a form of insurance if divorce should occur. Divorce was frowned on but was always an option for the male and (if written into the marriage contract) could be initiated by the female.

The *Koran* recognized polygamy but limited the number of wives to four with the provision of equality for all four. Unlimited concubines were allowed unless prohibited in the marriage contracts. Today, according to Shabbas and Al-Qazzaz (1989), polygamy is illegal in many Arab countries and represents only about 5 percent of all marriages. Where polygamy *is* permitted, approval of the first wife and proof of ability to provide equal financial support are required—or a document certifying the first wife is sterile. The harem (meaning "forbidden"), composed of a family's womenfolk and dominated by the mother or grandmother of the eldest male, is almost nonexistent today, and in fact never was the prevailing living arrangement.

The Prophet Muhammad wrote of the importance of good and educated mothers, but due to political, historical, and economic reasons, the education of Arab women lagged in the past. Progress in women's education accelerated with the Arab World's independence from colonial rule. Greatly encouraged by the *Koran* and considered a duty of all Muslims, education became the key to advancement for Arab women. Presently, the education of women is given high priority, and the rapid rate of women's enrollment in all levels of education is evident. According to Shabbas and Al-Qazzaz (1989), in 1985 there were 20 million Arab women enrolled in education programs of all levels. Today, Arab women are more likely to enroll in all-girl schools and to study science and math. They score higher on national examinations than do Arab boys and compete for top places in medical and engineering schools. Women also hold key positions in teaching and administration, especially in universities, and are greatly recognized as writers, journalists, painters, sculptors, poets, reporters, doctors, lawyers, and engineers. However, they are still isolated from government in many areas, except as elected officials and cabinet ministers.

Modernization has taken root, but for most Arabs, life is still organized around their religion, and their values are expressed in relation to the family. Some Arab countries still adhere to the very strict limitations for women that evolved during ancient times. Saudi Arabia still forbids women to drive, prohibits coed educational institutions, and demands complete modesty by women when they are outside the home. In both Iraq and Saudi Arabia, the women must be veiled and cover their arms and legs when in public or in the presence of most nonfamily males. All Arab families, even the poorest, guard their daughter's honor with the greatest circumspection. In 1974, the advanced family law finally gave both women and men the freedom to choose their own marital partners. Marriage is still based on contract, however, and both may have to pay alimony. Women can sue for divorce, but they stand to lose the dowry agreed upon in the marriage contract. The Arab woman living in seclusion is rare; today she is educated and works in the professions. The modern Arab woman helped greatly during the struggle for independence from colonial rule and continues to be active in the resistance movement, especially in Palestine (Kayal & Kayal, 1975).

In the final analysis, despite common and dominant strands of culture throughout the Arab World, there are also vast differences. During the nineteenth and twentieth centuries, the separate Arab countries have often responded in their own chosen ways to the influences of the various Western powers. Even without the influence of foreign intrusion, notable dissimilarities in cultures, ideologies, languages, and religions already existed. As Naff (1985) has noted, it is difficult to define and describe an Arab culture that is characteristic and common to *all* Arabs. Indeed, the separate Arab countries reflect unique cultural differences, and individuals in each of these separate countries are as different from each other as are individuals of Western countries.

ARAB IMMIGRATION: TRIALS, TRIUMPHS, AND ASSIMILATION

Knowledge about the Arabic-speaking immigrants in the United States was virtually nonexistent until the 1970s, when independent Arab immigration research efforts were initiated. Further accurate data on incoming Arab immigrants were obtained in the 1980 census, the first ever to ask Americans to declare ancestry. Three distinct emigration waves have been identified: (1) the first wave, 1890 to 1940, was influenced by the Arab immigrants' strong desire for economic security; (2) the second wave, or post–World War II group, emigrated for political and economical security and educational opportunities; and (3) the third wave was a result of the Israeli occupation of Jerusalem in 1948 and 1967, which led to the exile of approximately 4.4 million Arab Palestinians (Shabbas & Al-Qazzaz, 1989). Originally, Arabic-speaking immigrants generally did not consider themselves to be Arabs, but rather

Turks. The Arabic Christians never considered themselves Turks; instead, they were identified on the basis of religious affiliation rather than nationality. The term *Syrians* came gradually to convey a geographic and ethnic meaning, and was the term officially adopted by the United States to identify Arabic-speaking immigrants from the Ottoman Empire Syria. The term remained a mark of identification until the 1940s, when the term *Arab* became more acceptable (Hooglund, 1987).

From the Arab World, the region where most prominent Islamic civilizations once existed, young generations of Arabs, motivated by political reasons and the hope of living in a land where dreams come true, began the first wave of migration to America. Between 1890 and 1940, the era of tremendous industrial growth in the United States, more than 250,000 Arab immigrants from the provinces of the Turkish Ottoman Empire, now known as Lebanon and Syria, came to America to seek better economic opportunities and to escape the impending military draft for Christians (Khalaf, 1987). Some 90 percent of the first wave were Arab Christians of the Middle Eastern Rite sects—mainly Maronite, Melkite, and Eastern Greek Orthodox—with the remaining 10 percent being Muslim and Druze Syrians (Zogby, 1990). They were barely perceptible in the great wave of all immigrants, approximately 27 million, who entered America during the high (1881 to 1914) and low (1915 to 1925) tides of immigration (Hooglund, 1987). The historical tendency of the Arab people in their original homelands to integrate with, rather than reject or destroy, other cultures augmented the development of a rich heritage of their own. This tendency appeared to carry over as they quickly entered the mainstream of American culture with relative ease, placing assimilation above ethnic identification.

First Wave

The majority of the first-wave Arab immigrants were fairly young unmarried males, not well educated. They came to America with little capital, limited skills, and speaking little or no English. Female immigration increased during the 1900s as the males realized that wives and relatives could facilitate the accumulation of wealth. Bureau of Immigration accounts indicate that illiteracy was high, particularly for the women (Naff, 1985). They struggled hard to achieve success as laborers, peddlers, shopkeepers, merchants, and workers in grocery stores and restaurants. Few entered the industrial labor force, although some did take factory jobs (Zogby, 1990). The majority who were peasants provided the human power that helped to transform the United States from a semiagricultural economy to one of the world's prominent industrial powers by 1914. The immigrants mainly worked diligently as pack peddlers, a trade they knew both before and after the rise of Islam in the Arab World.

Individualism, loyalty, pride, determination, hard work, perseverance, resourcefulness, conservatism, close family relationships, and traditional values allowed the Arab immigrants to endure the hardships of America when they first arrived in the 1800s. To succeed in the United States was a matter of family honor, the main impetus for their hard work and hardships.

Peddling hastened the acculturation process—but it also contributed to its demise. With the accumulation of capital also came new values and aspirations to enter occupations of greater prestige and to become permanent citizens. It took time for the immigrants to reach a level of comfortable success; they often lived clustered together in ghettos and appeared to other Americans as clannish. However, throughout these difficult times the first-generation wave of Arab immigrants never lost sight of the value of family, both within America and at home in the Arab World. Age and wisdom were highly regarded, as was the tradition of giving help to the extended family. Much of the money they accumulated was sent back home to provide for the needs of their extended families or to provide passage for them to come to America—a culturally induced commitment to make a better life for all of their family members, both near and far.

The earliest Arab American communities were predominantly in fast-growing urban and industrial areas, such as Toledo and Detroit-Dearborn, and were built around a network of peddlers selling their wares and achieving a great degree of affluence quickly. Within the settlements, commonly known to many as the "Little Syrias," the Arab immigrants reveled in a sense of belonging and lapsed back into time through fellowship and the legacy of Arabic food, drink, song, and dance. The settlements offered a touch with the past. Contacts with other Arab immigrants provided not only a social network but also an economic one that helped newer immigrants to secure employment and housing and to maintain ties with their Arab language and culture.

The relatively high degree of Americanization among the first generation and the rather low degree of ethnic consciousness in the second generation of first-wave immigrants are two indications that the assimilation process penetrated sectors of Arab communities more deeply than expected (Zogby, 1990). Although many of the first generation enjoyed the prosperity that was now afforded them in America, their bliss was not without personal conflict as they watched many of their old customs dissipate. The first generation experienced many changes in their way of life as they struggled emotionally to maintain loyalty to the values and customs of the old country, while justifying the changes that seemed inevitable. In contrast to the Arab Christians, the assimilation was much more difficult for the Arab Muslims because of their strong adherence to Islamic faith and law.

The establishment of the first Islamic mosque in 1926 in Highland Park (Detroit) finally provided a place for the Arab Muslims to gather and to discuss the problems they were experiencing. The Mosque was a place to study the *Koran* and to reinforce their cultural ties to the mother country. Through the compulsory system, intimate contacts with classmates and teachers, the acquisition of a language other than Arabic, and an opportunity to compare two different cultures and ways of life, the second and third generations (American born and American reared) played a transitional role between the old and the new cultures and became agents of social change in Arab communities. These generations acquired more naturally and with less effort the language tools of the U.S. culture. Knowledge of the harsh socioeconomic conditions experienced by their parents in the old country made their assimilation into the now culture much easier.

The second generation often walked a fine line in trying to balance religious and social pressures exerted on them by the home and ethnic community and by the school and larger community. The Arabic values of family honor, and obedience to and respect for parental authority, became less restrictive for many Arab families, but still remained more of a source of control than did comparable values in most American families. The formal institution of education gradually replaced the role of the patriarchal head in providing knowledge and wisdom to succeed in the American society, and the devout adherence to the practice of Islam was influenced by cries for Islamic reform. As the assimilation process took place, the revered habits of fasting during Ramadan, prayers five times a day, and abstaining from the eating of pork were often difficult and impractical. The Islamic rituals of *qada* and *kafara* (meaning respectively "to satisfy a claim or duty" and "atonement") made it easier to make certain changes with respect to some traditional Muslim practices because prayers, acts of penance, and sacrifices could be performed as acts of forgiveness. Being different just made life too difficult in America, which gradually accelerated abandonment of a number of the cherished ancient Arab and Islamic customs.

Thus, the traditional Arab family was forced to change in the American setting. Personal attitudes toward such complex cultural matters as interethnic marriages were altered as a more liberal attitude was accepted. Many Arab Americans, males in particular, married Americans from other cultural and ethnic ancestries, which in turn affected the social structure of the Arab family. The restrictive customs pertaining to marriage (such as parallel cousin weddings, parental choice of the bride's husband, and the wife's role within the social hierarchy of the family) quickly underwent significant change as Arab women entered the work force in order to help provide economic security for the family. A breakup of the traditional patriarchal, extended family also reinforced both the rise of the Arab woman's status within the family and the beginning of the nuclear family unit. The notions of female obedience, sacrifice, and chastity, and the idea of male superiority, however, were preciously slow to change.

Eventually, the vagaries of change were such that even divorce was no longer viewed by the Arab American woman as equivalent to social and economic death. In time, diverse responsibilities even compelled working Arab women and homemakers alike to have fewer children and to cook many less time-consuming Arabic meals. Visiting, an important function in the Arab World practiced for the sake of reinforcing and creating relationships, became practically impossible to continue due to the newly imposed time constraints. The art of following a specific clocked schedule soon precluded hours formerly spent with a special friend or relative.

As Arab Americans experienced assimilation into the American culture, newly created paradigms continued to impact traditional and revered practices. For example, according to Naff (1985), "Even the time-honored preference for male children began to lose much of its force" (p. 287). Furthermore, the Arab American children were no longer prepared to live a life of dependency, or expected to be a means of security for the aged parents or extended-family members, as in the old country. The American spirit of competition and independence had become yet another new way of life for the Arab American.

Naturally, the assimilation process of the Arab immigrants was not without pain or agony of choice regarding the preservation of their culture and traditions. Additionally, many suffered the prevailing ethnic and racial discrimination directed to minorities in America in general. Many of the dark-complexioned Arabs experienced extreme prejudice while perceived as being non-White and adherents of suspect religions (Hooglund, 1987). Ironically, the discrimination served in the main to solidify Arab unity and reinforce their identity. Through churches, clubs, and neighborhood functions, the immigrants reaffirmed their roots and preserved their customs as best they could under the enticing pressures to assimilate quickly within the U.S. culture.

The fairytale images of America and the American people that the immigrants held before they arrived, coupled with the wonder and awe they experienced in accumulating economic security, only heightened their desire to remain in America come what might. Their food, customs, and norms had been Arab, and great energy was expended to preserve them in that mode. As their economic status and adjustment improved, they united to combat racial ostracism and to preserve their cultural heritage. The introduction of Arabic newspapers helped greatly to preserve the language and opened lines of communication for the Arab immigrants. While the immigrants simultaneously struggled to prevent what they thought might become the amalgamation (and perhaps the complete destruction) of their native traditions and values, there abound among them nevertheless an acceptance of American assimilationist views of patriotism, citizenry, and hard work.

Second Wave

A second wave of immigrants, nationals of various—and often competing—Arab nations known collectively as the Arab World, flourished following

World War II, sparked to a large degree by political turmoil, civil war, foreign invasion, the creation of Israel, and poverty in the Middle East. This wave continues even now, and its members are recognized as being more educated, more ethnically conscious, more politically vocal, and more determined to retain their cultural heritage than were first-wave Arabs.

According to Zogby's (1990) study, the second wave is predominantly concentrated in the Northeastern and Midwestern urban areas of America and as a group are younger than the U.S. population as a whole and than other ethnic groups. Zogby documented that the age level for the second influx of immigrants is (or at least was, as of the time of his study) between twenty and forty-four years of age, with the median age being twenty-five. He further described their communities as more likely to be foreign born and less likely to be assimilated with respect to both marriage outside their ethnic group and/or speaking a language other than Arabic in the home. This post–World War II group emigrating from independent Arab nation-states is made up of many individuals with college degrees, those who come to earn degrees, and people seeking professional positions—again, characteristics differing from those of the farmers and artisans who migrated during the first wave. The second wave is also more affluent and better educated than both the U.S. national average and many other ethnic groups. They continue to show a degree of independence with a much higher rate of self-employment and participation in retail trades.

Indeed, the postwar wave of immigrants do differ—greatly—from the first group who made that long journey to follow their dreams for a better life economically. The second group is dominated by Muslims, in contrast to the first wave of Arab Christians. They are less likely to assimilate at the cost of losing their ethnic identity, and they reflect a more active political disposition. A growing concern for the crisis situation in the Middle East, a resurgence in the study of Arabic in community schools and universities, and a more devout adherence to the practice of Islam have greatly deepened the interest of second- and third-generation Arab Americans in both their Arab culture and their ties to the Arab World. Although the newer immigrants appear to hold stronger ties to Islam and Arabic customs, the second- and third-generation Arab American descendants of the first-wave immigrants still tend to be greatly removed in both tradition and religion as recognized and practiced in the present-day Arab World. At times, they even lack a meaningful grounding within the Arabic language and cultural practice.

Third Wave

A third wave can be identified among post–World War II immigrants who continue to arrive in America due to the escalating Palestinian-Israeli wars (Orfalea, 1988). Arab Palestinians have flocked to America's shores since

1967, when the Israelis took full control of the remaining sectors of Palestine, the West Bank, and Gaza. Between 1968 and 1985, close to 350,000 Arabs migrated to the United States. According to the U.S. Immigration and Naturalization Service's records, Palestinians account for a majority of the combined second and third waves of Arabs entering America. Mixed emotions over support given by the United States and Britain during the initial 1948 Zionist occupation has remained a continuous source of resentment among Arab Americans, and indeed the Arab World. In recent times, the United States has rejected Israel's actions of 1967 to place Jerusalem under Israeli jurisdiction, the rejection based on an interpretation of international law that posits that there can be no legal settlement by an occupying power in the territory it holds. It is somewhat of a paradox that so many Palestine refugees would come to the country that supported the forces they consider the cause of their exile.

According to the 1980 United States Census, Arab Americans, both native born and foreign born, have a higher educational achievement level and a significantly higher number of high school and college graduates than the United States population as a whole and than most other ethnic groups. Many of the second-wave immigrants have come already educated, or specifically for the purpose of obtaining higher education. Presently, most of the third-wave Arab Americans are Muslims, as are the majority of Middle Eastern students that come to the United States to study. Religious mandates of ancient origin such as "God will raise up in the rank those of you who believe and have been given knowledge" (*Koran,* 58:11) and the Prophet Muhammad's "Seeking knowledge is the duty of every Muslim" (*Al-Ghazaly Minaret Newsletter,* 1991) are powerful motivational forces that drive educational achievement in the Arab culture. The data contradict the general American perception that Arab Americans are uneducated and are politically and globally naive. Educational achievement is abundantly evident among recent Arab immigrants, despite their having endured during most of their lifetime the tragedies of war.

Today, Arab Americans constitute a growing, sizable minority group in the United States. Zogby's (1990) study notes Arab immigration as a main source of new Americans and provides information on Arab immigration trends. For example, in the 1980s, the Arab nations accounted for 3.7 percent of the total of naturalized citizens, ranking tenth in the total number of immigrants coming into the United States, superseded in number only by that of the Western Hemisphere and other parts of Asia. Lebanon was the primary nation of origin of immigrants coming over from the Arab World during the 1980s. Immigrants from Egypt and Iraq recently surpassed Syrian immigrants. Many of the immigrants from Jordan and (to a lesser degree) other Arab nations are Palestinians. Additionally, a considerable number of non-immigrants are university students who come to the United States to study and then return home, although some from the war-torn countries, particularly Lebanon and Iraq, choose to remain. The Lebanese and Syrians, however, still account for nearly 9 of every 10 Arab Americans. Regardless of the specific countries of origin, the collective Arab American population is predicted to increase in number and so warrants increasing recognition—and inclusion—in U.S. society.

IMPLICATIONS FOR EDUCATION

The presence of 3 million Arab Americans, increasing numbers of visiting Arab students, and a burgeoning population of new immigrants from Arab countries all have noteworthy implications for the U.S. educational system. In general, students of Arab heritage face problems similar to those of students from other nonmainstream cultures in the United States. That is, cultural and behavioral norms, and the curricula of U.S. schools, have been based primarily on Western traditions. In addition, according to Law and Lane (1986), classroom teachers are "no more accepting of various ethnic groups than the national samples spanning six decades" (p. 8). Furthermore, there exist extreme displays of overt and covert prejudice and discrimination toward people of color (Oakes, 1990). In this context, then, the first general implication is that education that is multicultural should become the rule rather than the exception in the U.S. school system. Second, teachers must learn to become culturally responsive to the unique needs of students of Arab descent.

To accomplish outcomes implicit in these two general implications, and to better understand Arab American students, teachers require first a broad and in-depth command of both the ancient and the modern histories that undergird today's Arab and Arab American culture. Thus, the histories, cultures, religions, and contributions of Arab Americans, which are largely ignored in the pages of American textbooks, must be placed alongside those of other previously excluded groups in the school curricula. Respect for and acceptance of diversity and the inclusion of multicultural education within our educational institutions are the life support systems to enable all students to define their role in history and to legitimize their own cultural values, beliefs, customs, and ideas—improving the education and economic and social survival of all students. While understanding Arab cultures broadly, it is equally important that teachers at the same time recognize the great diversity within Arab culture and see the child of Arab descent as an individual. Indeed, what Naff (1985) wrote about the Arab World is also true for the persons of Arab descent in America: "No one religion, ideology, national identity, or sense of history and heritage defines all Arabs...[and] one cannot overlook the complexities imposed on any generalization by Arab history, geography, and society" (p. 15). To keep in mind individual differences and also be culturally responsive to students of Arab descent, teachers need to be cognizant of a number of factors that may characterize their students.

Teachers should know, for instance, that Arab American and Arab "foreign" students often face social and psychological displacement when confronted with a new language, methods, and curriculum that are foreign to the culture they know. Many students feel that it is their responsibility, their duty, to maintain their native culture; yet they need to feel comfortable with the culture of their new target language, English. In addition, behaviors reinforced within the Arab home are often not regarded in the same way outside the home, especially in school settings. The learning required by two different cultures (home and school) may lead to a lack of "fit," which may have detrimental effects on the development of adolescent self-esteem. For example, an important characteristic of Arab culture concerns the idea of "face." Teachers may very often find that the parents of Arab students are very sensitive to public criticism. Consequently, criticism should be shared in a way that will minimize loss of "face" and honor for both the student and the family.

Also, teachers of Arab American students and visiting Arab students should realize the problems of acculturation. Many Arab children are bilingual or trilingual and so may speak Arabic, French, and/or English. Matters of religion, diet, hygiene, gender roles, proxemics (social distance), and punctuality reflect cultural differences that are often misunderstood. Arab Americans vary from adherence to total assimilation to rejection of almost everything that is Western in nature. In some instances, it is important for teachers to remember that visiting Arab students have already been dealing with cultural conflict in their own countries, as the opposing Western modernism and Islamic conservatism clash within the Arab World.

In addition, teachers should be aware of other problems unique to Arab assimilation into U.S. society. In efforts to retain aspects of their culture and religion, the foreign-born Arab American students, as well as the Arab visiting students, often feel insecure and experience feelings of loneliness, hostility, indecision, frustration, sadness, and homesickness. They are caught between cultures, not sure of which one they belong to, and may sense both a loss of membership in their original reference group and an increasing identification with the new group in an effort to become bicultural. Cultural stress or shock may pass rather quickly, but then, of course, it may also linger.

Similarly, in reference to cultural problems, Arab American students, and particularly Arab visiting students, must confront harsh American perceptions of their way of life and the differences that tend to isolate them from the mainstream. For example, Arab Americans are a people who enjoy close proximity to one another when talking, and members of the same gender are often known to walk arm-in-arm or hold hands—a behavior normal for them yet often unaccepted within mainstream America. Additionally, features of their language, such as loudness, and intonation patterns—perfectly acceptable in their own mother tongue—unfortunately can have connotations of rudeness, anger, and/or hostility as they attempt to speak in a new language.

Teaching within a pluralistic society further entreats educators to realize that traditional Arab customs and values, especially among students from a Muslim heritage and sometimes other cultural religious heritages, pose unique circumstances in typical U.S. school settings. For instance, male students who have never been exposed to female authority figures may have difficulty following orders from female teachers and administrators. Also, a lack of familiarity with deodorant has often led to the practice of washing hands and face with cologne, usually reinforcing the U.S. perception of being unclean when in reality cleanliness is greatly valued, but culturally addressed from a different perspective. Punctuality, in contrast to the value placed on it by most middle-class Americans, may also present a problem. Some Arabs may place little significance on being a little late—tardiness is not considered a sign of disrespect. Forbidden to eat pork, Muslims often find it served as a main entree in school cafeterias.

Again, their differences are often brought to the forefront without any attempt to understand the rationale that gives value to them. Furthermore, many Muslim students fast during the month of Ramadan and may appear tired or irritable during this period. Teachers should be understanding of the strength and endurance required by these young people to commit to the doctrines of their faith. Ramadan is a chance for them to reaffirm their cultural traditions and values that maintain important links to their home culture. Non-Muslim teachers need an extra measure of patience and should provide support during this period when some students may withdraw from or be isolated by classmates who perceive differences as being strange, wrong, or unacceptable.

Furthermore, it is instructive for teachers to recognize the differences and similarities among previous and new immigrant groups within the larger Arab community. As Zogby (1990) has noted, the first wave is now both older and more affluent in contrast to the newer immigrants, some of whom are struggling near poverty. However, employment status of the second wave reflects the greater exposure to the professions, management, and student status. Whereas household income averages for Arab Americans tend to be higher than the national average, there is a greater percentage of Arab American households below the poverty level than for the U.S. population as a whole. This paradox exists because a large number of Arab immigrants are earning less than poverty income and have a higher unemployment rate.

Early images of Arab immigrants as peddlers or merchants standing in front of a grocery store, adorned in a white apron, contrast greatly with the present Arab Americans' unparalleled need for independence. As noted, new immigrants are more likely to be self-employed entrepreneurs, or work as corporate, health-care, or educational professionals—all sharing a demonstrative success orientation. In contrast, adherents of Islam are found in increasing numbers among the new immigrants, when compared to the second-wave immigrants who were predominantly of the Christian faith (Shabbas & Al-

Qazzaz, 1989). Nevertheless, both the "newcomers" and the "established" Arab Americans are bound by a common ancient heritage, language, and culture. Indeed, in spite of the effects of enculturation and acculturation in U.S. life-styles, it is clear that family unity, honor, religious beliefs and practices, strong feelings of identity with their homelands, in addition to many other traditional values and customs, remain strong symbols of reverence in the Arab American culture.

CONCLUSION

Recognizing the great importance of preparing young people for their roles as thoughtful and informed citizens of the twenty-first century challenges society to acknowledge that the U.S. involvement with the Middle Eastern nations and the world of Islam is certain to remain significant for many years. As Americans, we must realize that "we" and "they" are in a state of mutuality and interdependence. For example, the Arab countries provide the United States with 80 percent of its oil, serve as a market for American goods and services, and provide a place for employment for many Americans in the Persian Gulf area, Saudi Arabia, and other countries in the region. In turn, the United States opens its schools to provide quality education for the Middle Eastern youths and continues to be a country that, for many reasons, draws thousands of Middle Eastern immigrants to its shores annually. If the current trends of immigration, birth rates, and family sizes continue to rise, the Middle Eastern Americans population and culture will become ever more visible.

Thus, an essential goal for educators ought to be to increase awareness and understanding of the Middle Eastern peoples through the study of their history, culture, religion, and contributions. An equally important educational goal should be to dispel the misconceptions and stereotypes about the Middle Easterners—Arabs and Arab Americans or Iranians and Iranian Americans, for example—that continue to be promoted through the media. In truth, the Arab caricature in the United States, for instance, continues to be dehumanizing, depriving the Arab Americans of much-deserved respect and ethnic pride. We as educators have a great opportunity, as well as a moral and ethical responsibility, to address aggressively these heinous forms of bigotry.

Finally, living within a pluralistic society should make it virtually impossible for ordinary people and highly sensitized educators alike to ignore the value of any of its citizens as contributing and distinctive members. Education must become the vehicle for eliminating stereotypes and replacing them with understandings. Educators are fortunate indeed to be in a position that allows them to reach out to all cultures in order to form bonds of friendship, savor shared memories, and create mutual respect for cultural traditions. In truth, the embracing of diversity is and will remain essential to America's social health and prosperity. Thus, teachers should not fear diversity; rather, they should enjoy its gifts.

REFERENCES

Al-Ghazaly Minaret Newsletter. (1991 October). 1(1).

Hooglund, E. J. (Ed.). (1987). *Crossing the Waters: Arabic-Speaking Immigrants to the United States before 1940.* Washington, D.C.: Smithsonian Institution Press.

Kayal, P. M. & Kayal, J. M. (1975). *The Syrian-Lebanese in America.* Boston: Twayne.

Khalaf, S. (1987). The Background and Causes of Lebanese/Syrian Immigration to the United States before World War II. In E. J. Hooglund (Ed.). *Crossing the Waters* (pp. 17–35). Washington, D.C.: Smithsonian Institution.

Law, S., & Lane, D. (1986, April). Multicultural Acceptance by Teacher Education Survey of Attitudes toward Thirty-Two Ethnic and National Groups. Paper presented at the annual meeting of the American Educational Association, San Francisco.

Naff, A. (1985). *Becoming Americans: The Early Arab Immigrant Experience.* Carbondale: Southern Illinois University.

Najda. (1975, April). Women in Ancient Egypt. *Najda Newsletter.*

Oakes, J. (1990). *Multiplying Inequalities: The Effects of Race, Social Class and Tracking and Opportunities to Learn Mathematics and Science.* Santa Monica, Calif.: Rand Corporation.

Orfalea, G. (1988). *Before the Flames: A Quest for the History of Arab Americans.* Austin: University of Texas Press.

Salah, N. (1979). *Costumes and Customs from the Arab World.* Altamonte Springs, Fla.: International Promoters of Art, Inc.

Shabbas, A. & Al-Qazzaz A. (Eds.). (1989). *Arab World Notebook.* Berkeley, Calif.: Women Concerned about the Middle East.

Shaheen, J. G. (1984). *TV Arab.* Bowling Green, Oh.: Bowling Green State University.

Zogby, J. G. (1990). *Arab Americans Today: A Demographic Profile of Arab Americans.* Washington, D.C.: Arab American Institute.

ANNOTATED BIBLIOGRAPHY

Books for Teachers

Abraham, S. Y. & Abraham, N. (Eds.) (1983). *Arabs in the New World: Studies on Arab-American Communities.* Detroit: Wayne State University, Center for Urban Studies.

This collection of papers focuses primarily on the Arab American communities in Detroit. Several papers at the beginning describe the historical context for the other papers.

Aswad, B. (Ed.). (1974). *Arabic Speaking Communities in American Cities*. New York: Center for Migration Studies.

> *This is one of the first projects supported by the Association of Arab-American University Graduates. It is a collection of essays by social scientists who examine subcultural groups of Arab Americans in communities throughout the United States.*

Hagopian, E. C. & Paden, A. (Eds.). (1969). *The Arab-Americans: Studies in Assimilation*. Wilmette, Ill.: The Medina University Press International.

> *This monograph is the first in a series supported by the Association of Arab-American University Graduates (AAUG). It is a collection of papers that provide an overview of the Arab American experience in various communities throughout the United States. One paper discusses the role of women.*

Haiek, J. (Ed.). (1992). *Arab American Almanac*. Glendale, Calif.: News Circle Publishing House.

> *This 448-page book includes Arab American organizations, leaders, and other useful information.*

Hooglund, E. J. (Ed.). *Crossing the Waters: Arabic-Speaking Immigrants to the United States before 1940*. Washington D.C.: Smithsonian Institution Press.

> *This collection of papers and case studies provides detailed descriptions of the Arab American immigration experience from 1890 to 1940.*

Hourani, A. (1991). *A History of the Arab Peoples*. Cambridge: The Belknap Press/ Harvard University Press.

> *A comprehensive, well-researched, and informative history of the Arab peoples by a first-rate English historian.*

Kayal, P. M. (1985). *An Arab-American Bibliographic Guide* (Bibliography Series No. 4). Belmont, Mass.: The Association of Arab-American University Graduates, Inc. (AAUG).

> *A comprehensive and useful but dated guide to books about Arab Americans.*

Kayal, P. & Kayal, J. (1975). *The Syrian-Lebanese in America: A Study in Religion and Assimilation*. Boston: Twayne.

> *This book traces the history of the Syrian-Lebanese in America. It discusses immigration and the struggle by Arab Americans from Syrian and Lebanon to develop their identities.*

McCarus, E. (Ed.). (1994). *The Development of Arab-American Identity*. Ann Arbor: The University of Michigan Press.

> *This is a collection of scholarly papers about Arabic speaking people in the United States. Chapters include "The Early Arab Immigrant Experience," "Arab-Americans and the Political Process," "Issues of Identity: In Theater of Immigrant Community," and "Anti-Arab Racism and Violence in the United States."*

Medhi, B. T. (1978). *The Arabs in America, 1492–1977: A Chronology and Fact Book*. Dobbs Ferry, N.Y.: Oceana Publications.

> *This book contains a comprehensive chronology and a plethora of documentation of the Arab American experience. It is modestly published, but is a useful reference book.*

Naff, A. (1980). Arabs. In S. Thernstrom, A. Orlov, & O. Handlin (Eds.). *Harvard Encyclopedia of American Ethnic Groups* (pp. 128–136). Cambridge: Harvard University Press.

A dated but informative overview of the experiences of Arabs in the United States.

Naff, A. (1985). *Becoming American: The Early Arab Immigrant Experience.* Carbondale: Southern Illinois University Press.

This is a scholarly account of Arab immigration from the mid-1870s to about World War I. The data collected for the book are based primarily on interviews, but documents and accounts of events in the Arab-language press are used as well. The strengths of the book are the author's clarity and intellectual honesty.

Orfalea, G. (1988). *Before the Flames: A Quest for the History of Arab Americans.* Austin: University of Texas Press.

This is a historical account of Arab immigration to the United States and the Arab American experience. It is primarily based on the author's own experiences and on interviews with family members and other Arab Americans.

Shaheen, J. (1984). *The TV Arab.* Bowling Green, Oh.: Bowling Green State University.

A media specialist describes the ways in which Arabs are depicted on television.

Books for Students

Ashabranner, B. K. (1991). *An Ancient Heritage: The Arab-American Minority.* New York: HarperCollins.

This book, designed for young readers, is based on personal interviews with Arab Americans.

Geha, J. (1990). *Through and Through: Toledo Stories.* St. Paul, Minn.: Graywolf Press.

Three generations of Arab Americans are portrayed in these short stories.

Harik, E. M. (1982). *The Lebanese in America.* Minneapolis: Lerner Publications.

An informative book that is illustrated with photographs.

Kadi, J. (Ed.). (1994). *Food for Our Grandmothers: Writings by Arab-American and Arab-Canadian Feminists.* Boston: South End Press.

This collection of essays explores diverse dimensions of being Arab in America.

Naff, A. (1988). *The Arab Americans.* New York: Chelsea House.

A book written for young readers by a leading historian who specializes in Arab American history.

MULTICULTURAL UNITS
AND EVALUATION

P art I discusses the goals and trends in the multicultural curriculum. It also discusses key concepts and ways to organize and plan the multicultural curriculum. Parts II through V present content about ethnic groups and strategies plus materials that can be incorporated into the school curriculum. Part VI highlights and summarizes the major points discussed in the previous chapters and illustrates how you can use the information and strategies in Parts I through V to develop and teach multicultural units and curricula that focus on several different ethnic and cultural groups.

The major components of a sample multicultural unit are presented in the first part of chapter 15, the chapter that constitutes Part VI. The second part of the chapter highlights the need for planned evaluation within an effective multicultural curriculum and discusses strategies for evaluating the components of decision making and the total school environment.

CHAPTER 15

MULTICULTURAL UNITS AND EVALUATION STRATEGIES

IDENTIFYING KEY CONCEPTS

When planning a multicultural unit, you should first decide which key concepts you will use to organize the unit. As stated in chapter 3, these concepts should be higher-level ones that are capable of encompassing a wide range of data and information. Concepts chosen for the multicultural unit should also be *interdisciplinary.* Interdisciplinary concepts are capable of encompassing facts, generalizations, and examples from several disciplines and content areas. Concepts drawn from the various behavioral sciences, such as *culture, social protest,* and *intercultural communication,* can be used effectively to organize interdisciplinary units and lessons. The rationale for an interdisciplinary curriculum is presented in chapter 3. I have selected the following key concepts for the sample unit discussed in this chapter:

Key Concept	*Disciplines*
cultural assimilation	anthropology
economic status	economics
ethnic community	geography-sociology
immigration	geography-history-sociology
social protest	political science
identity	psychology
discrimination	sociology

IDENTIFYING KEY AND
INTERMEDIATE-LEVEL GENERALIZATIONS

After you have identified organizing concepts, key generalizations related to each of the concepts should be chosen. Ideally, you should identify a key or universal generalization for each concept and then an intermediate-level generalization for each concept. A universal generalization applies to all cultures, times, and peoples (see pages 44–48). An intermediate-level generalization is limited in its application to a particular nation, subculture, or time period. Thus, a generalization that applies only to the United States is an intermediate-level generalization. In the following examples, I identify a universal generalization and an intermediate-level generalization for the first concept, *cultural assimilation,* but only intermediate-level generalizations for the other key concepts.

KEY CONCEPT: Cultural Assimilation

Key or Universal Generalization: Whenever a minority group comes into contact with a dominant culture, it is usually expected to acquire the culture and values of the dominant group.

Intermediate-Level Generalization: In the United States, ethnic minority groups are expected to acquire the culture and values of the mainstream American culture.

KEY CONCEPT: Economic Status

Intermediate-Level Generalization: Because of racial discrimination and other factors, members of U.S. minority groups of color are often paid low wages for their work. Consequently, most of them are members of the lower socioeconomic classes.

KEY CONCEPT: Ethnic Community

Intermediate-Level Generalization: U.S. ethnic groups that have strong ethnic identities and characteristics often live in ethnic neighborhoods and communities.

KEY CONCEPT: Immigration

Intermediate-Level Generalization: Most ethnic groups came to the United States or moved within it to improve their economic conditions. However, some ethnic groups were either forced to come to the United States or were forced to move from one region of it to another.

KEY CONCEPT: Social Protest

Intermediate-Level Generalization: Throughout their experiences in the United States, ethnic minorities have resisted discrimination and oppression in various ways.

KEY CONCEPT: Identity

Intermediate-Level Generalization: During the 1960s and 1970s, ethnic groups in the United States became increasingly aware of their ethnic identities and expressed them in various ways.

KEY CONCEPT: Discrimination

Intermediate-Level Generalization: Most ethnic groups in the United States have been the victims of various kinds of discrimination. Ethnic groups of color still experience discrimination in contemporary U.S. society.

DETERMINING WHICH ETHNIC GROUPS TO INCLUDE IN THE UNIT

After the key and intermediate-level generalizations have been identified, you should decide which ethnic groups will be included in the unit. It is neither possible nor desirable to include every U.S. ethnic group within a particular unit or curriculum. For each unit, you should select several ethnic groups that best illustrate the particular concepts you are trying to teach. In conceptual teaching, the major goal is to help students master higher-level concepts and generalizations. *Which particular ethnic groups are selected to illustrate the concepts chosen for study is a secondary but important consideration.*

As pointed out earlier, it is essential that certain concepts be taught in an effective multicultural curriculum. These concepts include *racism, discrimination, prejudice, social protest,* and *culture.* In each unit, you should not only include groups that best exemplify particular concepts but should also be sure that a range of ethnic groups is selected for study. Groups that vary in cultural characteristics, geographical location, socioeconomic status, racial characteristics, history, time of immigration, conditions of immigration, income characteristics, and level of assimilation should be selected for study. During the course of the year, a variety of ethnic groups should be studied, although only several will be studied within a particular unit. In one unit, for example, you may wish to focus on African Americans, Anglo-Americans, Chinese Americans, and Jewish Americans. In another, the focus may be on Mexican Americans, Anglo-Americans, Japanese Americans, and Arab Americans. I am including African Americans, Mexican Americans, Puerto Ricans, Jewish Americans, and American Indians in the exemplary unit outlined in this chapter.

IDENTIFYING LOW-LEVEL GENERALIZATIONS

After the ethnic groups to be included in the unit have been identified, you should then identify low-level generalizations (see Table 4-2) related to each key concept and to each ethnic group chosen for study. Low-level generalizations are low-level statements that explain how the experiences of specific groups are related to the key concepts and generalizations. In the examples that follow, I have identified low-level generalizations for each of the key concepts as they relate to African Americans, one ethnic group chosen for study in our sample unit. However, in an actual unit, you should identify low-level generalizations for each group chosen for study.

Ethnic Group: African Americans

Cultural Assimilation: To attain economic and social mobility, African Americans must usually acquire the behavior, values, and norms of the dominant middle-class culture in the United States.

Economic Status: Because of job discrimination, low educational levels, and other factors, about one-half of African Americans are members of the lower socioeconomic classes. However, there is a significant Black middle class.

Ethnic Community: Many African Americans live in ethnic communities called "ghettos" by the dominant society. However, as individual African Americans attain higher social status and higher levels of cultural assimilation, they tend to move out of their ethnic communities.

Immigration: Ethnic groups who immigrated to America came voluntarily to improve their economic conditions; most African Americans were forced to come to America as slaves.

Social Protest: Since they were first captured on the west coast of Africa, African Americans have systematically protested against oppression and discrimination. Their forms of protest have reflected the times in which they occurred.

Identity: In the 1960s, African Americans attempted to shape a new identity and to reject the view of themselves that had been perpetuated by the dominant society.

Discrimination: Since they landed in America, African Americans have been the victims of racism and discrimination. Discrimination against African Americans has taken different forms in various historical periods.

DEVELOPING TEACHING STRATEGIES

When the low-level generalizations for each ethnic group have been identified, you are then ready to write the strategies and identify the materials for teaching each of the low-level generalizations. One helpful format is for you to divide a sheet of paper as illustrated in Table 15-1 and list the concepts and generalizations on one side and the activities and materials on the other. In the lesson plan in Table 15-1, I illustrate how content about Mexican Americans, one of the ethnic groups chosen for study in our sample unit, can be used to teach the concept of social protest at the senior high school level.

Helping Students to Derive the Key Generalizations

In order to formulate the key generalizations in the unit, the students must be given opportunities to compare and contrast the experiences of different ethnic groups. Students cannot derive key generalizations by studying one ethnic group. Rather, high-level generalizations can be derived only when students use data from several groups. At various points during the teaching of multicultural units, the teacher should give the students ample opportunities to compare and contrast the experiences of various ethnic groups and to formulate the key generalizations.

A simple device that enables students to compare and contrast the experiences of various ethnic groups and to derive key generalizations is the data retrieval chart. This device allows students to log in the data they have found in answer to a series of questions related to the key concepts in the unit. Its chief value is that it can be easily expanded to include two or more data samples. The data retrieval chart enables students to ask the same kinds of questions about a number of ethnic groups. Thus, comparisons and contrasts can be readily made. A data retrieval chart related to our sample unit is presented in Table 15-2.

Determining Unit Objectives

Multicultural units should have clearly stated objectives so that the teacher can effectively evaluate instruction and student learning. Multicultural units should have two major kinds of objectives, *cognitive* and *affective*. Cognitive objectives are related to the mastery of knowledge. Affective objectives are related to student attitudes and values. Multicultural units should also have objectives that are related to the student's ability to relate knowledge and values when making decisions on ethnic and other social issues. I call these kinds of objectives *synthesis* objectives.

Writing Cognitive Objectives

Throughout this book, I recommend the conceptual approach to instruction, in which the teacher determines the key concepts and generalizations to be taught and then selects content related to ethnic groups to be used in teach-

Table 15-1 KEY IDEAS AND TEACHING STRATEGIES

Key Ideas	Activities

KEY CONCEPT: Social Protest *Key Generalization:* When individuals and groups are victims of oppression and discrimination, they tend to protest against their situation in various ways.
 	
Intermediate-Level Generalization: Throughout their experiences in the United States, ethnic minorities have resisted discrimination and oppression in various ways.
 	
Low-Level Generalization: Mexican Americans have resisted Anglo discrimination and oppression since Anglo-Americans conquered and occupied the Southwest.
	1. To give the students a general overview of Mexican American history, show them a videotape, such as *Mexican Americans* (a videotape in the *Multicultural Peoples of North America* series listed in Appendix B). After showing the videotape, ask the students to discuss the questions:
	  a. What major problems have Mexican Americans experienced in the United States?
	  b. What actions have been taken by Mexican American individuals and groups to eliminate the discrimination they have experienced?
	
	2. Ask a group of students to prepare reports that reveal the ways in which the following men led organized resistance to Anglo-Americans in the 1800s:
	  Juan N. Cortina
	  Juan Jose Herrera
	  Juan Patron
	The class should discuss these men when the reports are presented. A good reference for this activity is Julian Samora and Patricia V. Simon (1993), *A History of the Mexican American People.* Notre Dame, Ind.: University of Notre Dame Press.
	
	3. Ask a group of students to prepare a report to be presented in class that describes Chicano involvement in strikes and unions between 1900 and 1940. When this report is presented, the students should discuss ways in which strikes and union activities were forms of organized resistance.
	
	4. Ask the students to research the goals, tactics, and strategies used by the following Mexican-American civil rights groups: Order of the Sons of America, League of United Latin-American Citizens, The Community Service Organization, The American G.I. Forum, Federal Alliance of U.S. Cities, and Crusade for Justice. Ask the students to write several generalizations about the activities of these groups.
	
	5. Ask the students to research the following questions:
	  a. How is the "Chicano" movement similar to other Mexican American protest movements?
	  b. How are its goals and strategies different?
	  c. When did the movement emerge?
	  d. What long-range effects do you think the movement will have? Why?

Table 15-1   *CONTINUED*

Key Ideas	Activities
	6. Ask the students to read and dramatize the epic poem of the Chicano movement, *I Am Joaquin,* by Rodolfo Gonzales.
	7. Ask the students questions that will enable them to summarize and generalize about how Mexican Americans have resisted Anglo discrimination and oppression in both the past and in contemporary U.S. society.
	8. Conclude the unit by viewing and discussing the film *I Am Joaquin,* distributed by El Teatro Campesino, San Juan Bautisa, CA.

ing the concepts and generalizations. In the conceptual approach, the teacher emphasizes the mastery of concepts and generalizations rather than the mastery of specific facts. Facts are important only to the extent that they are necessary to help students learn key concepts and generalizations.

When you identify the key concepts and generalizations for a unit, you have already largely determined the cognitive objectives of the unit, although they have not been specifically stated. In the sample unit discussed in this chapter, the key concepts chosen for study are *cultural assimilation, economic status, ethnic community, immigration, social protest, identity,* and *discrimination.* A major objective of this unit is for the students to demonstrate their understandings of each of these concepts. However, because *understanding* is a word that means different things to different people, we must state the objective in behavioral terms so that its meaning will be more precise. To do this, we use an action word in the objective. Action words often used in behavioral objectives include the following:

recall	analyze
identify	describe
apply	construct
recite	observe
compare	

Our two conceptual objectives for this unit can be stated as follows:

1. The student will be able to identify examples and non-examples of the key concepts in the unit.

Table 15-2 COMPARATIVE STUDY OF ETHNIC GROUPS

Key Concepts and Questions	American Indians	Mexican Americans	African Americans	Jewish Americans	Puerto Ricans
Cultural Assimilation Level: Within group?					
Economic Status: High or low?					
Ethnic Community: To what extent?					
Immigration: Reasons?					
Social Protest: Forms?					
Identity: Kinds of expressions?					
Discrimination: What kinds does group experience?					

2. The student will be able to state examples and non-examples of the key concepts in the unit.

Other major unit objectives relate to the key generalizations in the unit and the method of inquiry used to derive them. At the conclusion of the unit, the students should be able to state or write the key generalizations in their own words, as well as to use the method of scientific inquiry to derive them. The objective related to the method of inquiry is a skill objective. The method of inquiry involves the following five basic steps (Banks with Clegg, 1990, p. 79):

1. Problem statement.
2. Statement of hypotheses.
3. Definition of terms (conceptualization).
4. Evaluation and analysis of data.
5. Testing hypotheses (deriving generalizations).

You can write objectives that relate to any or all of the skills involved in the process of inquiry. Presented below are objectives related to the basic steps of scientific inquiry.

When presented a problem such as, "What are the basic causes of racial and ethnic discrimination?" the student will be able to do the following:

1. State relevant hypotheses.
2. Collect pertinent data.
3. Evaluate the data (tell whether they are valid and reliable; state whether they are related to the problem).
4. Write a tentative generalization.
5. Revise the generalization when presented with additional data related to the problem.

Writing Affective Objectives

Objectives related to feelings, attitudes, and values pose special problems for the teacher. Although teachers in traditional classrooms usually had as one major objective the development of democratic attitudes in students, current theory and research about value teaching and learning have raised some serious questions about traditional approaches to value education (Shaver & Strong, 1982). Contemporary value education theorists argue that traditional approaches to value education have not been successful in helping students attain a system of clarified beliefs on which they are willing to act (Fraenkel, 1977; Kohlberg, 1968; Shaver & Strong, 1982).

Most students have many negative, confused, and/or conflicting feelings and attitudes toward racial and ethnic groups (Banks, 1995a). The goals of the affective component of the multicultural curriculum should be to help students determine how their values conflict, to identify value alternatives, to predict the consequences of alternative values, to freely choose a set of values on which they are willing to act, and to learn how to defend their moral choices reflectively.

Like cognitive objectives, affective objectives should be stated in behavioral terms so that they can be evaluated successfully. The following nine value objectives are based on the author's valuing model that is presented in outline form in chapter 4 (Banks with Clegg, 1990, pp. 435–448).

1. The students will be able to define and recognize value problems.
2. The students will be able to describe value-relevant behavior.
3. The students will be able to list values exemplified by behavior described.
4. The students will be able to identify conflicting values in behavior described.
5. The students will be able to state hypotheses about the sources of values analyzed.
6. The students will be able to list alternative values to those exemplified by behavior observed.
7. The students will be able to state hypotheses about the possible consequences of the values analyzed.
8. The students will be able to state value preferences.
9. The students will be able to state reasons, sources, and possible consequences of their value choices.

Writing Synthesis Objectives

Synthesis objectives are designed to increase the student's ability to use knowledge (facts, concepts, generalizations, and theories), to identify alternative courses of action, predict the possible consequences of each alternative, order those alternatives according to personal values, and take effective action consistent with his or her value positions. Examples of synthesis objectives follow.

An open-ended story like "Boycott, Yes or No" can be used to attain synthesis objectives. In this story Judy, age sixteen, tries to convince her family to stop buying lettuce after hearing an emotional and effective speech by Juan Garcia, a Mexican American social activist, at school earlier that day. Garcia told the students that people who refused to join the lettuce boycott were helping to exploit Mexican American field workers. Unable to convince her family to stop buying lettuce, the story ends with Judy frustrated and about to cry. When given such a story, the student will be able to do the following:

1. Identify and state the decision problem that Judy faces in the story.
2. State what courses of action Judy might take to solve her problem.
3. State the possible consequences of each course of action stated in objective.
4. State the facts, concepts, and generalizations that will help the student predict the possible consequences of each course of action stated in objective.
5. State the values that would play a part in each possible course of action.
6. State which course of action the student would take if he or she were Judy and why.
7. State how the action the student would take relates to personal values (whether it is consistent or inconsistent with the values he or she professes).

Using Multimedia Resources

Previous chapters stress the use of written materials in the exemplary teaching because books are the easiest resources for most teachers to obtain. However, whenever possible, you should use other media when teaching ethnic content, such as records, films, videotapes, photographs, and slides. Many multimedia materials are available that can be used to teach ethnic content. Many professional organizations, as well as commercial publishers, issue catalogs that list, and often annotate, available multimedia resources related to ethnic groups. The Anti-Defamation League of B'nai B'rith publishes an annual catalog that includes a rich collection of videotapes and other teaching materials. This publication can be obtained free from either the national office or a regional office of the League. The National Education Association also publishes a list of multimedia resources it produces. The Public Broadcasting Service (PBS) airs many excellent and informative programs that deal with ethnic groups and race relations. One of its most effective for teaching purposes is *Eyes on the Prize* (Parts I and II) (see Appendix B). PBS Video publishes a comprehensive catalog of videotapes that is available free by calling their toll-free telephone number: 800–344–3337.

The Southern Poverty Law Center, publisher of the magazine *Teaching Tolerance* (which it distributes free to teachers), also produces videotapes that it sends to teachers without charge. Its videotapes include *A History of Intolerance in America* and *America's Civil Rights Movement*. The AACP, Inc. (Asian American Curriculum Project), publishes a comprehensive catalog annually that includes multimedia materials for teaching about Asian Americans (AACP, P. O. Box 1587, San Mateo, CA 94401). These magazines include reviews of videotapes and films that are appropriate for school, college, and university use: *Teaching Tolerance, Multicultural Education,* and *Multicultural Review*. Some excellent multimedia resources are listed in the catalogs of commercial firms. The Social Studies School Service (Culver City, California) publishes an annual catalog that contains an excellent selection of multiethnic audiovisual materials. An annotated list of videotapes is found in Appendix B.

Some publishers publish excellent photographs and wall charts related to diversity in the United States that can be used in lessons and units. The New Press, a nonprofit publisher in New York City, publishes many excellent multicultural materials, including sets of photographs and wall charts. "Art of the American Indian Frontier" and "African Art Portfolio" are two of its sets of teaching photographs. The New Press also publishes an excellent set of wall charts, including one based on Howard Zinn's popular and transformative book, *A People's History of the United States* (Zinn & Kirschner, 1995).

Even though catalogs and bibliographies are helpful in locating multimedia resources, it is essential that you preview multimedia materials before using them in class. Most commercial firms will send materials for examination on a trial basis. Previewing multimedia resources is a time-consuming task. Unfortunately, however, there is no other way to make sure that they will contribute to your instructional goals and depict ethnic groups accurately and sensitively. Multimedia resources are often expensive to rent or purchase and are frequently difficult to obtain when they are needed by the teacher. However, in most metropolitan areas there is at least one good public library that has an excellent collection of audiovisual materials that can be borrowed without charge. You should take advantage of the many excellent services provided by the public libraries in your community. Photographs are usually easier to obtain than films, videotapes, and sound recordings. They can be cut from magazines such as *Ebony, Black Enterprise, Essence,* and *Hispanic* and can be purchased from publishers for a reasonable price. There are many sets of commercial photographs available that include American ethnic groups.

Using Community Resources

Every community has resources you can use to enrich the multicultural curriculum. One of the most helpful community resources is the ethnic organization. Ethnic organizations such as the Anti-Defamation League of B'nai B'rith, the National Association for the Advancement of Colored People, the Japanese American Citizenship League, and ASPIRA of America, Inc., provide services, many of them without charge, that can help enrich your curriculum. These organizations issue publications that describe and annotate teaching materials (usually available free on request) and will often provide speakers for a class or school who are specialists on particular ethnic groups.

Some ethnic organizations, such as the AACP (Asian American), the Association for the Study of Afro-American Life and History, and the Indian Historian Press, exist solely for the purpose of developing books and other materials that can be used as teacher references and as student resources. Materials published by ethnic organizations, and annotated bibliographies issued by them, merit special attention in the multicultural curriculum. Within every ethnic community, there is a wide diversity of opinions and attitudes. However, there are certain feelings and points of view that are usually shared within the ethnic community but that are frequently unknown by authors of books about ethnic groups or by librarians and teachers who select books for the school or public library. Paying close attention to the publications issued by ethnic organizations can enable you to select books and materials that reflect ethnic cultures and perspectives.

There are other community resources you should use when teaching ethnic content. Many colleges and universities have academic programs that focus on particular ethnic groups such as African Americans, Mexican Americans, Puerto Ricans, and Asian Americans. The professors who teach in these types of programs are academic specialists on the various ethnic groups and are often persons of color. You can draw on the services of these specialists when planning and teaching ethnic content. They are an important human resource that should not be overlooked. Heads of ethnic organizations, who are social activists, can also be invited to speak to the class or the school. They can present knowledge and points of view that are essential in a sound multicultural curriculum.

EVALUATING COGNITIVE AND AFFECTIVE OUTCOMES

If both the cognitive and affective objectives have been stated in behavioral terms, the evaluation of multicultural units will be greatly facilitated. To determine whether students can recognize examples and non-examples of such concepts as *racial discrimination* and *social protest,* you can give the students lists containing examples and non-examples of discrimination and social protest and ask them to indicate which are examples of the concepts and which are non-examples. Below is a list containing examples and non-examples of racial discrimination. Note that the student must have a mastery of factual knowledge about the court cases and events in order to be able to determine which items on the list are examples and non-examples of racial discrimination. However, the major goal of the exercise is to test the student's ability to recognize examples and non-examples of one key concept, *racial discrimination.*

Directions

Below are some events and court cases we have studied. Indicate those that are examples of racial discrimination by placing an "X" in front of them. Mark those which are non-examples of discrimination with "N."

_____ the Civil Rights Act of 1964

_____ the *Plessy* v. *Ferguson* decision, 1896

_____ the March on Washington, 1963

_____ Jim Crow laws

_____ the Brown decision, 1954

_____ the Detroit race riot, 1943

_____ the Immigration Act of 1924

_____ the Civil Liberties Act of 1988

To determine whether students can use the method of social inquiry to derive key generalizations related to such concepts as *immigration, social protest,* and *ethnic community,* you can give them graphs, statistics, maps, selected readings, and other kinds of data and ask the students key questions that will enable them to formulate and write generalizations.

Many types of sources and exercises, a number of which are described by Simon, Harmin, & Raths (1991), can be used to determine whether students are able to recognize value problems, to identify value conflicts, and to state their own values. These include the valuing sheet, the values grid, the value survey, role playing exercises, literary selections, photographs, open-ended stories, and essays written by the students. Some of these types of materials and exercises are discussed in chapter 4 in the section dealing with valuing goals and strategies.

EVALUATING DECISION-MAKING AND SOCIAL ACTION SKILLS

To evaluate the students' abilities to make decisions and to plan effective social action, they can be given a case study that presents an unresolved problem related to race and ethnicity and asked to do the following:

1. List the facts, concepts, and generalizations needed to make a sound decision regarding the issue.

2. List alternative values that are related to the issue, and the values that the student would endorse.

3. List alternative courses of action that could be taken regarding the issue, and their possible consequences (data should support each alternative listed).

4. Order the alternatives in a way most consistent with his or her values identified earlier.

5. List the course of action he or she would take on the issue.

6. State the possible consequences of taking that particular action.

In their book *Role Playing in the Curriculum,* Fannie and George Shaftel (1982) present several open-ended stories related to racial and ethnic problems. These stories can be used to help students develop decision-making and social-action skills, as well as to test their mastery of these skills. "No Trespassing" deals with a situation in which a boy is the victim of anti-Semitism. However, the story can be adapted to relate to problems encountered by other ethnic individuals. In "Second Prize," a donor of a school prize wants to withdraw it when he learns that the winner of the prize is African American. A Mexican American girl faces a personal dilemma when an Anglo boy asks her for a date in "Josefina."

Some of the open-ended stories in previous chapters of this book can be used successfully to evaluate decision making and the skill to develop social-action plans, especially "Trying to Buy a Home in Lakewood Island," "Father and Son," and "Mr. Diaz and Mr. Seda on the Mainland." You can also use pictures without captions, as well as case studies related to racial and ethnic incidents that have occurred within your school or community.

In a testing situation, you can ask the students to read "Trying to Buy a Home in Lakewood Island" (see page 234), and to respond briefly to each of the following questions.

1. What knowledge (facts, concepts, generalizations, and theories) would the Greens need in order to make an effective decision in this case?

2. What are some values that are involved in the case? What value do you think should guide the Greens' decision? What is the most important value to you in this case?

3. What are possible actions that the Greens can take? What are the possible consequences of each possible course of action?

4. Which of the courses of action you identified above are most consistent with your own values?

5. What should the Greens do? If you were the Greens, what would you do? Why?

6. What are some of the possible consequences that might result from the course of action you would take? Are you willing to accept them?

When you evaluate a student's response to a decision-making testing exercise, such as the one above, you should determine whether the knowledge the student identifies is accurate and whether it is related to the particular case study. Knowledge about prejudice, discrimination, civil rights laws, and how real estate is traditionally sold will help the Greens make a reflective decision in the case in our example. You should also determine how well the student can identify values implicit in the case. This case, for example, raises two conflicting values—the rights of the property owner versus the rights of the buyer.

ou should determine how well the student can identify and state realistic alternatives and their possible consequences. The students should also be judged on how well they can state and defend a personal value position.

EVALUATING THE TOTAL SCHOOL ENVIRONMENT

Multicultural teaching can best occur within an educational environment that has institutional norms that recognize and are sensitive to cultural and ethnic diversity. Thus, to change the school climate so that the school reinforces and promotes the concept of cultural diversity, changes must occur in all the major variables of the school environment, including teacher attitudes and expectations, the "hidden curriculum," school policy, the counseling program, and the assessment and testing procedures. Figure 15-1 illustrates these and other variables that must be reformed in order to make the school a multicultural institution. In other words, effective multicultural teaching can best occur within a multicultural school environment.

When trying to determine the quality of multicultural education in their school, the instructional and administrative staffs can use the rating scale in Table 15-3. When completed, this scale will give the staff a rough estimate of the general quality of the school's multicultural education program. This information will enable the staff to identify recommendations that will guide actions to make the school environment more culturally pluralistic. In areas where the school program is already outstanding, the findings derived by using the scale can provide the staff with needed positive reinforcement.

Schools or districts that wish to use a more detailed evaluation instrument may use the Multiethnic Education Program Evaluation Checklist developed by the National Council for the Social Studies Task Force on Ethnic Studies Curriculum Guidelines. It is designed to encourage and assist in the assessment of specific school environments to determine the extent to which they reflect the standards for multicultural education presented in the Task Force's publication, *Curriculum Guidelines for Multicultural Education* (Banks, Cortés, Gay, Garcia, & Ochoa, 1991). This publication was issued as a position statement by the National Council for the Social Studies.

THE TEACHER AND THE MULTICULTURAL CURRICULUM

The teacher is the most important variable in the multicultural curriculum. His or her attitudes toward ethnic content and ethnic cultures are crucial. Many teachers, especially mainstream American teachers, may fear teaching ethnic content, particularly if their classes include students of color. This problem might be compounded if minority students in their classes express or show

Figure 15-1 THE TOTAL SCHOOL ENVIRONMENT

In this figure, the total school environment is conceptualized as a system that consists of a number of major identifiable factors, such as school policy, the institutionalized norms, and the formalized curriculum or course of study. In the ideal multicultural school, each factor reflects ethnic pluralism. Even though any one factor may be the focus of initial school reform, changes must occur in each of them to create and sustain an effective multicultural educational environment.

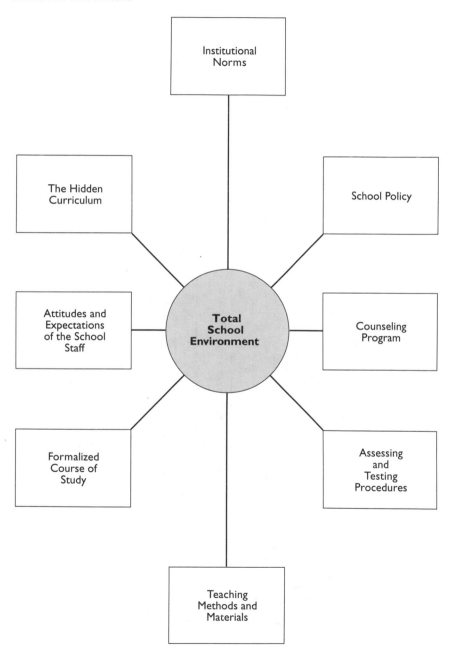

Table 15-3 EVALUATING THE TOTAL MULTICULTURAL PROGRAM

Directions for using this rating scale:

Check "NA" if the answer to the question is "not at all." Check "1" if the answer is "yes but very little." Check "5" if the answer is "yes, that aspect of our program is outstanding." Check the numbers from 2 to 4 if the response is somewhere between the extremes. By adding the points when you have finished rating your school, you can obtain a rough estimate of the general quality of your total multicultural educational program ("NA" = 0 points). The total number of points possible is 90.

1. Is information about U.S. ethnic groups included in *all* the courses in the school, including social studies, English, literature, physical education, home economics, and science?	NA	1	2	3	4	5
2. Is there a procedure for evaluating the treatment of ethnic groups in textbooks before they are adopted for use in the school? If so, to what extent is it effective?	NA	1	2	3	4	5
3. Are there pictures of minority groups in the classrooms and in the halls of the schools?	NA	1	2	3	4	5
4. Do the calendars in the school include information about ethnic holidays and outstanding Americans of ethnic origin?	NA	1	2	3	4	5
5. Do the foods served in the school cafeteria reflect the ethnic diversity of American life? If so, in what ways?	NA	1	2	3	4	5
6. Do school assemblies and plays reflect the ethnic diversity of American life? If so, to what extent?	NA	1	2	3	4	5
7. Are the teachers and administrators provided inservice workshops and activities where they can acquire content about American ethnic cultures and ways to teach about them?	NA	1	2	3	4	5
8. Does the school's professional library include books about American ethnic groups and ways to teach about them?	NA	1	2	3	4	5
9. Does the school's library include an ample number of books about American ethnic groups for all grade levels? If so, have the books been evaluated for their sensitivity to ethnic groups?	NA	1	2	3	4	5
10. Does the school library subscribe to ethnic magazines such as *Ebony, Indian Historian, Amerasia Journal, Hispanic,* and *El Grito?*	NA	1	2	3	4	5

	NA	1	2	3	4	5
11. Is there, or has there been a curriculum committee created to devise ways to integrate the entire school curriculum with ethnic content? If so, did the committee solicit the help of specialists in ethnic studies?	NA	1	2	3	4	5
12. Are individuals from the various ethnic organizations within the community or in nearby communities frequently invited to speak to classes and in school assemblies?	NA	1	2	3	4	5
13. Does the school offer elective courses in ethnic studies? If so, what are they?_____ Do they provide the student with a range of courses that include information about all American ethnic groups, including Puerto Ricans, Filipino Americans, Cuban Americans, and Mexican Americans?	NA	1	2	3	4	5
14. Do school holidays and celebrations reflect the ethnic diversity of American life? If so, what specific ethnic holidays are celebrated?_____ How are they celebrated?_____	NA	1	2	3	4	5
15. Do bulletin boards and other displays in the school reflect the ethnic diversity of American life? If so, in what ways?_____	NA	1	2	3	4	5
16. Does the school district have an ample supply of films, videotapes, records, and other multimedia resources on American ethnic groups? If so, have they been evaluated for ethnic sensitivity?	NA	1	2	3	4	5
17. Has the school (or the school district) developed and implemented a policy to hire staff members who represent a range of racial and ethnic groups?	NA	1	2	3	4	5
18. Does the school encourage and support dialect and language diversity?	NA	1	2	3	4	5

Total School Score _____

Recommended Actions:

1.

2.

3.

4.

5.

negative attitudes toward learning about their cultural heritages, which sometimes happens. Teachers might also be intimidated by those who argue that White teachers cannot and should not teach about African Americans, American Indians, and Mexican Americans, and that they can never know the experiences of people of color who are victims of institutional racism in America.

The teacher should clarify his or her attitudes toward people of color before attempting to teach about them. Teachers who have negative or condescending attitudes toward people of color may do more harm than good when they teach ethnic content. Research suggests that teacher attitudes are revealed to students even when teachers are unaware of their negative feelings (Banks, 1972; Henderson, 1974). Teachers who are unsure about their racial and ethnic attitudes should test them by reading some of the books recommended in earlier chapters and by enrolling in a human relations or multicultural education workshop or course. A multicultural education workshop or course will give the teacher the opportunity to express personal feelings and perceptions, compare them with the attitudes of other teachers, and clarify racial feelings.

Once a teacher is keenly aware of personal racial attitudes and is satisfied that they are basically positive toward people of color, that teacher should staunchly defend his or her right and responsibility to teach ethnic content. It is true that White teachers will never fully know what it means to be African American, Puerto Rican, or Indian in contemporary American society, just as members of these groups will never fully know what it means to be White. It is also true that teachers of color can present students with perspectives and points of view that the White teacher will be unable to present to them. However, ethnic content is legitimate knowledge that should be taught in the school. We should approach the teaching of ethnic content the way in which we approach the teaching of other content in the social sciences and humanities. We do not assume that a teacher must have lived during medieval times in order to teach medieval history effectively, or that a teacher has to be Italian in order to teach about the Renaissance in Italy. African American teachers have successfully taught European history for many years. Likewise, we are not justified in arguing that only African Americans can teach about Blacks or that only Chicanos can teach about Mexican Americans. Although it is desirable, for many reasons, for school districts to recruit and hire as many teachers of color as possible, White teachers, as well as African American and Mexican American teachers, have a professional and, I feel, moral responsibility to teach about American ethnic groups and to integrate ethnic content into their regular curricula and courses.

A teacher who is sensitive and knowledgeable, regardless of his or her ethnic or racial group, can teach any subject effectively. *However, it is important for students to be exposed to the points of view and perceptions of members of the various ethnic groups.* This can be done by selecting sensitive and powerful teaching materials written by ethnic authors, using powerful videotapes such as *Eyes on the Prize* and *How the West Was Lost* (see Appendix B) and using the types of community resources discussed earlier in this chapter. Many excellent books written by authors of color are annotated in chapters 5 through 14. Records, films, videotapes, and ethnic periodicals can also be used to present the perspectives of ethnic groups to students. Knowledgeable and informed teachers can also interpret many of these viewpoints to students. However, there is no substitute for students' reading and listening to such viewpoints themselves.

Sensitive and knowledgeable teachers who approach teaching with integrity and openness can defend their right to teach ethnic content to any individual or group. Such teachers can convince ethnic students that they have a right and a responsibility to teach about ethnic cultures. When a teacher claims that students of color are resisting ethnic content, it is usually because the teacher has presented ethnic content in a condescending way, has not clarified his or her feelings toward groups of color, or has not established a norm in the classroom that respects and tolerates cultural and ethnic differences. It is unrealistic to expect minority group students to be eager to study and examine their cultural heritages in a school and classroom atmosphere in which the mainstream American culture is held up as the ideal and in which their cultures are demeaned in subtle or overt ways.

The need for teachers to be intellectually competent before they embark on teaching ethnic content cannot be overemphasized. The teacher who is serious about wanting to teach ethnic content should read at least one book or comprehensive chapter on each major American ethnic group and one general source on race and ethnicity in American society. Every school should have a multicultural library for its professional staff. The "Books for Teachers" section at the end of this chapter contains appropriate and recommended books.

I do not mean to suggest that teachers can read a few books and become experts in ethnic studies or specialists on a particular ethnic group. Becoming an ethnic studies specialist, in any sense, takes many years of study, research, and reflection. Even though I am recommending that all classroom teachers integrate ethnic content into their regular courses, I feel that specialized courses on ethnic groups or particular ethnic groups, such as a Black studies course or a Chicano studies course, should be taught only by a teacher who has specialized in ethnic studies. A person who has successfully functioned within an ethnic culture is more likely to have the kind of sensitivity needed to teach a specialized ethnic studies course effectively.

The Challenge of Ethnic Studies

No one who has seriously studied American ethnic groups can underestimate the difficulties involved in learning about them. Trying to learn the truth about American ethnic groups involves much unlearning of facts and interpretations that we learned in school and much new learning. It involves a kind of personal transformation, in both attitudes and conceptual understandings. A good part of the knowledge that most of us learned in school contained myths created by social scientists and historians who strongly identified with the mainstream culture and who felt a need, whether conscious or not, to justify the discrimination and racism that groups of color in the United States experienced (Banks, 1995b). Studying and teaching about ethnic cultures will involve, for most teachers, intellectual and emotional confrontations with many of the feelings and beliefs they cherish about U.S. society.

To understand fully the nature of American society and the role that ethnicity plays within it, teachers will have to reconceptualize their views of America. This will involve conceptual transformation and re-envisioning America. For example, the United States is usually studied as an extension of European social and political institutions. However, American Indians were in America centuries before Columbus. To view America merely as an extension of European institutions ignores American Indian institutions and cultures. Ethnic studies demands that teachers and students reconceptualize their views of the winning of the West, the meaning of slavery, the purpose of American expansion in the late 1800s, and the nature of democracy as it is practiced in contemporary U.S. society (Todorov, 1982).

The intellectual and emotional confrontations that ethnic studies will require of teachers and students will help them attain more humanistic views of people of color and break out of their own ethnic encapsulations. Ethnic studies will teach them that there are other ways of living and being, and that to be racially and ethnically different does not mean that one is inferior or superior. More humanistic views of other cultures are imperative within our increasingly interdependent and ethnically polarized world. Humanistic views of other groups and cultures may help to create the kind of racial and ethnic harmony that our society must have to survive and prosper in the new century.

REFERENCES

Banks, J. A. (1972). Racial Prejudice and the Black Self-Concept. In J. A. Banks & J. D. Grambs (Eds.). *Black Self-Concept: Implications for Education and Social Science* (pp. 1–35). New York: McGraw-Hill.

Banks, J. A. (1995a). Multicultural Education: Its Effects on Students' Racial and Gender Role Attitudes. In J. A. Banks & C. A. M. Banks (Eds.). *Handbook of Research on Multicultural Education* (pp. 617–627). New York: Macmillan.

Banks, J. A. (1995b). The Historical Reconstruction of Knowledge about Race: Implications for Transformative Teaching. *Educational Researcher*, 24 (2), 15–25.

Banks, J. A. with Clegg, A. A., Jr. (1990). *Teaching Strategies for the Social Studies* (4th ed.). New York: Longman, Inc.

Banks, J. A., Cortés, C. E., Gay, G., Garcia, R. L., & Ochoa, A. (1991). *Curriculum Guidelines for Multicultural Education*. Washington, D. C.: National Council for the Social Studies.

Fraenkel, J. R. (1977). *How to Teach about Values: An Analytic Approach*. Englewood Cliffs, N.J.: Prentice-Hall.

Henderson, G. (1974). *Human Relations: From Theory to Practice*. Norman: University of Oklahoma.

Kohlberg, L. (1968, September). The Child as a Moral Philosopher. *Psychology Today 2*, No. 4, 24–30.

Shaftel F. R. & Shaftel, G. (1982). *Role Playing in the Curriculum* (2nd ed.). Englewood Cliffs, N.J.: Prentice-Hall.

Shaver, J. P. & Strong, W. (1982). *Facing Value Decisions: Rationale Building for Teachers* (2nd ed.). New York: Teachers College Press.

Simon, S. B., Harmin, M. & Raths, L. E. (1991). *Values and Teaching: Working with Values in the Classroom* (Rev. ed.). Columbus, Oh.: Merrill.

Todorov, T. (1982). *The Conquest of America: The Question of the Other*. New York: HarperCollins.

Zinn, H. & Kirschner, G. (1995). *A People's History of the United States: The Wall Charts*. New York: The New Press.

ANNOTATED BIBLIOGRAPHY

Books for Teachers

Andersen, M. L. & Collins, P. H. (Eds.). (1995). *Race, Class and Gender: An Anthology* (2nd ed.). Belmont, Calif.: Wadsworth.

An excellent and thoughtful collection of articles designed for use by college and university students.

Aponte, J. F., Rivers, R. Y., & Wohl, J. (Eds.). (1995). *Psychological Interventions and Cultural Diversity*. Boston: Allyn and Bacon.

The chapters in this book discuss a range of issues related to mental health and ethnic minorities, including "Clinical Issues and Intervention with Ethnic Minority Women," "Community Approaches with Ethnic Groups," and "Group Interventions and Treatment with Ethnic Minorities."

Banks, J. A. (1994). *Multiethnic Education: Theory and Practice* (3rd ed.). Boston: Allyn and Bacon.

The author describes theories, paradigms, and strategies for implementing multicultural education.

Banks, J. A. & Banks, C. A. M. (Eds.). (1993). *Multicultural Education: Issues and Perspectives* (2nd ed.). Boston: Allyn and Bacon.

Experts in multicultural education provide diverse perspectives and conceptual frameworks for implementing multicultural education.

Banks, J. A. & Banks, C. A. M. (Eds.) (1995). *Handbook of Research on Multicultural Education.* New York: Macmillan.

Scholars from a variety of disciplines and fields discuss the history, philosophy, practice, and future of the field. An essential reference for the school, college, or university library or teacher resource collection. The Handbook *consists of 47 chapters and 882 oversized pages.*

Carnoy, M. (1994). *Faded Dreams: The Politics and Economics of Race in America.* New York: Cambridge University Press.

An economist argues that politics to a great extent explain the economic problems and loss of progress among minorities of color in contemporary U.S. society.

Cyrus, V. (Ed.). (1993). *Experiencing Race, Class and Gender in the United States.* Mountain View, Calif.: Mayfield Publishing Co.

A rich and excellent collection of articles designed for college students. Many of the selections are suitable for use with senior high school students.

Delpit, L. (1995). *Other People's Children: Cultural Conflict in the Classroom.* New York: The New Press.

A beautifully and sensitively written collection of essays about effective ways to teach children from diverse racial, ethnic, and cultural groups. The last chapter in this engaging book is titled "Education in a Multicultural Society."

Dines, G. & Humez, J. M. (Eds.). (1995). *Gender, Race, and Class in Media: A Text-Reader.* Thousand Oaks, Calif.: Sage Publications.

This comprehensive anthology will help teachers to implement lessons and units related to the treatment of women and minorities in the media.

Feagin, J. R. & Vera, H. (1995). *White Racism: The Basics.* New York: Routledge.

This well-researched and readable book deals with a topic that deserves more attention in multicultural education.

Funderburg, L. (1995). *Black, White, Other: Biracial Americans Talk about Race and Identity.* New York: William Morrow.

The biracial author of this book presents the lives and views of forty-six adult children of Black–White unions. Interest in this topic is growing.

Gay, G. (1994). *At the Essence of Learning: Multicultural Education.* West Lafayette, Ind.: Kappa Delta Pi.

This well-crafted and thoughtful book by a multicultural education veteran describes how the goals of multicultural and general education intersect.

Gillan, M. M. & Gillan, J. (Eds.). (1994). *Unsettling America: An Anthology of Contemporary Multicultural Poetry.* New York: Penguin.

Color, language, ethnicity, and religious diversity are reflected in this rich anthology that is very useful for teaching social studies and language arts.

Goldberg, D. T. (Ed.). (1994). *Multiculturalism: A Critical Reader.* Cambridge, Mass.: Basil Blackwell.

Contributors to this stimulating and informative reader that focuses on multicultural issues in higher education include Peter McLaren, Ramón A. Guitiérrez, Henry Louis Gates, Jr., Michele Wallace, Sandra Harding, and Henry Giroux.

Grant, C. A. & Gomez, M. L. (Eds.). (1996). *Making Schooling Multicultural: Campus and Classroom.* Englewood Cliffs, N.J.: Merrill.

This volume includes chapters on multicultural issues in a variety of subject areas.

Gutiérrez, R. A. & Fabre, G. (Eds.). (1995). *Feats and Celebrations in North American Ethnic Communities.* Albuquerque: University of New Mexico Press.

This book consists of twelve essays that discuss the cultural and historical meanings of ethnic feasts and celebrations.

Igoa, C. (1995). *The World of the Immigrant Child.* New York: St. Martin's.

Written by an author who was an immigrant child, this book presents important perspectives on the world of immigrant children.

Johnson, L. & Smith, S. (1993). *Dealing with Diversity through Multicultural Fiction: Library-Classroom Partnerships.* Chicago: American Library Association.

A helpful source for implementing a literature-based instructional program.

Nieto, S. (1996). *Affirming Diversity: The Sociopolitical Context of Multicultural Education* (2nd ed.). White Plains, N.Y.: Longman.

This thoughtful book by a leading scholar in multicultural education uses a case-study approach.

Perkins, D. (1995). *Outsmarting IQ: The Emerging Science of Learnable Intelligence.* New York: The Free Press.

A hopeful book about the intellectual potential of all children. It provides a needed antidote to the doom prophets who write about the limited intellectual potential of children of color.

Rico, B. R. & Mano, S. (Eds.). (1995). *Multicultural Readings in Context* (2nd ed.). Boston: Houghton Mifflin.

This comprehensive anthology includes readings that focus on early immigrants, Chinese immigrants, African Americans, Puerto Ricans, Japanese Americans, Chicanos, American Indians, and new immigrants. Designed for college students, many of the selections can be used successfully with high school students.

Seller, M. S. (Ed.). *Immigrant Women* (rev. 2nd ed.). New York: State University of New York Press.

This rich resource includes diaries, oral history, and fiction, as well as other genres.

Sleeter, C. E. & McLaren, P. L. (Eds.). (1995). *Multicultural Education, Critical Pedagogy, and the Politics of Difference.* Albany: State University of New York Press.

The contributors to this book, including Geneva Gay, Sonia Nieto, and Cameron McCarthy, discuss the intersections between multicultural education and critical pedagogy.

Stephan, W. G. & Stephan, C. W. (1996). *Intergroup Relations.* Madison, Wisc.: Brown & Benchmark.

An excellent summary of the research on stereotypes, theories of prejudice, the contact hypothesis, and intergroup conflict and its resolution.

Takaki, R. (Ed.) (1994). *From Different Shores: Perspectives on Race and Ethnicity in America* (2nd ed.). New York: Oxford University Press.

These historical and sociological articles are organized into six parts: patterns, culture, class, gender, public policy, and prospects. The last part focuses on the curriculum cultural wars.

Ungar, S. J. (1995). *Fresh Blood: The New Immigrant Experience.* New York: Simon & Schuster.

Ungar argues that immigrants still "enrich our national character and experience." This book includes a discussion of the Hmong, Cubans, Poles, Ethiopians, Koreans, and other new immigrant groups.

Wang, M. C. & Gordon, E. W. (Eds.). (1994). *Educational Resilience in Inner-City America: Challenges and Prospects.* Hillsdale, N.J.: Lawrence Erlbaum.

The contributors to this important book focus on the strengths of inner-city youth, a needed perspective in education.

Zinn, H. (1995). *A People's History of the United States: 1492 to Present* (rev. and updated ed.). New York: Harper.

This transformative work presents perspectives on U.S. history that should be incorporated into the social studies curriculum.

Books for Students

Series That Focus on Ethnic Groups and Cultures

American Voices. (1991). Vero Beach, Fla.: Rourke Publications.

Each of these illustrated books describes the history of one ethnic group and its experiences in the United States. Each book is about 100 pages in length. Titles in the series include Chinese Americans; German Americans; Italian Americans; Japanese Americans; Mexican Americans; *and* Vietnamese Americans. *(Middle School and up)*

In America Series. (1987–1993). Minneapolis: Lerner Publications.

This valuable series consists of more than fifteen books that describes the historical experiences of ethnic groups in the United States. Titles in the Series include Cubans in America; Filipinos in America; Koreans in America; America Indians in America *(2 volumes);* The Jews in America; Italians in America; *and* The Lebanese in America. *Each book is written by a different author. (Intermediate and up)*

Ethnic America. (1991). Brookfield, Conn.: Millbrook Press.

This series of six books, organized by regions in the United States, describe the contributions of diverse ethnic groups to each region. Titles are North Central States; Northeastern States; Northwestern States; South Central States; Southeastern States; *and* Southwestern States. *Each book consists of sixty-four pages. (Intermediate/Middle School)*

Hoobler, D. & Hoobler, T. (1994–1995). *The American Family Album Series.* New York: Oxford University Press.

Each of the books in this excellent, exciting, and well-written series simulates a family album and includes period photographs and original documents such as diaries, letters, and newspaper excerpts. These books are beautifully illustrated with photographs. The series includes these titles: The African American Family Album; The Cuban American Family Album; The German American Family Album; The Irish American Family Album; The Japanese American Family Album; The Jewish American Family Album; The Chinese American Family Album; The Italian American Family Album; *and* The Mexican American Family Album. *(Intermediate and up)*

Katz, W. L. (1993). *A History of Multicultural America.* Austin, Tex.: Raintree Steck-Vaughn.

This excellent and well-written series of seven books was authored by a veteran writer. The books are well-researched and are illustrated with black-and-white photographs. Titles in the series are Exploration to the War of 1812, 1492–1814; The Westward Movement and Abolitionism, 1815–1850; The Civil War to the Last Frontier, 1850–1880s; The Great Migrations, 1880s-1912; The New Freedom to the New Deal, 1913–1939; World War II to the New Frontier, 1940–1963; The Great Society to the Reagan Era, 1964–1990; *and* Minorities Today. *(Intermediate and up)*

The Peoples of North America (1986–1993). New York: Chelsea House.

The thirty-three books is this series have color and black-and-white photographs and describe a wide range of ethnic groups. Titles in the series include The Arab Americans; The Chinese Americans; The Filipinos Americans; The Korean Americans; The Italian Americans; The Puerto Rican Americans; *and* The Ukrainian Americans.

Takaki, R. (1994). Adapted by R. Stefoff. *The Asian American Experience.* New York: Chelsea House.

The fifteen books in this valuable and well-researched series are based on the author's popular history of Asian Americans, Strangers from a Different Shore *(Little Brown, 1989). The text from the author's book was adapted for young readers by Rebecca Stefoff, a writer and editor who has published fifty nonfiction books for young readers. Titles in the series include* Spacious Dreams: The First Wave of Asian Immigration; Journey to Gold Mountain: The Chinese in Nineteenth Century America; Issei and Nisei: The Settling of Japanese America; From the Land of Mourning Calm: The Koreans in America; In the Heart of Filipino America: Immigrants from the Pacific Isles; India in the West: South Asian Immigrants in America; *and* Breaking Silences: Asian Americans Today. *The books are amply illustrated. (Intermediate and up)*

Publishers That Specialize in Books for Children and Young Readers on Multicultural Topics

A few publishers specialize in publishing books on multicultural issues for children and young people or have a division that does. Below is a short list of such publishers who responded to my letter of inquiry. Readers are invited to send me the names of other publishers. The addresses and phone numbers are correct for early 1996. However, it is best to double-check addresses and phone numbers. They change frequently in the publishing world.

Children's Books Press
246 First Street, Suite 101
San Francisco, CA 94105
Phone: 415–995–2200

Lee & Low Books
95 Madison Avenue
New York, NY 10016
Phone: 212–779–4400

The New Press
450 West 41st Street, 6th Floor
New York, NY 10036
Phone: 212–629–8802

Northland Publishing
P.O. Box 1389
Flagstaff, AZ 86002
Phone: 520–774–5251
Toll free: 800–346–3257
Northland specialize in books on Native Americans and the West.

Piñata Books
A Division of Arte Público Press
University of Houston
Houston, TX 77204–2090
Phone: 713–743–2841
Piñata Books deal with Hispanic topics.

ETHNIC GROUPS IN U.S. HISTORY

A CHRONOLOGY OF KEY EVENTS

*Indicates an important immigration act.

Date	Event
1513	Juan Ponce de León landed on the Florida peninsula while on route from Puerto Rico. The relationship between Europeans and Indians north of Mexico began.
1519	Hernán Cortéz, the Spanish conquistador, and a group of Spaniards arrived in the region that is now Mexico.
1565	The Spaniards established the St. Augustine colony in Florida, the first settlement organized by Europeans in present-day United States.
1619	The first Africans arrived in the English North American colonies.
1620	The Pilgrims came to America from England on the *Mayflower* and established a settlement at Plymouth, Massachusetts.
1637	More than 500 American Indians were killed by the colonists in a massacre known as the Pequot War.
1654	The first Jewish immigrants to North America settled in New Amsterdam to escape persecution in Brazil.
1683	German immigrants settled in Pennsylvania.
1718	The Scots-Irish began immigrating to North America in large numbers.
1754–63	The French and Indian War occurred.

Date	Event
1798	A Federalist-dominated Congress enacted the Alien and Sedition Acts to crush the Republican party and to harass aliens.
1812	The War of 1812, a war between the United States and Britain, caused deep factions among the Indian tribes because of their different allegiances.
1815	The first mass immigrations from Europe to North America began.
1830	Congress passed a Removal Act, which authorized the removal of Indians from east to west of the Mississippi.
1831	Nat Turner led a slave revolt in which nearly 60 Whites were killed.
1836	Mexico's President Santa Anna and his troops defeated the Texans at the Alamo. Six weeks later Santa Anna was defeated by Sam Houston and his Texan troops at San Jacinto.
1845	The United States annexed Texas, which had declared itself independent from Mexico in 1836. This was one key event that led to the Mexican-American War.
1846–48	A series of potato blights in Ireland caused thousands of its citizens to immigrate to the United States.
1846	On May 13, 1846, the United States declared war on Mexico and the Mexican-American War began.
1848	The United States and Mexico signed the Treaty of Guadalupe Hidalgo that ended the Mexican-American War. Mexico lost nearly one-third of its territory, and the United States acquired most of the territory that comprises its southwestern states.
1850	The California legislature passed a discriminatory Foreign Miner's Tax that forced Chinese immigrants to pay a highly disproportionate share of the state taxes.
1855	Castle Garden, an immigration station, opened in New York City. The antiforeign Know-Nothing Movement reached its zenith and had a number of political successes in the 1855 elections. The movement rapidly declined after 1855.
1859	Juan N. Cortina, who became a U.S. citizen under the provisions of the Treaty of Guadalupe Hidalgo, led a series of rebellions against Anglo-Americans in the Southwest.
1863	On January 1, 1863, President Abraham Lincoln issued the Emancipation Proclamation, which freed slaves in those states still fighting the Union.
1864	Nearly 300 Cheyennes were killed in a surprise attack at Sand Creek, Colorado. This event is known as the Sand Creek Massacre.

Date	Event
1869	The transcontinental railroad, linking the West to the East, was completed. Chinese laborers did most of the work on the Pacific portion of the railroad.
	The unsuccessful Wakamatsu Colony, made up of Japanese immigrants, was established in California.
1871	A White mob in Los Angeles attacked a Chinese community. When the conflict ended, 19 Chinese were killed and their community was in shambles.
1876	In the disputed Hayes-Tilden election, the Democrats and Republicans made a political bargain that symbolized the extent to which northern Whites had abandoned southern Blacks.
	Sioux tribes, under the leadership of Sitting Bull, wiped out Custer's Seventh Cavalry at Little Big Horn. This was one of the last victories for American Indian tribes.
*1882	The Chinese Exclusion Act was enacted by Congress.
	Another congressional immigration act established a head tax of fifty cents and excluded lunatics, convicts, idiots, and those likely to become public charges.
1885	A serious anti-Chinese riot occurred in Rock Springs, Wyoming. Twenty-eight Chinese were killed, and many others were wounded and driven from their homes.
1886	The Apache warrior Geronimo surrendered to U.S. forces in September 1886. His surrender marked the defeat of the Southwest tribes.
	The Haymarket Affair in Chicago increased the fear of foreign "radicals" and stimulated the growth of nativistic sentiments in the United States.
	The Statue of Liberty was dedicated as nativism soared in the United States.
1887	Congress passed the Dawes Severalty Act, which was designed to terminate partially the Indian's special relationship with the U.S. government.
1888	The Scott Act prohibited the immigration of Chinese laborers and permitted only officials, teachers, students, merchants, and travelers from China to enter the United States.
1890	Three hundred Sioux were killed in a conflict at Wounded Knee Creek in South Dakota.
1891	Eleven Italian Americans were lynched in New Orleans during the height of American nativism, after being accused of murdering a police superintendent.

Date	Event
1892	Ellis Island opened and replaced Castle Garden as the main port of entry for European immigrants.
1893	Queen Liliuokalani of Hawaii was overthrown in a bloodless revolution led by American planters. The Republic of Hawaii was established, with Stanford B. Dole as president.
1896	In a historic decision, *Plessy* v. *Ferguson,* the Supreme Court ruled that "separate but equal" facilities were constitutional.
1898	Hawaii was annexed to the United States. Under the terms of the Treaty of Paris, the treaty that ended the Spanish-American War, the United States acquired Puerto Rico, Guam, and the Philippines. Cuba became independent of Spain but was placed under U.S. tutelage.
1900	With the Foraker Act, the United States established a government in Puerto Rico to which the president of the United States appointed the governor and the Executive Council.
1901–10	Almost 9 million immigrants entered the United States, most of whom came from southern and eastern Europe.
1908	The United States and Japan made the Gentlemen's Agreement, which was designed to reduce the number of Japanese immigrants entering the United States.
1910	The National Association for the Advancement of Colored People (NAACP) was organized. A Mexican revolution caused many Mexican peasants to immigrate to the United States looking for jobs. Other immigrants came to escape political turmoil and persecution.
1913	The California legislature passed a land bill that made it difficult for Japanese immigrants to lease land.
*1917	Thirty-nine African Americans were killed in a bloody riot in East St. Louis, Missouri. A comprehensive immigration bill was enacted that established a literacy test for entering immigrants. The Jones Act was passed by the U.S. Congress. It made Puerto Ricans U.S. citizens and subject to the U.S. draft.
1920	The Hawaiian Homes Commission was started to benefit the native Hawaiian. Very little of the land involved was used for its stated purpose. The number of persons born in Puerto Rico and living in the United States was 11,811. That number increased to 58,200 in the year 1935.
*1924	The Johnson-Reed Act established extreme quotas on immigration and blatantly discriminated against southern and eastern European and non-White nations.

Date	Event
1925	A large number of Filipinos began to immigrate to Hawaii and the U.S. mainland to work as field laborers.
1927	The Filipino Federation of Labor was organized in Los Angeles.
1928	The League of United Latin American Citizens was formed in Harlingen, Texas.
1929	An anti-Filipino riot occurred in Exeter, California, in which more than 200 Filipinos were assaulted.
1930	The Japanese American Citizenship League was organized.
*1934	Congress passed the Tydings-McDuffie Act. This act promised the Philippines independence and limited Filipino immigration to the United States to 50 per year.
1935	President Franklin D. Roosevelt signed the Repatriation Act. The act offered free transportation to Filipinos who would return to the Philippines. Those who left were unable to return to the United States except under a severe quota system.
1942	On February 19, 1942, President Franklin D. Roosevelt issued Executive Order 9066, which authorized the internment of Japanese Americans who lived on the West Coast. The United States and Mexico made an agreement that authorized Mexican immigrants to work temporarily in the United States. This project is known as the *bracero* program.
1943	White violence directed at African Americans led to a serious riot in Detroit, in which 34 people were killed. The anti-Mexican zoot suit riots occurred in Los Angeles during the summer.
1946	On July 4, 1946, the Philippines became independent.
*1952	The McCarran-Walter Immigration and Nationality Act was passed by Congress. It eliminated race as a factor in immigration. However, the national origins quota system remained but was liberalized.
1954	The Refugee Relief Act permitted 5,000 Hungarian refugees to enter the United States. In a landmark decision, *Brown v. Board of Education,* the Supreme Court ruled that school segregation was inherently unequal. The U.S. Immigration and Naturalization Service began Operation Wetback, a massive program to deport illegal Mexican immigrants.
1959	Fidel Castro took over the reins of power in Cuba from the government of Fulgencio Batista. After this revolution, many Cuban refugees entered the United States. Hawaii became the fiftieth state of the United States.
1960	On February 1, 1960, the sit-in movement, which desegregated public accommodation facilities throughout the South, began in Greensboro, North Carolina.

Date	Event
1961	The National Indian Youth Council was organized.
1962	Commercial air flights between the United States and Cuba ended. Immigration from Cuba to the United States became strictly clandestine.
1963	More than 200,000 people participated in a "March on Washington for Freedom and Jobs."
1964	The Civil Rights Act of 1964, the most comprehensive civil rights bill in American history, was enacted by Congress and signed by President Lyndon B. Johnson.
1965	With the passage of the Civil Rights Act of 1965, Puerto Ricans were no longer required to pass an English literacy test to vote in New York state. *The Immigration Reform Act of 1965 was passed by Congress. This act, which became effective in 1968, abolished the national origins quota system and liberalized American immigration policy. Immigration from Asia and Latin America increased after this act was passed. A grape strike led by César Chávez and the National Farm Workers Association began in Delano, California, a town in the San Joaquin Valley. Rodolfo "Corkey" Gonzales formed the Crusade for Justice in Denver. This important civil rights organization epitomized the Chicano movement that emerged in the 1960s. The Cuban Refugee Airlift program began. Flights from Cuba to Miami, Florida, were sponsored by the U.S. government. The program was terminated in 1973.
1965–68	A series of riots occurred in U.S. cities in which African Americans expressed their frustrations and discontent.
1966	Stokely Carmichael issued a call for Black Power during a civil rights demonstration in Greenwood, Mississippi.
1970	Herman Badillo was elected to the U.S. House of Representatives. He was the first Puerto Rican elected to Congress.
1973	African Americans were elected mayors in Detroit, Atlanta, Los Angeles, and other cities.
1974	The U.S. Supreme Court ruled in the *Lau* v. *Nichols* case that schools should provide students with instruction in their native language. This ruling gave bilingual-bicultural education in the United States a tremendous boost.
1975	U.S. participation in the Vietnam War had ended (1973), and communist governments took control of Vietnam and Cambodia (Kampuchea). Many Indochinese refugees settled in the United States. Between 1971 and 1978, 110,200 Vietnamese refugees immigrated to the United States.

Date	Event
1978	In the case of *Regents of the University of California* v. *Bakke,* the Supreme Court of the United States upheld the idea of affirmative action but ruled against strict racial quotas. The Court concluded that the affirmative action program at the Medical School of the University of California at Davis was unconstitutional.
1980	The 1980 U.S. Census indicated that the population of some ethnic groups in the United States increased dramatically in the decade between 1970 and 1980. Mexicans, Koreans, and Chinese were among the groups whose population increased the most. While the White population increased only 6% between 1970 and 1980, the population of Asian and Pacific islanders more than doubled (from 1.5 million to 3.5 million) and the Hispanic population increased more than 60%. The Refugee Relief Act of 1980 was enacted. It enabled more refugees to enter the United States.
*1986	The Immigration Reform and Control Act of 1986 was passed by Congress and became law. The act imposed severe penalties on employers who knowingly hired illegal immigrants, and it gave amnesty to many illegal immigrants who had been living in the United States since January 1, 1982.
1988	The Civil Liberties Act of 1988 was passed by Congress and signed by President Ronald Reagan. The act provided compensation for the Japanese Americans and the Aleuts of the Pribilof Islands and the Aleutian Islands for the losses they incurred for being forcibly relocated during World War II.
*1990	The Immigration Act of 1990 made some significant changes in immigration law. It set immigration to 675,000 annually (beginning in 1995) to consist of 480,000 family-sponsored, 140,000 employment-based, and 55,000 "diversity immigrants." It revised grounds for exclusion and deportation, rewriting political and ideological grounds.
1994	Nativistic sentiments throughout the nation were epitomized by the passage of Proposition 197 in California. This proposition denied undocumented workers and their children schooling and nonemergency medical care.

VIDEOTAPES ON MULTICULTURAL EDUCATION AND U.S. ETHNIC GROUPS

For Teachers and Teacher Education

A Class Divided. Producer/Distributor: Arlington, VA: PBS Video.

> *An innovative teacher who discriminated against her class on the basic on eye color to teach them about the pain of prejudice is united with them after twenty years in this powerful presentation. This videotape shows how this teacher, Jane Elliott, made a difference. She is an inspiration to us all.*

Learning in America: Schools That Work. Arlington, VA: PBS Video.

> *This interesting and involving videotape profiles elementary schools in Kansas, Maryland, Massachusetts, and Texas that have implemented educational programs that are working. Several of the schools are populated by students of color. Teacher education students like this videotape because it shows them educational practices that work.*

Many Voices, Many Dreams. Produced by Jeff Spitz Productions/Chicago: Distributor: Oak Brook, IL: North Central Educational Laboratory.

> *Perceptively conceptualized and filmed by Jeff Spitz, this videotape is a thoughtful and excellent introduction to multicultural education. It stimulates rich discussion.*

Multicultural Education. Producer/Distributor: Knoxville, TN: Whittle Educational Network.

> *This program presents a town meeting discussion of multicultural education narrated by Judy Woodruff. A panel of experts and an audience of educators interact*

on various issues related to education for diversity. This program was taped in Chicago in 1991.

School Colors. Producer/Distributor: Arlington, VA: PBS Video.

This 143-minute videotape describes efforts at Berkeley (California) High School to implement ethnic diversity into the curriculum. Originally shown on PBS, the videotape evoked considerable controversy and discussion when it was aired. Some educators with whom the author talked stated that the presentation exaggerated racial and ethnic tensions at Berkeley High.

Status Treatments for the Classroom. Producer/Distributor: New York: Teachers College Press.

This videotape is based on the book Designing Groupwork: Strategies for the Heterogeneous Classroom *(2nd ed.) by Elizabeth Cohen (Published by Teachers College Press). This excellent videotape demonstrates how teachers can create equal status among students in the classroom and consequently enhance the academic achievement of students of color. Both the videotape and the book are highly recommended for staff development.*

For Students

Act of War: The Overthrow of the Hawaiian Nation. Distributor: San Francisco: CrossCurrent Media.

The struggle of Native Hawaiians to reclaim their land and the historical events that led to their current situation are described in this one-hour program.

The American Story. Producer/Distributor: New York: Anti-Defamation League of B'nai B'rith:

The lives of twelve families from different ethnic groups are profiled in this series. Titles in the series include families from these U.S. ethnic groups: Puerto Rican, Japanese, Polish, Mexican, Native American, Jewish, Greek, and Italian. This series is excellent for involving students in discussion. The range of ethnic groups covered in the series is another strong characteristic.

The Americans: The Latin American and Caribbean Presence in the U.S. Producer: WGBH, Boston: Distributor: Annenberg/CPB Collection.

The 60-minute videotape examines the Hispanic experience in the United States by focusing on three groups: Cubans in Miami, Puerto Ricans in New York City, and Mexican Americans in Southern California.

Becoming Americans. Producer/Distributor: Honokus, NJ: New Day Films.

This documentary film focuses on the Hmong refugees from Laos. It is a powerful presentation that is excellent for stimulating discussion. Available in both 30-minute and 60-minutes versions.

Before Columbus: Native Americans Tell Their Own Story. Producer/Distributor: Princeton, NJ: Films for the Humanities & Sciences.

Each of the five parts of this program consists of 28 minutes. Titles in the series are Invasion; The Right to Their Own Land; Temples into Churches; Teaching Indians to Be White; Rebellion; *and* The Indian Experience in the 20th Century.

Black Athena: A Film on the Controversy. Producer/Distributor: San Francisco: California Newsreel.

This videotapes chronicles the controversy that surrounded the publication of Black Athena: The Afroasiatic Roots of Classical Civilization *by Martin Bernal (Rutgers University Press, 1987, 1991, 2 vols.). Bernal argues that the debts that European civilizations owes to African and Semitic civilizations have been deliberately hidden by classical historians. His argument has become important in the Afrocentric movement. This videotape is somewhat pedantic, but it provides a powerful lesson on the factors and forces that shape the construction of knowledge. It is best used in staff development, with advanced juniors and seniors, and with college and university students.*

Chicana. Distributor: New York: Women Make Movies.

The important roles and contributions of Mexican American women are described in this 23-minute videotape.

Different and the Same. Producer/Distributor: Pittsburgh, PA: Family Communications, Inc.

This series of videotapes is designed to teach children in grades 1 through 3 about racial and ethnic differences and to develop respect for differences. The nine program segments are contained within three videotapes. Puppets are central characters in these effective and useful videotapes for use with young children. Programs segment titles include Sticks and Stones, Proud to Be Me, *and* I Am American, Too.

Dollar a Day, Ten Cents a Dance: A Historic Portrait of Filipino Farmworkers in America. Distributor: San Francisco: CrossCurrent Media.

This thirty-minute program describes the Filipino immigrants who settled in the United States in the 1920 and 1930s. Their community consisted primarily of men.

Eyes on the Prize: America's Civil Rights Years. Series I and II. Producer/Distributor: Alexandria, VA: PBS Video.

This is an outstanding series of fifty-seven-minute color videotapes that cover the civil rights movement in depth from 1954 through the mid-1980s. Part I (six videotapes) covers the period from 1954 to 1965. Part II (eight videotapes) covers the period from 1965 through the mid-1980s. Every school system, as well as college and university media centers, should purchase this outstanding series.

Hidden Heritage: The Roots of Black American Painting. Distributor: Falls Church, VA: Landmark Films.

African American art from the American Revolution to World War II is described in this 52-minute videotape.

How the West Was Lost. Distributor: Landover, MD: Discovery Enterprises Group.

This powerful series of three videotapes (100 minutes each) poignantly describes the conquering of the Native Americans by the Europeans. The titles of the three videotapes are A Clash of Cultures: I Will Fight No More Forever; Always the Enemy: The Only Good Indian Is a Dead Indian; *and* A Good Day to Die; Kill the Indian; Save the Man.

Ida B. Wells. Distributor: New York: William Greaves Productions.

The life of the crusader against lynching is described in this 53-minute program.

In Black and White: Conversations with African American Writers. San Francisco: California Newsreel.

This set of six videotapes (151 minutes) features six African American authors: Charles Johnson, Gloria Naylor, Toni Morrison, Alice Walker, August Wilson, and John Wideman.

In No One's Shadow: Filipinos in America. Distributor: San Francisco: CrossCurrent Media.

This 28-minute videotape describes the historical saga of Filipinos in the United States, with emphasis on the twentieth century.

In the White Man's Image. Distributor: Arlington, VA: PBS Video.

The Carlisle School for Indian Students founded in the early part of this century is profiled in this 58-minute videotape.

The Latino Family. Distributor: Princeton, N.J.: Films for the Humanities & Sciences.

Changes in the traditional Mexican American family are revealed by depicting three generations of one family.

Japanese American Women: A Sense of Place. Distributor: New York: Women Make Movies.

Japanese American women describe the conflict of cultures and identity they experience in America (27-minute videotape).

The Longest Hatred: The History of Anti-Semitism. Distributor: New York: Anti-Defamation League of B'nai B'rith.

This comprehensive history of anti-Semitism consists of three 45-minute segments on two cassettes. Titles in the series are From the Cross to the Swastika, Enemies of the Nation, *and* Between Moses and Mohammed.

Malcolm X: Make It Plain. Arlington, VA: PBS Video.

The life of the civil rights leader is the subject of this 60-minute videotape.

More Than Bows and Arrows. Producer/Distributor: Seattle, WA: Camera One.

The contributions that Native Americans have made to American culture are highlighted in this 53-minute program.

Multicultural Peoples of North America. Producer: Library Video. Distributor: Culver City, CA: Social Studies School Service.

This series of fifteen 30-minute videotapes is based on the Chelsea House series of books, The Peoples of North America. *Titles are* African Americans; The Amish; Arab Americans; Central Americans; Chinese Americans; German Americans; Greek Americans; Irish Americans; Italian Americans; Japanese Americans; Jewish Americans; Korean Americans; Mexican Americans; Polish Americans; *and* Puerto Ricans. *Each videotape is 30 minutes.*

Power, Politics and Latinos. Distributor: Los Angeles: Producer: National Latin Communication Center. Distributor: PBS Video.

The political participation of Latinos is the subject of this 56-minute program, with emphasis on the 1992 election.

Racism 101. Producer/Distributor: Alexandria, VA: PBS Video.

This 57-minute color video explores the reasons for the racial unrest that flared up on many college and university campuses during the 1980s. It is from the PBS program "Frontline."

The Road to Freedom. Distributor: San Francisco: California Newsreel.

In this 58-minute videotape, the historical events that culminated in the landmark Brown *vs.* Board of Education *Supreme Court decision are described.*

Roll of Thunder, Hear My Cry. Distributor: New York: Macmillan/McGraw-Hill Schooling Publishing.

A 46-minute dramatization of the powerful novel by Mildred Taylor. The novel chronicles events in the life of the Logan family, a family that lived in Mississippi in the 1930s.

The Shadow of Hate: A History of Intolerance in America. Producer/Distributor: Montgomery, AL: Teaching Tolerance.

This 40-minute program uses historical footage, photographs, and voices of individuals who participated in historical events to depict the intolerance directed against various ethnic, cultural, and minority groups in American society. This teaching package consists of the video, a 128-page text, Us and Them, *and a Teacher's Guide.*

Slaying the Dragon. San Francisco: CrossCurent Media.

The Hollywood and television images of Asian American women are described in this 60-minute videotape.

A Time for Justice: America's Civil Rights Movement. Producer/Distributor: Montgomery, AL: Teaching Tolerance.

This 38-minute program describes the civil rights movement with the use of actual historical footage and the voices of people who participated in it. This teaching package consists of the videotape, a book, Free At Last, *and a teacher's guide.*

Unfinished Business: The Japanese Internment Cases. Distributor: San Francisco: CrossCurrent Media.

The stories of three Japanese American men who resisted the military orders to be interned are told in this 60-minute videotape.

A Weave of Time: The Story of a Navajo Family 1838–1986. Distributor: Los Angeles: Direct Cinema.

This 60-minute documentary describes four generations in the life of a Navajo family.

Winds of Change, Part 1: *A Matter of Promises.* Distributor: Arlington, VA: PBS Video.

> *The Onondaga Nation, the Navajo Nation, and the Lummi Nation strive to attain rights guaranteed by treaties in this powerful and thought-provoking videotape narrated by N. Scott Momaday. Recommended for advanced high school students and college and university students.*

World of Difference Training Program (Video Vignettes). Producer/Distributor: New York: Anti-Defamation League of B'nai B'rith.

> *The World of Difference Program is a nationally implemented prejudice reduction program implemented by the Anti-Defamation League of B'nai B'rith. This 11-minute videotape presents three reenactments of real-life situations. The vignettes are* Ethnic Humor, The Art Exhibit, *and* Routine Check. *Includes a discussion guide.*

Addresses and Telephone Numbers (as of January 1, 1996)

Annenberg/CPB Project
P.O. Box 2345
South Burlington, VT 05407–2345
Phone: 800–LEARNER

Anti-Defamation League of B'nai B'rith
823 United Nations Plaza
New York, NY 10017
Phone: 800–343–5540

California Newsreel
149 Ninth Street, Suite 420
San Francisco,CA 94103
Phone: 415–621–6196

Camera One Productions
431 North 34th Street
Seattle,WA 98103
Phone: 206–547–5131

CrossCurrent Media
346 Ninth Street, 2nd Floor
San Francisco, CA 94103
Phone: 415–552–9550

Direct Cinema, Ltd.
P.O. Box 10003
Santa Monica, CA 90410
Phone: 310–396–4774

Discovery Channel
8201 Corporate Drive, Suite 1200
Landover, MD 20785
Phone: 301–577–1999

Family Communications
4802 Fifth Avenue
Pittsburgh, PA 15213
Phone: 412–687–2990

Films for the Humanities & Sciences
P.O. Box 2053
Princeton, NJ 08543–2053
Phone: 800–257–5126

William Greaves Productions, Inc.
230 West 55th Street, 26th Floor
New York, NY 10019
Phone: 800–874–8314

McGraw-Hill School Publishers
1221 Avenue of the Americas
New York, NY 10020
Phone: 212–512–3328

New Day Films
22D Hollywood Avenue
Hohokus, NJ 07423
Phone: 201–652–6590

North Central Educational Laboratory
1900 Spring Road
Suite 300, Oak Brook, IL 60621
Phone: 1–800–356–2735.

PBS Video Public Broadcasting Service
1320 Braddock Place
Alexandra, VA 22314–1698
Phone: 800–344–3337

Social Studies School Services
10200 Jefferson Blvd., Room 1221
P.O. Box 802
Culver City, CA 90232–0802
Phone: 800–421–4246

Teachers College Press
1234 Amsterdam
New York, NY 10027
Phone: 212–678–3929

Teaching Tolerance
400 Washington Avenue
Montgomery, AL 36104
Fax: 334–264–3121
Phone: 334–264–0286

Whittle Communications
600 Madison Avenue, 6th Floor
New York, NY 10022
Phone: 212–508–6800

Women Make Movies, Inc.
462 Broadway, Suite 500B
New York, NY 10013
Phone: 212-925-0606

APPENDIX C

BOOKS ABOUT WOMEN OF COLOR

Agosin, M. (Ed.) (1994). *These Are Not Sweet Girls: Poetry by Latin American Women.* Fredonia, N.Y.: White Pine Press.

Alarcón, N., Castro, R., Pérez, E., Pesquera, B., Riddell, A. S., & Zavella, P. (Eds.). (1993). *Chicana Critical Issues.* Berkeley, Calif.: Third Woman Press.

Albrecht, L. & Brewer, R. M. (Eds.). (1990). *Bridges of Power: Women's Multicultural Alliances.* Philadelphia: New Society Publishers.

Benedek, E. (1995). *Beyond the Four Corners of the World: Navajo Woman's Journey.* New York: Knopf.

Buss, F. L. (Ed.). (1993). *Forged under the Sun/Forjada bajo el Sol: The Life of María Elena Lucas.* Ann Arbor: The University of Michigan Press.

Castillo-Speed, L. (Ed.). (1995). *Latina: Women's Voices from the Borderlands.* New York: Touchstone/Simon & Schuster.

Córdova, T., Cantú, N., Cardenas, G., García, J., & Sierra, C. M. (Eds.). (1990). *Chicana Voices: Intersections of Class, Race, and Gender.* Albuquerque: Univeristy of New Mexico Press.

Crawford, V. L., Rouse, J. A., & Woods, B. (Eds.). (1993). *Women in the Civil Rights Movement: Trailblazers and Torchbearers, 1941–1965.* Bloomington: Indiana University Press.

Dog, M. C. and Erdoes, R. (1990). *Lakota Woman.* New York: HarperCollins.

DuBois, C. & Ruiz, V. L. (Eds.). (1994). *Unequal Sisters: A Multicultural Reader in U.S. Women's History* (2nd ed.). New York: Routledge.

Frankenberg, R. (1993). *White Women, Race Matters: The Social Construction of Whiteness.* Minneapolis: University of Minnesota Press.

Garrow, D. J. (Ed.). (1987). *The Montgomery Bus Boycott and the Women Who Started It: The Memoir of Jo Ann Gibson Robinson.* Knoxville: The University of Tennessee Press.

Golden, M. & Shreve, S. R. (Eds.). (1995). *Skin Deep: Black Woman and White Woman Write about Race.* New York: Doubleday.

Green, R. (1992). *Women in American Indian Society.* New York: Chelsea House.

Hemenway, R. E. (1980). *Zora Neale Hurston: A Literary Biography.* Urbana: University of Illinois Press.

Higginbotham, E. B. (1993). *Righteous Discontent: The Women's Movement in the Black Baptist Church, 1880–1920.* Cambridge: Harvard University Press.

555

Hine, D. C. (Ed.). (1993). *Black Women in America: An Historical Encyclopedia.* Brooklyn, N.Y.: Carlson Publishing.

Hine, D. C. (Ed.). (1995). *"We Specialize in the Wholly Impossible": A Reader in Black Women's History.* Brooklyn, N.Y.: Carlson Publishing.

hooks, b. (1995). *Killing Rage, Ending Racism.* New York: Henry Holt.

Houston, V. H. (Ed.). (1993). *The Politics of Life: Four Plays by Asian American Women.* Philadelphia: Temple University Press.

Katz, J. (Ed.) (1995). *Messengers of the Wind: Native American Women Tell Their Life Stories.* New York: Ballantine Books.

Klein, L. F. & Ackerman, L. A. (1995). *Women and Power in Native North America.* Norman: University of Oklahoma Press.

Mankiller, W. & Wallis, M. (1993). *Mankiller: A Chief and Her People.* New York: St. Martin's Press.

Mills, K. (1994). *This Little Lite of Mine: The Life of Fannie Lou Hamer.* New York: Penguin.

Nakane, M. (1990). *Japanese American Women: Three Generations 1890–1990.* Berkeley, Calif.: Mina Press Publishing.

Schmitz, B., Butler, J. E., Rosenfelt, D., & Guy-Sheftall, B. (1995). Women's Studies and Curriculum Transformation. In J. A. Banks & C. A. M. Banks (Eds.). *Handbook of Research on Multicultural Education* (pp. 708–728). New York: Macmillan.

Telgen, D. & Kamp, J. (Eds.). (1993). *Notable Hispanic American Women* (1st ed.). Detroit: Gale Research.

Vaz, K. M. (Ed.). (1995). *Black Women in America.* Thousand Oaks, Calif.: Sage Publications.

Watanabe, S. & Gruchac, C. (Eds.). (1990). *Home to Stay: Asian American Women's Fiction.* Greenfield Center, N.Y.: The Greenfield Review Press.

Women of South Asian Descent Collective (1993). *Our Feet Walk the Sky: Women of the South Asian Diaspora.* San Francisco: Aunte Lute Books.

THE CARTER G. WOODSON AWARD BOOKS

The Carter G. Woodson Award is presented each year by the National Council for the Social Studies in honor of the distinguished Black historian and educator who wrote books for adults and young people, founded and edited the *Journal of Negro History,* and contributed in many significant ways to interracial understanding. The Award is designed to "encourage the writing, publishing, and dissemination of outstanding social science books for young readers that treat topics related to ethnic minorities and race relations sensitively and accurately."

1974

Eloise Greenfield, *Rosa Parks* (New York: Thomas Y. Crowell).

1975

Jesse Jackson, *Make a Joyful Noise unto the Lord: The Life of Mahalia Jackson* (New York: Thomas Y. Crowell).

1976

Laurence Yep, *Dragonwings* (New York: Harper and Row).

1977

Dorothy Sterling, *The Trouble They Seen* (Garden City, N.Y.: Doubleday).

1978

Jane Goodsell, *The Biography of Daniel Inouye* (New York: Thomas Y. Crowell).

1979

Peter Nabokov, *Native American Testimony* (New York: Thomas Y. Crowell).

1980

Nancy Wood, *War Cry on a Prayer Feather* (Garden City, N.Y.: Doubleday).

Outstanding Merit Books

John Bierhorst, *A Cry from the Earth: Music of North American Indians* (New York: Four Winds Press).

Jim Haskins, *James Van Derzee: The Picture Takin' Man* (New York: Dodd, Mead).

Eloise Greenfield and Lessie Jones Little, *Childtimes: A Three Generation Memoir* (New York: Harper and Row).

1981

Milton Meltzer, *The Chinese Americans* (New York: Thomas Y. Crowell).

Outstanding Merit Book

Pamela Bullard and Judith Stoia, *The Hardest Lesson: Personal Accounts of a School Desegregation Crisis* (Boston: Little, Brown).

1982

Susan Carver and Paula McGuire, *Coming to North America from Mexico, Cuba and Puerto Rico* (New York: Delacorte Press).

1983

Brent Ashabranner, *Morning Star, Black Sun: The Northern Cheyenne Indians and America's Energy Crisis* (New York: Dodd, Mead).

1984

E. B. Fincher, *Mexico and the United States* (New York: Thomas Y. Crowell).

1985

Brent Ashabranner, *To Live in Two Worlds: American Indian Youth Today* (New York: Dodd, Mead).

Outstanding Merit Book

David Adler, *Our Golda: The Story of Golda Meir* (New York: Viking).

1986

Brent Ashabranner, *Dark Harvest: Migrant Farm Workers in America* (New York: Dodd, Mead).

Outstanding Merit Book

Elaine Pascoe, *Racial Prejudice: Issues in American History* (New York: Franklin Watts).

1987

Arlene Hirschfelder, *Happily May I Walk* (New York: Scribner's & Sons).

Outstanding Merit Books

Brent Ashabranner, *Children of the Maya* (New York: Dodd, Mead).

Maxine B. Rosenberg, *Living in Two Worlds* (New York: Lothrop Publishers).

1988

James Haskins, *Black Music in America: A History through Its People* (New York: Harper and Row).

1989

Elementary Category

Jeri Ferris, *Walking the Road to Freedom* (Minneapolis: Carolrhoda Books, Inc.).

Secondary Category

Charles Patterson, *Marian Anderson* (New York: Franklin Watts).

Outstanding Merit Books

Elementary

Russell Freedman, *Buffalo Hunt* (New York: Holiday House).

Secondary

Judith Harlan, *Hispanic Voters* (New York: Franklin Watts).

Joseph Thomas Moore, *Pride against Prejudice: The Biography of Larry Doby.* (New York: Praeger).

1990

Elementary

Aylette Jenness and Alice Rivers, *In Two Worlds: A Yup'ik Eskimo Family* (Boston: Houghton Mifflin Co.).

Elementary Outstanding Merit Books

Corrin Codye, *Wilma Martinez* (Milwaukee: Raintree Publishers).

Jeri Ferris, *Arctic Explorers* (Minneapolis: Carolrhoda Books).

Secondary

Rebecca Larsen, *Paul Robeson* (New York: Franklin Watts).

Secondary Outstanding Books

Janet Bode, *New Kids on the Block* (New York: Franklin Watts).

Patricia and Frederick McKissack, *A Long Hard Journey* (New York: Walker and Co.).

1991

Elementary

Catherine Scheader, *Shirley Chisolm* (Hillside, N.J.: Enslow Publishing).

Elementary Outstanding Merit Books

Peter Bolenback, *Teammates* (San Diego: Gulliver/Harcourt, Brace & Jovanovich).

Joan Hewett, *Hector Live in the U. S. Now* (Philadelphia: Lippincott).

Secondary

Mary Lyons, *Sorrow's Kitchen: The Life and Folklore of Zora Neal Hurston* (New York: Scribner's Books for Your Readers/Macmillan)

Secondary Outstanding Books

Patricia and Frederick McKissack, *W. E. B. DuBois* (New York: Franklin Watts).

William Katz, *Breaking the Chains* (New York: Atheneum).

1992

Elementary

Fay Stanley, *The Last Princess: The Story of Princess Ka'Iolani of Hawai'i* (illustrations by Diane Stanley) (New York: Macmillan).

Elementary Outstanding Merit Books

Diane Hoyt-Goldsmith, *Pueblo Storyteller* (photographs by Lawrence Migdale) (New York: Holiday House).

Patricia and Frederick McKissack, *Carter G. Woodson: The Father of Black History*, illustrated by Ned Ostendorf. (Hillside, N.J.: Enslow Publishers).

Secondary

Jeri Ferris, *Native American Doctor: The Story of Susan LaFlesche Picotte* (Minneapolis: Carolrhoda).

Secondary Outstanding Books

James Haskins, *Outward Dreams: Black Inventors and their Inventions* (New York: Walker Publishing Group).

Walter Dean Myers, *Now Is Your Time: The African-American Struggle for Freedom* (New York: HarperCollins).

1993

Elementary

Patricia and Frederick McKissack, *Madam C. J. Walker: Self-Made Millionaire* (Springfield, N.J.: Enslow Publishers).

Elementary Outstanding Merit Books

Diane Hoyt-Goldsmith, *Hoang Anh: A Vietnamese-American Boy* (New York: Holiday House).

Susan Kuklin, *How My Family Lives in America* (New York: Bradbury Press / Macmillan).

Secondary

Mildred Pitts Walker, *Mississippi Challenge* (New York: Bradbury Press).

Secondary Outstanding Books

James Haskins, *Thurgood Marshall: A Life for Justice* (New York: Henry Holt).

Beatrie Siegal, *The Year They Walked* (New York: Four Winds Press/Simon & Schuster).

1994

Elementary

Mary Lyons, *Starting Home: The Story of Horace Pippin, Painter* (New York: Scribner's).

Elementary Outstanding Merit Books

Diane Hoyt-Goldsmith, *Celebrating Kwanzaa* (New York: Holiday House).

Paintings by Jacob Lawrence, *The Great Migration: An American Story* (New York: HarperCollins).

Secondary

James Haskins, *The March on Washington* (New York: HarperCollins)

Secondary Outstanding Merit Books

Virginia Hamilton, *Many Thousand Gone: African Americans from Slavery to Freedom* (New York: Knopf).

Janet Klausner, *Sequoyah's Gift: A Portrait of the Cherokee Leader* (New York: HarperCollins).

1995

Elementary

Jeri Ferris, *What I Had Was Singing: The Story of Marian Anderson* (Minneapolis: Carolrhoda Books).

Elementary Outstanding Merit Books

Mary E. Lyons, *Master of Mahogany: Tom Day, Free Black Cabinetmaker* (New York: Scribner's).

Andrea Davis Pinkey, *Dear Benjamin Banneker* (San Diego: Gulliver Books, Harcourt Brace).

Secondary

Zak Mettger, *Till Victory Is Won: Black Soldiers in the Civil War* (New York: Lodestar Books).

Secondary Outstanding Merit Books

Roger C. Echo-Hawk and Walter R. Echo-Hawk, *Battlefields and Burial Grounds: The Indian Struggle to Protect Ancestral Graves in the United States* (Minneapolis: Lerner Publications).

Norma Johnston, *Harriet: The Life and World of Harriet Beecher Stowe* (New York: Four Winds Press, Macmillan).

APPENDIX **E**

TWENTY CLASSIC AND LANDMARK BOOKS IN ETHNIC LITERATURE

Adamic, L. (1932). *Laughing in the Jungle: The Autobiography of an Immigrant in America.* New York: Harper and Brothers. (Slavic American)

Anaya, R. A. (1972). *Bless Me, Ultima.* Berkeley, Calif.: Tonatiuh International. (Mexican American)

Banks, J. A. & Banks, C. A. M. (Editors). (1996). *Handbook of Research on Multicultural Education.* New York: Macmillan.

Bulosan, C. (1973). *America Is in the Heart.* Seattle: University of Washington Press. (Filipino American)

Ellison, R. (1952). *Invisible Man.* New York: New American Library. (African American)

Galarza, E. (1971). *Barrio Boy.* Notre Dame, Ind.: University of Notre Dame Press. (Mexican American)

Haley, A. (1976). *Roots: The Saga of an American Family.* Garden City, N.Y.: Doubleday. (African American)

Handlin, O. (1951). *The Uprooted: The Epic Story of the Great Migrations That Made the American People.* New York: Grosset and Dunlap. (European American)

Howe, I. (1976). *World of Our Fathers: The Journey of the Jews to America and the Life They Found and Made.* New York: Simon & Schuster. (Jewish American)

Kingston, M. H. (1976). *The Woman Warrior: Memories of a Girlhood among Ghosts.* New York: Vintage. (Chinese American)

Momaday, N. S. (1966). *House Made of Dawn.* New York: Signet. (American Indian)

Morrison, T. (1987). *Beloved: A Novel.* New York: Knopf. (African American)

Novak, M. (1973). *The Rise of the Unmeltable Ethnics.* New York: Macmillan. (European American)

Okada, J. (1976). *No-No Boy.* San Francisco: Combined Asian American Resources Project, Inc. (Japanese American)

Rolvaag, O. E. (1927). *Giants in the Earth: A Saga of the Prairie.* New York: Harper and Row. (Norwegian American)

Takaki, R. (1989). *Strangers from a Different Shore: A History of Asian Americans.* Boston: Little, Brown. (Asian American)

563

Takaki, R. (1993). *A Different Mirror: A History of Multicultural America.* Boston: Little, Brown.

Walker, A. (1982). *The Color Purple.* New York: Harcourt Brace, 1982. (African American)

Wong, J. S. (1945). *Fifth Chinese Daughter.* New York: Harper and Row. (Chinese American)

Wright, R. (1966). *Black Boy: A Record of Childhood and Youth.* New York: Harper and Row. (African American)

INDEX